When should I travel to get the best airfare?
Where do I go for answers to my travel questions?
What's the best and easiest way to plan and book my trip?

frommers.travelocity.com

Frommer's, the travel guide leader, has teamed up with **Travelocity.com**, the leader in online travel, to bring you an in-depth, easy-to-use resource designed to help you plan and book your trip online.

At **frommers.travelocity.com**, you'll find free online updates about your destination from the experts at Frommer's plus the outstanding travel planning and purchasing features of Travelocity.com. Travelocity.com provides reservations capabilities for 95 percent of all airline seats sold, more than 47,000 hotels, and over 50 car rental companies. In addition, Travelocity.com offers more than 2,000 exciting vacation and cruise packages. Travelocity.com puts you in complete control of your travel planning with these and other great features:

Expert travel guidance from Frommer's - over 150 writers reporting from around the world!

Best Fare Finder - an interactive calendar tells you when to travel to get the best airfare

Fare Watcher - we'll track airfare changes to your favorite destinations

Dream Maps - a mapping feature that suggests travel opportunities based on your budget

Shop Safe Guarantee - 24 hours a day / 7 days a week live customer service, and more!

Whether traveling on a tight budget, looking for a quick weekend getaway, or planning the trip of a lifetime, Frommer's guides and Travelocity.com will make your travel dreams a reality. You've bought the book, now book the trip!

Travelocity.com
A Sabre Company

D1227090

A New Star-Rating System & Other Exciting News from Frommer's!

In our continuing effort to publish the savviest, most up-to-date, and most appealing travel guides available, we've added some great new features.

Frommer's guides now include a new **star-rating system.** Every hotel, restaurant, and attraction is rated from 0 to 3 stars to help you set priorities and organize your time.

We've also added **seven brand-new features** that point you to the great deals, in-the-know advice, and unique experiences that separate travelers from tourists. Throughout the guide look for:

Finds	Special finds—those places only insiders know about
Fun Fact	Fun facts—details that make travelers more informed and their trips more fun
Kids	Best bets for kids—advice for the whole family
Moments	Special moments—those experiences that memories are made of
Overrated	Places or experiences not worth your time or money
Tips	Insider tips—some great ways to save time and money
Value	Great values—where to get the best deals

We've also added a **"What's New"** section in every guide—a timely crash course in what's hot and what's not in every destination we cover.

Other Great Guides for Your Trip:

Frommer's England *Frommer's Greece* *Frommer's Portugal*
Frommer's Europe *Frommer's Greek Islands* *Frommer's Scandinavia*
Frommer's France *Frommer's Ireland* *Frommer's Scotland*
Frommer's Germany *Frommer's Italy* *Frommer's Spain*
and other great city, regional, and budget guides

Other Great Frommer's Cruise Guides:

Frommer's Alaska Cruises & Ports of Call
Frommer's Caribbean Cruises & Ports of Call

Frommer's®

European Cruises

& Ports of Call

2nd Edition

by Fran Wenograd Golden
and Jerry Brown

Here's what the critics say about Frommer's:

"Amazingly easy to use. Very portable, very complete."

—*Booklist*

"The only mainstream guide to list specific prices. The Walter Cronkite of guidebooks—with all that implies."

—*Travel & Leisure*

"Complete, concise, and filled with useful information."

—*New York Daily News*

"Hotel Information is close to encylopedic."

—*Des Moines Sunday Register*

"Detailed, accurate and easy-to-read information for all price ranges."

—*Glamour Magazine*

Hungry Minds™

Best-Selling Books • Digital Downloads • e-Books • Answer Networks
e-Newsletters • Branded Web Sites • e-Learning
New York, NY • Cleveland, OH • Indianapolis, IN

About the Authors

Fran Wenograd Golden is a columnist for concierge.com and the *Boston Herald* travel section, author of *Cruise Vacations For Dummies,* co-author of *Frommer's Alaska Cruises & Ports of Call,* a contributor to *Frommer's Greece* and *Honeymoon Vacations For Dummies,* and author of *TVacations: A Fun Guide to the Sites, the Stars and the Inside Stories Behind Your Favorite TV Shows.* She lives north of Boston with her husband, Ed, and two teenagers, Erin and Eli, who love traveling and join her on the road (and on the high seas) whenever school and job commitments permit.

Jerry Brown was born in Edinburgh, Scotland, and worked in Scottish newspapers and then in the news department of the *London Daily Mail.* Later, for 31 years, he was the West Coast bureau chief of a leading travel trade publication, and he's the other co-author (with Fran) of *Frommer's Alaska Cruises & Ports of Call.* He and Margaret, his wife and best editor, have two grown sons, Mark and Paul, and as a family unit and individually they have sailed the waters of Europe on numerous occasions. Recently, the group was enlarged by one—his first granddaughter, Victoria Rose, whom he hopes someday to introduce to the joys of a European cruise vacation.

Published by:

Hungry Minds, Inc.

909 Third Ave.
New York, NY 10022

ISBN 0-7645-6556-7
ISSN 1527-1641

Editor: Lorraine Festa
Production Editor: Heather Wilcox
Cartographer: Nicholas Trotter
Photo Editor: Richard Fox
Production by Hungry Minds Indianapolis Production Services

Front cover photo: Santorini, in the Greek Cyclades, is noted for its whitewashed architecture.
Back cover photo: Villefranche harbor, Côte d'Azur

Special Sales

For general information on Hungry Minds' products and services, please contact our Customer Care department; within the U.S. at 800-762-2974, outside the U.S. at 317-572-3993, or fax 317-572-4002. For sales inquiries and reseller information, including discounts, bulk sales, customized editions, and premium sales, please contact our Customer Care department at 800-434-3422.

Manufactured in the United States of America

5   4   3   2   1

Contents

Part 1: Planning, Booking & Preparing for Your Cruise

Part 2: The Cruise Lines & Their Ships

List of Maps

An Invitation to the Reader

In researching this book, we discovered many wonderful places—hotels, restaurants, shops, and more. We're sure you'll find others. Please tell us about them, so we can share the information with your fellow travelers in upcoming editions. If you were disappointed with a recommendation, we'd love to know that, too. Please write to:

Frommer's European Cruises & Ports of Call, 2nd Edition
Hungry Minds, Inc. • 909 Third Avenue • New York, NY 10022

An Additional Note

Please be advised that travel information is subject to change at any time—and this is especially true of prices. We therefore suggest that you write or call ahead for confirmation when making your travel plans. The authors, editors, and publisher cannot be held responsible for the experiences of readers while traveling. Your safety is important to us, however, so we encourage you to stay alert and be aware of your surroundings. Keep a close eye on cameras, purses, and wallets, all favorite targets of thieves and pickpockets.

New! Frommer's Star Ratings & Icons

We use seven icons to highlight insider information, useful tips, special bargains, hidden gems, memorable experiences, kid-friendly venues, places to avoid, and other useful information:

| Finds | Fun Fact | Kids | Moments | Overrated | Tips | Value |

The following abbreviations are used for credit cards:

| AE | American Express | DISC | Discover | V | Visa |
| DC | Diners Club | MC | MasterCard | | |

FROMMERS.COM

Now that you have the guidebook to a great trip, visit our website at **www.frommers.com** for travel information on nearly 2,000 destinations. With features updated regularly, we give you instant access to the most current trip-planning information available. At Frommers.com, you'll also find the best prices on airfares, accommodations, and car rentals—and you can even book travel online through our travel booking partners. At Frommers.com, you'll also find the following:

- Daily Newsletter highlighting the best travel deals
- Hot Spot of the Month/Vacation Sweepstakes & Travel Photo Contest
- More than 200 Travel Message Boards
- Outspoken Newsletters and Feature Articles on travel bargains, vacation ideas, tips & resources, and more!

Europe

Norwegian Sea

NORTH ATLANTIC OCEAN

Bergen

NORWAY

GRAMPIAN
Aberdeen
TAYSIDE
Perth
Edinburgh

North Sea

DENMARK

Belfast

IRELAND
DINGLE PENINSULA
KERRY COUNTY
Dublin

Liverpool

U.K.

COTSWOLDS
Bath
Oxford
Stonehenge ■
Salisbury
London

THE NETHERLANDS
Amsterdam
Hamburg

Bruges
BELGIUM
GERMANY
Brussels
Bonn
Liège
Frankfurt
LUX.
Rothenburg ob der Tauber

English Channel

Le Havre

Paris
Strasbourg
Augsburg
Munich
BAVARIAN

LOIRE VALLEY

FRANCE
Bern
Innsbruck
SWITZERLAND
Geneva
BERNER OBERLAND

Bay of Biscay

Bordeaux

Milan

Arles
PROVENCE
MONACO
Marseille
Nice
Florence
Côte d'Azur
TUSC

Bilbao

CORSICA

Porto

ANDORRA
Barcelona

Madrid

PORTUGAL

Lisbon

SPAIN

Córdoba
Valencia

SARDINIA

Cagliari

ALGARVE
Seville
ANDALUSIA
Granada
Malaga
Costa del Sol

Mediterranean Sea

0   150 mi
0   150 km
N

SWEDEN
ndheim
Sundsvall
Gulf of Bothnia
Gavle
Stockholm
Göteborg
Baltic Sea
Copenhagen
rlin
Poznan
Berlin

FINLAND
Tampere
Helsinki
St. Petersburg

RUSSIA
Moscow

Tallinn
ESTONIA

Riga
LATVIA

LITHUANIA
Vilnius
RUSSIA
Kaliningrad
Minsk

BELARUS

Gdansk
Warsaw

POLAND
lovy Vary
arlsbad)
Prague
Krakow
Lvov
Kiev

UKRAINE

CZECH
REPUBLIC
BÜHEL ALPS
Vienna
Bratislava
DANUBE
Salzburg VALLEY
Budapest

SLOVAKIA

MOLDOVA
Chisinau
Odessa

AUSTRIA
HUNGARY
bljana
LOVENIA
Zagreb
CROATIA
nice
Lake Balaton
Cluj-Napoca

ROMANIA

BOSNIA
Sarajevo
Belgrade
SERBIA

Bucharest
Constanta
Black Sea

Varna

BULGARIA
Sofiya

Adriatic Sea
ALY
ome
MONTENEGRO
Titograd
Skopje
MACEDONIA
Tirana

Istanbul

Naples
Pompeii
ALBANIA

TURKEY

rhenian
Sea
GREECE
Delphi
Aegean Sea

Palermo
SICILY
Ionian Sea
Athens
CYCLADES

CYPRUS

PELOPONNESE

Mediterranean Sea
MALTA
CRETE

Introduction

Fran first cruised in Europe—or more exactly, *to* Europe—in 1959 when she was 3 years old and her mother, brother, and she traveled transatlantic from New York to Southampton on the old *United States*. She remembers nothing of the trip by sea, but obviously something stuck since she loves to visit Europe, loves to cruise, and finds it great fun to combine the two. She explores Europe's waters as often as she can, usually in the company of friends (both American and European) or her family (her teenagers and husband fight over who gets to go along).

Although he was born and raised in Europe (in Scotland), Jerry didn't cruise the region until much later than Fran, in 1984, on the *Pacific Princess,* which happens to be leaving Princess Cruises' fleet after this summer. The cruise still evokes happy memories and laughter in the Brown household. The cabin steward delighted and amused Jerry's sons (then ages 14 and 9) by deliberately exaggerating his Cockney accent to make himself virtually unintelligible to them. And there is, in the Brown family album, a classic photograph of Jerry's sons on that cruise looking utterly bored among the ruins of Pompeii. (Remember that if you're dragging teens to sites of ancient civilizations. Take them, by all means. Just don't be surprised if they pretend not to be enjoying it!) The kids, now grown, agree that cruising Europe is by and large a joy, and the Browns individually and

as a group have cruised to and in Europe umpteen times since.

Whether you are a first-time visitor to the region or are returning to see countries you've visited before from a new oceanview perspective (many European cities were built to be seen from the sea) and at a different pace, cruising in Europe can be a wonderful experience.

The ports in Europe hold treasures of antiquities and natural beauty, fascinating history (you'll quickly realize how young 1776 is in the scheme of things), and enchanting cultural experiences.

From your ship, depending on the route you choose, you will have easy access to such delights as the ancient cities of Pompeii and Ephesus; Europe's historic and cultural capitals, including London, Paris, and Rome; modern port cities; gorgeous islands; scenic fjords; rugged coastlines; and glamorous resorts.

You can visit museums, cathedrals, palaces, and monuments and learn about the region's history. Or you can concentrate on the Europe of today, checking out the latest trends in food and fashion before they hit the shores of the U.S.

WHY A CRUISE?

Europe is a popular cruising region, second only to the Caribbean (and followed by Alaska in third place), and it's really a no-brainer to see why. The region truly offers something for everyone: great sights, shopping, beaches, museums, a diversity of cultural and natural attractions, and a decent climate.

The **ports** are close together, meaning you can visit several in a limited period of time; the seas relatively calm; the opportunities interesting and diverse. Europe has a seafaring tradition that goes back to ancient times—you can even choose an itinerary that follows the exact route of the ancient mariners—so is it any wonder a European cruise sounds so exciting and romantic?

A cruise is also one of the most practical, comfortable, and economical ways to see Europe. You only have to unpack once, your floating hotel takes you to different ports in different countries, and you don't have to deal with the hassle and expense of getting around Europe by plane or train.

On a cruise you are fed, pampered, and taken care of in a stress-free environment. You don't have to worry about things like currency fluctuations and their effect on your hotel, entertainment, and meal costs, since all of these are included in your cruise fare. Food offerings will be familiar—you can even sip a piña colada while viewing, say, St. Petersburg—and you don't have to deal with potential language problems, since there will be personnel on the ship who speak English.

A downside to cruising is that you might not have as much time as you'd like in port to experience the local culture, although some lines overnight in cities like Venice, Monte Carlo, and Istanbul, and smaller ships may overnight in smaller cities. The cruise lines do their best, through their organized shore excursions, to get passengers to the major sights. And if you'd rather sit at a cafe and check out the local scene than do an organized tour, you can just head off on your own.

We've found that when cruising in Europe, it's best to think of your cruise as a **sampler package.** If you fall in love with a city, plan on visiting again later.

EUROPEAN CRUISING 2002

Cruise lines—including major American lines like Princess, Holland America, Royal Caribbean, Norwegian Cruise Line, and Celebrity—have steadily been increasing their presence in Europe, although in 2002 they won't have as many ships in Europe as they originally planned (all scaled back after the tragedies of Sept 11, 2001). And Carnival, the big kahuna of the cruise industry, will inaugurate its new *Carnival Legend* in Europe in 2002—even though the line is offering only one sailing of the 2,100-passenger ship in Europe (in addition to a transatlantic voyage), the development is significant as it marks the first time the Caribbean cruise giant has entered the European market.

In Europe, the cruise lines offer all sorts of itinerary options and a variety of ships to suit everyone's tastes. And the European cruising season has expanded from April to October to March to December; there are even cruises offered now in the winter, mostly in the Mediterranean.

In 2001 (the latest year for which there are statistics), North Americans could choose from an estimated 1,233 Mediterranean sailings, up 8.35% from the year before. And for travelers interested in cruising other parts of Europe, there were some 899 cruising options, an increase of 15.85% from 2000. (Figures provided by the Cruise Line Coalition.)

A record 1.3 million North Americans were expected to hit the European seas in 2001, representing a 14% increase over the number of passengers in 2000, also a record-breaking year.

Because of this popularity and to encourage even more business, cruise companies are putting some of their most impressive ships in the market in 2002. Princess, for instance, has the 2,600-passenger *Golden Princess,* one of the biggest ships in the world, spending the entire summer in

A Note to Our Readers

In the wake of the tragic events of September 11, 2001, the cruise map of Europe in 2002, of the itineraries—of even the cruise *lines* themselves—has been significantly altered. European cruise itineraries, especially those in the eastern Mediterranean, were severely curtailed. One line, Renaissance Cruises, quickly announced its closure. Another, Silversea, put one of its ships in mothballs for the entire year of 2002. Some ships that were supposed to be in Europe in 2002 were redeployed to the Caribbean and Alaska. Other ships (although not all) were redeployed away from places like Greece and Turkey and instead put on itineraries in the Western Mediterranean, the Baltics, and Norway.

Cruise lines have scaled back their operations in Europe in 2002, but they have by no means abandoned it. Europe will rebound. Its hold on the hearts and minds of cruise aficionados will not be denied. In the meantime, there is still a grand array of itineraries and classes of ships in the market. As a precaution, though, check with your travel agent, or the cruise line itself, to confirm itineraries.

Europe. Holland America Line will introduce its newly acquired *Prinsendam* (formerly the *Seabourn Sun*) in Europe this year. Celebrity will do the same with its brand-new *Constellation,* and those on Europe cruises will be the first to see Royal Caribbean's new *Brilliance.* Posh Silversea will have three ships in Europe this summer, including its new 388-passenger *Silver Shadow* and *Silver Whisper.* And Radisson Seven Seas will have three ships in the market, including its biggest ship, the 700-passenger *Seven Seas Mariner,* which boasts cabins that are all suites with balconies.

You can see Europe on a giant floating **American resort ship** with Las Vegas–style entertainment, a lavish casino and spa, and a mostly American clientele; choose a ship that's more like a **floating European hotel** where multiple languages will be spoken, Americans will be the minority, and meals will be a form of entertainment; see the continent in posh **luxury** with the very best in service and cuisine; or pick a small, **casual ship** where you can jump off a platform at the stern for a swim.

And you can choose **itineraries** as diverse as the Rivieras, where the sun shines on cafes and beaches in places like St-Tropez; or the Norwegian fjords, where the midnight sun may shine all day and night, but you'll use that light to spot whales and reindeer rather than the rich and famous in their skimpy bikinis.

You can easily extend whatever itinerary you choose with a **land stay,** which the cruise lines can arrange for you, usually at reasonable rates, or which you can arrange on your own.

The lines are also expanding into different cruise regions in Europe and introducing more 1-week options in addition to more traditional 10- and 12-day Europe itineraries. For instance several lines have added 1-week Baltics itineraries.

Cruising in Europe has been a rather big-ticket item in the past, but a flurry of discount offers in 2001 helped bring **prices** down, and that trend is expected to continue in 2002, making cruising in Europe more affordable. And while Europe has traditionally drawn a senior crowd, the cruise lines, through shorter itineraries and a greater diversity of product, have done a good job of late in attracting families, younger couples, singles, and honeymooners.

BON VOYAGE!

Just the fact that you've bought the book means you've got a hankering to cruise; now it's our job to find the cruise that's just right for you from among the huge selection of ships and cruise experiences in the market. In the following chapters, we'll detail the various and diverse itinerary options in Europe and the types of ships that can take you there. And we'll give you a taste of what you can expect from your European cruise experience.

Whichever cruise option you choose, we're sure your Europe cruise will be an enlightening experience that will leave you wanting to come back again for more.

Frommer's Favorites

Whether you're looking for pampering and resort amenities or an off-the-beaten-track experience, cruise ships offer it in Europe. To make it easier for you to see what's what, we've put together a list of Frommer's Favorites—our picks for the best cruise experiences and offerings. You'll find full details on the ships in part 2, and full details on ports in part 3.

1 Best Ships for Luxury

- **Seabourn:** Small and intimate, Seabourn's sleek modern ships are floating pleasure palaces bathing all who enter in doting service and the finest cuisine at sea. You'll luxuriate in unprecedented amounts of onboard space and an almost 1 to 1 passenger/staff ratio, with service worthy of the grand hotels of Europe.
- **Silversea:** A little less high-brow than Seabourn and operating ships that are a little bigger (296 to 382 passengers against Seabourn's 204), Silversea still offers one of the most luxurious experiences around.
- **Crystal:** Crystal's dream ships offer the best of two worlds: pampering service and scrumptious cuisine on ships large enough to offer lots of outdoor deck space, generous fitness facilities, four restaurants, and over half a dozen bars and entertainment venues. Crystal's California ethic tends to keep things more mingly and chatty than aboard the more staid Seabourn.

2 Best Mainstream Ships

- **Celebrity:** While everyone's new ships are beautiful, Celebrity has proved itself above the norm, and we have no reason to doubt that the line's newest ship, *Constellation,* debuting in Europe this year, will carry on the tradition. We particularly like the fact that these ships have cutting-edge art collections. The dining rooms are stunning and feature wonderful French-inspired cuisine, and there are plenty of plush getaway areas including cigar and champagne bars.

3 Best Small Alternative Ships

- **Star Clippers:** These real sailing vessels offer a fun, wind-in-your-face experience in an environment that's surprisingly nice (you won't be roughing it!).
- **Clipper Cruise Line's *Clipper Adventurer:*** The *Clipper Adventurer* is another solid contender in this category—again, usually attracting an older crowd.

4 Best Ships for Families

- **Princess's *Golden Princess:*** Nothing beats the giant *Golden Princess* in this category. The 109,000-ton vessel has a spacious children's playroom, a fenced-in outside deck area designated as kids' space (with a kiddie pool and a fleet of red tricycles), and for older kids a teen center complete with computers, video games, a sound system, and even a teens-only hot tub and sunbathing area. Supervised activities are offered for those ages 2 to 17. The ship also has amenities designed to please adults and kids alike, including a pizzeria, basketball and volleyball courts, and a virtual-reality game room (including a motion-simulator ride).

5 Best European Ships

- **Costa:** Italian line Costa does the best overall package with interesting entertainment, fun activities, comfortable surroundings, and wonderful itineraries. The line's ownership by Carnival Corp. hasn't hurt it one bit.
- **P&O:** The British P&O—parent company of Princess Cruises—has a fleet of classy, beautiful ships sailing interesting itineraries. Entertainment is high quality, the onboard atmosphere is generally low-key, and dining is more varied than you'd expect, owing to infusions from the cuisines of Britain's former colonies (curries from India, for example).
- **Fred. Olsen:** British Fred. Olsen caters to a professional and/or early retired class of mostly British Europeans and offers a friendly atmosphere, fairly priced, aboard a couple of older ocean liner–style ships.
- **Swan Hellenic:** Swan Hellenic provides one of the strongest enrichment programs on the high seas, with four or five lecturers giving talks aboard, dining with the passengers, and accompanying them ashore. The non-repeating itineraries, generally lasting 2 weeks, attract a very loyal and generally well-educated British clientele for whom a standard cruise would never do. Good manners and a quiet approach to life reign.

6 Most Romantic Ships

- **Windstar:** Got to go with the sails here. Windstar's large sailing ships offer a product that's hard to beat for romance. You can snuggle in your comfy cabin watching movies on the VCR or on the deck, enjoy a romantic dinner for two in the open-seating restaurant, and go off hand-in-hand to explore the lovely ports.
- ***Sea Cloud:*** The gorgeous, historic sailing yacht *Sea Cloud* offers some of the most lavish fantasy-suites at sea.

7 Best Value

- **Orient Lines:** Orient Lines' product is solid, port-focused, and popular with an older clientele. Pre- and/or post-cruise hotel stays, airfare, sightseeing, and transfers are all included in the price.
- **First European:** This line's older ships (*Azur* and *Flamenco*) are

geared towards a budget-conscious crowd (1-week sailings are priced from only $700), and even the line's state-of-the-art newer vessels offer an informal and inexpensive way to see a bunch of neat European locales.

• **Norwegian Coastal Voyage:** Norwegian Coastal Voyage gives passengers a close-up view of Norway on working ships (they also carry cargo and vehicles) that are both comfortable and budget-priced.

8 Best Ships for Pampering

• **Crystal Cruises:** Crystal pampers all around, including in its nice spas.
• **Celebrity Cruises:** Celebrity's ships, including the new *Constellation,* offer AquaSpas with indoor thalassotherapy pools and a wealth of soothing and beautifying treatments that are hard to beat.
• **Royal Caribbean:** The *Splendour of the Seas* and *Brilliance of the Seas*

offer wonderful, soothing Ship-Shape spas with adjacent spacious solarium pool areas.

• **Princess's *Golden Princess:*** The *Golden Princess* reserves a good portion of the Sun Deck for pampering.
• **Costa's *CostaAtlantica:*** The spa on this stunning ship offers a big indoor whirlpool and sunning area.

9 Best Ships for Entertainment

• **Royal Caribbean:** The Las Vegas–style shows are well produced, with music provided by a big live band. You'll also find headliners, a variety of cabaret and lounge acts, and even classical music presentations.
• **Celebrity:** Aboard Celebrity's elegant modern ships you'll find well-produced musical reviews of the Broadway-show-tune variety, interactive entertainment like a magician who does card tricks at your table, and good cabaret acts.
• **Holland America:** Holland America offers some of the glitziest costumes afloat (in the show lounge), as well as a variety of cabaret acts including magicians, comedians, and illusionists. An added bonus is the crew talent show, which usually features folk song and dance from the Philippines and Indonesia.

• **Norwegian:** Ambitious show productions, sometimes featuring scenes from Broadway musicals, comedians, and juggling acts are the regular offerings, and excellent local entertainers, including folk dance troupes, come on board in some ports.
• **Princess:** The Las Vegas–style show productions are well executed and the cabaret singers excellent (sometimes including known performers). There are also quiet delights like pianists and jazz performers and fun acts like puppeteers and hypnotists.
• **Costa:** Show lounge presentations are creative and include attempts at modern ballet, plus lots of nighttime participatory activities like dance contests, a carnival, and even a Mr. Universe competition.

10 Best Cuisine

- **Crystal:** Crystal's cuisine is well-prepared and creative in the dining rooms and at buffets, but the very best is served in the alternative Asian restaurant, where the offerings include sushi. There's also a specialty Italian restaurant.
- **Seabourn:** The culinary experience on these ships—creative, flavorful, and well-presented—rivals any fine dining you can find on land.
- **Silversea:** Silversea offers excellent dining, not only in the main dining room but also at the informal buffets and in theme dinners like Italian, Chinese, and Southwestern.
- **Radisson:** The *Radisson Diamond* has one of the nicest dining rooms afloat and fine cuisine to match, with an emphasis on the regions where the ship is cruising. Cuisine on the *Mariner,* especially in the specialty Signatures restaurant, operated with Le Cordon Bleu, is among the best at sea.
- **Windstar:** Renowned Los Angeles chef Joachim Splichal advises on Windstar's creative "California cuisine" menus and wonderful presentation.
- **Celebrity:** Though it's not of the same caliber as the luxury lines, Celebrity, with its cuisine overseen by celebrity French chef Michel Roux, is certainly tops among the mainstream lines, offering elegant French-inspired dishes.
- **The French river barges:** The closest many of us can come to having a private chef, the French-trained chefs aboard these barges have the advantage of being able to incorporate great local ingredients in their menus.

11 Best Itinerary

- *Royal Princess:* For a comprehensive look at Western Europe, we like the *Royal Princess's* 12-day itinerary, round-trip from Dover, with port calls in Bilbao (Spain), Bordeaux (France), Glasgow (Scotland), Devon (England), Dublin and Cork (Ireland), Le Havre/Paris (France), Amsterdam (The Netherlands), and Zebrugge/Brussels (Belgium). For the off-the-beaten-path, try the Star Clipper's 7-day all Italy cruises, round-trip from Civitavecchia/Rome, with port calls in Paestum, Taormina, Lipari, Sorrento, and Palmarola.

12 Best Adventure Itineraries

- **Lindblad Expeditions:** Europe is not traditionally an adventure destination, but Special Expeditions has made inroads, including its offering of a soft adventure experience in the British Isles.
- **Norwegian Coastal Voyage:** Norwegian Coastal Voyage's ships sail as semi-cruise/semi-ferry ships between Bergen and Kirkenes (Norway), visiting no fewer than 34 ports (though sometimes the stops are incredibly short). There are also a few really adventurous itineraries offered by the company to Spitsbergen, an archipelago lying 360 miles north of Norway, in the Arctic.

13 Best Ports

- **Overall:** There are so many great ports in Europe it's hard to choose, but Fran's personal favorite is **Venice,** a city where every view is museum-quality. Jerry's is **London,** which he says is the greatest city in the world; it is visited by small ships (or you can get there on excursion from other ports including Southampton and Dover).
- **For Ancient History:** You can't top Athens or Rome and the ancient cities of Ephesus in Turkey and Pompeii in Italy.
- **For Shopping:** Fran heads to the French Riviera (Nice, Cannes, and Monaco) or ports in Italy (including Venice). Jerry hates to shop.
- **For Fun:** The French Riviera offers great art museums and, of course, beaches. Fun times can be had in Copenhagen, home of the famous Tivoli Gardens amusement park, and Amsterdam, a youthful city and happening place.
- **For Quaintness:** It's hard to beat Portofino, Italy.
- **For Drama:** The most dramatic port scene has to be Santorini, Greece.
- **Other Faves:** Barcelona is looking awful spiffy since it was fixed up for the Olympic Games; Lisbon is a perpetual favorite; and Istanbul's exotic (yet crowded) ambience always impresses. Bergen, Norway, is a surprise with its excellent museums and historic waterfront, and Edinburgh and Dublin offer the best of the British Isles (except for London).

14 Best Shore Excursions

- **Medieval walled cities:** St-Paul-de-Vence or Eze (France), Lindos on Rhodes (Greece), and Mdina (Malta) all offer medieval walled cities with cobblestone streets and quaint homes located on hilltops with gorgeous ocean views—and art galleries and other shopping options to boot.
- **City tours:** If you are at one of the ports close to London, Paris, Berlin, Rome, or Florence, take the shore excursion (or at the very least the bus transfer) to explore the city.
- **Ephesus, Turkey:** For ancient history, nothing beats Ephesus, the ancient city found under a mountain near Kuşadasi, Turkey.
- **Pompeii, Italy:** Tour this once-prosperous ancient city of 20,000, which was buried when Vesuvius erupted in A.D. 79. Today, nearly two-thirds of the city has been excavated, and the ruins are amazing.
- **Excursions from St. Petersburg, Russia:** In Russia, you can't tour without a visa unless you book a shore excursion. The best are the summer palaces of Peterhof or Pushkin, or the Hermitage (Winter Palace).
- **Zeeland and the Delta, the Netherlands:** For something totally different, Zeeland and the Delta give you a look at how the Netherlands has developed water management techniques, with a massive project of dams, canals, and dikes.
- **Nordkapp, Norway:** The excursion to the North Cape (Nordkapp), Norway, gives you the chance to see the northernmost accessible point in Europe.

Part 1

Planning, Booking & Preparing for Your Cruise

With advice on choosing and booking your ideal cruise and tips on getting ready for the cruise experience.

1 Choosing Your Ideal Cruise
2 Booking Your Cruise & Getting the Best Price
3 Things to Know Before You Go
4 The Cruise Experience

1

Choosing Your Ideal Cruise

There are many things you should consider before plunking down big bucks for the perfect European cruise. What kind of itinerary are you looking for and when do you want to go? What size ship will make you most comfortable and will its age matter? What special things should you know if you are a family traveler, a honeymooner, or a person with disabilities? European cruises come in all different styles to suit all different tastes, so the first step in ensuring that you'll have the best possible vacation is matching your expectations to the appropriate itinerary and ship. In this chapter, we'll explore the differences between your various European cruise options.

1 The European Cruise Season

The European cruise season is generally considered to be April to November, although some lines operate into December, and even year-round in the Mediterranean. April, early May, and November/December are considered shoulder season, and lower fares are usually offered during these months. High season is the summer months.

If you are considering traveling in the shoulder season, keep in mind that some visitor facilities will operate during more limited hours, and some—say, in the Greek Isles—may not be open at all. The least expensive cruises are typically the first and last runs of the season, though these have their own charm: Specifically, you'll avoid the big tourist crush, which can really make a difference in some port towns. During the high season in Venice, for instance, you can't swing a stick without hitting a family from Duluth.

WEATHER

Europe is a continent of distinct seasons, but, just as in the U.S., there can be great variations in temperature from one part to another. The warmest months are July and August. August is the month when many Europeans go on vacation, and when beaches and other resort facilities will be particularly packed.

Here's the typical summer weather you can expect to encounter by region (all temperatures are measured in °F):

- **Britain & Ireland** Average temperatures in the low- to mid-60s (may be milder in Ireland). August, September, and October tend to be the sunniest months.
- **Scandinavia** Average temperatures above the Arctic Circle in the mid-50s; in the south, in the 70s (Denmark tends to be the mildest). It may be rainy in the fjords.
- **Holland & Belgium** Average temperatures in the high 60s in Holland and Germany (may be rainy in May); in the low 70s in Belgium (sunniest in July and Aug).

What Time Is It?

Want to know what time it is at home? Based on U.S. Eastern Standard Time, Britain, Ireland, and Portugal are 5 hours ahead, Greece and Estonia are 7 hours ahead, and western Russia is 8. The rest of the countries in this book are 6 hours ahead. The European countries observe daylight saving time, but not necessarily on the same day or in the same month as in the U.S.

- **France**   Average temperatures in the mid-70s in Paris; can be hot in the Riviera (high 80s or above).
- **The Baltics**   Average temperatures in the 70s (the best weather is in late summer).
- **Italy, Greece, Spain, Portugal & Turkey**   Temperatures in the high 80s or higher, but there may be nice breezes along the coast. Portugal tends to be cooler (more like mid-70s), but also rainier. Greece and Turkey are the hottest, and if you're not a hot-weather lover, you're better off visiting these countries in mid-April to June or mid-September to the end of October.

2 European Cruise Itineraries

There's really no such thing as a standard European itinerary. Instead, the cruises focus on specific regions and sometimes more than one region. And there are many variations on each theme. A cruise of the Norwegian fjords, for instance, may depart from Bergen, Norway. Or it may depart from London or Copenhagen.

TYPICAL CRUISE ITINERARIES

The Greek Isles/Eastern Mediterranean   The Aegean Sea and sometimes the Adriatic as well, with port calls in the Greek islands (Rhodes, Santorini, Mykonos, etc.), in Athens, in Kuşadasi, Turkey, and sometimes in Istanbul. Some of the cruises also visit Dubrovnik or other ports in Croatia.

Western Mediterranean   The area from Barcelona or Lisbon to Rome and including port calls in Spain, France, and Italy.

The Rivieras   The French Riviera (with ports such as St-Tropez), Monte Carlo, and small Italian Riviera ports (such as Portofino). May also include Rome.

Scandinavia & Russia   The Baltic Sea; Copenhagen, Denmark; Stockholm, Sweden; Helsinki, Finland; Tallinn, Estonia; and St. Petersburg, Russia. May also include Oslo.

The British Isles   England, Scotland, Wales, and Ireland, and sometimes France; sailing in the North Sea, Irish Sea, and English Channel.

Norway & the Fjords   Norway from Bergen up to Honningsvag and the North Cape.

The Black Sea   The area from Athens or Istanbul to Yalta, with port calls in Bulgaria, Romania, and the Ukraine. May be combined with the Red Sea (Egypt and Israel).

SPECIAL ITINERARIES

THE BEST OF EUROPE   One of the best ways to see Europe if you've never been here before is on one of the 2-week cruises that visit the major cities. These cruises tend to combine aspects of the above itineraries to give passengers a comprehensive (albeit quick) look at Europe. Princess, for example, does a 12-day Western Europe itinerary, round-trip from Dover (England) with port calls in Bilbao (Spain), Bordeaux (France), Glasgow (Scotland), Devon (England), Dublin and Cork (Ireland), Le Havre/Paris (France), Amsterdam (The Netherlands), and Zeebrugge/Brussels (Belgium).

And there are some Grand Mediterranean–type sailings that include the *Royal Princess*'s 12-day Med: from Venice to Barcelona, with port calls in Monte Carlo (Monaco), Livorno and Naples (Italy), Athens (Greece), and Kuşadası and Istanbul (Turkey). You can extend your stay with hotel nights in Venice and Barcelona.

RIVER CRUISES   Europe's inland waterways offer a wealth of cruise opportunities on smaller vessels specifically designed for river and canal travel, including luxurious barges that ply the waterways of inland France, Holland, Belgium, and England, offering a close-up view of the local culture.

There are also larger river ships in France, Holland, Belgium, Germany, Austria, and the former Soviet counties, as well as in Italy and Portugal.

COMPARING ITINERARIES
LENGTH OF CRUISE

In choosing a region or regions to visit, you will obviously have to consider the length of cruise you want to take. Itineraries in Europe range from a few days to several weeks. The shortest cruises, **3- and 4-day offerings,** can be found mostly in the Greek Isles and on inland waterways. Norwegian Coastal Voyages also does 5- and 6-day cruises in Norway. **One-week cruises** are regularly offered in the Greek Isles/Eastern Mediterranean, in the Western Mediterranean, in the British Isles, in Norway, in the French and Italian Rivieras, and on Europe's inland waterways. There are also 1-week sailings in the Baltics and other regions. But more common in most parts of Europe are **10- and 12-day cruises.** The longest cruise itineraries include several different regions.

TIME IN PORT & TIME AT SEA

It's important when comparing the various itineraries to make sure there will be enough time in port for what you came to see and do. Some ships even overnight in key ports such as Venice, Monte Carlo, or Istanbul to give you time to both explore and enjoy the local nightlife. Alternative ships may spend most evenings in port.

Keep in mind that visiting a port a day in an exciting region like Greece, where there are so many ancient sites to see, can be exhausting. And some of the ships make more than one port call a day. Experienced cruisers will know some of the most relaxing times to be had on ships are lazy days at sea, and consequently often choose an itinerary that spends a day or two without a port call.

MATCHING YOUR HABITS TO YOUR DESTINATION

Some ports are better for certain things than others. Here's a short rundown (see part 3, "The Ports of Call," for more detailed information).

PORTS FOR SHOPPERS

London, Paris, Rome, and all the other major cities; Nice and Cannes, France; Venice, Italy.

PORTS FOR BEACH LOVERS

Cannes and St-Tropez, France; Mykonos and Rhodes, Greece; Málaga and Palma, Spain.

PORTS FOR ANTIQUITIES

Kuşadasi, Turkey (Ephesus); Sorrento (Pompeii); Athens (the Parthenon); Rome (the Colosseum, etc.).

PORTS FOR NATURE BUFFS

Norway (especially above the Arctic Circle); British coastal areas.

SHORE EXCURSIONS: THE WHAT, WHY & HOW

No matter what size ship you're on or what its itinerary is, you can choose from a variety of shore excursions at any given port, ranging in price from around $30 to more than $200 per person. The most popular are city tours, which typically highlight the historic and scenic attractions in each port city. Other, pricier tours take you beyond the port city to inland attractions.

We enjoy exploring port cities on our own and take only those tours that go further inland, but that's just us. It's a personal choice.

On the big ships, excursions can sell out quickly, so don't dawdle if you know what you want; sign up before the trip (if the cruise line allows you to do so), or on the first or second day of the cruise. Because of the large numbers of passengers on large ships, be prepared for some waiting around as each jumbo-sized tour group is herded from the ship to the waiting fleet of buses or minivans.

On smaller ships, there's usually room on the excursions to accommodate all passengers on board, and the excursions may even be included in your cruise fare (in which case 100% attendance is not uncommon). The whole process is saner, and group sizes are most likely smaller.

Whatever the size of the ship, the attraction itself, quality of the tour guide, and execution of the tour are what determine whether you have an enjoyable time.

Indulging Your Obsessions at Sea: Theme Cruises

As cruise lines look for more ways to attract passengers with unique onboard activities, theme cruises—focused on everything from food and wine to song and dance—are growing in popularity. **Crystal,** for instance, features an annual series of food and wine cruises where well-known chefs and sommeliers conduct demonstrations and tastings on board. **Fred. Olsen's** ships host sailings themed on wine, bridge, photography, Latin dance, antiques, and other topics. **Holland America** does an annual big band cruise in Europe. **Cunard** offers an impressive roster that includes such topics as art, jazz, literature, comedy, classical music, film, theater, opera, cooking, antiques, and dance, especially on its transatlantic *QE2* sailings. **Silversea** features golf-themed cruises with play on courses throughout Europe (including St. Andrews in Scotland) and designated cruises themed on culinary arts or classical music.

In chapter 2, we list the pros and cons of taking shore excursions, and in chapters 11 and 12, we list both the best shore excursions and the top sights you can see on your own.

3 Choosing Your Ship

After choosing your itinerary, picking the right ship is the number-one factor in ensuring you get the vacation you're looking for. As we've said, cruise ships operating in Europe range from **small alternative-type vessels** to **resort-like megaships,** with the cruise experience varying widely depending on the type of ship you select. There are casual cruises and luxury cruises; educational cruises where you attend lectures; soft adventure cruises that explore remote areas and offer water-sports opportunities; and resortlike cruises where massages and Las Vegas–style shows are the order of the day.

You'll need to decide what overall cruise experience you want. Type of cruise is even more important than price. After all, what kind of bargain is a party cruise if what you're looking for is a quiet time? Your fantasy vacation may be someone else's nightmare, and vice versa.

BIG SHIP OR SMALL?

When comparing ship sizes, think of the difference between a small New England inn and a big resort hotel in Miami. A ship's size, like that of a hotel, greatly determines its personality and the kind of vacation you'll have. Big ships tend to be busy, exciting affairs, while the smaller ships are most often low-key retreats with unique personalities.

THE BIG SHIPS

Big ships operating in Europe vary in size and scope, and include everything from classic cruise ships to massive new megaships. They all offer a comfortable cruising experience, with virtual armies of service employees overseeing your well-being. Ship stabilizers assure smooth sailing and all have plenty of deck space from which you can take in the coastal sights.

Due to their deeper drafts (the amount of ship below the waterline), the biggest of the big ships can't get to some of the islands and small ports that smaller ships may visit. However, the more powerful engines on these ships allow them to visit more ports during each trip, and shore excursions allow you to more closely explore different aspects of the port's history and culture. (A downside, however, is that disembarkation at ports can be a lengthy process because there are so many passengers wanting to visit the ports.)

The itineraries of these ships tend to be the tried-and-true routes sailed by many other vessels.

The classic-style ships (some of which are really mid-sized in today's market) embrace their nautical history and don't look as much like floating Hyatt hotels as the bigger megaships (see below). Classic-style ships may be older vessels (and some tattered ones at that) or they may be modern ships designed to appeal to those who don't want everything quite so big and glitzy. These ships, operated by both European and American companies, range from budget to luxurious. On the more expensive of these ships, the crowd will be older and more refined, and take formal nights seriously. On the more moderately priced ships in Europe you'll find lots of middle-class Europeans and family travelers (as well as value-conscious Americans) and generally a more casual atmosphere.

Megaships are newer, are bigger (the biggest cruising in Europe holds more than 2,600 passengers), and offer the latest and greatest. They're glitzy American-style floating resorts and, with the exception of those operated by Costa, attract more Americans than Europeans. The atmosphere is casual during the day, with a few formal nights so you can really put on the ritz.

Both the classic-style ships and the megaships have all the facilities you can imagine on a cruise ship. There are swimming pools, health clubs, spas (of various sizes), nightclubs, movie theaters, shops, casinos, bars, and children's playrooms. In some cases—especially on the megaships—you'll also find sports decks, virtual golf, computer rooms, and cigar clubs, as well as quiet spaces where you can get away from it all. There are so many rooms you won't likely feel claustrophobic.

These ships have big dining rooms and buffet areas serving more food with more variety and at more times (including midnight) than you can think about, much less eat. There might also be additional eating venues such as pizzerias, hamburger grills, ice-cream parlors, alternative restaurants, wine bars, champagne bars, caviar bars, and patisseries.

In most cases, these ships have lots of onboard activities to keep you occupied when you're not in port, including games and contests, classes, children's programs, and lectures (possibly by archaeologists and historians). The activities are somewhat lower key than they would be in, say, the Caribbean, where the crowd is more party-hearty. These ships also offer a variety of entertainment options that might even include celebrity headline acts, and usually include stage show productions, some quite sophisticated (particularly on ships run by American companies).

Cabins, in many cases, offer modern comforts such as TVs and telephones, and some even have personal safes and minibars. The cabins themselves might be cubbyholes or large suites, depending on the ship and the cabin level you book. On most of these ships, options will include picture windows and private verandas.

These ships carry a lot of people, and as such can at times feel crowded—and there may occasionally be lines at the buffets and in other public areas. On the other hand, you aren't stuck with the same faces for your whole cruise.

THE SMALL & ALTERNATIVE SHIPS

Just as big cruise ships are mostly for people who want every resort amenity, small or alternative ships are best suited for people who prefer a casual, crowd-free cruise experience that gives them a chance to get up-close-and-personal with Europe's coastal offerings.

Thanks to their smaller size, these ships can offer a yacht-like experience (some of them even have sails) and can go places that larger ships can't, such as islands and smaller ports that cater mostly to yachts and small fishing vessels. The decks on these ships are closer to the waterline, too, giving passengers a more intimate view than from the high decks of the large cruise ships. These ships tend to hug the coast, and in Europe they usually visit a port a day (although some spend a day or two at sea exploring areas of natural beauty).

The alternative ship experience comes with a sense of adventure, although it's usually adventure of a soft rather than rugged sort, and offers a generally casual cruise experience: There are usually no dress-up nights, the food may be rather simply prepared, and because there are so few public areas to choose from—usually only one or two small lounges—camaraderie tends to develop more

SHIP SIZE COMPARISONS

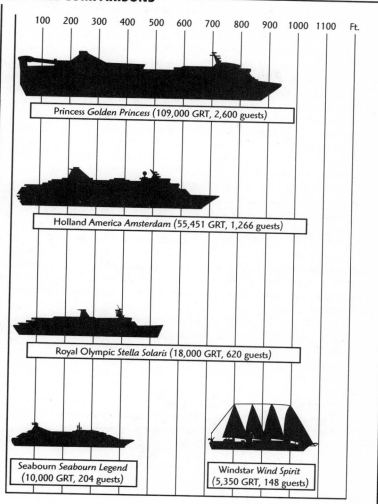

100   200   300   400   500   600   700   800   900   1000   1100   Ft.

Princess *Golden Princess* (109,000 GRT, 2,600 guests)

Holland America *Amsterdam* (55,451 GRT, 1,266 guests)

Royal Olympic *Stella Solaris* (18,000 GRT, 620 guests)

Seabourn *Seabourn Legend*
(10,000 GRT, 204 guests)

Windstar *Wind Spirit*
(5,350 GRT, 148 guests)

Ships selected for this chart are representative of the various size vessels sailing in Europe for 2000. See the specifications tables accompanying every ship review in chapters 5–9 to see the approximate comparative size of all the ships not shown here. (GRT = gross register tons, a measure that takes into account interior space used to produce revenue on a vessel. One GRT = 100 cubic feet of enclosed, revenue-generating space.)

Leading Websites for Cruise Planning

Check out the cruise line sites for information on their products. Some are amazing, giving you everything from their ships' itineraries and prices (the site for Peter Dielmann EuropeAmerica Cruises is particularly impressive in this regard; **www.deilmann-cruises.com**) to virtual tours (the Holland America site, for instance, at **www.hollandamerica. com**). Be aware, though, that most cruise lines do not accept bookings on their sites, preferring that you make your actual reservation through a travel agent (see more in chapter 2).

This aside, the cruise line sites (listed in chapters 5–9 in the individual cruise line reviews) will give you some great visual reference points, and the following independent sites can provide other valuable information as you plan your cruise.

- **www.cdc.gov/travel**   Twice each year, the Centers for Disease Control's Vessel Sanitation Program rates sanitary conditions aboard all ships that have foreign itineraries and carry 13 or more passengers. Access this link for the latest test results. (*Note:* Since the CDC is a U.S. agency, some ships in this book won't be rated in their listings.)
- **www.cruising.org**   Cruise Lines International Association (CLIA), the U.S. cruise industry's marketing arm, maintains a website that lists CLIA-affiliated travel agencies, links to the member cruise lines, and more.
- **www.cruise-news.com**   Cruise News gives news on seasonal and themed cruises and information about upcoming launches of new ships. You'll also find links to agents who specialize in selling cruise vacations.
- **www.cruisemates.com**   The Cruisemates site contains ship reviews, information for first-time cruisers, bargain offers, and lots of opportunities to chat with other cruise aficionados.
- **www.cruiseopinion.com**   The most valuable part of CruiseOpinion. com is the section of passenger reviews. Most people who comment include their age, occupation, and number of cruises they've taken, and some add their e-mail address so you can send follow-up questions. This site is a fine example of travelers getting online to help one another.
- **www.porthole.com**   The website of *Porthole* cruise magazine offers light feature articles on cruising and a great list of cruise links.
- **www.cruisecritic.com** (or AOL keyword: cruise critic)   This site offers reviews, useful tips, chat opportunities, and postings of cruise bargains.
- **www.sealetter.com**   This well-stocked website, managed by a husband-and-wife travel agent team, features a lot of reader ship reviews, cruise tips, and loads of great cruise links.
- **www.steinerleisure.com**   Steiner runs most of the onboard spas in the cruise industry. Via their site, you can get a preview of the spa treatments you'll find aboard ship.

quickly between passengers on these ships than aboard larger vessels, which can be as anonymous as a big city.

Cabins may not offer TVs or telephones and tend to be very small, and in some cases downright spartan. Meals are generally served in a single, open seating, and dress codes are usually nonexistent.

Instead of aerobics and pool games (featured on the big ships), these ships may offer a brisk walk around the deck or, on some ships, the opportunity to enjoy water sports right from the ship. And the alternative ships more frequently feature expert lectures on archaeology, history, and other intellectual pursuits.

There are no stabilizers on most of these smaller ships, and the ride can be bumpy in open water. There are also often no elevators, making cruises on most of these ships a bit difficult for travelers with disabilities. And the alternative ship lines do not offer specific activities or facilities for children, although you still may find a few families on some of these vessels.

4 Matching the Cruise to Your Needs

CRUISES FOR FAMILIES

European cruises have become increasingly popular with families, including intergenerational gatherings: parents traveling with their kids and the grandparents, too. The lines are responding with youth counselors and supervised programs, fancy playrooms, and even video game rooms to keep the kids entertained while their parents relax. At night, most ships offer babysitting (for an extra charge). Some lines offer reduced rates for kids, though it's important to note that most lines discourage passengers from bringing infants.

ACTIVITIES   Ask whether a supervised program will be offered when you plan to cruise; sometimes such programs are only operated if there are a certain number of kids on board. Depending on the program, the youngest children may frolic in toy- and game-stocked playrooms, listen to stories, and go on treasure hunts; older kids have options like arts and crafts, computer games, lip-synch competitions, pool games, and volleyball; and teenagers can mingle at teen parties or hang out at the video arcade. The megas have large playrooms with computer stations and video games as well as shelves of toys. There's usually a TV showing movies throughout the day and, for the younger ones, there are ball bins and plastic jungle gyms. Many megaships have shallow kiddie pools, sometimes sequestered on an isolated patch of deck.

BABYSITTING   Babysitting is offered on most large cruise ships from around 8pm to 2am. Private in-cabin babysitting by a crew member is a steep $8 to $10 per hour for two kids (and there may be a 4-hr. minimum). There may also be a group babysitting option.

FAMILY-FRIENDLY CABINS   A family of four can share a cabin that has bunk-style third and fourth berths, which pull out of the walls just above the pair of regular beds (some even have a fifth berth), but there's no two ways to slice it: A standard cabin with four people in it will be cramped. However, when you consider how little time you'll spend in the cabin, it's do-able. The obvious incentive to share one cabin is the price: Whether children or adults, the rates for third and fourth people sharing a cabin with two full-fare (or even discounted) passengers are usually about half of the lowest regular rates. On occasion there are special deals and further discounts. If you can afford it, and if space equals sanity in your book, consider booking a suite, many of which have

Family Cruising Tips

Here are some suggestions for smoother sailing on your family cruise.

- **Ask about children's amenities.** Check in advance with the cruise line to make sure the ship you're sailing offers things your child might need. Are cribs available? Children's menus?
- **Pack some basic first-aid supplies plus any medications your doctor may suggest, and even a thermometer.** Cruise lines have limited supplies of these items (and charge for them, too) and can quickly run out if the ship has many families aboard. If an accident should happen aboard, virtually every ship afloat has its own infirmary staffed by doctors and/or nurses. Keep in mind, first aid can usually be summoned more readily aboard ship than in port.
- **Warn younger children about the danger of falling overboard and make sure they know not to play on the railings.**
- **When in port, prearrange a meeting spot.** If your child is old enough to go off on his or her own, pick a meeting spot either on board or on land, and meet there well before the ship is scheduled to depart to make sure no one is still ashore.
- **Make sure your kids know their cabin number and what deck it's on.** The endless corridors and doors on the megas look exactly alike.
- **Prepare kids for TV letdown.** If your kids are TV addicts, you might want to make sure your cabin will have a TV and VCR. And even if it does, they should be prepared for a little bit of withdrawal, since televisions on ships just don't have 200 channels of cable—you'll be lucky to get five or eight channels. On the bright side, big ships are likely to have nightly movies and a video arcade.

a pullout couch in the living room. Families with older kids can always consider booking two separate cabins with connecting doors. Lots of ships, big and small, have them. You'll be close to each other, but separate.

TAKING THE KIDS ON SMALL SHIPS   The big new ships are certainly most prepared for families, but if your children are at least 10 or 12, some of the casual, alternative cruises can be loads of fun and educational to boot. While you won't find a kids' playroom stuffed with toys, the experience of visiting a culturally rich port of call every day or learning (on sailing vessels) about nautical knots and winches will help keep you and the kids from going stir-crazy on board.

CRUISES FOR SINGLE TRAVELERS

For singles, a nice thing about cruises is that you needn't worry about dining alone, since you'll be seated with other guests (if you don't want to be, seek a ship with alternative dining options). You also needn't worry much about finding people to talk to, since the general atmosphere on nearly all ships is very congenial and allows you to easily find conversation, especially during group activities. And the ship may even host a party to give singles a chance to get to know one another and/or offer social hosts as dance partners.

The downside is that you may have to pay more for the cruise experience than those sharing a room. Since cruise line rates are based on two people per cabin, some lines charge a "single supplement" rate (which sounds like a deal, but it's *you* who pays the supplement) that ranges from 110% to an outrageous 200% of the per-person, double-occupancy fare. As a single person, you have two choices: Find a line with a reasonable single supplement rate or ask if the line has a cabin-share program, under which the line will pair you with another single so you can get a lower rate. You may not be able to get much information about your roommate before the sailing, although all lines match gender and most also try to match age. Some lines also offer a single guarantee program, which means if they can't find you a roommate, they'll book you in a cabin alone but still honor the shared rate. On some older ships (including the *QE2*) and a few small ships, there are special cabins designated for single travelers, and in some cases they carry no additional charge. But keep in mind that these cabins, originally designed on the older ships for nannies or maids accompanying passengers, are really, really small, and that they tend to sell out fast.

To increase your chances of meeting other singles, book a cruise through a travel company that specializes in bringing singles together. These companies include **Cruiseman** (℃ 800/805-0053; www.cruiseman.com) and **Discount Travel Club** (℃ 800/393-5000; www.singlecruise.com). Such firms coordinate groups of as few as 30 or as many as 300 singles on specific sailings, and typically have a tour coordinator on board to organize mixers and make sure people get a chance to meet. Singles in these groups tend to be in their 30s to 50s (of course, some may be younger or older).

CRUISES FOR TRAVELERS WITH DISABILITIES

Cruise lines, due in no small part to public pressure, have made an effort in recent years to make their ships more accessible to travelers with disabilities. It is not uncommon on the newest ships to find two dozen or more wheelchair-accessible cabins with such features as wide doors, handrails, and low sinks.

On older ships, however, the shipboard experience remains a struggle. You may encounter doors that are too narrow and other frustrations such as entranceways with lips (to prevent flooding). You may even find that some public rooms are simply not accessible. And smaller ships might not have elevators, much less accessible cabins.

If you are a traveler with a disability, it is important to let the cruise line know your special needs when you make your booking. If you use a wheelchair, you'll need to know if wheelchair-accessible cabins are available (and how they're equipped), as well as whether public rooms are accessible and can be reached by elevator; I've noted this information in the cabin sections of the ship reviews in chapters 5 to 9. Be aware that the cruise line may also have special policies regarding travelers with disabilities—for instance, some require that you be accompanied by an able-bodied companion.

Travelers with disabilities should also inquire when they're booking whether the ship docks at ports or uses tenders (small boats) to go ashore. Tenders cannot always accommodate wheelchairs. Also, once on board, travelers with disabilities will want to seek the advice of the tour staff before choosing shore excursions, as not all will be wheelchair-friendly.

If you have a chronic health problem, we advise you to check with your doctor before booking the cruise, and, if you have any specific needs, to notify the cruise line in advance. This will ensure that the medical team on the ship is properly prepared to offer assistance.

A handful of experienced travel agencies specialize in booking cruises and tours for travelers with disabilities. **Accessible Journeys,** 35 W. Sellers Ave., Ridley Park, PA 19078 (© **800/846-4537;** www.disabilitytravel.com), publishes a newsletter and can even provide licensed health-care professionals to accompany those who require aid.

CRUISES FOR GAY & LESBIAN TRAVELERS

There are a number of gay-friendly cruises and special charter sailings for gay men and lesbians. For details, contact these specialists:

- **RSVP Cruises,** 2800 University Ave. SE, Minneapolis, MN 55414 (© **800/328-7787;** www.rsvp.net)
- **Pied Piper Travel,** 330 W. 42nd St., Ste. 1804, New York, NY 10036 (© **800/TRIP-312;** www.piedpiper.com)
- **Olivia Cruises and Resorts,** 4400 Market St., Oakland, CA 94608 (© **800/631-6277;** www.oliviacruises.com); caters specifically to lesbians

You can also contact the **International Gay & Lesbian Travel Association,** 52 W. Oakland Park Blvd. no. 237, Wilton Manors, FL 33311; © **800/ 448-8550;** www.iglta.org, which has over 1,000 travel industry members. You might want to check out *Frommer's Gay & Lesbian Europe,* the well-known *Out & About* travel newsletter ($49 for 1 yr.; to subscribe, call © **800/ 929-2268** or visit www.outandabout.com), or *Our World* travel magazine ($35 a yr.; to subscribe, call © **904/441-5367** or visit www.ourworldpublishing. com), for articles, tips, and listings on gay and lesbian travel.

CRUISES FOR HONEYMOONERS

Most 1-week cruises depart on either Saturday or Sunday, although there are some exceptions. You'll want to look carefully at sailing times as you plan your wedding weekend. You will also want to make sure that the ship offers double, queen-, or king-size beds, and you may want to book a cabin with a tub or Jacuzzi. Rooms with private verandas are particularly romantic. You can take in the sights in privacy, and even enjoy a private meal, assuming the veranda is big enough for a table and chairs (some are not) and that the weather doesn't turn chilly. If you want to dine alone each night, make sure the dining room offers

---

Weddings at Sea

Cruise ship captains generally only conduct marriage ceremonies in movies and on television, but Princess's *Golden Princess* is an exception. The ship has its own wedding chapels and a captain who is willing and able to lead the proceedings. And your friends back home can even watch the ceremony via the Internet thanks to the line's special Wedding Cam. Princess offers wedding packages that include a ceremony, flowers, music, cake, champagne, and other niceties, priced from $1,400 (plus your cruise fare). Keep in mind that you will need to make the ceremony and party arrangements and get a license in advance (a spur-of-the-moment wedding at sea is another thing that only exists on movies and television).

Already married? Check out the lines' romantic vow-renewal ceremony packages.

tables for two and/or that the ship offers room service (your travel agent can fill you in on these matters). You may also want to inquire as to the likelihood that there will be other honeymooners your age on the ship. Some ships—among them those of Princess, Royal Caribbean, Costa, Celebrity, and Holland America—offer add-on honeymoon packages that provide champagne, a fruit basket, and the like. Most lines will offer special perks, like an invitation to a private honeymooners' cocktail party, if you let them know in advance that you will be celebrating your special event on the ship.

High-end lines, such as Windstar, Radisson Seven Seas, Seabourn, Cunard, and Crystal, don't offer special cocktail parties, but their ultra-deluxe amenities are especially pleasing to honeymooners. From terrycloth bathrobes and slippers that await you in walk-in closets to whirlpool bathtubs, five-course dinners served in your cabin, stocked minibars, and high crew-to-passenger ratios (meaning more personalized service), extra-special touches are business as usual on these upscale lines.

2

Booking Your Cruise & Getting the Best Price

Cruise prices are not always the easiest things to figure out, and cruises in Europe can run you big bucks, but the first important rule to remember is that **few people pay full price.** The retail price quoted in the brochure is the optimum price the cruise line hopes to get for the cruise—like the sticker price on a new car—rather than the price it really *expects* to get. There are all sorts of deals out there, and virtually all the lines offer early-booking discounts, which can offer huge savings if you book at least 3 months in advance of your sailing date. The best way to find the best deals is through an experienced cruise travel agent.

In this chapter, we'll point you in the right direction for finding the best fare, keeping costs down, and choosing a good agent, and clue you in on what's included in your "all-inclusive" fare and what's not. We'll also provide some guidance about choosing a cabin and dining-room seating time.

1 The Scoop on Cruise Fares

FINDING THE BEST FARE

The best way to save on a European cruise is to **book in advance.** Cruise itineraries are usually printed 10 to 12 months ahead of the season, so there's ample time to find the right cruise; most lines offer early-bird discounts that generally amount to 10% to 50% off, but sometimes reach as high as 60% (for a limited number of cabin types). Policies for the rates also vary, but generally you have a good chance of qualifying for the deals (which are offered in limited numbers on a first-come, first-served basis) by booking at least 3 months in advance (though some cabin categories may even sell out 6–9 months in advance). If cabins aren't selling, the lines may even extend the early-booking deadlines closer in to the sailing dates.

Booking early gives you the advantage of getting first pick on cabins (the cheapest and most expensive ones tend to sell out first). And, if you are booking your own air, you have a better chance of getting a deal from the airlines.

If cabins are still not filled up as the season begins, the cruise lines will start marketing **last-minute deals,** usually through their top-producing travel agents. One couple we heard about booked a last-minute 12-day cruise for two for $700! Keep in mind, though, that last-minute deals require a certain amount of flexibility. Your desired sailing date may sell out, and even if it doesn't, you will have to take whatever cabin is still available. Also, you may have trouble getting a good last-minute deal on your airfare. And most last-minute deals are completely nonrefundable.

You can also save by booking a cruise in the **shoulder months** of April, early May, and November or early December, when pricing is usually less than in the

Price Protection

It's a little-known fact that if the price of your cabin category goes down after you've booked it, most cruise lines will make up the difference, in effect giving you the lowest rates. The cruise lines won't call you with this information, but a diligent travel agent will monitor the rates and contact the cruise line for you if the rates go down.

summer peak season. For lines that operate in Europe year-round, winter, with the exception of the Christmas and New Year's holiday periods, is bargain time.

And keep in mind that the lines also tend to offer cut rates when they are **introducing a new ship** or **new itinerary** in a market. So it pays to keep track of what's happening in the industry—or to have your agent do so. You should be aware, though, that several new ships have experienced construction delays and have had to cancel their maiden voyages and inaugural sailings, sometimes only weeks ahead of time. Of course passengers on those cancelled sailings were well compensated with refunds, big discounts on their rebooked cruise, and the like, but if you want to try a brand-new ship, some flexibility may be required.

STANDARD SAVINGS FOR THIRD & FOURTH PASSENGERS

Most ships offer standard discounts for third and/or fourth passengers sharing a cabin with two full-fare passengers. These discounts are designed for families and others who don't mind the closeness sharing a cabin brings. Generally, the first two in a cabin are booked at a regular fare, with the third and fourth passengers booked at a highly discounted rate. If you are four adults traveling together, you can add the four rates together and divide by four to get your per-person fare.

Some lines offer **special rates for kids,** usually on a seasonal or select-sailings basis, that may include free or discounted airfare. Kids under age 2 usually cruise for free.

GROUP RATES

One of the best ways to get a cruise deal is to book as a group (generally at least 16 people in a minimum of 8 cabins), so you may want to get a family reunion together or convince your friends or colleagues that they need a vacation, too. The savings include not only a discounted rate, but at the least, the cruise portion of the 16th ticket will be free (on some upscale ships you can negotiate a free ticket for groups of eight or more). The gang can split the proceeds from the free ticket, or, just for the fun of it, hold a drawing for the ticket, maybe at a cocktail party on the first night. If your group is large enough you may be able to get that cocktail party—or perhaps some other onboard amenities—for free as well.

SENIOR DISCOUNTS

Seniors may be able to get extra savings on their cruise. Some lines will take 5% off the top for those 55 and up, and the senior rate applies even if the second person in the cabin is younger. Membership in groups such as AARP is not required, but may bring additional savings.

Tour operators who sell cruise packages to seniors may book blocks of cabins and offer group discounts. One well-known operator is **Grand Circle Travel,** 347 Congress St., Boston, MA 02210 (© **800/955-1034** or 617/350-7500;

www.gct.com). You can write to them for a free booklet called "101 Tips for the Mature Traveler."

GOOD DEALS FOR THOSE WHO CAN'T GET ENOUGH

If you've been on a cruise before and are traveling with the same line, you may qualify for a **repeat-passenger discount** or other perks. Policies vary by line, but repeat-passenger discounts generally range from 5% to 20% (you may have to take several cruises to qualify); repeaters might also get invitations to private shipboard cocktail parties, priority check-in, and cabin upgrades (and nearly every line sends its repeaters enticing direct-mail pieces). *Note:* If you sail on any of Carnival Corporation's lines, which include Carnival, Holland America Line, Seabourn, Cunard, Costa, and Windstar, you can qualify for a past-passenger discount on a sister line.

If you want to visit more than one region, you can usually get a good deal by booking two cruises **back-to-back** (you stay on the ship for more than one sailing).

Or, if you like your European cruise so much you decide you want to vacation here again, consider **booking another cruise on the ship.** Cruise lines, making the most of their captive audiences, may pitch you to make future vacation plans while still on board, with discounts—usually 5%. Before you sign on the dotted line, though, *make sure the on-the-spot discount can be combined with other offers you might find later.* Keep in mind if you do choose to book on board you can still do the reconfirmation and ticketing through your travel agent by giving the cruise line his or her name.

MORE DEALS

Cruise lines market Europe cruises with **free hotel** stays and, in some cases, **free airfare** offers. You may also see **two-for-one** deals or offers that tack a few **free days** on to a cruise (such as 14 days for the price of 12). Be sure to evaluate these deals carefully by adding up the total amount you would spend with the line for your cruise, hotel, and airfare and comparing it to offers by competing lines. Make sure you are comparing apples and apples.

Repositioning cruises, such as when a ship repositions from the western Mediterranean to the Greek Isles, may be value-priced. Because these cruises tend to cover greater distances than standard cruises they usually offer more days at sea and last longer than 1 week. On these cruises you get to see more than one region, which is a particular advantage to those trying to see as much of Europe as possible.

Some of the more upscale lines will reward customers willing to **pay their full fare in advance** (thus giving the cruise line cash in hand). The discounts—sometimes as much as 15%—are significant enough that it could pay to go this route rather than putting a comparable sum in a CD.

AIRFARE & PRE- AND POST-CRUISE OFFERINGS

Your cruise package might include airfare, but if not, you will be offered an air add-on. As a general rule, if you are offered air transportation from the cruise line, it's best to take it. Why? First of all, as big customers of the airlines, the cruise lines tend to get very good (if not the best) discounted airfare rates, which they pass on to their customers.

Secondly, booking air with the cruise line also allows the line to keep track of you. If your plane is late, for instance, they might even hold the boat. And most cruise lines include **transfers** from the airport to the ship, saving you the hassle of getting a cab. (If you do book on your own, you may still be able to get the transfers separately—ask your travel agent.)

The only time it may pay to book your own air transportation is if you are using frequent-flyer miles and can get the air for free. Also, book your own if you are particular about which carrier you fly or route you take (you are more or less at the mercy of the cruise line to make these choices if you take their air offers, and may end up on chartered aircraft).

Some lines offer special **deviation programs,** which allow you to request specific airlines and routing for an extra fee. The deadline for these requests is usually 60 days prior to the sailing date or the day your cruise reservation is made if you book later.

Be aware that once the ticket is issued by the cruise line, you will be charged a fee if any changes are made.

If you choose not to book your air transportation with the cruise line, and said airfare is part of the cruise deal, you will be refunded the air portion of the fare.

Note: If you are not booking airfare through the cruise line, make sure to allow several hours between the plane's arrival and when you need to get on the ship. It may be best, in terms of reducing anxiety anyway, to arrive a day before and spend the night in a hotel.

PRE- & POST-CRUISE PACKAGES

All sorts of add-on programs are offered by the cruise lines in Europe, and many people will want to stretch their cruise vacation by adding a hotel stay, before or after the cruise, in a port city. These hotel stays are typically booked at the same time you book your cruise, to create what's known as pre-cruise or post-cruise offerings.

Just like air add-ons, the cruise lines negotiate **special deals with hotels** at port cities. An advantage to coming in a day or two early is that you don't have to worry if your flight is running late—you won't miss the boat. Plus, the extra evening gives you time to recover from jet lag before your cruise begins.

Some lines, including Orient Lines, include a hotel package in the cruise fare. When evaluating a cruise line's hotel offering, consider the following:

- does the offer include transfers (airport to hotel *and* hotel to cruise ship);
- does the deal offer a hotel that you will be happy with in terms of location and room style;
- does the offer include escorted tours, car-rental deals, or meals.

CRUISETOURS

Most of the cruise lines also offer some **escorted land tours,** usually in major cities like London, Paris, Madrid, Lisbon, Venice, Athens, or Istanbul, to complement your cruise vacation.

The land portion is typically 4 to 6 nights, and may be offered before or after the cruise. The package usually includes hotel accommodations, sightseeing, admission to attractions, and some meals, as well as ground transportation (usually by bus) and all transfers (between the airport, the hotel or hotels, and the ship).

2 Extra Costs to Consider

While your cruise price typically includes accommodations on the ship, meals and snacks, activities, and entertainment, there are some added costs that arise during your cruise; before your trip, you may want to make a tentative budget.

Additional expenses usually include shore excursions, bar drinks, dry cleaning and laundry services (some ships have coin-operated machines for passenger use as well), phone calls, massage and other spa services, beauty parlor services, photos taken by the ship's photographer, wine at dinner, souvenirs, and crew tips. Such extras can easily add up to $50 to $60 per person per day, or more if you really indulge.

SHORE EXCURSIONS

The most expensive addition to your cruise fare in Europe will likely be shore excursions. With some lines, shore excursions are included in your cruise fare, but with most lines they are an added (though very worthwhile) expense. Ranging from about $30 for a 3-hour city tour to more than $200 for a long excursion to a city far from the port, these sightseeing tours are designed to help cruise passengers make the most of their time at the ports the ship visits, but they can add a hefty sum to your vacation costs. Sometimes, you'll actually be in port long enough to take more than one excursion.

Our advice? Don't discount the excursions on the basis of cost. Think about it this way: You probably don't get to Europe very often, so it would be a shame to limit your experience just to save a few bucks. We've highlighted the best of these tours in chapters 11 and 12.

In general, you get the biggest bang for your buck by taking tours that go beyond the port city (in many cases, it's easy to walk around the port city on your own).

Shore excursions are generally booked on board, not in advance, and you will have an opportunity on board to ask questions of the ship's tour staff, who will even offer lectures on the subject, before you make your decision. Keep in mind that popular tours sell out fast.

GRATUITIES

You'll want to add to your calculations tips for the ship's crew. Of course, tipping is at your own discretion—Holland America even makes a point of this, with their "no tipping required" policy—but with the cruise lines being so forthcoming with their tipping advice (they even have special envelopes and cheat sheets prepared to help you out), you'll feel like a crumb for not obliging.

Tipping is usually paid at the end of the cruise, and passengers should reserve at least $9 per person, per day, or $63 a week, for tips for the room steward, waiter, and busboy (in practice, people to tend to nudge it up to $10 or $12).

Additional tips to other personnel, such as the head waiter or maitre d', are at your discretion. Most lines automatically add 15% to bar bills, so you don't have to tip your bartender, though some people will slip a bartender they really like a few bucks at the end of the cruise anyway. You aren't asked to tip crew members who bring you room service, or bring back your clean laundry, but you can if you want to (having a few dollar bills on hand is useful). On some European and small-ship lines, the crew pools tips, with the recommended contribution $10 to $12 per person, per day. Other lines suggest you pay your tip based on a percentage of what you paid for your cruise (usually 5%). Norwegian Cruise Line automatically adds tips of $10 per passenger, per day to your shipboard account (you can adjust the amount up or down as you see fit). Some luxury lines, including Radisson and Silversea, include tips in the cruise fare.

For more on tipping, see "Wrapping Up Your Cruise—Debarkation Concerns," in chapter 4, "The Cruise Experience."

What's Not Included in Your Cruise Fare   U.S. $

To help you calculate what you'll need to cover onboard costs, we've put together this chart:

Babysitting (per hr., for two kids)	
Private	$10
Group	$6–$8
Bar drinks	
Soda	$1.50–$2
Mixed drinks	$3.25–$5
Beer	$2.95–$3.95
Wine	$10–$300/bottle
Alternative dining (service charge)	$5–$20
Haircuts*	
Men's	$29
Women's	$52–$70
Massage (50 min.)*	$89–$109
Cruise line logo souvenirs	$3–$50
Dry cleaning (per item)	$2.50–$7.50
Phone calls (per min.)	$6.95–$16.95
Photos (5 x 7)	$6.95–$7.95
E-mail (per min.)	50¢–$1.50

Standard prices of Steiner, which has contracts to provide spa and beauty services on most ships.

BOOZE

Most ships charge extra for alcoholic beverages (including wine at dinner) and for soda. Nonbubbly soft drinks such as lemonade and iced tea are typically included in your cruise fare.

PORT CHARGES & OTHER FEES

Port charges, taxes, and other fees are usually included in your cruise fare but not always, and these charges can add as much as $200 per person onto the price of a European cruise. We've noted in the cruise reviews when ships do not include port charges and taxes in their rates.

PHONE CALLS FROM THE SHIP

Making phone calls from any ship is extremely expensive (up to $16.95 per min.), so you're much better off waiting until you're at a port. However, making calls from a port in Europe can also be tricky. You should bring along an AT&T, Sprint, or other **phone-service card** from home, and make sure you know the local access number for the card in advance (you can call your phone service for the numbers for each country you will be visiting).

On some pay phones in Europe you can drop in a coin (in the local currency) to connect to your local access number, but others require the use of prepaid phone cards (not coins). In either case, you usually can't just pick up the receiver and dial the local number for your phone service, even if that number is toll-free. If the phone requires a prepaid card, you can buy one at a newsstand or tobacco shop. If you are using the prepaid card just to connect to your phone service's local number, buy the card in the smallest denomination available.

If you don't want to hassle with the prepaid cards or figuring out local coinage, we've found that most hotels will let you use a phone to call AT&T or your other phone service if you walk in and ask nicely (looking lost helps). They may charge you a small fee.

Another, more convenient, option is to bring along a worldwide cellular phone. If you don't own one, you can rent one from **Nextel** (© **800/754-6905;** www.nextel.com) for $9.95 a day, $49.95 a week, or $199 a month, plus usage charges (usually 99¢–$1.99 per min. in Europe). With 48 hours' notice, the company will ship you the phone. And if you really like it, you can apply your rental costs to a purchase (the phones retail for $199). Keep in mind that the phone is more likely to work when you are on land than when you are at sea.

OTHER ONBOARD COSTS

Cruise lines make a substantial amount of their revenue on board, meaning you'll find enticements at every turn (especially on the big ships)—from the friendly bar staff offering the drink of the day (the largest source of onboard revenue for the cruise lines is drinks), to the roving photographer snapping that must-have photo, to the glass snow globe with the cruise ship inside.

There may be additional extras as well, depending on the ship, such as caviar at the champagne bar (if your ship has one), or cigars at the cigar bar (if your ship has one). Some ships charge extra for afternoon ice-cream sundaes. All ships that offer babysitting (as opposed to the organized kids' programs) charge for it.

You'll also pay extra for such activities as golf simulators or minigolf, and video games. And some lines charge a small service fee for dinner in the ship's alternative restaurant. If you have teenagers or are a Type A personality who needs to stay in touch, you may find that you tally up an impressive e-mail bill.

Don't underestimate the lure of items in the gift shop in your budget planning. The shops offer frequent sales, and are especially attractive during days at sea (when you can't shop in port). And don't think you won't be tempted by the photos snapped onboard by the ship's photographer. Even if you're a reluctant poser they'll get you, and you'll find them offered the next day not only in regular pictures but also as key chains and other nifty souvenirs.

3 Booking Through a Travel Agent

You may wonder whether the traditional travel agent has been replaced by the Internet or gone the way of typewriters and eight-track tapes. Well, not exactly. Booking a cruise is a complicated process, with lots of nuances. That's why the vast majority of cruise passengers book through agents, particularly those who specialize in cruises (see below). The cruise lines are happy with the system, have only small reservations staffs themselves (unlike the airlines), and actually discourage direct sales. Even if you do try to call a cruise line to book yourself, you may be advised to contact an agent in your area (the cruise line may even offer you a name from its list of preferred agencies). And while lines like Royal Caribbean, Celebrity, and Norwegian Cruise Line have begun taking bookings over their websites, they also offer links to their preferred agents (and any Web specials the lines offer on the sites are also typically available through agents).

The process of booking a cruise is probably more involved than you think, and a good travel agent can save you both time and money. By working with an agent, you don't have to hassle with calling cruise lines for brochures; agencies have them in stock. Plus, agents usually work for you *for free* (the bulk of their fee is paid by the cruise lines). Your agent will also help you make decisions on the type of **cabin** best suited for your needs, help you arrange your **dining-room seating preference** and **travel insurance,** and handle any **special requests** you may have such as meal requirements or notifying the cruise line of a birthday or anniversary that will be celebrated on board.

Your agent will discuss with you optional **airfare programs** offered by the lines, **transfers** from the airport to the pier, and any pre- or post-cruise **hotel or tour programs.** Some lines also let you purchase **shore excursions** in advance (for more on shore excursions, see above). And there may also be pre-bookable spa packages available.

However, if you are computer savvy and have a good idea of what you're looking for in a cruise (which you probably will after reading this book), **websites** are a great way to trawl the seas at you own pace and check out last-minute deals. But keep in mind that you won't get much in the way of personalized service when you book a cruise online. And if something does go wrong or you need help getting a refund, you're on your own. That's why we recommend you go ahead and do research on the Web if you want, but make your actual booking through an experienced agent.

If you don't have a good travel agent, try to find one through your friends, preferably those who have cruised before. For the most personal service, look for an agent in your local area, and for the most knowledgeable service, look for an agent who has cruised him- or herself, preferably on one of the lines you're considering. It's perfectly okay to ask an agent questions about their experience, such as whether they have ever cruised in Europe.

It really doesn't matter whether your agent is at a small agency or works for a large national agency. And it's a personal choice whether you prefer to work with an agent face-to-face or over the phone. What is important is that the agent gets to know you and understands your vacation desires. He or she should ask you questions about your lifestyle and past vacation experiences (if the agent doesn't ask you such questions, be wary of using him or her).

It is important to realize that **not all agents represent all cruise lines.** In order to be experts on what they sell, and to maximize the commissions the lines pay them (they're paid more based on volume of sales), some agents may limit their product to, say, one luxury line, one mid-priced line, one mass-market line, etc. If you have your sights set on a particular line or have it narrowed down between a couple, make sure the agent you choose can handle your choices. As we mentioned above, you can contact the lines directly to get the name of an agent near you.

It's perfectly okay to **shop around,** calling a few different agents to compare rates. Some agents will even offer perks to keep your business (such as a free cabin upgrade or a bottle of champagne).

CRUISE AGENCIES & CRUISE SPECIALISTS

The easiest way to ensure the agent is experienced in booking cruises is to work with an agent at a **cruise-only agency** (all cruises, all the time) or to find an agent who is a **cruise specialist.** If you call a **full-service agency** (that handles all types of travel), ask to speak to someone on its **cruise desk.**

The easiest way to find reputable cruise agents is to check the membership rosters of the **Cruise Lines International Association** (CLIA; ℂ 212/ 921-0066; www.cruising.org) or the **National Association of Cruise Oriented**

Keeping an Open Hot Line to Your Agent

Since you'll be traveling on Europe time, it's particularly important to make sure your agent has some sort of 24-hour service in case you run into any problems. Many agencies contract with outside firms for this coverage, which is perfectly okay. The bottom line is, you want someone you can call for assistance no matter what time it is back home.

Agencies (NACOA; ✆ 305/663-5626; www.nacoaonline.com). Members of both groups are cruise specialists.

Membership in the **American Society of Travel Agents (ASTA; ✆ 800/ 275-2782;** www.astanet.com) ensures that the agency is monitored for ethical practices, although it does not in itself designate cruise experience.

Cruise Specialists with the Certified Travel Counselor (CTC) designation have completed a professional-skills course offered by the **Institute of Certificated Travel Agents (ICTA),** and the designation is another guarantor of in-depth knowledge of the industry. You can find the institute's website at www.icta.com.

GETTING EXTRA-SPECIAL DEALS THROUGH AGENTS

Agents, especially those who specialize in cruises, are in frequent contact with the cruise lines, and are alerted by the lines, either by e-mail or fax, about the latest and greatest deals and **special offers.** The cruise lines tend to communicate such deals and offers to their top agents first, before the general public, and some of these will never appear in your local newspaper.

Depending on the agency you choose, you may run across additional incentives for booking through an agent.

- **Newsletters:** To keep their clients alert to specials, agencies may offer newsletters or have other means of communication, such as postcards, e-mail, or posting the specials on their Internet sites.
- **Group Rates:** Some agencies buy big blocks of space on a ship in advance and offer it to their clients at a group price only available through that agency. These are called group rates, although "group" in this case means savings, not that you have to hang around with the other people booking through the agency.
- **Rebates and Incentives:** Some agencies are willing to give back to the client a portion of their commissions from the cruise line in order to close a sale, in what is known as rebates or incentives. This percentage may be monetary, or it may take the form of a perk such as a free bottle of champagne or a cabin upgrade.

ROUNDING UP ADDITIONAL INFORMATION

The **glossy brochures** produced by all the cruise lines are basically advertisements, but they do contain valuable information—such as deck layouts and schematics (and sometimes photos) of the different cabin categories—that'll help you when selecting and booking your cruise. Of course, the verbiage in these brochures may not be all that straightforward. For instance, "comfortable cabins" can be another way of saying "small." The lines put a lot of money into these brochures, and they all show off their ships in a beautiful light. Rarely are lower-end cabins shown, for instance.

TAKING ADVANTAGE OF THE INTERNET

The Internet is another good source for gathering information on cruises. Most major lines have their own sites, which typically offer information on cabin configurations and public rooms, and sometimes feature a virtual tour of the ships. Most of the cruise lines' sites also have links to that line's preferred agents.

Only a few cruise-line sites offer online booking capability. And as we said above, while you may find **special deals** at the sites, these are usually the same deals your travel agent can get you. When Internet-only deals are offered, they tend to come from agencies rather than the cruise lines themselves. *Tip:* If you do find a better rate online than your land-based agent is offering, you can always ask your agent to match the price.

Websites selling cruises include online travel agencies that sell all types of travel (travelocity.com, expedia.com, mytravel.com, uniglobe.com), agencies that specialize in cruises (icruise.com, cruise.com, cruise411.com), travel discounters (bestfares.com, 1travel.com, lowestfare.com), and auction houses (all cruiseauction.com, onsale.com). For a listing of other sites that will be valuable in researching and planning your trip, see "Leading Websites for Cruise Planning," in chapter 1, "Choosing Your Ideal Cruise."

WATCH OUT FOR SCAMS

As the adage warns, if you hear a deal that just sounds to good to be true, then it probably is. If you get a solicitation by phone, fax, mail, or e-mail that just doesn't sound right, or if your agent gives you the creeps, contact your state consumer protection agency or local office of the Better Business Bureau (www.bbb.org). Or you can check with the cruise line to see if they've ever heard of the agency in question. Find more ways to avoid scams at the American Society of Travel Agents' website, www.astanet.com.

4 Choosing Your Cabin

The cruise lines have improved accommodations a bit since Charles Dickens referred to his stateroom as a coffin, but cramped, windowless spaces can still be found. On the other hand, so can penthouse-size suites with expansive verandas, Jacuzzis, and hot and cold running butler service.

What kind of cabin is right for you? Price will likely be a big factor here, but so should the vacation style you prefer. If, for instance, you plan to spend a lot of quiet time in your cabin, you should probably consider booking the biggest room you can afford, and you should also consider taking a cabin with a picture window or a private veranda. If, conversely, you plan to be off on tours or out and about the ship's public areas and will only be using your cabin to change clothes and collapse in at the end of the day, you might be just as happy with a smaller (and cheaper) cabin.

Most cabins on cruise ships today have a private bathroom with a shower and twin beds that are convertible to queen-size (you can request which configuration you want), though some ships also have a limited number of double beds. Some cabins have bunk beds.

Many ships have cabins designed for three or four people that will include bunks. In some, it is possible to add a fifth, portable bed. Some lines offer special cabins designed for families. Families may also be able to book connecting cabins (although they'll have to pay for two cabins to do so).

MODEL CABIN LAYOUTS

Typical Outside Cabin Configurations
- Twin beds (can often be pushed together)
- Upper berths for extra passengers fold into walls
- Bathrooms usually have showers only (no tub)
- Usually (but not always) have TVs and radios
- May have portholes or picture windows

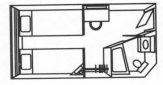
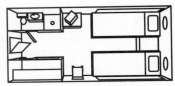

Typical Suite Configurations
- Queen-size or double beds
- Sitting areas (sometimes with sofa beds for extra passengers)
- Large bathrooms, usually with tub
- Refrigerators (sometimes stocked, sometimes not)
- Stereos and TVs with VCRs are common
- Large closets
- Large windows or outside verandas

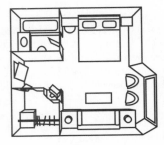
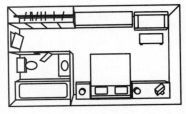

Figure 2-1: Sample cabin layouts.

Some cabins have televisions. Some also have such extra amenities as safes, mini-refrigerators, VCRs, bathrobes, and hair dryers. A bathtub is considered a luxury on ships and will usually only be offered in more expensive rooms.

CABIN TYPES

The typical ship offers several types of cabins, as outlined by floor plans in the cruise line's brochure. The cabins are usually described by **price** (highest to lowest), **category** (suite, deluxe, superior, standard, economy, and others), and **furniture configuration** ("sitting area with two lower beds," for example). Diagrams of the various cabin types are typically included (p. 36).

The cabins will also be described as being **inside** (without windows or portholes) or **outside** (with). Outside cabins are more expensive since windows allow natural light into the cabin and may allow ocean views—though some may be obstructed (usually by a lifeboat) or look out onto a public area, which will be an issue if you crave privacy. An experienced travel agent should be able to advise you on these matters.

THE SOUNDS OF SILENCE

Noise can be a factor that may influence your cabin choice. If you take a cabin on a lower deck, you may hear engine noises; in the front of the ship, anchor noises; and in the back of the ship, thruster noises. A cabin near an elevator may bring door-opening and -closing sounds. Cabins on the Promenade Deck may sound great, but you may hear passengers walking or talking outside or even peeking into your cabin. And a cabin above or below the disco may pulse until all hours of the night. You may also want to avoid cabins near the laundry area or galley. If noise is a problem for you, make your cabin choice accordingly. A ship's deck plan can clue you in to potential problems.

On the big ships, the more deluxe outside cabins may also come with **verandas** that give you private outdoor space to enjoy sea breezes. But the verandas vary in size, so if you're looking to do more than stand on your balcony, make sure the outdoor space is big enough to accommodate deck chairs, a table, or whatever else you require. And before you step out in your birthday suit, realize that private doesn't necessarily mean your neighbors can't see you.

Usually, the higher on the ship (by deck) the cabin is located, the more expensive and nicer the cabin is. This is true even if there are cabins of the same size on lower decks (the decor changes).

Luxury suites are usually on upper decks, but a quirky thing about cabin pricing is that the most stable cabins during rough seas are those in the middle and lower parts of the ship.

On **small ships,** cabins can run to the truly spartan, though some can also give the big-ship cabins a run for their money. Generally, the difference lies in the orientation of the line: Those promising a real adventure experience tend to feature somewhat utilitarian cabins.

CABIN SIZES

The size of a cabin is described in terms of square feet. This number may not mean a lot unless you want to mark it out on your floor at home. But to give you an idea: 120 square feet and under is low-end and cramped, 180 square feet is mid-range (and the minimum for people with claustrophobia), and 250 square feet and up is suite-size.

What Is Luxury?

Cruise lines freely use terms like *deluxe* and *luxury*, but these terms vary greatly from line to line, rendering them virtually meaningless. Instead, evaluate cabins based on size and amenities offered.

A FEW CABIN-CHOOSING TIPS

Make sure the **beds** in the cabin can be configured the way you want. Not all cabins offer double or queen-size beds. If you want a **bathtub** or **television,** make sure you choose a cabin that has one. If you are traveling by **wheelchair,** make sure the cabin and bathroom doors are wide enough to accommodate your chair. (Of course there will be other accessibility considerations if you are traveling by wheelchair; be sure to discuss them with the line before you book.) **Book early for first-choice of cabins** (the cheapest and most expensive cabins tend to sell out first).

5 Choosing Your Dining Options

In addition to choosing your cabin, you can also choose your preferred meal seating time, if you're on a ship that requires one. Smaller ships and luxury vessels usually serve dinner in an open seating, or restaurant-style, allowing you to sit at any table you want; if you plan to sail one of these lines, you can skip this section. Norwegian Cruise Line also offers open seating, and Princess Cruises has an open-seating option. But because most dining rooms on larger ships are not large enough to accommodate all passengers at once, these ships typically offer two seatings, or sittings, especially for dinner. All table space is on a reserved basis. Early or main seating is typically at 6pm. Late seating is at 8:30pm.

There are advantages and disadvantages to both times, and it basically comes down to personal choice. The **early seating** is usually less crowded and is the preferred time for families and seniors. The dining experience can be a bit more rushed (the staff needs to make way for the next wave), but food items may be fresher since they haven't had to wait under warmers. You can see a show right after dinner, and have first dibs on other nighttime venues as well. And you just may be hungry again in time for the **midnight buffet.**

The **late seating,** on the other hand, allows you time for a good long nap or late spa appointments before dining. Dinner is not rushed at all. You can sit as long as you want enjoying after-dinner drinks—unless, that is, you choose to rush off to catch the 10pm show.

If you choose to also eat **breakfast and lunch** in the dining room as opposed to at the more casual venues on the ship, theoretically you are also supposed to eat at assigned times as well. We've found, though, that most ships are fairly flexible in this area. Crowds in the dining room are typically only an issue at dinner (a lot of people eat lunch in the ports). If you show up other than at your assigned time for breakfast or lunch and your assigned table is full, the staff will probably just seat you elsewhere.

Typical meal times for breakfast are 7 or 8am for the early seating and 8:30 or 9am for the late. For lunch, it's usually noon for the early seating and 1:30pm or so for the late.

SPECIAL DIETARY OR MENU REQUESTS

Though many cruise lines these days offer vegetarian and low-fat meals as a standard feature, you should still arrange any special dietary needs through your travel agent at the time you make your reservation. Some lines offer kosher menus, and all will have vegetarian, low-fat, low-salt, and sugar-free options available.

Also have your agent let the cruise line know of any birthday or anniversary that will occur during the cruise so they can plan to help you celebrate accordingly.

TABLE SIZES

Do you mind sitting with strangers? Are you looking to make new friends? Your dinner companions can make or break your cruise experience. Most ships offer tables configured for 2 to 12 people. For singles or couples who want to socialize, generally a table of six to eight seats allows enough variety so you don't get bored and also allows you the ability to steer clear of any one individual you don't particularly care for (tables are assigned, not seats). Couples may choose to sit on their own, but keep in mind that the smallest tables are typically the hardest to come by. Singles may find the ship reluctant to offer a table for one. A family of four may want to choose a table for four, or request to sit with another family at a table for eight.

You need to state your preference in advance, but don't worry if you change your mind once you're on board. You'll probably be able to move around. Just tell the dining room maitre d' and he'll review the seating charts for an opening (greasing his palm will probably help).

Many ships now feature **smoke-free dining rooms,** but if smoking is a particular concern to you, check this out with your travel agent. If the room isn't nonsmoking, you can request a nonsmoking table. Vice versa for smokers.

6 Deposits & Cancellation Policies

DEPOSITS

You'll be asked by your travel agent to make a deposit, either of a fixed amount (usually $300–$1,000) or at some percentage of your total cruise cost. You'll be asked to pay the remaining fare usually 60 to 90 days before your departure date. Make sure before making any payment that you carefully review the line's refund policy. You'll find the policy listed in the back of the cruise line's brochure.

Cancellation penalties vary by line. Before paying a dime you should make sure you understand the payment schedule that you're agreeing to by putting down your deposit.

If at all possible, make your payment with a credit card. This gives you an additional avenue of recourse should you encounter any problems.

CANCELLATIONS

Cruise lines have varying policies regarding cancellations, and it's important to read the fine print. Most lines, but not all, allow you to cancel for a full refund on your deposit and payment anytime up to 76 days before the sailing. After that time, you'll have to pay a penalty, which increases as you get closer to your sailing date. If you cancel a month before the sailing, for instance, you might have to pay 50% of your fare as a penalty. If you cancel at the last minute, you may not be refunded any of what you've paid.

7 Your Cruise Documents

About 1 month before your cruise and no later than 1 week before, you should receive your cruise documents, including your **airline tickets** (if you purchased them from the cruise line), a **boarding document** with your cabin (and sometimes dining) choice on it, boarding forms to fill out, **luggage tags,** and your prearranged **bus transfer vouchers** and **hotel vouchers** (if applicable). There will also be information on shore excursions and additional material detailing things you need to know before you sail.

Read all of this carefully. Make sure your cabin category and dining preferences are as you requested and that your airline flight and arrival times are what you were told. If there are problems, call your agent immediately. Make sure there is enough time so you can arrive at the port no later than an hour before departure time.

You will be required to have a **passport** for your trip (see chapter 3 for more on this). You won't likely need a visa, but based on your itinerary, ask your travel agent if this applies.

We recommend that you **confirm your flight** 3 days before departure. Also, before you leave for the airport, tag your bags with the tags provided by the cruise line, and fill in your boarding cards. This will save you time when you arrive at the ship.

8 Travel Insurance

Three primary types of insurance are available: trip cancellation, medical, and lost luggage. Trip cancellation insurance, which we most recommend, is a good idea since you have paid a large portion of your vacation expenses up front, and want that investment protected. It typically costs 6% to 8% of the total value of your vacation. Make sure the policy covers bankruptcy or default of the cruise line. Medical insurance and lost luggage insurance don't make sense for most travelers since your existing health insurance should cover you if you get sick on vacation (though if you belong to an HMO, you might want to make sure you are fully covered when away from home), and your homeowner's insurance should cover stolen luggage if you have off-premises theft protection. Check your existing policies before you buy additional coverage, and don't buy more insurance than you need. If, for example, you only need trip-cancellation insurance, don't buy coverage for lost or stolen property. Also keep in mind the airlines are responsible for up to $2,500 on domestic flights and $640 on international flights if they loose your luggage; if you plan to carry anything more valuable than that, keep it in your carry-on bag.

Among reputable issuers of travel insurances are **Access America,** 6600 W. Broad St., Richmond, VA 23230 (℗ **800/284-8300;** www.accessamerica.com), and **Travel Guard International,** 1145 Clark St., Stevens Point, WI 54481 (℗ **800/826-1300;** www.travelguard.com).

Please note: Keep in mind that in the aftermath of the World Trade Center attacks, a number of airlines, cruise lines, and tour operators are no longer covered by insurers. *The bottom line:* Always check the fine print before you sign on; more and more policies have built-in exclusions and restrictions that may leave you out in the cold if something does go awry.

3

Things to Know Before You Go

You've bought your ticket and you're getting ready to cruise. Here are a few nuts and bolts, odds and ends, FYIs, and helpful hints to consider before you go.

1 Passports & Visas

Citizens of non-EU countries need a **passport** to enter any European country. Keep your passport in a safe place (don't pack it in your check-in luggage) and keep a photocopy in a separate place, just for backup. On some ships, you are required to turn your passport in to the purser's office for the duration of your cruise.

APPLYING FOR A NEW PASSPORT

U.S. CITIZENS   If you do not have a passport, you will have to apply for one in person at one of the 13 passport offices throughout the U.S., or at a federal or state court, probate court, or major post office. You need to bring a certified birth certificate as proof of citizenship; bringing along your driver's license, state or military ID, or social security card is also wise. You also need two identical passport-sized photos (2" × 2"), taken within the last 6 months at a photo shop or special passport photo venue (strip photos from photo machines are not acceptable).

For those over age 15, a passport is valid for 10 years and costs $60 ($45 plus a $15 handling fee); for those 15 and under, a passport is valid for 5 years and costs $40.

If you are replacing an expired passport that was issued within the past 12 years, you can renew it by mail and bypass the handling fee.

Make sure to allow plenty of time before your trip to apply, as processing takes about 3 weeks (but can take longer during busy periods). You may be able to expedite things by paying extra for FedEx delivery. For more information, contact the **National Passport Information Center** at © **900/225-5674** (there is a charge of 35¢ a min. for automated service or $1.05 a min. to speak to an operator). On the Web, check out www.travel.state.gov.

CANADIAN CITIZENS   You can pick up a passport application at one of the 28 regional passport offices or most travel agencies. Passports are valid for 5 years and cost $60. Children under 16 may be included on a parent's passport, but they need their own passport to travel unaccompanied by the parent. Applications must be accompanied by two identical passport-sized photos and proof of Canadian citizenship. Processing takes 5 to 10 days if you apply in person, about 3 weeks by mail.

For more information, contact the central **Passport Office,** Department of Foreign Affairs and International Trade in Ottawa (© **800/567-6868**). On the Web, check out www.dfait-maeci.gc.ca/passport.

What to Do if You Lose Your Passport

If you lose your passport, notify the ship's purser. He or she will help you arrange a visit to the nearest consulate of your home country as soon as possible to have the passport replaced.

U.K. CITIZENS   For passport information, call the **London Passport Office** (*C* 0171/271-3000); or check out www.open.gov.uk/ukpass/ukpass.htm.

AUSTRALIAN CITIZENS   You can apply for a passport at your local post office or passport office, or call *C* **131-232** (www.dfat.gov.au/passports/) for more information.

NEW ZEALAND CITIZENS   You can pick up a passport application at any travel agency or Link Centre. For information, contact the **Passport Office** (*C* **800/225-050**).

VISAS

Your cruise line will advise you if any visas are needed for the countries you will visit (if in doubt, call the line or ask your travel agent). In most cases, a visa is not required if you are visiting a country for a limited amount of time (less than 24 hr.). If you are visiting Russia, you do not need a visa to take a shore excursion, but you will need one to head off on your own. Visas need to be applied for well in advance of your trip. The easiest place to apply is through a **visa service,** and your travel agent can guide you to one in your area. A small fee is charged for the service. You can also apply by contacting the embassy of the country you will be visiting.

2 Money Matters

You have already paid the lion's share of your cruise vacation, but you will still need a credit card, traveler's checks, or cash to handle your onboard expenses such as drinks, shore excursions, photos by the ship's photographer, spa services, gift shop purchases, and so forth. Some ships (but not all) will take a personal check.

You will want cash for taxis, drinks, small purchases, and tips for guides in port. You may also need cash to pay crew tips at the end of the cruise, although some lines allow you to charge tips. And you'll want a few dollars on hand in case you want to tip a crewmember for room service or laundry delivery.

ABOARD SHIP

Cruise ships themselves operate on a cashless basis. Basically, this means you keep a running tab. You sign for virtually everything you want to buy all week long—drinks at the bar, shore excursions, and gift shop purchases—and pay up at the end of the cruise with cash or a credit card (you can use cash in the casino). Very convenient, yes—and also very easy to spend more than you would if you had to dole out cash each time you made a purchase.

On some European ships, the onboard items are priced in European currency such as Italian lira or Norwegian kroner, so you may want to bring a calculator with you to figure out what you are really spending for that nifty T-shirt with the ship's logo or that special drink of the day. First European Cruises was the first to use the euro to price onboard items (which is helpful to Europeans but not necessarily to Americans).

We've included a chart in chapter 10 showing relative currency values of the major European currencies at press time. For more current conversions, check out the currency calculator at **www.bloomberg.com**.

Shortly before or after embarkation, a purser or check-in clerk in the terminal or on board will request an imprint of one of your credit cards. (If you want to pay in cash or by traveler's check, you will be asked to leave a deposit, usually $250 for a 1-week sailing.) Larger ships will then issue you an **identification card** that you show whenever you board the ship after spending the day in port and that you also use when you sign for something. On the newest ships, this same ID card often serves as your room key. Smaller and older ships may not use these ID cards, and still issue regular room keys.

On the last day of your cruise, an **itemized account** of all you've charged throughout the cruise is slipped beneath your cabin door. If you agree with the charges, they are automatically billed to your credit-card account. If you are paying in cash or if you dispute any charge, then you need to stop by the ship's cashier or purser's office, where there's usually a long line.

We suggest you keep careful track of your onboard expenses to avoid an unpleasant surprise at the end of your cruise. Some ships make this tracking particularly easy by offering interactive TV, enabling you to check your account from the comfort of your own stateroom. On others, you have to visit the purser's or guest-relations desk to review your account. You can do so as often as you choose, but you may encounter lines of others doing the same.

IN PORT

The cashless system works just fine on board, but you will need some dough in port. Of course, you can put any shore excursions you sign up for on your room tab, and credit cards are accepted at most port shops (as are traveler's checks), but we do recommend having some real cash on you, ideally in small denominations, for taxi rides, snacks, and street-side souvenir vendors.

It is more expensive to exchange your money for foreign currency in your own country than it is once you've reached your destination. But it's a good idea to arrive in Europe with a bit of local currency, enough at least to buy a cup of coffee and a newspaper between flights or to get you to your hotel or ship. About $30 to $50 should do it.

Many of the larger ships operating in Europe offer **exchange services** where you can exchange your currency for the local currency of the country you're visiting. This is usually accomplished by a local bank official coming on board at the port. Some ships have special ATMs that do currency exchange (for a fee). Most ships do not offer exchange services at the purser's desk.

Your ship, if it's an American line, may also have an ATM that delivers greenbacks (usually for a hefty fee). Some lines will also cash personal checks up to a set amount (usually around $200).

See chapter 10 for exchange rates from U.S., Canadian, U.K., Australian, and New Zealand currencies into all the local currencies you'll use in port.

ATMS IN EUROPE

In nearly every town in Europe (even the tiny ones) you can find an **ATM** that will give you local currency (but not dollars) from your ATM or PIN-enabled Visa or MasterCard (contact the issuing bank to enable this feature and get a PIN). PLUS and Cirrus cards work on many ATMs in Europe and present what is really the fastest and easiest way to exchange your money. You get a good rate (better than banks or exchange services) and unless your home bank charges you for using a nonproprietary ATM you don't have to pay a fee or commission (which you usually do at banks and exchange services). We usually rely on ATMs, but we also find it's a good idea to have some cash or traveler's checks just in case of emergency (or in case the bank computer lines are down).

Before you leave home, make sure the PINs on your bank- and credit cards will work in Europe; you usually need a four-digit code (six digits may not work in Europe). And keep in mind you can only access your checking account (not savings) from ATMs abroad. Both the **Cirrus** (© **800/424-7787**) and **PLUS** (© **800/843-7587**) networks have automated ATM locators that list the banks in each country that will accept your card.

American Express card cash advances are usually only available from Amex offices, which you'll find in every major European city.

EXCHANGING MONEY

If you are not using ATMs, then try to exchange your money at a bank rather than the exchange services you will see in busy tourist areas or at your hotel. The rate of exchange is usually higher at banks, and the service fee less.

USING CREDIT CARDS

Most restaurants, shops, and hotels in Europe accept major credit cards such as American Express, Diners Club, MasterCard, and Visa (but not Discover). The most widely accepted cards are Visa and MasterCard.

USING TRAVELER'S CHECKS

Most banks in the U.S. sell traveler's checks, charging fees of 1% to 2% of the value of the checks. AAA members can buy American Express traveler's checks commission-free. The checks offer great insurance since, if you lose them—and have kept a list of the numbers and a record of which ones you cashed—you can get them replaced at no charge. Be aware, though, that you won't get as high a rate when you go to exchange them for foreign currency as you will for cash. Personal checks are pretty much useless in Europe, except as accepted on your ship (check your ship's policy before relying on this method of payment).

American Express (© **800/221-7282**) is one of the largest issuers of traveler's checks, and its checks are widely accepted. **Thomas Cook** (© **800/ 223-7373** in the U.S. or Canada, 0171/480-7226 in London) issues Master-Card traveler's checks. **Citicorp** (© **800/645-6556**) and other banks issue checks under their own name or under MasterCard or Visa. Checks issued in dollar amounts (as opposed to, say, French francs or Italian lira) are the most widely accepted in the world.

VALUE-ADDED TAX (VAT)

All European countries charge a Value-Added Tax (VAT) of 15% to 35% on goods and services, which is already included in the price you see. Rates vary from country to country, although most are moving toward a 15% rate. Citizens of non-EU countries can get back most of the tax on purchases (but not on services) if they spend a designated amount (usually $50–$200) in a single store.

Regulations vary by country (you should check when you get there or with your ship's purser), but generally you can collect your refund for goods purchased in any EU country at the airport as you leave Europe, or have it mailed to you. To do this, you will be required to have forms and receipts from the store where your purchases were made (make sure to ask for the forms), and may be required to show the items purchased to a VAT official at the airport. Allow an

Impressions

If there is one thing in the world that will make a man peculiarly and insufferably self-conceited, it is to have his stomach behave himself, the first day at sea, when nearly all his comrades are seasick.

—Mark Twain, *The Innocents*

extra 30 minutes at the airport to get through the process (if you've spent a lot, the wait will be worth it).

3 Health & Safety

It's a good rule of thumb to check with the **Centers for Disease Control** in Atlanta (© **877/FYI-TRIP;** www.cdc.gov/travel/) or your physician to see if there are any health precautions you should take before your trip. In the past, for instance, tetanus-diphtheria boosters have been recommended for travel in St. Petersburg, Russia.

TRAVELERS' ADVISORIES

The U.S. State Department issues advisories on areas travelers should be concerned about visiting. You can look up the advisories on the State Department's website (http://travel.state.gov) or call © **202/647-5225** for recorded information.

4 Packing

The great thing about packing for a cruise is that once you're aboard the ship, you only have to unpack once. The downside is you don't always get all that much storage space.

People (including us on some occasions) tend to overpack for cruises, but you don't have to. A cruise vacation is no different from any other, except that you will want to change your clothes for dinner, and there may be a formal night or two.

CLOTHING

Check your cruise documents for specifics on the types of nighttime dress codes (see more on these below) and to see if there are any theme nights you may want to dress specifically for (Greek night on Greek ships, for instance, means wearing blue and white, the national colors). The daily bulletin delivered to your cabin each day will advise you on the proper dress for the evening.

Obviously what you pack will be determined by when you plan to travel (summer is hotter than spring and fall) and where (Northern Europe and Scandinavia are cooler than the Mediterranean). Consult chapter 1 for average temperatures. The type of ship you are on also has some bearing on what you pack—some alternative ships are totally casual.

As a general rule, you are best off packing loose and comfortable cotton or other **lightweight fabrics.** If you are traveling in Northern Europe, bring clothing you can layer. Comfortable **walking shoes** are a must in Europe as many tours involve walking on cobblestones and other uneven surfaces.

Especially in the Med, you'll want to pack a swimsuit, a sun hat, sunglasses, and plenty of sunscreen (the sun reflects off the water and can be quite bright).

And you'll want to have a raincoat and umbrella, as well as a sweater (even in warm climates you'll want some protection against overactive air-conditioning).

If you plan on hitting the gym, don't forget sneakers and your workout clothes.

We recommend you leave valuable jewelry home and stick with costume. But if you must bring the real thing, be careful. If you're not wearing it, leave it either in your in-room safe (if there is one) or with the purser.

If you wear glasses or contact lenses, bring an extra pair. And remember to pack whatever toiletries you require (you probably won't be able to find your preferred brand in Europe if you forget).

DAYTIME CLOTHES

Across the board, daytime wear is the same as casual resort wear, meaning T-shirts, polo shirts, bathing suits, jeans, khakis, jogging suits, and sundresses. Remember to bring a cover-up and sandals if you want to go right from your deck chair to lunch in one of the restaurants or to some activity being held in a public room. Many ships ban swimsuits and tank tops from the dining room. When in port, the same dress code generally works. But keep in mind that some religious sites prohibit shorts and sleeveless shirts and require women to wear knee-length skirts. Also be aware of the local culture of the port you are visiting (at some, parading around in short shorts and a bathing suit top is simply not acceptable). And don't forget to wear comfortable shoes!

EVENING CLOTHES

When it comes to evening attire on most ships—with the exception of the casual alternative ships described in chapter 8—you'll want to pack some dressy duds. Most ships have casual, informal, and formal nights. What the cruise line means by these terms will be explained in your documents package, but as a general rule **casual** means that men can wear slacks (but jeans may be banned) and shirts with collars, women slacks, skirts, and sundresses. **Informal** (or semiformal) means men wear a jacket (but not necessarily a tie), and women wear something slightly fancier than a sundress. **Formal** means bring out the tuxes and dark suits for the men and cocktail dresses, gowns, or other fancy wear for women. As a woman, Fran finds that at night the best approach is to pack simple outfits that can be dressed up or down with scarves or other accessories. And if you stick to one or two colors, you don't have to pack as many shoes.

In spite of the suggested dress codes, which are usually described in the back of a cruise line's brochure, you'll still find a wide variety of outfits being worn. Invariably, one person's "formal" is quite different from another's. So, like hemlines and everything else these days, to a large extent, anything goes.

Tips Tuxedo Rentals

If you are on a cruise with formal nights and don't own a tux or don't want to bother lugging one along, you can often arrange a rental through your travel agent for about $75. In some cases, a rental offer arrives with your cruise tickets. If you choose this option, your suit will be waiting for you in your cabin when you arrive.

SUNDRIES

Like hotels, many ships (especially the newest and the high-end ones) come equipped with hair dryers and supply bathroom amenities such as shampoo, conditioner, lotion, and soap, although you might still want to bring your own products. If you bring your hair dryer, electric razor, curling iron, or laptop, you might want to bring an adapter, since not all ships in Europe run on 110 (the cruise line will provide you with this information).

No need to pack a **beach towel** as they're almost always supplied on board. Bird-watchers will want their **binoculars** and manuals, golfers their clubs (although they can always be rented), and snorkelers their gear (which can also be rented).

If you forget to pack a personal effect or two, don't worry. Most ships offer items like razor blades, toothbrushes, sunscreen, and film on board (but you'll pay a premium price).

Most ships have **laundry service** and some offer **dry-cleaning** service as well (there will be a price list in your cabin). Some ships also offer **self-service laundry rooms** (you'll find them on Royal Caribbean, Crystal, and Holland America, among others) so you can wash, dry, and iron your own clothes.

If you like reading but don't want to lug three or four hefty novels on board, there are options. Most ships of all sizes have **libraries** stocked with books and magazines. Some libraries are more extensive than others, of course; the *QE2*'s is huge, for example. Also, most ships stock paperback bestsellers in their shops.

LUGGAGE RESTRICTIONS

Keep in mind that there may be limitations on the number of bags you can take on the plane (usually two checked bags and one carry-on per person). Checked baggage should not weigh more than 70 pounds. It's a good idea to make sure your baggage is sturdy. Before you use it, make sure there are no rips and that the handles are still firmly attached.

You should plan on bringing a piece of **hand luggage** in which you should pack all valuables, prescription and over-the-counter medication, and your cruise documents, passport, and air tickets. You should also keep in your hand luggage your credit cards, house and car keys, and claim checks for airport parking, as well as a change of clothes, chewing gum, and reading materials.

With all the tempting things for sale in Europe, it's important to remember to **save room in your luggage for your souvenirs.** You may even want to pack an extra foldable suitcase for your treasured finds.

4

The Cruise Experience

Unlike their more utilitarian ancestors, today's cruise ships aren't just about transportation. Rather, they're attraction-filled destinations themselves, bustling resorts at sea where there are countless things to do, people to meet, good food and drink, and entertainment.

While the cruise experience varies from ship to ship, the common denominator is choice. You can run from an aerobics class to an art auction and then play bingo, all before lunch, or you can choose to watch the seascape from a quiet deck chair. Whether you like to do it all or do nothing at all, cruising is a convenient and leisurely way of traveling from one exotic port to another. While ports may be the focus for most of us on European cruises, you'll have plenty of time to sample shipboard life as well.

1 Getting Started: Checking In & Boarding

Most people hire a travel agent to plan their cruise vacation, and with good reason: Given all the details—flights, transfers, cabin selection, dining preferences—it makes sense (and can save you money) to hire an experienced professional. But once the plans are made, there are a few details left for you.

AIRPORT CHECK-IN

For starters, be sure to confirm your flight before the trip. Since you are flying to Europe, you should get to the airport at least 3 hours before your scheduled flight time. This will give you time to check in your bags, get your seat assignments, and pick up a magazine for the long flight.

Make sure your bags are tagged properly with your name and address. If you are checking your bags through to the ship or a hotel booked through the cruise line, make sure your bags are also appropriately tagged with the tags provided by the cruise line.

Remember to bring in your carry-on any valuables (including jewelry and camera equipment), your cruise documents, airline tickets and passport, claim checks for airport parking, house and car keys, eyeglasses, all prescription medications, and any other items you can't do without. It's also a good idea to pack a change of clothes so you can freshen up when you get to the ship or hotel, even if your bags haven't yet arrived. You may also want to pack gum, a snack, a book, a magazine, and Dramamine (in case it's a bumpy flight).

WHAT TO DO IF YOUR FLIGHT IS DELAYED

If your flight is delayed, and you are sailing that day, tell airline personnel. They may be able to get you onto another flight. Also call the cruise line to advise the ship of your delay (there should be an emergency number in your cruise documents). Keep in mind that you may not be the only passenger delayed, and the line might just hold the ship until you arrive. If your ship does leave without you, you'll be flown or driven to the next port. If you booked your air through the cruise line you will not be charged for this service, but if you booked air on your own you may have to pay.

ARRIVAL

Assuming you booked air and transfer through the cruise line, you will be met at the airport, after you clear Customs and Immigration, by a cruise line representative. You will probably have to identify your luggage in the baggage area before your bags are transferred to the ship (you won't see them again until they are delivered to your cabin). You will then be escorted to buses to take you to the cruise terminal (or your hotel if you've booked a pre-cruise hotel stay).

If you booked air on your own, you will have to claim your bags and arrange your own transportation to the hotel or ship (you may have to negotiate with a cab driver for a good rate). Make sure you find out in advance exactly which terminal the ship is departing from, since some ports are quite busy and your cab driver may not know exactly where to go. If you need a porter at the terminal, tip him $1 per bag (U.S. dollars will be gladly accepted).

CHECKING IN

What happens as you enter the terminal depends on the cruise line and the size of the ship, but generally at this point you can expect to wait in line. Despite the best efforts of the cruise line, the scene at the pier may be zoolike.

You will not be able to board the ship before the scheduled embarkation time, usually about 3 or 4 hours before sailing. That's because the ship has likely had to disembark passengers from the previous cruise earlier that day, and the crew needs time to clean and prepare and take care of the various paperwork and Customs documents that need to be completed. If you fly in on an early flight on the day of departure, the ship may let you board early and wait in a lounge or restaurant until your cabin is ready.

European ships are very strict about boarding times. If the last boarding is scheduled for 5pm, you better be there by 5pm, even if the ship doesn't leave the dock until 6pm. You have up until a half-hour (on some ships, it's 1 hr.) before departure to board, but there are some advantages to boarding earlier, like getting first dibs on prime dining room tables (if you haven't been assigned a table in advance) and spa treatment times. Plus, if you get on early enough you can eat lunch on the ship (depending on the ship and departure time, lunch may be served until 3pm or even 4pm the first day).

⌜Fun Fact⌝ Birthplace of the Pleasure Cruise

Hamburg, Germany, claims to be the place where traveling on a ship dedicated to cruising (as opposed to transporting cargo) was invented. In 1845, the Sloman Shipping Line placed an ad in a Hamburg newspaper promoting that "A fully rigged ship is to go on a voyage of the world which will not have as its aim any mercantile purposes, but the ship's whole facilities and accommodation, the fixing of the times of sojourn in the towns and countries to be visited, the overriding aim of the whole voyage will only be consideration for the security, comfort, entertainment and information of the travelers."

The ad further stated that the cruise was only for people "of good reputation and education."

Either right before or right after you get to the check-in desk, you will likely have to pass through an X-ray machine (like those at the airport).

During check-in, your **boarding documents** will be checked and your passport will likely be taken for immigration processing. You will get it back sometime during the cruise (you might want to carry a photocopy as backup). If you have booked a suite you may get priority boarding at a special desk. Special-needs passengers may also be processed separately.

Depending on the cruise line, you may establish your **onboard credit account** at this point by turning over a major credit card to be swiped or by making a deposit in cash or traveler's checks (usually $250). On other ships you need to report to the purser's office once on board to establish your onboard credit account. You may also be given your cabin key at check-in (in some cases your onboard credit card doubles as your room key and boarding card), though on some ships your cabin key will be waiting for you at your cabin.

Protocol for establishing your **dining room table assignment,** if one is required (on open-seating ships, it's not) also varies by ship. You may be given your assignment in advance of your sailing (on your tickets), or advised of your table number as you check in. Or a card with your table number may be waiting for you in your stateroom. If you do not receive an assignment by the time you get to your stateroom, you will be directed to a maitre d's desk set up in a convenient spot on board. This is also the place to go to make any changes if your assignment does not meet with your approval.

Make sure your seating time (early or late) and table size are as you requested and that you are in the smoking or nonsmoking section you requested (where applicable). Special dietary requests can also be confirmed at this time.

A bevy of cruise line employees will be on hand to make sure your check-in goes smoothly. Don't be afraid to ask them questions.

After you clear the check-in area, you will likely be corralled into posing for the ship's photographer. These pictures sell for about $7 or $8 a pop and will be displayed later for your perusal at the ship's photography shop. Of course, you are under no obligation to buy them. Ditto for any drinks you may be offered as you board.

STEPPING ABOARD

As you exit the gangplank, a crew member will probably escort you to your cabin, probably offering to help carry your hand luggage. No tip is required, but would be accepted.

Either immediately or a short time later, your steward, the person responsible for the upkeep of your cabin, will stop by to introduce him or herself. He or she will point out the various cabin amenities and controls, such as air-conditioning and light switches, advise you on how they can be reached when you need them (usually by phone or buzzer), and answer any immediate questions you have. The steward will also make you aware of the ship's safety drill procedures (see below) and advise you of the location of your muster (assembly) station for the drill.

It's important to alert the steward immediately if the beds are not configured to your liking or if there are any other problems you can see. If the cabin itself is not what you thought you booked, go right to the hotel manager with your complaint.

You can also make the steward aware of any special needs you might have, such as a preference for foam as opposed to feather pillows (extra pillows and blankets should already be in your closet).

What Happens if Your Bags Get Lost?

Before you start to panic, keep in mind that on big ships, some 4,000 bags need to be loaded and distributed. But if you're hours into the sailing and getting concerned, don't hesitate to call the guest relations desk (or purser's office). If your luggage really is lost, the cruise line customer relations folks are supposed to spring into immediate action. They, not you, will contact the airline and ground operators to see what's what.

Usually, missing bags will arrive at the ship the next day. They will be either driven or flown to the first port-of-call.

If your baggage is lost, the cruise line will likely provide an overnight kit with such items as a toothbrush and toothpaste. The first night of a cruise is always casual dress, so you don't have to worry about wearing what you have on in the dining room.

If the baggage is still lost the next day, your baggage insurance, if you purchased any, will kick in and you get to go shopping in the ship's shops for proper attire. If you do not have insurance, the line may, at its discretion, offer you cash compensation—usually $50 a day.

If the second night is a formal night, the line may be able to provide a tux for a man and may also have a small selection of clothes available that a woman can borrow.

In your cabin, on most ships, you will find a **daily program** detailing the day's events, meal times, and so forth, as well as important information on the ship's safety rituals.

There may also be a hotel-like **menu of services** notebook, including room service options, and a phone directory. Your room should also be outfitted with a DO NOT DISTURB sign (important for nappers), order forms for room-service breakfast (if offered), and forms and bags for dry cleaning and laundry services.

You may want to try the TV, safe, and other gadgets to see how they work, check out the bathroom, etc. The loud whoosh of the toilet is normal (most ships use a vacuum system). Note that you are not supposed to put any objects other than paper in the bowl.

There may be bottles of water provided in your cabin (although the water on most ships is perfectly drinkable). Just because the bottles are there doesn't mean they are free. If you don't know, ask before you open them. Items in the mini-bar are not free.

There should be directions near the phone advising you how to make calls to other passengers on the ship and to ship personnel, as well as how to request wake-up calls. There should also be directions on dialing outside. Note the cost of outside calls, which can be really expensive (as much as $16.95 per min.).

Your **luggage** probably won't have arrived yet, but if it has, go ahead and unpack. If not, after you've exhausted your tour of your room, we recommend checking out the rest of the ship.

Before you do this, though, don't forget to put your cash, ID, air tickets, and other valuables in the **cabin safe.** If there is no safe in your room, take this all down to the purser's office where there will be one available. Don't forget to take your shipboard credit card (in case you want to buy a drink) and key with you.

You may find a **deck map** of the ship in your cabin. If not, you should be able to get one at the purser's office, so find your way there. There are usually deck plans and directional signs at main stairways and elevators. You probably won't need the map after the first day (part of the fun of being on a big ship is getting lost, anyway), but it's a good way to establish the layout in your mind.

Begin your tour on the top deck and work your way down, checking out the main public rooms. That way, you can stop at the beginning of your tour at the **"welcome aboard" buffet,** which is usually set up in the casual dining area, near the pool deck.

If you plan to use the spa services, stop by and make appointments so you can get your preferred times (the best times go fast, and some popular treatments sell out). The staff may be offering an introductory **spa tour.** Also stop by at the gym, especially if you plan on taking fitness classes. The fitness staff will likely be on hand to pass out schedules and answer any questions you might have.

Note the ship's casino and shops are always closed when the ship is in port. While in the port, the swimming pool(s) will also likely be tarped—to be filled with either fresh or salt water after the ship sets sail.

Some ships offer **escorted tours** of the public rooms. If you aren't comfortable roaming on your own, check the daily program in your cabin for details.

LIFEBOAT/SAFETY DRILL

In your room you will find, either waiting on your bed or in the closet or a drawer, bright orange **life jackets.** If you are traveling with kids there should be special jackets for them (if not, alert your steward). Ships are required by law to conduct safety drills within the first 24 hours. Most do it either right before the ship sails or shortly thereafter. Attendance is mandatory, and the crew often takes attendance. A notice on the back of your cabin door will list the procedures and advise as to your assigned **muster station** and how to get there. You will also find directions to the muster station in the hallway. You will be alerted as to the time in both the daily program and in repeated public announcements (and probably by your steward as well).

To start the drill, the ship will broadcast its emergency signal. At this time you will be required to return to your cabin, grab your life jacket, and report to your assigned muster station (this will be in a lounge, the casino, or another public room). Some drills last only a few minutes, while others are quite detailed. At the muster station, a crew member will review how to put on your life vest. He or she will also point out the features of the vest, including the whistle to call for help (don't try it out here!) and the light that turns on when it hits the water. The drill may also include a visit to the **lifeboats** and even a discussion of how to jump into the water.

In some cases guests will be required to put on the life jacket so a crew member can check and make sure it's being worn correctly; on other ships you just need to bring it with you on the drill.

If you have additional questions about safety procedures, you can address them to a crew member or officer at this time. On some ships, in addition to the drill, a safety video will also be broadcast on the TV in your cabin.

After the drill, return to your cabin and put your life jacket back in its place.

2 An Introduction to Onboard Activities

In Europe, you will probably want to spend most of your time exploring the ports. But from morning till night, most big ships also offer an extensive schedule of onboard activities, especially during days at sea (when the ship isn't visiting a port). All the contests, lessons, and classes will be listed in the ship's **daily program,** which is placed in your cabin the previous evening, usually while you're at dinner. A **cruise director** and his or her staff are in charge of the festivities and do their best to ensure a good time is had by all. Smaller ships offer activities, too, but often with less hoopla; there may be wine-tastings, port talks by the cruise director and captain, and maybe presentations by guest lecturers.

Many lines encourage passengers to let their hair down. Hence you will find group contests (remember *Family Feud?*), bingo, shipboard horse racing, pool games, and the like.

If you're a performer at heart, volunteer for the weekly **passenger talent show** or head to the nightclub one evening for **karaoke.** Brainy types can sign up for trivia quizzes, and there will also likely be chess, checkers, bridge, or backgammon tournaments.

Winners of any of the above get prizes like champagne, T-shirts, mugs, or key chains, maybe even a massage from the spa, all of which add to the fun.

SHIPBOARD CASINOS

For all you high-rollers out there, all but the smallest, adventure-oriented ships have casinos. Not surprisingly, the megas have the biggest, flashiest, Vegas-style casinos, full of neon, with literally hundreds of slot machines and dozens of blackjack, poker, and craps tables as well as roulette. Smaller ship lines, like Windstar and Seabourn, have casinos as well, albeit scaled-down ones, with maybe a dozen slots and a couple of blackjack and poker tables. European ships tend to have smaller casinos than American ships (it's a cultural thing). Stakes aboard most ships are relatively low, with maximum bets rarely exceeding $200. Average minimum bets at blackjack and poker tables are generally $5; the minimum at roulette is typically 50¢ or $1. Children are not allowed in onboard casinos.

CLASSES, LESSONS & DEMONSTRATIONS

There are plenty of learning opportunities available on ships in Europe. Most feature a lecturer, usually a university professor, author, or museum curator well versed in the art, architecture, and history of the regions you will be visiting.

For those seeking less cerebral pursuits, there are likely to be **line dancing and ballroom dancing lessons** held a few times a week on big ships in the main show lounge, and taught by one of the onboard entertainers. There may also be informative **seminars** on subjects like cooking, bartending, arts and crafts, and wine tasting; there is usually a $5 to $15 charge for the wine tasting and sometimes there's a cost for arts and crafts materials. There may even be classes on topics such as **personal investing** or **handwriting analysis.**

The chef might do a food-decorating demonstration and share tips on how to carve flowers and animals out of fruits and vegetables. Demonstrations by the salon and spa staff on hair and skin care are common too (not to mention free advertising for their not-so-cheap spa treatments).

QUIET DIVERSIONS

For those seeking quieter times, there is always the option of planting yourself in a deck chair with a good book. Many ships have **libraries** (some are nice plush retreats) stocked with classic books and new releases. Some of the libraries also have chairs specially equipped with CD players and headphones and a collection of CDs. Some ships also have **video libraries** (you can take the movie back to your cabin to play on your VCR) and/or offer both standard TV movies and pay-per-view first-run movies on in-cabin TVs. **Cinemas** on some ships also show classic and first-run movies. Some ships offer **computers** preprogrammed with both reference materials and games. Usually adjacent to the library you'll find the **card room,** a nice quiet place to play (usually with bridge as the top attraction). Here you'll often also find board games like Monopoly, backgammon, and Scrabble.

ART AUCTIONS

Many large ships offer art auctions, which are fun and entertaining but not necessarily guaranteed to give you a bargain price. Outside concessionaires with really entertaining salespeople run the auctions, with the artwork fetching anywhere from $50 to $85,000 or more. The auctions are big business on ships these days, and you'll see a lot of pieces sold.

The auctions are held several times during the cruise in a lounge, with the salesperson briefly discussing each painting before opening the floor up to bids. The offerings will include some big names like Peter Max, Marc Chagall, Joan Miró, Walt Disney, and Salvador Dalí, plus some absolute schlock. They're usually sold duty-free, with or without frames, and can be packed and mailed home to the winner for an additional fee (it will take several weeks to arrive).

On vessels including the *Golden Princess* and Radisson's *Seven Seas Mariner* you can also bid on some of the art that's displayed aboard the ship if something really catches your eye.

ONBOARD SPORTS & FITNESS OPTIONS

If you're into sports, the megaships pack the most punch. In addition to well-equipped gyms rivaling those on shore, they boast outdoor volleyball, basketball, and paddle tennis courts as well as outdoor jogging tracks and several pools for water polo, volleyball, aqua-aerobics, and swimming.

WATER SPORTS

For water-sports enthusiasts, small ships are the best equipped. Windstar, Radisson Seven Seas, Club Med, and Seabourn have retractable water-sports platforms that, weather permitting, can be lowered from the stern into calm waters when the ship is anchored, allowing passengers to almost step right from their cabins to snorkel, windsurf, kayak, sail, water-ski, go on banana boat rides, and swim. Star Clippers also has an extensive water-sports program, and you can start your PADI diving certification program on board the vessels.

GOLF

If you're a golfaholic, you'll be happy to find that more and more cruises are offering the opportunity to tee off, both on board and on shore. For the casual golfer, a few ships—Royal Caribbean's *Brilliance of the Seas* and Princess's *Golden Princess*—have **miniature golf courses** on board. For more serious players, Crystal's *Symphony,* Royal Caribbean's *Brilliance of the Seas,* and Princess's

Golden Princess, among others, have **golf simulators.** These state-of-the-art virtual-reality machines allow you to play the great courses of the world without ever leaving the ship (for about $20 per half-hour). Full-size clubs are used, and a virtual-reality video screen allows players to watch the electronic path of a ball they've actually hit soar high over the greens or land flat in a sand trap.

Many more lines, including Celebrity, Costa, Crystal, Cunard, Norwegian, Princess, and Radisson Seven Seas, have on at least some of their ships **outdoor golf cages,** areas enclosed in netting where you can swing, putt, and whack at real golf balls.

More and more lines are offering **golf programs** that include instruction and tips by golf pros who sail on board, videotaping lessons and going over technique with passengers. Half-hour lessons are about $30 to $40, and hour-long lessons are $60 to $70. In port, Silversea, Crystal, and Radisson are among lines that offer **golf excursions** to well known courses.

SPORTS FOR COUCH POTATOES

No need for those sports-loving couch potatoes out there to be deprived. NCL's *Norwegian Dream* and Princess's *Golden Princess* are among the vessels that, in Europe, have dedicated sports bars with large-screen televisions broadcasting ESPN International (which features a lot of soccer). On some ships, you may also be able to watch ESPN International on your in-cabin TV.

3 An Introduction to Onboard Entertainment

The cruise lines offer a vast repertoire of exciting entertainment. As you'd expect, the biggest ships offer the most variety, from Vegas-style cabaret to magicians, soloists, pianists, dance bands, quartets, jugglers, DJs, puppeteers, and comedians.

ENTERTAINMENT ON THE MEGASHIPS

Entertainment is a big part of the cruise experience on the biggest ships, particularly those in the fleets of Royal Caribbean, Celebrity, Costa, Princess, Norwegian Cruise Line, and Holland America. Not surprisingly, they have an extensive variety of options throughout the day. Afternoons, you can dance the day away on deck with the live dance band playing Caribbean melodies (yes, even in Europe).

By about 5pm, before the first-seating dinner (and again at 7pm before the late seating begins), the entertainment choices really kick in. Head to the piano bar for a cocktail or do some pre-dinner, big-band style dancing.

After both the early and the late dinner seating, 2 or more nights during your cruise, the main show lounge will feature **Vegas-style musicals,** where a flamboyant troupe of anywhere from 4 to 16 male and female dancers decked out in feather boas, sequins, and top hats slide and kick their way across the stage (and lip-synch to the songs' choruses) as a soloist or two belts out show tunes. You'll hear favorites from *Phantom of the Opera, Cats, Hair, Grease, A Chorus Line,* and all the Gershwin and Rodgers and Hammerstein classics. Elaborate stage sets and frequent costume changes on the biggest ships make these shows the entertainment highlight of the week. On some of the European ships, these shows can be downright amateurish, but are no less amusing.

When the Broadway show stuff isn't scheduled, entertainment may be a **magic show,** complete with rabbits in hats and scantily clad assistants getting sawed in half, **acrobatic acts** (always a big hit), and **headlining soloists** (some are quite good). In Europe some ships bring on **local performers** at ports for special performances (held in the afternoon or evening) usually of the folkloric variety. You might, for instance, be entertained by flamenco performers, or an Irish step-dancing group.

The **disco** will probably get going around 9 or 10pm (later on European ships) and continue until 2 or 3am or later. Shake your booty to the best of '70s, '80s, '90s, and Y2K pop and rock music; often a live band plays until about midnight, when a DJ takes over until the wee hours.

An alternative to the disco or the main show might be a **1950s sock hop** held in another lounge, or a **jazz trio** in yet another romantic nightspot. Show-offs, or those who just like to embarrass themselves, will probably be able to find a **karaoke lounge.**

ENTERTAINMENT ON THE SMALL SHIPS

Ships carrying 100 to 400 passengers have fewer entertainment options, but are no less appealing if you like things mellow. On the high-end lines, there may be a quartet or pianist performing before dinner and maybe afterward, a small-scale **Broadway dance revue,** and dancing in a quiet lounge. The more casual small ships might have taped music or a synth-piano player before and after dinner; or no entertainment at all (you can go off to a club at a port for that). Expect a crew and passenger **talent show** to be scheduled during the cruise, too. While in port, small-ship lines like Windstar and Star Clippers might bring **local performers** on board for an afternoon or evening of entertainment. Some small ships also offer movie evenings when a movie is shown in a lounge.

4 Shipboard Gyms & Spas

If your idea of a perfect vacation includes a run on a treadmill or a relaxing seaweed facial, the newest big ships have the biggest and best-equipped fitness and spa facilities. Since the early 1990s, cruise lines have prioritized their spa and fitness areas, moving them out of windowless corners of bottom decks and into prime top-deck positions with oodles of space and lots of glass for soothing views of the ocean. They offer **state-of-the art workout machines** and a host of **spa treatments.**

GYMS: AN ANTIDOTE TO THE MIDNIGHT BUFFET

The well-equipped fitness centers on the megaships may feature a dozen treadmills and just as many stationary bikes, step machines, upper- and lower-body machines, and free weights.

The roomy **aerobics studios** on most big ships built in the last decade or so are the kind you have at your gym back home, with mirrors and special flooring. There are at least a couple of aerobics and stretch classes per day. Certified instructors teach the classes, which usually range from the traditional to the trendy—high- and low-impact, funk, step, body sculpting, stretch and tone, and abdominals.

Older ships often do not devote nearly as much space and resources to sports and fitness. The gyms are generally smaller and more spartan, but on all but the smallest alternative ships you'll find at least a couple of treadmills and a stationary bike or step machine or two, plus some free weights. On ships with limited gym facilities, aerobics classes tend to be held out on deck or in a lounge.

ONBOARD SPAS: TAKING RELAXATION ONE STEP FURTHER

If your idea of a heavenly vacation is spending half of it under a towel being massaged and kneaded with some soothing mystery oil, choose a cruise ship with a well-equipped spa.

Shipboard spas are big business. On post-1990 big ships, they've been given spacious quarters on top decks. The largest spas have several treatment rooms, a sauna and a steam room or two, and full locker rooms with showers. On ships built pre-1990 the spas, like the gyms, are generally going to be small; the large spa on the *QE2* is an exception. Even most of the smaller upscale ships have some semblance of a spa and a beauty salon. Windstar Cruises' *Wind Surf* carries only 300 passengers but boasts a particularly big spa facility (not so on the other Windstar ships, though). As with gyms, you won't find spas at all on the smaller alternative ships.

Some of the best spas and fitness facilities at sea are on board Celebrity Cruises' vessels. Called the AquaSpa, these spacious health meccas are as pleasing to the eye as they are functional. The focal point is a giant thalassotherapy pool, a bubbling cauldron of warm, soothing seawater that's a great place to relax before a massage. Other impressive spas can be found on Costa Cruise Lines' *CostaVictoria*, which includes such accoutrements as tile mosaics, rattan lounge chairs, and a small plunge pool; and *CostaAtlantica*, which offers a dozen treatment rooms and an indoor sunning area with a whirlpool.

Spa treatments range in price from about $30 to over $150, plus the 10% to 15% tip that's expected (some lines add this on automatically) and can be charged to your onboard account. Celebrity and Windstar allow you to **prebook spa packages** with your travel agent, but appointment times cannot be reserved until you board the ship.

 The Ubiquitous Steiner

The spas and hair salons on most ships are staffed and operated by a firm called Steiner, a London-based company with a hands-down corner on the market. You'll find most of the prices are steep—for instance, a 55-minute facial is $89 to $130, and a 50-minute massage is $84 to $99.

The young women, mostly Brits, who do the massages, facials, manicures, pedicures, reflexology, and other services are professional and charming, but they don't always deliver consistent service. A best bet is the massages, which are nearly always well executed. The manicures, pedicures, and facials can be disappointing. And you can't usually get your nails done unless you also submit to a pricey hand (or foot) softening and massaging treatment.

Be aware that Steiner isn't shy about pushing its extensive and expensive collection of creams, exfoliants, moisturizers, toners, and masks, either. Get a facial and you'll wind up with an itemized list of four or five products, easily adding up to over $200, that they recommend you buy to get the same effect at home (of course you can just say no). The shameless promotion of the fancy ointments on some ships, which occurs just as you're coming out of your semi-conscious post-massage trance, certainly brings you back to reality. That said, people rave about the quality of the products.

5 An Introduction to Shipboard Dining

Food takes on Fellini-esque proportions on cruise ships. With meals a major part of the cruise experience, they are served with much pomp and circumstance, particularly on the bigger ships.

Forget your standard breakfast, lunch, and dinner. You will be offered, on a daily basis, an early-riser's continental breakfast, choice of breakfast in the dining room or a lavish breakfast buffet, a mid-morning snack, lunch in the dining room or a lavish luncheon buffet, afternoon tea, dinner in the dining room or in an alternative venue such as an intimate, reservations-only restaurant or more casual Lido restaurant, and an unbelievable midnight buffet or trays of late-night snacks.

And if that's not enough, some ships also have pizza parlors, poolside grills, 24-hour room service, and specialty food venues such as caviar bars, ice-cream parlors, and gourmet coffee shops. And you may even be offered fresh fruit daily in your cabin.

DINNER IS SERVED

The nighttime meal on most ships is one of the main social events of the day. The table setup is quite formal, with china, silver, fresh flowers, and starched linens, and serving will be at a leisurely pace. You will likely sit with other passengers (tables for one or two are hard to come by) and should enjoy some lively conversation which no doubt will center on some of the sights you have visited that day.

On most ships, you'll find at least five courses, with three to six options for each course, and you can choose from a wide array of international fare like escargot, vichyssoise, veal scaloppini, poached salmon, prime rib, and pastas. There will also likely be **vegetarian choices** as well as **healthier entrees** that are lower in fat, calories, cholesterol, and sodium.

It's considered good etiquette to arrive at the dining room on time, to show up dressed according to the dress code of the day, and to wait until everyone at your table has arrived before you order.

You are not required to order every course. Conversely, if two appetizers or main courses catch your fancy, you can order both. If you do not like something you ordered, send it back and ask for another selection.

DINNER TABLE DIVORCES

If you get stuck with a couple of yahoos who seem to offend every bone in your body or there just isn't any chemistry, no need to suffer in silence. It's best to explain to the maitre d' as courteously and as soon as possible that your table assignment simply won't do, and request a change. You will usually be accommodated (a greasing of the palm will help).

SPECIAL DIETS

If you follow any special diet, inform the cruise line as early as possible, preferably when booking your cruise. **Vegetarian dishes** and **kosher food** are commonly available, and almost all cruise lines now feature a selection of healthier, **lighter meals,** labeled as such on the menu. On all but the most cost-conscious lines, the kitchen usually tries to satisfy reasonable culinary requests.

CASUAL DINING

If you'd rather skip the formality of the main dining room, all but the tiniest ships serve breakfast and lunch in a casual **buffet-style cafe restaurant.** Usually located on the Lido Deck, with indoor and outdoor poolside seating, these restaurants serve an extensive spread of both hot and cold food items. On the megaships, nearby may be a **grill** where at lunch you can get hamburgers, hot dogs, and often chicken. Veggie burgers are also showing up regularly at the grills these days. On most ships, **breakfast and lunch buffets** are generally served for a 3- to 4-hour period, so guests can stroll in and out whenever they desire. Princess Cruises has the Lido cafe open around the clock on its newest ships.

If you're not in the mood for the fuss of formal dining in the evening, either, many big ships now offer dinner as well in the casual Lido restaurant (sometimes not every night). Most serve casual dinner buffet-style, but some do a combination of sit-down service and buffet. Wear what you want, stroll in when you please, and, in most cases, sit where you please (most are open seating). After soup and salad, two or three entrees are offered, like prime rib, salmon, or stir-fry, followed by dessert.

If you do want the fine dining and formality, but with fewer fellow diners in tow, several lines have added intimate, **reservations-only alternative restaurants,** usually seating less than 100. In some, but not all cases, there's a cover charge to dine in these special venues, usually $5 to $20. (See specifics on alternative dining options in the ship reviews in chapters 5, 6, 7, and 8.)

6 Onboard Shopping Opportunities

Even the smallest ships have at least a small shop on board selling T-shirts, sweatshirts, baseball caps, and the like bearing the cruise line's logo. The big new megaships, though, have the most extensive onboard shopping. Like mini malls, there may be as many as 10 different stores selling everything from **toiletries and sundries** like film, toothpaste, candy, and paperback books (and even condoms) to totes, T-shirts, mugs, toys, key chains, and other **cruise line logo souvenirs.** You'll find **formalwear** like sequined dresses and jackets, silk dresses and scarves, purses, satin shoes, cummerbunds, ties, and tuxedo shirts, as well as **perfume, cosmetics, jewelry** (costume and the real stuff), and **porcelain figurines.**

All merchandise sold on board while a ship is at sea is tax-free; to maintain that tax-free status, the shops are closed whenever a ship is in port. Though tax-free, prices aren't always deals, though some good deals can be had on alcohol, and by mid-cruise there are often good sales on a selection of T-shirts, tote bags, and jewelry as well. Some ships stock **local arts and crafts items** at great prices. Things that usually cost you more on board than off are disposal cameras, sunscreen, and candy and snack foods. Prices on clothing and good jewelry vary.

7 Sundry Shipboard Services & Facilities

RELIGIOUS SERVICES
Some ships, including those in the Costa fleet, have priests on board who lead Catholic Mass. Most ships have a nondenominational service on Sunday and a Friday-night Jewish Sabbath service, usually run by a passenger. On holidays, whether Jewish or Christian, clergy is typically aboard large ships to lead services. The services are usually held in a library or conference room, although some ships have chapels, and the *QE2* has its own synagogue.

MEDICAL CARE
Unless you're on a very small ship, your vessel will have a medical facility staffed by a doctor and a nurse, ready to handle medical emergencies that may arise at

Tips   **Seasickness; or, How to Avoid Getting Green Around the Gills**

Unless you're particularly prone to seasickness, you probably don't need to worry much if you're on a big ship (small ships can be bumpier). But if you are, there are medications that can help, including Dramamine, Bonine, and Marezine (although it's recommended that if you use these medications you not drink alcohol; and they can make you drowsy). All can be bought over the counter, and most ships have supplies available on board—the purser's office may even give them out free. Another option is the Transderm patch for seasickness, available by prescription only, which goes behind your ear and time-releases medication. The patch can be worn for up to 3 days, but comes with a slew of side-effect warnings. Some people have also had success in curbing seasickness by using ginger capsules available at health-food stores, and with the acupressure wrist-bands available at most pharmacies.

sea. Some facilities are quite elaborate. The *Grand Princess,* for instance, has high-tech medical equipment that, using cameras and a live video system, links the ship's medical team to doctors at Cedars-Sinai Medical Center in Los Angeles. The medical center will typically be open during set office hours, with the medical team available on a 24-hour basis to deal with emergencies (on some ships, the doctor can handle everything up to and including an appendectomy, but more typically, he or she dispenses seasickness shots and antibiotics and treats sprained muscles). If there is a major medical emergency, the passenger will be taken off the ship either at the nearest port or by helicopter.

If you have a chronic health problem, it's best to check with your doctor before booking your cruise; and if you have any specific needs, notify the cruise line in advance. This will ensure the ship's medical team is properly prepared to meet your needs.

GETTING THE NEWS

Most newer ships offer **CNN International** on their in-room TVs, and nearly every ship will post the latest news from the wire services outside the purser's office. Some lines even excerpt information from leading newspapers and each day deliver the printouts to your cabin.

STAYING IN TOUCH

In addition to the **telephone** in your cabin (which will cost you big bucks if you use it to call home), you may be able to send **faxes** home via your ship's business center. And many ships in the past year or so have added **e-mail.** In some cases, the ship has a real Internet cafe setup where you can go on the Internet and check your mail at home. In other cases, however, you set up a shipboard account, and while you can send and receive e-mail from that account, you can't actually get on the Internet. Standard fees for e-mail are 50¢ to $1.50 a minute, although on some ships, such as First European's *European Vision* and *European Stars,* the fee can run as high as $15 (in such cases, you may be better off finding an Internet cafe at one of the ports of call).

Where the ship does offer e-mail, you can also usually send your friends back home nifty **e-postcards.** For those into more traditional modes of communications, the purser's office on your ship should have **postcards,** local stamps (U.S. stamps don't work in Europe), and a mailbox that is emptied at each port of call.

8 Wrapping Up Your Cruise—Debarkation Concerns

Hardly anybody likes to get off the ship at the end of his or her cruise, but it's part of the deal. To make it easier, here are a few matters you'll have to take care of before heading back to home sweet home.

THE DEBARKATION TALK

On the last full day of your cruise, the cruise director will offer a debarkation talk covering areas such as tipping, settling your onboard account, packing, dealing with Customs and Immigration, and debarkation procedures, all as they apply to your specific ship. You or a member of your party should attend the talk, particularly if you are a first-time cruiser. You might also be able to catch a broadcast of the session on your in-room TV, and procedures will also be printed in your daily bulletin, but the talk is your chance to ask any questions you might have. Some lines even offer a prize drawing to encourage your attendance at the session.

TIPPING

Tipping is an area that some people find confusing. First, let's establish that on almost all lines (the exceptions being the ritzy lines of Seabourn, Radisson, and Silversea) you are expected to tip the crew—in particular your cabin steward, waiter, and busboy—and to not do so is bad form, since these people rely on tips for the better part of their income. How much you tip is totally up to you, though the cruise line will make suggestions in the daily bulletin and in the cruise director's debarkation briefing. Keep in mind that these are just suggestions.

Generally speaking, each passenger should tip his or her cabin steward and waiter a minimum of about $3.50 per day each, and the busboy $1.50 to $2. In practice, many people nudge it up a bit more so the total tips are $10 to $12 a day per person. On some European lines, suggested tips may be lower (Europeans are not as used to tipping as much as Americans do). On some ships you are also encouraged to tip the waiter and maitre d', plus your butler, if you have one. Recently, in an attempt to make the whole process less confusing, Norwegian Cruise Line began adding tips of $10 per passenger per day automatically to shipboard accounts (you can adjust the amount up or down as you see fit). It's our guess other lines may follow suit.

Tips to the crew are paid at the end of the cruise, and you may have to pay tips in cash (U.S. dollars are okay), in which case the ship will probably offer you envelopes you can distribute to the appropriate crew person. Some lines alternatively (and in our opinion, more conveniently) let you put the tips on your shipboard charge account. Occasionally, tips are pooled and distributed among the crew after the cruise (in which case you just put a lump sum into the pot).

Bar bills automatically include a 15% tip, but if a bartender or wine steward has served you exceptionally well, you can slip him or her a bill, too.

Don't tip the captain or other officers, since they're salaried employees, and tipping them is gauche, if not embarrassing.

If a porter carries your bags at the pier, he'll likely expect a tip.

Tip-Free Cruising

A few lines—for example, Holland America Line and Windstar, have a no-tipping-required policy, meaning you're under no obligation, though staff on these ships will gladly accept tips if proffered. Some other lines, however, have a no-tipping-allowed policy that is strictly enforced.

Note: The above tipping policy is standard for most cruise lines. Guidelines for cruise lines with alternative policies are listed in the "Services" sections of individual ship reviews in part 2.

SETTLING UP

Your shipboard account will close in the wee hours before departure, but prior to that time you will receive a preliminary bill in your cabin. If you are settling your account with your credit card, you don't have to do anything but make sure all the charges are correct. If there is a problem, you will have to report to the purser's office, where you will likely encounter long lines.

If you are paying by cash or traveler's check, you will be asked to settle your account during either the day or night before you leave the ship. This will require that you report to the purser's office.

A final invoice will be delivered to your room before departure.

Keeping receipts for shipboard purchases during your cruise will help you with your tallying efforts, and also ensure you're not surprised when the bill arrives.

PACKING UP

With thousands of suitcases to deal with, big ships have established the routine of requiring guests to pack the night before departure. You will be asked to leave your bags in the hallway before you retire for the night (or usually by midnight). The bags will be picked up overnight and removed from the ship before passengers are allowed to disembark. (If you party late and end up putting your bags out after other bags on your deck have already been collected, advise the purser's office so they can send someone to get your bags; if you don't leave your bags in the hall you will have to carry them off the ship yourself.) You'll see them again in the cruise terminal, where they'll most likely be arranged by deck number.

It's important to make sure your bags are tagged with the **luggage tags** given to you by the cruise line. These tags are color-coded to indicate deck number and disembarkation order. If you need more tags, ask your cabin steward.

A good rule of thumb is to begin packing before dinner. Usually the last night of your cruise will be a casual night to make things easier. When packing, remember to leave out any clothes and toiletries you will need the next day, and don't pack your valuables, breakables, travel documents, or medication. Make sure everything you keep out fits in your overnight bag.

Pack all your purchases made during the trip in one suitcase. This way you can easily retrieve them if you are stopped at Customs (see below).

DEBARKATION ORDER

You'll know it's the day you have to get off the ship because loudspeaker announcements will start blaring particularly early in the morning.

You won't be able to get off the ship until it is cleared by Customs and other authorities, a process that usually takes 90 minutes.

Even so, in most cases you will be asked to vacate your cabin early in the morning (as early as 8am) to give the crew time to prepare the space for the next load of passengers. Before you leave the cabin, check all the drawers to make sure you don't leave anything behind.

On disembarkation day, breakfast may be served earlier than usual, and there may be limited room service or no room service at all. Check your daily bulletin for details.

It takes about 2 hours to get everyone off the ship, and people will be given departure numbers. Those with earlier flights will be allowed to leave first. Everyone will want to leave the ship at the same time, but unless you have an early number, you don't have to rush. Grab a book and head up to the deck, catch a movie or other ship offering, or find another way to occupy yourself. Clogging the hallways doesn't help anyone get off faster.

If things drag on and you're concerned about missing your flight, tell a crew member.

MORE BAGGAGE

If you booked your air through the cruise line and are heading right home, you will collect your bags—there should be porters to help—and proceed to the bus to the airport.

If you booked your own air, you're on your own. You can retrieve your bags—again, there should be porters to help—and catch a cab to the airport or your next destination.

If you're on a post-cruise tour, special instructions will be given by the cruise line.

CUSTOMS
CLEARING CUSTOMS & IMMIGRATION

Make sure you allow enough time at the European airport to check in, collect any Value-Added Tax refunds owed you on the purchases you have made (see chapter 3 for more on VAT) and clear Immigration (you'll need to show your passport).

You may also want to allow time to check out the airport's duty-free offerings.

When you return to the U.S., you will again have to show your passport at Immigration, collect your bags, and clear Customs. You will be handed a Customs form on the plane to fill out.

CUSTOMS   For U.S. citizens, standard Customs allowances are $400 in goods duty-free, including 1 liter of alcohol per person over age 21 and 1 carton of cigarettes. The same goes for green-card holders and non–U.S. residents staying more than 72 hours in the U.S.

On the first $1,000 worth of goods over $400 you pay a flat 10% duty. Beyond that, duty is charged on an item-by-item basis.

You don't have to pay duty on fine works of art, antiques more than 100 years old, and some other luxury items. And you do not have to pay duty on items you mail home.

Is the Earth Moving, or Is It Me?

When you get off the ship, and especially when you close your eyes, you might experience a feeling of rocking, as if you're still on the water. Don't worry—this is perfectly normal and should go away by the next day.

Tips **No Cuban Cigars**

Got a hankering for those Cuban cigars you'll see for sale throughout Europe? Buy them to enjoy in Europe, but don't try to bring them home. If the government can make a case that you bought, sold, traded, or otherwise engaged in transactions involving illegally imported Cuban cigars, you may face civil penalties of up to $55,000, and even criminal charges.

If you do go over your limit, you will have to report to a Customs official. If you are in doubt about whether you have gone over the limit, you can ask a Customs officer for help in filling out the form.

If you go over your allowance, fail to declare it, and get caught, you can get in a heap of trouble, and you might have to pay stiff fines.

Remember, you can't bring into the U.S. anything fresh including fruit, seeds, animals, plants, or meat. This includes any leftovers from the fruit basket in your cabin.

For more information and to help you understand the rules, which are really quite complicated, check out the U.S. Customs Service website (www.customs.ustreas.gov) or write for the department's booklet, "Know Before You Go," P.O. Box 7407, Washington, DC 20044.

FOR BRITISH CITIZENS   You can bring home almost as much as you like of any goods from any EU country (there are limits, in theory at least, of 90l of wine). If you are returning home from a non-EU country or if you buy goods in a duty-free shop, you're restricted to 200 cigarettes, 50 cigars, 2 liters of still table wine, plus 1 liter of spirits or 2 liters of fortified wine. For more information, contact **Her Majesty's Customs & Excise Office,** Passenger Enquiry Point, Wayfar House, 2nd Floor, Great South West Road, Feltham, Middlesex, TW14 (© **020/8910-3744**).

FOR CANADIAN CITIZENS   Canada allows a $750 exemption, and you're allowed to bring back 200 cigarettes, 2.2 pounds of tobacco, 40 imperial ounces of liquor, and 50 cigars. In addition, you're allowed to mail gifts to Canada (with some restrictions). *Note:* The $750 exemption can only be used once a year and only after an absence of 7 days. For more information, write for the booklet "I Declare," issued by **Revenue Canada,** 2265 St. Laurent Blvd., Ottawa, ONT K1G 4KE (© **800/461-9999** or 506/636-5064).

FOR AUSTRALIAN CITIZENS   The duty-free allowance is A$400, or, for those under 18, A$200. Citizens can also bring in 250 cigarettes or 250 grams of loose tobacco, and 1,125 milliliters of alcohol. A helpful brochure, "Know Before You Go," is available from Australian consulates and Customs offices. For more information, contact the **Australian Customs Services,** GPO Box 8, Sydney, NSW 2001 (© **02/9213-2000**).

FOR NEW ZEALAND CITIZENS   The duty-free allowance is NZ$700. Citizens over 17 years of age can bring in 200 cigarettes or 50 cigars, or 250 grams of tobacco, plus 4.5 liters of wine and beer or 1.125 liters of liquor. Most questions are answered in a free pamphlet, "New Zealand Customs Guide for Travellers," which is available at New Zealand consulates and Customs offices. For more information, contact **New Zealand Customs,** 50 Anzac Ave., P.O. Box 29, Auckland (© **09/359-6655**).

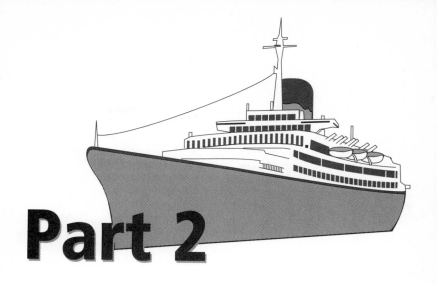

Part 2

The Cruise Lines & Their Ships

Detailed, in-depth reviews of all the cruise lines in Europe, with discussions of the experiences they offer and the lowdown on their ships.

About the Ratings

The cruise industry today offers such a profusion of experiences that it makes comparing all lines and ships by the same set of criteria impossible. The typical, across-the-board ratings used by most cruise guidebooks don't offer the kind of comparisons you need to make your decision. For that reason, our "Frommer's Ratings" system, based on the classic customer satisfaction survey, judges the cruise lines on the following important considerations, rating them either *poor, fair, good, excellent,* or *outstanding.*

- Enjoyment Factor
- Dining
- Activities
- Children's Program
- Entertainment
- Service
- Overall Value

Again, though, you can't compare the experiences you'll have aboard an ultra-luxury line like Seabourn, an exploratory alternative line like Lindblad Expeditions, and a megaship line like Royal Caribbean. They're different animals. For that reason, **we've graded the cruise lines on a sliding scale,** comparing ships *only with the other ships in their category*—mainstream with mainstream, luxury with luxury, alternative with alternative.

Note that since the river ships and barges described in chapter 9 are marketed mostly through brokers rather than cruise lines that strive to present a consistent product identity, categorical ratings for these vessels are not possible.

THE SHIP REVIEWS

We've listed some of the ships' vital statistics—ship size, year built and most recently refurbished, number of cabins, number of officers and crew—to help you compare, then rated such things as cabin comfort, decor, etc., on a scale of 1 to 5, which you can read just like the Frommer's Ratings at the beginning of each line review (i.e., 1 = poor, 2 = fair, 3 = good, 4 = excellent, 5 = outstanding).

Size is listed in tons. Note that these are not actual measures of weight, but **gross register tons (GRTs),** which is a measure of the interior space used to produce revenue on a ship. One GRT equals 100 cubic feet of enclosed, revenue-generating space.

CRUISE PRICES

As we discussed in chapter 2, rates listed in the cruise line brochures are inflated and, with the exception of holidays, you can **expect to pay anywhere from 10% to 60% less if you book your cruise early** (generally 3 to 6 months in advance). The rates listed in this book are the starting rates listed in the cruise lines' brochures. We have not added in any discounts that may be applied.

In each ship review, we offer prices for a seven-night cruise (in cases where only longer cruises are available that is so noted, and priced accordingly) for the following three basic types of accommodations:

- inside cabins (without windows)
- outside cabins (with windows)
- suites

Remember that cruise ships generally have several different categories of cabins within each of these three basic divisions, all priced differently, which is why you'll find a range of prices in each category. In general, the cost of a top-level inside cabin will probably be very close to the rate for a low-level outside cabin, and the cost of a top-level outside may be very close to the rate for a low-level suite.

Rates listed include port charges and taxes unless otherwise noted. Other extras that are included, such as airfare and hotel stays, are also noted.

Cruise lines have various ways of expressing the number of days or nights of the itinerary. When calculating the number of days, we have eliminated the disembarkation day, since you usually leave the ship in the morning. So when we describe an itinerary as 7-day, that means you spend 7 nights on the ship.

5

The American Mainstream Lines

The American mainstream ships offer a little something for almost everyone—all ages, backgrounds, and interests. The more elegant and refined of the lot are commonly referred to as **premium,** a notch up from **mass-market** in the sophistication department. Of the ships we review below, Celebrity, Holland America, and Princess are premium lines, while Norwegian and Royal Caribbean are mass-market lines and Orient falls somewhere in between.

Since the mainstream category is the most popular, it's the one that's seen the most growth, innovation, and investment in recent years. This is the category where the **megaships** reside, those hulking floating resorts that offer the widest variety of activities and entertainment.

The mainstream ships as a whole offer a broad range of cabins—outside (with windows), inside (no windows), suites, and cabins with private verandas. They have both formal and informal dining options, a wide array of entertainment (heavy on the Vegas-style stuff), and more activities than you can possibly squeeze into one day. Overall, the atmosphere is very social, and passengers tend to enjoy mingling.

Even the smaller mainstream ships, like those of Orient Lines, offer lots of choice in accommodations, dining venues, activities, and entertainment. Offering variety to make your onboard experience as pleasant as possible is what these ships are really about.

When these ships, especially the larger ones, visit ports, their presence does not go unnoticed. Since these ships mean so much to the local economy of the ports they are visiting, they are sometimes greeted with much pomp and circumstance, including marching bands and onlookers waving from the shore. It's often a festive affair for both passengers and locals.

DRESS CODES   On most week-long cruises aboard mass-market and premium ships, there are 2 formal nights calling for dark suits or tuxedos for men and cocktail dresses, sequined numbers, or fancy pantsuits for women. The other 5 nights are some combination of semi-formal and casual, and call for suits or sport jackets and slacks for men, and dresses, pantsuits, or skirts and tops for women. Daytime is casual. But keep in mind that some lines—Norwegian Cruise Line, for instance—scheduled only one formal night in a weeklong voyage. On all ships, guests are asked not to wear shorts and T-shirts in the formal dining rooms at night.

Carnival's European Debut

Carnival Cruise Lines, the big kahuna of the cruise industry, makes its European debut in 2002. The "Fun Ship" line will offer one cruise to introduce its new *Carnival Legend* (which will be fresh from a shipyard in Helsinki). The 12-day Northern Europe sailing will depart from Harwich (England) on August 24, visiting Copenhagen (Denmark), Warnemunde (Germany), Helsinki (Finland), St. Petersburg (Russia), Tallinn (Estonia), and Amsterdam (The Netherlands) before returning to London on September 5. The ship will then make its way across the Atlantic on a 15-day transatlantic sailing that includes port calls in Europe at Le Havre (France), Cobh (Ireland), and Greenock (Scotland).

If the cruises are successful (as in sold out), Carnival will likely increase its presence in Europe in 2003, a spokesman said.

The *Carnival Legend* is a sister ship to the *Carnival Spirit* (introduced in April 2001) and *Carnival Pride* (introduced December 2001). The 88,500-ton, 2,124-passenger vessel offers a wide variety of resort-style amenities and facilities including 18 bars, lounges, and nightspots; a duty-free shopping mall; a big multitiered gym and health spa (with the latest and greatest equipment); an Internet cafe; and an expansive casino. Kids get a 2,400-square-foot play area and a video arcade, and the ship also has four swimming pools (including a kiddie splash pool and one pool with a removable dome for all-weather use) as well as a freestanding water slide.

Dining options will include a reservations-only supper club featuring excellent steaks and other treats for a cover charge of $20. A patisserie offers specialty coffees and sweets, and there's a 24-hour pizzeria, standard on Carnival ships. Carnival redid its cuisine recently, and it's surprisingly good, including treats like soft-shell crab in the main dining room, and Chinese food and deli stations in the main buffet area.

The interior design scheme, orchestrated by legendary Carnival designer Joe Farcus, will focus on the "legend" of the ship's name with interiors to reflect some of the world's most famous figures. No doubt it will be a glitzy, fabulous affair.

The ship will have 1,062 cabins, 80% of which feature a sitting area and ocean views. And 80% of the outside cabins have balconies.

Fares for the 12-day cruise are $1,999 to $2,099 inside, $2,299 to $2,999 outside, and $3,999 to $5,127 suites. For reservations, call ℭ **866/204-2979**; or visit www.carnival.com.

Cruise Lines Reviewed in This Chapter
- Celebrity Cruises
- Holland America Line
- Norwegian Cruise Line
- Orient Lines
- Princess Cruises
- Royal Caribbean International

1 Celebrity Cruises

SHIPS IN EUROPE   Constellation (preview)

1050 Caribbean Way, Miami, FL 33132. ℂ **800/327-6700** or 305/539-6000. Fax 800/722-5329. www. celebrity-cruises.com.

Celebrity is simply the best of the American mainstream lines. With the most elegant mainstream ships in the industry, Celebrity offers the best of both worlds: a refined cruise experience with pampering and fine food, yet one that is fun at a price normal people can afford.

Each of the line's ships is spacious, glamorous, and comfortable, mixing sleekly modern and updated classic styles, and throwing in astoundingly cutting-edge art collections to boot.

The genteel service on board is exceptional for a mainstream product. Staff members are exceedingly polite and professional, and contribute to the elegant shipboard mood. Dining-wise, Celebrity shines, offering innovative cuisine with a French influence that's a cut above what's offered by all the other mainstream lines.

There's plenty to do on Celebrity ships, but the focus is on mellower, more relaxing pursuits. Innovative programming helps set the line apart from the pack. Niceties such as roving a cappella bands and magicians who sidle up to your table to entertain during pre- and post-dinner drinks lend a personal touch.

Celebrity gets the "best of" nod in a lot of categories: The AquaSpas, with their indoor thalassotherapy pools, are the best at sea; the art collections the most compelling; the cigar bars the most plush; and the onboard activities among the most varied. Cabins are good-size (there is really not a bad cabin in the house) and Celebrity pampers suite guests with butler service. Guests in any cabin can get in-cabin pizza delivery.

Pros

- **Spectacular spas and gyms.** Beautiful to look at and well stocked.
- **Fabulous food.** Consistently high-rated cuisine is tops among mainstream ships.
- **Innovative everything.** Entertainment, art, cigar bars, service, spas, and cuisine are some of the most innovative in the industry.

Cons

- **Semi-private verandas.** Many of the huge "private" verandas are really only semi-private (keep that robe on!).
- **Occasional crowding.** Pack a couple thousand people onto a ship (pretty much any ship) and you'll get crowds sometimes, such as at buffets and when debarking.

Compared with other American Mainstream lines, here's how Celebrity rates:

	Poor	Fair	Good	Excellent	Outstanding
Enjoyment Factor					✓
Dining					✓
Activities				✓	
Children's Program			✓		
Entertainment				✓	
Service					✓
Overall Value					✓

THE FLEET

With their crisp navy-blue and white hulls and rakishly angled funnel decorated with a giant *X* (actually the Greek letter for *ch,* as in *Chandris,* the line's founding family), the profiles of Celebrity's ships rank among the industry's most distinctive. Inside, the ships are just as innovative and modern, offering, among other things, the most impressive and striking art collections at sea, featuring works by artists including Robert Rauschenberg, Damien Hirst, Jasper Johns, David Hockney, Pablo Picasso, Andy Warhol, and Helen Frankenthaler.

As the line never tires of pointing out, it has among the youngest fleets in the industry—all of its ships having been built since 1990. The line's ship in Europe this year is its newest—the 2,000-passenger, 91,000-ton **Constellation**—and one of the largest ships in the Celebrity fleet. With its distinctive exterior, large cabin size, innovative spa, and fine dining, there's no mistaking which line the *Constellation* sails for. Like its sister ships *Millennium, Infinity,* and *Summit,* the *Constellation,* which, at press time, was scheduled to debut in May 2002, is a product of the Chantiers de l'Atlantique shipyard in St-Nazaire, France.

PASSENGER PROFILE

Celebrity vessels attract a wide range of ages and backgrounds, although the common denominator among passengers is that they want a toned-down, elegant brand of fun cruise: lots of activity, without the wild or nutty atmosphere you get aboard some other megaships. The line focuses on middle- to upper-middle-income cruisers.

Celebrity entered the Europe market just 3 years ago, first with the *Mercury* and then with the *Millennium,* attracting mostly Americans but some European passengers as well. This year, the significance of the Europe market is underscored by Celebrity's deployment of its newest ship here. The line is currently operating on a reduced schedule.

DINING

Celebrity has poured lots of time and money into creating a culinary format that consistently provides well-orchestrated, well-presented, and good-tasting meals.

In the mid-1990s, the line signed on as its culinary consultant internationally known chef **Michel Roux,** whose most visible successes were his direction of Le Gavroche, one of London's best restaurants, and the Waterside Inn (in Bray, Berkshire), which has attracted the attention of well-heeled European foodies—including the queen of England—for many years. While some people consider Roux's cuisine a bit overrated and only slightly better than that of other mainstream lines, we personally find it quite tasty.

Dine Ashore

Celebrity, in partnership with *Gourmet* magazine, offers two land-based dining programs. The first, Gourmet Valet, allows passengers to browse the menus of in-port restaurants chosen by the magazine and then make table reservations through the ship's shore excursions desk (which can also help arrange transportation to your restaurant of choice). The other program, Gourmet Privileges, allows Celebrity's Sea and Stay package cruisers (pre- and post-cruise stay-over buyers) to enjoy a complimentary glass of champagne or a free dessert at *Gourmet*-recommended restaurants.

A dinner menu is likely to feature something along the lines of escargots a la bourguignon, pheasant mousseline with blueberry vinaigrette, pan-fried salmon with parsley potatoes, pad Thai (noodles and veggies in a peanut sauce), tournedos Rossini with foie gras and Madeira sauce, or a well-seasoned slab of prime rib with horseradish and baked potato. At every meal, Celebrity also offers **lighter "spa" fare,** like a seafood medley in saffron sauce or oven-roasted rack of veal with steamed veggies (calories, fat, cholesterol, and sodium are listed on the back of the menu), and **vegetarian entrees** such as curried Indian vegetables or linguini with shiitake mushrooms and herbs.

An **alternative casual dining venue** is available in the Lido restaurant, where those who don't want to dress up can get a simple five-course meal, with a choice of main entrees like salmon, steak, pasta, or chicken. Serving dinner between 6:30 and 8:30 by reservation only, it's a good place to bring the kids, and a good option if you want to skip the hustle and bustle (and formality) of the main restaurant. It's open every night but formal nights. The menu features options such as fresh fruit cocktail, soup du jour, salad, and entrees like pasta, broiled salmon steak, spit-roasted chicken, and grilled sirloin steak, as well as pizza and dessert selections. The *Constellation* also has one of those upscale **alternative restaurants** that are becoming so popular in cruise circles these days. Celebrity has themed all its specialty restaurants to the palmy days of the great Transatlantic liners. In such ornate, nostalgic settings, guests will be able to experience something of the elegance of early–20th-century luxury liners, and the cuisine reflects Roux at his finest. It's worth the rather steep $25 cover charge. (The name of the *Constellation's* specialty restaurant was unavailable at press time.)

The *Constellation,* in common with other Celebrity ships will feature at its **lunch buffets** all-American favorites like salads and stir-fries, grilled hamburgers and hot dogs, fish-and-chips, cheeses and breads, omelets, pizza, smoked salmon, shrimp cocktail, and French onion soup.

A nice touch that appears on all formal nights is a late-night culinary soirée known as **Gourmet Bites,** where a series of upscale canapés and hors d'oeuvres are butler-served in the public lounges between midnight and 1am. On other nights, themed **midnight buffets** might offer Oriental, Italian, Tex-Mex, or tropical smorgasbords, with a spread of fancifully carved fruits.

Chef Roux's wine selections are offered in a wide price range to suit every budget. Interestingly, a few of the wines featured on board are produced by French vineyards with which Roux has a direct link and, in some cases, of which he is the owner.

Room service is available 24 hours a day and offers a limited menu with complete breakfasts, hot and cold sandwiches, pizzas, salads, desserts, and beverages. **Gourmet pizzas** are available from room service from 3 to 7pm and 10pm to 1am.

ACTIVITIES

On Celebrity, there's a lot to do and a lot, well, not to do.

If you like to stay busy, activities during days at sea are fairly standardized across the fleet, and may include one of the fascinating **enrichment lectures** often offered by experts on topics such as personal investing, handwriting analysis, and body language. There are also the tried-and-true wine tastings, horse racing, bingo, art auctions, trivia games, arts and crafts, spa and salon demonstrations, and line-dancing lessons. During days at sea, a live pop band plays a couple of sets on the Pool Deck.

Preview: *Constellation*

This is Celebrity's newest and largest ship, weighing in at 91,000 tons, carrying 1,950 guests, and offering a host of onboard activity and entertainment options that expand on the line's core strengths: relaxed elegance, fine food, exceptional spa facilities, and modern flair.

Eighty percent of the *Constellation*'s cabins are outside (about 780 units), of which about 580 have verandas. They range from the average-size inside room of 170 square feet all the way up to the massive Penthouse Suite, with more than 2,500 square feet, including a 1,098 square feet veranda. Now *that's* a veranda! All cabins offer television, voice-mail telephone capability, safe, hair dryer, bathrobes, and mini-bar. Butlers are available to suite guests, providing full meal service, complimentary hors d'oeuvres daily, in-suite afternoon tea, shoeshine, and a variety of other pampering services. Suites guests also enjoy in-cabin whirlpools, walk-in closets, and VCRs. Twenty-six cabins are wheelchair accessible.

The *Constellation*'s alternative restaurant is designed to be on a par with those on the other ships in its class—which is to say, very elegant and very good. Decorated in the rich, Edwardian style of the great liners, the restaurant is designed to transport guests back to the golden days of ship travel. Other innovative features carried forward from her sister ships to the *Constellation* include a music library with thousands of digital recordings available for guests at individual listening stations; the largest spa facilities at sea; elevators that offer ocean views; and a botanical conservatory up top. (Pull up a rattan chair, sit under a ceiling

If you prefer curling up with a good book in some quiet nook, you'll have no problem finding one. On the *Constellation*, you can grab a lounge chair at the spa's thalassotherapy pool or duck into one of the many lounges, including the quiet, clubbish Michael's Club cigar bar, which offers the atmosphere of a British men's club—for both sexes, of course.

Although managed by Steiner like the spas on most other ships, Celebrity **spas** offer more exotic treatments than most—for example, mud packs, herbal steam baths, and a variety of water-based treatments involving jet massages and "aquameditation," in which you're caressed by light, whirling showers while lying on a soft mat. Certain procedures are offered in a partner arrangement, whereby you and your significant other can apply medicinal muds to each other and share an herbal steam bath. The whole shebang ends with a warm shower and the application of an aromatic "potion" to the skin. Exotic, huh?

The *Constellation* has an Internet cafe, with access available for 95¢ a minute. There are no self-service laundry rooms, but laundry service is available.

CHILDREN'S PROGRAMS

Although it did not originate that way, Celebrity has evolved into a cruise line that pampers kids as well as adults. Each ship has a **playroom** and **supervised activities** as well as private and group **babysitting.**

Activities are geared to those 3 to 17, and include treasure hunts, arts and crafts, dancing, movies, ship tours, ice-cream-sundae-making and pizza parties, fan, and enjoy a drink while you check out the views through two-story-high windows.)

The ship's striking, three-story Celebrity Theater showroom has excellent sight lines and comfortable seating, and when you tire of Broadway-style entertainment, you'll find the *Constellation* has an array of **cozy lounges** and **piano bars** where you can retreat for a romantic nightcap (there's even a coffee bar for teetotalers). The ship has late-night disco dancing. And you'll also find **karaoke** and **first-run movies** in the theater. All this, plus a spacious **casino** and the line's trademark Michael's Club, decorated like the parlor of a London men's club and devoted to fine cigars and cognac.

As on all of the later-model Celebrity ships, the AquaSpa facility on the *Constellation* is spectacular. The treatment menu is an international affair with options such as heated aromatic stones borrowed from Asia; a milk-and-ginger bath treatment from Egypt; a Tahitian jasmine flower bath; a Hawaiian massage given by not one but *two* therapists working in unison. The AquaSpa doesn't miss a thing.

Next door to the spa there's a very large and well-equipped cardio room and an aerobics floor. On the top decks there are facilities for basketball, volleyball, quoits, and paddle tennis, and a jogging track (three laps equal 1km). The ship also has a golf simulator, two pools (one with a waterfall), four whirlpools, and sunning space on various decks.

Rates for a 7-day cruise are $1,694 to $1,769 inside, $1,949 to $2,629 outside, and $5,849 to $14,099 suite.

karaoke, and computer games, as well as theater productions and junior Olympics contests. For teens ages 14 to 17 who don't think themselves too cool to participate, there are talent shows, karaoke, pool games, and trivia contests.

A once-weekly, complimentary parents' night out program allows mom and dad to enjoy dinner alone while the kids dine with counselors. The line's Family Cruising Program (not operational on all sailings) provides for group slumber party–style babysitting in the playroom from 10pm to 1am for children ages 3 to 12, for $3 per child per hour or $5 per hour for two or more children from the same family. Private in-cabin babysitting by a crew member is available on a limited basis for $8 per hour for up to two children (must be arranged on board through the ship's cabin services or guest relations departments).

ENTERTAINMENT

Although entertainment is not a prime reason to sail on a Celebrity ship, the line does offer a varied selection of innovative performances. For instance, Celebrity Cruises fleetwide feature a strolling a cappella group as well as a wandering magician, who perform in lounges and public areas in the afternoons and before and after dinner. The four-man troupe of singers delight passengers with well-known songs old and new, performed in a fun, entertaining style. Meanwhile, the tuxedo-clad magician dazzles guests with card tricks and disappearing acts.

Celebrity also offers the popular favorites, like Broadway-style musicals led by a sock-it-to-'em soloist or two and a team of lip-synching dancers in full

Celebrity Fleet Itineraries

Ship	Home Ports & Season	Itinerary
Constellation	**7-day W. Med,** from Barcelona (May); **14-day Baltics,** from Dover (England) (June–Aug); **10- and 11-day W. Med,** Barcelona (Sept)	**7-day W. Med:** Port calls include Villefranche (France), Ajaccio (Corsica), Civitavecchia/Rome (Italy), Valletta (Malta); **14-day Baltics:** Port calls include Stockholm (Sweden), Helsinki (Finland), St. Petersburg (Russia), Tallinn (Estonia), Rostock (Germany), and Copenhagen (Denmark); **10- and 11-day W. Med:** Port calls may include Marseille and Villefranche (France); Livorno, Civitavecchia, and Naples (Italy); Valletta (Malta); and Malaga (Spain).

Vegas-esque regalia. Other nights in the showroom, you'll find magicians, comedians, cabaret acts, and passenger talent shows. Showrooms aboard all Celebrity ships have excellent acoustics and sight lines praised as among the most panoramic and unobstructed at sea.

SERVICE

Service is polite, attentive, cheerful, and especially professional. Waiters have a poised, upscale-hotel air about them, and are able to think on their feet. On one sailing, when Fran mentioned to her cabin steward that she was disappointed that there were chairs but no deck chair on her cabin balcony, he promptly snuck one off the Pool Deck for her. There are very professional sommeliers in the dining room, and in the Lido breakfast and lunch buffet restaurants, waiters are on hand to carry passengers' trays from the buffet line to a table of their choice.

If you occupy a suite on any of the ships, you'll get a tuxedo-clad **personal butler** who serves afternoon tea and complimentary hors d'oeuvres from 6 to 8pm, bringing them right to your cabin. If you ask, he'll handle your laundry, shine your shoes, make sewing repairs, deliver messages, and do many other errands and favors. For instance, on a recent sailing Fran's butler brought her mother a glass of juice each night, which she needed to take her medication. Your butler will serve you a full five-course dinner if you'd rather **dine in your cabin** one night, and if you're in the mood to compile a guest list and pay for the drinks and hors d'oeuvres everyone will consume, your butler will even organize a cocktail party for you and your list of cruising friends, either in your suite or in any of several suitable public areas on board the ship.

Other hedonistic treats bestowed upon suite guests include a bottle of champagne on arrival, personalized stationery, terry-cloth robes, a Celebrity tote bag, oversized bath towels, priority check-in and debarkation, express luggage delivery at embarkation, and complimentary use of the soothing thalassotherapy pool. Suite guests can even get an **in-cabin massage** daily between the hours of 7am and 8pm.

2 Holland America Line

SHIPS IN EUROPE   Noordam • Prinsendam (preview)

300 Elliott Ave. W., Seattle, WA 98119. ℂ **800/426-0327** or 206/281-3535. Fax 800/628-4855. www. hollandamerica.com.

More than any other line today (except Cunard), Holland America has managed to hang on to some of its seafaring history and tradition, offering an affordable, classic, ocean liner–like cruise experience. The line consistently delivers a worthy and solid product for a fair price, and is unique for offering mid-size to large ships with an old-world elegance that remains appealingly low-key and not stuffy. These ships aren't boring, but they're sedate, so it's no surprise that the line attracts predominantly passengers in their 50s and up (the age range has widened a bit as the line has introduced new vessels).

The line's well-maintained ships are mid-size, creating a cozy atmosphere, understated, and with excellent layouts to ease passenger movement. HAL's older ships, including the *Noordam* in Europe, are the most humble, with plainish one-level dining rooms and pleasing, but simple, public rooms. The newer ships are more lavish, but still in an understated way.

Holland America emphasizes tradition, and that's what sets it apart. In the public areas you'll see antiques, trophies, and memorabilia, and the very names of the vessels hark back to ships in the line's past. For example, the line's flagship, the 62,000-ton *Rotterdam,* is the sixth HAL ship to bear that name.

Pros

- **History and tradition.** The impressive collection of artifacts and artwork on the ships reflect Holland America's important place in seafaring history and lend the ships more of a traditional ocean liner ambience than can be found on nearly any other line.
- **Great gyms.** For their size, the ships offer some of the most attractive, roomy, and well-stocked gyms and aerobics areas at sea.

Cons

- **Sleepy nightlife.** While there's always a few stalwarts and a couple of busyish nights, if you're big on late-night dancing and bar hopping, you may find yourself partying mostly with the entertainment staff.
- **Homogenous passenger profile.** Although this is changing to a certain degree, passengers tend to be a pretty homogenous group of 50+, low-key North American couples who aren't overly adventurous.

Compared with other American Mainstream lines, here's how Holland America rates:

	Poor	Fair	Good	Excellent	Outstanding
Enjoyment Factor					✓
Dining			✓		
Activities			✓		
Children's Program		✓			
Entertainment		✓			
Service					✓
Overall Value					✓

THE FLEET

Holland America currently has 9 ships (the *Westerdam* left the fleet in Mar) and will soon have 10 (the *Zuiderdam* is scheduled to debut in Nov). In Europe in 2002, it is positioning the *Noordam,* at age 17 among the older and plainer of the line's ships, and the 38,000-ton, 794-passenger *Prinsendam,* which joined the fleet just in May, and was previously operated by Seabourn as the *Seabourn Sun.*

PASSENGER PROFILE

Before its acquisition by Carnival in 1989, HAL passengers tended overwhelmingly to be in their 60s and 70s, but Carnival's influence has moved the demographics toward a somewhat younger market, although any kind of real transformation is slow as molasses in coming and far from complete (if indeed it ever will be). HAL's passenger rosters typically include some graying, 50-ish members of the baby-boom generation, mixed in with many passengers of their parents' age.

Passengers tend to be hospitable and amiable, and sensible with their money. They tend to be fairly set in their ways and not especially adventurous.

The line attracts many groups traveling together, from incentive groups to social clubs on a lark together. If you're a 40-something member of such a group and are worried about finding company aboard, don't abandon hope, particularly if you happen to be a divorcée, widow, or widower: You won't be alone.

DINING

Joining the trend, Holland America recently began offering a casual **dinner option** several times during every sailing in its buffet-style Lido restaurant, which also serves breakfast and lunch.

Of course, an elegant dinner in the main dining room is still the preferred venue. As its executive chef, HAL employs the renowned Reiner Greubel, formerly of Westin Hotels, New York's Plaza Hotel, and his own Reiner's Restaurant in Seattle. Instead of daring experimentation, Greubel recognizes that some of the world's finest cuisine comes from classics prepared with fresh and high-quality ingredients, and that some sophisticated palates still prefer traditional favorites: osso buco, cassoulet, Alaskan king crab, and Caribbean snapper, for instance. Dinner items might be as straightforward as roast prime rib of beef with baked Idaho potatoes and horseradish cream, or as esoteric as warm hazelnut-crusted brie with a compote of apples and onions. Children can enjoy tried-and-true staples like pizza, hot dogs, burgers with fries, chicken fingers, and tacos.

Value The Generous Line

Holland America is generous with its complimentary treats (a rarity in today's nickel-and-diming industry), serving hot canapés in some of the bar/lounges during cocktail hour, offering freshly popped popcorn in the movie theater, doling out espresso and cappuccino at no charge in the Java Cafes, and serving lemonade on deck on all warm-weather cruises. Unlike other lines, there's no cover charge in the small, alternative restaurant on the *Rotterdam.* Stewards replenish a bowl of fruit in your cabin daily, and each guest is given a Holland America canvas tote bag.

Greubel has also expanded the line's **light and healthy cuisine,** and he serves what he calls **fun foods,** such as spring rolls and sushi. And he did a major league improvement in the area of desserts, moving away from grandmother's favorite cakes to things more sophisticated, including many desserts based on tropical fruit and delicate sauces.

Buffets for breakfast and lunch, with the inevitable queues, are bountiful and frequent, and include separate stations for omelets, tacos, and pasta. **Indonesian dishes** are the theme of at least one buffet a week. There are also theme dinners in Europe reflecting European regions.

Dutch influences prevail with Gouda cheese offered at breakfast and, at least once during each cruise, a **Dutch Chocolate Extravaganza,** a Holland-themed midnight buffet where the calories stack up so fast you might as well give up trying to count them.

Room service is available 24 hours a day. Mid-morning bouillon and **afternoon teas** are well-attended events. Hot canapés are served in some of the bar/lounges during the cocktail hour.

On the *Prinsendam* there is also a reservations-only alternative restaurant. It was unclear at press time whether there would be a service charge to dine there.

ACTIVITIES

Activities are varied, relatively nontaxing, and fun. The Flagship Forum **lecture series,** featuring knowledgeable lecturers on such topics as culture, history, art, and architecture, is particularly popular in Europe, and offered on all cruises of 12 days or more. You can learn how to dance cheek-to-cheek, be taught the fine art of vegetable carving or creative napkin folding, or play bingo or bridge. A member of the cruise will take interested passengers on **art tours,** discussing the ship's impressive art collection and giving passengers a handout about the collections. Gentlemen hosts are on board to escort ladies on cruises of 14 days or longer.

HAL, like its competitors, has an incentive-based fitness program in which passengers are awarded points every time they take an aerobics class or do some other fitness activity. Points can be redeemed at the cruise's end for T-shirts, souvenirs, and so on.

For those whose activities include keeping up with the stock market or the office gossip, all HAL ships are now equipped with Internet facilities, at 75¢ a minute for an Internet hookup and $3.95 for each e-mail sent.

CHILDREN'S PROGRAM

Whenever demand warrants it (usually during the summer months), HAL offers supervised programs for children, called **Club HAL.** The menu of activities is not anywhere as extensive as on lines like Disney, Carnival, Celebrity, Royal Caribbean, and Princess, and HAL never pretends it is. When enough kids are on board, programs are designated for three different age brackets: 5- to 8-year-olds, 9- to 12-year-olds, and teens. However, based on the number of young people aboard, these barriers sometimes blur.

Regardless of the age of the attendees, young people are diverted with pizza and soda parties, as well as tours of the bridge, the galley, and other areas below deck. There might also be movies, ice-cream parties, arts and crafts, storytelling sessions, games, karaoke, golf lessons, disco parties, charades, bingo, and Ping-Pong. On the first night of each cruise, parents meet and mingle with staff responsible for the care, counseling, and feeding of their children. Activities are not scheduled while a ship is in port.

Holland America Fleet Itineraries

Ship	Home Ports & Season	Itinerary
Noordam	**10-day W. Med,** Lisbon to Civitavecchia/Rome (Aug–Nov); **14-day N. Europe,** Amsterdam to Copenhagen (Aug–Nov)	**10-day W. Med:** Port calls may include Lisbon (Portugal), Casablanca (Morocco), Gibraltar, Barcelona (Spain), Marseille (France), Monte Carlo (Monaco), Livorno and Roma (Italy); **14-day N. Europe:** Port calls may include Copenhagen (Denmark), Kristiansand, Bergen, Hellesylt, Trondheim, Honningsvag, Tromso, Vik, and Stavanger (all Norway)
Prinsendam	**13-day W. Med,** Lisbon to Civitavecchia/Rome (June, Aug, Sept); **14-day N. Europe,** Southampton to Copenhagen (Aug–Nov)	**13-day W. Med:** Port calls may include Monte Carlo, Sete, Bonifacio, and Marseille (France), Barcelona, Gibraltar, Portofino and Livorno (Italy), and Casablanca; **14-day N. Europe:** Port calls may include Copenhagen (Denmark), Kristiansand, Bergen, Hellesylt, Trondheim, Honningsvag, Tromso, Vik, and Stavanger (all Norway)

There are **playrooms** on all ships (on the *Noordam,* the room does double duty as a meeting or card room when there aren't many kids on board).

Babysitting is sometimes (but not always) available from volunteers among a ship's staff. If a staff member is available—and be warned, their availability is never guaranteed—the cost is usually around $7 per child per hour.

ENTERTAINMENT

Onboard entertainment has improved since HAL's acquisition by Carnival, which really understands how cabaret shows should be presented. Each ship features small-scale glittery **Broadway-style shows** with live music, singers, dancers, and laser lights. There are also musicians, comedians, illusionists, and the like performing in the various lounges.

Regular offerings on Europe sailings include a '50s and '60s dance party, a talent show by the crew (with Indonesian and Filipino songs and folk dancing), and first-run movies (complete with popcorn) in the movie theaters.

Pre-dinner cocktails and **dancing** are a major event of the day. And on cruises 14 days and longer, women traveling alone or those whose escorts have two left feet need not fear for lack of dance partners: A complement of "gentlemen hosts" sail on board and are available for a whirl or two around the dance floor.

On the *Noordam,* the disco is in a larger lounge and sees more action than you might expect a few nights a week.

SERVICE

Onboard service is permeated with nostalgia for the Netherlands' past and its genteel traditions. During lunch, a uniformed employee might hold open the door of a buffet, and a steward ringing a chime will formally announce the two dinner seatings.

Holland America is one of the few cruise lines that maintains a training school (a land-based facility in Indonesia dubbed in HAL circles SS *Jakarta,* also known as HAL U.) for the selection and training of its staff. On the ships, the soft-spoken, mostly Indonesian staff members are quick to offer a warm smile and attentive service.

Although Holland America proudly touts its no-tipping-required policy, it's more lip service than anything else. In fact, like most other ships, tips are expected; it's just that on Holland America ships you won't be bombarded by guidelines and reminders—you can feel as though you're tipping because you truly enjoyed the service. HAL's no-tipping required policy includes bar tabs, which, unlike on most lines, do not automatically include a 15% gratuity (if you want, you can tip a bar waiter in cash or handwrite a tip onto your tab).

Onboard services include **laundry** and **dry cleaning.** Each ship also has a **self-service laundry.**

Noordam

The Verdict

This mid-sized '80s ship is among the oldest and coziest in the fleet, offering a comfortable, calm, glitz-free cruise experience and a slice of the past.

Noordam *(photo: HAL)*

Specifications

Size (in tons)	33,930	Officers	Dutch
Number of Cabins	607	Crew (Indonesian/Filipino)	530
Number of Outside Cabins	413	Passenger/Crew Ratio	2.2 to 1
Cabins with Verandas	0	Year Built	1984
Number of Passengers	1,214	Last Major Refurbishment	N/A

Frommer's Ratings (Scale of 1–5)

Cabin Comfort & Amenities	4	Decor	4
Ship Cleanliness & Maintenance	4	Pool, Fitness & Spa Facilities	3
Public Comfort/Space	3	Children's Facilities	2

The *Noordam* provides the amenities most passengers associate with a classic ocean liner. Inside and out there are lots of nooks and crannies that create a cozy and intimate atmosphere that's much different than the wide-open, sprawling spaces on newer ships. This ship is pared down in scope and scale from its newer rivals, and consequently, cabins go at a commensurately pared-down price. It's a great ship for those looking for value.

The vessel was built at the Chantiers de l'Atlantique shipyard in St-Nazaire, France, and the basic design is classic, almost nostalgically evocative of the pre-megaship age of cruising.

Overall, passengers aboard this vessel tend to be more low-key than those aboard the line's larger ships, though they're certainly not opposed to a good time.

If you plan on traveling with children, it's wiser to opt for the larger, newer HAL ships, although the *Noordam* does have children's programs during holidays and on sailings that have a lot of kids on board. At these times, an all-purpose room is converted to a children's playroom.

Cabins & Rates

Cabins	Brochure Rates*	Bathtub	Fridge	Hair Dryer	Sitting Area	TV
Inside	$1,612–$1,859	no	no*	no	no	yes
Outside	$1,931–$2,304	some	no*	no	some	yes
Suite	$2,801	yes	yes	no	yes	yes

Fridges can be requested through your travel agent and placed in cabins for a nominal fee.

Preview: *Prinsendam*

The *Prinsendam* will be in Europe for its maiden season in the Holland America livery. At 39,000 tons and carrying just 794 passengers, it is an extraordinarily spacious ship with eight passenger decks. It was built in 1988 (as the *Royal Viking Sun*) and underwent an extensive renovation in the spring of 2002 as it joined the HAL fleet. Teak decks, quiet corners, many public rooms furnished with fine antiques and Dutch art—all hallmarks of this venerable cruise line—are much in evidence.

About 36% of the cabins have private balconies, which is now the norm for a newly built ship. All the cabins are good-size (the smallest are about 185 sq. ft.; the largest suite is 725 sq. ft.) and tastefully decorated. All of the outside cabins have both tub and shower. Eight of the cabins are wheelchair accessible.

The ship has some 17 public rooms, including the sophisticated Explorer's Lounge and the more intimate Ocean Bar, as well as a coffee bar. For the drive and bustle of shipboard life, music and dancing, and lively conversation, the Crow's Nest Bar, topside, is the place to be.

Unlike those of many of its recent competitors, the *Prinsendam*'s dining room, La Fontaine Room, is built on only one level, occupying the entire rear portion of the Promenade deck and much of the port side as well. The ship offers a fine alternative dining facility, the Odyssey Restaurant, which promises elegant service and a superb eclectic menu. At press time there was no cover charge, but the line was considering adding one. Casual meals are available in the Lido Deck restaurant.

The *Prinsendam* has two swimming pools, one with a swim-up bar, and a wraparound promenade that walkers will enjoy. The Ocean Spa is elegantly decorated, with appropriately moody lighting to enhance the wide range of spa and beauty treatments.

Rates for a 13-day cruise are $4,890 to $5,865 inside, $6,233 to $10,263 outside, and $12,636 to $25,625 suite.

CABINS   Standard outside cabins are a decent size (measuring 177 sq. ft.), while lower-end inside cabins are still comfortable at 152 square feet. All are furnished in HAL's low-key style. Mirrors make the space seem larger than it is, storage space is more than adequate, and bathrooms are compact and well designed. The highest category of cabin is the minisuite, which is about 294 square feet.

Most cabins on the Boat and Navigation Decks have views obstructed by lifeboats, and those on the Upper Promenade Deck overlook an unending stream of joggers, walkers, and passersby. Cabins near the stern are subject to more than their share of engine noise and vibration. Many cabins have bathtubs and all have TVs, music channels, and a fruit bowl. (There are no in-cabin safes, but valuables can be kept at the purser's desk.)

Four cabins in the B category—deluxe outside double rooms on the Boat Deck—are suitable for people with disabilities. Elevators are wheelchair accessible.

PUBLIC AREAS   The decor is discreet and pleasant, with bouquets of fresh flowers liberally scattered through public areas. A 15-foot-wide teak-covered promenade allows plenty of room for deck chairs, strollers, joggers, and voyeurs to mingle under the open sky. Some passengers consider it the ship's most endearing feature and it's a lovely reminiscence of the classic ocean liner.

There are some other unfortunate design flaws, however. For example, the show lounge is not large enough to seat all passengers. And, in general, the ship's choppy clusters of public areas and decks can leave you disoriented at times. The one-story main-dining room, while pleasant, is rather plain when compared to the more glamorous ones on the line's newer ships (but it does boast floor-to-ceiling windows and fresh flowers on the tables).

The Crow's Nest is the best place to enjoy a pre-dinner cocktail, and the Explorer's Lounge is a nice venue for after-dinner drinks and coffee (and after-noon tea as well).

ALTERNATIVE DINING   None.

POOL, FITNESS & SPA FACILITIES   There are two outside pools, a wading pool, and a hot tub. The classic aft tiered decks offer many nooks and crannies for sunbathing or a snooze in a deck chair. You can walk or jog on the broad, unobstructed Promenade Deck. The gym and spa are small, but the gym, located on one of the topmost decks, has windows and is equipped with rowing machines, weight machines, and stationary bicycles. The spa is really just a cou-ple of treatment rooms for massages and facials, plus a steam room and sauna and a beauty salon. Aerobics classes are held on the decks or in a public room.

3 Norwegian Cruise Line

SHIPS IN EUROPE Norwegian Dream

7665 Corporate Center Dr., Miami, FL 33126. ℂ **800/327-7030** or 305/436-4000. Fax 305/436-4126. www.ncl.com.

Norwegian Cruise Line, under new management and a new owner (it was purchased in 2000)—Star Cruises of Malaysia—offers affordable, down-to-earth cruises that attract seasoned travelers and first-timers alike. In Europe, the line's alternative dining and sports offerings set it apart.

NCL excels at activities—if it offered any more, passengers would be exhausted. Recreational and fitness programs are among the best in the industry, including programs where attendance at fitness events earns you points you can cash in for prizes. Also top-notch are the line's children's program and entertainment.

The company instituted a program it calls "Freestyle Cruising," which is highlighted by a relaxed attitude about dining (eat when and with whom you want, with more restaurants to choose from), tipping (automatically charged to your room account), and dress (the emphasis is on casual). As an added bonus at the end of the voyage, guests will be permitted to remain in their cabins until their time comes to disembark rather than huddling in lounges or squatting on luggage in stairwells until their lucky color comes up. New ships will be built according to this cruising concept—which has been standard operating procedure for the Star Cruises for years—while existing ships will adapt to the plan to whatever extent possible.

Pros

- **Flexible dining.** NCL's dining policy lets you sit where and with whom you want, dress as you want, and dine when you want (within certain hours).
- **Sports.** NCL is a leader in this regard. You can play basketball and even watch a football game on ESPN International (usually on tape delay in Europe).
- **Activities.** From cha cha lessons to computer learning classes, there's a wider range and a greater number of activities on NCL ships than on most.

Cons

- **Unmemorable food.** Despite the improvements in choice, the line's cuisine is not its strong point. As long as you don't crave sophisticated cuisine, you'll be fine.
- **Inconsistent service.** Service isn't always as sharp as it could be, even though crew has been added to handle the new and more labor-intensive "Freestyle" cruising concept.

Compared with other American Mainstream lines, here's how Norwegian Cruise Line rates:

	Poor	Fair	Good	Excellent	Outstanding
Enjoyment Factor				✓	
Dining		✓			
Activities					✓
Children's Program			✓		
Entertainment				✓	
Service		✓			
Overall Value			✓		

THE FLEET

NCL is a cruise company in the midst of dramatic changes in more ways than one: After several years spent claiming (some would say defending) that its fleet of older, mid-size ships offer a more personal experience, it has moved into the megaship age with the 80,000-ton flagship *Norwegian Sky,* sister ship *Norwegian Sun,* and brand new, ultra-modern, and bigger (at 91,000 tons) *Norwegian Star.* The *Norwegian Dream,* the line's only ship in Europe in 2002, is not quite of that caliber. But for a mid-size ship built in 1993, it offers a good number of megaship-type facilities and amenities.

PASSENGER PROFILE

In Europe, NCL attracts mostly an older crowd, with an average age of around 60. About 90% are from North America, and they tend to be more affluent than the line's crowd in the Caribbean and—as is true with American passengers on most European cruises—are more experienced: The majority have cruised before. The atmosphere aboard all NCL ships is informal and down-to-earth and well-suited to first-timer cruisers, including families and honeymooners.

This is the cruise line for sports nuts who can't be without access to major sports events. But it's also a good choice for those looking for value who don't want to be on a big, brand-new megaship, but don't want to be on a budget ship either.

DINING

None of the NCL vessels is particularly distinguished for its cuisine, but the way they handle the business of dining these days is pretty darn innovative. Two years ago, the company's management introduced a new flexibility concept called **Freestyle Cruising.** All restaurants offer open seating every evening, allowing you to dine when and with whom you like, strolling in any time between about 5:30 and 10 pm (you can linger over your meal until midnight), rather than at a set table at a set time. And, you can dress pretty much however you like, too: Resort casual is perfectly acceptable. Only one restaurant is formal on the night of the captain's cocktail party.

The *Norwegian Dream* has six restaurants, including two main restaurants, an Italian alternative restaurant, a French alternative restaurant, a pizzeria, and a Sports Bar & Grill. There is a service charge of $10 to dine in the Sun Terrace Italian Trattoria or Le Bistro French Restaurant.

Meals in Europe include regional favorites, and that means the addition of Norwegian salmon, schnitzel, and the like. One of the main restaurants one night on each 7-day sailing features a menu created by Chef Henry Haller, former White House executive chef. There is always a **light spa cuisine** option, as well as a **vegetarian entree** at lunch and dinner, and fresh fruit is often offered throughout the day. There are also **children's menus,** featuring the popular standards: burgers, hot dogs, spaghetti and meatballs, and ice cream sundaes.

NCL is also proud of its **midnight buffets,** which include, on the *Dream,* the always popular Chocoholic Extrav-

> **Value Add-on Savings**
>
> Book your NCL Europe cruise at least 180 days in advance and get two pre- or post-cruise nights in a first-class hotel in Rome or London for free.

aganza on each sailing. For sugar addicts, an ice-cream bar is open a few hours a day; in the afternoon you can enjoy **English high tea, a coffee bar** that serves

NCL Fleet Itineraries

Ship	Home Ports & Season	Itinerary
Norwegian Dream	12-day W. Europe, from Civitavecchia (Italy) to Dover (England) (Apr); 12-day Baltics, round-trip from Dover (England) (May–Aug); 12-day North Cape/Fjords, round-trip from Dover (England) (June)	12-day W. Europe: Port calls include Livorno and Genoa (Italy), Cannes, Le Havre and Marseille (France), Barcelona and Cadiz (Spain), and Lisbon (Portugal); 12-day Baltics: Port calls include Tallinn (Estonia), St. Petersburg (Russia), Helsinki (Finland), Stockholm (Sweden), Copenhagen (Denmark), and Oslo (Norway); 12-day North Cape/Fjords: Port calls include Flam, Kristiansand, Honningsvag, Trondheim, Hellesylt, Geiranger, Bergen, and Stavanger (all Norway)

specialty coffees as well as other beverages, and a pizzeria. **Room service** is offered 24 hours a day.

ACTIVITIES

Activities are one of the line's strongest points. You can take cha-cha lessons; play duplicate bridge, shuffleboard, or basketball; attend an art auction or spa or beauty demonstration; learn to tie scarves; or listen to a band at the pool. There are galley and bridge tours, trapshooting, makeovers, talent shows, wine tasting, and trivia contests. In Europe, the line also offers an enrichment program with **guest lecturers** including university professors who present lectures on such topics as religion, ancient history, earth sciences, and astronomy.

Spa treatments are run by Mandara spa, and include a variety of offerings with an Asian influence (Mandara was founded in Bali, Indonesia), such as a Balinese Coffee Scrub or Coconut Body Polish. Ironically, NCL switched spa operators late in 2000, from Steiner to Mandara, looking for an improved product. And then Steiner bought Mandara! The new owners have allowed Mandara to continue with their own specialized treatments.

All the ships have Internet cafes, with access available at 75¢ a minute.

CHILDREN'S PROGRAM

Although the program and playroom are not as well-stocked as those on many other lines, NCL has expanded its Kids Crew program to offer year-round **supervised activities** for children ages 3 to 17. The program divides children into four age groups: junior sailors, ages 3 to 5; first mates, ages 6 to 8; navigators, ages 9 to 12; and teens, ages 13 to 17.

Activities may include sports competitions, dances, face painting, treasure hunts, magic shows, arts and crafts, cooking classes, and even a Circus at Sea, which provides an opportunity for the kids to learn circus acts, most of them humorous or magic (like card tricks) rather than the athletic variety, which they share with their parents in a performance towards the end of the cruise. Children get their own "Cruise News" detailing the day's events. The *Norwegian Dream* also has a video arcade and an ice-cream parlor, sure to be a hit with the young set.

Private, in-cabin babysitting by a member of the crew may be available from noon to 2am aboard all NCL's ships for $8 per hour for the first child and $2 per hour for each additional child. But check with the reception desk because availability of babysitting depends on staff numbers and needs.

ENTERTAINMENT

NCL has found a nice balance between theme-related events and general entertainment that keeps everyone happy. In Europe, **local performers** come on board and in the past have included a Spanish flamenco group, a Portuguese folkloric troupe, and Irish dancers from the Cowhie-Ryan troupe, whose members have also been selected to perform in *Riverdance.*

The casino on the *Dream* is small, but lively. There are several bars where you can slip away for a quiet rendezvous, and small tucked-away corners for more intimate entertainment, like **pianists** and **cabaret acts** that include comedy, magic, juggling, vocalists, ventriloquists, concert and classical pianists, and other instrumentalists (including the occasional banjo player). Live big-band and ballroom-style music for dancing is popular before or after the big **production shows,** which are expensive, lavish, and artistically ambitious.

SERVICE

"Uneven" was the word that used to crop up to describe service aboard NCL vessels. That's not as true nowadays. Personalized service is an increasing area of focus for the line since its change of management. Each ship has added about 100 crew members. Generally, room service and bar service fleetwide are speedy and efficient, and cabin attendants win passenger approval. But there are still problems in the main dining rooms. The breakfast and lunch buffet restaurants often seem understaffed and hectic, especially if you're there at prime times. The Norwegian officers are generally smooth and charming. Tips of $10 per passenger, per day ($5 for kids 3–12; and no charge for children under 3) are automatically added to shipboard accounts (you can move that amount up or down as you see fit). Passengers in top Owner's Suites get butler service. Dry cleaning and laundry service are offered, but there is no self-service laundry.

Norwegian Dream

The Verdict

Despite its 1,748-passenger capacity, this ship doesn't feel like a megaship, though it offers most of the amenities and facilities of one.

Norwegian Dream *(photo: NCL)*

Specifications

Size in Tons	50,760	Officers	Norwegian
Number of Cabins	874	Crew	700 (International)
Number of Outside Cabins	716	Passenger/Crew Ratio	2.4:1
Cabins with Verandas	48	Year Built	1992
Number of Passengers	1,748	Last Major Refurbishment	1998

Frommer's Ratings (Scale of 1–5)

Cabin Comfort & Amenities	4	Pool, Fitness & Spa Facilities	4
Ship Cleanliness & Maintenance	4	Children's Facilities	3
Public Comfort/Space	3	Decor	4

If your heart isn't dead set on a cruise aboard a brand-new megaship, you may find this modern mid-size ship very appealing. It's a quality, moderate-cost ship known for its innovative designs (by Bjorn Storbatten, the Scandinavian designer who also designed the much more upscale Seabourn twins).

In 1998, both the *Dream* and its sister, the *Wind*, sailed into the Lloyd Werft shipyard in Bremerhaven, Germany, where they were "stretched" by grafting a 130-foot midsection into each, an operation that raised the ships' tonnage and increased their capacity from the 1,200-passenger range to over 1,700. Other improvements made possible by the stretch included the addition of a casual restaurant, another gift shop, lounges, a library, a card room, a cigar bar, and improved spas, health clubs, and children's facilities (designed to gain NCL additional market share in the families-with-children niche).

The design makes the *Dream* appear more spacious than it really is. Both forward and aft, the ship's upper decks cascade down in evenly spaced tiers, resulting in panoramic views both ahead and behind the moving ship. Walls of glass line the length of the vessel, and 85% of the contemporary cabins are outside. However, in an attempt to save money, low-grade materials were used in the passageways and stairways (and in the cabins, too), so you know you're not on anything close to a luxury yacht (or even any Celebrity, Holland America, or Princess ship).

Cabins & Rates

Cabins	Brochure Rates*	Bathtub	Fridge	Hair Dryer	Sitting Area	TV
Inside	$1,603–$1,878	no	no	yes	no	yes
Outside	$1,803–$5,027	no	no	yes	some	yes
Suite	$6,227–$7,827	yes	yes	yes	yes	yes

Rates shown are for a 12-day W. Europe cruise.

CABINS   The big draw is that nearly all cabins are outside, and about 80% of them have picture windows. Standard outside cabins measure 160 square feet, which is okay but not large (Carnival's standard cabins, for instance, are 185 sq. ft.). The inside cabins are small, ranging in size from 130 to 150 square feet.

The accommodations have a breezy, pastel-based decor evocative of the West Indies. Unfortunately, bathrooms are tiny and storage space is minimal. Two people can just barely manage, but when a third or fourth person shares a cabin, it can get truly cramped.

Most cabins have a separate sitting and sleeping area, but to accommodate this feature, the area around the beds was made smaller and now requires the grace of a dancer to negotiate without stubbing toes and banging knees. Most cabins have twin beds that can be converted to queen size, and cabins on the port side are for nonsmokers. Note that lifeboats block the views of the Category 4 cabins amidships on the Norway Deck, and early morning joggers might disturb late sleepers who have cabins on the Promenade Deck.

Suites are rather luxurious and decent-sized, with floor-to-ceiling windows and mini-fridges; many have private balconies. The dozen-plus Owner's Suites are the most dramatic, followed by penthouse suites with private balconies. The 10 Superior Deluxe Penthouse suites amidships on Norway Deck have partially obstructed views because of the overhang from the restaurant above. Avoid them.

All cabins have TVs showing ESPN and CNN. Nearly a dozen cabins are wheelchair accessible, and an additional dozen or so are equipped with doorbell/phone/emergency alert lights and vibrating alarm clocks for those with hearing impairments, an innovation aboard cruise ships. Passengers in the Owner's Suites get the services of a butler.

PUBLIC AREAS The ship has a tiered design, making for roomier lower-level public areas, generous amounts of deck space on upper levels, and good passenger flow.

The ship has two main restaurants serving separate menus and offering open seating, as well as a pizzeria, and a Sports Bar & Grill that doubles as a buffet area. The Terraces is the most cozy and attractive of the dining rooms, rising three levels and evoking a supper club in a 1930s movie.

The casino is of the glitzy variety, but it's on the small side. There is a good variety of bars and lounges, including the Observatory Lounge for views and a Coffee Bar. Lucky's Bar and the Dazzles disco on the Star Deck see the most late-night action. The sports bar, with its giant big-screen TVs, is the most popular bar on the ship.

ALTERNATIVE DINING The *Norwegian Dream's* reservations-only Le Bistro restaurant is smaller and more intimate than the main dining room (a service fee of $10 is charged for dinner here). The menu includes such dishes as filet mignon with foie gras, salmon in sorrel cream sauce, and Caesar salad prepared tableside. Try the chocolate fondue for dessert. There's also an Italian venue, Sun Terrace Italian Trattoria, serving dishes like buffalo mozzarella with tomatoes, shrimp scampi, and a trio of risotto, again with a $10 cover charge.

POOL, FITNESS & SPA FACILITIES The ship's spa, now run by the Mandara Spa company, which originated in Bali, Indonesia, is small but its offerings have been beefed up since the new organization took over.

The ship's Pool Deck is gorgeous, with dark wood and crisp blue-and-white striped canvas umbrellas making you feel like you're at some stylish beach resort on the French Riviera. There are two hot tubs and two pools, the more theatrical of which is on the International Deck, where semicircular rows of chaise lounges and deck chairs surround a small and almost purely decorative keyhole-shaped pool at the ship's stern. The view—whether of the ocean or of your fellow passengers—is panoramic. A larger pool lies two decks above on the Sun Deck. A great pool bar allows you to sip a drink while bobbing happily in the shallow pool.

The 24-hour fitness center is equipped with state-of-the-art exercise equipment. Aerobics and exercise classes are part of the activity-filled agenda. On the Sports Deck, there are also Ping-Pong tables and a golf-driving range, while upstairs on the Sky Deck are a jogging track and basketball/volleyball court.

4 Orient Lines

SHIPS IN EUROPE   **Crown Odyssey • Marco Polo**

1510 SE 17th St., Ste. 400, Fort Lauderdale, FL 33316. (C) **800/333-7300** or 954/727-6660. Fax 954/527-6657. www.orientlines.com.

Orient Lines, owned and operated by Star Cruises, caters to an English-speaking clientele looking for a classically styled ship, serious destinations, better-than-average food, and a fair price. A good-valued cruisetour is Orient Lines' great strength, pairing a cruise on a mid-size ship and land tour to make a more in-depth travel experience.

Orient's *Marco Polo* has an interesting history: It was built 35 years ago and sailed as the transatlantic liner *Aleksander Pushkin,* but in the early 1990s, it was completely rebuilt from the ice-strengthened hull and engines up and is now a sturdy and graceful cruise liner, both modern and traditional—it's a young ship, yet able to boast the graceful profile of a classic liner. The *Crown Odyssey* was built in 1988 and offers a roomier onboard atmosphere and only a slightly larger passenger capacity, with a more contemporary ambience. A cruise aboard either is social and fairly low-key, without the glitz typical of much larger ships or the pulsating round of activities. The ships perform destination-oriented cruises concentrating on the ports and well-run shore excursions. A third ship is to be added by Star Cruises in 2003.

Pros
- **Great cruisetour packages.** It is easy to plan a longer vacation by combining land extensions either side of the cruise.
- **Service-oriented staff.** The ship's Filipino crew aims to please.
- **The price is right.** Orient Lines has been a value-oriented company since its inception.

Cons
- **Limited handicapped access.** These ships do not offer the facilities available on newer vessels, with only a few cabins able to handle wheelchairs.
- **Some design quirks.** The *Marco Polo*'s show lounge is awkwardly arranged, and viewing can be limited.

Compared with other American Mainstream lines, here's how Orient rates:

	Poor	Fair	Good	Excellent	Outstanding
Enjoyment Factor					✓
Dining				✓	
Activities				✓	
Children's Program	N/A				
Entertainment			✓		
Service				✓	
Overall Value					✓

THE FLEET

The *Marco Polo,* with its black hull, pronounced sheer, and traditional lines, has a graceful ocean liner look and is one of the most handsome ships afloat today. Because she appears to reflect the past, many think she is an old ship, but in fact everything but the ice-strengthened hull and engines dates from the early 1990s. In today's growing fleets of megaships with lengthy passenger lists, the 850-passenger *Marco Polo* provides one of a dwindling number of mid-size ship experiences, one that is neither a high-priced all-suite vessel, nor a pulsating city at sea. While touted as an elegant liner with Art Deco flourishes, she is actually rather simple in decor and for some lacks a distinctive character. The outer decks are pure ocean liner style, and she is a delight to explore from stem to stern.

Bigger than the *Marco Polo,* the 1,050-passenger **Crown Odyssey** was built in 1988 for Royal Cruise Line, a Greek company based in California. The ship was once the pride of the Greek merchant marine until the company was sold and the fleet disbanded. With a name change to *Norwegian Crown* under the Norwegian Cruise Line banner, few changes were made to her post-war Art Deco style that features wood paneling, brass, smoked glass, mirrors, and chrome. Built for longer voyages, the ship has reverted to her original name of *Crown Odyssey* and her hull will get a handsome black paint job, becoming a fitting partner to the *Marco Polo.*

PASSENGER PROFILE

The shorter Mediterranean itineraries attract the youngest passenger list, and the Northern European and positioning cruises an older crowd. Still, Orient Lines' demographic is 50 and up, sometimes way up. Most passengers on these European cruises are experienced cruisers, and the line has also been successful in attracting British and Australian passengers along with the majority of Americans. Repeaters are a major chunk of Orient's business. This is not a big late night crowd; people exhaust themselves seeing the ports (which is why most choose this line in the first place).

DINING

Meals are at two sittings, and the festive atmosphere and low ceilings unfortunately make for a noisy room. On the bright side, dinner offers four main courses, with the Continental and American menu offering dishes along the lines of Surf & Turf (grilled tenderloin and baby rock lobster), Chardonnay-poached shrimp, tournedos of beef, honey-roasted Long Island duck, New Zealand lamb, and pan-fried snapper. **Vegetarian and health-oriented choices** are also available, preparation and presentation are uniformly good, and portions are sensible. The Filipino stewards provide friendly, helpful service. Wines are very reasonably priced, and the list encompasses far-reaching parts of the world from California to France and Chile.

Casual venues on both ships serve enticing and varied breakfast and luncheon buffets with indoor/outdoor seating. The outdoor grill on the Marco Polo turns out kebabs, hamburgers, and hot dogs, and Café Italia on the *Crown Odyssey* al fresco dining, weather permitting, from a self-service menu that includes pizza, pasta, and grilled specialties. Well over half the passengers dress on formal nights. The *Marco Polo's* Palm Court fills up quickly for a substantial afternoon tea service on days when the bulk of the passengers are not ashore, with afternoon tea also popular on the *Crown Odyssey.*

Orient Lines Fleet Itineraries

Ship	Home Ports & Season	Itinerary
Crown Odyssey	**5-day Greece and Turkey,** Piraeus/Athens to Istanbul (Apr–Oct); **5-day W. Med,** Civitavecchia/Rome to Barcelona (May–Oct); **7-day Med,** Barcelona to Piraeus/Athens (Apr–Oct); **7-day E. Med,** Istanbul to Civitavecchia/Rome (May–Oct); **12-day Med,** Istanbul to Barcelona (May–Oct)	**5-day Greece and Turkey*:** Port calls include Mykonos, Santorini, and Rhodes (Greece) and Kuşadasi (Turkey); **5-day W. Med*:** Port calls include Livorno and Portofino (Italy), Cannes (France), and Palma de Mallorca (Spain); **7-day Med*:** Port calls include Monte Carlo (Monaco), Civitavecchia/Rome and Sorrento (Italy), Valletta (Malta), and Aghios Nikolaos (Greece); **7-day E. Med*:** Port calls include Kuşadasi (Turkey), Mykonos and Piraeus/Athens (Greece), Valletta (Malta), and Sorrento (Italy); **12-day Med*:** Port calls include Kuşadasi (Turkey), Mykonos and Piraeus/Athens (Greece), Valletta (Malta), Sorrento, Civitavecchia/Rome, Livorno, and Portofino (Italy), Cannes (France), and Palma de Mallorca (Spain)**
Marco Polo	**5-day W. Med,** between Civitavecchia/Rome and Barcelona (Apr); **7-day Baltics,** between Copenhagen and Stockholm (June–Aug); **7-day Norway,** round-trip from Copenhagen (May–July); **14-day Norway and Baltics,** between Copenhagen and Stockholm (May–July)	**5-day W. Med*:** Port calls include Livorno and Portofino (Italy), Cannes (France), and Palma de Mallorca (Spain); **7-day Baltics*:** Port calls include Tallinn (Estonia), St. Petersburg (Russia), and Helsinki (Finland); **7-day Norway*:** Port calls include Flam, Gudvangen, Hellesylt, Geiranger, Bergen, and Oslo (Norway), and Aarhus (Denmark); **14-day Norway and Baltics*:** Port calls include a combination of the 7-day Baltics and 7-day Norway itineraries

*Sold as part of a cruisetour package with 2–9 hotel nights (depending on the itinerary).
**Crown Odyssey also does Holy Lands itineraries; Marco Polo also does a limited number of E. Med, and other Europe itineraries.

ACTIVITIES

The European itineraries are destination-oriented so daytime activities are fewer than on the longer cruises elsewhere. Still, on Scandinavian itineraries there are lecturers on board from fields including politics, education, and journalism. There are Ping-Pong, shuffleboard, bingo, and cooking demonstrations (the line prides itself on its cuisine). You can enjoy Asian-influenced spa treatments such as a Coconut Body Polish ($99) or sit in a whirlpool or by the pool. The card room tends to be a busy place, attracting lots of bridge players. E-mail and Internet access is available for 75¢ a minute from computer terminals set up on both ships.

CHILDREN'S PROGRAMS

There are no special facilities on these ships, and the line has historically carried very few children.

ENTERTAINMENT

Big-time shows and revues are not a feature of the line; instead, the show lounges stage more low-key performances like cabaret acts, classical concerts, the Filipino crew show, and some local entertainment brought aboard at some ports. The show lounge on the Marco Polo is one gently sloping level with poor sight lines.

Further, it can get crowded because of the tightly packed banquettes and moveable seating and structural columns. There are also piano lounges and small casinos on these vessels. The late-night disco gets as many cruise staff as passengers. Gentlemen hosts are on board to dance with single ladies.

SERVICE

Overall, the line has a loyal, hardworking staff, some who have been around since the line opened for business. Orient recently introduced 24-hour room service from a limited menu on both ships. No coin-operated laundry on either ship. But there is laundry and dry cleaning service.

Crown Odyssey

The Verdict

The *Crown Odyssey* has a roomier onboard atmosphere and only a slightly larger passenger capacity than the *Marco Polo.*

Crown Odyssey *(photo: Orient Lines)*

Specifications

Size	34,242	Officers	Scandinavian/
Number of Cabins	526		European
Number of Outside Cabins	412	Crew	470 (Filipino)
Cabins with Verandas	16	Passenger/Crew Ratio	2.24 to 1
Number of Passengers	1,026	Year Built	1988
Last Major Refurbishment	2000		

Frommer's Ratings (Scale of 1–5)

Cabin Comfort & Amenities	4	Pool, Fitness & Spa Facilities	3
Ship Cleanliness & Maintenance	4	Children's Facilities	N/A
Public Comfort/Space	4	Decor	3

This handsome, 34,242-ton ship was refurbished to the tune of almost $10 million when she came into the Orient Lines fleet in 2000, and offers decent cabins and a good variety of public rooms, as well as an interesting Roman-style indoor pool space and a full teak wraparound promenade.

Cabins & Rates

Cabins	Brochure Rates*	Bathtub	Fridge	Hair Dryer	Sitting Area	TV
Inside	$1,750–$2,350	some	no	no	no	yes
Outside	$2,275–$3,050	some	no	no	some	yes
Suite	$2,995–$4,450	yes	yes	yes	yes	yes

For 5-day Greek Isles cruise, plus 5 or 6 hotel nights, some sightseeings, and transfers.

CABINS   The 526 wood-trimmed cabins are larger than the *Marco Polo's* (standard cabins are 165 sq. ft.) and most have picture windows and marble bathrooms. Accoutrements include TVs, hair dryers, safes, phones, and spacious closets. Many cabins have bathtubs, though some are not full size. The 12 penthouse suites have floor-to-ceiling windows, living room, veranda, VCR, walk-in closet, refrigerator, marble bath, and whirlpool tub. Some intriguing rooms have bay windows allowing a view fore and aft as well as directly out to sea.

PUBLIC AREAS   The range of public rooms, which all boast lots of light, marble, and glass, is extensive. Like on the *Marco Polo,* most public rooms occupy one full deck. The main show lounge has steeply sloped seating for good views, a much better design than aboard the *Marco Polo.* There's also a two-story theater. The Top of the Crown lounge is a wraparound disco at night, and a quiet observation lounge with views in three directions during the day. The card room offers lots of tables, but the library is small, and so is the casino. The main dining room, with two sittings, is arranged on two levels with a stained-glass raised ceiling in the central portion. Because of its hard stainless steel and glass surfaces, it's as noisy as that aboard the *Marco Polo.* Café Italia offers alfresco dining on top of the ship, weather permitting. And casual buffets are offered for breakfast, lunch, and dinner at The Yacht Club, a nautically themed restaurant with indoor/outdoor seating. This is also the spot for afternoon tea.

ALTERNATIVE DINING   None.

POOL, FITNESS & SPA FACILITIES   The ship has a very good Mandara Spa (now owned by Steiner) with a columned indoor pool that harks back to the ocean liner era. The facilities include a mirrored gym, separate men's and women's sauna and massage, two whirlpools, and a full-service beauty salon. In addition, there is an outdoor pool, and a splash pool and two whirlpools all the way aft.

Marco Polo

The Verdict

The *Marco Polo* is a comfortable ship that is well-suited to both longer itineraries and shorter, port-intensive cruises. It's an all-around winner.

Marco Polo *(photo: Orient Lines)*

Specifications

Size (in tons)	22,080	Officers	Scandinavian/
Number of Cabins	425		European
Number of Outside Cabins	294	Crew	350 (Filipino)
Cabins with Verandas	None	Passenger/Crew Ratio	2.43 to 1
Number of Passengers	850	Year Built	1993
Last Major Refurbishment	1993		

Frommer's Ratings (Scale of 1–5)

Cabin Comfort & Amenities	3	Pool, Fitness & Spa Facilities	4
Ship Cleanliness & Maintenance	4	Children's Facilities	N/A
Public Comfort/Space	3	Decor	3

The *Marco Polo,* a former transatlantic liner, was completely rebuilt from the hull and engines up in the early '90s and is now a sturdy and graceful cruise liner, both modern and traditional.

Cabins & Rates

Cabins	Brochure Rates	Bathtub	Fridge	Hair Dryer	Sitting Area	TV
Inside	$2,250–$2,825	no	no	yes	no	yes
Outside	$2,950–$4,095	some	no	yes	some	yes
Suite	$4,450–$5,250*	yes	yes	yes	yes	yes

For 7-day Baltics cruise, plus 2 hotel nights, some sightseeing, and transfers.

CABINS   The 425 cabins (294 outside) are mostly average-size, twin-bedded staterooms ranging between 115 and 158 square feet, with light wood trim, TVs, three-channel radios, phones, good storage, and hair dryers. Higher-category staterooms and junior and deluxe suites have tubs. The cabins are found on all passenger decks apart from Belvedere, the level for the public rooms.

PUBLIC AREAS   The forward Ambassador Lounge spotlights after-dinner shows, large parties, and lectures, but seating is tight, and sight lines are poor. The Polo Lounge is a delightful setting with a pianist playing before meals and in the evening, and is a pleasant option for those not taking in the show. Tea is served in the Palm Court, and the tiny bar there is a snug hideaway. The casino offers blackjack, roulette, and slot machines; and a card room, good library with limited hours, and two boutiques share an adjacent area. Aft of the buffet is an open and partly covered deck, a favorite gathering place at the end of a day ashore. One deck up is a disco, and above that are the well-equipped health club and the beauty salon.

ALTERNATIVE DINING   None.

POOL, FITNESS & SPA FACILITIES   The cluster of three hot tubs looks over tiered decks aft, and below are several quiet areas to enjoy a snooze or a good book from the comfort of a deck chair. Handsome wooden deck chairs line wide teak promenades, and the Upper Deck has a wraparound walking track. Because of narrow side sections, however, most walkers prefer to stroll the promenade below. There's an outdoor pool and a mirrored aft-facing fitness center and spa two decks above the Lido, offering aerobics and tai chi classes. Fitness equipment includes rowing machines, stationary bikes, treadmills, and weight machines, and a Steiner-managed Mandara spa provides beauty treatments, facials, hydrotherapy, and massage.

5 Princess Cruises

SHIPS IN EUROPE   Golden Princess • Royal Princess

24305 Town Center Dr., Santa Clarita, CA 91355-4999. © **800/421-0522** or 661/753-0000. Fax 611/753-1535. www.princesscruises.com.

These lovely ships—especially our favorite, the *Royal Princess*—offer a cruise experience that's both glamorous and fun. The Royal deserves a special mention all of its own.

Owned by British firm Peninsular & Oriental Steam Navigation Company (also known as P&O), Princess achieved worldwide fame as the line portrayed in the TV series *The Love Boat.* It's a company that strives, successfully, to please a wide variety of passengers. It offers more choices in terms of accommodations, dining, and entertainment than nearly any other line.

The line's ships in Europe for 2002 are diverse. The *Royal Princess,* the oldest of the ships, was christened by Princess Di, whose portrait hangs prominently on board. The ship was cutting-edge when built. Today it looks almost out of place alongside the behemoths in this and other fleets, but it is still a most appealing ship. The *Golden Princess* is the second of Princess's Grand-class ships of which there are to be four, all of 109,000 tons. Like its sister, the *Grand Princess,* it manages to offer both massive, dramatic spaces out on deck (particularly in the stern) and remarkably cozy lounges, restaurants, and bars.

Overall, the Princess ships are one notch above mainstream competitors like Royal Caribbean. But they are not luxury vessels. They offer a consistent product, and serve the upper-middle ground of the market in a very consistent manner. You get a well-functioning, semiformal product delivered on a large (and in the case of the *Golden Princess,* massive) scale, and a good value for your vacation dollar.

Pros
- **Verandas.** The Princess ships have a lot of them.
- **Personal Choice Dining.** All the ships offer 24-hour casual dining, pizza, and 24-hour room service, and the *Golden Princess* also has three main dining rooms, two intimate alternative dining restaurants, and flexible dining times.
- **Efficient onboard tour desk.** Princess tour desk people always seem to us to do a better job of getting people on and off the ship for shore excursions.

Cons
- **No free ice cream (outside the dining room).** It may sound petty, but it's irritating that Princess sells only Häagen-Dazs ice cream—at $1.90 a scoop and $3.75 for a sundae—in lieu of the free frozen yogurt and soft ice cream most all other lines offer from self-serve machines.

Compared with other American Mainstream lines, here's how Princess rates:

	Poor	Fair	Good	Excellent	Outstanding
Enjoyment Factor					✓
Dining			✓		
Activities				✓	
Children's Program				✓	
Entertainment				✓	
Service				✓	
Overall Value				✓	

Major Merger

In November 2001, Royal Caribbean and P&O Princess Cruises (see chapter 6, "The European Lines") announced plans for a monumental merger that would create the world's largest cruise vacation company, with 41 ships and more on the way. The deal was to close in the second quarter of 2002.

Officials said they would continue to operate Princess and Royal Caribbean brands as separate entities; at press time, it was unclear what they would do in terms of their other brands, which include Celebrity Cruises, P&O Cruises, and Swan Hellenic. Future plans include the creation of a new joint venture company, A'Rosa, which is to offer cruises targeting the Italian market beginning in 2003.

THE FLEET

Princess has a diverse fleet of 10 ships. It has the two ships in Europe this year: the 45,000-ton *Royal Princess* and the 109,000-ton *Golden Princess*. Elsewhere, it has the 109,000-ton *Grand Princess*, four others at 77,000 tons, and two more at 70,000 tons. And there are several more giants in various stages of construction. The futuristic-looking twins, the *Regal Princess* and *Crown Princess*, were on order for Sitmar when P&O acquired that company in the late 1980s.

In May 1998, Princess made giant waves throughout the travel industry with the launching of what was to date the largest cruise ship in the world, the *Grand Princess*. She's since been matched in the Princess fleet and, late last year, eclipsed by the 142,000-ton *Voyager of the Seas* of Royal Caribbean International.

PASSENGER PROFILE

In the past, most Princess passengers were middle-aged middle Americans, but the new megas, including the *Golden Princess*, are attracting younger, more active 30- and 40-something cruisers and honeymooners. The *Golden Princess* has extensive kids' facilities, making it ideal for families (including several generations traveling together). The vessel also attracts lovebirds with its wedding chapel, in which its captain conducts official marriage ceremonies at sea by pre-arrangement.

All the ships strike a nice balance between formal and informal. They draw a relatively affluent but not overly wealthy crowd that appreciates the traditional cruise experience, as well as a dose of bells and whistles.

DINING

The *Golden Princess* offers the most dining options, including three main dining rooms; and two reservations-required alternative restaurants, Mexican and Italian, that have a $8 and $15 cover charge, respectively. There's also a Häagen-Dazs ice-cream parlor (selling its sweet treats for several dollars a pop).

Both ships in Europe have 24-hour casual dining (in the Lido restaurant), pizzerias, and 24-hour room service; and the *Golden Princess* also has outdoor grills, patisseries, and wine and caviar bars.

Princess's food is on par with that of competitor Holland America, though not as good as that of competitor Celebrity. Some of the food is, frankly, mediocre; but you'll occasionally get a dish that really makes you smile. The pastas are usually the best bet.

The dining rooms offer two seatings in addition to the Personal Choice option, and are open for breakfast, lunch, and dinner. The menus include a choice of four or five entrees, featuring halibut with saffron mayonnaise, broiled

Princess Fleet Itineraries*

Ship	Home Ports & Season	Itinerary
Royal Princess	**12-day W. Europe,** round-trip from Dover (May and Aug); **12-day Norway,** round-trip from Dover (June); **12-day British Isles/Iceland,** round-trip from Dover (July); **12-day Med,** Venice–Barcelona and reverse (Sept); **10- and 12-day Med,** between Barcelona and Istanbul (May–Aug, Oct)	**12-day W. Europe:** Port calls include Bilbao (Spain), Bordeaux (France), Glasgow (Scotland), Devon (England), Dublin and Cork (Ireland), Le Havre/Paris (France), Amsterdam (The Netherlands), and Zeebrugge/Brussels (Belgium); **12-day Norway:** Port calls include Hellesylt, Geiranger, Trondheim, Honningsvag, Tromso, Fram, and Bergen (Norway); **12-day British Isles/Iceland:** Port calls include Bergen (Norway), Lerwick (Scotland), Akureyi and Reykjavik (Iceland), Londonderry and Dublin (Ireland), Glasgow, Cornwall (England); **12-day Med:** Port calls include Monte Carlo (Monaco), Livorno and Naples (Italy), Athens (Greece), Kuşadasi and Istanbul (Turkey); **10- and 12-day Med:** Ports of call may include Rome, Naples, Valletta, Athens, Santorini (Greece), and Kuşadasi*
Golden Princess	**10-day Grand Med,** Barcelona–Venice (May); 12-day Grand Med Barcelona–Venice (June–Aug)	10-day Grand Med: Port calls include Athens (Greece), Venice, Naples, Livorno, Civitavecchia (Italy), Valletta (Malta); **12-day Grand Med:** Port calls include Monte Carlo, Athens (Greece), Livorno, Naples, Civitavecchia, and Messina (Italy)

*Royal Princess *also does some Holy Lands itineraries.*

lobster tail, royal pheasant in pan juices, and beef Wellington, plus a pasta dish like ravioli con salsa di funghi porcini (pasta squares filled with meat in a creamy mushroom sauce). There's also always **"healthy" choices** and **vegetarian options.**

A touch we really like: On request, a bowl of fresh fruit will be delivered to your cabin.

ACTIVITIES
The line that wants to be all things to all people is expert at programming activities to please a wide range of tastes. In Europe, the *Golden Princess* offers the most elaborate and extensive repertoire, the *Royal Princess* is much more sedate.

Activities include your typical shuffleboard and bridge tournaments, lectures, games like Passenger Feud, art auctions, and exercise classes.

If you participate in aerobics classes or other sports activities, you receive chits you can cash in for prizes, like water bottles and T-shirts, at the end of your cruise.

Princess devotes a lot of attention and space to its onboard libraries. And the ships all have movie theaters offering first-run movies.

Internet access on Princess ships costs 75¢ a minute, with a 15-minute minimum. The ships have laundromats.

CHILDREN'S PROGRAM
Supervised activities are offered for ages 2 to 17, and are divided into two groups: "Princess Pelicans," ages 2 to 12, and teens, ages 13 to 17. The *Golden Princess* has a spacious **children's playroom** and a sizable area of fenced-in outside deck dedicated for kids only, with a shallow pool and tricycles. **Teen centers** have computers, video games, and a sound system (and the one on the *Golden Princess* even has a teen's hot tub and private sunbathing deck).

The *Golden Princess* has a playroom and teen center and offers a children's program year-round. The *Royal Princess,* on the other hand, does not have a dedicated children's playroom and only offers activities when there are 15 or more kids on board.

Kids' activities include karaoke, movies, tours of the galley and bridge, scavenger hunts, arts and crafts, coloring contests, and teenage versions of *The Dating Game.*

In late 1998, Princess lowered its minimum age requirement to 6 months; previously a child had to be at least a year old to sail. Princess does not offer private in-cabin babysitting at all, but does provide **slumber party–style group babysitting** in the playroom for $4 an hour (10pm–1am nightly, and 9am–5pm when in port).

> **Fun Fact Cruise History**
>
> Princess Cruises originated in 1962, when the company's founder, Stanley McDonald, chartered the long-gone *Princess Patricia* as a floating hotel for the Seattle World's Fair.

ENTERTAINMENT

There's a lot going on, and the quality of the overall package ranks way up there. From glittering, well-conceived, and well-executed **Vegas-style production shows** to New York cabaret singers on the main stage; from a wonderfully entertaining **cabaret piano/vocalist** in the Atrium Lounge (a throwaway space for many ships) to a rocking disco, this line offers a terrific blend of musical delights, and you'll always find a cozy spot where some soft piano or jazz music is being performed. Hypnotists, puppeteers, and comedians are also part of the act. The Princess **casinos** are sprawling and exciting places, too, and are bound to keep gamblers happy for hours (or until the cash runs out).

SERVICE

Overall, service is efficient and lines miraculously aren't much of a problem (even on the *Golden Princess*). Staff and crew are friendly, well intentioned, and generally good. (We've seen waiters deal with even the rudest of guests in an even manner.) Suites and minisuites on the *Golden Princess* come with butler service. And every cabin on all the ships gets turndown service, including chocolates, at night. The ships offer **laundry** and **dry cleaning** services, and have their own **self-service laundromats.**

Golden Princess

The Verdict

The ship is a winner. Despite its size, it doesn't often feel as though you're surrounded by thousands of others. There are plenty of opportunities to "get away from it all."

Golden Princess *(photo: Princess Cruises)*

Specifications

Size (in tons)	109,000	Officers	Italian/British
Number of Cabins	1,301	Crew	1,200 (Internat'l)
Number of Outside Cabins	992	Passenger/Crew Ratio	2.1 to 1
Cabins with Verandas	710	Year Built	2001
Number of Passengers	2,600	Last Major Refurbishment	n/a

Frommer's Ratings (Scale of 1–5)

Cabin Comfort & Amenities	4	Pool, Fitness & Spa Facilities	4
Ship Cleanliness & Maintenance	4	Children's Facilities	4
Public Comfort/Space	5	Decor	5

The 109,000-ton, 2,600-passenger *Golden Princess* is one of the world's biggest and most expensive (call it $450 million) cruise ships. With 15 towering decks, the ship—like its predecessor *Grand Princess* and the brand new *Star Princess*—is taller than the Statue of Liberty (from pedestal to torch) and too wide to fit through the Panama Canal. In fact, it's so big that the line's *Pacific Princess,* the original *Love Boat,* could easily fit inside its hull and still have lots of room to spare.

Inside and out, the *Golden Princess* is a marvel of size and design. Its massive white, boxy body with its spoiler-like aft poking up into the air cuts a bizarre, space-age profile and is like nothing else at sea. It might look a bit scary, but the ship's well-laid-out interior is very easy to navigate and, amazingly, the ship never feels crowded—a characteristic, we've found, of Princess's new Grand Class ships.

The *Golden Princess* offers an amazing variety of entertainment and dining options and recreational activities. There's no question it's designed to be a floating resort. There are six restaurants (plus a pizzeria and outdoor grill), four swimming pools, and three show lounges, as well as expansive deck space.

Even the ship's medical center is grand: It boasts a high-tech "telemedicine" program that, via a live video hook-up, links the ship's doctors to the emergency room at Cedars Sinai Medical Center in Los Angeles.

Cabins & Rates

Cabins	Brochure Rates*	Bathtub	Fridge	Hair Dryer	Sitting Area	TV
Inside	$2,720–$3,350	no	yes	yes	no	yes
Outside	$3,465–$4,290	no	yes	yes	no	yes
Suite	$4,840–$8,790	yes	yes	yes	yes	yes

Rates for 10-day cruises.

CABINS The *Golden Princess* has 707 cabins with verandas of a total room count of 1,301. (*Be forewarned:* The verandas are tiered, so passengers in levels above may be able to look down on you. So, while they might be said to be private, they're really rather exposed. Don't do anything out there you wouldn't want the neighbors to see!) Cabins are nicely decorated and all have safes, hair dryers, refrigerators, robes (for use during the cruise), and TVs broadcasting CNN, ESPN, Nickelodeon, BBC programming, and TNT (as well as *Love Boat* reruns). Storage is adequate and features more closet shelves than drawer space.

A standard outside cabin (including veranda) ranges from 215 to 255 square feet; minisuites run as big as 325 square feet, and full suites are anywhere from 515 to 800 square feet, including verandas.

The suites and minisuites (the entire Dolphin Deck is nothing but minisuites) have tubs as well as showers (suite tubs have whirlpools), separate sitting areas with sofa beds, private balconies, and two TVs (which really seems unnecessary). In addition to the room stewards, all suites and minisuites come with the services of white-gloved butlers who wear beepers so they're at passengers' beck and call to help with unpacking, deliver nightly canapés, make sure the minibar is stocked with beverages (it's stocked one time on a complimentary basis, including alcohol), arrange shore excursions, and make spa appointments.

Getting Married at Sea

Talk about the Love Boat: Aboard the *Golden Princess,* the captain can actually marry you in a charming wedding chapel adorned with fresh flower arrangements (there are two full-time florists on board), ribbons strung along the aisle, and stained glass. There's seating for a few dozen friends and family members, and assistant pursers, decked out in their handsome dress blues, are available to escort a bride down the mini-aisle. Call for details on the ceremony packages.

The views from many cabins on the Emerald Deck are obstructed by lifeboats.

The ship has 28 wheelchair-accessible cabins. (The Skywalkers disco has a wheelchair lift up to the elevated dance floor, too.)

PUBLIC AREAS You'll wonder where everyone is. The *Golden Princess* is a huge ship with a not-so-huge-ship feeling. Thanks to its smart layout, with lots of small rooms rather than a few large rooms, passengers are dispersed rather than concentrated into one or two main areas; you'll have no problem finding a quiet retreat.

The public areas have a contemporary and upscale appeal, thanks to pleasing color schemes and touches like wood, marble, and brass. Two full-time florists create and care for impressive flower arrangements and a large variety of live plants.

There are three main dining rooms, all named for famous sculptors—Bernini, Donatello, and Canaletto—all decorated with the appropriate artwork (reproductions, of course). The rooms are purposely not very large (the largest is actually smaller than the main dining room on the *Royal Princess*), so you don't feel you're dining with crowds and so the acoustics are good (although you may also feel like the ceiling is closing in on you a bit). In Europe, there are specialty theme nights including a Greek night featuring Greek music and national cuisine. Passengers are assigned to the dining room closest to your cabin. This means women don't have to trek a mile in high heels to get to dinner. There's also a 24-hour Horizons restaurant, and Princess's usual poolside pizza parlor (Prego), hamburger/hot dog joint (The Trident Grill, also near the pool), ice-cream sundae stand, and, oh yes, in case you're still hungry, 24-hour room service.

What it all adds up to, according to the company, is options, lots and lots of options—four dining options for breakfast, seven for lunch, and eight for dinner or evening snacks.

Gamblers will love the sprawling and dazzling 13,500-square-foot Atlantis Casino, one of the largest at sea. Near the casino are Castaways and Meridian Bay, two lounge areas ideal for whiling away a few moments while awaiting friends coming to join you to attack the gaming tables.

The ship's most striking design feature is the disco, which juts out the back, and is suspended, scarily in our opinion, some 155 feet above the water. From this space you can literally look back at the rest of the ship, as if you were in a helicopter behind the vessel. It's really quite spectacular. Smoke machines and other high-tech gizmos add to the effect at night. During the day its banquettes make a particularly cozy spot to snuggle up with a good book, away from the sun-worshiping gang, but with passing scenery in good view. Kids are hardly ignored on this vessel. There are two-tiered children's and teen's centers, the latter with its own disco. The kiddies have access to computers, games, a wading pool, and even a fleet of bright red tricycles. Teens get their own whirlpool.

The ship's large virtual reality center, with interactive games and a motion-based simulator "ride," is designed to please kids and adults alike (all for an extra fee, of course).

The *Golden Princess* also has a library, small writing room, card room, and business center with computers, from which e-mails can be sent and received ($7.50 for 15 min. of use).

ALTERNATIVE DINING   The alternative eating areas are the Desert Rose, an excellent Southwestern-style establishment replete with Mexican tile, where the $8 cover charge includes a margarita, Mexican beer, or other beverage of choice; and Sabatini's Trattoria, which serves fine Italian food in a setting that will remind you of Italy, for a cover charge of $15. Both require reservations.

POOL, FITNESS & SPA FACILITIES   This ship has something like 1.7 acres of open deck space, so it's not hard to find a quiet place to soak in the sun (in some of the more remote areas, it's said that you may find a few women discreetly going topless—although Jerry claims never to have seen that!). There are four great swimming pools, including one with a retractable glass roof so it can double as a sort of solarium, another touted as a swim-against-the-current pool (although truth be told, there really isn't enough room to do laps if others are in the pool), and a third, aft under the disco, that feels miles from the rest of the ship (and is the least crowded).

A large, almost separate part of the ship, on the forward Sun Deck, is reserved for pampering the body. Surrounding the lap pool and its tiered, amphitheater-style wooden benches is the large Plantation Spa, with a layout we personally find a bit weird (for instance, there are no showers in the dressing area). The complex includes a very large oceanview beauty parlor and an oceanview gym, which is surprisingly small and cramped for a ship of this size (although there is an unusually large aerobics floor). Unfortunately, the sports decks are just above the spa, and if you're getting a relaxing massage when someone is playing basketball, you'll hear it.

Other active diversions include a jogging track, basketball, paddle tennis, a fun nine-hole putting green, and computerized simulated golf.

Royal Princess

The Verdict

This ship, christened by Princess Diana in 1984, was ahead of its time, with all oceanview cabins and more cabins with verandas than ever before. It's still a lovely vessel—one of Jerry's all-time personal favorites—offering a traditional cruise experience.

Royal Princess *(photo: Princess Cruises)*

Specifications

Size (in tons)	45,000	Crew	520 (International)
Number of Cabins	600	Passenger/Crew Ratio	2.3 to 1
Number of Outside Cabins	600	Year Built	1984
Cabins with Verandas	152	Last Major Refurbishment	1999
Number of Passengers	1,200		

Frommer's Ratings (Scale of 1–5)

Cabin Comfort & Amenities	4	Pool, Fitness & Spa Facilities	4
Ship Cleanliness & Maintenance	4	Children's Facilities	N/A
Public Comfort/Space	4	Decor	4

Princess Cruises set standards for the industry with its classy *Royal Princess*. The ship's 152 cabins with verandas was by far the highest number of veranda cabins on any ship at the time, and Princess has reflected the success of that concept with every vessel it's built since.

Even today, the *Royal Princess* is in some ways ahead of its time. But that's not its greatest claim to fame; it's the fact this ship was christened by Princess Diana. Somehow, it seems entirely fitting that a ship this elegant would be christened by a person of Princess Di's stature.

The interior design concept at work on this vessel was to create a simple yet elegant atmosphere. Carpets and wall coverings are in mostly neutral tones, and traditional nautical touches such as teak and brass enhance an otherwise contemporary ambience. The sea is never far from sight, since all public areas boast floor-to-ceiling windows (the vessel has some 16,000 sq. ft. of windows all told). The art collection (all original) reflects both British and American artists. For sheer elegance, this ship, with its traditional, sleek lines, has not been topped in its tonnage range. Crystal's two ships might be said to have matched it, but nobody has improved on *Royal's* elegance or overall level of service.

Cabins & Rates

Cabins	Brochure Rates*	Bathtub	Fridge	Hair Dryer	Sitting Area	TV
Outside	$2,790–$4,590	yes	yes	yes	no	yes
Suites	$5,815–$9,745	yes	yes	yes	yes	yes

*Rates for 12-day cruises

CABINS   All cabins have large picture windows, and a quarter of them have private verandas. They are comfortably laid out, with a standard cabin 168 square feet, and suites 336 square feet, including verandas. Twin beds can be combined to make a queen, and in standard cabins one bed can be folded into the wall during the day to create more room to walk around. The cabins all have bathtubs and showers. The two penthouse suites are very large (more than 800 sq. ft.) and each has a separate sitting/dining area with a sofa bed, table, and chairs, as well as a queen-size bed, large closets, and Jacuzzi tub.

Cabins on the Baja and Caribe decks, and some on the Dolphin Deck, have obstructed or partially obstructed views. Since the cabins on Promenade Deck are located directly above the public areas, you're best off avoiding them if you're a light sleeper.

In-cabin amenities in all cabins include safes, hair dryers, refrigerators, robes for use during the cruise, and color TVs broadcasting CNN, ESPN, Nickelodeon, BBC programming, and TNT.

Ten cabins are wheelchair accessible.

PUBLIC AREAS   Most of the ship's public rooms are on the Riviera Deck, including the show lounge, nightclub, theater, and casino, and all are good-size, creating an overall feeling of spaciousness. The Princess Court is a circular lounge amidships that overlooks The Plaza, the ship's elegant and comfortable two-story lobby. The two-level restaurant has floor-to-ceiling windows. As mentioned earlier, keep in mind that *Royal Princess* does not have the same variety of alternative dining opportunities as some of its newer fleetmates.

The Horizon Lounge on the top deck offers a panoramic view that makes it the best place to catch the passing scenery. The space is used as an observation lounge during the day and a disco at night.

The ship has lots of teak deck space, including a Promenade Deck you can walk all the way around.

ALTERNATIVE DINING   None.

POOL, FITNESS & SPA FACILITIES   The ship has three pool areas, including one of the largest lap pools at sea. The pool on Lido Deck is actually a combination of several pools grouped together in a circular pattern.

The ship's small spa and oceanview gym (with Lifecycles, an 11-station multi-gym, and two massage rooms) are on the top deck, where there are also two saunas, an indoor hot tub, and a beauty salon, as well as table tennis and shuffleboard. You can jog on the Promenade Deck.

6 Royal Caribbean International

SHIPS IN EUROPE   Splendour of the Seas • Brilliance of the Seas (preview)

1050 Caribbean Way, Miami, FL 33132. *©* **800/327-6700** or 305/539-6000. Fax 800/722-5329. www. royalcaribbean.com.

On its own, Royal Caribbean International was one of the most successful cruise companies in the world. In November 2001, the company announced a merger with P&O Princess, making it also part of the world's largest cruise company (see "Major Merger," p. 97). Royal Caribbean sells a big-ship cruise experience that's reasonably priced and designed to please everyone, except, perhaps, those who hate crowds. The ships are well-run and provide a consistent product, overseen by an army of service employees who pay close attention to detail. Bringing to Europe the mass-market American experience that's proven so popular in the Caribbean, these ships are contemporary, attractive, and glamorous without being overly glitzy.

Most passengers in Europe are couples in their 40s to 60s, but you'll also find honeymoon couples, younger singles, and families. The majority of passengers are North American, although these ships also attract Europeans.

The company's vessels in Europe are megaships with multistory atria, mall-like shopping complexes, multi-level dining rooms and show lounges, wide-open public areas, indoor (with retractable roof) and outdoor pools, and relatively small cabins (although those on the brand-new *Brilliance* are a little bigger than on the other vessels).

Pros

- **Entertainment.** The line's entertainment offerings are among the best at sea, and include both flashy show productions and headliner acts.
- **Attractive public rooms.** They are witty and classy, with lots of greenery and artwork, and just the right amount of glamour. And there's lots of glass, most notably the line's trademark Viking Crown Lounges, for viewing the scenery outside.

Cons

- **Cabin categories.** These ships have 16 to 19 different cabin categories, which can be very confusing, and cabins aren't very big (but they do all offer sitting areas).
- **Crowds.** Hey, these are big ships, so there are going to be lines at times, especially in the buffet restaurants, at bars, and getting on and off the ship in port.

Compared with other American Mainstream lines, here's how Royal Caribbean rates:

	Poor	Fair	Good	Excellent	Outstanding
Enjoyment Factor					✓
Dining			✓		
Activities				✓	
Children's Program				✓	
Entertainment					✓
Service			✓		
Overall Value				✓	

Fun Fact   Size Matters

Back in 1988, Royal Caribbean was the first line to introduce megaships. The 73,192-ton *Sovereign of the Seas* was the largest passenger ship built in the previous 50 years, and introduced features that have become industry standards, including the multistory atrium. In late 1999, Royal Caribbean grabbed headlines again by introducing the largest ship in the world, the 142,000-ton *Voyager of the Seas,* which among other innovations offers, for the first time on a cruise ship, interior cabins with views of the atrium (think Hyatt hotels).

THE FLEET

Royal Caribbean will have 17 ships in its fleet by the end of 2002, including three of the world's largest, the 3000-plus-passenger *Voyager of the Seas* and its equally mammoth sisters *Explorer of the Seas* and *Adventure of the Seas.* The *Splendour of the Seas* isn't quite as large, but it's still a giant ship in the scheme of things. The brand-new *Brilliance of the Seas* is the second ship of a new generation of 2,100-passenger vessels the company introduced with the *Radiance of the Seas* in 2001.

More vessels are under construction or on order.

PASSENGER PROFILE

Most passengers in Europe are couples in their 40s to 60s, but there are also honeymoon couples, younger singles, and families (including three generations—children, parents, and grandparents—traveling together). About half of the guests have cruised before; more than half will be on their first trip to Europe. The majority of passengers come from somewhere in North America, although these ships also attract Europeans. Whenever there are more than 200 non-English speakers of a particular language on board, announcements are made in that language (usually Spanish, French, German, or Russian).

DINING

Royal Caribbean has changed and upgraded its dining options, but the cuisine is still rather pedestrian. Entrees may include prime rib, grilled medallions of veal, deviled crab, and Chinese roast duck, as well as a pasta option, such as ravioli. There's always a **ShipShape healthy menu option** (along the lines of pan-seared salmon) as well as a **vegetarian option** such as Indian spiced curry. Cuisine is often presented in different themes, with table settings, menus, and waiters' costumes reflecting the theme, including Latin Night.

The **formal dining room** on each ship offers two seatings, and an alternative casual evening dining option is offered in the poolside Windjammer Cafe most nights of the cruise. The *Brilliance* also has alternative dining options including a steakhouse and an upscale Italian restaurant (for a fee of $20, and with reservations required; kids are not allowed). You can eat breakfast and lunch in the main dining room or in the buffet-style Windjammer Cafe, and the *Brilliance* also has the option of a cafe with a light menu. Lines, unfortunately, can grow long. **Ice cream** and a couple of toppings are available throughout the day from a station in the Windjammer. There's also a **midnight buffet** nightly, and sandwiches are served throughout the night in the public lounges. Pizza is served in the afternoon and late night for those after-partying munchies.

Royal Caribbean Fleet Itineraries

Ship	Home Ports & Season	Itinerary
Brilliance of the Seas	12-day Baltics, Harwich (England) (July and Aug)	12-day Baltics: Port calls include Oslo (Norway), Stockholm (Sweden), Helsinki (Finland), St. Petersburg (Russia), Tallinn (Estonia), Copenhagen (Denmark)*
Splendour of the Seas	7-day W. Med, Barcelona (Spain) (Apr–Oct)	7-day W. Med: Port calls include Villefranche (France), Livorno, Civitavecchia/Rome, and Naples (Italy) and Valletta (Malta)

*The Brilliance also does one 12-day British Isles cruise in July.

An extensive **kids' menu** features items like fish sticks, burritos, oven-fried lemon chicken, spaghetti and meatballs, and pizza; the standard burgers, hot dogs, and fries; plus lots of yummy desserts.

Room service is available 24 hours a day from a fairly routine, limited menu. However, during normal lunch and dinner hours, your cabin steward can bring anything being served in the restaurant to your cabin.

ACTIVITIES

Daytime activities are typical cruise line fare: bingo, shuffleboard, horse racing, line-dancing lessons, crafts lessons, spa and beauty demonstrations, contests and games, and art auctions. Destination-type lectures focus on the itinerary. The *Splendour of the Seas* and *Brilliance of the Seas* even feature **miniature golf courses,** right on board!

If you participate in the line's **ShipShape fitness program,** which includes aerobics and other classes, you'll get chits you can turn in at the end of the cruise for prizes like T-shirts and baseball caps.

If **shopping** can be considered an activity, Royal Caribbean offers a particularly impressive selection of shops clustered around the atrium. You can surf the Web and check your e-mail at the Internet cafe for 50¢ a minute.

CHILDREN'S PROGRAM

Year-round, Royal Caribbean offers **supervised kids' programs** fleetwide for children ages 3 to 17. Male and female youth staff all have college degrees in education, recreation, or a related field. The "Adventure Ocean" program offers fun and games for four age groups: Aquanauts, ages 3 to 5; Explorers, ages 6 to 8; Voyagers, ages 9 to 12; and Navigators, ages 13 to 17.

Each ship has a **children's playroom,** a **teen center and disco,** and a **video arcade.** The fun includes talent shows, karaoke, pizza and ice-cream parties, bingo, scavenger hunts, and game shows.

Slumber party–style **group babysitting** is available nightly and also when the ship is in port. The charge is $4 per child. Private, **in-cabin babysitting** by a crew member is available and must be booked at least 24 hours in advance through the purser's desk. The charge is $8 per hour for up to two children in the same family, and $10 per hour for a maximum of three kids in the same family.

ENTERTAINMENT

The line doesn't scrimp on entertainment. There is something happening on these ships from before dinner until late at night, including lavish Las

Vegas–style show productions done on sprawling high-tech stages, music acts, comedians, and sometimes even big-name performers.

Royal Caribbean uses 8- to 10-piece bands for its main showroom, and its large-cast revues are among the best you'll find on a ship. Show bands and other lounge acts, who keep the music playing all over the ship, are all first-rate.

SERVICE

Overall, service in the restaurants and cabins is friendly, accommodating, and efficient, despite some language-barrier problems (sign language often comes in handy). You're likely to be greeted with a smile by someone polishing the brass in a stairwell, a greeting that supervisors encourage on the part of even the lowest-ranking employees. That said, big, bustling ships like Royal Caribbean's are no strangers to crowds, lines, and harried servers not able to get to you exactly when you'd like them to. While laundry and dry cleaning services are available, the ships do not have self-service laundries, which can be an annoyance on a longer cruise.

Splendour of the Seas

The Verdict

This contemporary cruise ship is a truly floating resort (think Hyatt Hotels on the high seas) and offers just the right amount of glamour and excitement, without going overboard—so to speak.

Splendour of the Seas *(photo: Royal Caribbean International)*

Specifications

Size (in tons)	69,130	Officers	Norwegian/Int'l
Number of Cabins	902	Crew (International)	720
Number of Outside Cabins	575	Passenger/Crew Ratio	2.5 to 1
Cabins with Verandas	231	Year Built	1996
Number of Passengers	1,804		

Frommer's Ratings (Scale of 1–5)

Cabin Comfort & Amenities	4	Pool, Fitness & Spa Facilities	5
Ship Cleanliness & Maintenance	4	Children's Facilities	4
Public Comfort/Space	5	Decor	5

This was one of the first in the Vision class, marking the beginning of a highly successful series of ships. The contemporary vessel is quite spectacular, from its chrome, glass, and marble multistory atria to its dazzling casino and high tech theatre, and will no doubt elicit a fair number of "Ahs." Glass and light are everywhere (there are about 2 acres of glass canopies, glass windbreaks, skylights, and floor-to-ceiling windows with sweeping views). The decor is enhanced by impressive art collections and lots of greenery.

Preview: *Brilliance of the Seas*

Based on sister ship *Radiance of the Seas* (introduced in 2001), the brand-new *Brilliance of the Seas,* due in July 2002, will be a spectacular floating resort featuring walls of glass, including a bank of ocean-facing, 12-story glass elevators. With this new class of 2,100-passenger vessels, Royal Caribbean is going for a slightly more upscale, contemporary look, with the airy ships successfully borrowing a page from upscale sister line Celebrity; these are very pretty vessels.

The *Brilliance,* like the *Radiance,* will boast trendy coffeehouse/bookstore space, as well as some features made popular on earlier Royal Caribbean vessels, including a nine-hole mini-golf course and a rock-climbing wall. But what really sets this new class of ship apart is the amount of glass on the exterior (some 110,000 ft. in all)—plus, nearly every public room including the Internet cafe will boast floor-to-ceiling windows from which you can watch the passing European scenery.

Like its sister, the *Brilliance* will offer cushy lounges including a champagne bar and a nautically themed Schooner Bar. And passengers will have no problem finding a comfortable spot to sit with a book if they prefer not to participate in the plethora of onboard activities. The multilevel main dining room is designed to be an elegant space with a grand staircase (but on the *Radiance* the room was a bit noisy). The Windjammer buffet area will have stations for hot and cold offerings and the bonus of plenty of outdoor seating, and the *Brilliance* will also boast two alternative dining venues: an upscale steakhouse and an excellent Italian restaurant (both operated on a reservations-only basis, for a cover charge of $20). There will also be the Seaview Café, where you can order from a casual menu that includes chili, burgers and fries, fish-and-chips, clam chowder, nachos, and brownies (for no cover charge).

The *Brilliance*'s theater will rise three levels. The line's trademark, glass-enclosed Viking Crown Lounge (a flying saucer-shaped space on top of the ship) on this vessel will hold a disco and an intimate cabaret area. The vessel's oceanview fitness center will offer dozens of machines and a large exercise floor. Kids will have a decent-size playroom space equipped with computers and crafts stations, and there will be both a video arcade and separate hangout area for teens. Teens will get their own pool with a water slide and there will be a splash pool for little kids. The ship will offer plenty of areas for quiet sunning away from the main pool area, including a solarium pool with removable dome.

Cabins will be larger than cabins on other Royal Caribbean vessels, although they are still not particularly big. All will offer hair dryers, computer jacks, minibars, and vanities.

Brochure rates for 12-day sailings are $3,299 to $3,449 inside, $3,899 to $4,579 outside, $9,749 to $22,499 suite.

Cabins & Rates

Cabins	Brochure Rates	Bathtub	Fridge	Hair Dryer	Sitting Area	TV
Inside	$1,499–$1,799	yes	no	no	no	yes
Outside	$1,949–$3,599	no	some	no	yes	yes
Suite	$4,199–$13,499	yes	yes	no	yes	yes

CABINS To be polite, cabins are compact. Inside cabins measure 138 square feet and outsides 153 square feet. For big, check out the Royal Suite—it measures a mammoth 1,150 square feet. Nearly one-fourth of the cabins aboard each ship have private verandas and about a third can accommodate third and fourth passengers. All have beds convertible to queen-size, phone, interactive TV (with some 20 channels), safe, radio, and individually controlled air-conditioning. Bathrooms, while not the largest, have good storage space, including a multilevel built-in shelf in the shower stalls. Seventeen cabins are accessible for travelers with disabilities.

PUBLIC AREAS Warm woods and brass, luxuriant fountains and foliage, glass and crystal, buttery leathers, and carefully chosen artwork and textures highlight the well laid-out public areas. A soaring seven-story "Centrum" atrium crowned by a sloped two-deck-high skylight is the focal point of the ship. Glass elevators, a la Hyatt, take passengers up through the Centrum into the stunning Viking Crown Lounge, a glass-sided spaceship-like area high above the waves.

There is an array of other hideaway refuges, including cocktail bars, a well-stocked library, and card rooms. The Schooner Bar is a casual piano bar, and is a great place for a pre-dinner drink or late-night unwinding. Ditto the Champagne Terrace at the foot of the atrium. The large dining room spans two decks and is interconnected with a very grand staircase. A pianist plays a massive grand piano throughout dinner service.

The ship has a two-story theater and there's not a bad seat in the house. The casino is Vegas-style flashy and offers hundreds of gambling stations. The vessel's conference rooms can hold up to 200 people. Regrettably, there are no self-service laundromats.

ALTERNATIVE DINING None.

POOL, FITNESS & SPA FACILITIES The ShipShape spa is a wonderful, soothing respite from the hubbub of ship life. It offers a wide selection of treatments, as well as the standard steam rooms and saunas. Adjacent to the spa is a spacious solarium with a pool (with a retractable roof), lounge chairs, and floor-to-ceiling windows. This spot is a peaceful place to repose before or after a spa treatment, except in the afternoon when pizza is being served (for some reason pizza draws loud people). The gym is not particularly large, but is well equipped.

Overall, there's more than enough open deck area, plus a jogging track, shuffleboard, Ping-Pong, and a 6,000-square-foot, 18-hole miniature golf course complete with trees, sand traps, and water hazards. The main pool area has two whirlpools, and there are two more in the Solarium.

The European Lines

These mostly mid-size ships are European-owned and operated and offer a different cruise experience than the mainstream American vessels. Most in this category are older, classic ships that hold a lot of appeal for ship buffs, though some have not been kept up as they should be (the teak deck may be covered with outdoor carpet to hide its splinters). There are also some new ships in this category, designed to continue the classic cruise tradition but with more modern amenities (see First European Cruises' *Mistral,* later in this chapter).

We've included the British lines P&O and Swan Hellenic in this chapter, though the experiences on these ships are more upmarket and somewhat different than on the other lines mentioned, most of which are in the budget- to moderate-price category. Similarly, the Italian line Costa Cruises offers more of a megaship, mainstream cruise experience.

The Euro lines tend to attract those looking for an affordable cruise, including older couples, families, and singles sharing a cabin. The crowd on these ships is mostly European, and that means lots of languages spoken on public address systems (because of this, announcements may seem to go on forever). It also means, especially on the non-British ships, there may be plenty of people who do not speak English (brush up on your sign language!) and lots of smokers, though some lines, like First European, now ban smoking in the dining rooms. To really enjoy these cruises, American travelers have to be really comfortable with people from other countries.

The vessels will appeal to the more adventurous American traveler who wants something different, the type who stays at European hotels (and not Marriotts or Hiltons) when in Europe. The moderate prices and friendly atmosphere are the big attractions. But keep in mind that these vessels tend to have lots of passengers and can feel crowded.

Onboard activities may be conducted in several languages. For shore excursions, there are usually separate buses for each language, but if there aren't enough English speakers to fill a whole bus, you might have to hear another translation as well.

Cabins tend to be smaller than what Americans are used to (just like rooms in European hotels tend to be smaller than those in American hotels) and you're best off booking a deluxe room or suite if you can afford it. Cabins are likely to have portholes rather than large windows, and few of these vessels have private verandas in any cabin categories.

These ships may be difficult for travelers with disabilities, with few wide-door cabins and, quite often, high doorway sills that would be a major roadblock to wheelchairs.

The **itineraries** of these ships tend to be port-intensive (usually a port a day), so for many people the nighttime meal will be all the entertainment they need before bed. People at the late seating may mingle till the wee hours. Discos usually quiet down early, and Europeans just aren't as casino-crazy as Americans.

A Word About SOLAS

The future of some of these older ships will depend on compliance with a set of international safety regulations known as the Safety of Life at Sea (SOLAS), which are predominantly concerned with issues like fire prevention. Ships built after 1994 automatically incorporate SOLAS safety features, such as alarm and sprinkler systems, while ships built before 1994 have been required to add them by a progressive set of deadlines. The most sweeping changes were completed by a 1997 deadline, and another series of changes must be implemented by 2005. You may want to inquire in advance whether a ship is fully equipped for fire safety with smoke detectors, alarms, sprinklers, and low-level emergency lighting for escape pathways. The changes required could prove too costly for the lines that operate some of these old-timers and seal their fate forever—so enjoy them while you can.

Entertainment tends to be much more amateurish than on the American vessels, and to appeal to a multi-language crowd, the ships may feature more magicians, singers, and dancers than, say, comedians. Most of these vessels do not have fancy **alternative dining** options: Some Costa and First European vessels are exceptions.

DRESS CODES Like the mainstream American lines, weeklong cruises on these ships generally feature two formal nights, but you won't find too many passengers in tuxedos or fancy sequined dresses. Overall, ships in this category are somewhat more casual, with guests preferring suits or sport coats to tuxes, and pantsuits or sundresses to gowns (although it's not unheard of to see a tux and a shimmery dress). Guests are asked not to wear shorts and T-shirts in the formal dining room. Daytime is casual.

Cruise Lines Reviewed in This Chapter
- Costa Cruises
- First European Cruises (Festival Cruises)
- Fred. Olsen Cruise Lines
- Mediterranean Shipping Cruises
- Norwegian Coastal Voyage/Bergen Line Services
- P&O Cruises
- Royal Olympic Cruises
- Swan Hellenic Cruises

1 Costa Cruises

SHIPS IN EUROPE CostaAllegra • CostaRomantica • CostaClassica • CostaVictoria • CostaAtlantica • CostaTropicale (preview) • CostaEuropa (preview)

200 South Park Rd., Hollywood, FL 33021. ☎ **800/33-COSTA.** www.costacruises.com.

Fun, food, and Italian-style ambience is what these mid- and mega-size European ships are all about. They offer good value, too, with airfare from New York or other selected gateways included in the cruise fare.

Even though it's now owned by Carnival Corporation, the line—with an illustrious history stretching back almost 90 years to Genoa, Italy—has managed to hold onto its heritage, and that's what sets this cruise line apart from so many others.

Costa's Europe cruises attract a majority of Italians, but also French, Germans, British, and others. Americans represent only about 20% of the clientele on any given sailing, but that's part of the fun: meeting new people and trying out a few remembered words from high school language classes.

Costa does an excellent job catering to its diverse clientele, but announcements are delivered in five languages on the loudspeakers and at entertainment and activities gatherings, which can get a bit tiring. In the past, smoking has also been a problem—Europeans smoke more than Americans these days—but in 2002 the line is introducing a new policy banning smoking at least in the main dining room and main showroom on European cruises.

The onboard currency is Italian lira. Currency exchange services are offered, but it can get confusing translating your money to lira and then to the other currencies.

Pros

- **Italian flavor.** The whole onboard atmosphere shows a festive Italian flair.
- **The pasta.** While the rest of the food is fairly standard (but tasty), the handmade pasta really shines.
- **Late-night action.** Despite port-intensive itineraries, people stay up late and party on these vessels. The disco gets going at midnight.

Cons

- **Very few cabins with private verandas.** The *CostaAtlantica* has verandas on the majority of its outside cabins. But the *CostaVictoria* has none at all, and the other ships just have a few.
- **Lots of languages.** Activities and entertainment are geared to a five-language audience.

Compared with other European lines, here's how Costa rates:

	Poor	Fair	Good	Excellent	Outstanding
Enjoyment Factor				✓	
Dining		✓			
Activities				✓	
Children's Program			✓		
Entertainment			✓		
Service			✓		
Overall Value			✓		

THE FLEET

The Costa fleet is diverse, from gleaming megas to old, rebuilt liners from the 1960s. Of its current fleet of seven, there are two megaships, the 1,928-passenger *CostaVictoria,* built in 1996; and the 2,680-passenger *Costa-Atlantica,* built in 2000; a pair of mid-size 1,300-passenger ships, the *Costa-Romantica* (built in 1993) and the *CostaClassica* (built in 1991); and the 800-passenger *CostaAllegra,* built in 1969 as a container ship and rebuilt as a cruise ship in 1992. Perhaps a sign of its faith in the brand, Carnival also moved two other ships over to the Costa fleet this year, the 1,022-passenger *CostaTropicale,* built in 1981 and previously operated as the Carnival *Tropicale* in the Caribbean; and the 1,494-passenger *CostaEuropa,* built in 1986, and pre-viously Holland America's *Westerdam.* All the ships spend the summer in Europe.

Costa's first new build since the launch of the *CostaVictoria* in 1996, the 2,112-passenger, 85,000-ton *CostaAtlantica* in many ways represents a new chapter for Costa. It's the first Costa ship to have a substantial number of pri-vate verandas; 78% of the ship's cabins will be outfitted with them. A sister ship to *CostaAtlantica,* the *CostaMediterranea,* is due in the summer of 2003. Costa also has two even bigger 105,000-ton ships, the *CostaFortuna* and *CostaMagica,* under construction and due in late 2003 and 2004, respectively.

PASSENGER PROFILE

This line attracts passengers of all ages, with a good number of couples in their 40s and 50s. Americans on board will be older, experienced travelers, many of whom deliberately avoid all-American megaships and are attracted by Costa's port-intensive itineraries. Costa passengers appreciate a sense of cultural adven-ture and fun, and like the atmosphere of casual, sophisticated elegance and a sense of romance at which the Italians excel.

The line is a favorite of European honeymooners, and on some sailings from Italy there may be dozens of honeymoon couples on board (an older friend who was on one of these cruises reported it was great fun watching the young cou-ples enjoy their special vacation). Families are also attracted to these cruises, although the number of kids on board is rarely overwhelming (Aug cruises attract the highest numbers). In the summer, the ships that depart from Italy often fill up with the Italian equivalent of the Carnival "Fun Ship" crowd, which can lead to some lively times.

DINING

Food is well-prepared Continental with Italian influences. Most memorable are the **pastas,** prepared fresh and served with lovely sauces.

The six-course dinners might feature appetizers like fried calamari and Parma ham and melon, as well as a vegetarian appetizer selection, along with soup, salad, and a choice of two pasta dishes such as cannelloni and spaghetti. Among the main courses are roast rack of lamb with an herb crust, salmon with dill sauce, and beef tenderloin in puff pastry. We have heard Americans complain about the quality of the beef, which comes from Argentina rather than the U.S., but we've found it acceptable. Also available on every menu is a **vegetarian entree** such as a vegetable-stuffed artichoke. There is also a **regional choice,** such as deer and juniper berry sauce, a Scandinavian specialty offered as a special one night on a Baltic itinerary.

Costa goes out of its way to cater to a number of international tastes and make everyone happy. Hence a table of Americans may be offered off-menu items popular in the States, such as fettuccine Alfredo and Caesar salad.

The **dessert menu** is limited to a few selections, but includes such Italian delights as tiramisu, gelato, and cannelloni siciliani, as well as chocolate soufflé.

Entertainment is part of the dining experience: Much emphasis and a few theatrics are placed on head waiters tossing a pasta or energetically seasoning a salad while diners look on. And most evenings have a theme, with the waiters donning special costumes and singing or dancing. On Mediterranean night, for instance, staff members don the native dress of cultures around the Mediterranean and present a red rose to each woman passenger during dessert.

Most of the ships have a single dining room; the bigger *CostaVictoria* has two, the one on the *CostaAtlantica* is two stories. Meals are offered in two seatings, breakfast including a choice of a buffet or menu, lunch served at noon and 1:30pm, and dinner at 7pm and 9pm or 9:15pm. (*Note:* Late seating on these ships is later than on American ships.) Lavish midnight buffets include a Grand Buffet that takes up half the dining room and includes a half-dozen elaborate ice sculptures and a unique galley buffet (a combination midnight buffet and galley tour).

The Lido restaurant is the venue for fairly standard **casual breakfast and lunch** each day; a few nights during each cruise an informal, buffet-style dinner is also offered in the Lido for those too exhausted from a day in port to sit through a more formal dinner in the dining room (the same menu is offered at the buffet). As a nice touch, tablecloths are put on the tables of the casual eatery for the occasion.

Between meals, a patisserie serves espresso, chocolates, and pastries aboard the *CostaAtlantica, CostaVictoria,* and *CostaRomantica;* and **Romeo's Pizzeria** offers pizza throughout the day and night. On the other ships, pizza, sweets, and other treats are offered during afternoon tea, served in the Lido restaurant.

As on most lines, cappuccino and espresso count as bar drinks and appear on your bar tab at the end of the cruise. There is no brewed decaf coffee available (instant only). The wine list is not extensive and there are no wine stewards.

Room service is offered on a 24-hour basis, but the selection is spartan at best, and there is a charge (about $2) for delivery.

Costa offers a **gourmet alternative restaurant** on the *CostaVictoria, CostaAtlantica,* and *CostaTropicale.* A fee of $23 is charged for the experience. The specialty cuisine is Italian on the *CostaAtlantica* and *CostaVictoria,* and Brazilian on the *CostaTropicale.*

(*Value* Special Deals

Passengers booking 90 days before the cruise receive a discount of up to $2,300 per couple, and there's also an early-booking bonus of two free post-cruise hotel nights on select sailings. All Costa fares include airfare from New York and selected other gateways.

Costa Fleet Itineraries

Ship	Home Ports & Season	Itinerary
CostaAllegra	7-day Norway, round-trip from Copenhagen (June–Aug); 7-day Baltics, round-trip from Copenhagen (June–Sept)	7-day Norway: Flam, Vik, Hellesylt, Geiranger, Bergen, Kristiansand, and Oslo (Norway); 7-day Baltics: Stockholm (Sweden), Helsinki (Finland), St. Petersburg (Russia), Tallinn (Estonia)
CostaAtlantica	7-day Greece and Turkey, round-trip from Venice (May–Oct)*	7-day Greece and Turkey: Bari (Italy), Katakolon and Piraeus/Athens (Greece), and Kuşadasi and Istanbul (Turkey)
CostaClassica	7-day Greek Isles, round-trip from Venice (Apr–Nov)*	7-day Greek Isles: Bari (Italy), Katakolon, Santorini, Mykonos, Rhodes (Greece), and Dubrovnik (Croatia)
CostaEuropa	11-day Black Sea, round-trip from Savona (Italy) (May, Aug, Sept)*	11-day Black Sea: Naples (Italy), Istanbul (Turkey), Odessa and Yalta (Ukraine), Piraeus/Athens and Katakolon (Greece)
Costa-Romantica	10- and 14-day Norway/North Cape, round-trip from Amsterdam (May–Aug); 10- and 12-day Baltics, round-trip from Amsterdam (June–Aug)*	11- and 12-day Norway/North Cape: Port calls may include Olden, Aleslund, Honningsvag, Tromso, Trondheim, Gravdal, Hellesylt, Geiranger, and Bergen (Norway); 10- and 12-day Baltics: Port calls may include Ronne (Denmark), St. Petersburg (Russia), Helsinki (Finland), Stockholm and Visby (Sweden), Oslo (Norway), and Copenhagen (Denmark)
Costa-Tropicale	7-day Greek Isles, round-trip from Venice (May–Nov)*	7-day Greek Isles: Bari (Italy), Katakolon, Santorini, and Mykonos (Greece), Kuşadasi (Turkey), and Dubrovnik (Croatia)
CostaVictoria	7-day W. Med, round-trip from Genoa (Italy) (May–Nov)*	7-day W. Med: Naples and Palermo (Italy), Tunis (Tunisia), Palma de Mallorca and Barcelona (Spain), Marseille (France)

*CostaAtlantica, CostaClassica, CostaTropicale, and CostaVictoria also do a limited number of 5-day sailings; and CostaClassica, CostaEuropa, and CostaRomantica offer some Holy Lands itineraries. The CostaEuropa also does some Canary Islands sailings.

ACTIVITIES

Activities on the ships are overseen by a team of "animators" who don costumes like clown suits and Hawaiian shirts and try their best to get everyone involved in the action.

Nights include **theme nights** such as Carnivale, when people are encouraged to create and wear Venetian-style masks, and a Circus night, when passengers are given tokens and participate in games set up in the lounges, such as throw-the-ball-at-the-target. Popular events also include a night-time Mr. Universe contest, musical chairs, and Samba Night (lessons are given during the day to prepare for the event). Daytime activities include Italian language and cooking classes as well as such traditional cruise staples as bingo, bridge, napkin-folding, dance classes, Ping-Pong tournaments, exercise classes, beauty demonstrations, trivia games, and fun pool-side competitions. Sports offerings include shuffleboard, paddle tennis, and Ping-Pong, and on some of the ships Foosball and pool tables. Each ship also has a library (although it may not have many English selections) and a card room.

A full-time Catholic priest conducts mass almost every day in the ship chapel.

CHILDREN'S PROGRAM

Compared to other cruise lines, Costa places less emphasis on separating children from adult passengers. Only about 10% of passengers are traveling with their families, so there are not throngs of children on board (except sometimes in July and Aug, popular family travel times), and the kids' programs and facilities are not nearly as extensive as those available on the American mainstream lines.

There's a full-time **youth counselor** aboard each Costa ship, with additional staff pressed into service whenever more than a dozen children are on the passenger list. Costa offers three children's clubs tailored to specific age groups: The Baby Club (3–6), featuring a story hour, crafts, games, and ice-cream parties; The Junior Club (7–12), with jogging and aerobics, a puppet theater, mini-Olympics, and treasure hunts; and The Teen's Club (13–17), offering sports and fitness programs, guitar lessons, video show productions, and a rock-and-roll hour. The *Victoria* has a teen disco.

Group **babysitting** is available, at no charge, for children ages 3 (out of diapers) and up, every night until 11:30pm (but the hours can be extended until 1am if you make arrangements at least 24 hr. in advance).

ENTERTAINMENT

Entertainment directors program amusements such as concerts, magic and mime acts, acrobatics, and cabaret that, although produced with an Italian bent, do not require audiences to actually know the language.

If you're not looking for Las Vegas–style glitter, you'll likely find the shows amusing. Particularly notable is the fact the dancers attempt something approaching modern ballet (with some degree of success, too). Costumes and lighting are particularly creative, and the repertoire includes everything from folk music to techno-pop (not necessarily on the same night).

The *CostaAtlantica, CostaVictoria, CostaClassica,* and *CostaRomantica* have particularly notable showrooms, multitiered affairs that evoke the half moon–shaped amphitheaters of an 18th-century opera house. The other ships have more typical showrooms with pillars blocking some sight lines.

In addition to live shows, the theaters are used for movie screenings that include Pavarotti concerts.

The **casinos** on these ships are large by European standards, and include dozens of slot machines, roulette tables, poker, and blackjack. The **discos** are popular places, and there's always dancing into the wee hours.

SERVICE

While far from pampering, service is more than adequate in both the dining room and cabins. The crew is friendly and quick-witted, though not all speak great English. Dining-room staff is composed of charming Italian waiters, but special culinary requests sometimes get lost in translation.

So as not to offend Italian passengers, who are less used to tipping than Americans, suggested tips are incredibly low by industry standards. Daily recommended tips per passenger are $1.50 for the cabin steward, $2.50 (combined) for the waiter and his assistant, and 50¢ for the maitre d'. No self-service laundry, but the ships do offer laundry and dry-cleaning services.

CostaAllegra

CostaAllegra *(photo: Costa Cruises)*

The Verdict

This ship is small enough so you don't get lost, comfortable, and lively, in a special Italian way.

Specifications

Size (in tons)	30,000	Officers	Italian
Number of Cabins	410	Crew	450 (International)
Number of Outside Cabins	205	Passenger/Crew Ratio	2 to 1
Cabins with Verandas	10	Year Built	1992
Number of Passengers	800	Last Major Refurbishment	N/A

Frommer's Ratings (Scale of 1–5)

Cabin Comfort & Amenities	3	Pool, Fitness & Spa Facilities	3
Ship Cleanliness & Maintenance	3	Children's Facilities	2
Public Comfort/Space	4	Decor	4

The *CostaAllegra* was originally built in the 1960s and was completely reconstructed in the early '90s as a cruise ship with modern, Italian decor. The ship has a slightly formal atmosphere, and with most public rooms on Deck 6, guests know where to go to find the action.

The ship offers lots of windows, including a wall of glass in the stern. The dining room has windows on three sides, and the ship looks striking from the rear with its three-deck wall of glass, domed disco on top, and trademark Costa cluster of yellow smokestacks.

Cabins & Rates

Cabins	Brochure Rates*	Bathtub	Fridge	Hair Dryer	Sitting Area	TV
Inside	$3,049–$3,179	no	no	yes	no	yes
Outside	$3,449–$3,749	no	no	yes	no	yes
Suite	$4,049–$4,349	yes	some	yes	yes	yes

All rates include airfare from New York and selected other U.S. gateways.

CABINS   Standard cabins are not particularly large (145–160 sq. ft.), but are comfortable and offer twin beds, good storage space, desk, phone, safe, TV, and hair dryer. Decor is nothing special, with plain white walls and colorful banners added for color.

The *Allegra* has three large (575 sq. ft.) Grand Suites that can sleep five or six and have forward-facing windows. Ten minisuites have verandas. All have a whirlpool bathtub, a sitting area, and two lower or a queen-size bed; the Grand Suites also have a wet bar.

The ship has eight cabins accessible for travelers with disabilities.

PUBLIC AREAS   There is one dining room, located on Deck 5, enclosed by glass on three sides. The best seats are in the rear of the room, where the windows are larger than even the large portholes on the sides.

Most public rooms are located on Deck 6, are large enough to handle the crowd, and flow easily into each other. There's a large lounge/ballroom at one end, a large showroom at the other, and a large casino (with dozens of slot machines) in between, as well as a bar area with live music. Above the lounge/ballroom, the ship offers a funky round-windowed disco with a glass dome. During the day, the disco, with its panoramic views, doubles as an observation lounge.

Other public rooms include an oceanview library (really just a room with one wall of books, few in English) and card room, plus a fully equipped meeting/conference room. The Murano Bar features striking walls of smoked blue Murano glass illuminated from behind.

The children's room is small, and the show lounge is your typical old-fashioned showroom, with poor sight lines in the rear. If you want to see the dancers' feet, get there early and get a seat in the front, and don't sit behind a pillar.

ALTERNATIVE DINING   None.

POOL, FITNESS & SPA FACILITIES   The *Allegra* has a jogging deck and a small but well-equipped gym and spa with steam rooms and sauna. The swimming pool has a Jacuzzi and waterfall, as well as a pool bar, and a second Jacuzzi area is located aft behind the disco.

CostaRomantica •
CostaClassica

The Verdict

Italophiles will adore these mid-size ships that deliver an authentic slice of *la dolce vita.*

CostaRomantica *(photo: Costa Cruises)*

Specifications

Size (in tons)	54,000/53,000	Officers	Italian/International
Number of Cabins	678/654	Crew	610/650 (Internat'l)
Number of Outside Cabins	462/428	Passenger/Crew Ratio	2 to 1
Cabins with Verandas	10	Year Built	1993/1991
Number of Passengers	1,356/1,308	Last Major Refurbishment	N/A

Frommer's Ratings (Scale of 1–5)

Cabin Comfort & Amenities	4	Pool, Fitness & Spa Facilities	3
Ship Cleanliness & Maintenance	4	Children's Facilities	3
Public Comfort/Space	3	Decor	4

These ultra-modern sister ships have a cool, European interior design that some people find almost clinical and that contrasts sharply with the lively shipboard atmosphere. The *Classica* is so knock-you-in-the-head modern with its white marble, hip art, metal accents, and glass walls that Costa mellowed its act when building sister ship *Romantica,* adding some wood paneling and warmer colors.

The vessels were the largest and most stylish ships in the Costa armada until 1996, when the *CostaVictoria* supplanted them. Many passengers are repeat customers, drawn to these vessels for their emphasis on comfort and a contemporary Italian design accented with the best of Italy's traditions. The relatively small size means you'll begin to recognize your fellow passengers after a few days at sea. And with the public rooms located on the upper four decks, it's hard to get lost.

Cabins & Rates

Cabins	Brochure Rates*	Bathtub	Fridge	Hair Dryer	Sitting Area	TV
Inside	$3,149–$3,379/	no	no	yes	no	yes
	$3,599–$3,899					
Outside	$3,449–$3,749/	no	no	yes	no	yes
	$3,999–$4,219					
Suite	$4,349/$4,999–$5,299	yes	yes	yes	yes	yes

First-listed rates are for 7-day cruises on CostaClassica, second are 10-day cruises on CostaRomantica. All rates include airfare from New York and selected other U.S. gateways.

CABINS   In a word, big. At 200 square feet, standard outside cabins are among the largest available on any mainstream cruise line and much bigger than those on most European lines. The well-designed modern cabins are attractively paneled with polished cherrywood and done up in warm colors. Each cabin is furnished with twin beds (some convert to queens), two armchairs, a small table and desk, good-size closets, safes, hair dryers, TV, and music channels.

Lower-end inside cabins are still large at 175 square feet. Ten suites on each ship have verandas. The *CostaRomantica* also has six suites with panoramic, forward-facing windows and 18 minisuites that measure 340 square feet. The suites can all accommodate up to six passengers and are furnished with a queen bed, single sofa bed, and Murphy bed along with sitting area, minibar, double vanity, and whirlpool bath.

Six inside cabins on the *Romantica* and five on the *Classica* are wheelchair-accessible.

PUBLIC AREAS   Public areas take their names from the heritage of Italy, and sometimes sport decors to match—for instance, in the *CostaRomantica*'s Botticelli Restaurant, murals and window blinds evoke themes from the Renaissance. Classic Italian touches in different areas include chandeliers from Murano, intricate mosaics, pear-wood inlays, and lots and lots of brilliant white Carrara marble, while a modern Italian design esthetic shows in an abundance of steel, mirrors, and sharp, efficient edges.

Both ships have an outdoor cafe, with access to a frequently replenished buffet that sometimes gets a bit overcrowded, as do some of the other public areas aboard the ship.

One of the most stunning public spaces is the *CostaRomantica*'s L'Opera Showroom, which resembles a Renaissance amphitheater complete with tiered seating. Rising two decks high, it contains 6 miles of fiber optics and mosaics inspired by 14th-century models.

The neat, glass-walled circular discos on each ship are high up, affording an opportunity to dance close to the stars.

ALTERNATIVE DINING   None.

FITNESS, POOL & SPA FACILITIES   These are definitely not ships for fitness fanatics, as facilities consist of a small albeit pleasant gym with a wall of windows, a handful of Stairmasters and treadmills, and sauna, steam, and massage rooms. Because of a lack of exercise space, it's often necessary to conduct aerobics classes in the disco. It's obvious that working out is not a top priority for most passengers, whose only trips to the fitness area, it seems, are to weigh themselves on the scale.

On both ships, the Caracalla Spa has a Turkish bath as well as treatment rooms offering a wide range of massages, wraps, facials, and hydrotherapy baths, but it pales in comparison to the *CostaVictoria's* Roman-styled spa.

There are two outdoor pools, one with a fountain, and four hot tubs (two on the *CostaClassica*), as well as a jogging track on Deck 11.

CostaVictoria

The Verdict

A sleek megaship with a European ambience and stunning decor, this ship is an all-around beauty.

CostaVictoria *(photo: Costa Cruises)*

Specifications

Size (in tons)	76,000	Officers	Italian/International
Number of Cabins	964	Crew	800 (International)
Number of Outside Cabins	573	Passenger/Crew Ratio	2.4 to 1
Cabins with Verandas	0	Year Built	1996
Number of Passengers	1,928	Last Major Refurbishment	N/A

Frommer's Ratings (Scale of 1–5)

Cabin Comfort & Amenities	4	Pool, Fitness & Spa Facilities	4
Ship Cleanliness & Maintenance	4	Children's Facilities	3
Public Comfort/Space	4	Decor	5

The ship that launched Costa Cruises into the megaship era was built in Bremerhaven, Germany, and inaugurated in the summer of 1996. With an impressive cruising speed of between 21 and 23 knots, it has a streamlined, futuristic-looking design with four tiers of glass-fronted observation decks facing the prow. Its mammoth size allows for more spacious and dramatic interior features and more options for dining and after-dark diversions than any other Costa ship. When built, it was the largest and most technologically sophisticated ship ever launched by Costa, though in 2000 the *CostaAtlantica* bested it.

The interior is splashier and more colorful than those of other Costa vessels (it feels a bit more like an American ship). Signature design elements include an abundant use of stainless steel, teak, suede, leather, tile mosaics, and Italian marble in swirled patterns of blues and greens—for instance, brilliant royal blue suede covers the tops of card tables, and deep, salmon-colored suede is used on the walls of the Concorde Plaza lounge. The Bolero Buffet features teak floors, and a wraparound tile mosaic creates eye-catching walls in the Capriccio Lounge.

The sleek, seven-story Planetarium Atrium—a Costa first—features four glass elevator banks and is punctuated by a thin string of ice-blue neon subtly spiraling toward the glass ceiling dome. Also a new concept in the Costa fleet is the

Victoria's two dining rooms, with two seatings and an abundance of seating for couples (ideal for honeymooners).

Cabins & Rates

Cabins	Brochure Rates*	Bathtub	Fridge	Hair Dryer	Sitting Area	TV
Inside	$3,149–$3,379	no	yes	yes	no	yes
Outside	$3,549–$3,799	no	yes	yes	no	yes
Suite	$4,099–$4,349	yes	yes	yes	yes	yes

Rates include airfare from New York and selected other U.S. gateways.

CABINS   Ironically, the cabins on this second biggest of Costa ships are smaller than those on the *Romantica* and *Classica*. At 120 to 150 square feet, standard inside and outside cabins certainly won't win any awards for their size (the smallest are like walk-in closets), but their sleek, minimalist design and decor bring a delicious European touch to the cruise experience. Decorative fabric panels hang on the wall above headboards, matching the bedspreads. Bedside tables and dressers have sleek styling. Stainless steel is used for all bathroom sinks, and for dressers and mirrors in the minisuites. All cabins have TVs, music channels, hair dryer, minibar, and safe. Some 60% of them feature oversized round portholes opening onto sea views. None have verandas.

Especially desirable are 14 minisuites, which have separate living rooms, reading areas, and tubs with hydro-massage equipment. Each is outfitted with one queen-size bed and two Pullman-style beds. What makes them a bargain is that they contain many of the same amenities and interior design features as the more expensive suites, and their space is very generous at 301 square feet. For those with imperial taste, six full-size suites raise the beam on luxury, with one queen and two Pullman-style beds and generous 430-square-foot proportions that make them feel roomy even if they're bunking four passengers. Furnishings in these suites are made of pear wood, with fabrics by Laura Ashley, who is not even remotely Italian, and whose particular patterns in this case are relatively bold and not particularly frilly looking. Some of the suites have floor-to-ceiling windows.

Four of the ship's cabins are specifically outfitted for passengers with disabilities. Cabins on Deck 6A don't benefit from direct elevator access, and require that guests climb a half-flight of stairs from the nearest elevator bank.

PUBLIC AREAS   Public areas throb with color and energy, especially the big and brassy Monte Carlo Casino, which is linked to the Grand Bar Orpheus one floor below by a curving stairway whose glass stair treads are illuminated in patterns that are almost psychedelic. This bar is the preferred spot aboard for sampling an espresso or cappuccino, or, if it's late enough, a selection of grappas.

Designed to re-create an Italian piazza, the four-story Concorde Plaza is one of the *Victoria's* signature public areas. Seating over 300, it boasts a four-story-high waterfall on one end and a wall of windows facing the sea on the other, and is a great venue for evening dancing and music or for a relaxing drink by day.

Other public rooms include a play area for children, a club for teens, three conference rooms, an array of boutiques, a card room, a library, a disco, and an observation lounge that serves as a grand arena for socializing and special shipboard events and as a theater for evening entertainment.

ALTERNATIVE DINING   The multifunction Tavernetta Lounge on Deck 12 is a gourmet restaurant inspired by the famous Zeffirino restaurant in Italy (where guests including Frank Sinatra and Pope John Paul II have dined). The cost to eat here is $23 per person.

POOL, FITNESS & SPA FACILITIES   The *Victoria's* Pompeii Spa includes its own indoor pool. It's done with richly colored mosaic tiles and Roman columns. You can release your tensions in a steam bath, a sauna, or a Turkish bath, or sit and soak in the spa's Jacuzzi, which is perched artfully within the larger waters of the heated swimming pool. The attractive but smallish workout room shares a glass wall with the spa and pool area and features over a dozen exercise machines.

Out on deck, there's a pair of swimming pools as well as a "misting pool" that cools off overheated sunbathers with fine jets of water. Further decks wrap around the pools and their sunbathing area, providing plenty of space for passengers to stretch out and soak up the rays, even when the ship is fully booked. It looks like a resort on the Italian Riviera with its bright yellow and blue deck chairs and its nautical blue-and-white-striped lounges. There are four Jacuzzis, a tennis court that does double-duty as a half-size basketball court, and a jogging track, four circuits of which equal 1 mile. There's also a beauty salon aboard.

CostaAtlantica

The Verdict

The biggest and best ship in the Costa fleet, it adds all the American-style amenities to Costa's Italian cruise experience.

CostaAtlantica *(photo: Costa Cruises)*

Specifications

Size (in tons)	85,000	Officers	Italian/International
Number of Cabins	1,057	Crew	920 (International)
Number of Outside Cabins	845	Passenger/Crew Ratio	2.3 to 1
Cabins with Verandas	678	Year Built	2000
Number of Passengers	2,112	Last Major Refurbishment	N/A

Frommer's Ratings (Scale of 1–5)

Cabin Comfort & Amenities	5	Pool, Fitness & Spa Facilities	5
Ship Cleanliness & Maintenance	4	Children's Facilities	4
Public Comfort/Space	5	Decor	5

Costa officials were downright gleeful about the arrival of the 2,112-passenger, 84,000-ton *CostaAtlantica,* the line's first new ship since the *CostaVictoria* in 1996, and with good reason: The ship, which was built in Finland, is big and brash in the style of Carnival Cruise Line's highly successful "Fun Ships." In fact, it's the exact same design as the Carnival *Spirit* (and sister ships *Legend* and *Pride*). The *CostaAtlantica* cost a cool $400 million, and offers American-style resort amenities including an indoor/outdoor pool space, a big gym and spa, and a big choice of entertainment options.

Preview: *CostaTropicale* and *CostaEuropa*

The 36,000-ton *CostaTropicale* comes to Costa from the Carnival fleet, where it was one of that line's oldest and smallest vessels. As part of its move to Costa, the ship, which was built in 1982, got a $25-million refurbishment, which included complete, floor-to-ceiling upgrades of all public areas and cabins. Some decks were widened, and a new pizzeria, and a reservations-only alternative dining restaurant, Club Bahia, which will serve Brazilian cuisine (for a cover charge of $23), were added. The ship's dolphin-shaped Carnival funnel was also replaced with Costa's signature yellow smokestack.

The ship carries 1,022 passengers, and offers 511 cabins including 12 suites with private verandas.

The decor is based on the music, rhythms, and ambience of the tropics; how that will play in Europe remains to be seen. Public rooms include the Habana Casino, Miami Ballroom, Casablanca Bar, and Tropicana Showroom. The ship has three swimming pools including a kiddie pool, and also offers an Internet cafe, children's playroom, and Technogym fitness center/spa.

The *CostaEuropa* was also expected to undergo a multimillion-dollar renovation, but details weren't available at press time. The ship, which was built in 1986, transfers to the Costa fleet from Holland America, where it operated as the *Westerdam.* As the *Westerdam,* the ship offered an old-time ocean liner ambience, with portholes on some decks, a wide wraparound promenade, a lovely showroom, and spacious cabins (standard outside cabins are a roomy 189 sq. ft.) and lounges. Due to a stretching in 1989 (the ship was cut in half and a new midsection inserted), the layout is a bit confusing with the dining room and the gym/spa sitting pretty much alone on their respective decks.

Brochure rates for 7-day sailings on *CostaTropicale* are $3,149 to $3,379 inside, $3,449 to $3,749 outside, $4,349 suite. Brochure rates for 11-day sailings on the *CostaEuropa* are $3,649 to $3,949 inside, $4,049 to $4,449 outside, and $4,999 to $5,399 suite. All rates include airfare from New York and select other U.S. gateways.

From the moment you step on board, the ship elicits wows. The decor, as overseen by legendary Carnival designer Joe Farcus, is quite colorful, modern, and glitzy, created with Italian materials such as Murano glass, Carrara marble, and mosaic tile. The tall atrium area boasts funky leather chairs, including king and queen chairs with 6-foot backs (they reminded us of chess pieces).

A gallery of photos by noted Italian press photographer Tazio Secchiaroli is displayed in the Paparazzi and Via Veneto Lounges, and drawings by Italian cartoonist Milo Manara are displayed throughout the ship.

Despite its size, it's fairly easy to find your way around to the numerous bars and lounges and various activities offerings.

Cabins & Rates

Cabins	Brochure Rates*	Bathtub	Fridge	Hair Dryer	Sitting Area	TV
Inside	$3,249–$3,379	no	no	yes	no	yes
Outside	$3,599–$3,949	no	no	yes	no	yes
Suite	$4,199–$4,799	yes	yes	yes	yes	yes

All rates include airfare from New York and selected other U.S. gateways.

CABINS   The *Atlantica* adds something that Costa has been lacking: lots of cabins with verandas. In fact, nearly 78% of the ship's cabins offer them, starting with mid-priced cabins and including three levels of suites: regular, Panorama, and Grand. And the cabins are decently sized at that. All cabins come with hair dryers, minibars, safes, phones, and TVs, as well as sitting areas featuring leather sofas with nifty storage drawers underneath and large vanity areas. Bathrooms offer plenty of shelf space and bigger showers than on the earlier Costa ships. All the suites will also come with whirlpool baths and sitting areas.

PUBLIC AREAS   The ship's 12 passenger decks are all named for Fellini films, such as *Fred & Ginger, 8½, Roma, La Strada, Amarcord,* and *La Dolce Vita.* Claudia Cardinale, the star of *8½,* even christened the vessel. Public rooms are big, from the two-deck disco to the two-deck dining room (with 1,300 seats). A favorite space, Caffe Floran, is a Venetian-style cafe modeled on the famous 18th-century Caffe Florian in Venice's St. Mark's Square; it serves specialty coffees and drinks. Among the numerous bars and lounges, the Madame Butterfly Grand Lounge comes complete with geisha waitresses, and the Coral Lounge has fake coral on the walls. The library doubles as an Internet cafe, but the computers are clearly more the focus than books (in fact, it's downright annoying to read with all the clicking).

Kids get a big video arcade and a play area with a tunnel system they can climb through.

ALTERNATIVE DINING   There is an alternative, reservations-only restaurant in a two-deck space on top of the ship, known as Club Atlantica. Dinner there is an extra $23 per person. Cuisine is Italian and based on recipes of Gualtiero Marchesi, a famous Italian chef.

POOL, FITNESS & SPA FACILITIES   There are three swimming pools, one with a retractable glass roof, as well as a separate kiddie pool and a stand-alone water slide. The ship's oceanview spa and fitness center is two decks high and offers the latest equipment, including Technogym machines that have keys to remember your settings. The interesting tiered design offers equipment on several levels, all facing a wall of glass windows so you won't miss any views when you work out. The spa offers a dozen treatment rooms, a nice beauty salon, and a sunning area with a large whirlpool. The ship offers lots of open deck space for outdoor sunning.

2 First European Cruises (Festival Cruises)

SHIPS IN EUROPE Azur • Flamenco • Mistral • European Stars (preview) • European Vision (preview)

95 Madison Ave., Ste. 1203, New York, NY 10016. © 888/983-8767 or 212/779-7168. www.first-european.com.

A popular line in Europe, First European operates mid-size ships (older, but well-maintained) with a friendly, informal atmosphere and first-rate itineraries. Cruises are always a good value. And the company is now armed with three new vessels, offering the same on contemporary and more resort-like ships. To differentiate the options, the line has branded the cruises on the state-of-the-art ships—the *Mistral, European Vision,* and *European Stars*—as "Premium Cruises," with the emphasis on an onboard experience that includes fancy spas, alternative dining, golf simulators, and Internet cafes. The older vessels, *Azur* and *Flamenco,* offer "Discovery Cruises," with more destination-focused itineraries.

The older ships can seem crowded at times, particularly in high season; lines at disembarkation and at buffets are not uncommon. Cabins on all the ships tend to be small, so if you've got the bucks you're best off booking a deluxe cabin or suite.

The ships cater to both Europeans and Americans, with the newer vessels attracting a larger share of Americans and other English-speaking guests. All prices for drinks, shore excursions, gift shop purchases, and so forth are listed in euros.

Due to the pan-European clientele aboard, communication with fellow passengers can get tricky, and announcements in English, German, French, Italian, and sometimes Spanish as well are near constant, since it takes so long to get through all the languages. Onboard activities and shore excursions are also conducted in a variety of languages.

The ships offer particularly good onboard duty-free shopping opportunities.

Pros
- **Cuisine.** Great food, designed to please a variety of palates.
- **Public rooms.** There's a good variety for ships of this size.
- **Unusual itineraries.** Itineraries go beyond the norm. For instance, the *Mistral*'s 7-day Med itinerary from Marseille, France, visits Genoa and Naples, Italy; Katakolon and Mykonos, Greece; and Kuşadasi, Turkey.

Cons
- **No verandas on the older ships.** No cabins on the *Azur* and *Bolero* have private balconies (suites on the newer ships do). Of course, this is a "con" only if you want a veranda cabin.
- **Incessant announcements.** There's a constant babble of public address announcements in multiple languages.

Compared with other European lines, here's how First European rates:

	Poor	Fair	Good	Excellent	Outstanding
Enjoyment Factor				✓	
Dining				✓	
Activities			✓		
Children's Program			✓		
Entertainment		✓			
Service		✓			
Overall Value			✓		

THE FLEET

The *Azur,* the line's first ship, was built in 1971 as a ferry and later remodeled into a classic-style cruise ship. The *Flamenco,* built in 1972, underwent a $10 million refurbishment in 1997 and offers more in the way of amenities than the *Azur.*

The *Mistral* is a mid-sized vessel that's very contemporary, and the line's best ship yet. Cabins include 80 suites with verandas, and there is a good variety of public rooms. The *European Stars* and *European Vision* were built for the line at Chantiers de l'Atlantique shipyards in St-Nazaire, France. The line **Bolero** is on long-term charter to a Spanish company.

PASSENGER PROFILE

The passenger mix aboard is mostly a middle-class, budget-conscious European one, and includes everyone from kids and young singles to retirees. The most-represented nationalities are Italian and German. The line draws about 20% of its passengers from the U.S., but wants to see those numbers increase. Its fairly recent offering of some Caribbean cruises should help that cause.

Passengers tend to enjoy the open deck space when the ship is not in port, and the majority goes to bed pretty early at night. Because we're talking Europeans, there will be lots of smokers.

DINING

The line handles well the differing food tastes of its international crowd, offering a good variety of meat, chicken, and fish dishes. Pastas are particularly tasty.

The main dining rooms on the *Flamenco* and *Azur* are large and can get noisy. Those on the newer ships are an improvement; the *Mistral,* *European Vision,* and *European Stars* also each boast an **alternative dining** venue that offers both indoor and outdoor dining and cuisine cooked to order for a fee of 19€ ($17; suite guests get to eat there free every night).

> **Value Special Deals**
>
> Book at least 120 days in advance and save 15%. Also special highly reduced rates for kids ages 2 to 17 and under sharing a cabin with their parents.

Most people prefer to take three meals a day in the dining rooms, but there are also **deck buffets** for breakfast and lunch, as well as midnight buffets and afternoon tea. *European Stars* and *European Vision* also have 24-hour cafes.

There is 24-hour room service, but from a limited menu. Pizza is served late at night at the bars. **Vegetarian and light items** are available, but are not always on the menu. You should notify the maitre d' of your needs when you get aboard.

Smoking is not permitted in the dining rooms.

ACTIVITIES

Daytime activities include multi-language quiz games, scavenger hunts, volleyball and basketball, dance lessons, lectures, bingo, pool games, and aerobics classes, but most people are happy to just stretch out on the generously sized decks. Bargain hunters will want to give the onboard gift shops a workout (the duty-free prices are great).

The **spas** on the *Mistral, European Vision,* and *European Stars* are operated by Steiner, and offer well-established standard services and prices. Massage and beauty treatments on the other ships (*Azur* and *Flamenco*) are independently operated and a bargain compared to Steiner's rates.

First European Cruises Fleet Itineraries

Ship	Home Ports & Season	Itinerary
Azur	7-day Greek Isles, round-trip from Venice (May–Nov); 10-day E. Med, round-trip from Venice	7-day Greek Isles: Port calls include Korcula (Croatia), Santorini, Mykonos, Rhodes, and Piraeus/Athens (Greece); 10-day E. Med: Port calls include Dubrovnik (Croatia); Rhodes, Katakolon, Piraeus/Athens (Greece); Limassol (Cyprus); Antalya (Turkey); Alexandria (Egypt)
European Stars	7-day W. Med, round-trip from Barcelona (Mar–Dec)	Port calls include Marseille (France), Genoa, Naples, and Messina (Italy), Valletta (Malta), and Palma (Spain).
European Vision	7-day E. Med, round-trip from Venice (May–Nov)	Port calls include Dubrovnik (Croatia), Corfu, Santorini, Mykonos, Rhodes, and Piraeus/Athens (Greece)
Flamenco	7-day Norway, round-trip from Kiel (Germany) (June–Aug); 7-day Baltics, round-trip from Kiel (Germany) (June–Sept)	7-day Norway: Port calls include Flåm, Gudvangen, Molde, Andalsnes, Hellesylt, Geiranger, and Bergen (Norway), and Copenhagen (Denmark). 7-day Baltics: Port calls include Visby (Sweden), Tallinn (Estonia), St. Petersburg (Russia), and Copenhagen (Denmark)*
Mistral	7-day Med, round-trip from Marseille (June–Nov)	Port calls include Genoa and Naples (Italy), Katakolon and Mykonos (Greece), and Kuşadasi (Turkey)

* *The* Flamenco *also does 10-day Canary Islands itineraries, round-trip from Genoa (Jan–May and Oct–Dec).*

One English-language film is shown in each ship's cinema each day, and on the new ships there are also movie choices on TV. TVs on the newer ships are interactive, and an activity in themselves (you can check your onboard account, book your shore excursions, etc.).

The **casinos** are small by U.S. cruise ship standards (Europeans aren't as into gambling as Americans), and offer roulette, blackjack, poker, and slots. The *European Vision* and *European Stars* boast Internet cafes (the *Mistral* also has a few computer stations) but the fee is a steep $15 per minute.

CHILDREN'S PROGRAM

These ships are family-friendly, and kids get a variety of supervised daily activities, including crafts and games. All the ships, except for the *Azur,* feature kiddie pools.

Keep in mind the multinational ambience on these ships translates to the kids' programs as well. It can be a great experience for kids to mingle with their peers from other countries, but they should be forewarned that not everyone will speak English.

Babysitting is available on all the ships.

ENTERTAINMENT

Entertainment includes acts that are musical or visual—for instance, dancers and magicians—and thus can appeal to people speaking a variety of languages.

These ships offer a variety of nightclubs and bars (including a cigar bar on the new ships) and discos. Karaoke is a popular offering.

SERVICE

Service is warm and friendly but not very refined. The crew is well versed in English, and a good crew-to-passenger ratio means you can nearly always find a helping hand. The European officers can be downright charming. Gratuities of 7€ ($6.25) per day are automatically added to shipboard accounts to cover tips for the cabin and dining room crew (you can adjust the amount up or down at the end of your cruise as you see fit). No dry cleaning service is available. A laundry-cleaning service is available, but there are no self-service machines.

Azur

The Verdict

This older ship offers a friendly, informal cruise experience well suited to first-timers and those who don't care much about big-ship amenities.

Azur *(photo: First European)*

Specifications

Size (in tons)	15,000	Officers	French/Greek
Number of Cabins	360	Crew	330 (International)
Number of Outside Cabins	178	Passenger/Crew Ratio	2 to 1
Cabins with Verandas	0	Year Built	1971
Number of Passengers	800	Last Major Refurbishment	1996

Frommer's Ratings (Scale of 1–5)

Cabin Comfort & Amenities	2	Pool, Fitness & Spa Facilities	3
Ship Cleanliness & Maintenance	3	Children's Facilities	3
Public Comfort/Space	3	Decor	2

Built as a ferry in 1971 and remodeled shortly thereafter into a cruise ship, the *Azur* is a friendly ship with classical appeal. There's plenty of open deck space, spacious public rooms, several bars, and lots of activities to keep passengers happily occupied.

Cabins & Rates

Cabins	Brochure Rates*	Bathtub	Fridge	Hair Dryer	Sitting Area	TV
Inside	$700–$1,440	no	no	no	no	no
Outside	$1,130–$1,720	no	no	no	no	no
Suite	$1,510–$2,030	yes	no	no	some	no

Rates do not include port charges of $100.

CABINS   The cabins are well-designed but small by American standards, with bright, mod appeal (think oranges and bright blues). The suites, at 204 square feet, have picture windows, bathtubs, and sitting areas. All cabins have two music channels and phones, but no TVs.

Two cabins are accessible to passengers with disabilities.

PUBLIC AREAS   Large is the word. There's a large, bright, and sometimes noisy restaurant and two large lounges. The Tahiti Disco faces one of two swimming pools, while the Pacific Lounge has picture windows on three sides for nice views. There are also a number of bars, a small casino (with blackjack, slots, and roulette), a children's playroom, a library, and a nice cinema with real theater seats and even a balcony. The ship, in general, has a nice warm feel.

ALTERNATIVE DINING   None.

POOL, FITNESS & SPA FACILITIES   There are two swimming pools, one with a retractable roof. The ship has a small fitness center, sauna, and massage rooms. Deck sports include volleyball, basketball, and Ping-Pong. Aerobics classes are also offered.

Flamenco

The Verdict

A warm and friendly yet sometimes crowded ship, the *Flamenco* is particularly well suited for first-timers and families.

Flamenco *(photo: First European)*

Specifications

Size (in tons)	17,000	Officers	Greek
Number of Cabins	392	Crew	350 (International)
Number of Outside Cabins	262	Passenger/Crew Ratio	2 to 1
Cabins with Verandas	0	Year Built	1972
Number of Passengers	800	Last Major Refurbishment	1997

Frommer's Ratings (Scale of 1–5)

Cabin Comfort & Amenities	2	Pool, Fitness & Spa Facilities	2
Ship Cleanliness & Maintenance	3	Children's Facilities	3
Public Comfort/Space	4	Decor	3

The *Flamenco* underwent a $10 million refurbishment before it entered the First European fleet in 1997, and offers public rooms done up in a warm and tasteful decor, and a nice relaxed atmosphere. The Greek officers and international crew keep the ambience friendly, but there are a lot of passengers on this ship and there are occasionally crowds, like at buffet lines and disembarkation.

Cabins & Rates

Cabins	Brochure Rates*	Bathtub	Fridge	Hair Dryer	Sitting Area	TV
Inside	$790–$1,550	no	no	no	no	yes
Outside	$1,380–$1,880	no	no	no	no	yes
Suite	$1,840–$2,190	some	no	no	some	yes

Rates do not include port charges of $100.

CABINS   Deluxe outside cabins are on the small side at 153 square feet, and are simply furnished and rather spartan, with bright-colored fabrics and dull-colored walls, phones, music channels, and TVs. Cabins have good storage space, however, with big closets with built-in drawers. Bathrooms are compact. There are no tubs or verandas. Four good-size suites offer sitting areas and picture windows.

Two cabins are wheelchair-accessible.

PUBLIC AREAS   The public rooms on this ship are contemporary and comfortable. The Universe show lounge has okay sight lines, but for the best views you'll want to grab the seating in the raised areas on the sides. The Starlight Lounge, a favorite hangout spot at the top of the ship, is a circular room offering panoramic views and dancing at night (everything from ballroom to disco).

The casino is not very large; the health club is downright tiny. But the ship does offer a variety of bars and lounges, plus a piano bar, a cinema, a children's playroom, and a library (which attracts a lot of smokers and has few English titles), plus the large (main) Galaxy Restaurant and a small Lido restaurant on pool deck, with indoor and outdoor seating for casual breakfast and lunch buffets (most passengers prefer to eat in the dining room).

There is lots of sun deck space, but it can get crowded.

ALTERNATIVE DINING   None.

POOL, FITNESS & SPA FACILITIES   The tiny (though windowed) gym has only a few treadmills and an assortment of weights. Gold's Gym it's not.

There's one outdoor pool for adults and a shallow pool for kids. The "Sports Deck," located on Galaxy Deck aft, behind the galley, and accessible via stairs from the Lounge Deck above, has only a basketball court. Beauty services and massages at the spa are offered at really low rates.

Mistral

The Verdict

This ship moved First European way up the evolutionary ladder, offering a lot of the amenities you'd only expect to find on a larger ship, but in a friendly and intimate setting.

Mistral *(photo: First European)*

Specifications

Size (in tons)	48,000	Officers	Greek
Number of Cabins	598	Crew	500 (International)
Number of Outside Cabins	362	Passenger/Crew Ratio	2.4 to 1
Cabins with Verandas	80	Year Built	1999
Number of Passengers	1,200	Last Major Refurbishment	N/A

Frommer's Ratings (Scale of 1–5)

Cabin Comfort & Amenities	4	Pool, Fitness & Spa Facilities	4
Ship Cleanliness & Maintenance	5	Children's Facilities	4
Public Comfort/Space	4	Decor	5

Launched in the summer of 1999, and built at Chanters de l'Atlantique in St-Nazaire, France, the $240 million *Mistral* offers a friendly and smart interior designed by a Greek firm that also worked on Celebrity Cruises' vessels. Each deck is named after a European city: Paris, Rome, London, Berlin, Brussels, Athens, Cannes, and Madrid.

The ship offers several dining options including an alternative restaurant, and boasts an outdoor thalassotherapy center (a big whirlpool tub) and 80 large

Preview: *European Stars* and *European Vision*

These state-of-the-art ships come from France and hold 1,500 passengers each (the *Vision* was introduced in June 2001, and the *Stars,* at press time, was scheduled to be introduced in March 2002). They offer a pleasant, informal atmosphere, with onboard amenities such as a thalassotherapy health spa, fully equipped gym and beauty salon, golf simulator, mini-golf course, rock climbing wall, volleyball and basketball courts, and two outdoor pools, as well as an Internet cafe.

The 651 cabins are equipped with minibars, interactive TVs, radios, hair dryers, and safes. The 132 suites offer private verandas, walk-in wardrobes, living room areas, and bathtubs. Other offerings include a beer bar, English Pub, piano bar, and *Gelateria* (for ice cream), as well as a shopping arcade. Kids get a Virtual Reality game room, a children's playroom, two splash pools, and a Teen's Club. Dining areas include a main dining room, intimate Italian alternative restaurant (free to suite guests, and open to others for a fee), and Venetian-inspired cafe. As on the *Mistral,* the medical centers on these ships offer dialysis treatment on select dates.

Brochure rates for 7-day Western Mediterranean sailings on *European Stars* are $820 to $1,840 inside, $1,260 to $2,240 outside, $1,840 to $2,720 suites; for 7-day Eastern Mediterranean sailings on *European Vision,* $910 to $1,840 inside, $1,390 to $1,910 outside, $2,040 to $2,720 suites. Port charges are an additional $100.

suites with verandas, both unusual offerings on a moderately priced, mid-size vessel.

Cabins & Rates

Cabins	Brochure Rates*	Bathtub	Fridge	Hair Dryer	Sitting Area	TV
Inside	$890–$1,790	no	yes	yes	no	yes
Outside	$1,360–$2,180	no	yes	yes	no	yes
Suite	$1,980–$2,650	yes	yes	yes	yes	yes

Rates do not include port charges of $90–$100.

CABINS   All the cabins are a comfortable 150 square feet, and the 80 mini-suites with verandas are 236 square feet (including veranda). All cabins are nicely decorated and have interactive TVs, phones, radios, minibars, safes, hair dryers, and writing areas, as well as a good amount of storage space. The lowest category cabins have bunk beds, making them suitable for families or singles trying to save a buck. The suites have sitting areas, bathtubs, and VCRs.

Two cabins are wheelchair-accessible.

PUBLIC AREAS   The ship was designed for Europeans, but with Americans in mind as well. For instance, there's a small casino that can be expanded by using the conference room next door. The ship has a two-story atrium with a grand piano and black granite waterfall sculpture.

The main restaurant boasts an Art Deco style. There are numerous bars and lounges. The multideck show lounge was built without pillars for great sight lines, and there's a cigar bar and library cleverly tucked under its slope.

The vessel also has both children's and teens' playrooms, a coffee bar, and several shops, as well as a particularly well-equipped medical center with dialysis machines (as required by French regulations).

ALTERNATIVE DINING   The Rialto alternative restaurant is particularly lovely, done up with Portuguese tile and offering both indoor and outdoor dining, and made-to-order cuisine. Passengers in the ship's minisuites dine there every night, while other passengers can book tables in the restaurant on a reservations-only basis, for a fee of 19€ ($17).

POOL, FITNESS & SPA FACILITIES   This vessel boasts spa offerings including an outdoor thalassotherapy pool, and inside the spa a rain-forest shower, thermal suites, and an aromatic steam room, as well as sauna and massage areas and a beauty salon—all operated by Steiner.

The *Mistral* also has two swimming pools and a good-sized gym with up-to-date machines.

3 Fred. Olsen Cruise Lines

SHIPS IN EUROPE Black Prince • Black Watch • Braemar

Fred. Olsen House, White Horse Road, Ipswich, Suffolk, England IP1 5LL. ✆ **01473/292200.** Fax 01473/292410. USA Sales Representative: EuroCruises, 33 Little West 12th St., Ste. 106, New York, NY 10014. Reservations ✆ **800/688-3876** or 212/691-2099. Brochures 800/661-1119. Fax 212/366-4747. www.eurocruises.com.

Homeported in Dover, England, and largely catering to British passengers, the *Black Watch* and *Black Prince* have long offered the kind of value that's hard to beat. Now, a third vessel, already well known in the U.S. as the *Crown Dynasty,* has joined the fleet and promises to do the same. The company bought the ship last year and, after a lengthy refit, it was relaunched in August as the *Braemar.*

The line's fairly priced ships cater to a professional and/or early retired class of mostly British Europeans, though the line is trying to attract Americans, as this excerpt from the "Cruising British Style" section of its promotional brochure makes clear: "The British have fabulous sea manners. All say Good Morning, are orderly on line, ask before interrupting, and are most cordial. Formal tea, between 3 and 4, includes scones and tasty biscuits. . . . You'll meet others who are generally well versed in world history, politics, and geography. And they are fun—in a contained sort of way. When you score at carpet boule (like Italian bocce ball with a nautical slant) they exclaim 'lovely' or 'brilliant.'" The last line of the little promotional item concludes: "Best of all, everybody speaks English."

It's likely North Americans who sail aboard will find themselves seated with the Brits at one of the big round dining room tables where conversations may turn to Tony Blair, the late Princess Di and the two young princes, or their favorite programmes (not "shows") on the telly.

Pros
- **British ambience.** A chance to view Europe with affable British passengers and through a British sensibility.
- **The *Black Prince*'s indoor swimming pool.** A rare find in a vessel this size. The vessel's drop-down marina also makes for easy access to water sports.
- **The *Black Watch*'s public rooms.** All tastefully restored with an eye towards tradition.

Cons
- **British ambience.** Some Americans may feel out of place among so many British passengers.
- **Some small spaces.** The *Black Prince* has small cabins and rather dark public rooms.

Compared with other European lines, here's how Fred. Olsen rates:

	Poor	Fair	Good	Excellent	Outstanding
Enjoyment Factor				✓	
Dining		✓			
Activities			✓		
Children's Program		✓			
Entertainment		✓			
Service		✓			
Overall Value					✓

THE FLEET

Fred. Olsen Cruise Line's flagship vessel is its new pride and joy, the **Braemar.** The ship was built for Cunard Line at the Union Navale de Levante yards in 1993 and launched as the *Crown Dynasty.* Later, it joined Crown Cruise Line and, eventually, the Fred. Olsen fleet. Its refurbishment—which involved some structural as well as cosmetic work—saw many of its public spaces reconfigured. Among the innovations installed was a fully integrated management system, which helps the ship's staff expedite passenger check-in/checkout and to control guest invoicing and shore excursion procedures. *Crown Dynasty* had its followers; Fred. Olsen is betting that this updated version will satisfy many of them and help the line develop a whole new market into the bargain. At less than 20,000 tons, it is considerably smaller than the *Black Watch,* much bigger than the *Black Prince.*

Black Watch, built in 1972 at the Wartsila shipyard in Finland for Royal Viking Line as the *Royal Viking Star,* was acknowledged at the time to be one of the finest passenger vessels afloat, along with its sister ships *Royal Viking Sky* and *Royal Viking Sea.* With their sleek lines, cheerful decor, and understated elegance, they brought a feeling of sophistication to cruising.

In 1996, Fred. Olsen acquired and completely retrofitted the ship, stretching it to 630 feet. At 28,492 tons, it's a smallish liner with classical lines, generously sized cabins, an open and airy feeling, a wide teak deck for walkers and joggers, a serious library, and expansive public rooms and lounges that were restored and decorated with taste.

The company's other ship, the 11,209-ton, 412-passenger **Black Prince,** is even smaller and correspondingly more intimate. She was built for Olsen at the Lubecker Fender Werft shipyard in Lubeck, Germany, in 1966 and served for a while as a car ferry and cargo carrier with a rear opening and an auto-truck ramp, doing heavy duty in the North Sea between England and Norway. At the ship's latest retrofit, the auto ramp was eliminated and what had formerly been a large cargo and car-carrying area was converted to an inside recreation area with a sizable indoor heated pool, rare in a vessel this size.

PASSENGER PROFILE

Given the company's home base in Dover, Fred. Olsen vessels attract a largely British clientele, but as the ships become better known in the Americas, the passenger mix is changing slightly. On *Black Watch,* non-Europeans traditionally have amounted to about 10%. The figure is half that on the *Black Prince.* With its Crown Cruises background and extensive North American exposure, *Braemar* may do even better in this regard than the other two. Fred. Olsen hopes so.

The cruise line has stated outright that its target market is middle-class, aged 50+, retired professionals, self-employed small business people, and civil servants. (Demographics differ. The *Black Watch* hitherto has attracted a slightly younger clientele than the *Black Prince* in a two-ship fleet. The *Braemar* may reach an even younger crowd.) The line concedes the high end of cruising to others, but thinks of its passengers as pleasant people attracted by a reasonable price on a venerable ship far removed from the megaship experience.

DINING

While the food is not memorable, it is perfectly acceptable and sometimes served with élan. Dinner is in two seatings on all three ships, and there are breakfast and lunch **buffets** as an alternative to taking all three meals in the dining rooms. **Afternoon tea** is served in the lounges and on deck. The ships also offer

Fred. Olsen Fleet Itineraries

Ship	Home Ports & Season	Itinerary
Black Prince	**14-day Med,** round-trip from Dover (Apr); **10-day Norway,** between Leith (Scotland) and Greenock (Scotland) (May); **14-day Europe/ Morocco,** round-trip from Greenock (June)	**14-day Med:** Port calls include Malaga (Spain), Cagliari (Sardinia), Tunis (Tunisia), Cartagena (Spain), Gibraltar and Lisbon (Portugal); **10-day Norway:** Port calls include Bergen, Kristiansand, Gravdal, Hellesylt, Geiranger, Balestrand (all Norway) and Lerwick (Scotland); **14-day Europe/Morocco:** Port calls include Gibraltar, Mahon and Barcelona (both Spain), Tangier (Morocco), La Coruna (Spain), and Dublin (Ireland)
Black Watch	All cruises round-trip from Dover (England) **14-day W. Med** (Apr); **18-day Med** (May); **8-day Norway** (May); **13-day Norway** (June); **13-day Baltics** (July–Aug); **15-day Norway** (July); **10-day Norway** (Aug); **14-day Baltics** (Aug); **23-day Med** (Sept)	**14-day Med:** Port calls include Almeria, Ibiza, Barcelona and Palma (all Spain), Gibraltar, St. Peter Port (Guernsey); **18-day Med:** Port calls include Lisbon, Cartagena, Salerno, Civitavecchia and Livorno (Italy), Villefranche (France), Mahon, Gibraltar, and La Coruna; **8-day Norway:** Port calls include Maloy, Olden, Flam, Gudvangen, Bergen (Norway), and Amsterdam (Netherlands); **13- & 15-day Norway:** Port calls may include Bergen, Belestrand, Alesund, Nordfjordeid, Gravdal, Honningsvag, Tromso, Longyearbyen, Barentsberg, Ny Alesund, Geiranger, Trondheim, Andalsnes and Belstrand (Norway), and Skagen (Denmark); **13- and 14-day Baltics:** Port calls may include Oslo (Norway), Copenhagen, Helsingborg and Stockholm (Sweden), Helsinki (Finland); Tallinn (Estonia), St. Petersburg (Russia), Travemunde, Holtenau and Burnsbuttel (Germany), and Antwerp (Belgium); **10-day Norway:** Port calls include Skagen (Denmark), Oslo, Kristiansand, Ulvik, Eldfjord, Bergen, Flam, and Gudvangen (Norway), and Lerwick (Scotland); **23-day Med:** Port calls include Malaga (Spain), Syracuse (Sicily), Mykonos and Santorini (Greece), Istanbul and Dikili (Turkey), Valletta (Malta), Tunis (Tunisia), Gibraltar, and Lisbon (Portugal)
Braemar	Cruises are round-trip from Dover unless other-wise stated. **13-day Med** (May); **13-day Baltics** (June); **8-day Norway** (June); **13-day North Cape** (July); **13- and 14-day Med** (13-day is Dover to Southampton) (Aug–Sept)	**13-day Med:** Port calls include Lisbon, Malaga, Barcelona, La Coruna, Mahon, Ceuta (Spanish Morocco), and Gibraltar; **13-day Baltics:** Port calls include Amsterdam, Oslo, Copenhagen, Tallinn, St. Petersburg, Stockholm, Holtenau, Brunsbuttel, and Hamburg (Germany); **8-day Norway:** Port calls include Amsterdam, Stavanger, Olden, Flam, Gudvangen, and Bergen (Norway); **13-day North Cape:** Port calls include Amsterdam, Flam, Gudvangen, Olden, Tromso, Honningsvag, Gravdal, Bergen (Norway), Invergordon (Scotland); **13- and 14-day Med:** Port calls may include Alicante (Spain), Barcelona, Sete and Brest (France), Ajaccio (Corsica), Ceuta, Cagliari, Palma, and St. Peter Port

a late-night buffet, but it is sometimes sparsely attended. **Vegetarians** are provided for at meals, but service isn't seamless: They must sometimes wait for their "special" soup or meal from the kitchen while others are served, which makes for awkwardness at a large table. And yes, as aboard so many ships, the tired last-night **baked Alaska** routine is honored here, too.

ACTIVITIES

Daytime activities include deck sports (the *Black Watch* has a golf net and deck tennis), carpet boule (somewhat like Italian bocce ball), card games (including bridge), lectures, and classes in subjects like clay modeling and ceramics. The *Black Prince* has a marina from which passengers can enjoy a variety of watersports offerings. The bridge aboard both ships is often open for visits.

Besides its fair share of sports activities, the *Braemar* has something that you don't find on many ships built in the 1990s—a full wraparound promenade deck, one that you can walk all the way round without back-tracking. We like that.

The ship also has an Internet room, available to passengers for Web surfing or e-mailing postcards to friends, for $16 for a half-hour (plus a $16 refundable deposit).

CHILDREN'S PROGRAM

The *Black Watch* and *Braemar* have small children's playrooms, with the plastic-ball bins that kids like to jump around in, among other attractions. The *Braemar* also has a video arcade. Kids' activities are supervised and include a lot of pizza and ice-cream parties. The *Black Prince* is not geared for kids.

ENTERTAINMENT

The entertainment is pleasant but many of the jokes are Brit-oriented, with references to members of Parliament or the game of snooker. There is a nightly show in the show lounge with cabaret-style song and dance, headline acts, and local performers brought on at ports of call, followed by live band music for dancing. Piano music is also offered in several lounge areas. The *Black Watch* and *Braemar* have cinemas.

SERVICE

Service is adequate on Fred. Olsen ships. Waiters are not obsequious. Virtually everyone on the table staff speaks English.

The *Black Watch* has a self-service laundry and ironing room, as does the *Braemar.* Dry cleaning is available on all three ships.

Black Prince

The Verdict

An intimate and comfortable ship with a mostly British clientele and a nifty drop-down marina, as well as an indoor swimming pool.

Black Prince *(photo: Fred. Olsen)*

Specifications

Size (in tons)	11,209	Officers	Norwegian
Number of Cabins	241	Crew	200 (British/
Number of Outside Cabins	145		Filipino/Malaysian)
Cabins with Verandas	0	Year Built	1966
Number of Passengers	451	Last Major Refurbishment	1996

Frommer's Ratings (Scale of 1–5)

Cabin Comfort & Amenities	2	Pool, Fitness & Spa Facilities	3
Ship Cleanliness & Maintenance	3	Children's Facilities	N/A
Public Comfort/Space	3	Decor	3

A much smaller ship than either the *Braemar* or the *Black Watch,* this intimate, comfortable vessel, which holds 451 passengers when all of the family cabins are filled, attracts a slightly younger clientele, 90% of whom are European, largely from the U.K. Many people aboard will know the ship is named for none other than the *Black Prince* (Edward of Woodstock) born in the 14th century and son of Edward III of England.

The ship underwent a multimillion-dollar refurbishment in 1996, and offers a relaxed atmosphere. It's fully stabilized, with a sizable indoor pool and adjacent health fitness center in what once was a cargo hold and garage when, decades ago, the ship was a car ferry on the North Sea sailing from England to Norway.

Cabins & Rates

Cabins	Brochure Rates*	Bathtub	Fridge	Hair Dryer	Sitting Area	TV
Inside	$2,040–$2,448	no	no	yes	no	yes
Outside	$2,040–$3,072	no	some	yes	no	yes
Suite	$4,080	yes	yes	yes	yes	yes

Prices shown are for 10-day cruise.

CABINS   Some outside and all inside cabins come with either a Pullman bed or sofa bed that you can put away to have more space during the day. Category G outside cabins have upper and lower berths. The cabins are small (some less than 70 sq. ft.) with the exception of the junior suites, the highest cabin category, which offer 220 square feet of living space and have bathtubs and fixed beds. Family cabins offer a double bed and one upper and one lower berth. All cabins have telephones, TVs, and hair dryers. The five top-level cabins are junior suites, with sitting areas, bathtubs, and refrigerators.

Special cabins for singles have a Pullman or sofa bed. Two cabins are designed for passengers with disabilities.

PUBLIC AREAS   Public rooms are small, which can be a plus (more intimate) or a minus (if one is looking for large and airy spaces). The ship has three restaurants: Fleur de Lys, the Royal Garter, and the conservatory-style Balblom Restaurant with retractable ceiling, as well as several lounges and bars. The Aquitaine Lounge is smaller, with relaxing piano music, while the Neptune Lounge is brighter and livelier, with "Showtime" held here nightly. There is also a small casino.

ALTERNATIVE DINING   None.

POOL, FITNESS & SPA FACILITIES   Few passenger vessels this size have such a formidable heated inside pool and fitness area, all made possible by the space vacated when the ship no longer ferried cars and trucks. There are also a small outdoor pool, two Jacuzzis, a sauna, and Steiner spa and beauty services. The ship has a drop-down marina from which passengers can enjoy water sports such as water-skiing and windsurfing while the ship is at anchor in calm seas.

Black Watch

The Verdict

Ocean-liner ambience with an appeal
that's decisively British.

Black Watch (photo: Fred. Olsen)

Specifications

Size (in tons)	28,492	Officers	Norwegian
Number of Cabins	427	Crew	330 (British/ Filipino/Malaysian)
Number of Outside Cabins	375		
Cabins with Verandas	9	Year Built	1972
Number of Passengers	798	Last Major Refurbishment	1998

Frommer's Ratings (Scale of 1–5)

Cabin Comfort & Amenities	3	Pool, Fitness & Spa Facilities	2
Ship Cleanliness & Maintenance	4	Children's Facilities	2
Public Comfort/Space	4	Decor	4

The *Black Watch* is an ocean liner in the tradition of ships built in the seventies, before megaships came along. If the ship's pianist around tea time is playing some classic tunes, one can feel a bit of nostalgia and be satisfied that this once-acclaimed vessel, after an elaborate retrofit when it joined the fleet, is still sailing the seas as it was intended to, carrying cruise passengers out of Dover. Call it historic preservation. After all, cruise ships, like fine homes, can be preserved and updated to enjoy a new life.

Despite the fact that this ship entered service in 1972, there's nothing dowdy about the interior. Bright colors in good taste are employed throughout. There's nothing garish, and no kitsch.

Cabins & Rates

Cabins	Brochure Rates*	Bathtub	Fridge	Hair Dryer	Sitting Area	TV
Inside	$2,344–$2,554	no	no	yes	no	yes
Outside	$2,704–$4,240	some	no	yes	no	yes
Suite	$4,570–$6,688	yes	yes	yes	yes	yes

Prices shown are for 10-day cruise.

CABINS Cabins range from small insides to spacious suites. About 90% are outside. Cabins in the upper categories and some lower categories as well come with bathtubs. All cabins have TVs, telephones, and hair dryers, and upper categories (junior suites on up) offer refrigerators and sitting areas. Suites also offer VCRs and stereos, floor-to-ceiling windows, and verandas. All cabins have taped television programming and, when the ship is within range, live reception.

There are four categories of cabins designed for singles, and four cabins are available for passengers with disabilities.

PUBLIC AREAS Many passengers appreciate the staffed Explorers Library with its nautical motif and large stock of up-to-date books. Just off this room is a small smoking room where the smell of cigar smoke is evident, some of it drifting into the library. Adjacent to the library on the Bridge Deck is the Dalreoch Card Room for card games, bridge, Scrabble, and special presentations.

There is a small casino on the Lido Deck, along with the Star Night Club and several bars. Nightly shows are held in the Neptune Lounge, with smoking restricted to one side of the lounge, and movies are shown at the 150-seat cinema.

ALTERNATIVE DINING None.

POOL, FITNESS & SPA FACILITIES There's a large outdoor pool, an outdoor splash pool, and Jacuzzis, as well as a spa operated by Steiner, a beauty salon, and a good-size fitness center with saunas and some sophisticated exercise equipment. On the Sun Deck are golf nets and a deck tennis court.

Braemar

The Verdict

The *Braemer* adheres closely to the Fred. Olsen philosophy that highlights intimacy and not a lot of glitz.

Braemer *(photo: Fred. Olsen)*

Specifications

Size (in tons)	19,089	Officers	Norwegian
Number of Cabins	381	Crew	300 (International)
Number of Outside Cabins	270	Year Built	1993
Cabins with Verandas	18	Last Major Refurbishment	N/A
Number of Passengers	825		

Frommer's Ratings (Scale of 1–5)

Cabin Comfort & Amenities	3	Pool, Fitness & Spa Facilities	3
Ship Cleanliness & Maintenance	4	Children's Facilities	N/A
Public Comfort/Space	4	Decor	4

Fred. Olsen has a slogan: "You didn't want bigger ships—so we got you a bigger fleet." The *Braemar* subscribes beautifully to that philosophy. Since joining the fleet, the ship has been sailing in the Caribbean primarily, earning a high degree of acceptance from its primarily North American clientele—exactly the kind of response Fred. Olsen hopes it will generate among cruisers on the other side of the Atlantic. The ship diligently follows the Olsen master plan: smallish, intimate, a good value, not glitzy, and so on.

Cabins & Rates

Cabins	Brochure Rates	Bathtub	Fridge	Hair Dryer	Sitting Area	TV
Inside	$3,032–$3,496	no	no	yes	yes	yes
Outside	$3,712–$5,024	no	no	yes	yes	yes
Suites	$6,112–$7,865	no	yes	yes	yes	yes

CABINS   The color scheme throughout the ship seeks to convey a feeling of elegance, not least in the staterooms. The wall hangings and carpeting tend to be in muted pastel colors, very little of the bolder patterned stuff that we're seeing in many ships nowadays. Only the suites have verandas; the superior outside rooms (all of which have twin beds that don't really combine well into one) have large picture windows. Some of the lesser outside rooms have good old-fashioned portholes.

PUBLIC AREAS   A four-story atrium, sweeping panoramic windows, and plenty of open deck space and terraces give the *Braemar* a roomy, airy feel. And one good thing (possibly a product of Olsen's desire to appeal to more North American guests) is that smoking is prohibited in any indoor public area. The Thistle Restaurant, one of those panoramic window rooms we mentioned, caters comfortably to the dinner crowd in two seatings. The *al fresco* buffet-style eatery is the Palms Café.

A favorite hangout on board is the Braemar Room, in which that original figurehead reposes. Another "in" place with the after-dinner crowd seeking a libation and a cha cha is the Skylark Club—after you've taken in the show in the Neptune Lounge, that is.

The ship has a library and a small casino, which can get a little claustrophobic.

ALTERNATIVE DINING   None.

POOL, FITNESS & SPA FACILITIES   The Steiner-managed spa isn't the biggest you ever saw, and services have been reduced accordingly. But Steiner gets plenty of mileage out of it nonetheless. A small fitness center is well stocked with weights, pulleys, stationary bicycles, and the rest.

The pool is on the top deck—known on this ship as the Marquee Deck.

4 Mediterranean Shipping Cruises

SHIPS IN EUROPE Melody • Monterey • Rhapsody

420 Fifth Ave., New York, NY 10018. © 800/666-9333 or 212/764-4800. Fax 212/764-8593. www.msccruisesusa.com.

The ships of this Swiss/Italian line aren't the fanciest afloat but they're all friendly and informal, and offer a decent range of amenities and activities at a low price.

The ships—including the *Melody* (formerly Premier Cruises' *Big Red Boat*)—are all mid-size, older vessels that have been updated with modern decor that's comfortable rather than plush. The ships offer lots of open deck space, port-intensive itineraries, and an experience that's friendly and fun, thanks in large part to the Italian crew members. Expect a European ambience and an experience that sometimes leans further toward creakiness than toward over-the-top elegance.

Mediterranean Shipping Cruises doesn't offer the range of activities and entertainment you'll find aboard the big new megaships, but they do offer good variety, with distractions like volleyball, Italian lessons, sunset cocktail parties with dance music, poolside contests, casinos, discos, and small spas.

You'll find few Americans aboard, and many, many Italians and Germans, as well as a goodly number of Brits. Announcements are made in multiple languages depending on the passenger manifest.

The onboard currency on all the ships is the Italian lira, and the crew includes a good number of Italians, who add much to the onboard ambience.

Pros

- **Affordable rates.** That's what really makes these cruises so attractive.
- **Informal international flair.** The ships offer an appealing Italian flavor and an international passenger mix.
- **Well laid-out and spacious public rooms.** There's a pretty good variety in the offerings.

Cons

- **Un-fancy dining.** The dining rooms are loud and a bit cafeteria-like.
- **Crowds.** These ships are sometimes densely packed, and that means longer lines.

Compared with other European lines, here's how Mediterranean Shipping rates:

	Poor	Fair	Good	Excellent	Outstanding
Enjoyment Factor				✓	
Dining		✓			
Activities		✓			
Children's Program		✓			
Entertainment		✓			
Service			✓		
Overall Value			✓		

Mediterranean Shipping Fleet Itineraries

Ship	Home Ports & Season	Itinerary
Melody	Round-trip from Genoa (May–Oct)*	**7-day W. Med:** Port calls include Naples and Palermo (Italy), Tunis (Tunisia), Palma de Mallorca and Barcelona (Spain), and Marseille (France)
Monterey	**11-day W. Med/Spain and Morocco,** round-trip from Genoa (May–Oct).*	**11-day W. Med/Spain and Morocco:** Port calls include Port Mahon, Valencia, Cadiz, and Barcelona (Spain), Lisbon (Portugal), Casablanca (Morocco), Gibraltar, and St-Tropez (France)
Rhapsody	**7-day Greek Isles,** round-trip from Venice (June–Oct)*	**7-day Greek Isles:** Port calls include Bari (Italy), Katakolon, Patmos, and Rhodes (Greece), Kuşadasi (Turkey), and Dubrovnik (Croatia)

*Melody *also does Holy Lands and Canary Islands itineraries;* Monterey *and* Rhapsody *also do Black Sea, Canary Islands, and Holy Lands itineraries.*

THE FLEET

The *Melody,* formerly *StarShip Atlantic,* sailed as the *Big Red Boat* for Premier Cruise Line. Aside from a paint job, MSC has made virtually no changes to the ship since its purchase.

The *Monterey,* built in 1952, and the *Rhapsody,* built in 1974 and formerly the *Cunard Princess,* were modernized by MSC.

PASSENGER PROFILE

MSC is an Italian entity that's only recently begun marketing in North America, so there will be few Americans aboard. Italians and Germans make up the largest percentage of passengers, but since the line is also popular with Brits you will find plenty of English speakers. The line's affordable prices draw from Europe's middle class, and include some families, young singles, and honeymooners, though mostly couples in their 40s on up.

These ships are particularly well suited to first-time cruisers.

DINING

The main dining room on each ship offers two seatings at lunch and dinner and one at breakfast. On the Pool Deck there's also buffet-style breakfast and lunch, the latter including pastas and salads.

The cuisine is primarily Italian. For the captain's dinner you can expect choices including lobster and baked Alaska, and for each meal you can choose fish, fowl, meat, vegetarian, and pasta (the latter especially good). The wine list is mostly made up of well-chosen Italian vintages.

Special diets are catered to on request. There is also 24-hour **room service** from a limited menu.

ACTIVITIES

These ships don't offer the range of amenities and state-of-the-art distractions you'll find on the big new megaships, but they do offer good variety, with table tennis, volleyball, and shuffleboard, plus activities like bridge, cards, jigsaw puzzles, Italian lessons, aperitif parties before lunch, sunset cocktail parties with dance music, poolside contests, visits to the beauty salon, stretch-and-tone aerobics classes, and movies in the cinema. Each ship also has both a **casino** and **disco.** The small **spas** are concessions and offer reasonably priced massages and beauty services.

Despite all these options, most passengers will head to the Sun Deck (spacious on all the ships) when their ship isn't in port.

Some news in English is printed out and made available every day. There is no e-mail available for passenger use on these vessels.

CHILDREN'S PROGRAM

There are children's programs on all the ships, and a **children's center** including a wading pool on the *Melody.* The *Rhapsody* also has a kiddie pool. Activities are of the low-tech, low-key variety like games, crafts, and Italian lessons.

Babysitting by crew members is available for a modest fee.

ENTERTAINMENT

There is at least one singer and a **musical group** that trots out danceable show tunes and favorites from both sides of the Atlantic, as well as an amateurish song and dance show presented nightly.

In the Italian tradition, passengers will spend a lot of time at meals, considering that a form of nighttime entertainment.

SERVICE

Overall, the Italian career staffers are fine examples of that country's superb tradition of attentive service. What they deliver is not all that refined, but is warm and genuine. Recommended tipping is a little less than standard, totaling only about $6.50 per passenger, per day.

Laundry and dry cleaning service is offered. There are no coin-operated laundry facilities.

Melody

The Verdict

This friendly, well-laid-out ship offers lots to do and decent-size spaces in which to do it.

Melody *(photo: MSC)*

Specifications

Size (in tons)	36,000	Officers	Italian
Number of Cabins	538	Crew	539 (International)
Number of Outside Cabins	371	Passenger/Crew Ratio	2 to 1
Cabins with Verandas	0	Year Built	1982
Number of Passengers	1,076	Last Major Refurbishment	1997

Frommer's Ratings (Scale of 1–5)

Cabin Comfort & Amenities	3	Pool, Fitness & Spa Facilities	3
Ship Cleanliness & Maintenance	3	Children's Facilities	2
Public Comfort/Space	3	Decor	3

This medium-size ship was built in the style of a classic ocean liner, with a layout of decks and public areas originally conceived for long-haul cruises. Teakwood decks and heavy doors with the traditional raised sill are commonplace. Real round portholes—an increasing rarity in these picture-window days—have been retained in many instances, and provide a nice reminder of traditional ship design.

Many thousands of nautical miles have washed beneath this ship's hull, and it experienced lots of wear and tear in its days as Premier's *Big Red Boat*. Very few cosmetic or architectural changes have been made since the ship's acquisition by MSC in 1997.

Cabins & Rates

Cabins	Brochure Rates*	Bathtub	Fridge	Hair Dryer	Sitting Area	TV
Inside	$1,099–$1,729	no	no	on request	no	yes
Outside	$1,399–$2,029	some	no	on request	some	yes
Suite	$2,199–$2,629	yes	some	yes	yes	yes

Port charges are an additional $99 for a 1-week sailing.

CABINS   Cabins come in many different configurations, the smallest of which tend to be somewhat cramped; the others, averaging 185 square feet, are relatively comfortable. Suites are a bit more plush and good-sized (280–440 sq. ft.) and can accommodate four or five people, which is great for families. Each cabin is equipped with music channels, telephone, and TV (with a satellite feed). Hair dryers are available from the purser on request. Most outside cabins and all suites have a bathtub/shower combination.

Four cabins have been configured to allow a collapsible wheelchair to go through (the chair can be no more than 29 in. wide, though).

PUBLIC AREAS   The decor is cheerful, but definitely feels a little dated—early '80s, with lights twinkling along metallic surfaces and bright but not jarring color schemes. The Blue Riband room is, by contrast, a deliberately darkened and artsy-looking jazz pub.

Cabaret and comedy acts are presented at Club Universe. There are also a few bars, a video arcade, and an unmemorable casino that's set amidships on the Lounge Deck. There's no library, per se, just a small collection of books. The Mercury Theater shows movies from both sides of the Atlantic, and kids get their own playroom.

ALTERNATIVE DINING   None.

POOL, FITNESS & SPA FACILITIES   The *Melody* has two swimming pools (one with a retractable roof), a kids' wading pool, and two whirlpools, all of which can get quite full. The ship's tiered aft decks offer lots of prime spots for sunbathing.

There's a small gym with updated equipment, a couple of massage rooms, and a beauty salon. The Sun Deck has a jogging track, and there are setups for aerobics classes, Ping-Pong, and shuffleboard.

Monterey

The Verdict

This one-time cargo ship works well as a classic cruise vessel, with lots of open deck space and pleasing public rooms.

Monterey *(photo: MSC)*

Specifications

Size (in tons)	20,000	Officers	Italian
Number of Cabins	290	Crew	200 (International)
Number of Outside Cabins	163	Passenger/Crew Ratio	2.8 to 1
Cabins with Verandas	0	Year Built	1952
Number of Passengers	576	Last Major Refurbishment	1998

Frommer's Ratings (Scale of 1–5)

Cabin Comfort & Amenities	2	Pool, Fitness & Spa Facilities	2
Ship Cleanliness & Maintenance	3	Children's Facilities	N/A
Public Comfort/Space	2	Decor	2

Built in 1952, this old workhorse of a ship (it was originally a U.S.-built cargo ship) is friendly, if not as packed with things to do as newer ships. The decor features some Art Deco styling, with some wood and brass, plus lots of open deck space.

Cabins & Rates

Cabins	Brochure Rates*	Bathtub	Fridge	Hair Dryer	Sitting Area	TV
Inside	$1,499–$2,199	no	no	on request	no	no
Outside	$2,199–$3,199	no	no	on request	no	no
Suite	$3,599–$3,799	yes	yes	yes	yes	yes

Rates are for 11-day cruise; additional port charge of $159.

CABINS   Cabins are comfortably furnished and come in a variety of sizes and configurations. Standard cabins vary from a tiny 100 square feet to a comfortable 180 square feet. All cabins have radios, phones, and writing areas, and some have bathtubs, sitting areas, and double beds. Hair dryers are available upon request through the purser's office. The two suites and two junior suites are very large (up to 400 sq. ft.) and have TVs, minibars, sitting areas, and picture windows. Some of the cabins on the Boat Deck have obstructed views.

There are no cabins for travelers with disabilities.

PUBLIC ROOMS   MSC recently updated the *Monterey's* decor. The two-level dining room can be noisy but is otherwise pleasant. The Palm Court has piano music for pre-dinner drinks, then cabaret and dancing. The vessel also has a disco, cinema, library, and casino (with blackjack, slots, and roulette).

The ship has a good amount of deck space, although the Promenade Deck is not of the wrap-around variety.

ALTERNATIVE DINING   None.

POOL, FITNESS & SPA FACILITIES   There's one outdoor pool, one whirlpool, and a modest gym and spa with a sauna and massage rooms. Deck sports include paddle tennis, Ping-Pong, volleyball, shuffleboard, and aerobics and exercise classes. The ship does not have a children's room, but does offer both children's and teens' activities.

Rhapsody

The Verdict

The *Rhapsody* used to be a Cunard vessel, and still shows signs of elegance even though the atmosphere today is less formal. Though friendly, the vessel can sometimes feel crowded.

Rhapsody *(photo: MSC)*

Specifications

Size (in tons)	16,852	Officers	Italian
Number of Cabins	384	Crew	250 (Italian/Int'l)
Number of Outside Cabins	257	Passenger/Crew Ratio	3 to 1
Cabins with Verandas	0	Year Built	1977
Number of Passengers	768	Last Major Refurbishment	1997

Frommer's Ratings (Scale of 1–5)

Cabin Comfort & Amenities	2	Pool, Fitness & Spa Facilities	3
Ship Cleanliness & Maintenance	3	Children's Facilities	N/A
Public Comfort/Space	3	Decor	3

The *Rhapsody,* a sister ship to Royal Olympic's *Olympic Countess,* is a nicely laid out ship that was previously operated as the *Cunard Princess.* The vessel's cabins are small and its public rooms big (including a two-story atrium and a neat indoor/outdoor nightclub), and there's lots of open deck space.

Cabins & Rates

Cabins	Brochure Rates*	Bathtub	Fridge	Hair Dryer	Sitting Area	TV
Inside	$1,099–$1,729	no	no	on request	no	no
Outside	$1,399–$2,029	no	no	on request	yes	no
Suite	$2,199–$2,629	yes	yes	yes	yes	yes

Port charges are an additional $99 for a 1-week sailing.

CABINS   Standard cabins are nicely furnished but very small—the largest cabin on the ship can only hold three people, maximum. The 20 junior suites (at 160 sq. ft.) are most appropriate for Americans. There are also two suites, each about 250 square feet. Only the suites have bathtubs, but both suites and junior suites have sitting areas. All cabins have phones, music channels, and writing areas, with hair dryers available on request.

There are no cabins for travelers with disabilities.

PUBLIC AREAS   The 8 Bells Nightclub is an indoor/outdoor entertainment venue that allows you to dance under the stars. The Top Sail Lounge is an observation area and nightclub on the Sun Deck and includes a piano bar.

The dining room has nice ocean views, but can be noisy. There's also a cinema, library area, and small casino with blackjack, roulette, and slots.

ALTERNATIVE DINING   None.

POOL, FITNESS & SPA FACILITIES   There is no wraparound promenade, but there is a jogging track on the Sun Deck. The ship has a good-size swimming pool, a kiddie wading pool, and two whirlpools. There's a small gym and spa and a beauty shop, and aerobics and stretch classes are offered. There is no children's playroom. Deck sports are of your typical Ping-Pong and shuffleboard variety.

5 Norwegian Coastal Voyage

SHIPS IN EUROPE   Kong Harald • Lofoten • Midnatsol • Narvik • Nordkapp • Nordlys • Nordnorge • Polarlys • Richard With • Vesteralen

405 Park Ave., New York, NY 10022. ℭ **800/323-7436** or 212/319-1300. Fax 212/319-1390. www. coastalvoyage.com.

The Norwegian Coastal Voyage offers a comfortable, moderately priced way to visit normally expensive Norway and get to know its people, towns, and wonderful mountain and island scenery. The line's relatively small ships operate year-round and offer 12-day round-trip itineraries that begin in Bergen and call at 34 coastal ports, from tiny villages to sizable cities, en route to Kirkenes at the very top of Norway. Short, one-way north- or southbound trips are also available. These ships carry cargo and vehicles as well as passengers and are considered a daily lifeline to some coastal and island regions.

The entertainment on these voyages is the scenery, the port arrivals and departures, and your fellow passengers; there are no evening shows or casinos aboard. Open stretches of sea, some lasting up to 24 hours long and others for just a few hours, can produce swells and even quite stormy weather, especially just north of Bergen at the North Cape. Temperatures are typical of a cool maritime climate, so prepare for cool weather.

Pros

- **A thrifty way to see Norway.** The voyages are moderately priced compared to a land itinerary in this expensive country.
- **Shows you beautiful Norway up close.** As these are coastal ships, they stay near to land and stop frequently.
- **Every season has its attractions.** In the late spring to early summer you see 24 hours of daylight (plus, above the Arctic Circle, the midnight sun in a narrower band of time), in the late summer and early fall you get the changing colors, and in the winter you can see the Northern Lights.

Cons

- **Ships do not penetrate the deepest fjords.** Unlike cruise ships that visit the most famous Norwegian fjords, the coastal fleet, while navigating some narrow passages, hugs the coast and threads a route among the islands.
- **The food is somewhat repetitious.** If you take the complete 12-day voyage, the food takes on a certain sameness.
- **Little time in port.** A lot of the port calls are for less than an hour (just enough time allowed to unload and load).

Compared with other European lines, here's how Norwegian Coastal Voyage rates:

	Poor	Fair	Good	Excellent	Outstanding
Enjoyment Factor					✓
Dining			✓		
Activities	N/A				
Children's Program	N/A				
Entertainment	N/A				
Service			✓		
Overall Value				✓	

Scandinavian Cruise Ferries

Norwegian Coastal Voyage also markets the Silja Line, operating large overnight Scandinavian cruise ferries, some of which gross up to 50,000 and 60,000 tons, on routes between Sweden and Finland and Finland and Germany. Contact Norwegian Coastal for information.

THE FLEET

The NCV fleet is divided into three distinct groups: the new ships (*Kong Harald, Nordkapp, Nordlys, Nordnorge, Polarlys,* and *Richard With*), the mid-generation ships (*Midnatsol, Narvik,* and *Vesteralen*), and two remaining traditional ships (*Lofoten* and *Nordstjemen,* the latter recently renovated). Gradually, the small, older, traditional passenger cargo ships, which still use cranes and pallets to lift on the cargo, have been replaced by newer tonnage that rolls on the cargo and vehicles through side doors. The first of the new breed appeared in the early 1980s, and they were enlarged later in the decade when they were found to be too small.

In the 1990s, an even larger class began to arrive, until only two classic ships now remain in service. The newest ships—those we've concentrated on in this review—have almost completely changed the character of the shipboard experience, approaching cruise ship standards in the variety of public rooms and attractive decor offered. Their cabins remind one of Carnival's older ships—functional and plain. However, there is little organized entertainment, gambling, or hoopla. There is also, unfortunately, little of the rugged maritime atmosphere of the older ships, and the sheer size of the new ships translates into a more remote connection to the port activities and cargo handling. (See "Norwegian Coastal's Older Ships: A Retro Coastal Adventure," below, for details on the line's older vessels.) New in 2002 are two new 15,000-ton Millennium ships that enter service in April, the 674-berth *Trollfjord* and the 643-berth *Finnmarken.* These are larger and more luxurious than the last generation of ships, offering 40% more overnight passenger capacity and 50% more deck space. And they will introduce to the fleet for the first time suites and private balconies. Three additional Millennium-class ships are scheduled to be launched in 2003, 2004, and 2005, respectively.

In the summer, a series of special expedition cruises will be offered, including Lofoten Islands sailings on the *Lofoten,* and Spitsbergen cruises on the *Nordstjemen.* Also being introduced in 2002 are sailings in Greenland and Antarctica and the Chilean Fjords.

PASSENGER PROFILE

Coastal Voyage passengers making one-way or round-trip passages are generally 50 and up, as the trip is seen as a sedentary, scenic cruise. In summer, there will be some younger passengers. Germans are the most numerous nationality, followed by British, Norwegians, and other Scandinavians and Europeans. Most Americans book as part of a tour operator's package, but some independent travelers will be aboard in the warmer months.

As the ships do provide basic transportation between ports, you'll find Norwegians aboard as deck passengers (on for the day or sleeping overnight in chairs or banquettes) or occupying a cabin for a night or two, and also lots of youthful backpackers during the summer holidays. The newer ships have conference facilities, and with oodles of available space in the off-season, the Norwegian meetings market is growing.

Announcements are kept to a minimum, but are repeated in five or six languages, with English always one of the languages. In the high season, there's a courier aboard to handle shore excursions and passenger information, and he or she will likely speak many languages. On shore excursions, English-speaking passengers get an English-speaking guide but may be assigned to a bus with another group, meaning you may have to hear the tour in English and French, or English and Italian.

DINING

The food is geared to Norwegian and European tastes and is prepared and presented in a straightforward manner. Breakfast and lunch are buffets, and dinner is served by the young Norwegian wait staff. There are two sittings when the complement is large enough, and tables are assigned at embarkation according to language.

Breakfast includes fruits, cereals, cold meats and cheese, various breads and toast, and often boiled or fried eggs and bacon or sausage. **Lunch** is the best meal, with several hot entrees, soup, salad fixings, cold meats, herring served about a half-dozen ways, and cakes and pies. **Dinner** is a set (there is no menu selection) three-course meal with soup, main course (often fish, chicken, or veal), and dessert. You can head forward to the bar for free coffee service after dinner (at other times if you want a cup of java between meals you have to buy it at the cafeteria). **Special diets** can be catered to with advance notice. After a week aboard, the food may become somewhat monotonous, but it has improved with the coming of the new ships and the need to attract cruise-type passengers. And you can enjoy red, yellow, and sometimes black caviar at nearly every meal (a bonus for caviar lovers).

Norwegian Coastal's Older Ships: A Retro Coastal Adventure

While most American passengers will book Norwegian Coastal's newer ships, there are other options.

Built in the early 1960s, the very traditional *Lofoten* is reminiscent of old steamships, and has been declared a Norwegian national landmark. Taking less than 200 passengers, it offers the atmosphere of a small, intimate country hotel with traditional wood-paneled walls. Most passengers who book this ship have little or no interest in the larger cruise-style ships, preferring these ships' old seagoing feel. Watching the cargo being lifted by crane into the ships' holds is like stepping back into a Humphrey Bogart movie. Similar but recently renovated is the *Nordstjemen*. When these ships are gone, there will be nothing like them left anywhere in the world.

The 4,200-ton mid-generation ships *Midnatsol*, *Narvik*, and *Vesteralen* take 325 passengers in functional cabins with private facilities. These three ships have an attractive dome-style lounge on the top deck and a small forward observation lounge, plus a dining room, a cafeteria, and a small shop.

Norwegian Coastal Voyage Fleet Itineraries

Ship	Home Ports & Season	Itinerary*
ENTIRE FLEET	Between Bergen and Kirkenes (most ships year-round).	**5- and 6-day:** 35 coastal ports northbound, 34 coastal ports southbound, with shore excursions offered at Geiranger, Trondheim, Ornes, Tromso, Honningsvag, and Kirkenes on northbound; at Honingsvag, Tromso, Harstad, Svolvaer, Trondheim, and Kristiansand, southbound; **12-day round-trip:** Visits the same 34–35 ports.

The northbound voyage has much better timing for the most interesting ports such as Alesund, Bodo, Trondheim, Tromso, and Honningsvag (for the North Cape). Passengers may join or alight at any port. Cabin berths sell out far in advance between late May and Aug.

As this is a domestic service, and taxes on alcohol are high, you can expect to pay a minimum of about $6 for a bottle of beer and $25 for wine. Some passengers bring their own supplies but, of course, they are not permitted to bring them into the dining room.

All the ships have **cafeterias,** mainly catering to the shorter port-to-port passenger, and if you get hungry between meals you have to pay to get snacks here. Three full restaurant meals a day are included for the full one-way or round-trippers.

ACTIVITIES

The main activity while under way is viewing the passing scenery. The ships stop in their 34 ports at all hours of the day and night—at which point passengers flock ashore for a walk or to buy newspapers and souvenirs—and if you take the complete 12-day round-trip you'll eventually visit all the ports at a convenient hour. Calls may be as short as 15 minutes or as long as a few hours. There is a package of reasonably priced **shore excursions** that provide a most worthwhile way to see some of interior Norway and several fjords by bus. They are booked through the onboard courier or in advance as a package (which we suggest you buy).

There are no activities offered otherwise—you have to be self-motivated, playing a game of cards or reading. There is no e-mail access onboard for passengers.

CHILDREN'S PROGRAM

Children come aboard with families making short hauls but generally not for the longer voyages. There's a video arcade on the newer ships, as well as a small, unstaffed children's playroom with a ball jump and climbing apparatus. Kids also get a 25% discount on shore excursions.

ENTERTAINMENT

In the summer season, there may be a band and dancing on selected evenings, but it's hit or miss. The **Arctic Circle crossing ceremony** is great fun if you enjoy being baptized with ice water, and the 180-degree turn in the tight Trollfjord basin amidst cascading waterfalls is also diverting.

SERVICE

The crew is all Norwegian (or at least people living in Norway), and ranges from long-time employees to recent recruits in their early 20s. On the smaller ships, service can be personal and friendly, but on the larger ones it is efficient and matter-of-fact. Tips are generally left with the dining room manager and pooled

---

Tips Prime Time Cruising

The best time to make the Norwegian Coastal Voyage is just before the middle of May, when you have 24 hours of daylight, fewer crowds, and lower fares. The only drawback may be snow still blocking the road to the North Cape.

---

among the staff, with the recommended amount $5 per passenger, per day. There is a laundry room with coin-operated washers and dryers (detergent is free).

Kong Harald • Nordkapp • Nordlys • Nordnorge • Polarlys • Richard With

The Verdict

These six similar (but not identical) ships are attractive, comfortable, and serviceable vessels providing a moderately priced, casual, low-key cruise.

Nordnorge *(photo: Bergen Line)*

Specifications

Size (in tons)	11,200–12,000	Officers	Norwegian
Number of Cabins	230	Crew	60 (Norwegian)
Number of Outside Cabins	203	Passenger/Crew Ratio	8.2 to 1
Cabins with Verandas	None	Year Built	1993–1997
Number of Passengers	464–490	Last Major Refurbishment	N/A

Frommer's Ratings (Scale of 1–5)

Cabin Comfort & Amenities	3	Pool, Fitness & Spa Facilities	N/A
Ship Cleanliness & Maintenance	4	Children's Facilities	3
Public Comfort/Space	4	Decor	4

These are attractive, comfortable, and low-key ships, but curiously, for vessels that are marketed as sightseeing-intensive, they don't provide much incentive to spend time out on deck: Space there is limited and less cozy than aboard the older ships (when you're passing a major sight such as the narrow Trollfjord it can seem downright crowded out on deck as people jockey for a view and photo op). On the plus side, though, these ships have cheerful and comfortable public rooms, lounge TVs, and lots of activities. Those seeking peace and quiet should sail in the shoulder season, when things aren't so busy on board. A warning about bar areas: They tend to attract lots of smokers.

Cabins & Rates

Cabins	Brochure Rates	Bathtub	Fridge	Hair Dryer	Sitting Area	TV
Inside	$874–$1,350*	no	no	yes	no	no
Outside	$902–$1,919*	no	no	yes	no	no
Suite	$1,223–$2,891	no	no	yes	yes	yes

For 6-day cruise.

Value **Some Special Deals**

There are off-season rates, and various packages combining the cruise with transatlantic air on SAS, hotel stays, sightseeing, and the scenic train ride between Oslo and Bergen.

CABINS   The cabins, mostly outside, are nearly all standardized and vary mostly by location. All are plainly furnished, with bunks that become bench-type sofas during the day, and many have an upper fold-away berth. The mattresses are foam and not particularly comfortable, but the addition of comfy duvets is nice. There is sufficient stowage space, plus a small shower, basin, and toilet compartment. The lowest passenger deck cabins have portholes while the rest have windows, and some facing the lifeboats will have obstructed views. Outside cabins on Deck 6 overlook the promenade and can be peered into by joggers and those out for a stroll (keep your curtains drawn). Room service is limited to bed-making and cleaning.

PUBLIC AREAS   The ships excel in Norwegian art, with specially commissioned sculpture and paintings depicting maritime scenes such as fishing boats, village life, and older coastal steamers in stormy seas. The furnishings feature bold colors and patterns, and there are lots of shiny surfaces in steel, brass, and glass. These offer great appeal, especially during the long, dark Norwegian winters.

The forward observation lounge is the most popular daytime spot, with comfortable seating and wraparound windows, and getting a seat here during the high season can become a blood sport (you are asked not to reserve seats). Aft of this space is a large bar and lounge (which tends to attract a good number of smokers). On the restaurant deck, the main dining room is aft with wraparound windows, and is reached by a long starboard side galley lounge where you can catch the views from tall windows while sitting in comfortable leather chairs. Forward are an entertainment lounge and bar (again popular with smokers), a small library, and a conference room. Amidships are a 24-hour cafeteria, shops, and a game room for children.

With generally cool temperatures, deck space is limited to a large enclosed area aft on the highest deck, smaller afterdecks, and a wraparound, narrow promenade, some of the spaces offering deck chairs.

ALTERNATIVE DINING   None.

POOL, FITNESS & SPA FACILITIES   There's a small gym with a few machines (such as a treadmills and bikes), a bench press, and a weight machine. Each ship also has a sauna, but no pool. There's a wraparound promenade, which is nice for jogging and strolling.

6 P&O Cruises

SHIPS IN EUROPE   Arcadia • Oriana • Victoria • Aurora

77 New Oxford St., London WC1A 1PP, England; in the U.S., contact Princess Tours, 2815 Second Ave., Ste. 400, Seattle, WA 98121-1299. ℂ **800/340-7074.** Fax 206/336-6100. www.pocruises.com.

P&O, the parent company of Princess Cruises, has been around since 1837 and is one of the most legendary British shipping lines. The ships themselves resemble those of Princess Cruises, with the same clean lines and smooth, modern feel, though public rooms in particular display a distinct British sensibility, often resembling the rooms of an Edwardian men's club, with dark wood paneling, heavy, overstuffed chairs and sofas, low lighting, portraits and paintings of old oceangoing vessels on the walls, and large wooden display cases.

Since P&O caters primarily to British passengers, the line's vessel and its operations have all been designed with their tastes in mind. For an American, it's like taking two vacations: one geographical and the other sociological. Overall, you're more likely to find kippers on your breakfast plate than pancakes, *Fawlty Towers* on the TV rather than *Friends,* and a droll attitude in place of the usual cruise ship whoopee.

Pros

- **British sensibility.** For Anglophiles or anyone who enjoys immersing themselves in another culture, an experience with P&O is fantastic—and without the language barrier (generally speaking!) See Passenger Profile, below.
- **Interesting passenger mix.** P&O was one of the great shipping lines of the British Empire, and aboard its ships you're likely to encounter passengers from former British colonies like India and Singapore mixed in among the Brits. The passenger talent shows are wonderful.
- **Beautiful ships.** The three newest P&O ships mix modern ship design with an old-world sensibility, while the smaller *Victoria* is more of an old-style cruiser.

Cons

- **British sensibility.** If you're an American, you're a foreigner here—a cultural student, as it were. If that's not what you want from your vacation, sail with an American line.
- **Few totally nonsmoking areas.** As on most European ships, smoking is either unrestricted or the enforcement is lax. Nonsmokers can have a tough time finding a totally clear space.

Compared with other European lines, here's how P & O rates:

	Poor	Fair	Good	Excellent	Outstanding
Enjoyment Factor				✓	
Dining				✓	
Activities				✓	
Children's Program				✓	
Entertainment					✓
Service				✓	
Overall Value				✓	

P&O Fleet Itineraries

Ship	Home Ports & Season	Itinerary
Arcadia	All sailings round-trip from Southampton. 7-day Europe (May and Oct); 4-day Europe (May); 13-day Med (May); 14-day Baltics (July); 14-day Med (July); 10-day Scandinavia (Aug); 13-day Med/Italy (Sept); 17-day Adriatic (Sept); 14-day Med (Oct)	7-day Europe: Port calls include Vigo (Spain), Lisbon (Portugal), La Rochelle (France), and St. Peter Port (Guernsey); 4-day Europe: Port calls include Amsterdam (Netherlands) and St. Peter Port; 13- and 14-day Med: Port calls may include Gibraltar, Calvi, Toulon, and St-Tropez (France), Livorno and Santa Margherita (Italy), Ajaccio (Corsica), Monte Carlo (Monaco), and Barcelona, Cadiz, and Palma de Mallorca (Spain); 14-day Baltics: Port calls include Oslo (Norway), Gdynia (Poland), St. Petersburg (Russia), Helsinki (Finland), Stockholm (Sweden), Copenhagen (Denmark), and Amsterdam; 10-day Scandinavia: Port calls include Bergen, Stavanger, Oslo (Norway), Copenhagen, Aarhus (Denmark), and Amsterdam. 13-day Med/Italy: Port calls include Palma, St-Tropez, Elba, Naples (both Italy), Cartagena (Spain), and Gibraltar. 17-day Adriatic: Port calls include Gibraltar, Malta, Venice (Italy), Dubrovnik (Croatia), Messina (Sicily), and Ciudadela (Spain)
Aurora	All sailings round-trip from Southampton. 16-day Med/Italy (Apr); 12-day Med (May); 14-day Baltics (May); 12-day Norway (July); 14-day Med (July); 16-day Adriatic (Aug); 7-day W. Europe I and 2 (July, Sept); 13-day Med (Oct); 17-day Greece/ Turkey (Oct); 13-day Med (Oct); 18-day E. Med (Nov)	16-day Med/Italy: Port calls include Vigo, Palma, Cagliari (Sardinia), Dubrovnik, Venice, Malta, Alicante (Spain), and Gibraltar; 12-day Med: Port calls include Barcelona, Cannes (France), Elba, Civitavecchia (Italy), and Gibraltar; 14-day Baltics: Port calls include Oslo, Copenhagen, Stockholm, Helsinki, St. Petersburg, Tallinn (Estonia), Warnemunde (Germany), and Amsterdam; 7-day W. Europe 1: Port calls include Vigo, Lisbon, La Rochelle and St. Peter Port; 12-day Norway: Port calls include Andalsnes, Tromso, Trondheim, Olden, and Bergen (all Norway); 13- and 14-day W. Med: Port calls may include Gibraltar, Ajaccio (Corsica), Civitavecchia/Rome, Livorno, Naples, and Messina (Italy), Villefranche and St-Tropez (France), Barcelona and Cadiz; 16-day Adriatic: Gibraltar, Palma, Cagliari, Dubrovnik, Venice, Naxos de Giardini (Sicily), Cartagena (Spain), and Vigo; 7-day W. Europe 2: Port calls include St. Peter Port, Cork (Ireland), Bilbao (Spain), Brest (France), and La Rochelle; 17-day Greece/Turkey: Port calls include Gibraltar, Athens (Greece), Istanbul and Kuşadasi (Turkey), Palma de Mallorca and Vigo (Spain)
Oriana	All sailings round-trip from Southampton. 13-day Med (Apr, Aug); 14-day Med (May); 14-day Baltics (June); 7-day Norway (July); 7-day Spain/Portugal (Sept); 12-day Italy (Oct)	13- and 14-day Med, 12-day Italy: Port calls may include Gibraltar, Ajaccio (Corsica), Calvi, Civitavecchia, Santa Margherita, Livorno, and Elba (Italy), Villefranche, Toulon, and Cannes (France), Barcelona and Palma de Mallorca (Spain); 14-day Baltics: Port calls include Oslo, Copenhagen, Stockholm, Helsinki, St. Petersburg, Tallinn, Warnemunde, and Bruges (Belgium); 7-day Norway: Port calls include Stavanger, Olden, Geiranger, and Bergen; 7-day Spain/Portugal: Port calls include Vigo, Lisbon, La Rochelle, and St. Peter Port

P&O Fleet Itineraries (continued)

Ship	Home Ports & Season	Itinerary
Victoria	All sailings round-trip from Southampton. **14-day Italy** (Apr); **4-day Europe** (May); **9-day Norway** (May); **13-day Baltics** (June); **15-day Norway** (June); **14-day Med** (July); **14-day Baltics** (July); **7-day W. Europe** (Aug); **14-day Europe/Baltics** (Sept); **14-day Med** (Sept); **23-day Adriatic** (Sept); **11-day Med** (Oct)	**14-day Italy:** Port calls include Gibraltar, St-Tropez, Portofino (Italy), Civitavecchia, La Maddelena (Sardinia), Port Mahon and La Coruna (Spain); **4-day Europe:** Port calls include St. Peter Port and Amsterdam; **9-day Norway:** Port calls include Andalsnes, Olden, Bergen, Stavanger, and Oslo; **13-day Baltics:** Port calls include Amsterdam, Stockholm, Helsinki, St. Petersburg, Tallinn, Copenhagen, and Bergen; **15-day Norway:** Port calls include Andalsnes, Alesund (Norway), Longyearbyen (Norway), Trondheim, and Geiranger; **11- and 14-day Med:** Ports of call may include Port Mahon, Cadiz, and Barcelona (Spain), Ajaccio and Propriano (Corsica), Sorrento, Santa Margherita, Livorno, and Civitavecchia/Rome (Italy), Sete, Toulon, and St-Raphael (France), Villefranche, Barcelona and Gibraltar; **14-day Europe/Baltics:** Ports of call may include Bruges, Stockholm, Helsingborg (Sweden), Turku (Finland), Helsinki, St. Petersburg, Gdynia, Travemunde and Warnemunde (both Germany), Fredericia (Denmark), Copenhagen and Kristiansand (Norway); **7-day W. Europe:** Port calls include St. Peter Port, Vigo, Lisbon, and La Rochelle; **23-day Adriatic:** Barcelona, Monte Carlo, Civitavecchia, Dubrovnik, Korcula (Croatia), Piraeus/Athens and Zakinthos (Greece), Ajaccio (Corsica), Palma de Mallorca and Cadiz (Spain) and Lisbon (Portugal)

All the ships also do some Canary Islands itineraries; Oriana also does Holy Lands and Black Sea itineraries.

THE FLEET

The *Arcadia* was launched in 1988 as the *Sitmar Fairmajesty* of Sitmar Cruises before P&O's buyout of that line, then sailed for a time as Princess's *Star Princess* before joining the P&O fleet under its new name in late 1997. Weighing in at 63,500 tons and carrying 1,475 passengers, the *Arcadia* has the look of a modern cruise ship but some of the posh interior feel of a classic old-time liner—a distinction shared by the 69,000-ton, 1,810-passenger *Oriana*, which entered service in 1995. The *Victoria*, on the other hand, really *is* a classic, having been launched in 1965 as the *Kungsholm* for the Swedish American Line and acquired by P&O in 1978, sailing first as the *Sea Princess*, then under its current name. Weighing in at 27,670 tons and carrying only 745 passengers, the *Victoria* is by far the line's most intimate vessel. If you're hoping to sail the "Old Vic" again, though, you'd better do it now. When it sails off into the sunset after its October 22, 2002, Med cruise, the venerable and much loved ship will be retired.

In May 2000, P&O debuted its newest ship, the 76,000-ton, 1,850-passenger *Aurora*. Though a sister ship to the *Oriana*, the vessel has several features that put it in league with the most modern American ships, amenities-wise.

PASSENGER PROFILE

Americans tend to think the differences between ourselves and the British are minimal—which ain't necessarily so. When you're an American put down in the midst of 1,300 of them, you know it. The British have different traditions, habits, history, psychology, manners—and vocabulary. Jerry was once at sea on the *Oriana* on January 25—the night Scots everywhere celebrate the life and works of their national poet, Robert Burns. Jerry was seated at a table of mostly Americans and spent the evening translating the menu for them. Burns Night specials included such items as "Neeps and Chappit Tatties"—turnip and mashed potatoes, the vegetables traditionally eaten with haggis, a Scottish dish. Then, too "wee bickies" were available with the after-dinner coffee. That's "biscuits" to the British, "cookies" to Americans. Of course, P&O's menus are not always that incomprehensible. That was, after all, a special event. But it's worth recalling the words of George Bernard Shaw, who described Britain and America as "two countries divided by a common language."

Aboard P&O, you'll likely meet many passengers who are of an age to remember when the sun never set on the British Empire, some of whom served in World War II and a small number of whom hail from former colonies such as India and Singapore.

DINING
Food aboard ship is, as you'd expect, extremely British, something Americans will notice first thing in the morning when they spot the kippered herring on the breakfast menu or buffet. Lunchtime might be the traditional fish-and-chips, followed a few hours later, naturally, by **afternoon tea.**

Dinner sees some wonderfully prepared dishes served in low-key, quietly elegant dining rooms (two each on the *Oriana* and *Aurora,* one each on the *Victoria* and *Arcadia*). In addition to British classics like beef Wellington, cream of Stilton and leek soup, and smoked Scottish salmon, you'll also find **vegetarian** and **health-conscious dishes** as well as international entrees popularized during the days of the Empire. As the line's publicity says, "We've been making and serving our famous curries since the days of the Raj." The *Oriana, Arcadia,* and *Aurora* all have a Lido-style buffet restaurant, plus other options like pizzerias and ice-cream stations. The *Victoria* has only its single dining room, plus a buffet area on the Lido Deck. Sandwiches and snacks are available through room service, as well as morning coffee/tea and biscuits.

ACTIVITIES
P&O onboard activities run the gamut from bingo and bridge to some of the best **port lectures** in the business, with dances, dance lessons, arts and crafts, cricket and tennis, exercise classes, and art auctions among the other offerings. The *Arcadia, Oriana,* and *Aurora* have cinemas for showing feature films (the *Victoria* shows films in its combination show lounge/cinema), plus a **casino,** a **library,** and the usual array of bars and lounges. There is no e-mail access on board for passengers.

Each ship has a gym and Steiner-managed spa. The *Victoria* boasts an indoor spa. Both the *Oriana* and *Aurora* have wraparound promenades that get a lot of use from the British passengers, and the *Aurora* will feature a golf simulator. Cricket matches between passengers and officers are always well-attended.

CHILDREN'S ACTIVITIES
The *Aurora* and the *Oceana* have children's **playrooms** and extensive children's programs. The *Victoria* has a teen center and outdoor play/pool area. As of 2002, the *Arcadia* will have, well, nothing for kids; it is to become an adults-only (16 and over) ship.

The *Aurora* also has a virtual reality center, as well as separate playrooms for kids under 5, ages 6 to 9, and ages 10 to 13. The *Aurora* and *Oceana* offer a staffed night nursery, and kids can attend separate early dinner seatings, with or without their parents.

When there are few children aboard, some areas may be converted for their use. On the *Oriana*, the door to the teen center is marked "You are about to enter outer space." A friend pushed it open to find two elderly British gentlemen playing Ping-Pong.

ENTERTAINMENT

Here's where the British-American cultural divide pops up again. While **production shows** are first-rate, there's only a fifty-fifty chance Americans will feel in the cultural loop, as the shows will feature either recognizable fare or British favorites that are so distinctly homegrown that Americans will be left scratching their heads.

Outside the show lounge, entertainment may feature a pianist, a big band (which sometimes provides accompaniment for ballroom dancing), and other combos, plus **comedians** who play up their British humor to the hilt. The **passenger talent shows** are a must-do, typically going far beyond the usual off-key karaoke (though you'll hear some of that, too).

SERVICE

Staff aboard all P&O ships is generally a mixture of British, other European nationalities, and Indian, all of whom tend toward the formal, crisp, and efficient. Brits tend to predominate in the "front office" jobs. The ships have self-service laundromats, and dry cleaning is available.

Arcadia • Oriana

The Verdict

Though modern and up-to-date in every way, both these ships also boast warm, old-fashioned, very British public rooms that evoke the classic steamship era.

Arcadia *(photo: P&O Cruises)*

Specifications

Size		Officers	British
Arcadia	63,524	Crew	British/Indian/Int'l
Oriana	69,153	*Arcadia*	650
Number of Cabins		*Oriana*	760
Arcadia	748	Passenger/Crew Ratio	
Oriana	914	*Arcadia*	2.25 to 1
Number of Outside Cabins		*Oriana*	2.4 to 1
Arcadia	583	Year Built	
Oriana	594	*Arcadia*	1988
Cabins with Verandas		*Oriana*	1995
Arcadia	50	Last Major Refurbishment	
Oriana	118	*Arcadia*	1997
Number of Passengers		*Oriana*	N/A
Arcadia	1,475		
Oriana	1,810		

Frommer's Ratings (Scale of 1–5)

Cabin Comfort & Amenities	4	Pool, Fitness & Spa Facilities	4
Ship Cleanliness & Maintenance	5	Children's Facilities	4
Public Comfort/Space	4	Decor	4

The handsome *Oriana* and *Arcadia* bear more than a passing resemblance to their cousins in the Princess fleet. It's evident that both vessels were designed with British passengers in mind. While cabins are modern, with the same kind of light wood design and modern fixtures that you find aboard Princess's megaships, public rooms like the *Oriana's* Anderson's Lounge and Monte Carlo Club have the warm atmosphere of an old London club, with comfortably soft couches and high-backed chairs, oil portraits on the walls, ship models, and faux bookcases. All that's missing is the fireplace.

CABINS No old-world nostalgia furnishings here. Cabins differ in size and decor. Those on the *Oriana* are far more sleek and modern, decorated in light, Scandinavian-type woods designed to make them look more spacious than they are (in reality, standard cabins are only about 150 sq. ft.—comfortable, but not huge). By contrast, cabins on the *Arcadia* are approximately 190 square feet, though their decor is not as contemporary. All cabins on both ships offer TV and music channels, refrigerator, telephone, safe, hair dryer, and vanity table/writing desk. All bathrooms have showers.

Cabins are available with two lower twin beds convertible to king-size, and a number of cabins have third and fourth berths. Both ships also offer minisuites (approximately 220 sq. ft. on *Oriana*, 372 sq. ft. on *Arcadia*) and full suites (414 sq. ft. on *Oriana*, 538 sq. ft. on *Arcadia*). Both suite levels have private verandas, two wardrobes, bar, and bathrooms with bathtubs (Jacuzzi bathtubs on *Oriana*). Full suites on *Oriana* have separate bedrooms and living areas; those on *Arcadia* have a small separate sitting area, though the bedroom and large main sitting area share the same space.

Accommodations aboard *Arcadia* are more spacious, but the *Oriana* offers far more cabins with balconies, as well as about twice as many single cabins—though the number on both (64 on *Arcadia*, 108 on *Oriana*) represent real rarities in such modern cruise ships, which typically have no singles at all, or very few. Eight cabins on *Oriana* and 10 on *Arcadia* are wheelchair accessible.

Cabins & Rates for *Arcadia*

Cabins	Brochure Rates*	Bathtub	Fridge	Hair Dryer	Sitting Area	TV
Inside	$2,395–$2,556	no	yes	no	no	yes
Outside	$2,571–$3,010	no	yes	yes	no	yes
Suites	$4,820–$5920	yes	yes	yes	yes	yes

Rates are for Arcadia's *10-day cruises.*

Cabins & Rates for *Oriana*

Cabins	Brochure Rates	Bathtub	Fridge	Hair Dryer	Sitting Area	TV
Inside	$2,688–$2,718*	no	yes	no	no	yes
Outside	$2,982–$4,775	no	yes	yes	no	yes
Suites	$5,922–$6,950	yes	yes	yes	yes	yes

Rates are for Oriana's *11-day cruises.*

PUBLIC AREAS   Public rooms aboard *Oriana* are mostly concentrated on two decks with spacious corridors. Aboard *Arcadia,* they're spread among several decks, most on Deck 7. On both ships, rooms have been designed like an idealized England in miniature. Many lounges have a clubby, dark wood ambience, and a pub on each features some of the best draught beer selections we've seen aboard any ship. A pub on each ship is themed to that most English of sporting passions—cricket. Each is named after a famous London cricket stadium—on *Oriana* it's Lord's Tavern, and on *Arcadia,* it's The Oval—and done out with cricket memorabilia of all sorts: bats, balls, pads, stumps, a mural of a cricket field, cricket-themed photos and paintings, and carpeting that looks like grass. All terribly English, but you don't need to know the difference between a googly and a maiden over to enjoy the atmosphere.

Both ships feature well-designed two-deck theaters, cinemas, 8 to 10 bars, pizzerias serving *very* tasty pizza and garlic bread, nightclubs, discos, libraries, card rooms, and lovely traditional-looking casinos. *Arcadia* has one main dining room and a buffet restaurant, while *Oriana* has two smaller main dining rooms and a buffet that's not terribly well-designed, traffic-wise—it gets chaotic.

ALTERNATIVE DINING   None.

POOL, FITNESS & SPA FACILITIES   Both ships have sizable pool decks, with Jacuzzis and twin pools (one of which, on *Arcadia,* features a swim-up bar—no need to leave the pool for that martini) and facilities for tennis or cricket, trapshooting, and more. For children, there's a "paddling pool" on an outside deck by the children's center. Each ship has a gym, the *Arcadia*'s buried, in the old style, low down on Deck 2, while the *Oriana*'s is in the more modern, accessible position, way up on the Lido Deck, just forward of the pools (and, as noted above, almost attached to the pizzeria). P&O, incidentally, claims that the main pool on the *Oriana* is the biggest on any cruise ship anywhere. The spas on both ships are run by Steiner Leisure, which operates the spas on most cruise ships, offering a vast arsenal of massage and beauty therapies.

Victoria

The Verdict

A real ocean liner of the old school, this beautiful, classic vessel carries only 745 passengers, allowing a more intimate, less crowded cruise experience.

Victoria *(photo: P&O Cruises)*

Specifications

Size (in tons)	27,670	Officers	British
Number of Cabins	379	Crew	417 (British/
Number of Outside Cabins	291		Indian/Internat'l)
Cabins with Verandas	0	Passenger/Crew Ratio	1.8 to 1
Number of Passengers	745	Year Built	1966
		Last Major Refurbishment	1997

Frommer's Ratings (Scale of 1–5)

Cabin Comfort & Amenities	3	Pool, Fitness & Spa Facilities	3
Ship Cleanliness & Maintenance	4	Children's Facilities	3
Public Comfort/Space	4	Decor	3

One of the last of a steadily decreasing number of classic ocean liners, the *Victoria* ends its illustrious career this season. It was built as the *Kungsholm* for the now-defunct Swedish American Line, and was purchased by P&O in 1978, at which time the number of cabins aboard was increased (meaning about half the cabins today are tiny at only 126 sq. ft.—see more on cabin size below). For a time, the ship sailed as the *Sea Princess,* partially for Princess cruises. Throughout, *Victoria* is a lovely old ship, retaining much of her fine original design and workmanship, and offers a real old liner experience in these megaship days.

CABINS   As noted above, approximately half the standard cabins, both inside and outside, are very tight at 126 square feet (those are designated by the line as "two bedded cabins"); "staterooms," on the other hand, are more spacious at 180. All offer two lower beds (in the "two bedded cabins" one folds away during the day), TV and music channels, wardrobes, vanity table/writing desk, safe, and phone. Many cabins have bathrooms with bathtubs—a rarity for which we can thank the ship's vintage—while the rest have only showers. Cabins designated "two berth" are truly Lilliputian at 95 square feet, with upper and lower berths, though they otherwise offer the same amenities as the other two standard categories. Suites are relatively large at 306 square feet, with living and bedroom areas sharing the same space, and additional amenities like a king-size bed, bathroom with Jacuzzi tub, stereo system, refrigerator/bar, and two large picture windows. (Windows in other categories are generally portholes.) There are 10 cabins for singles, and eight cabins that are wheelchair accessible.

Cabins & Rates

Cabins	Brochure Rates*	Bathtub	Fridge	Hair Dryer	Sitting Area	TV
Outside	$3,423–$4,775	some	no	no	some	yes
Suite	$7,128	yes	yes	no	yes	yes

Prices are for 11-day cruise.

PUBLIC AREAS   Many public areas on *Victoria,* especially the indoor pool and the lovely enclosed promenade decorated with potted plants, reveal the ship's former life sailing transatlantic voyages on the North Atlantic. Three lounges and four bars (including the very nice International Bar, attached to the show lounge, and our favorite, the plush yet understated Riviera Bar) ensure variety, while a disco and nightclub join the show lounge in offering after-dinner entertainment. Other rooms include a small casino, a library/writing room, and a card room.

ALTERNATIVE DINING   None.

POOL, FITNESS & SPA FACILITIES   The ship's small Lido pool is perched in a small area—a crater, almost—between the funnel and what used to be the forward funnel, which was purely decorative and was removed when P&O acquired the vessel. The pool and attached buffet area are nicely decorated and cozy. Another pool, this one with a Jacuzzi, sits farther astern on the same deck.

The real news, though, is that *Victoria* has one of the cruise world's only remaining indoor pools, which were once common when ships regularly sailed the cold North Atlantic. The *Victoria's* is very classy and nicely tiled, with a Jacuzzi, a small gym, and massage and sauna rooms opening off the same main pool area. *Victoria* offers no other spa facilities or services aside from the massage rooms and a hairdresser/beauty salon on a different deck. Indoor and outdoor promenade decks offer lots of space for walkers.

Aurora

The Verdict

Since its 2000 debut, the *Aurora* has proved to be just as popular as its older sibling, the *Oriana*.

Aurora *(photo: P&O Cruises)*

Specifications

Size (in tons)	76,000	Officers	British
Number of Cabins	939	Crew	850 (British/Int'l)
Number of Outside Cabins	655	Passenger/Crew Ratio	1.8 to 1
Cabins with Verandas	406	Year Built	2000
Number of Passengers	1,874	Last Major Refurbishment	n/a

Frommer's Ratings (Scale of 1–5)

Cabin Comfort & Amenities	4	Pool, Fitness & Spa Facilities	5
Ship Cleanliness & Maintenance	5	Children's Facilities	4
Public Comfort/Space	5	Decor	4

This grand vessel has made quite a name for itself since its debut in 2000, proving to be as innovative and as popular as its late-model sister ship, the *Oriana*. While remaining totally British in ambience, *Aurora* boasts several new features that should put it in a league with the very best of the mainstream ships, whether British or American. This is a ship that could be slotted instantly into any major American fleet. It has lots of verandas and interconnectable cabins for parents traveling with youngsters.

CABINS   With its high ratio of veranda cabins (well over a third), the *Aurora* has established itself as a favorite of the romantically inclined (or relaxation-minded) types. At 150 square feet for the lower-end rooms (the inside and some of the outside units), they're hardly overly spacious, but they do have a two-seater sofa and coffee table. Balcony staterooms run from 175 to 207 square feet. It's perhaps in the suites that *Aurora* impresses most, in terms of size and amenities. The minisuites are 325 square feet and the full suites range from 445 to 885 square feet. The Penthouse Suite, an 865-square-foot duplex feet, offers a huge living area; guests have their choice of one that contains a grand piano or one that has a fully stocked library. All suites have Jacuzzi baths.

Cabins & Rates

Cabins	Brochure Rates	Bathtub	Fridge	Hair Dryer	Sitting Area	TV
Inside	$1,880–$2,085*	some	yes	some	yes	yes
Outside	$2,159–$3,453	yes	yes	yes	yes	yes
Suites	$4,305–$6,510	yes	yes	yes	yes	yes

*Prices are for 9-day cruises.

PUBLIC AREAS   It's not much of an exaggeration to suggest that *Aurora* has carried British cruising into a new era. From the first exposure to its three-story atrium, dominated by a soaring waterfall, throughout its lounges, dining rooms, and bars, the ship really is an eye-catcher. Its public rooms include a range of lounges and bars, some reminiscent of the tried-and-true British-style rooms on the other vessels, some new, including P&O's first champagne bar, chocolate bar, and coffee bar. Other rooms include a West End–style theater (The Curzon Theatre), a large concert hall (Carmen's Show Lounge), a cinema, a virtual reality center, a sports bar, a business center, two dining rooms (as on *Oriana*), and a number of dining options, including a 24-hour bistro-style restaurant.

ALTERNATIVE DINING   None.

POOL, FITNESS & SPA FACILITIES   The ship's pools are worthy of note. One, aft, can be reserved for families during certain times of the year (although demand may be too great to allow it to be done a lot in Europe); another can be covered by a sliding roof for use in inclement weather; and a third will feature a waterfall descending from the tiered decks that surround it. All three pools, by the way, have their own bars alongside.

The Steiner-run spa offers the predictable wide range of services and the gym is kitted out with the latest equipment.

7 Royal Olympic Cruises

SHIPS IN EUROPE   Odysseus • World Renaissance • Olympia Countess •
Stella Solaris • Triton • Explorer (preview)

850 Third Ave., New York, NY 10022-7513. ℭ **800/872-6400** or 212/688-7555. Fax 212/688-2304.
www.royalolympiccruises.com.

These casual, friendly, and affordable ships offer a Greek-flavored cruise like no other line out there.

The Royal Olympic mid-size vessels focus on the destination as much as the shipboard experience. Passengers typically want to see as much of the islands as they can in 3, 4, or 7 days, so most of the itineraries are pretty jam-packed, some including visits to as many as two ports a day.

The line's European-based ships are old and low-key, staffed by very professional crews. There's no glitz or razzmatazz, no neon lights or lavish atriums. For their size, though, they offer a good variety of public rooms, although they can at times (particularly in midsummer) feel crowded. For the most part, decor is modern, bright, and cheery, with modern Greek artwork and an overall European ambience, in an older setting. Unfortunately, due to recent financial turmoil at the line, upkeep has not been what it should be, and you may see some signs of wear and tear on the ships.

As with other lines in this category, the international crowd aboard means announcements are made in many languages, which can get a bit monotonous.

Pros

- **Great service.** Dining room and cabin service are delivered with a friendly, personal touch.
- **Well-organized and diversified shore excursions.** It's clear this line knows the Greek Isles.
- **Good variety of public rooms.** These ships have their fair share of quiet nooks and crannies, even though they are pretty small, high-density vessels.

Cons

- **The ships show their wrinkles.** While the crews work diligently to keep everything clean and polished, evidence of deterioration cannot be camouflaged.
- **Small gyms and spas.** On the plus side, the spas are operated by the line and reasonably priced.
- **A lack of TVs and verandas.** On the older ships, there are no verandas, and TVs can only be found in top suites.

Compared with other European lines, here's how Royal Olympic rates:

	Poor	Fair	Good	Excellent	Outstanding
Enjoyment Factor				✓	
Dining					✓
Activities			✓		
Children's Program		✓			
Entertainment		✓			
Service					✓
Overall Value				✓	

Tips **Buyer Beware!**

Royal Olympic has been experiencing both financial troubles and frequent changes in management. At press time, at least one major travel insurer was refusing to insure travelers against default of the line (meaning if the line goes out of business before your cruise, you may have trouble getting your money back). Royal Olympic has also been known to cancel cruises on short notice.

THE FLEET

Royal Olympic's fleet includes five older, classic vessels, all built between 1953 and 1976. There is also a new ship, *Olympia Voyager*, which debuted in 2000 but was moved to Houston for year-round Caribbean and Central America itineraries. A sister ship, the *Olympia Explorer*, was to debut in 2001 but due to a legal dispute with the shipbuilder was delayed. *Stella Solaris*, in service since 1953, is a classic ocean liner, while the *Olympia Countess* and *Triton* are more sleek and contemporary. The *World Renaissance* and *Odysseus* are comfortable older vessels, but not classic. Both joined the fleet in 1998. The ships with the Olympia names, by the way, were previously called Olympic, as in *Olympic Voyager, Olympic Explorer,* and *Olympic Countess,* but the names were changed in deference to the 2004 Olympics scheduled for Athens. The line had also planned to change its name to Royal Olympia, but apparently backed off from that move.

PASSENGER PROFILE

The cruises are affordably priced, and unlike some of the other European lines, attract about 60% Americans plus 40% Europeans and others (including Australians and Japanese). Most tend to be seasoned travelers with an intellectual interest in the places they are visiting. But these ships, with their affordable rates, are also suitable for first-timers and families. And they also attract groups (Fran cruised on the *World Renaissance* once, when it was about 50% filled with French doctors and their spouses). The age range is across-the-board, with most in their 40s on up. Younger travelers looking for energetic nightlife may be disappointed. For the most part, passengers tend to go to bed rather early, saving their energy for exploring the ports. There's rarely more than a handful of people in the midnight disco. The *Stella Solaris* gets the oldest crowd, with many in the over-55 category. Activities for children and teens are offered on the ships based on need (if there are enough kids booked, the line will put a youth counselor on board).

DINING

No one ever goes hungry on these ships and the quality and presentation of the **Greek cuisine,** featured as specials on the continental menu, really stand out. Offerings include *tash kebab* (chunks of tender beef simmered with tomatoes and herbs served with rice pilaf), *sfyrida all spetsiota* (baked sea bass in tomatoes with potatoes), and *spanakopita* (spinach pie).

Dinner is served in two seatings, and menus also offer three continental entrees, plus **vegetarian dishes, spa cuisine** (low cholesterol, reduced salt), and Pacific Rim cuisine (dishes with the flavor and spices of Asia). Following the entree is a choice of four desserts (including homemade baklava) plus a sugar-free dessert and an assortment of domestic and international cheeses and fresh fruit.

Passengers can eat breakfast and lunch in either the dining room or on Lido Deck. Those who choose the dining room have the option of a buffet breakfast

Royal Olympic Fleet Itineraries

Ship	Home Ports & Season	Itinerary
Odysseus	Round-trip from Piraeus/ Athens (Mar–Nov)	**3- to 7-day Greek Isles:** Port calls may include Mykonos, Amorgos, Rhodes, Patmos, Santorini (Greece), Heraklion (Crete), Kuşadasi, Bodrum, and Istanbul (Turkey)
Olympia Countess/ Stella Solaris/ World Renaissance	Round-trip from Piraeus/ Athens (Mar–Nov)	**3- to 7-day Greek Isles:** Port calls may include Mykonos, Rhodes, Patmos, Santorini (Greece), Heraklion (Crete), Kuşadasi and Istanbul (Turkey)
Triton	Round-trip from Piraeus/ Athens (Mar–Nov)	**3- to 7-day Greek Isles:** Port calls may include Mykonos, Rhodes, Patmos, Katakolon, Santorini (Greece), Heraklion (Crete), Kuşadasi and Istanbul (Turkey), Messina (Taormina), Naples, and Civitavecchia (Italy).

and/or ordering from a breakfast menu, while the Lido offers an extensive buffet. Similarly, a full five-course lunch is served in the dining room, whereas the Lido has a choice of several wonderful salads, cold cuts and cheeses, sandwiches, several meat and fish dishes, and various desserts. While the food at the deck buffets is plentiful, getting a seat can be a problem, so your best bet is to get there early.

The ships also offer afternoon tea either on deck or in a bar, snacks are served at midnight, and there's very limited 24-hour room service.

ACTIVITIES

The ships offer pretty standard fare: exercise classes, dance lessons, deck sports (Ping-Pong and shuffleboard), arts and crafts classes, backgammon, bingo, and bridge.

What sets the line apart are its special enrichment programs, most prevalent on longer sailings. Royal Olympic boasts of having hosted more Pulitzer Prize–winning authors as guest lecturers than any other line, as well as specialists in various fields including astronomers, archaeologists, historians, and ambassadors.

On all Greek Isles sailings, a licensed guide offers lectures on the ports, as well as on topics such as archaeology, architecture, art, and mythology.

All the ships have a saltwater swimming pool (in some cases two), small gym, spa, and beauty parlor. (Unlike the vast majority of lines, who employ the London-based Steiner to run and staff their spas, Royal Olympic runs its own beauty services program, and the spa and beauty treatments are very reasonably priced.) Each ship in the fleet also offers expansive deck space for taking in the Greek sun, and the *Olympia Countess* offers tennis and a golf-driving range as well.

CHILDREN'S PROGRAM

The *Olympia Countess* is the only ship in the fleet with a dedicated children's playroom. All the ships offer kids' activities when there are enough kids on board. The program includes pool games, disco dancing, magic tricks, contests, movies, and breakfast with the captain and his officers on the bridge.

ENTERTAINMENT

The song and dance team tries its best to perform light cabaret shows on the dance floors of the main lounges. Headline performers such as Leroy Schultz, formerly of The Platters, and acts like magicians, are part of the line's repertoire. Each ship also has a disco, but don't expect too much action there.

By far, the most popular and exciting entertainment event is **Greek Night,** when the crew joins in with each ship's resident Greek musicians and other entertainers to create a lively party atmosphere. Guests are encouraged to wear blue and white (the colors of the Greek flag), and festivities begin at sunset with an ouzo party accompanied by bouzouki music, followed by a dinner featuring a five-course, all-Greek meal. The evening culminates with a gala celebration of Greek music and dance in the show lounge, with passengers invited to come on stage at the end of the show to join the crew and performers in some lively Greek folk dancing.

Nightly dancing in the show lounge is another popular activity, and many sailings feature gentlemen hosts (to dance with single ladies).

SERVICE

While many cruise lines have a rapid turnover in personnel, some of the crew on these ships have been with the company for years (especially on the *Stella Solaris*). It's not uncommon to see them greet repeat passengers like old friends—a greeting the passengers return in kind. Service aboard the ships is warm and very good; Fran had a doting female cabin steward on one ship who was downright grandmotherly. The waiters take pride in their job and are very attentive to individual passenger requests. They also tend to have a great sense of humor, making mealtime a pleasure all around.

The ships do not have self-service laundry or dry cleaning, but do offer laundry and pressing services.

The crew pools tips, with a recommended contribution of $9 per person, per day.

Odysseus • World Renaissance

The Verdict

These are older ships, but they get the job done, transporting you to the Greek islands in friendly and comfortable surroundings.

Odysseus *(photo: Royal Olympic)*

Specifications

Size (in tons)		Officers	Greek
Odysseus	12,000	Crew	(Greek/Filipino)
World Renaissance	12,000	*Odysseus*	200
Number of Cabins		*World Renaissance*	235
Odysseus	224	Passenger/Crew Ratio	2 to 1
World Renaissance	243	Year Built	
Number of Outside Cabins		*Odysseus*	1962
Odysseus	183	*World Renaissance*	1966
World Renaissance	178	Last Major Refurbishment	
Cabins with Verandas	0	*Odysseus*	1998
Number of Passengers		*World Renaissance*	1997
Odysseus	400		
World Renaissance	457		

Frommer's Ratings (Scale of 1–5)

Cabin Comfort & Amenities	3	Pool, Fitness & Spa Facilities	2
Ship Cleanliness & Maintenance	3	Children's Facilities	N/A
Public Comfort/Space	3	Decor	3

These ships are friendly and relaxed, but not at all fancy. They do what they are supposed to do, providing passengers with a comfortable way to see as many islands as is humanly possible in a limited amount of time. The decor is tasteful, but the ships are still old-fashioned in a 1960s kind of way without being classic (maybe if you think of it as "retro" you'll be happiest).

Cabins & Rates

Cabins	Brochure Rates	Bathtub	Fridge	Hair Dryer	Sitting Area	TV
Inside	$1,545–$1,990	no	no	no	no	no
Outside	$1,845–$2,480	no	no	no	some	no
Suite	$2,890–$4,130	some	no	no	some	some

CABINS   Cabins on the *Odysseus* are on the small side (a superior is about 130 sq. ft.), while those on the *World Renaissance* are larger (about 165 sq. ft.). All cabins come with a writing area, phone, and four-channel radio. Some suites on each ship have sitting areas, bathtubs, double beds, and TVs. On the *Odysseus,* some cabins offer sofa beds, allowing you to tuck away your bed and have sitting space during the day. A handful of cabins on both are equipped with upper and lower bunks. There are no wheelchair-accessible cabins nor any cabins with verandas on either ship.

PUBLIC AREAS   The ships both have an old-fashioned main show lounge with raised seating on the side and a dance floor in the center, that serves as the ship's hub (it's a gathering place for shore excursions and so forth). Both ships have various other bars and lounges, most on the same deck, as well as a cinema and a small casino. One of the more lively rooms is the Taverna bar on the *Odysseus,* a popular social venue that sometimes features Greek musicians.

Special attention seems to have been paid to the decor in the dining rooms, which are plush, bright, and pleasant, with nice fabrics, an intimate ambience, and glass-fronted wine display cases that make for a more upscale decor than that in the rest of the ships' public rooms. The other rooms are done up, in most cases, in cheerful colors, although the *World Renaissance* has some rooms, like the main show lounge, that are a tad dark.

ALTERNATIVE DINING   None.

POOL, FITNESS & SPA FACILITIES   The *Odysseus* has one outdoor pool and the *World Renaissance* has two; neither has a hot tub. The ships also have small gyms, saunas, beauty shops, and massage rooms.

Both ships have a good amount of deck space for sunning and lounging, although the pool areas can feel crowded at times, particularly when the buffet lunches are served. The *Odysseus* also has sheltered teak-deck promenade areas for walking, though there's no unobstructed wraparound deck.

Olympia Countess

Olympia Countess *(photo: Royal Olympic)*

The Verdict

This lovely ship, formerly owned by Cunard, is slightly more elegant and more modern than the others.

Specifications

Size (in tons)	18,000	Officers	Greek
Number of Cabins	423	Crew	350 (Greek/Int'l)
Number of Outside Cabins	281	Passenger/Crew Ratio	2 to 1
Cabins with Verandas	0	Year Built	1976
Number of Passengers	840	Last Major Refurbishment	1996

Frommer's Ratings (Scale of 1–5)

Cabin Comfort & Amenities	2	Pool, Fitness & Spa Facilities	3
Ship Cleanliness & Maintenance	3	Children's Facilities	2
Public Comfort/Space	3	Decor	3

The *Olympia Countess,* a sister ship to Mediterranean Shipping Cruise's *Rhapsody,* was built for Cunard, which was at the time trying to create an informal line to complement its traditional upscale cruises, a concept it later abandoned. The vessel later sailed in Indonesia as the *Awani Dream II* for now defunct Awani Dream Cruises. It's a nice, airy ship that has a more hotel-like feel than the other Royal Olympic vessels, with a larger reception area, casino, and pleasant cinema.

Cabins & Rates

Cabins	Brochure Rates	Bathtub	Fridge	Hair Dryer	Sitting Area	TV
Inside	$1,715–$1,990	no	no	no	no	no
Outside	$2,060–$2,480	no	no	no	no	no
Suite	$3,210–$4,130	yes	yes	no	yes	yes

CABINS   Cabins are small but decorated attractively. Bathrooms are rather tight. The 58 deluxe suites average 215 square feet and have windows, tubs, sitting areas, and TVs. Superior cabins are tiny at 125 square feet. Some have double beds, and some cabins have sofa beds, allowing you to tuck away your bed and have sitting space during the day. There are connecting cabins for families, and a few with upper and lower bunks. Only the suites have safes and TVs. None of the cabins is wheelchair accessible.

PUBLIC AREAS   This ship has a good-size, hotel-like reception area and a more modern feel than some of the other ships in the fleet. It's light and airy with lots of windows and a pleasant decor. Public rooms include a 487-seat restaurant, a main show lounge done up in tasteful fabrics (and featuring oval windows), and a large indoor/outdoor disco where the decor includes (bizarrely) suits of shining armor. Other public rooms include a casino, piano bar, tea-room, card room, and new and larger children's playroom (added in 1998).

ALTERNATIVE DINING   None.

POOL, FITNESS & SPA FACILITIES   While the *Countess* has no wrap-around promenade, it does offer a good amount of open deck space, including two levels of decking surrounding the one swimming pool. There's also a kiddie pool, a hot tub, and even an outdoor practice tennis court, a rare find on a ship of this size.

The *Countess* has a larger gym than most of the other ships in the fleet (it's about the same size as the one on the *Stella Solaris*) and it has a dozen exercise machines.

Two massage rooms are located nearby. The ship also has a small beauty salon.

Stella Solaris

The Verdict

Calling all culture vultures! This warm, hospitable Greek ship offers a comfortable, old-fashioned way to see the Greek Isles.

Stella Solaris *(photo: Royal Olympic)*

Specifications

Size (in tons)	18,000	Officers	Greek
Number of Cabins	329	Crew (Greek/Filipino)	320
Number of Outside Cabins	250	Passenger/Crew Ratio	1.9 to 1
Cabins with Verandas	0	Year Built	1953
Number of Passengers	620	Last Major Refurbishment	1999

Frommer's Ratings (Scale of 1–5)

Cabin Comfort & Amenities	3	Pool, Fitness & Spa Facilities	3
Ship Cleanliness & Maintenance	3	Children's Facilities	N/A
Public Comfort/Space	4	Decor	3

After almost half a century of service, the *Stella Solaris*—which began life as the French liner *Cambodge* and was extensively refitted in 1973—continues to run smoothly. The ship is a true classic ocean liner, one of the oldest cruise vessels around today. It's got a classic wraparound teak Promenade Deck (unfortunately rather weathered at this point), polished hardwood railings, and a traditional profile.

Most passengers who choose to sail on the *Stella Solaris* don't seem to mind the ship's wear and tear, however, and the vessel continues to maintain a strong, loyal following. Waiters remember the repeaters and warmly welcome them. When you choose this ship, you choose a vessel with heart and soul, repeaters say; something, they add, big new ships just don't seem to provide.

Cabins & Rates

Cabins	Brochure Rates	Bathtub	Fridge	Hair Dryer	Sitting Area	TV
Inside	$1,715–$1,990	no	no	no	no	no
Outside	$2,060–$2,480	yes	no	no	yes	no
Suite	$3,210–$4,130	yes	no	no	yes	yes

CABINS   Cabins are brightly colored and comfortable but not at all fancy, and come in 11 price categories. Top-of-the-line accommodations are the 34 deluxe suites located on the Boat Deck, which measure a spacious 215 square feet and offer picture windows looking out onto the classic promenade. The 100 deluxe outside cabins measure 182 square feet. The lowest-level inside cabins have bunk beds. Suites, deluxe cabins, and superior outside cabins have bathtubs, and suites alone also have walk-in closets and TVs, which screen four movies daily plus national news, weather, sports, and financial reports.

All cabins come with four music channels featuring Greek, classical, easy-listening, and American Armed Services radio news, and are also equipped with telephones and hair dryers.

There are no cabins with verandas, and none of the cabins are equipped for wheelchair users.

PUBLIC AREAS   The all-purpose, 550-seat Solaris Lounge is the ship's largest public space and serves as gathering place, activity hub, and entertainment center. During the day it accommodates everything from lectures to dance classes to bingo, and in the evening it hosts before- and after-dinner dancing and cocktails, as well as nightly cabaret-style shows. Situated at one end of the lounge is the Solaris piano bar, which along with a grand piano has three gaming tables (two blackjack, one roulette); the rest of the casino is made up of 19 slot machines located in a separate room off the Solaris Foyer, near the shore-excursion desk. While there's a late-night disco, it rarely sees much action.

Just steps away from the Solaris Lounge is the dining room, an expansive, cheerful space surrounded by large picture windows. Around the corner is a richly appointed piano bar with leather chairs—it's the ship's favorite evening watering hole.

The Lido Cafe opens directly onto the Pool Deck and, weather permitting, offers passengers the option of eating inside or at one of the tables around the pool.

Other public areas include a cinema that screens daily movies and occasional documentaries and also serves as the venue for lectures. There is also a combination card room/library.

ALTERNATIVE DINING   None.

POOL, FITNESS & SPA FACILITIES   The small gym has only a few exercise machines crammed into one room; the spa offers five massage/treatment rooms plus sauna and steam rooms. There's also a beauty parlor.

The wide, shaded promenade encircling the Boat Deck provides plenty of space for walkers and joggers and is one of the ship's most attractive features. On days at sea it's an ideal place to relax in a deck chair with a good book and immerse yourself in the balmy breezes. There is a single pool just aft of the Lido Bar, but no hot tubs.

Triton

The Verdict

The destination is the main objective on these cruises, not the ship, and the *Triton* does a decent job of offering a comfortable place to relax in between ports.

Triton *(photo: Royal Olympic)*

Specifications

Size (in tons)	14,000	Officers	Greek
Number of Cabins	353	Crew (Greek/Filipino)	315
Number of Outside Cabins	236	Passenger/Crew Ratio	2 to 1
Cabins with Verandas	0	Year Built	1971
Number of Passengers	620	Last Major Refurbishment	1992

Frommer's Ratings (Scale of 1–5)

Cabin Comfort & Amenities	2	Pool, Fitness & Spa Facilities	3
Ship Cleanliness & Maintenance	3	Children's Facilities	N/A
Public Comfort/Space	3	Decor	3

The ship was built by Cunard for informal cruising, and later sailed for Norwegian Cruise Line as the *Sunward II*. It joined Royal Olympic in 1992. The look is contemporary inside and out; the decor is bright and cheery. That said, the ship can feel crowded. The standard cabins are particularly narrow, and there are no suites on this vessel, although there are some good-size deluxe cabins.

Cabins & Rates

Cabins	Brochure Rates	Bathtub	Fridge	Hair Dryer	Sitting Area	TV
Inside	$1,545–$1,795	no	no	no	no	no
Outside	$1,448–$2,230	some	no	no	some	no
Suite	$2,890–$3,310	yes	no	no	yes	yes

CABINS   The Triton has 26 suites, including 16 deluxe suites measuring 219 square feet each. Cabins on the Venus Deck have windows, while those on the Dionysos Deck have portholes. All cabins come with phones and radios, as well as writing desks, while some deluxe cabins have bathtubs, sitting areas, and picture windows. Some lower-end cabins have upper and lower bunks. There are no wheelchair-accessible cabins nor cabins with verandas.

PUBLIC AREAS   Public rooms are located on the top four decks, with most cabins below. The dining room is light and bright, with a contemporary feel. The Nefeli Bar is located under a canopy on the top deck, next to the Nine Muses Nightclub, where panoramic windows also allow use as an observation lounge. One deck below is the Theatron cinema with theater seating, and the smallish Monte Carlo Casino.

ALTERNATIVE DINING   None.

POOL, FITNESS & SPA FACILITIES   There's a large oval-shaped swimming pool and a small fitness center. Wide teak decks around the pool and a wraparound promenade above offer ample deck space.

Preview: *Explorer*

Royal Olympic began the millennium by launching its first new builds, *Olympic Voyager,* introduced in 2000 and now cruising year-round from Houston, and *Olympic Explorer,* which begins cruising in spring 2002 (after being held up in a legal dispute between the cruise line and ship's builder).

Like its sister ship, the 836-passenger *Olympic Explorer* is 25,000 tons and features a unique mono-hull design with a pointy bow, which gives it a yacht-like appearance and makes it one of the fastest cruise ships afloat (up to 28 knots).

The ship, like its sister, is more upscale than the older ships in the fleet, but it's still a mainstream rather than luxury product. The design theme is "Precious Earth," with the ship's stylish public spaces inspired by the planet's precious stones, with color schemes to match.

This is a ship where you are best off splurging on accommodations (standard cabins are a small 140 sq. ft.), with top-of-the-line accommodations including 52 suites (ranging from 183–258 sq. ft.). Twelve deluxe Sky Suites (Category SA) and 12 deluxe Suites (Category SB) have verandas, but the 28 junior suites do not. The top suites come with butler service).

All cabins have minibars, hair dryers, and TV. Four cabins are fully accessible to passengers with disabilities.

Public rooms include a dining room and separate casual dining venue, a casino, a cushy cigar bar, and a comfortable library. The spa offers treatment rooms for mud baths, facials, massages, and water therapies.

From May to October, the ship will offer Grand Mediterranean Cruises round-trip from Athens/Piraeus and Venice (you can get on at either port). Port calls include Corfu, Katakolon, Mykonos, and Santorini (Greece), Dubrovnik (Croatia), and Istanbul (Turkey), as well as Athens/Piraeus and Venice.

Pre- and post-cruise packages are offered in both Greece and Italy.

Brochure rates are $1,885 to $2,190 inside, $2,355 to $2,730 outside, and $3,530 to $4,545 suite.

8 Swan Hellenic Cruises
SHIPS IN EUROPE   Minerva

U.S. Reservation Office, 631 Commack Rd., Ste. 1A, Commack, NY 11725. ℭ **877/219-4239.** Fax 631/858-1279. www.swanhellenic.com.

Swan Hellenic has always been in a class by itself, where mostly British passengers, and a minority of Americans, come aboard to be as active in mind and body as they are at home, sometimes more so.

The line offers one of the strongest, if not the best, enrichment programs on the high seas, with four or five top-notch lecturers giving talks aboard, dining with the passengers, and accompanying them ashore. The non-repeating itineraries, generally lasting 2 weeks, attract a very loyal and generally well-educated British clientele for whom a standard cruise would never do. There is a Swan code of behavior, and good manners and a quiet approach to life reign throughout the ship. Local entertainment in port, two crew shows, and classical concerts are the extent of organized evening activities.

The *Minerva,* a small ship by today's standards, takes just 344 passengers double occupancy and usually fewer, because there are many single travelers. Most cabins are a good size, and the public-room atmosphere is like that of a genteel English country house. Dining for all three meals is a choice between the formal and informal, and the focus is on lively conversation.

Pros
- **Well thought-out itineraries.** They're destination-oriented, yet provide enough time at sea to introduce the lecture program and catch up on reading and napping.
- **One of the best libraries afloat.** Offers a large selection of fiction, nonfiction, travel guides, and other reference books, and plenty of lounge chairs for reading.
- **An unusual dining policy.** The maitre d' seats passengers at shared tables (different ones each night), which facilitates social interaction. You can, though, often request a table for two.

Cons
- **Service varies in the formal restaurant.** Some waiters are friendly, others very matter of fact, perhaps the result of the gratuities being included in the fares.
- **It's best to play by the rules.** This is not a cruise geared for Americans who want to stick together as a group or who like to make lots of individual demands on the crew.

Compared with other European lines, here's how Swan Hellenic rates:

	Poor	Fair	Good	Excellent	Outstanding
Enjoyment Factor					✓
Dining				✓	
Activities					✓
Children's Program	N/A				
Entertainment			✓		
Service			✓		
Overall Value					✓

THE FLEET

The company has never operated more than a single oceangoing ship at any one time, and the latest ship was built up from the hull of an uncompleted Ukrainian nuclear submarine maintenance vessel. Completed in 1996, the ship was named by the duchess of Gloucester in a ceremony that took place on the Thames just above London's Tower Bridge, and made her first cruise in April. The *Minerva* sets a new high standard for Swan.

PASSENGER PROFILE

The passenger list is overwhelmingly British with a high percentage of repeat passengers on every voyage—often, the first questions asked will be "Have you cruised with Swan before?" And if so: "How many times and on which ships?" Once that is established, the social interaction begins. The age range is 55 and up, with many passengers in their 70s and 80s, but they tend to be as active in mind and spirit as those 20 years younger. Single women, traveling alone or with a friend, make up a significant minority. The northern European cruises will have a higher average age than the Mediterranean cruises. Most are well educated, and if not possessing university degrees or higher, then they are keenly interested in the cruise destinations. Swan Hellenic has snob appeal, and many of its patrons would never go on a standard cruise. American guests will likely be Anglophiles, at least to some extent. Everything aboard ship and ashore operates to military precision, and the passengers like it that way. Children are not part of the scene.

DINING

When passengers appear at the entrance to the main restaurant, they are escorted to a table with seats available; thus, in the course of 2 weeks, a couple may meet upwards of 100 passengers. One may request a table for two, and a few do, but they will not be available at peak dining times on a full sailing. The sophisticated formal dining room requires a jacket and tie for men every evening. Service from a Filipino wait staff and Ukrainian wine stewards ranges from friendly to abrupt. Menus reflect the countries the ship is visiting, with dinner hours generally 7:30 to 9pm (most people are seated by 8pm). Breakfast and lunch are also served here.

The Bridge Cafe, one deck up, serves all three meals, and is generally full at breakfast and lunch, especially at meals before tour departures. The food is buffet style with separate stations for salads, cold meats, hot entrees, and desserts. Coffee and tea are waiter served. Additional seating is available around the pool on fine days. The dinner hour does not require a jacket and tie but many still do adhere to the main restaurant's policy. As there is less demand here at dinner, those who like a table for two will find one easily. The service here is more consistently friendly than in the main restaurant.

⎛*Value* Some Special Deals

Besides the typical advance booking discounts, special offers include a repeat-passenger discount, discounts for combining two cruises, special offers on slow-selling sailings, and a program of standby fares and half-price fares for passengers under 26.

Swan Hellenic Fleet Itineraries

Ship	Home Ports & Season	Itinerary
Minerva	**7- or 14-day Greece and Turkey,** Piraeus/Athens to Kuşadasi or Istanbul to Venice (Apr–May), Naples to Kuşadasi, Naples to Piraeus/Athens, or Piraeus/Athens to Kuşadasi (Aug), Kuşadasi to Istanbul, Kuşadasi to Piraeus/Athens, or Piraeus/Athens to Istanbul (Sept), Thessaloniki to Kuşadasi (Oct); **14-day Spain and France,** Seville to London (July), London to Naples (Aug); **5-day France,** round-trip from London (July); **11-day Baltics,** London to Copenhagen (July); **14-day Norway,** Copenhagen to London (Aug)*	**7- or 14-day Greece and Turkey:** Port calls may include Gulluk, Kos, Canakkale, Dikili, Knidos, Fethiye, and Kuşadasi (Turkey), Rhodes, Ios, Limnos, Samothrace, Mykonos, Piraeus/Athens, Ithaca, Nauplion, Aghios Nikolaos, Itea, Gythion. Katakolon, Gythion, Cephalonia, Volos, Santorini, Heraklion (Greece), Dubrovnik (Croatia), Naples, Lipari, and Catania (Italy); **14-day Spain and France:** Port calls may include Lisbon and Oporto (Portugal), Bilbao, Cadiz, Malaga, Mahon (Spain), Bordeaux, Lrient, and La Rochelle (France), Cagliari (Italy); **5-day France:** Port calls include Rouen and Honfleur (France); **11-day Baltics:** Port calls include Kiel (Germany), Ronne (Denmark), Gdansk (Poland), St. Petersburg (Russia), Tallinn (Estonia), Helsinki (Finland), and Stockholm (Sweden); **14-day Norway:** Port calls include Flam, Geiranger, Tromso, Trondheim, Runde, Kristiansand, and Bergen (Norway)

Also does some Holy Lands and Black Seas itineraries.

The food is not as important to Swan passengers as on comparably priced ships catering to the American market. In the beginning, the menus were disappointing, as they tried to achieve something complex and missed the boat, probably an overreaction to the Anglo-Greek food of the *Orpheus* days. Now, however, there is a nice balance between British and continental menus, with themed Scottish or Indian dinners.

At dinner, there are generally three appetizers, two soups, one salad, three main courses plus a vegetarian selection, and three desserts plus a good selection of cheeses, fresh fruit, and a savoury (like a pickled fish or brandied fruit). The chef has the flexibility to buy fresh produce locally, hence there is no set rotation for the menus, and as often as possible, local dishes are prepared. Catering to upscale but not necessarily risk-taking British passengers, the menus include entrees such as roast sirloin of beef, steamed tuna, grilled swordfish, loin of venison, and guinea fowl casserole. Salads at dinner are less varied than on a ship catering to Americans.

Lunch and dinner in the Bridge Cafe generally have a pared-down menu of what is available in the main dining room. The salad selections and desserts are more extensive, especially at lunch. Breakfast offers the usual range of hot and cold selections, plus cold meats and cheeses for European tastes, and freshly prepared omelets. The croissants are fresh and light.

Wines, mostly from European countries, are moderately priced, and many passengers who regularly drink wine with dinner choose the French red or Italian white house wines priced at $12 a bottle. Bottles are marked with cabin numbers for those who wish to save the remains for the next evening.

ACTIVITIES

The *Minerva* is a smallish ship, so the range of activities is limited but also geared to what Swan passengers want. Lectures are an integral part of all Swan cruises, and there are usually four or five lecturers aboard covering subjects appropriate to the destination, such as archaeology, anthropology, architecture, history, politics, and religion. Most are men who hail from British universities, but there may also be a newspaper columnist on gardens, an ornithologist from the Royal Society for the Protection of Birds, and a priest or bishop from the Anglican church. Names and brief biographies are listed in the brochure. Talks are formal presentations scheduled twice in the morning or afternoon on sea days. They are very well attended and last no more than 40 minutes, with questions taken after the talk in the adjacent Wheeler Bar. Guest speakers are expected to be available on the shore excursions, and may actually lead some tours in countries where it's allowed. A program of complimentary shore excursions is included for every port, with no sign-up required. Some ports will offer supplementary tours, some lasting all day with lunch, and they are generally fairly priced. You're encouraged to book alternate tours (such as a ballet performance, for which you'd pay the ticket price) before the cruise, but may also be able to book on board based on availability. Swan prides itself on organization and the high quality of the tours, deservedly so. Disembarkation rotates from day to day according to deck.

The card room is popular for bridge games, and an instructor is aboard for some cruises. The large library may be considered a major activity center for reading, researching, and sharing in the ubiquitous puzzle with usually three completed each cruise. The moderate-size gym sees limited use and is taken over by the crew in the evenings. The cinema shows a film usually once a day. There are no bingo, horse racing, casino, or pool games, and no one seems to mind; in fact, many would object to their presence.

CHILDREN'S PROGRAMS

Children are generally not part of the scene, and if aboard, they need to enjoy adult company.

ENTERTAINMENT

All entertainment, which is limited by design, takes place in the main forward lounge. In the evening, there may be dancing to a small band, a popular place after dinner for coffee and liqueurs. Shows are limited to the Filipino and Ukrainian crew performances and local folkloric groups in a few ports. Classical concerts may be a feature on several evenings.

SERVICE

Cabin service is taken care of by Ukrainian stewardesses who are generally excellent at keeping the cabins clean and tidy. Coffee, tea, and light snacks are available free of charge, but there is a charge for cabin meals, and few passengers opt for this service. There are laundry and dry cleaning services and a small passenger laundrette with no charges. Restaurant service ranges from excellent to good enough to matter-of-fact. In the Bridge Cafe waiters are on hand to help passengers with trays. Bar service is excellent. The ship carries a British doctor and there is no charge for consultations. Tips are included in the cruise fare.

Minerva

The Verdict

The *Minerva* offers a high standard of comfort in an English country hotel setting for serious destination cruising.

Minerva *(photo: Swan Hellenic)*

Specifications

Size	12,500	Officers	British/European
Number of Cabins	170	Crew	155 (mostly Filipino and Ukrainian)
Number of Outside Cabins	136		
Cabins with Verandas	12	Passenger/Crew Ratio	2.2 to 1
		Year Built	1996
		Last Major Refurbishment	N/A

Frommer's Ratings (Scale of 1–5)

Cabin Comfort & Amenities	3	Pool, Fitness & Spa Facilities	3
Ship Cleanliness & Maintenance	4	Children's Facilities	N/A
Public Comfort/Space	5	Decor	5

Swan Hellenic was able to design the *Minerva* for its specific market of destination-oriented cruises for mostly British passengers. The ship incorporates a first-rate library, lecture facilities, a roomy variety of public rooms, and a good standard of cabin accommodation for passengers who only expect to sleep and rest there.

The interiors, designed for the British market, set new standards for Swan Hellenic, which had previously chartered first a Turkish and then a Greek ship. The public rooms combine the formal with the informal and provide a range of settings for different kinds of uses with plenty of room, even when passengers are driven inside by the weather.

Past passengers were asked to donate artwork and photographs, and the result is a potpourri collection that reflects the regions through which the ship travels as well as recalls the past. In addition, there are some very fine sets of drawings of Roman and Greek artifacts and statesmen, and maps of the Ancient World.

Cabins & Rates

Cabins	Brochure Rates*	Bathtub	Fridge	Hair Dryer	Sitting Area	TV
Inside	$1,555–$1,575	no	no	yes	no	yes
Outside	$1,579–$2,549	some	some	yes	some	yes
Suite	$3,005–$3,149	yes	yes	yes	yes	yes

Rates are based on a 7-day Greek and Turkey cruise, and include air between London and the ship, transfers, a program of shore excursions, and tips to personnel aboard and on trips ashore.

CABINS   Cabin accommodations are comfortable, but not huge, with most rooms between 140 and 162 square feet, all equipped with a two-seat sofa, writing/vanity table, direct-dial telephones, TV and radio, hair dryer, binoculars (so you won't miss any sights), and set of company-produced reference guides. Superior grade and up categories have full tub baths. Deluxe cabins (226 sq. ft.) and up have refrigerators, and suites have private verandas (suites measure 290 sq. ft., including veranda). Two Owners' Suites (360 sq. ft.) also have verandas. Insulation is good, and four cabins are wheelchair accessible.

PUBLIC AREAS   The public rooms are extensive and spacious, decorated like an English country house and spread over two decks. The main lounge, furnished with bold colors, has a large wooded dance floor, and with the furniture rearranged, serves as the main lecture hall. Walking aft from here is the Wheeler Bar, with a clubby, wood-paneled lounge atmosphere and furnished with sofas and chairs arranged in conversational groupings. A pianist plays before lunch and before and after dinner. The paneled library is one of the largest on any ship and is heavily used by readers and researchers. Next door are a large card room with suede walls and a true smoking room with leather chairs. The small auditorium screens films. The bright and cheerful Orpheus Bar, a cocktail venue before meals, and a sitting lounge at other times, also takes the overflow from the Bridge Cafe next door at peak periods. The Bridge Cafe is decorated in light colors and is located right above the formal dining room, designed with dark furnishings and chandeliers.

Deck space is more than adequate, with a wide-open Funnel Deck, a teak wraparound promenade, and covered deck aft. Shaded sections are limited and the outdoor pool area is set up for drinks and meals in good weather.

ALTERNATIVE DINING   None.

POOL, FITNESS & SPA FACILITIES   The outdoor swimming pool is surrounded by a Lido area on Bridge Deck. The small and spare gym on the Promenade Deck is adequate for a Swan passenger who gets most exercise taking constitutional walks on deck and going ashore. There is also a room for massages.

For Access Numbers not listed, ask any operator for **AT&T Direct** Service.

In the U.S. call 1-800-222-0300 for **AT&T Direct** Service information.

Visit us at **www.att.com/traveler**

Bold-faced countries permit country-to-country calling.

▲ Available from select locations.

● Pay phones may require coin or card to place call.

✔ From N. Ireland, use U.K. Access Number.

▽ Includes "Ladatel" public phones.

★ From St. Maarten or phones at Bobby's Marina, use 1-800-USA-ATT1.

❮ Includes "Lenso" public phones.

* Credit card calling subject to availability. Payment terms subject to your credit card agreement.

When placing an international call *from* the U.S., dial 1-800-CALL-ATT.

WW   ©3/01 AT&T

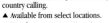
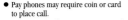

AT&T Direct®Service

1. Just dial the AT&T Access Number for the country you are calling from.
2. Dial the phone number you're calling.
3. Dial your card number.*

AT&T Access Numbers

Anguilla▲	1-800-USA-ATT1
Antigua (hotels)▲	1-800-USA-ATT1
Aruba▲	800-8000
Australia	**1-800-881-011**
Austria●	**0800-200-288**
Bahamas	**1-800-USA-ATT1**
Barbados▲	1-800-USA-ATT1
Belgium●	**0-800-100-10**
Bermuda▲	1-800-USA-ATT1
British V.I.▲	1-800-USA-ATT1
Canada	**1-800-CALL-ATT**
Cayman Islands▲	1-800-USA-ATT1
China, PRC▲	10811
Cook Islands	09-111
Costa Rica	0-800-0-114-114
Czech Republic▲	**00-42-000-101**
Denmark	**8001-0010**
Dominica▲	1-800-USA-ATT1
Dominican Republic▲	**1-800-USA-ATT1**
Egypt (Cairo)●	**510-0200**

AT&T Direct® Service

1. Just dial the AT&T Access Number for the country you are calling from.
2. Dial the phone number you're calling.
3. Dial your card number.*

AT&T Access Numbers

Fiji	004-890-1001
Finland●	0-8001-10015
France	0800-99-00-11
French Antilles▲	0800-99-00-11
Germany	0-800-2255-288
Greece●	00-800-1311
Grenada▲	1-800-USA-ATT1
Hong Kong	800-96-1111
Hungary●	06-800-01111
Ireland✓	1-800-550-000
Israel	1-800-94-94-949
Italy●	172-1011
Jamaica▲	1-800-USA-ATT1
Jamaica▲	872
Japan ●▲	005-39-111
Japan ●▲	0066-55-111
Korea●	0072-911
Malaysia▲	1-800-80-0011
Mexico●▽	01-800-288-2872
Mexico▽	001-800-462-4240

AT&T Direct® Service

1. Just dial the AT&T Access Number for the country you are calling from.
2. Dial the phone number you're calling.
3. Dial your card number.*

AT&T Access Numbers

Netherlands●	0800-022-9111
Neth. Antilles★ ▲	001-800-USA-ATT1
New Zealand●	000-911
Norway	800-190-11
Portugal▲	800-800-128
Puerto Rico/U.S. V.I.	1-800-CALL-ATT
St. Kitts/Nevis▲	1-800-USA-ATT1
St. Lucia▲	1-800-USA-ATT1
St. Vincent▲	1-800-USA-ATT1
Singapore	80-0001-0001
Singapore	800-0111-111
South Africa	0-800-99-0123
Spain	900-99-00-11
Sweden	020-799-111
Switzerland●	0-800-890011
Thailand ‹	001-999-111-11
Trinidad & Tobago▲	1-800-USA-ATT1
Turkey●	00-800-12277
U.K.	0800-89-0011
U.K.	0500-89-0011

ALPS   ASPEN

AT&T Direct® Service

The easy way to call home from anywhere.

Global
connection
with the AT&T
Network

AT&T
direct
service

or the easy way to call home, take the attached wallet guide.

 **AT&T**

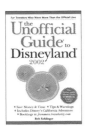
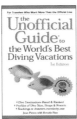
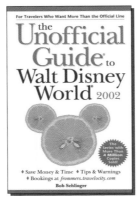
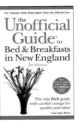

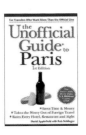
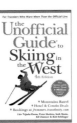
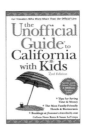

9 Other Lines

The following lines cater predominantly to European passengers: Peter Dielmann to Germans, the others to Brits. We decided to include them here mostly for European readers (and for Americans looking to avoid other Americans). Upscale Dielmann has made efforts to attract Americans to its new *Deutschland.* While the ship, which is one of the prettiest afloat, did draw a few Americans on its North America sailings, the numbers at this point still keep the vessel in the Other Ships category.

AIRTOURS

SHIPS IN EUROPE   Carousel • Seawing • Sunbird • Sundream

Airtour Holidays, Ltd., Holiday House, Sandbrook Park, Sandbrook Way, Rochdale, Lancashire OL11 1SA. Reservations agents ℂ **800 028 6302** (toll-free in U.K.) or 011 44 1 706 74 2000. www.airtours.co.uk.

Airtours offers down-to-earth cruises geared to those who have not cruised before. The average Airtours passenger is around 48 years old, 7 years below what the Passenger Shipping Association in London reports as the UK industry average, and more than one-third are repeat passengers. Overall, its product is mainstream, but it has recently introduced a premium product, the *Sunbird.*

The line's aim is to take the perceived formality out of cruising. Because the small size of the ships limits what can be done, the entertainment is mediocre and not of the standard of the big American megaships. While there are onboard activities, the cruises are geared towards the ports of call and shore excursions. Each ship has a children's club, though catering to kids is not the line's top priority.

Dining on these ships, which naturally tends to be British in taste, is better than on comparable lines, with better presentation and more inventive choices.

Being older, Airtours' ships have a traditional appeal. Three vessels are almost 30 years old while the fourth, *Sunbird,* was built in 1982. Three of the ships were bought from Royal Caribbean: *Carousel* was the *Nordic Prince, Sunbird* was the *Song of America,* and *Sundream* was the *Song of Norway. Seawing* was formerly NCL's *Southward.*

Sunbird (built in 1982; 37,580 GRTs; 1,595 passengers) has nine public decks, two outdoor swimming pools, two bars, restaurant, gymnasium/sauna, sports deck, library, beauty salon, and casino. There are TVs in all cabins and the vessel has nine penthouse suites (the first in the fleet). Cabins come in superior and standard inside and outside categories. There are elevators to each deck.

Sundream (built in 1970; 22,945 GRTs; 1,190 passengers) has seven public decks all served by elevators and all decorated in clean, bright Scandinavian style. There are an outdoor pool, a poolside bar, another deck bar and gym, a casino, and several public rooms.

Carousel (built in 1971; 23,149 GRTs; 1,160 passengers), *Sundream*'s sister, also has seven decks served by elevators. There's an outdoor pool and gym, and entertainment is offered in the Carousel lounge, the Show Boat Lounge, and the casino.

Seawing (built in 1971: 22,945 GRTs; 916 passengers) was Airtours' first ship. The vessel has seven public decks (all served by elevators), plunge pool, poolside bar, and gym. There is entertainment in the Clipper Lounge, Crows Nest nightclub, Riviera bar, piano bar, and casino.

Cabins on all ships have air-conditioning, telephone, music channels, power socket (U.S. adapter required), dressing table, drawers, and wardrobe space.

Seawing is based in Cyprus, and offers two different 7-day eastern Mediterranean cruises that visit the Greek islands and Turkey; the two can be combined to make a 14-day sailing. *Carousel* and *Sunbird* cruise from Mallorca, each on two western Mediterranean itineraries that can be combined. *Sundream* sails from Southampton on 14-day sailings that include the western Mediterranean, Scandinavia and Russia, and the North Cape. Fares for 7-day sailings are from $784 for inside cabins ($959 on the *Sunbird*), and from $1,267 for outside cabins.

HEBRIDEAN ISLAND CRUISES

SHIPS IN EUROPE   Hebridean Princess • Hebridean Spirit

Griffin House, Broughton Hall, Skipton, North Yorkshire, BD23 3AN England. © 800/659-2648 or 011 44 1756 704 704. Fax 011 44 1756 704 794. www.hebridean.co.uk.

Hebridean Island Cruises' *Hebridean Princess* and new *Hebridean Spirit* are posh floating country houses for 50 (on the *Princess*) or 79 (on the *Spirit*) mostly British passengers who consider the ships to be their territory. The owners feel the optimal mix is to have two to five North American couples in among the Brits. Anglophilia greatly enhances passengers' enjoyment of these superb small vessels whose crew is also British. The British passengers may include lords and ladies; retired army, navy, and colonial personnel; and the new rich who wish to partake of the genteel atmosphere. Children are not normally aboard, and there are no special facilities for them. Nor is there a pool.

With such a small passenger capacity, fares are very high, with 7-day cruises ranging from $2,100 to more than $12,000 (for suites on some itineraries). Included in the fares are port charges, shore excursions and gratuities, soft drinks and bottled water, and water-sports equipment). But these ships are one-of-a-kind treasures appealing to well-heeled Anglophiles, many of whom come back year after year.

The *Hebridean Princess* operates on mostly 7-day itineraries from Oban, in northwest Scotland, and explores British waters, with the Scottish coast and the Inner and Outer Hebrides the principal destinations. The *Hebridean Spirit* ventures farther afield to Norway, the Baltics, the Western Med, and the Eastern Med, where it again offers mostly 7-day sailings.

A guide accompanies all cruises, and excursions include visits to stately homes and country gardens (some not on the normal tourist run), fishing villages, and remote islands. The season begins in early March and lasts through early November. On some itineraries the ships anchor or tie up at night.

The *Princess* started life as a 600-passenger Scottish ferry before its major conversion, and today the cozy public rooms evoke the feel of comfy country inns, nowhere more so than in the forward observation lounge, with its upholstered armchairs and settees and rustic brick and timber fireplace. Likewise, the *Spirit* has a country-house hotel feel, complete with a fireplace and fine fabrics. Libraries on the ships feature travel books, afternoon tea is served in lounges, and there's even a special lounge for cigar smokers. Passengers relax on open and protected decks on wooden deck chairs.

The restaurants on these vessels are like hotel dining rooms. Passengers have their choice of tables, but singles are seated with fellow singles. Fresh ingredients produce excellent seafood and Scottish specialties, with the fine cuisine including wild game and haggis. Presentation and service are top-notch. At breakfast and lunch, varied buffets and table service are offered. Some evenings are formal, and on warm evenings, passengers gather on deck for champagne receptions with hot hors d'oeuvres. The ships are also outfitted with small gyms, and the vessels carry bicycles, fishing tackle, water-sports equipment, and small boats for passengers' use.

Cabins are individually designed and furnished. The 30 cabins (24 outside) on the *Princess* vary widely, but most show chintz frills above headboards and around windows that open. TVs, minibars, teamakers, irons and ironing boards, trouser presses, hair dryers, dressing tables, and ample stowage are standard throughout.

The better staterooms are as plush as any afloat, some boasting private balconies. The lavish suites and balcony cabins on the *Spirit* even come with Jacuzzi tubs. The ship is not air-conditioned, but this is seldom a problem in these northerly waters. A good number of inside and outside cabins are set aside for singles.

PETER DEILMANN EUROPEAMERICA CRUISES
SHIPS IN EUROPE   Deutschland • Lili Marleen

1800 Diagonal Rd., Ste. 170, Alexandria, VA 22314. ☎ **800/348-8287** or 703/549-1741. Fax 703/549-7924. www.deilmann-cruises.com.

This German line's handsome new flag ship, **Deutschland** (built in 1998; 22,400 GRTs; 505 passengers) carries passengers and crew hailing largely from the German-speaking countries of Germany and Austria, though the line is looking to develop the same kind of North American following for this ocean-going cruise ship that they have for their European riverboat fleet that plies the waters of Germany, Austria, Hungary, France, and Holland (see chapter 9), as well as the 50-passenger luxury sailing yacht **Lili Marleen** (built in 1994; 750 GRTs; 50 passengers), which now operates in the Galápagos year-round. The company's 420-passenger oceangoing cruise ship *Berlin* is not marketed in North America.

Thanks to its marketing efforts, which have included free and low-cost air, transfers, and discounts on pre-arranged shore excursions for American travelers, the line now attracts about 10% to 20% American passengers on any given cruise. And for a sophisticated American who is truly looking for a European ship experience, this is a very nice product. The English spoken by staff at the purser's desk, in cabin service, and in the restaurants, bars, and on deck is as good or even better than on some ships with international crews catering to North American passengers; and communication between Americans and the ship's German-speaking passengers is generally good, as many of the Germans speak English, and some even enjoy putting it to use.

Within, the *Deutschland* is, without qualification, absolutely beautiful, extremely well designed and with a public room layout that suits many different occasions and moods. The decor is richly Edwardian, with Art Nouveau and Art Deco flourishes on the paneling and elevator doors and in the styles of lighting fixtures. For quiet reading, playing games, and having afternoon tea, the Lido Terrace, an observation lounge, provides a light-filled atmosphere with wicker chairs and views outside to the surrounding open decks.

For a drink before meals, the Lili Marleen Salon (dedicated to Marlene Dietrich) is a cozy space with polished paneling and warm lighting. A trio provides music to drink to. The room looks through open colonnades to the port and starboard side galleries and out to sea.

Two lounges have specialized functions with very popular followings at different times of the day. Zum Alten Fritz replicates a dark-paneled tavern with its etched-glass mirrors and button leather curved banquettes, and offers live music, hot snacks such as bratwurst (frankfurters) and weiss wurst (white veal sausage), and beer by the stein. The tiny Adlon Lounge serves as a sophisticated wine and cigar bar and smoking room, though smoking is also permitted in many more locations than is the case on North American ships.

Outside, varnished wooden deck chairs with royal blue cushions are arranged in settings that include open and protected venues forward, aft, high up, around the Lido pool, and along an old-fashioned covered promenade. "Das Traum Schiff" (The Dream Ship), written on the funnel overlooking the Lido, refers to the popular German TV show set on the *Deutschland* and copied in concept from North America's *Love Boat*.

Dining takes place in a two-sitting main restaurant, the Berlin; in the Four Seasons with reservations but no extra charge; and in the Lido Gourmet buffet, which offers indoor and outdoor seating. Menus are continental with German specialties, and the preparation is good to excellent, with the exception being a handful of bland dishes. Some of the more interesting presentations are air-dried beef with fresh horseradish; mild French goat cheese with grapeseed oil and baguette; cream of asparagus with baby shrimp; black noodles with lobster and scallops; grilled lemon sole with lime sauce; Maine lobster; veal loin with morels and dates in a cream sauce; and white chocolate mousse with basil.

Lunchtime buffets offer hot and cold meats, a fair salad variety, lots of cheeses, excellent desserts, and, from the grill, freshly prepared shrimp, lamb chops, rib-eye steaks, and chicken. At breakfast, the menu caters to European and American tastes, but the main criticism here was finding a table with clean place settings, as the system was to reset the tables only after someone was seated. The service in the main dining room, and especially in the Four Seasons, was generally professional but very slow, with dinner sessions ranging from 2½ to 3 hours, making you nearly always late for the 10:15 show times.

For English-speaking passengers, the entertainment is more successful when the program is a singing group and a big band than one that features German-language banter. The Kaisersaal is an extraordinarily opulent cabaret lounge (one of the most stunning at sea) furnished in a 1920s bordello style with comfortable chairs, small table lamps, a huge glass chandelier, and a mezzanine with tables for two set next to the railing.

Of the 286 cabins, 224 are outside (including 17 singles) and 50 inside, and all have white wood-tone paneling, handsomely framed reproduction oil paintings, color TVs, music channels, safes, stocked refrigerators (selections are charged to your account), and good closet, storage, and counter space. Only two suites have verandas.

The *Deutschland* sails in Europe from April to December, before making a transatlantic crossing for a series of South America cruises. Its Europe itineraries include 8- to 12-day Western Med departing from Venice and Barcelona; 11-day Med, departing from Malaga (Spain); 7- and 11-day Norway, departing from Cuxhaven (Germany); 16-day North Cape, departing from Kiel (Germany); 9- to 13-day Baltics, departing from Kiel (Germany); and 14-day British Isles, departing from Cuxhaven (Germany). The ship also does Holy Lands and Canary Islands itineraries.

Fares for an 8-day Western Med cruise are $2,285 to $3,330 inside, $2,975 to $4,395 outside, $5,140 to $7,065 suite.

THOMSON CRUISES
SHIPS IN EUROPE   Emerald • Topaz

Greater London House, Hampstead Road, London NW1 7SD, United Kingdom. Direct bookings © **011 44 870 164 7012.** www.thomson-holidays.com.

Thomson, Britain's largest holiday group, now offers mass-market cruises as an extension of its vast package tour program, particularly aiming at first-time cruisers. Prices are competitive, even allowing for discounts offered by established operators.

On these ships, cruisers should expect to share their holiday with mostly British passengers. Dining is good enough (especially considering the low-end nature of the line), but won't soon be winning any awards. The British-slanted entertainment does not compare with that of American ships. There is a full range of onboard activities, but the main focus is port calls and shore excursions. Families would not feel out of place in this environment.

As Thomson is a tour operator rather than a cruise line, they use chartered vessels. The *Emerald* and *Topaz* are both more than 40 years old and therefore traditional in character. The company also books space and actively sells other ships such as the *Stella Solaris* (part of the Royal Olympic fleet).

The *Emerald* (built in 1958; 26,431 GRTs; 1,198 passengers) has two restaurants, five bars, and two lounges. There are also a discotheque, casino, swimming pool, two whirlpools, beauty salon, boutiques, children's playroom, fitness center, sauna, library, and card area in the Starlight Lounge. The ship has 10 decks, and cabins come in six grades from single inside to premier.

Topaz (built in 1956; 31,482 GRTs; 1,050 passengers) has five grades of cabins ranging from two-berth inside up to superior outside. In many, the sink is in the bedroom. There are three restaurants, four bars, two lounges, a discotheque, a swimming pool, a whirlpool, a hairdresser and massage parlor, a shopping arcade, a teen area, a children's playroom, a gymnasium, and laundry facilities at an extra charge. There are seven decks in all.

Topaz sails mostly 7-day western Mediterranean itineraries from Mallorca that include ports in the French and Italian Rivieras, and 7-day Western Med sailings that include port calls in Tunisia, Italy, France (Corsica), and Spain. The *Emerald* offers the same.

7

The Ultra-Luxury Lines

These cruise lines are the top shelf, the best (and most expensive) of the best, catering to discerning travelers who want to be pampered with fine gourmet cuisine and wines and ensconced in spacious suites with marble bathrooms, down pillows, sitting areas, and walk-in closets. Caviar is served on silver trays and chilled champagne in crystal glasses. Elegant dining rooms are dressed in the finest linens, stemware, and china, and guests dress in tuxedos and sparkling dresses and gowns on formal nights and suits and ties on informal nights. (An exception to this is Windstar Cruises, which offers a much more casual kind of luxury and a more laid-back decor. Radisson Seven Seas also tends toward the casual, but not to Windstar's degree.)

Exquisite French, Italian, and Asian cuisine on these ships rivals that of the best shoreside restaurants and is served in high style by doting, gracious waiters. A full dinner can even be served to you in your cabin, if you like.

Entertainment and organized activities are more limited as guests tend to amuse themselves, and enjoy cocktails and conversation in a piano bar more than they would flamboyant Vegas-style shows.

Ship capacity ranges from just a few hundred passengers to nearly 2000 (on the *QE2*). All are big on service, with almost as many staff as passengers. You're not likely to feel lost in the crowd, and staff will get to know your likes and dislikes early on. The onboard atmosphere is much like that of a private club, with guests trading traveling tales and meeting for cocktails or dinner.

Although the high-end lines are discounting more than ever, they still can cost twice as much as your typical mainstream cruise. Besides early-booking discounts, many high-end lines give discounts to repeat cruisers and those booking back-to-back cruises, and sometimes offer two-for-one deals and free airfare. Many extras are often included in the cruise fares (see chart below).

Most people attracted to these types of cruises are sophisticated, wealthy, relatively social, and used to the finer things in life. While most are well traveled, they've most likely not done overly adventurous or exotic traveling, sticking instead to the five-star kind.

These ships are not geared to children except for the *Crystal Symphony* and *QE2*, which do have children's play centers. Every so often kids show up on the other ships, and babysitting can sometimes be arranged privately with an off-duty crew member.

DRESS CODES   On Seabourn, Silversea, Cunard, and Crystal, bring the tux and the gown—guests dress for dinner on the two or three formal nights on these cruises. Informal nights generally call for suits and ties for men and fancy dresses or pantsuits for ladies. Sports jackets for men and casual dresses or pantsuits for women are the norm on casual nights. Windstar espouses a "no jackets required" policy during the entire cruise, so men, bring nothing but dress slacks, chinos, and nice collared shirts (short or long sleeves); women, leave the pantyhose at home—casual dresses and slacks are fine for evenings. Radisson is somewhere in between, so bring the suit and nice dresses, but no need to lug the tux or fancy full-length gown on board if it's not your style.

Cruise Lines Reviewed in This Chapter

- Crystal Cruises
- Cunard Line
- Radisson Seven Seas Cruises
- Seabourn Cruise Line
- Silversea Cruises
- Windstar Cruises

 Freebies for the Ultra-Luxury Set

It's a fact: The ultra-luxury ships treat passengers like royalty. The following is a sampling of what they offer their guests on a complimentary basis (or at least what they've already figured into their cruise rates).

Tips: Radisson, Seabourn, Silversea

All Booze: Seabourn, Silversea, Radisson (*Song of Flower* only)

Wine with Lunch & Dinner: Radisson, Seabourn, Silversea

Free Stocked Minibar: Radisson, Crystal (top suites only), Cunard (top suites only), Seabourn (upon request), Silversea

Unlimited Soda Water/Mineral Water: Radisson, Seabourn, Silversea

Some Shore Excursions: Seabourn, Silversea

Transatlantic Airfare: Seabourn, Silversea, Cunard (one-way with transatlantic cruises)

Water Sports: Radisson, Seabourn, Windstar

1 Crystal Cruises

SHIPS IN EUROPE   **Crystal Symphony**

2049 Century Park E., Ste. 1400, Los Angeles, CA 90067. ℂ **800/446-6620** or 310/785-9300. Fax 310/785-3891. www.crystalcruises.com.

Fine-tuned and fashionable, Crystal's dream ships offer the best of two worlds: pampering service and scrumptious cuisine on ships large enough to offer lots of outdoor deck space, generous fitness facilities, four restaurants, and over half a dozen bars and entertainment venues.

Crystal has the two largest truly upscale ships in the industry. Carrying 960 passengers each, they aren't huge, but they're big enough to offer much more than their high-end peers. You won't feel hemmed in, and you likely won't be twiddling your thumbs. Service is excellent, and the cuisine, which includes Asian offers, is very good and close to par with that of Seabourn, Silversea, and Radisson.

Unlike Seabourn, which tends to be more staid, Crystal's California ethic tends to keep things mingly and chatty. Passengers are social and active, and like dressing for dinner and being seen.

Pros

- **Four restaurants.** Only the megaships offer as many options—and none so sophisticated. There are two alternative restaurants as well as a formal dining room and a casual Lido restaurant. Crystal recently affiliated itself with Valentino, a fabulous Los Angeles restaurant, to create a new menu for Prego, the onboard Italian eatery.
- **Fitness choices.** No need to sit around and simply be pampered all day long if you'd rather get a workout in. There's a nice-size gym, a paddle-tennis court, shuffleboard, Ping-Pong, an uninterrupted jogging circuit, golf-driving nets, and a putting green.
- **Computer learning.** No other ship has such an extensive computer lab, with over 20 computer stations, complimentary training classes during sea days, and e-mail.

Cons

- **Price.** Be prepared to shell out more than $6,000 per person for a 12-night Mediterranean cruise. That's rack rates, of course; early booking and other discounts may knock that down considerably.
- **Formality.** If you're not nuts about dressing up nearly every night, think twice about a Crystal cruise. Some passengers even get gussied up during the day.
- **Rigid dining schedule.** Like most biggish ships, it has two seatings at dinner, locking passengers into 6:30 or 8:30pm appointments in the main dining room.

Compared with other Ultra-Luxury lines, here's how Crystal Cruises rates:

	Poor	Fair	Good	Excellent	Outstanding
Enjoyment Factor					✓
Dining					✓
Activities					✓
Children's Program					✓
Entertainment					✓
Service				✓	
Overall Value					✓

> **Fun Fact** **Crystal Facts**
>
> Cruise Crystal is the North American spin-off of Japan's largest container shipping enterprises, Nippon Yusen Kaisa (NYK). Based in Tokyo, NYK is responsible for hauling large quantities of raw materials and finished goods around the Pacific. Despite its parentage, a passenger aboard Crystal could conceivably spend an entire week at sea and not even be aware that the ship is Japanese owned, built, and funded—but one hint might be the excellent Asian cuisine found on board.

THE FLEET

Crystal's fleet comprises two nearly twin 960-passenger ships. The *Crystal Harmony,* built in 1990, weighs 49,400 tons and cruises in Alaska as well as the Caribbean/Panama Canal, South America, and the South Pacific. (Pressed to choose his favorite ship of any on the seas, Jerry would opt for *Crystal Harmony.*) The *Crystal Symphony* was built in 1995 and is slightly bigger (at 51,044 tons), with a larger atrium and some expanded public rooms. One thing the company did, unfortunately, which prevents Jerry from offering the *Symphony* the same high degree of affection as he does its fleet mate, is to reduce the size of the Palm Court which, on *Crystal Harmony,* he considers to be the prettiest public room afloat. In addition to spending May through November in the Mediterranean and Europe, *Crystal Symphony* does Panama Canal cruises and a world cruise from Los Angeles to London, visiting the South Pacific and Asia.

PASSENGER PROFILE

Few other cruise lines attract as loyal a crop of repeat passengers, many of whom hail from affluent areas of California and most of whom step aboard for a second, third, or fourth cruise with a definite sense of how they want to spend their time on board. There's commonly a small contingent of passengers from Japan, Australia, Europe, and South America who make up about 10% to 15% of the passenger mix. Most passengers are well-heeled couples, stylish but not particularly flamboyant, and over 55. A good number of passengers "step up" to Crystal from lines like Princess and Holland America.

Many Crystal passengers place great emphasis on the social scene before, during, and after mealtimes, and many enjoy dressing up (sometimes way up) for dinner and adorning themselves with the biggest and best diamonds they own. You'll see no shortage of big rocks and gold Rolexes. On formal nights, the majority of men wear tuxes and many women wear floor-length gowns (although your classic black cocktail dress is just fine). Passengers tend to be well traveled, although not particularly adventurous. They're not likely to be candidates for shooting the Colorado River rapids or backpacking in the Himalayas.

The onboard jewelry and clothing boutiques do a brisk business, and it's obvious that women on board have devoted much care and attention to their wardrobes and accessories. Although, as on most ships, dress codes are much more relaxed during the day, after 6pm men are usually dressed as you'd expect conservative Fortune 500 board members would be. On formal nights (at least 3 per 10- or 11-day cruise) virtually every male aboard opts to wear a dinner jacket or tux.

There may be 20 to 40 kids on board summer European sailings, traveling with their parents or grandparents (or both).

DINING

One of Crystal's best features is its diverse and high-quality cuisine. Its themed, reservations-only **alternative restaurants**—known as Jade Garden, a pan-Asian restaurant on the *Symphony* (Kyoto, also Asian, on the *Harmony*), and Prego, an Italian restaurant, on both—are right up there with the best at sea (a $6 service fee is charged at these venues).

Overall, the galleys aboard Crystal's ships feature a light-textured, thoughtful, **California-style cuisine** with selections like roasted duck with apricot-sage stuffing served with a Grand Marnier orange sauce, broiled Black Angus sirloin steak, or seared sea scallops and jumbo shrimp served with a light lobster beurre blanc over a bed of pumpkin risotto. At lunch and dinner in the dining room there's a **low-fat selection,** such as broiled filet of Chilean sea bass served with steamed vegetables (with calories, fat, cholesterol, sodium, carbohydrates, and protein content listed), as well as an **entree salad**—like a mixed grill salad with grilled herb-marinated chicken breast, jumbo shrimp, and filet mignon. **Vegetarian** meals are available. In the Mediterranean, the chef will often feature more seafood and local specialties, like lamb.

In a kind of homage to the California wine industry, Crystal offers one of the most sophisticated inventories of **California wines** on the high seas. Extensive **French wines** are also offered. Prices begin at as little as $18 a bottle, with many selections in the $20 to $60 range, going as high as $800. In the Mediterranean, Crystal usually tries to have more local wines in the inventory.

The main dining room is chic and stylish, with white Doric columns, high-backed chairs, and mirrored ceilings with lotus-flower lighting fixtures. Tables are not too close together, and there are well over 20 tables for two, mostly along the side or near the oceanview windows.

Because of the size of the *Crystal Symphony,* dinner is served in **two seatings.** Lunches and breakfasts, however, are open seating in the dining room and the Lido buffet restaurant. Service by the team of ultra-professional, gracious European male waiters is excellent, and there seem to be more nattily attired staff than passengers. In the main dining room—and to a somewhat lesser degree in the alternative restaurants—table settings are lavish and include fine, heavy crystal and porcelain. Even in the Lido restaurant, waiters are at hand to serve you your salad from the buffet line, prepare your coffee, and then carry your tray to wherever you want to sit.

Themed luncheon buffets—Asian, Mediterranean, or a western barbecue, for instance—are excellent and are generously spread out at lunchtime by the pool and sometimes in the lobby/atrium, where the midnight buffet takes place. No expense or effort is spared to produce elaborate food fests, with heaps of jumbo shrimp, homemade sushi, Greek salads, shish kebabs, and more.

If you don't want to stroll much farther than your deck chair or if you've slept through lunch, between 11am and 6pm daily you can order something from the **Trident Grill** on the Pool Deck and have a seat, in your bathing suit if you so desire, at the counter or head back to your deck chair. The Grill serves beef, chicken, and salmon burgers; pizza; tuna melts; hot dogs; fries; fruit; and a special of the day, like a Caesar salad and chicken wrap.

Yet another place for a snack or a specialty coffee is the Bistro, open from 9:30am to 11:30am for a late continental breakfast and then between 11:30am and 6pm for complimentary grazing at the buffet-style spread of cheeses, cold cuts, fruit, cookies, and pastries. For a few dollars, you can also sip an almond mocha, hazelnut latte, espresso, or fruit shake, or a glass of pinot grigio or a nice merlot.

For **afternoon tea,** there's the ultra-chic Palm Court on Lido Deck (Deck 11). There is, of course, **24-hour room service.** If you've booked one of the suites, your room-service attendant will be a white-gloved butler who will bring you nightly pre-dinner treats like shrimp cocktail and caviar.

ACTIVITIES

While not overwhelming, Crystal offers an interesting selection of activities. Count on several **enrichment lectures** throughout a cruise, such as a professor of European history or geography presenting lectures on the region, or a movie critic talking to guests about Hollywood and movies. Most speakers are not celebrities, but well-known personalities do occasionally show up on Crystal cruises. In the past, some notables have included TV patriarch Walter Cronkite, glitz-meister Judith Krantz, Hollywood gossip enthusiast Bill Harris, NBC news commentator Edwin Newman, biographer David McCullough, and maritime historian Bill Miller.

Crystal also offers its **Wine & Food Festival** program during many of its cruises (23 in 2002, including, on the *Symphony,* a Baltics cruise departing June 1, and three Mediterranean sailings on Aug 13 and 25, and Sept 6), where a respected wine expert conducts two complimentary tastings, and a guest chef from a well-known restaurant conducts a pair of cooking demonstrations for guests and then presents those very entrees at dinner that night. Guests can ask questions of and mingle with the experts.

Dancing lessons are often taught by guest teachers as well, popular when offered. Learn to swing, or do the rumba and merengue. Group lessons are complimentary, and sometimes private lessons can be arranged with the instructors for about $50 per hour per couple.

Crystal is also big on organizing **bridge and paddle-tennis competitions,** game-show–style contests, and trivia games, as well as providing mid-afternoon dance music with the resident dance trio or quartet, serving tea to the accompaniment of a harpist, offering interesting arts and crafts like glass etching, and even presenting guest fashion shows. Commonly, a PGA-accredited golf pro sails, too, conducting complimentary **group golf lessons** several times per cruise (again, private lessons can be arranged for a fee).

Kudos to the line's **Computer University**—it's really something else. Each ship has a well-stocked computer lab with over 20 computer workstations. On cruises with at least 6 days at sea, complimentary classes are offered on topics like a basic introduction to using the computer, understanding the Internet and the Web, and how to buy a computer. Cruises with fewer sea days also offer guests the opportunity to learn about using e-mail. There's no other computer program at sea that's this extensive. On all cruises, e-mail access is readily available, as well, so passengers can send and receive e-mails to a special personal address they're given when they get their cruise documents. All computer use is free of charge, though e-mail carries a fee of $1.25 per minute with a 10-minute minimum, and a $5 set-up fee; or you can alternatively send or receive e-mails via a shipboard account for $3 each, plus a $5 set-up fee.

CHILDREN'S PROGRAM

Crystal is a sophisticated cruise line that focuses its attention on adults. That said, each ship does have a small but bright **children's playroom,** and there may be as many as 20 to 40 kids on board summer European sailings. At times like

Crystal Fleet Itineraries

Ship	Home Ports & Season	Itinerary
Crystal Symphony	10-day **Baltic** from Southampton (May); 12-day **Baltic** from Copenhagen (June and July); 14-day **Scandinavia** from Stockholm (July); 11-day **British Isles** round-trip from Dover (Aug); 12-day **Med 1** from Southampton (England) (Aug); 12/13-day **Med/Adriatic** from Athens, Civitavecchia or Venice (Aug–Oct); 12-day **Med 2** from Civitavecchia (Oct)*	10-day **Baltic:** Port calls include Oslo (Norway), St. Petersburg (Russia), Helsinki (Finland), and Copenhagen (Denmark); 12-day **Baltic:** Ports of call may include Oslo, St. Petersburg, Helsinki, Copenhagen, Warnemunde (Germany), Amsterdam (Netherlands), Stockholm and Helsingborg (Sweden), Kristiansand (Norway), and Dover (England); 14-day **Scandinavia:** Port calls include Oslo, Bergen, Flam, Gutvangen (Norway), Reykjavik (Iceland), and Dublin (Ireland); 11-day **British Isles:** Port calls include Edinburgh, Invergordon and Stornoway (Scotland), Londonderry (Ireland), Douglas (Isle of Man), Dublin and St. Peter Port (Guernsey); 12-day **Med 1:** Port calls include Bordeaux (France), Lisbon (Portugal), Taormina (Sicily), and Athens (Greece); 12/13-day **Med/Adriatic:** Ports of call may include Taormina, Sorrento (Italy), Cagliari (Sardinia), Tunis (Tunisia), Corfu, Thessaloniki (Greece), Dubrovnik (Croatia) and Venice, Bari, Portofino, Elba and Civitavecchia (Italy), Kuşadasi, Istanbul (Turkey). 12-day **Med 2:** Port calls include Sorrento, Valletta (Malta), Taormina, Portofino, Monte Carlo (Monaco), Palma de Mallorca, and Barcelona (Spain)

Also does a Canary Islands itinerary.

this, **counselors** are on hand to supervise activities for several hours in the morning and in the afternoon (on a recent Easter-time cruise, 6 counselors were on board to supervise about 35 kids). **Babysitting** can be arranged privately through the concierge, but Crystal is not shy about pointing out that they do not offer a day-care service and that parents are responsible for well-behaved kids. Generally, though, you'll find few if any kids on board the majority of Crystal cruises.

ENTERTAINMENT

Shows in the horseshoe-shaped, rather plain Galaxy Lounge encompass everything from **classical concertos** by accomplished pianists to **comedy.** A troupe of spangle-covered, lip-synching dancers and a pair of lead singers are likely to do a **Vegas-style performance.** Onboard entertainment is good, but certainly not the high point of the cruise. There sure are lots of options, though.

In addition to the Galaxy show lounge, a second large, attractive lounge is the venue for nightly after-dinner **ballroom style dancing** to a live band. There's also the Starlight **nightclub** that doubles as the **disco** for a few late-night revelers. Nightly, there's a pianist in the dark, paneled, and romantic Avenue Saloon (our favorite room) playing popular show tunes and pop hits from "New York, New York" to "My Funny Valentine" before and after dinner. A few nights per cruise the Avenue Saloon is the venue for **karaoke.** Next door, **cigar smokers** will enjoy the cozy and genteel Connoisseurs Club. A **movie theater** shows first-run movies several times a day, and cabin TVs feature a wonderfully varied and

---

---

full menu of movies each day, listed in the daily schedules under categories such as comedy, classics, arts and documentaries, concerts, and regular first-run movies. It's one of the best TV systems at sea.

Gamblers will have no problem feeling at home in the roomy **casino,** which is supervised directly by Caesar's Palace Casinos at Sea.

SERVICE

The hallmark of a high-end cruise like Crystal is its service, so the line's staff is better-trained and more attentive than that aboard most other cruise lines, and is typically of an international cast: The dining room and restaurant staffs hail from Italy, Portugal, and other European countries, and have trained in the grand restaurants of Europe and North America; the pool attendant who brings you a fresh towel and a glass of lemonade, as well as the bartender mixing your martini, is likely to be Filipino; and the cabin stewardess who tidies your stateroom is likely to be from Scandinavia or some other European country like Hungary. Overall, the dining/bar staff is best, outshining the room stewardesses. Without a doubt, service is a high point of the Crystal cruise experience. Even the staff manning the information and concierge desks in the lobby are endlessly good-natured and very helpful—a rare find, indeed.

We might note the Crystal ships have both a small pool and a hot tub for their crew members (located at the bow of the ship on Deck 5). It pays to keep the crew happy!

In addition to laundry and dry cleaning services, self-serve laundry rooms are available.

Crystal Symphony

The Verdict

This gracious ship is small enough to feel intimate and personal, yet large enough for a whole range of entertainment, dining, and fitness diversions.

Crystal Symphony *(photo: Crystal Cruises)*

Specifications

Size (in tons)	51,044	Officers	Norwegian/Japanese/International
Number of Cabins	480	Crew	545 (International)
Number of Outside Cabins	480	Passenger/Crew Ratio	1.7 to 1
Cabins with Verandas	276	Year Built	1995
Number of Passengers	960	Last Major Refurbishment	N/A

Frommer's Rating (Scale of 1–5)

Cabin Comfort & Amenities	4	Pool, Fitness & Spa Facilities	4
Ship Cleanliness & Maintenance	4	Children's Facilities	3
Public Comfort/Space	5	Decor	4

Plush, streamlined, extravagantly comfortable, and not as overwhelmingly large as the megaships being launched by less glamorous lines, the *Crystal Symphony* competes with the hyper-upscale Seabourn vessels, although Crystal's ships are almost five times as large as Seabourn's, with a broader choice of onboard diversions and distractions.

The hub of this ship is the atrium. Impressive and stylish, and less overwhelming than aboard some of the larger mainstream ships, it's where you'll find the concierge, the information and shore excursion desk, the Crystal Cove lounge, the ship's chic shops, and the site of the much-awaited midnight buffets, which are presented with fanfare every evening.

Cabins & Rates

Cabins	Brochure Rates*	Bathtub	Fridge	Hair Dryer	Sitting Area	TV
Outside	$6,645–$8,520	yes	yes	yes	yes	yes
Suite	$12,170–$22,680	yes	yes	yes	yes	yes

Prices shown are for 12-day cruise.

CABINS   The smallest cabins aboard the *Symphony* are 202 square feet, size large enough to incorporate a sofa, coffee table, and desk. Outside staterooms with verandas measure 246 square feet (including the veranda). Despite their high price tag, the majority of Crystal's cabins are smaller than the smallest aboard any of the Seabourn vessels (its smallest cabins measure 277 sq. ft.). Just over half the accommodations have small verandas, measuring about 6 by 8 feet. While drawer space is adequate, the hanging closets are smaller and tighter than you'd expect on ships of this caliber. Tiled bathrooms have double sinks and are smartly laid out.

Deck 10 holds the ships' spectacular, attractively styled penthouses; the two best measure nearly 1,000 square feet, including balconies. The other two categories are about 491 and 367 square feet, including balconies. All have walk-in closets and Jacuzzi bathtubs, and the penthouse suites and the Crystal Penthouses have bidets.

All of the *Symphony*'s cabins are outside, more than half with verandas; those without have large rectangular windows. The E category cabins on Deck 8 have views obstructed by lifeboats.

Overall, color schemes are pastels—pinks, mints, blues, and beiges—and golden-brown wood tones, and are cheerful, breezy, and light. All cabins have a sitting area; bathtub and shower; TVs broadcasting CNN, ESPN, and other channels; VCR; minibar; hair dryer; and safe.

PUBLIC AREAS   Throughout the ship, you'll notice an intensely cultivated sense of craftsmanship, with marble features and brass, glass, and hardwood paneling mingling with flowers and potted plants (especially palms). Although the Palm Court on the *Symphony* is smaller and configured differently from the one on the *Harmony,* it's nevertheless a strikingly handsome room, with its comfy, inviting chairs and sofas, large windows, and natural greenery. In that classic

California style, the color schemes are light and airy throughout with lots of white and very pastel furniture and walls.

Passenger throughways are wide and easy to navigate. The atrium/lobby area is a miniature, more subdued version of the glittery megaship atria, but still the most dazzling area of the ship.

Designed with curved walls and low, vaulted ceilings, the ship's main dining room is elegant and spacious and done up in light colors. The chunky silverware and heavy crystal glassware twinkle and shine and mirror a sophisticated land-based restaurant.

There are two large entertainment lounges, one for Vegas-style material and another for ballroom dancing to a live band (and disco dancing late at night).

The ship has a hushed, somewhat academically charming library that's outfitted with comfortable, upholstered chairs and a worthy collection of books, periodicals, and videos. There's also a large theater for movies and slide-lectures.

The ship has six-plus bar/entertainment lounges as well as a roaming staff that wanders the public areas throughout the day and much of the night, offering to bring drinks to wherever you happen to be sitting. The dark Avenue Saloon, where polished mahogany, well-maintained leather upholsteries, and a live pianist draw passengers in, is one of the prime before- and after-dinner cocktail spots (and Fran's personal favorite). The adjacent Connoisseurs Club (created in 1999 from a part of the Avenue Saloon) offers a similar ambience for cigar smokers and lovers of fine cognacs.

ALTERNATIVE DINING   The Jade Garden and Prego alternative restaurants are located on the main entertainment deck (think dining as entertainment) and are interesting and colorful spaces. Meals in these venues—Asian and Italian, respectively—require reservations, and a $6 per person service fee is charged.

POOL, FITNESS & SPA FACILITIES   The *Symphony* offers a lot of outdoor activities and spacious areas in which to do them. There are two outdoor swimming pools separated by a bar, ice-cream bar, and sandwich grill, as well as two hot tubs. One of the pools is refreshingly oversized, stretching almost 40 feet across one of the sun decks. The other has a swim-up bar and can be covered with a retractable glass roof. The gym and separate aerobics area are positioned for a view over the sea, and the adjacent Steiner-managed spa and beauty salon are sizable.

There's also a pair of golf driving nets, a putting green, a large paddle-tennis court, and Ping-Pong tables. Runners and walkers, note: Just under four laps equals 1 mile on the broad, uninterrupted teak Promenade Deck.

The ship's generous tiered afterdecks are gorgeous and provide quiet places for an afternoon spent dozing in a deck chair or for quiet repose leaning against the railing and allowing yourself to become entranced by the ship's wake.

2 Cunard Line

SHIPS IN EUROPE   Caronia • Queen Elizabeth 2

6100 Blue Lagoon Dr., Ste. 400, Miami, FL 33126. ℭ **800/728-6273.** Fax 305/463-3010. www.cunard.com.

Cunard may be the last truly traditional line still afloat, and for a true trans-atlantic crossing, there is no competition. The two ships in the fleet are lovingly looked-after treasures from the past.

In business since the mid–18th century and once the dominant British line on the north Atlantic, Cunard has had its ups and downs since the invention of the passenger aircraft, but in the past couple of years it has reemerged with its very classic, very British personality intact.

Interestingly, it may be the line's acquisition by the incredibly American Carnival Corporation (parent of Carnival Cruise Lines) that's responsible for this new focus on Cunard's core strengths. After the purchase, Cunard's fleet was trimmed to its core, leaving two traditional ships, the *Caronia* (formerly called the *Vistafjord*) and the *Queen Elizabeth 2,* the latter the most famous ocean liner in the world today. The atmosphere on board both ships is genteel and as formal as it gets today, and most passengers like it that way. Except on short cruises, or ones that fill up with deeply discounted fares, the passengers enjoy dressing up for dinner, creating an elegant atmosphere that lasts throughout the evening.

Pros

- **Cruising much the way the last well-heeled generation did.** The *QE2* is today the only ship sailing a full slate of transatlantic crossings part of the year while also operating a small cruise schedule (just three Europe/Med cruises this year, for instance).
- **Graceful ocean liner profiles.** This pair turns heads; they're handsome-looking ships, not apartment blocks on a squared-off hull with a blunt bow.
- **Most passengers feel at home aboard ship.** The atmosphere is social because Cunard passengers enjoy life at sea where ports often play a secondary role.

Cons

- **Neither ship is high-tech.** There are no multitiered show lounges.
- **Deck space is limited.** On "fun in the sun" cruises (which both ships do occasionally), the outer decks get crowded at midday.
- **The *QE2* gets mixed reports.** Some passengers who dine in the Mauretania Restaurant—one of five dining rooms on board—find the service uneven and sometimes quite slow.

Compared with other Ultra-Luxury lines, here's how Cunard rates:

	Poor	Fair	Good	Excellent	Outstanding
Enjoyment Factor					✓
Dining				✓	
Activities				✓	
Children's Program				✓	
Entertainment				✓	
Service			✓		
Overall Value				✓	

THE FLEET

The *QE2* makes a few cruises from Southampton, England, in addition to about a score of Atlantic crossings between Europe and New York. The *Caronia's* 2002 schedule is somewhat different from past years in that, rather than operating from Athens on one cruise and Barcelona the next, it will be home ported for all Europe cruises in Southampton for Med, Baltic, Norwegian fjords, and Iceland sailings. The aim, according to Cunard, is to spur interest in the product in the British market, something that management feels will be easier to do with a ship based in England than with one that flits around the Med.

The *Caronia* and *QE2,* while both having a traditional ocean liner look about them, are quite different in size and layout.

The 70,327-ton **QE2** takes up to 1,750 passengers at speeds generally not exceeding 24 knots, though she can make over 30 knots if behind schedule. Built as a semi-two-class liner, she has a wide variety of public rooms tucked around the ship and has undergone many changes to keep her up-to-date.

The 24,492-ton **Caronia,** known as the *Vistafjord* until late 1999, takes only 675 passengers and is elegantly furnished, like a fine British hotel, and is an easy ship on which to spend many sea days.

The powers that be at Carnival Corporation have indicated that they intend to develop the Cunard fleet, first by building the *Queen Mary,* which is on schedule in the Chantiers de L'Atlantique shipyard in St-Nazaire, France, for delivery to Cunard in December 2003. It is proposed that the new ship take over the bulk of the high-revenue transatlantic crossing and cruise the world in the off-season, while the *QE2* would be in Europe in the summer months and then do worldwide cruising the rest of the year.

PASSENGER PROFILE

The *Caronia's* well-heeled passengers have a simple profile that is older and hails from the United States, Britain (where most of the 2002 marketing effort for this ship is to take place), and Germany for the most part, with the German element much higher on Baltic cruises than on other itineraries. *Caronia* guests like traditional service and enjoy dressing up at night.

The *QE2's* mix varies considerably depending on whether you're sailing transatlantic voyages or cruising from England. On the Atlantic, there is still the traditional traveler who is visiting Europe or North America and prefers to go at least one way by sea. There are many repeaters in this group who would never consider taking the ship on a cruise. Especially in the summer months, passengers represent the age spectrum from small children looked after by English nannies to those who crossed the ocean as small children before World War II and are back for another try. On cruises from England, the number of British passengers increases enormously, though Americans are also given incentives to take a transatlantic crossing one way and then take a connecting cruise. As the fares for cruises from England are lower, the atmosphere is less formal and passengers are, for the most part, less well heeled. (Rates are higher on the North Atlantic because the ship has no competition there.)

DINING

Dining is formal on both ships, though formal attire is not requested every night. However, the middle 4 nights of a transatlantic crossing are designated formal and most passengers comply because they like it that way. It certainly makes dining, whether on the Atlantic or a European cruise, more elegant.

On the *QE2* there is a total of **five restaurants** with reserved seating, including three grills—Queens, Princess, and Britannia—and two large dining rooms—Caronia and Mauretania, the latter with two sittings. The 231-seat Queens Grill has its own kitchen, so preparation and presentation are of a higher standard. Passengers here may order items that aren't on the menu, and many do, especially game dishes such as pheasant or guinea fowl or a specially prepared rib roast of beef sliced tableside. Princess and Britannia Grill diners can also order items not appearing on the menu. Some regulars who book the highest cabin categories actually prefer to dine in one of these two grills rather than the larger, top-of-the ship Queens Grill.

Cruise Tip

The *QE2* often offers deep discounts for off-season transatlantic sailings.

The Caronia Restaurant was completely redesigned into an elegant London hotel dining room, and now uses the grand space into which one descends to its best advantage since the ship was completed in 1969. The room benefits from big side windows and some partitioning.

The lowest-priced cabin occupants eat in the Mauretania Restaurant, a very large, low-ceiling room but with attractive etched glass dividers that create more intimate spaces. A two-sitting policy operates here, and the continental menu is the same as for the Caronia Restaurant. Being a quasi-British ship catering mostly to British and American passengers, the menu reflects their tastes and runs from excellent beef and veal dishes, prepared many different ways, to daily changing salads, terrific fancy desserts, and a traditional cheese tray with lots of biscuits from which to choose.

The **casual dining** takes place in a large and somewhat noisy Lido Restaurant, located aft and with a low ceiling. Avoid the peak-hour queues and try finding a table near one of the big side windows or facing aft. In heavy, pitching seas, this room rises and falls, especially all the way aft. The buffet layout is good with separate sections for the salad bar, pizza, dessert, and ice cream (lots of toppings). Coffee and tea are also available at all times. The Lido is open at night, when it is frequented more on a European cruise than on the North Atlantic because the latter attracts a traditional crowd who prefers the main restaurant.

On the *Caronia,* there is one formal, single-seating dining room with highly polished European service that caters to a broader mix of Europeans and North Americans. The continental menu, featuring heavier sauces to accompany the veal and game dishes than aboard the *QE2,* also caters to lighter tastes with salmon, Dover sole, and shellfish dishes. The informal Lido buffet aft is small and can be cramped for seating at lunchtime, with the spillover on a rainy day taking up residence in the adjacent ballroom. The selections are well prepared, but the variety is less because of the tight space. At night, Italian dining is available in the **alternative restaurant,** the festive reservations-recommended 40-seat Tivoli Restaurant (no fee is charged), an intimate space facing aft over the afterdeck and pool. The menu is a set one, and the careful preparation takes place in a separate kitchen.

Vegetarian/spa choices are available on both ships.

ACTIVITIES

On the *QE2* there is no shortage of daytime activities as the ship spends a lot of time at sea, especially when sailing to and from Europe. The *QE2*'s well-received **lecture program** features a wide range of speakers, some well known and others

Cunard Fleet Itineraries

Ship	Home Ports & Season	Itinerary
Caronia	All sailings round-trip from Southampton. **18-day Med** (May); **5-day Belgium/ France** (May); **10-day Norwegian Fjords** (June); **25-day Norway** (June); **8-day Med** (June); **9-day Med** (July); **14-day Baltics** (July); **15-day Med** (Aug); **18-day Med** (Aug); **7-day Iberian Peninsula** (Sept); **18-day Med/Adriatic** (Oct); **14-day Med** (Oct)	**18-day Med:** Port calls include Gibraltar, Barcelona, Cadiz (Spain), Messina, Naples, Civitavecchia (Italy), Tunis, (Tunisia), Cartagena (Spain); **5-day Belgium/ France:** Port calls include Antwerp (Belgium), Cherbourg (France), St. Peter Port (Guernsey); **10-day Norwegian Fjords:** Port calls include Zeebrugge (Belgium), Bergen, Gudvangen, Flam, Olden, Hellesylt, Geiranger, Kristiansand (Norway); **25-day Norway:** Same ports as Norwegian Fjords cruise above plus Rosyth (Scotland), Trondheim, Spitzbergen, Honningsvaag (Norway); **8-day Med:** Port calls include La Coruna, Cadiz, Malaga, Alicante (Spain); **9-day Med:** Cartagena, Malaga, Gibraltar, Cadiz, Lisbon (Portugal), Vigo (Spain); **14-day Baltics:** Port calls include Zeebrugge, Stockholm (Sweden), Helsinki (Finland), St. Petersburg (Russia), Tallinn (Estonia), Warnemunde (Germany), Copenhagen (Denmark), Oslo (Norway); **15-day Med:** Port calls include Vigo, Lisbon, Palma de Mallorca (Spain), Villefranche (France), Livorno, Civitavecchia (Italy), Ajaccio (France), Gibraltar; **18-day Med:** Port calls include Gibraltar, Malaga, Tunis, Heraklion, Rhodes (Greece), Kuşadasi (Turkey), Valletta (Malta), Lisbon; **7-day Iberian Peninsula:** Port calls include La Coruna, Leixoes (Portugal), Bilbao (Spain), St. Peter Port; **18-day Med/Adriatic:** Port calls include Cadiz, Valletta, Venice, Messina (Italy), Dubrovnik (Croatia), Palma de Mallorca, Gibraltar; **14-day Med:** Port calls include Gibraltar, Barcelona, Cannes (France), Civitavecchia, Livorno, Mahon (Spain), Cadiz
Queen Elizabeth 2	Between Southampton and New York (Apr–Dec); Europe cruises round-trip from Southampton: **15-day Med** (May) and **12-day Norway** (July)	**6-day transatlantic crossings:** Sail between New York and Southampton; **15-day Med:** Port calls include Vigo, Lisbon, Palma de Mallorca, Ajaccio, Livorno, Marseille (France), Barcelona, Malaga, Gibraltar; **12-day Norway:** Port calls include Skarsvaag, Hammerfest, Tromso, Trondheim, Aalesund, Geiranger, Bergen (Norway)

just very good at what they do, on diverse topics such as an author's latest book (later made available for purchase and signing at the library); producing a movie; investing in the stock market; foreign affairs; and ocean liner history. The **Computer Learning Center** is terrific; classes are held regularly, and the facilities are available to all at other times. A staff member takes passengers on the ship's **Heritage Trail,** displaying Cunard's 160-year history in original oil paintings, trophies, and collected memorabilia, including a mesmerizing photo display of the famous passengers who have crossed on Cunard ships. Outdoors, there are a putting green, a golf range, basketball, paddle tennis, deck tennis, shuffleboard, and both indoor and outdoor pools.

On the *Caronia,* there are fewer activities because of the ship's size, but it still carries on the tradition of a good **enrichment program,** especially focusing on the destinations and cooking demonstrations by the chefs. The card room is popular for bridge players and for board games, and a proper cinema screens films.

Web junkies can hook up to the Internet on either ship for 95¢ a minute.

CHILDREN'S PROGRAMS

The structure of the *QE2*'s programs will depend on how many children are booked. For the young ones, there's a large children's room-cum-nursery with tiny furniture, staffed throughout the day. It's located high up, out of the way and near the pet kennels. Young children may choose from a kid's menu and have an early supper. The *QE2* has a private room for teenagers called Club 2000, with video games, Foosball, and board games. Most children from the U.S. will be aboard on the summer transatlantic trips.

The *Caronia* sees very few children and has no special programs.

ENTERTAINMENT

Compared to the newest large cruise ships, Cunard does not offer lavish shows as there simply is not the room to stage them. The *Caronia* has a ballroom with only a slightly raised stage and the *QE2* uses the Grand Lounge, which has a slightly better setup for shows. Hence the evening entertainment is **cabaret acts** such as singers, dancers, illusionists, and the like. However, both ships do offer ballroom dancing and provide dance lessons and male hosts. On the *QE2,* dancing takes place every night in the Queens Room to a large band, and on the *Caronia* on selected nights and before the after-dinner cabarets. In addition, the *Caronia* offers high-quality **after-dinner concerts** in the Garden Lounge. The *QE2*'s Golden Lion Pub and Yacht Club each have bands, and a pianist plays the old *Queen Mary*'s grand piano alternating with a harpist. The *QE2* has a large **cinema** with balcony; the *Caronia*'s is smaller, and on one level.

SERVICE

Cunard offers **24-hour cabin service,** but sometimes you need to ask if you want a particular service (morning tea, ice at 6, leaving the curtains open at night so you can see the dawn, etc.), after which it's willingly performed. The dining staff may be a little harried in the two-sitting Mauretania Restaurant, but excellent otherwise (though staff turnover may turn up a raw steward on occasion). The bad old days of inconsistent service are gone forever, hopefully, and the staff is friendlier and more willing than ever before. Both ships have laundry facilities and offer dry cleaning and pressing service.

Caronia

The Verdict

The *Caronia* provides a traditional, sophisticated, mid-size ship experience, a rarity on the high seas today.

Caronia *(photo: Cunard)*

Specifications

Size (in tons)	24,492	Officers	British
Number of Cabins	372	Crew (mostly European)	379
Number of Outside Cabins	333	Passenger/Crew Ratio	1.7 to 1
Cabins with Verandas	25	Year Built	1973
Number of Passengers	668	Last Major Refurbishment	1999

Frommer's Ratings (Scale of 1–5)

Cabin Comfort & Amenities	4	Pool, Fitness & Spa Facilities	3
Ship Cleanliness & Maintenance	4	Children's Facilities	N/A
Public Comfort/Space	4	Decor	4

The *Caronia* came on the scene just as the transatlantic trade was drying up, and while she resembled her earlier sister *Sagafjord* (now *Sage Rose*), the *Caronia,* then called *Vistafjord,* never made regular Atlantic crossings. However, she is one of the last surviving ocean liner–style ships, with unmatched traditional elegance and grace. Her recent refit is wonderful news, ensuring that she will be around for some years to come, offering the high-end market spacious European-style cruising.

Cabin & Rates

Cabins	Brochure Rates*	Bathtub	Fridge	Hair Dryer	Sitting Area	TV
Inside	$3,199–$3,519	some	yes	yes	some	yes
Outside	$3,799–$9,099	some	yes	yes	some	yes
Suite	$17,879–$19,099	yes	yes	yes	yes	yes

*Rates based on 10-day cruise.

CABINS Eighty percent of the 372 cabins are outside, and all are designed for longer voyages, with spacious floor plans and plentiful stowage. The detailed cabin plans are well worth studying because of the intriguing variety of arrangements. All cabins have light wood accents, TVs with VCRs, two music channels, phones, safes, minibars, robes, fresh fruit daily, and bottles of sparkling wine upon embarkation. Many cabins on Promenade Deck overlook the open side deck, but some views are obstructed by lifeboats. Some cabins in the top categories have verandas, and two Hollywood-style duplex suites are among the nautical world's best, featuring glass-enclosed lounges with treadmills and indoor-outdoor hot tubs on upper levels and bedrooms with hot tubs below.

PUBLIC AREAS *Caronia's* public rooms are paragons of understated British hotel elegance, from the forward circular Garden Lounge for afternoon tea and concerts to the spacious ballroom for shows and dancing. Gentleman hosts provide company on the dance floor for ladies traveling alone. Side galleries provide intimate spaces for a newly refitted bar (now a British-style pub), card room, mahogany-paneled library, and casino. The elegant dining room serves some of the best food afloat at one unhurried sitting. Passengers dress accordingly. Buffets are set up in the cafe and by the pool, and it's a bit cramped here on a fine day. Amidships is a cinema for first-run films and special-interest lectures, and the aft-facing nightclub doubles as a daytime retreat for readers, who revel in the views over the Veranda Deck pool.

ALTERNATIVE DINING Tivoli, a 40-seat restaurant with an all-Italian menu and wine list, is open for dinner on a reservations-recommended basis. It's popular, so book early.

POOL, FITNESS & SPA FACILITIES There is an outdoor pool aft and a second pool that lies deep within the hull in a complex that includes a gym and spa with aerobics, bikes, rowing machines, Stairmasters, sauna, steam bath, thalassotherapy, and massage facility. There is a wraparound deck for jogging and walking.

Queen Elizabeth 2

The Verdict

For the past 2 decades, the *QE2* has been the only game in town for a traditional transatlantic crossing, and she seems to get better doing it with each passing year.

Queen Elizabeth 2 *(photo: Cunard)*

Specifications

Size (in tons)	70,327	Officers	British
Number of Cabins	921	Crew	1,000 (International)
Number of Outside Cabins	625	Passenger/Crew Ratio	1.79 to 1
Cabins with Verandas	33	Year Built	1969
Number of Passengers	1,791	Last Major Refurbishment	1999

Frommer's Ratings (Scale of 1–5)

Cabin Comfort & Amenities	3	Pool, Fitness & Spa Facilities	4
Ship Cleanliness & Maintenance	3	Children's Facilities	3
Public Comfort/Space	4	Decor	4

The *Queen Elizabeth 2* is an unusual dual-purpose ship that makes both transatlantic crossings and cruises and has kept this balance for the last 3 decades. Since her re-engining and major subsequent refits she has simply become better and better in food, service, decor, and amenities. No ship has had a greater capital investment (Cunard claims to have spent $675 million on refits and refurbishment throughout the years) and it shows.

Cabins & Rates

Cabins	Brochure Rates*	Bathtub	Fridge	Hair Dryer	Sitting Area	TV
Inside	$2,249–$2,559	no	no	no	no	yes
Outside	$2,939–$13,619	some	some	some	some	yes
Suite	$18,119–$29,369	yes	yes	yes	yes	yes

Rates for 6-day transatlantic crossing, including one-way airfare.

CABINS   Being an older ship originally designed for two classes, the *QE2* has a huge range of cabin accommodations, and even layout and decorative variations within a single category. The high-up veranda cabins were added to the ship over the years, and they are located in a separate penthouse location, effectively cut off from the rest of the ship. The amidships One and Two Deck Q3 Grades were the top accommodations when the ship was new, and they remain the preferred choice for traditionalists who want an authentic steamship cabin. They have wood paneling, satin-padded walls, a large elliptical window or three elliptical portholes, walk-in closets-cum-dressing-rooms, a corner for a standing steamer trunk, and a large marble bathroom with full-size tub and bidet. On a rough North Atlantic crossing, these well-situated, middle-of-the-ship cabins are preferred by those in the know.

The mid-priced Princess and Caronia Grade rooms are also roomy for this level, while the lowest-priced are deep in the ship and relatively tight, with many inside, including some with upper and lower berths. However, they provide moderately priced accommodations for those who could otherwise not afford the ship. During rough weather conditions, the portholes on Five Deck may be sealed by metal covers called deadlights.

PUBLIC AREAS   Nearly all the public rooms range over two complete decks (Upper and Quarter Decks) and offer a great variety of venues for socializing, reading, and special functions. Every public room has been redone several times over the years, and today the decor is both traditional and up-to-date. The Queens Room, with its tapered white columns, comes alive at a formal afternoon tea with music and again after dinner for ballroom dancing with several gentlemen hosts at the ready. The most attractive bar lounge is the Chart Room, a two-section space with a cozy interior, seats next to the starboard side windows parallel to the path of the indoor promenaders, and a pianist or harpist in attendance.

Passengers dining in the three grill rooms have exclusive access to the Queens Grill Lounge high on the Boat Deck for reading, tea, or drinks. In the afternoon and evening, the Golden Lion Pub attracts the beer set, who come for the small-band sounds, while the Yacht Club is the late-night venue where the officers and staff mingle with passengers. The theater, a two-level room with a balcony, offers films and special-interest talks. The oft-bustling library is a two-room complex with two professional librarians, 7,000 books, and ocean liner books, videos, and memorabilia for sale.

ALERTNATIVE DINING   None.

POOL, FITNESS & SPA FACILITIES   Steiner runs the spa and fitness facilities. While they're complete in the range of offerings, they lie deep down in the hull, with the spa on Six Deck and the gymnasium and indoor pool on Seven Deck. The Spa offers a 10-station AquaSpa and treatment rooms, sauna, and massage. The gym positioned alongside the glassed-in pool has the typical range of treadmills, cycles, and machines, plus classes and daily forced-march hikes on deck. The outdoor pool is One Deck aft.

3 Radisson Seven Seas Cruises

SHIPS IN EUROPE Radisson Diamond • Seven Seas Mariner • Song of Flower

600 Corporate Dr., Ste. 410, Fort Lauderdale, FL 33334. ℭ **800/333-3333** or 954/776-6123. Fax 954/722-6763. www.rssc.com.

Radisson Seven Seas Cruises offers one of the most sophisticated, nearly all-inclusive cruising styles afloat, and the line takes its destinations seriously, offering a strong enrichment program.

Cruising European waters with Radisson Seven Seas is sea travel at its best, a culturally rich experience shared with a couple hundred rather than a couple thousand fellow passengers. While the 354-passenger *Radisson Diamond,* 700-passenger *Seven Seas Mariner,* and 180-passenger *Song of Flower* are quite different types of ships, they all provide many inclusive features in the overall cruise price, reducing the number of nagging extra charges at the end of the cruise. The ships offer a wide variety of port-intensive itineraries in northern Europe and the Mediterranean.

Pros
- **A nearly all-inclusive price.** Rates include gratuities, complimentary wines with dinner, complimentary soft drinks, and a stocked minibar. Rates for the *Song of Flower* also include drinks at the bar.
- **No crowds aboard.** With just 180 passengers aboard the *Song of Flower* and 354 aboard the roomy *Radisson Diamond,* it's a low-key, relaxed cruising atmosphere. The *Mariner* is bigger but crowds are never a problem.
- **Terrific menus and alternative dining.** All the ships pride themselves on fine dining that reflects the regions through which they are traveling. They offer single-seating dining, as well as reservations-only alternative dining (an impressive two reservations-only alternative restaurants on the *Mariner*).

Cons
- **Awkward public rooms on the *Radisson Diamond.*** The piano bar lacks windows, and the show lounge has poor sight lines beyond the first couple of rows.
- **The *Song of Flower* has a noisy afterdeck.** The aft engine uptakes are irritatingly noisy when you're seated between them at the outdoor buffet tables on the Sun Deck.
- **Slow nightlife.** People on these cruises tend to go to bed right after the shows. Don't look for much late-night action.

Compared with other Ultra-Luxury lines, here's how Radisson rates:

	Poor	Fair	Good	Excellent	Outstanding
Enjoyment Factor					✓
Dining					✓
Activities					✓
Children's Program	N/A				
Entertainment			✓		
Service				✓	
Overall Value				✓	

THE FLEET

Each Radisson ship is different in design, which is confusing to some prospective passengers, but the overall experience maintains much in common. The 354-passenger **Radisson Diamond** is a futuristic, one-of-a-kind twin-hulled ship (like a huge catamaran) that's stable and especially roomy. It was originally designed for the incentive and conference markets; hence, the public rooms have a hotel feel and lack communion with the sea. The 180-passenger **Song of Flower** has always been best known for its terrific value rather than high level of luxury, and for the well-run onboard operation that takes passengers to exotic and out-of-the-way destinations. Its small size results in a country-club-style atmosphere. Both ships have a loyal following, and the varied itineraries give passengers an incentive to come back. The 700-passenger **Seven Seas Mariner** is decisively bigger and more resort-like, and is the first ship to offer all-suite, all-balconied cabins.

The 184-passenger *Hanseatic* is chartered for a couple of cruises to Antarctica, where it's the most luxurious ship in the market. The 320-passenger *Paul Gauguin* is based year-round in the South Pacific, and the 490-passenger *Seven Seas Navigator* is spending the summer in Alaska.

PASSENGER PROFILE

Radisson passengers are usually a well-traveled lot with high incomes, some still working and some retired. The *Radisson Diamond* and *Mariner* get a more status-seeking clientele because of the luxurious accommodations and outstanding dining experience, with passengers tending to be 45 and up. The European itineraries are a big draw, but the ship's loyal following will follow her elsewhere to less culturally rich destinations. The *Song of Flower,* a step down in luxurious accommodations, attracts older (think gray-haired crowd) passengers who are the antithesis of status seekers. For the most part they like the ship's small size, the intimate feel of a seagoing club with no pretensions, and its serious destinations, be they in Europe or elsewhere. Most passengers hail from North America, though there are likely to be some Europeans and Australians aboard. The line has been trying to make this ship's itineraries more soft adventure, which should mean a younger crowd in the future.

DINING

The line prides itself on having some of the best food afloat and ever-changing menus. The *Radisson Diamond*'s dining room is one of the best settings for lunch or dinner on the high seas, and the Italian headwaiters run a very good show. Passengers in a romantic mood can usually obtain a table for two, and may also have full-service meals served in their suite or on the balcony. Meals in the *Mariner*'s Compass Rose are far above the norm, featuring Black Angus beef, lobster, and such unusual treats as ostrich, all creatively served on fine china in a nouvelle cuisine fashion (the portions are small, but there are enough courses that you won't leave hungry). The *Song of Flower*'s cuisine may not be so lavishly presented but it is fine nonetheless, with great attention to selections that reflect where the ship is cruising. **Vegetarian** and **light selections** are available. All the ships also offer wonderful **breakfast and lunchtime buffets** for those who don't want to have these meals in the formal dining room. The *Mariner* also offers the casual dinner option in the Lido dining area, La Veranda, by converting part of the space at night into a bistro featuring a waiter-served Mediterranean menu and an antipasto buffet. An alternative, reservations-only **Italian restaurant** is housed in a private room on the *Song of Flower* and in the Grill (part of the

Radisson Seven Seas Fleet Itineraries

Ship	Home Ports & Season	Itinerary
Radisson Diamond	7-day W. Med, roundtrip from Civitavecchia/Rome, Civitavecchia to Nice, Nice to Venice, Venice to Civitavecchia/Rome, and the reverse (Aug–Oct)	7-day W. Med: port calls may include Capri, Porto Cervo, Taormina, Livorno, Syracuse, Sorrento, and Portofino (Italy), Valletta (Malta), Dubrovnik and Split (Croatia), Nice and Cannes (France), and Monte Carlo (Monaco)
Seven Seas Mariner	7- and 11-day W. Med, Barcelona to Civitavecchia/Rome, Venice to Civitavecchia/ Rome (and the reverse), Monte Carlo to Civitavecchia/Rome (and reverse), Le Havre to Nice (May–June, Sept and Oct); 11-day E. Med, Monte Carlo to Venice (Oct); 11-day Baltics, Stockholm to Dover; 7-day W. Med/ Casablanca, Civitavecchia/Rome to Lisbon (June); 7-day Spain/France, Lisbon (Portugal) to Southampton (England) (June); 11-day British Isles, Southampton (England) to Hamburg (Germany) (June); 11-day Norway, Hamburg to Kiel (Germany) (July); 7- and 8-day Baltics, Kiel (Germany) to Copenhagen (Denmark), Copenhagen to Stockholm (Sweden) and the reverse (July– Aug); 11-day Baltics, Stockholm (Sweden) to Rouen (France) (Aug)	7- and 11-day W. Med: Port calls may include St. Malo, Nice, Marseille. St-Tropez, Sete, Bordeaux (France), Bilbao, Cadiz, Malaga, Barcelona (Spain), Lisbon (Portugal), Monte Carlo (Monaco), Portofino, Livorno, Taormina, Sorrento (Italy), Corfu (Greece), Valletta (Malta), Dubrovnik (Croatia); 11-day E. Med: Port calls include Monte Carlo (Monaco), Civitavecchia/Rome, Sorrento, Taormina (Italy), Rhodes, Piraseus/Athens, and Corfu (Greece), Kuşadasi (Turkey), Dubrovnik (Croatia); 7-day W. Med/Casablanca: Port calls include Monte Carlo (Monaco), St-Tropez (France), Barcelona and Malaga (Spain), and Casablanca (Morocco); 7-day Spain/ France: Port calls include Vigo (Spain), Bordeaux and St-Malo (France); 11-day British Isles: Port calls include Waterford and Dublin (Ireland), Holyhead (Wales), Glasgow, Edinburgh, Stornoway, Kirkwall, Invergordon (Scotland); 11-day Norway: Port calls include Bergen, Hammerfest, Honningsvag, Tromso, Svolvaer, Hellesylt, and Geiranger (Norway); 7- to 11-day Baltics: Port calls may include Visby and Stockholm (Sweden), Tallinn (Estonia), St. Petersburg (Russia), Helsinki (Finland)

indoor/outdoor buffet complex) on the *Radisson Diamond*. There is no cover charge, and on the *Diamond* you get the added bonus of waiters who sing. The *Mariner* offers two reservations-only dining venues, one French (with cuisine overseen by chefs from Le Cordon Bleu) and the other offering a creative menu with a slight Asian influence. And there is no cover charge at either.

Wines are complimentary at lunch and dinner and include choices that even wine connoisseurs will find impressive.

Radisson Seven Seas Fleet Itineraries *(continued)*

Ship	Home Ports & Season	Itinerary
Song of Flower	7- and 8-day W. Med, Civitavecchia/Rome to Monte Carlo (and the reverse) and Monte Carlo to Lisbon (and the reverse (May and Sept); **9-day W. Europe,** Lisbon (Portugal) to Rouen (France) (June), and London to Lisbon (Sept); **9-day British Isles,** Edinburgh to London (Sept); **11-day Baltics,** Rouen (France) to Stockholm (July); **7- and 9-day Baltics,** Stockholm (Sweden) to Hamburg (Germany), and reverse, and Stockholm to Copenhagen (Denmark) (July–Aug); **9-day Norway,** Copenhagen to Edinburgh (Aug)	**7- and 8-day W. Med:** Port calls may include Nice, Marseilles, Sete, and St-Tropez (France), Livorno and Portofino (Italy), Malaga and Barcelona (Spain); **9-day W. Europe:** Port calls include Vigo, La Coruna, Santander, and Bilbao (Spain), St-Malo, Honfleur, and Bordeaux (France), Guernsey and Sark (U.K.); **9-day British Isles:** Port calls include Kirkwall, Tobermory, and Iona (Scotland), Holyhead (Wales), Dublin (Ireland), Fowey (England), and St-Malo and Cherbourg (France); **7- to 9-day Baltics:** Port calls may include Zeebrugge (Belgium), Rostock (Germany), Copenhagen (Denmark), Tallinn (Estonia), St. Petersburg (Russia), Helsinki (Finland), Riga (Latvia), Gdynia (Poland), and Visby (Sweden); **9-day Norway:** Port calls include Oslo, Flam, Gudvangen, Olden, Kristiansand, Molde, and Bergen (Norway)

*Seven Seas Mariner *also does a Black Sea itinerary.*

ACTIVITIES

These ships are fairly low-key in this area, with the emphasis on the destinations. But that's not to say there's not plenty to do on board for those who want it. The **cultural enrichment lectures** are a big draw and include experts in the fields of European art, culture, wine and food, history, and current affairs. **Bridge instructors** offer instruction and lectures. There are shuffleboard and Ping-Pong tournaments, golf-putting competitions, an occasional guest chef offering a cooking demonstration or wine tasting, art auctions, computer classes, and even instruction in the fine art of pom-pom making. The ships have outdoor pools, casinos, and a good selection of free videos to take to the cabin. The *Radisson Diamond*'s spa is far more impressive than the one aboard the *Song of Flower,* and the *Mariner*'s is far more impressive than the *Radisson Diamond*'s. The spas on *Diamond* and *Song of Flower* are operated by ubiquitous Steiner, while that on the *Mariner* is operated by aromatherapy guru Judith Jackson and offers an interesting array of treatments. The *Song of Flower* has an open-bridge policy during daylight hours, a popular pastime when at sea. You can send and receive e-mails on all ships for roughly $1 a message.

CHILDREN'S PROGRAMS

None of these ships has special facilities for children, and you should only consider bringing children who enjoy adult company aboard.

ENTERTAINMENT

Entertainment is Broadway-style productions (more cabaret-style on the *Song of Flower*), and the ships carry pianists who play during afternoon tea and at the cocktail hour. Guest performers are featured on each cruise (on one *Mariner* sailing we were on, there were members of the Florida Philharmonic), and may include a comedian. A five-piece orchestra provides accompaniment for dancing. Only a few passengers stay up to the wee hours on these port-intensive cruises, although the *Mariner* and *Diamond* have spaces that function as late-night discos (they tend to attract more crew than passengers). Gentlemen hosts are on board the *Mariner* to dance with single ladies.

SERVICE

The personnel is primarily European, with some Filipinos, and all the ships are very service oriented. Room service is popular on all the vessels, and you can order a full meal from the dining room menu served course by course (if you book a veranda cabin you can even eat outside). Tips are included in the cruise fare. There are laundry and dry cleaning services on all the vessels, but no self-service facilities.

Radisson Diamond

The Verdict

A great ship for touring Europe in luxury and privacy, with low passenger capacity and a terrific enrichment program.

Radisson Diamond *(photo: Radisson Seven Seas)*

Specifications

Size (in tons)	20,295	Officers	Scandinavian
Number of Cabins	177	Crew	200 (European)
Number of Outside Cabins	177	Passenger/Crew Ratio	1.77 to 1
Cabins with Verandas	123	Year Built	1992
Number of Passengers	354	Last Major Refurbishment	1998

Frommer's Ratings (Scale of 1–5)

Cabin Comfort & Amenities	5	Pool, Fitness & Spa Facilities	4
Ship Cleanliness & Maintenance	4	Children's Facilities	N/A
Public Comfort/Space	3	Decor	3

The *Radisson Diamond* is the most unusual-looking cruise ship afloat, and by far the world's largest catamaran with overnight accommodations. Her cabins are roomy and meant for spending a quiet afternoon, and her dining, whether at the buffet or in one of the loveliest dining rooms afloat, is tops. However, her public rooms are an odd hotel design and lack connection to the sea.

Cabins & Rates

Cabins	Brochure Rates*	Bathtub	Fridge	Hair Dryer	Sitting Area	TV
Outside	$3,595–$4,495	yes	yes	yes	yes	yes
Suite	$7,395	yes	yes	yes	yes	yes

Rates include gratuities, wine with dinner, soft drinks, and in-room bar setup.

CABINS   Most staterooms have picture windows, spacious teak balconies, and solid partitions for privacy. Spacious sitting areas, TVs, VCRs, phones, stocked refrigerators, four complimentary bottles of liquor, safes, only adequate storage, queen beds, hair dryers, and combination shower baths are common to all.

PUBLIC AREAS   Entry is through the impressive Deck 6 lobby, replete with mirrors, walls of bird's-eye maple, and lovely rose-patterned carpeting. A circular staircase and two glass elevators rise through the five-story atrium. The sleek tri-level lounge on Deck 8 offers dancing and shows, but sight lines are good only from the first couple of rows, and the windowless piano bar draws few patrons at cocktail hour. The small casino contains three blackjack tables, one Caribbean stud poker table, one roulette wheel, and a sweep of slot machines. For conferences and incentive groups, there are meeting rooms, a business center, secretarial services, and computer hookups. The library has plenty of current books and videos. The stunning main dining room seats 230 with great views in three directions.

ALTERNATIVE DINING   Don Vito's Italian Trattoria is created every evening in The Grill (the same space used for breakfast and luncheon buffets), and features a set tasting menu and singing waiters. Reservations are required, but there is no cover charge.

POOL, FITNESS & SPA FACILITIES   The spa on Deck 11 offers facials, massages, herbal wraps, saunas, steam rooms, a full-service beauty salon, and a state-of-the-art fitness center. A jogging track and driving range are also on board. The retractable marina platform astern provides in-port access to water-skiing, jet-skiing, and sailing. Passengers congregate on Deck 10 to sunbathe, read, and chat around the small pool, whirlpool, and bar. The ship boasts more deck space per passenger than any other ship afloat and deck chairs are ample, as is protection from the sun. Waiters serve free soft drinks.

Seven Seas Mariner

The Verdict

There's something nicely democratic about Radisson's newest vessel: All guests get to sleep in suites with balconies. In fact, the spacious ship is the world's first to offer that feature.

Seven Seas Mariner *(photo: Radisson Seven Seas)*

Specifications

Size (in tons)	50,000	Officers	European
Number of Cabins	350	Crew	445 (European/Filipino)
Number of Outside Cabins	350	Passenger/Crew Ratio	.63 to 1
Cabins with Verandas	350	Year Built	2001
Number of Passengers	700	Last Major Refurbishment	N/A

Frommer's Ratings (Scale of 1–5)

Cabin Comfort & Amenities	5	Pool, Fitness & Spa Facilities	4
Ship Cleanliness & Maintenance	5	Children's Facilities	N/A
Public Comfort/Space	5	Decor	4

Some Radisson fans have complained the line has gone too big with the *Mariner*. We happen to like the ship and the extra space it affords. While it carries only 700 passengers, the vessel offers the same amount of space as some other line's ships provide for 1,600 guests, so you'll rarely feel part of a crowd. However, the vessel does at times feel, well, empty, especially after 11pm when the majority of passengers seem to go to bed.

Cabins & Rates

Cabins	Brochure Rates*	Bathtub	Fridge	Hair Dryer	Sitting Area	TV
Suite	$3,395–$15,195	yes	yes	yes	yes	yes

Rates include gratuities, wine with dinner, soft drinks, and in-room bar setup.

CABINS   Every cabin is a suite with ocean views and offers a balcony for enjoying ocean breezes, and a nice sitting area, as well as a walk-in closet. Of course some suites are bigger than others—the biggest are apartment-sized and very pricey. The balconies vary in size too, with those on standard suites big enough for just two chairs, while those on larger suites have room for two lounge chairs as well. In either case, before you step outside in your birthday suit keep in mind not all the balconies are really private (your neighbors may be able to see you). All suites come with a king-size bed or two twins done up with feather pillows and duvets, marble bathrooms with bathtubs, free bottles of liquor and soft drinks, TVs and VCRs, hair dryers, bathrobes, and such. The Category HS suites in the back of the ship offer lots of space and big balconies, and are a good deal for those not bothered by engine noise.

PUBLIC AREAS   The *Mariner*'s decor is low-key and elegant (some may find it a bit bland) with most rooms featuring windows that allow the ocean views to be the main attraction. There is artwork on display (much of it for sale), but not enough to liven things up. The most striking space is the eight-deck atrium, which includes glass elevators, a twisting metal and wood staircase, and a weird mesh sculpture of bodies floating in space that is so low key as to nearly be invisible.

The theater is appropriately plush with cozy seating and tables for drinks. Nicely executed productions are presented here and make good use of the facility. The ship's other lounges, including the Horizon Lounge and Observation Lounge on the top deck, while nice spaces, feel pretty empty at night (the Horizon Lounge is a popular venue for afternoon tea, however), and the disco rarely attracts more than a dozen revelers. A more popular space is the casino, which offers tables for blackjack, roulette, Caribbean stud poker, and craps, and some five dozen slot machines. The ship's cozy cigar bar is replete with fake fireplace and comfy leather chairs, and offers hand-rolled cigars for sale (but it is another space that is often empty). The vessel boasts two card rooms and a big, open library space with books and videos, as well as a popular classroom-style Internet cafe with 15 computers (there are three more in the library) that seem to be in almost constant use. The Compass Rose dining room is a nice space, although a bit awkwardly divided into two long, narrow sections; its success is that nearly everyone gets to dine with an ocean view.

ALTERNATIVE DINING   The *Mariner* boasts two reservations-only alternative dining venues with no cover charge at either. Signatures is a lovely space done up with red velvet and candlelight, with top-notch cuisine overseen by chefs from Le Cordon Bleu in Paris. The changing menu includes such treats as foie gras terrine with leek and truffle vinaigrette and roast breast of quail with turnips in a morel mushroom sauce. Latitudes offers a creative tasting menu in an Asian-influenced, modern setting. Some people choose to eat at these venues more than once, which you are free to do as long as you can get a reservation (make your plans early on in the cruise).

POOL, SPA & FITNESS FACILITIES   The *Mariner's* spa is run by Judith Jackson, and looks a bit medicinal beyond the pretty reception area. If offers treatments that include an 80-minute hydro bath and aromatherapy massage combo, fairly priced at $100. The locker room offers the nice feature of lockers pre-filled with a bathrobe, slippers, towel, and bottle of Evian. The oceanview gym offers about a dozen machines, weights, and an exercise area that fills up rather quickly. The roster of classes includes the unusual shipboard offerings of yoga, Fitball, and kickboxing, along with the more standard Stretch and Step classes. There's a track for joggers, and paddle tennis and golf-driving cages on the upper deck. The Sun Deck boasts a good-size heated swimming pool, three whirlpools, and a vast deck area sheltered with tinted glass.

Song of Flower

The Verdict

An intimate social experience, with a very low passenger capacity, a little luxury, and a great enrichment program.

Song of Flower *(photo: Radisson Seven Seas)*

Specifications

Size (in tons)	8,282	Officers	Scandinavian
Number of Cabins	100	Crew (European/Filipino)	144
Number of Outside Cabins	100	Passenger/Crew Ratio	1.39 to 1
Cabins with Verandas	10	Year Built	1986
Number of Passengers	200	Last Major Refurbishment	1998

Frommer's Ratings (Scale of 1–5)

Cabin Comfort & Amenities	4	Pool, Fitness & Spa Facilities	3
Ship Cleanliness & Maintenance	4	Children's Facilities	N/A
Public Comfort/Space	4	Decor	3

This efficiently run ship exudes the charm and character of a seagoing club full of like-minded travelers who enjoy a relaxed air of exclusivity. The decor is luxurious, with pastels and earth tones dominating the subtle color schemes. With a small passenger complement, the ship does not intrude on small European ports.

Cabins & Rates

Cabins	Brochure Rates*	Bathtub	Fridge	Hair Dryer	Sitting Area	TV
Outside	$2,895–$4,995	some	yes	yes	yes	yes
Suites	$7,195	yes	yes	yes	yes	yes

Rates include gratuities; complimentary bar drinks, wine, and soft drinks; and a stocked refrigerated minibar.

CABINS   Cabins come in six categories, and each supplies a TV, VCR, music channels, minibar, ample stowage, and shower or half-tub. Some cabins on Decks 5 and 6 have views partly blocked by lifeboats, but these rooms are all outside and lie forward, well away from noise. (Generators switching on and off are a problem in a few cabins.) Cabins on Deck 3 have double portholes instead of the windows found in higher categories. Two-room suites have sitting rooms and two bathrooms. Slightly smaller veranda cabins, by far the most popular category, feature sliding doors to private balconies.

PUBLIC ROOMS   Most public rooms are located aft and include the roomy tiered main lounge with a bar at the rear for shows and lectures, and a more intimate nightclub one deck below, adjacent to the casino with blackjack tables and slot machines. The library has over 1,000 books and 450 videos. The forward observation lounge is a delightful retreat for reading, meeting friends, afternoon tea, or taking in the views.

ALTERNATIVE DINING   Angelo's offers a intimate dining experience featuring the flavors of Northern Italy's Piedmont and Tuscany regions. Reservations are required, but there is no cover charge.

POOL, FITNESS & SPA FACILITIES   Deck space is generous and creatively designed for securing a chair in a quiet location. The main outdoor area is framed by twin funnels and is noisy with the ship underway. There is free use of jet skis, sailboards, snorkeling equipment, and inflatable motorboats. The 80-seat launch, *Tiny Flower,* can take passengers to the beach for dry landings. There's an outdoor pool, a sauna, and a fully equipped (though small) health club with upright and recumbent bicycles, stairclimbers, treadmills, free weights, and strength-training machines.

4 Seabourn Cruise Line

SHIPS IN EUROPE   Seabourn Legend • Seabourn Pride

6100 Blue Lagoon Dr., Ste. 400, Miami, FL 33126. ℂ 800/929-9595 or 305/463-3000. Fax 305/463-3010. www.seabourn.com.

Small and intimate, these sleek modern ships are floating pleasure palaces bathing all who enter in doting service and the finest cuisine at sea. They're genuine aristocrats, with perfect manners. Seabourn's small, luxurious ships have unprecedented amounts of onboard space and staff for each passenger, service worthy of the grand hotels of Europe, and the hushed, ever-so-polite ambience that appeals to prosperous, usually older passengers who appreciate the emphasis on their individual pleasures.

Although now owned by industry giant Carnival Corporation, the line maintains strong links with its Norwegian roots, registering each of its ships in Norway and preferring to restock many of its marine supplies there.

Pros

- **Top-shelf service.** Staff seem to know what you need before you ask, and there's more staff per passenger than on most other lines.
- **Excellent cuisine.** Rivaling the best land-based restaurants, cuisine is exquisite with creative, flavorful, well-presented dishes served with an extensive wine list.
- **Large cabins.** Cabins are not mere cabins, but roomy suites, with cushy features like walk-in closets, bathtubs, and complimentary stocked minibars.
- **Free booze.** Liquor and wines are included in the price.
- **A free shore excursion in one port per cruise.** This exclusive Seabourn outing might be a glass-roofed canal boat ride to the Historical Museum in Amsterdam or a visit to a private villa in Malta—always something not to be found in the shore excursion brochures of most lines.

Cons

- **Limited activities.** The Seabourn ships have limited organized activities on board, but what they do offer is good. For the most part, guests are content with socializing over cocktails and catching up on their reading.
- **Shallow drafts, rocky seas.** If you happen to be sailing through rough water, you'll know it. These small ships get tossed around more than the megas.
- **Few or no private verandas.** It's unfortunate that the Seabourn ships have only six private balconies apiece (the line tried to correct the situation by adding narrow French balconies onto 36 cabins on each ship, but it's not the same thing as having your own private outdoor space).

Compared with other Ultra-Luxury lines, here's how Seabourn Cruise Line rates:

	Poor	Fair	Good	Excellent	Outstanding
Enjoyment Factor					✓
Dining					✓
Activities		✓			
Children's Program	N/A				
Entertainment			✓		
Service					✓
Overall Value				✓	

Value **Seabourn Special**

Seabourn is offering free economy class air from 25 North American gateways with its 2002 European cruises. You can upgrade to Business Class at prices starting at $995.

THE FLEET

The Seabourn fleet comprises three globetrotting vessels, two of which will spend time in Europe this year—the *Seabourn Legend* (built in 1992) and the *Seabourn Pride* (built in 1988). The other is the *Seabourn Spirit.* All three weigh 10,000 tons and carry 204 passengers. Seabourn in 2001 sold two additional ships, the sailing yachts *Seabourn Goddess I* and *Seabourn Goddess II,* which it had inherited from Cunard; and transferred the *Seabourn Sun,* a 740-passenger vessel that never fit well into the Seabourn fleet (mostly because of its size), to Holland America.

PASSENGER PROFILE

Most passengers have more than comfortable household incomes, usually in excess of $250,000. Many are retired (or never worked to begin with), and many have net worths in the millions, and sometimes much higher. The majority of passengers are couples, and there is always a handful of singles as well, usually widows or widowers. Some come aboard for family reunions with children or grandchildren in tow.

In many ways, the passenger roster looks like the membership of a posh country club, where old money judges new money. Most passengers are North American, and dress expensively though not, of course, flashily. Many passengers are not excessively chatty, giddy, or outgoing. They are likely to have sailed aboard other luxury cruise lines and stayed in five-star hotels. Passengers expect to receive good service in an atmosphere of discreet gentility.

The line's history of repeaters is among the highest in the industry, sometimes as many as 50% aboard any given cruise.

DINING

Cuisine is one of Seabourn's strongest points, matching what you'd find in a world-class European resort hotel. Fleetwide, meals are offered in the dining rooms in a single seating, and the ships have an open-seating policy, allowing guests to dine whenever they choose and with whomever they want, within a window of several hours at each mealtime.

While tables seat up to 8 or 10, you'll almost never have a problem getting a table for two if that's your wish. Also, tables are spaced far enough apart so you'll never feel crowded.

Dinner service is high style and extremely formal. Men are expected to wear jackets and, on most evenings, neckties as well. Two formal evenings are held during the course of any 1-week cruise. Virtually every male present appears in a tuxedo, and the events are, indeed, very formal. Staff members almost run at a trot through the elaborate, six-course European service. It's all extremely civilized.

Seabourn cuisine is an eclectic mix. The *Legend* and *Pride* feature old favorites such as beef Wellington, Dover sole, and broiled lobster; ethnic dishes reflecting the itinerary of wherever the ship happens to be at the time; and a mixture of light Pacific Rim and California cuisine. Dishes are prepared to order, **spa menus** are available at every meal, and passengers can make virtually any special request they want. Every night features a flaming dessert served in individual portions or such choices as chocolate mousse with fresh berries or coconut crème brûlée. Lunch and dinner include **complimentary wines** from an impressive wine cellar, in fact Seabourn is so proud of its recently updated list of complimentary wine and spirits list it put out a press release on it (the list includes more than 50 quality wines from around the world, and some 75 brands of spirits).

What was already good has become even better. Seabourn's menus are now created under the supervision of Charlie Palmer, a two-time James Beard Award winner, and owner of New York's tony Aureole restaurant (and others).

If your mood doesn't call for the dining room, the ships have an **alternative dining option** at the Veranda Café—at no extra charge, of course. Here they serve bountiful breakfasts every morning, with omelets made fresh to your specifications. At lunchtime, you'll find salads, sandwich makings, fresh pasta, and maybe jumbo shrimp, smoked salmon, and smoked oysters on the cold side and hot sliced roast beef, duck, and ham on the carving board. On these ships, you'll find a **special of the day**—pizza with pineapple topping, chili, or corned beef—will also be available at the Sky Bar overlooking the Lido, for those who don't want to change out of their swimsuits. Dinner is served under the stars on the Lido Deck several evenings a week as well, offering a meal roughly equivalent to whatever's being whipped up in the main dining room. Dinners at the Café require reservations and are romantic candlelight affairs, often based on Italian, French, and seafood themes. In good weather it's a treat to eat at one of the arc of tables located aft overlooking the wake and under a protective canvas awning.

Room service is available 24 hours a day. During normal lunch or dinner hours, your private meal can mirror the dining room service, right down to the silver, crystal, and porcelain. After hours, the menu is more limited, with burgers, salads, sandwiches, and pastas. And whenever a cruise itinerary calls for a full-day stopover on a remote island, a lavish beach barbecue might be whipped up at midday.

ACTIVITIES

These small ships don't offer much in the way of organized activities, and that's what most passengers really love about the line.

You won't find the bingo, karaoke, or poolside contests featured by mass-market lines. The atmosphere is ever tasteful and unobtrusive. Activities include card games and tournaments, trivia contests, tours of the ship's galley, visits to the cozy library, and watching movies in your cabin. You'll soon realize that many passengers are aboard to read, quietly converse with their peers, and be ushered from one stylish spot to the next. As a nice bonus, the line offers complimentary Random Massage Moments, free mini-massages delivered by experienced hands for passengers sitting on deck or by the pool or Jacuzzi.

That said, you don't have to be sedate, either. The *Legend* and *Pride* have **retractable water-sports marinas** that unfold from the ships' sterns, weather and sea conditions permitting, and gracefully usher passengers into the sea for water-skiing, windsurfing, sailing, snorkeling, banana-boat riding, and swimming.

There are few, if any, public announcements to disturb your solitude, which is a relief when compared to the barrage of noise broadcast aboard many other lines.

Seabourn Cruise Line Fleet Itineraries

Ship	Home Ports & Season	Itinerary
Seabourn Legend	7- and 14-day Med, round-trip from Nice or from Nice to Cannes (Apr–Sept)	**7- and 14-day Med:** Ports of call may include Barcelona (Spain), Port Vendres, Cassis, Porquerolles, St-Tropez (France), Sorrento, Capri, Livorno, Porto Cervo, Portofino (Italy)
Seabourn Pride	14-day Med, from Malaga (Spain) (Apr); 14-day Italy/Dalmatian Coast/Greece, from Piraeus (Greece) (May); 7-day Dalmation Coast/ Greece, from Venice (Apr); 14-day W. Europe, from Barcelona (Spain) (May); 7-day W. Europe, from London (May); 14-day Baltics, round-trip from London (June–Aug); 14-day Scandinavia, round-trip from London (June–Aug)	**14-day Med:** Port calls include Cartagena, Alicante, Valencia, Palma de Mallorca (Spain), Nice, Porquerolles, Cannes (France), Monte Carlo (Monaco), Livorno, Civitavecchia (Italy); **14-day Italy/Dalmatian Coast/Greece:** Port calls include Navplion, Santorini, Corfu, and Cephalonia (Greece), Dubrovnik (Croatia), Venice, Taormina, Sorrento, Civitavecchia (Italy); **7-day Dalmation Coast/Greece:** Port calls include Corfu, Galaxidhi, Mykonos, Monemvasia, Piraeus (Greece), Kuşadasi (Turkey). **14-day W. Europe:** Port calls include Palma de Mallorca, Alicante, Malaga, Motril, Vigo (Spain), Lisbon (Portugal), Lorient (France), St. Peter Port (Guernsey), London; **7-day W. Europe:** St. Peter Port, Lorient, Vigo, Lisbon; **14-day Baltics:** Port calls include Hamburg (Germany), Tallinn (Estonia), St. Petersburg (Russia), Stockholm (Sweden); **14-day Scandinavia:** Port calls include Leith (Scotland), Bergen, Gudvangen, Flam, Oslo (Norway), Copenhagen (Denmark), Amsterdam (Netherlands).

On certain cruises there are **guest lecturers,** such as noted chefs, authors, or statesmen, or maybe a wine connoisseur, composer, anthropologist, TV director, or professor, who present lectures and mingle with guests. You can generally count on port lectures from resident travel experts.

Each ship has a small-scale, staid, and rather un-casino-like **casino** with a couple of blackjack tables and a handful of slots.

Passengers may send e-mails through the Radio Officer for $5 per message. Or they can do it themselves by using onboard computers, which also allow them to surf the Web. The cost: 95¢ a minute.

CHILDREN'S PROGRAM

These ships are not geared to children, although they are permitted. You may see a younger child occasionally—probably a very bored child, as the line provides no special programs, no special menus, and no special concessions for children.

In a pinch, you may be able to arrange babysitting by an available crew member.

ENTERTAINMENT

Entertainment is not Seabourn's strong suit, but if you're happy with a singer, pianist, or duo doing most of the entertaining, you'll be pleased enough. On all the ships, a resident dance band or music duo performs a roster of favorites, while the mellow piano bar is always a good option. The ships have small show lounges.

SERVICE

Seabourn maintains the finest service staff of any line afloat. Most are young northern Europeans, many Norwegian, who are recruited after they've gained experience at one of the grand hotels of Europe. They are, overall, universally charming, competent, sensitive, and discreet—among Seabourn's most valuable assets.

Laundry and dry cleaning are available. There are also self-service laundry rooms on the *Legend* and *Pride.*

All Seabourn ships provide Molton Brown toiletries. As part of its new "Pure Pampering" program, passengers will find in their suites a menu of personal well-being preparations (essentially, several kinds of bath salts) that may be ordered from their cabin attendants; if requested, the attendant will run and prepare the bath for you.

Cabin minibars are stocked with wine, liquor of the guest's choice, and soft drinks upon check-in. And they're kept that way upon request. Fleetwide, complimentary wine is served with lunch and dinner. All drinks in public bars and lounges are complimentary. Seabourn's cruise prices, though high, are about as all-inclusive as you can get.

Across the fleet, gratuities are officially included in the cruise fare, but staff is not prohibited from accepting additional tips, and some passengers do tip.

Seabourn Pride • Seabourn Legend

The Verdict

Hands-down these ships are top of the market in Europe, the cream of the crop. They're among the most luxurious ships at sea, designed to let you be as social, or as private, as you like.

Seabourn Legend *(photo: Seabourn)*

Specifications

Size (in tons)	10,000	Officers	Norwegian
Number of Cabins	100	Crew	140 (International)
Number of Outside Cabins	100	Passenger/Crew Ratio	1.5 to 1
Cabins with Verandahs	6	Year Built	1988/1992
Number of Passengers	204	Last Major Refurbishment	N/A

Frommer's Rating (Scale of 1–5)

Cabin Comfort & Amenities	5	Pool, Fitness & Spa Facilities	3
Ship Cleanliness & Maintenance	4	Children's Facilities	N/A
Public Comfort/Space	5	Decor	4

These two understated, beautifully designed ships represent luxury cruising at its very best; they travel everywhere one would ever want to cruise. Passengers who like to be social and meet others with similar interests will find plenty of opportunities to do so at open-sitting meals, in the intimate public rooms, and out on deck. On the other hand, if you want to get away from it all, you can also be completely private in your spacious suite, at a table for two in the restaurant, or in a quiet corner of the deck.

Cabins & Rates

Cabins	Brochure Rates	Bathtub	Fridge	Hair Dryer	Sitting Area	TV
Suite	$4,999–$13,639	yes*	yes	yes	yes	yes

The four handicapped-accessible suites have showers only.

CABINS   The great majority of the accommodations are handsomely designed "Type A" 277-square-foot one-room suites (for comparison, an average cabin on Carnival is 190 sq. ft.), varying only in location but priced at four different levels. Suites are popular for entertaining and dining, as the lounge area's coffee table rises to dining table height, and one can order hors d'oeuvres such as caviar and smoked salmon at no extra charge. Closet space is more than adequate for hanging clothes, but drawer space is more limited. The *Pride* has twin sinks in the all-white marble bathrooms; *Legend* has a single sink.

The two Classic Suites measure 400 square feet, and two pairs of Owner's Suites are 530 and 575 square feet. These six have the only (small) verandas on the ships. French balconies with sliding glass doors (read: no space for sitting or standing, but you can let in air) are to be found in some of the 36 suites on each ship (the 277-sq.-ft. Type A suites on the top two decks).

The Owner's Suites have dining rooms and guest powder rooms. As in any cabins positioned near the bow of relatively small ships such as these, these forward-facing suites can be somewhat uncomfortable during rough seas. The dark wood furnishings make the overall feeling more like a hotel room than a ship's suite. Regal Suites, at 554 square feet, are simply two combined 277-square-foot Seabourn suites with one room given completely over to a lounge.

Everything about a Seabourn cabin has the impeccably maintained feel of an upscale Scandinavian hotel. Each unit contains a stocked bar, walk-in closet, safe, hair dryer, VCR and TV broadcasting CNN and ESPN among other channels, crystal glasses for every kind of drink, terry-cloth robes, and fresh fruit daily. Videotape movies are available from the ship's library, and the purser's office broadcasts films from the ship's own collection. Color schemes are either tastefully ice-blue or champagne-colored, with lots of bleached oak or birch wooden trim, as well as mirrors and a sophisticated bank of spotlights.

Owner's Suites 05 and 06 have obstructed views. There are four wheelchair-accessible suites.

PUBLIC AREAS   An attractive double open spiral staircase links the public areas, which are, overall, a bit duller than you'd expect on ships of this caliber. For the most part, they're spare and almost ordinary looking. Art and ornamentation are conspicuous by their absence. It's almost as if in its zeal to create conservative decors, management couldn't decide on the appropriate artwork and so omitted it completely. (There are a few exceptions: The *Legend,* for instance, has an attractive curved ocean liner–motif mural in its stair foyers.)

The forward-facing observation lounge on Sky Deck offers an attractive, quiet venue all day long for reading, a drink before meals, cards, and afternoon tea. A chart and compass will help you find out where the ship is currently positioned, and a computerized wall map lets you track future cruises.

The Club lounge and bar, with an aft-facing position, is the ship's principal social center, with music, a small band, a singer and/or pianist, and fancy hot hors d'oeuvres before and after dinner. Next door, behind glass, is the ship's casino, with gaming tables and a separate small room for slot machines. The semicircular and tiered formal lounge on the deck below is the venue for lectures, pianists, and the captain's parties.

The formal restaurant, located on the lowest deck, is a large low-ceilinged room with an open-seating policy. The Veranda Café offers casual meals during the day and romantic meals at night (see below).

ALTERNATIVE DINING   The Veranda Café is open for dinner (except for formal nights) on a reservations-only basis (but with no extra fee), and offers an intimate setting under the stars—perfect for a romantic meal. The cuisine is often based on Italian, French, and seafood themes, and is served with candlelight. In good weather it's a treat to eat at one of the arc of tables located aft overlooking the wake and under a protective canvas awning.

POOL, FITNESS & SPA FACILITIES   The outdoor pool, not much used, is awkwardly situated in a shadowy location aft of the open Lido Deck, between the twin engine uptakes, and is flanked by lifeboats that hang from both sides of the ship. A pair of whirlpools are located just forward of the pool. There's a third hot tub perched on the far forward bow deck. It's isolated and a perfect spot (as is the whole patch of deck here) from which to watch the landscape or a port come into sight or fade away.

A retractable, wood-planked water-sports marina opens out from the stern of the ship so passengers can hop into sea kayaks or go windsurfing, water-skiing, or snorkeling right from the ship. An attached steel mesh net creates a saltwater pool when the marina is in use.

The gym and Steiner-managed spa are roomy for ships this small, and are located forward of the Lido. There is a separate aerobics area, plus two saunas, massage rooms, and a beauty salon.

5 Silversea Cruises

SHIPS IN EUROPE   Silver Cloud • Silver Shadow • Silver Whisper

110 E. Broward Blvd., Fort Lauderdale, FL 33301. © **800/774-9996** or 954/522-4477. Fax 954/468-3034. www.silversea.com.

No arguments: the last word in quality. These all-suite ships offer an impressively high degree of comfort, ambience, and elegance, supported by excellent, attentive service both at sea and ashore.

Guests enjoy spacious suites, complimentary beverages (alcoholic or otherwise), no tipping expected, careful baggage handling, smiles all around, and a bottle of good champagne (no cheap stuff on these ships) that greets passengers in their suites when they arrive.

The company's first two 296-passenger ships, *Silver Cloud* and *Silver Wind,* are small and intimate. Its latest two, the *Silver Shadow* (which debuted in 2000) and *Silver Whisper* (debuted summer 2001) are slightly larger but hardly less intimate. All four offer all-suite accommodations that run from 240 square feet up to a massive 1,435 square feet, including veranda—larger than some private homes. Public areas are small but are consequently more intimate and more likely to lead to new friendships.

Dining is a joy not merely because of the quality of the food but also because you are not confined to a seating time; you can go anytime from 6:30 to 9:30pm. Come alone, with a partner, or with two or three newfound friends, and the maitre d' will find you a table. There's also an alternative dining option—a theme dinner in the Terrace Cafe several nights during the cruise.

Pros

- **A surprisingly high degree of informality.** Considering the economic level of most of those on board there's very little stuffiness.
- **Golf.** The ships offer a huge selection of golf cruises involving play at some of Europe's best courses, from Valderrama to St. Andrews. (The golf packages are extra, of course.)
- **Many private verandas.** Balconies abound. Three-quarters of the units are so equipped on *Silver Wind* and *Silver Cloud,* and an even higher number on the two new ships.
- **Moët & Chandon is the "house" champagne.** Godiva chocolates are left on the pillow at turndown.

Cons

- **Limited space for entertainment.** Casino and entertainment facilities are limited and, because of the space restrictions, the resident performers don't get a chance to really show their talents.

Compared with other Ultra-Luxury lines, here's how Silversea rates:

	Poor	Fair	Good	Excellent	Outstanding
Enjoyment Factor					✓
Dining					✓
Activities			✓		
Children's Program	N/A				
Entertainment				✓	
Service					✓
Overall Value					✓

THE FLEET

The twin, ultra-deluxe, 16,800-ton ships, the *Silver Cloud* and *Silver Wind,* were built in Italy in 1994. The *Cloud* will be in Europe in the summer of 2002, joined there by its bigger and equally ultra-deluxe new fleetmates, the 28,258-ton, 382-passenger *Silver Shadow* and *Silver Whisper.*

PASSENGER PROFILE

On any of these ships, the passenger manifest is apt to include high-powered entertainment industry types, Fortune 500 executives, and wealthy retirees—people who like their cruising top drawer and can pay for the best. You are not likely to find a significant number of small children. This is not a younger crowd cruise line. One of the reasons that the ships' show lounges, small as they are, are adequate for the purpose is that half of the passengers are bound for bed by the time the entertainment starts.

DINING

Food is one of Silversea's strengths, and not just in the main meal services in the dining room (known on all the ships, rather prosaically, as The Restaurant) but also in the **breakfast and lunch buffets** in the Terrace Cafe on Deck 7, and in the **theme dinners** served (reservations, please) in the same room. Be it an Italian, Chinese, Southwestern U.S., or any other theme meal, the quality is tops.

In The Restaurant, the mixed menu offers excellent fish, steak cooked as requested (isn't that a novel thought!), a **vegetarian option,** and more than enough variety to satisfy any taste. On the two new ships, a **poolside grill** offers luncheon hamburgers, hot dogs, fries and the like.

If you want a very special bottle of wine at dinner, you'll have to pay the going rate. Otherwise, the very acceptable wines served in the dining room are on the house.

You can get croissants, juice, and coffee in the lounge in the very early morning.

ACTIVITIES

Activities tend toward the sedentary. There are the usual bridge, shuffleboard, and Scrabble setups, and the cruise director conducts a daily quiz in the lounge. There's no skeet, no putting tournaments, no knobby knees contests, and nothing organized for youngsters. These just aren't those kinds of ships.

Internet hookup is available on all ships for 75¢ a minute.

Silversea throws in for free a special shore excursion called **The Silversea Experience** on every cruise. In Norway, it might be a trip to a year-round ski jump (the surface in summer is straw matting) to view an exhibition by some Olympic hopefuls. In Italy, it might include a wine-and-cheese tasting at the town hall and a welcome by the mayor. Always, it is something that nobody else offers. Other shore excursions are at the passenger's expense, although Silversea always provides a shuttle from dockside to and from the city center.

CHILDREN'S PROGRAM

Silversea has no children's program whatsoever—which really says it all, doesn't it?

ENTERTAINMENT

The entertainers are energetic but the size of the facilities cramps their style even on the two new ships—they sing and dance Broadway show tunes well enough but can't be expected to do justice to the helicopters in *Miss Saigon* or the falling

Silversea Fleet Itineraries

Ship	Home Ports & Season	Itinerary
Silver Cloud	**14-day Greece/Turkey,** from Piraeus to Monte Carlo (Mar); **12-day W. Med,** Monte Carlo to Lisbon (Apr); **7-day W. Med,** Barcelona to Nice (May); **12-day Med,** Nice to Civitavecchia (May); **10-day Turkey/Med,** Istanbul to Lisbon (June); **10-day W. Med,** Lisbon to Rouen (June); **10-day W. Europe,** Dublin to Lisbon (July); **7-day W. Med/Casablanca,** Lisbon to Monte Carlo (July); **12-day Med/Adriatic,** Monte Carlo to Venice (Aug); **10-day E. Med,** Venice to Istanbul (Aug); **7-day Med,** Piraeus to Genoa (Oct)	**14-day Greece/Turkey:** Port calls include Antalya, Kuşadasi, Istanbul (Turkey), Rhodes, Nafplion, Katakolon (Greece), Sorrento, Portoferraio (Italy); **12-day W. Med:** Port calls include St-Tropez, St-Florent, Marseille (France), Tarragona, Palma de Mallorca, Malaga (Spain), Gibraltar; **7-day W. Med:** Port calls include Palma de Mallorca, Mahon (Spain), Bastia, Marseille, Cannes (France); **12-day Med:** Port calls include Portofino, Portovenere, Livorno, Taormina, Valletta (Malta), Bonifacio, Calvi (France), Sorrento (Italy), Portoferraio; **10-day Turkey/Med:** Port calls include Marmaris (Turkey), Aghios Nikolaos (Greece), Valletta (Malta), Tunis (Tunisia), Alghero (Italy), Malaga, Cadiz (Spain); **10-day W. Med:** Port calls include Leixoes (Portugal), La Coruna (Spain), Bordeaux (France), St. Peter Port (Guernsey); **10-day W. Europe:** Port calls include Waterford, Cork (Ireland), Amsterdam (Netherlands), Zeebrugge (Belgium), Honfleur (France), St. Peter Port, St-Malo (France), La Coruna; **7-day W. Med/Casablanca:** Port calls include Casablanca, Palma de Mallorca, Barcelona, Marseille; **12-day Med/Adriatic:** Port calls include Portofino, Portovenere, Livorno, Tunis, Valletta, Katakolon, Dubrovnik (Croatia); **10-day E. Med:** Port calls include Hvar, Dubrovnik (Croatia), Nafplion, Mykonos, Rhodes (Greece), Kuşadasi (Turkey); **7-day Med,** Piraeus to Nice (Sept); **7-day Med:** Port calls include Valletta, Siracusa (Italy), Ajaccio (France), Livorno; **9-day E. Med,** Nice to Istanbul (Sept); **9-day E. Med:** Port calls include Portofino, Taormina, Aghios Nikolaos, Rhodes, Kuşadasi; **7-day Med:** Port calls include Nafplion, Katakolon, Valletta, Palermo (Italy), Civitavecchia/ Rome
Silver Shadow	**10-day E. Med/Greece,** Istanbul to Genoa (May); **12-day W. Med,** Civitavecchia to Lisbon (May); **5-day Ireland,** Honfleur to Tilbury (June); **11-day Baltic,** Tilbury to Copenhagen (June); **7-day Baltics,** Copenhagen to Stockholm (July); **12-day Baltics,** Stockholm to Dover (July); 11-day Scandinavia, Dover to Hamburg (July); **10-day Baltics,** Hamburg to Copenhagen (Aug); **12-day Norwegian Fjords,** Copenhagen to Tilbury (Sept); **11-day British Isles,** Tilbury to Dublin (Aug)	**10-day E. Med/Greece:** Port calls include Dikili, Volos (Greece), Piraeus, Katakolon, Taormina, Livorno; **12-day Med:** Port calls include Livorno, Marseille, Palma de Mallorca, Tarragona (Spain), Gibraltar, Casablanca; **5-day Ireland:** Port calls include St. Peter Port, Cork, Dublin; **7- to 12-day Baltic:** Port calls may include Lubeck (Germany), St. Petersburg (Russia), Tallinn (Estonia), Stockholm (Sweden); Gdynia (Poland), Helsinki (Finland), Rostock (Germany), Zeebrugge (Belgium); **11-day Scandinavia:** Port calls include Amsterdam, Oslo (Norway), Gothenburg (Sweden), Copenhagen, Karlskrona (Sweden); **12-day Fjords:** Port calls include Flam, Gudvangen, Bergen, Alesund, Honningsvag, Trondheim (Norway); **11-day British Isles:** Port calls include Leith, Peterhead, Invergordon, Kirkwall (Scotland), Belfast (N. Ireland), Douglas (Isle of Man), Waterford

Silversea Fleet Itineraries *(continued)*

Ship	Home Ports & Season	Itinerary
Silver Whisper	7-day E. Med, Piraeus to Istanbul (Apr); 9-day Med, Istanbul to Barcelona (Apr); 7-day W. Med, Barcelona to Civitavecchia (May), Civitavecchia/Rome to Barcelona (June); 12-day Med/Adriatic, Rome to Piraeus (May), Istanbul to Genoa (June); 7-day Turkey, Piraeus to Istanbul (May); 7-day Med, Civitavecchia to Barcelona (June); 11-day Med, Barcelona to Athens (June); 7-day E. Med, Istanbul to Athens (July); 12-day E. Med/ Dalmatian Coast, Piraeus to Civitavecchia (July); 10-day Med, Civitavecchia to Barcelona (Aug); 8-day W. Med, Lisbon to Civitavecchia (Sept); 10-day W. Med, Civitavecchia to Barcelona (Sept); 14-day Med/Dalmatian Coast, Civitavecchia to Venice (Sept); 12-day Med, Venice to Barcelona (Oct)	7-day E. Med: Port calls include Santorini (Greece), Aghios Nikolaos, Kuşadasi, Nesebur (Bulgaria); 9-day Med: Port calls include Mykonos, Catania, Salerno (Italy), Civitavecchia, Livorno, Barcelona; 7-day W. Med: Port calls may include Marseille, Genoa, Sorrento, and Palermo (Italy), Bonifacio, Cannes, and Marseille (France), and Tunis (Tunisia); 12-day Med/Adriatic: Port calls may include Messina, Bari, Civitavecchia/Rome, and Venice (Italy), Corfu, Katakolon, Nafplion, Mykonos (Greece), Dubrovnik, Korcula, and Hvar (Croatia); 7-day Turkey: Port calls include Rhodes, Kas, Marmarios, Kuşadasi; 11-day Med: Port calls include Palma de Mallorca, Mahon, Ajaccio, Valletta, Aghios Nikolaos, Rhodes, Bodrum (Turkey), Santorini; 7-day E. Med: Port calls include Thessaloniki, Volos, Rhodes, Patmos (Greece); 12-day E. Med: Port calls include Monemvasia, Katakolon, Itea (Greece), Venice, Dubrovnik, Corfu, Taormina, Sorrento; 10-day Med: Port calls include Catania, Valletta, Tunis, Palermo, Portofino, Calvi, Marseille; 8-day W. Med: Port calls include Cadiz, Malaga, Mahon, Livorno; 10-day W. Med: Port calls include Valletta, Taormina, Sorrento, Portofino, St-Tropez, Marseille; 14-day Med/ Dalmation Coast: Port calls include Livorno, Valletta, Siracusa, Athens, Kuşadasi, Santorini, Corfu, Dubrovnik, Split (Croatia); 12-day Med: Port calls include Dubrovnik, Bari, Naples, Civitavecchia, Genoa, Marseille

*Silver Cloud *also does Black Sea and Canary Islands itineraries.*

chandelier of *The Phantom of the Opera* considering the relatively small stage they have to deal with.

Some of Silversea's onboard **lecturers** are well worth listening to, though.

SERVICE

Uniformly of the highest standard, and there's more than one crew member to every two passengers—a high ratio indeed. They seem forever to be not only willing, but anxious, to serve. The smiles are broad and genuine and requests are fulfilled promptly.

One surprising weakness, though, seems to be in the way the Italian officers on board interact with the passengers. They're polite and welcoming, of course, but they have a tendency to keep their own counsel. There is self-service laundry, and complete valet services including laundry are also available. Tips are included in the cruise fare.

Silver Cloud

The Verdict

Intimate, elegant, and warm, the ship is unquestionably among the leaders in its category.

Silver Cloud *(photo: Silversea)*

Specifications

Size (in tons)	16,800	Officers	Italian
Number of Cabins	148	Crew	210 (International)
Outside Cabins	148	Passenger/Crew Ratio	3 to 2
Cabins with Verandas	128	Year Built	1994/1995
Number of Passengers	296	Last Major Refurbishment	N/A

Frommer's Ratings (Scale of 1–5)

Cabin Comfort & Amenities	5	Pool, Fitness & Spa Facilities	3
Ship Cleanliness & Maintenance	4	Children's Facilities	N/A
Public Comfort/Space	4	Decor	5

Don't choose a Silversea cruise if you want nonstop activity, acres of gambling facilities, and lavishly choreographed stage presentations. But, if you require only plush surroundings, great service, and fine food—and can afford them—it might just be for you.

Cabins & Rates

Cabins	Brochure Rates*	Bathtub	Fridge	Hair Dryer	Sitting Area	TV
Suites	$7,795–$16,795	yes	yes	yes	yes	yes

*Rates are for 10-day cruise. All rates include 1 free hotel night in the port of embarkation.

CABINS   All the cabins are suites and all are outside. The smallest of them, the Vista Suites on Deck 4, are a spacious 240 square feet, though they lack a private veranda. All of the other suites have verandas and range from 295 square feet to the one-bedroom Royal Suite, with 1,031 square feet, and the one-bedroom Grand Suite, with an impressive 1,314 square feet. Non-balcony rooms have huge picture windows.

The cabin decor is easy on the eye with lots of pastel shades and good quality artwork on the walls. Stateroom refrigerators are stocked with soft drinks and liquor. Two cabins on each ship are accessible for travelers with disabilities.

PUBLIC AREAS   Public areas are small, as one might expect on a ship this size, but are consequently more intimate and more likely to lead to new friendships. One of the great gathering places on this ship is the midship's bar, a well laid-out, relaxing place to mingle and meet. The Observation Lounge, up top, is another inviting area.

ALTERNATIVE DINING   None.

POOL, FITNESS & SPA FACILITIES   The facilities are small, but they include just about everything you would want on a cruise. The pool is modest in size—about 30 feet long—and the ship has two Jacuzzis, men's and women's saunas, massage, hydrotherapy treatments, and aerobics classes. There's also a small jogging track. The beauty shop and salon offer manicures, pedicures, facials, and hair styling.

Silver Shadow • Silver Whisper

The Verdict

For space and comfort, service and cuisine, these two newcomers are hard to beat.

Silver Whisper *(photo: Silversea)*

Specifications

Size (in tons)	28,258	Officers	Italian
Number of Cabins	194	Crew	295 (International)
Number of Outside Cabins	194	Passenger/Crew Ratio	1.31 to 1
Cabins with Verandas	168	Year Built	2000/2001
Number of Passengers	382	Last Major Refurbishment	N/A

Frommer's Ratings (Scale of 1–5)

Cabin Comfort and Amenities	5	Pool, Fitness & Spa Facilities	4
Ship Cleanliness and Maintenance	5	Children's Facilities	N/A
Public Comfort/Space	5	Decor	4

These newcomers are like the *Silver Cloud* and the *Silver Wind,* only slightly bigger. They're slightly longer and wider and carry more passengers, but they outweigh their siblings by more than 11,000 tons.

There is one statistic that is of more than passing interest to cruise aficionados. The new ships' passenger/space ratio—a measurement of the vessel's interior space divided by the number of passengers—will be a whopping 74, one of the highest in the industry and almost a full eight points higher than even those of the spacious *Silver Cloud.*

Cabins & Rates

Cabins	Brochure Rates	Bathtub	Fridge	Hair Dryer	Sitting Area	TV
Suites	$5,995–$15,495	yes	yes	yes	yes	yes

CABIN On these great new vessels, of course, the Silversea standard applies: All cabins are suites and all are outside. The smallest—a handful of them on the two lowest passenger decks—have no verandas but they're plenty spacious at 278 square feet. From there, the suite sizes only get better and better. The next—with veranda—goes to 345 square feet rising all the way up to the top accommodations, the Grand Suites at anything from 1,286 to 1,435 square feet.

All suites have convertible twin-to-queen beds, walk-in closet, writing desk, sitting area, and dressing table with hair dryer. They have Italian marble bathrooms, double vanity basins, tubs and showers, entertainment center with satellite TV and VCR with remote control, safe, and refrigerator/minibar. Nothing is left to chance. Nothing has been overlooked.

The biggest suites (some of them with two bedrooms) have guest powder rooms, flat-screen TV, CD stereo system, and so on. Get the message?

PUBLIC AREAS The Athenian Show Lounge is a bi-level room and clearly a step up on that of the *Silver Cloud*. Once again these areas are small, but the quality of the performances and the staging are splendid, given what they have to work with.

An innovation for Silversea is a small (24-person) champagne and wine bar on each of the new vessels—the Moët & Chandon–inspired Le Champagne—and an even smaller cigar club, The Humidor.

The casino offers the usual menu of money-speculating opportunities—blackjack, roulette, craps, and slots. You can have a drink in the casino, and there's another, bigger bar called The Bar (who thinks up these names?).

ALTERNATIVE DINING None.

POOL, SPA & FITNESS FACILITIES More than half as big again as that found on the *Silver Cloud*, the facilities include just about everything you would want on a cruise. The Mandara Spa (now owned by Steiner) offers a range of hydrotherapy, massage and beauty treatments, men's and ladies' sauna and steam rooms, and two whirlpool baths. The pool is surprisingly large for ships this size. For fitness buffs there are aerobics classes and a small jogging track. The beauty salon and barber shop offer manicures, pedicures, and facials as well as hairstyling.

6 Windstar Cruises

SHIPS IN EUROPE   Wind Spirit • Wind Star • Wind Surf

300 Elliott Ave. W., Seattle, WA 98119. ✆ **800/258-7245** or 206/281-3535. Fax 206/281-0627. www.windstarcruises.com.

Windstar offers a truly unique cruise experience, giving passengers the delicious illusion of adventure on board its fleet of four- and five-masted sailing ships and the ever-pleasant reality of first-class cuisine, service, and itineraries. This is no barefoot, rigging-pulling, paper-plates-in-lap, sleep-on-the-deck kind of cruise, but a refined yet down-to-earth, yacht-like experience for a sophisticated, well-traveled crowd who despise big ships and throngs of tourists.

On board, fine stained teak, brass details, and lots of navy-blue fabrics and carpeting lend a traditional nautical ambience. While the ships' proud masts and yards of white sails cut an ever-so-attractive profile, the ships are ultra-state-of-the-art and the sails can be furled or unfurled at the touch of a button. The ships are so stable that at times the bridge may actually induce a modest tilt so passengers remember they're on a sailing ship. Under full sail, the calm tranquility of the cruises is utterly blissful.

Pros
- **Cuisine.** The ambience, service, and imaginative cuisine created by renowned Los Angeles chef Joachim Splichal is superb. Dining is an event much looked forward to each day. Seating is open, and guests can usually get a table for two.
- **Informal and unregimented days.** This line offers the most casual high-end cruise out there—an approach much loved by passengers who like fine service and cuisine but don't like the formality and stuffiness of the majority of high-end lines. It's the most unregimented experience in a class of cruising already known for its unregimented atmosphere.
- **Itineraries.** Besides 1 day at sea (on most routes), these small ships visit a port every day of a weeklong cruise, and many of the ports visited are wonderfully less touristy than those visited on the megaship routes.

Cons
- **No verandas.** If they're important to you, you're out of luck.
- **Limited activities and entertainment.** This is intentional, but if you need lots of organized hoopla to keep you happy, you won't find much on these ships.

Compared with other Ultra-Luxury lines, here's how Windstar rates:

	Poor	Fair	Good	Excellent	Outstanding
Enjoyment Factor					✓
Dining					✓
Activities		✓			
Children's Program	N/A				
Entertainment		✓			
Service				✓	
Overall Value				✓	

THE FLEET

Today, Windstar's fleet consists of four ships, the 148-passenger *Wind Star,* *Wind Song,* and *Wind Spirit,* all constructed originally for Windstar and built in 1986, 1987, and 1988, and the 312-passenger *Wind Surf,* built in 1990 and sailed until 1997 as the *Club Med I* for Club Med Cruises. The *Wind Surf* is the only one of the Windstar ships to have a spa and to offer a substantial number of suites (31). All but the *Wind Song* spend the summer in Europe.

PASSENGER PROFILE

People who expect high-caliber service and very high-quality cuisine but detest the formality of the other high-end ships and the mass-mentality of the mega-ships are thrilled with Windstar. Most passengers are couples in their 30s to early 60s (pretty evenly distributed across range, with the average age about 48), with a smattering of parents with adult children and the occasional single friends traveling together.

The line is not the best choice for first-timers, since it appeals to a specific sensibility, and is definitely not a good choice for singles or families with children under 15 or 16.

Overall, passengers are sophisticated, well traveled, and more down-to-earth than passengers on the other high-end lines. Most want something different from the regular cruise experience, and eschew the "bigger is better" philosophy of conventional cruising. These cruises are for those seeking a romantic escape, who like to visit European ports not bombarded by regular cruise ships, including Portofino and Messina, Italy, and Bodrum, Turkey.

About a quarter of all passengers have sailed with the line before, a figure that represents one of the best recommendations for Windstar, and about 20% are first-timers. There are often a few honeymooners on board (Windstar is an excellent choice for honeymooners, and was in fact voted as the top honeymoon choice on the "*Today Show* Throws a Wedding" series in 2001.)

DINING

A high point of the cruise, the cuisine is among the better prepared aboard any ship in Europe, although maybe not quite the caliber of Seabourn or Radisson.

The line's cuisine was the creation of the renowned chef/restaurateur **Joachim Splichal,** winner of many culinary awards (including some from the James Beard Society) and owner of Los Angeles's Patina Restaurant and Pinot Bistro. At its best, Splichal's food is inventive and imaginative, as reflected by such appetizers as a corn risotto with wild mushrooms and basil or a "Farinetta" bread and Parmesan griddle cake with roasted chicken and shallots, followed by a seafood strudel of lobster, scallops, mussels, king crab, and shrimp in a lobster sauce; or an artfully presented potato-crusted fish with braised leeks and apple-smoked bacon; or a salmon tournedo with an herb crust served with stewed tomatoes and garlicky broccoli rabe. Irresistible desserts such as banana pie with raspberry sauce and French profiteroles with hot fudge sauce are beyond tempting. A very good wine list includes California and European vintages.

Called the "Sail Light Menu," **healthy choices** and **vegetarian dishes,** designed by light-cooking expert Jeanne Jones, are available for breakfast, lunch, and dinner (fat and calorie content are listed on the menu).

The once-a-week **evening barbecues** on the pool deck are wonderful parties under the stars, and an ample and beautifully designed buffet spread offers more than you could possible sample in one evening. The setting is sublime, with tables set with linens and, often, live music performed by the ship's duo.

Windstar Fleet Itineraries

Ship	Home Ports & Season	Itinerary
Wind Spirit	Piraeus/Athens and Istanbul (May–Oct); Lisbon and Barcelona (Apr and Nov)	**7-day Greek Isles:** Mykonos, Santorini, Rhodes (Greece), and Bodrum and Kuşadasi (Turkey); **7-day Andalusia:** Portimao (Portugal), Tangier (Morocco), Marbella, Ibiza, and Palma de Mallorca (Spain)
Wind Star	Between Piraeus/Athens and Istanbul (May–Oct); Lisbon and Barcelona (Apr and Nov)	**7-day Greek Isles:** Mykonos, Santorini, Rhodes (Greece), and Bodrum and Kuşadasi (Turkey). **7-day Andalusia:** Portimao (Portugal), Tangier (Morocco), Marbella, Ibiza, and Palma de Mallorca (Spain)
Wind Surf	**7-day Rivieras,** Nice (May, June, July, Aug, Sept, Nov); **7-day Italy and Greece,** Civitavecchia/Rome and Malta (June, Aug, Oct); **7-day W. Med 1,** Lisbon and Barcelona (Apr, June, July, Sept, Nov); **7-day W. Med 2,** Barcelona (May, June, July, Sept, Nov)	**7-day Rivieras:** Port calls include Monte Carlo, St-Tropez, Portofino, Portovenere, and Portoferraio (Italy); **7-day Italy and Greece:** Port calls may include Capri, Sorrento, Amalfi, Taorrmina (Italy), Gythion, Nafplion, Corfu, and Cephalonia (Greece), Dubrovnik and Hvar (Croatia), Le Goulette (Tunisia); **7-day W. Med 1:** Port calls may include Portimao (Portugal), Tangier (Morocco), Marbella, Ibiza, and Palma de Mallorca (Spain); **7-day W. Med 2:** Port calls include Mahón (Spain), Port Vendres, Marseille, Sanary-sur-Mer, Porquerolles, and Cannes (France)

Each ship has **two dining rooms,** one casual and breezy and used during breakfast and lunch (The Veranda), and the other a more formal room (The Restaurant) that's the stage for dinner. On the *Wind Spirit,* The Veranda is a sunny, window-lined room whose tables extend from inside onto a covered deck (unfortunately, you do have to go outside on deck to get there, so if it's raining you get wet), while The Restaurant is enclosed and accented with nautical touches like teakwood trim and paneling and pillars wrapped decoratively in hemp rope.

At breakfast and lunch, meals can be ordered from a menu or selected from a buffet, so your choices are many. Made-to-taste omelets and a varied and generous spread of fruits are available at breakfast, and luncheons may feature a tasty seafood paella and a hot pasta dish of the day. There is **open seating for meals,** at tables designed for between two and eight diners. You can often get a table for two, but you might have to wait if you go during the rush.

Windstar's official dress code is "no jackets required," which is a big draw for guests. In The Restaurant, guests are asked to dress "casually elegant," which generally means trousers and nice collared shirts for men and pantsuits or casual dresses for women.

The **24-hour room service** includes hot and cold breakfast items (cereals and breads as well as eggs and omelets) and a limited menu that includes sandwiches, fruit, pizza, salads, and other snacks.

The *Wind Surf* also has an **alternative dining venue,** The Bistro, open evenings on a reservations-only basis. Here you might start off with Thai soup, follow that with a Caesar salad, enjoy an entree of seared scallops with red wine sauce and chive mashed potatoes, and finish off with a crème brûlée.

ACTIVITIES

Since these ships generally visit a port of call every day of the cruise and guests spend the day on shore exploring, there are few organized activities offered, and the daily schedules are intentionally unregimented—the way guests prefer it. Weather and conditions permitting, the ships anchor and passengers can enjoy complimentary kayaking, sailing, windsurfing, banana-boat rides, and swimming from the **water-sports platform** lowered at the stern. Optional scuba dives are offered in some locales (including Calvi, Corsica) for an additional charge. There will be a handful of scheduled diversions, such as gaming lessons in the casino and walk-a-mile sessions and stretch classes on deck. Chances are there may be a vegetable carving or food decorating demonstration poolside, as well as clothing or jewelry sale items on display by the pool. Before ports, brief orientation talks are held.

The pool deck, with its hot tub, deck chairs, and open-air bar, is conducive to sunbathing, conversations with shipmates, or quiet repose. There's an extensive video library and CD collection from which passengers can borrow for use in their cabins.

The company's **organized port tours** tend to be more creative than usual, and the cruise director/shore excursions manager/jack-of-all trades person or couple is knowledgeable and able to point passengers toward good spots for independent activities.

You can send and receive e-mails from an account set up on the ships for a rather steep $7.50 for outgoing messages and $5 for incoming messages. On the *Wind Surf* only you can also get on the Internet and check your account at home for 75¢ a minute.

CHILDREN'S PROGRAM

As children are not encouraged to sail with Windstar, there are no activities planned for them. There are often a handful of teenagers on board who spend time sunbathing or holed up in their cabins watching movies.

ENTERTAINMENT

For the most part, passengers entertain themselves. There's often a duo on board (a pianist and a vocalist) performing during cocktail hour before and after dinner in the ships' one main lounge. **Local entertainment,** such as a Turkish dance troupe, is sometimes brought aboard at a port of call. A very modest **casino** offers slots, blackjack, and "Ocean stud poker" (which is Caribbean stud poker with a different name). After dinner, passengers often go up to the pool bar for a nightcap under the stars, and sometimes after 10 or 11pm, disco/pop music is played in the lounge if guests are in the dancing mood.

SERVICE

Windstar is a class operation, as reflected in its thoughtful service personnel. The staff smiles hello and makes every effort to learn passengers' names. Dining staff is efficient and first-rate as well, but not in that ultra-professional, military-esque, five-star-hotel, Seabourn kind of way. That's not what Windstar is all about. Officers and crew are helpful, but not gushing. It's common for several married couples to be among the crew.

Laundry service is available (no self-serve or dry cleaning).

The line operates under a "tipping not required" policy, although generally guests do tip staff as much as on other ships; on Windstar, like Holland America, there's just less pressure to do so.

Wind Spirit • Wind Song • Wind Star

Wind Spirit *(photo: Windstar Cruises)*

The Verdict

Some of the most romantic, cozy, yet roomy small ships out there, these ships look chic and offer just the right combination of creature comforts and first-class cuisine, along with a casual, unstructured ethic.

Specifications

Size (in tons)	5,350	Officers	British/Dutch
Number of Cabins	74	Crew	89 (International)
Number of Outside Cabins	74	Passenger/Crew Ratio	1.6 to 1
Cabins with Verandas	0	Year Built	1988/1987/1986
Number of Passengers	148	Last Major Refurbishment	2001

Frommer's Rating (Scale of 1–5)

Cabin Comfort & Amenities	5	Pool, Fitness & Spa Facilities	2
Ship Cleanliness & Maintenance	4	Children's Facilities	N/A
Public Comfort/Space	3	Decor	4

Despite these ships' high-tech design and size—significantly larger than virtually any private yacht afloat—they nonetheless have some of the grace and lines of a clipper ship, with practically none of the associated discomforts. There's even a needle-shaped bowsprit jutting into the waves. Getting around is usually easy, except that there's no inside access to the breakfast and luncheon restaurant, so during high winds or rain, access via an external set of stairs can be moderately inconvenient.

Cabins & Rates

Cabins	Brochure Rates	Bathtub	Fridge	Hair Dryer	Sitting Area	TV
Outside	$5,020–$6,719	no	yes	yes	no	yes

CABINS   All cabins are very similar, with subtle nautical touches. They're roomy at 188 square feet, but nowhere near as large as your typical high-end ship suite. Beds can be adapted into either a one-queen-size or two-twin-size format. Each cabin has a VCR and TV showing CNN and lots of movies, a CD player, a minibar, a pair of large round portholes with brass fittings, bathrobes, fresh fruit, and a compact closet. Teakwood-decked bathrooms, largish for a ship of this size, are better laid out than those aboard many luxury cruise liners, and contain a hair dryer, plenty of towels, and more than adequate storage space. Like the ships' main public rooms, cabins have navy-blue fabrics and carpeting, along with wood tones—attractive but simple, well constructed, and utilitarian.

Although all the cabins are comfortable, cabins amidships are more stable in rough seas. Note that the ships' engines, when running at full speed, can be a bit noisy.

This line is not recommended for passengers with serious disabilities or those who are wheelchair bound. There are no elevators on board, access to piers is often by tender, and there are raised doorsills.

PUBLIC AREAS There aren't a lot of public areas on these small ships, but they're more than adequate since the ships spend so much time visiting ports. The four main rooms include two restaurants, a library, and the vaguely nautical-looking Lounge, with several cozy, somewhat private partitioned-off nooks and clusters of comfy caramel-colored leather chairs surrounding a slightly sunken wooden dance floor. In the corner is a bar and, in another, a piano and music equipment for the onboard entertainment duo. Here passengers congregate for port talks, pre- and post-dinner drinks, dancing, and any local dance performances. The second bar is the one out on the pool deck, which also attracts passengers before and after dinner for drinks under the stars. There's a piano in the corner of the deck (which doesn't get much play), but mostly this is your typical casual pool bar, and the place where cigars can be purchased and smoked.

The wood-paneled library manages to be both nautical and collegiate at the same time. Guests can read, play cards, or check out one of the hundreds of videotapes (CDs are available from the purser's office nearby).

The restaurant is elegant and dimly lit. The Veranda breakfast and lunch restaurant is light and airy. Throughout the ship, large glass windows, which are locked into a permanently closed position, allow in plenty of light if not air.

ALTERNATIVE DINING None.

POOL, FITNESS & SPA FACILITIES The swimming pool is tiny, as you might expect aboard such a relatively small-scale ship, and there's an adjacent hot tub. The deck chairs around the pool can get filled during sunny days, but there's always the crescent-shaped slice of deck above and more space outside the Veranda restaurant. On Deck 4, there's an unobstructed wraparound deck for walkers.

There's a cramped gym in a cabin-size room, and an adjacent co-ed sauna. Massages and a few other types of treatments are available out of a single massage room next to the hair salon on Deck 1.

Wind Surf

The Verdict

This sleek, sexy, super-smooth sailing ship is a gem, offering an extensive spa along with an intimate yacht-like ambience.

Wind Surf *(photo: Windstar Cruises)*

Specifications

Size (in tons)	14,745	Officers	English/Dutch
Number of Cabins	156	Crew	163 (International)
Number of Outside Cabins	156	Passenger/Crew Ratio	2 to 1
Cabins with Verandas	0	Year Built	1990
Number of Passengers	312	Last Major Refurbishment	2001

Frommer's Rating (Scale of 1–5)

Cabin Comfort & Amenities	5	Pool, Fitness & Spa Facilities	5
Ship Cleanliness & Maintenance	4	Children's Facilities	N/A
Public Comfort/Space	4	Decor	4

The newest member of the Windstar fleet of deluxe motor-sailers continues the line's tradition of delivering a top-of-the line cruise experience that's as chic and sophisticated as it is easygoing and unregimented. Previously sailing under the Club Med banner (it originally entered service as the *Club Med I*), the ship was designed by the same French architect who worked on the other three Windstar vessels, and for the most part is an enlarged copy of them. Purchased for $45 million and subsequently renamed, the *Wind Surf* underwent a major $8 million renovation in early 1998, which included an overhaul of all the public areas and the addition of 30 suites, a 10,000-square-foot spa complex, an alternative restaurant, and a casino.

As part of the conversion, many areas were gutted and all the grace notes of upscale, high-end life at sea were added to make what has emerged since then as a very elegant vessel. Despite a passenger capacity more than double her sister ships (312 versus 148), the *Wind Surf* maintains the feel of a private yacht.

Cabins & Rates

Cabins	Brochure Rates	Bathtub	Fridge	Hair Dryer	Sitting Area	TV
Outside	$5,020–$5,220	no	yes	yes	no	yes
Suite	$7,718	no	yes	yes	yes	yes

CABINS   Cabins are clones of those described in the *Wind Song/ Wind Spirit/Wind Star* review, above. The interiors of both suites and standard cabins feature generous use of polished woods (burled maple and teak), bedspreads and curtains in navy-blue and beige color schemes (suites are maroon and beige), white laminated cabinetwork, and plentiful storage space. All cabins have ocean views, and both standard cabins (188 sq. ft.) and suites (376 sq. ft.) are well supplied with creature comforts, including terry-cloth robes, hair dryers, well-stocked minibars, safes, VCRs and CD players, and satellite TVs with

CNN. Bathrooms have teakwood trim, and are artfully designed and more appealing than those aboard many luxury cruise ships. Extra-spacious suites have separate sleeping and living quarters and his-and-her bathrooms (each with a shower and a toilet).

As part of *Wind Surf*'s metamorphosis in 1998, cabins were completely reconfigured for a reduced passenger capacity of 312 instead of the *Club Med*'s 386. In addition, 30 suites were added on Deck 3 (its original layout had only one), making the *Wind Surf* the only vessel in the Windstar fleet to offer suites.

The ship has two elevators (unlike the other ships in the Windstar fleet, which have none), but still is not recommended for people with serious mobility problems. Access to piers is often by tender, and ramps over doorsills are not adequate.

PUBLIC AREAS   Since the *Wind Surf*'s passenger-space ratio is 30% greater than that of its sister ships, its two main public spaces—the bright and airy Wind Surf Lounge where passengers gather in the evening for cocktails and to listen to a three- to five-person band play your favorite requests, and the Compass Rose piano bar, popular for after-dinner drinks—are also roomier than comparable public spaces on the other ships. There's also the pool bar for a drink under the stars.

As on the other Windstar ships, breakfast and lunch are served in the glass-enclosed Veranda Cafe topside, but the *Wind Surf* offers an alternative dinner option that's unique—in addition to The Restaurant, the smaller, 90-seat Bistro (adjacent to the Veranda) serves dinner each night.

Also unlike the other Windstar ships, *Wind Surf* has a 2,100-square-foot conference center that lies amidships and just below the waterline (a company spokesperson says about 25% of the *Wind Surf*'s total business comes from charter and corporate incentive business; sometimes the whole ship is chartered, sometimes just half or less). Suitable for between 118 and 180 occupants, depending on the arrangement of tables and chairs, it contains technical amenities such as a photocopy machine and audiovisual equipment.

Other public areas include a casino that's nestled into one edge of the Windsurf Lounge, a library, and a gift shop.

ALTERNATIVE DINING   The Bistro, located on the ship's top deck, offers Joachim Splichal's brand of cuisine in a contemporary Mediterranean bistro setting. Reservations are required, but there is no cover charge.

POOL, FITNESS & SPA FACILITIES   The *Wind Surf* has the most elaborate fitness and spa facilities in the Windstar fleet (the line's three 148-passenger ships have no spa and a tiny gym) and, in fact, outclasses facilities on other similar-sized ships. There's a well-stocked windowed gym on the top deck, a "sports" pool for aqua-aerobics and scuba lessons (passengers can get resort certification), and an aerobics room one deck below that's also used for yoga and golf swing practice. The new Steiner-managed WindSpa offers a roster of exercise, massage, and beauty regimens that rival those available at many land-based spas. There's aromatherapy, a variety of massages and other treatments, a sauna, and a steam room. Spa packages—geared to both men and women—can be purchased in advance through your travel agent, with appointment times made once you're on board.

Besides the sports pool, there's another pool on the Main Deck as well as two hot tubs. For joggers, a full-circuit teak promenade wraps around the Bridge Deck.

8

The Alternative Lines

The ships in this chapter offer a much more personal experience than larger ships, carry fewer passengers than the big ships, and spend more time in port, which means you'll get to get off quicker and to know your destination better. The ships—some sailing ships and others motorized yachts—are small and intimate, many of them offering a measure of adventure mixed in with your sea voyage. Plus, with the exception of the *Sea Cloud,* which is more upscale than the other ships, these ships are resolutely casual, meaning you can leave the jackets, ties, pumps, and pearls at home.

These ships generally visit a port every day, and because they have shallow drafts (the amount of the ship that rides below the waterline), they're able to sail adventurous itineraries to small, out-of-the-way ports that the big cruise ships would run aground trying to approach. There is generally little time spent at sea, with the emphasis on giving you the maximum amount of time possible in each port.

Passengers tend to be well-traveled people who like to learn and explore and care little about plush amenities and onboard activities of the bingo and horse-racing variety. Don't expect doting service, but do expect very personal attention, as crew and passengers get friendly fast. Also, since there are so few passengers aboard (34–386 rather than 1,200–2,600), you'll get to know your fellow shipmates better—it's not uncommon for people on these ships to make friends and plan follow-up trips together.

The ships in this chapter are more like private yachts or summer camps at sea than floating resorts. You'll have fun, make lots of new friends, and be able to let your hair down. Food will be basic, hearty, and plentiful, but don't count on room service and midnight buffets, because there may not be any. There may not be TVs in the cabins, and you won't find a casino except aboard Club Med's *Club Med 2.*

These ships do not have elevators or cabins accessible to travelers with disabilities, and are therefore not a good choice for travelers in wheelchairs or others who would have problems walking up and down stairs a lot.

DRESS CODES   Dress code? What's a dress code? Aboard most of the ships in this chapter you can get away with a shirt and shorts during the day and a polo shirt and pants at night (sundresses for ladies).

- Clipper Cruise Line
- Club Med Cruises
- Lindblad Expeditions
- Sea Cloud Cruises
- Star Clippers

1 Clipper Cruise Line

SHIPS IN EUROPE   Clipper Adventurer

7711 Bonhomme Ave., St. Louis, MO 63105. ℰ **800/325-0010** or 314/727-2929. Fax 314/727-6576. www. clippercruise.com.

Clipper, an American-owned line, is highly experienced in offering expedition-style and destination-oriented cruises in an intimate seagoing setting with a top-notch enrichment program. It's an expanding small-ship operator carrying mostly American passengers who enjoy each other's company and who get along well with the ships' youngish crews. The European programs are destination-driven, with a good enrichment program that includes well-attended informal lectures. Company-wide, there are no in-cabin TVs.

A very shippy ship, the *Clipper Adventurer*—built in 1975 as the *Alla Tarasova* and converted into a cruise ship by Scandinavian craftsmen in 1997 to 1998—has an ice-hardened hull that allows it to follow exotic itineraries in the Arctic and Antarctic as well as its European sailings. At 4,575 tons, it's still a small ship, but it offers more public areas than most and an almost astounding amount of open deck space, considering the ship carries only 122 passengers. There are quiet areas throughout where passengers can get off on their own, plus places to congregate when one feels the urge to be social.

The *Clipper Adventurer*'s shore program is more ambitious and active than aboard the company's U.S.-flag coastal vessels, and the ship's shallow draft and nimble nature allow the captain to enter some very tight harbors and include a wider range of seldom-visited ports.

Pros

- **An intimate seagoing club.** The onboard atmosphere is informal, and camaraderie between passengers, staff, and crew comes easily.
- **Cozy, small-hotel–style public rooms.** From the comfy forward observation lounge to the bar amidships and cozy library one deck above, this is a fine ship on which to spend 2 weeks.
- **Serious enrichment program.** Clipper prides itself in hiring a good staff of guest lecturers who enjoy sharing their knowledge, experience, and time with passengers.

Cons

- **Ship bucks in choppy seas.** The ship is small and is subject to considerable movement in large swells and stormy seas, though side-to-side rolling is minimized by stabilizers.

Compared with other Alternative lines, here's how Clipper Cruise Line rates:

	Poor	Fair	Good	Excellent	Outstanding
Enjoyment Factor				✓	
Dining				✓	
Activities				✓	
Children's Program	N/A				
Entertainment			✓		
Service				✓	
Overall Value				✓	

Tips on Tipping

Tipping on small ships is a little different than on big ships. Gratuities are often pooled among the crew, and may not be the same amounts as recommended on big ships. Below is a rundown of suggested tips. Keep in mind these are just suggestions (tipping is always at your own discretion).

Clipper: $10, pooled, plus tips to bartenders at your discretion.
Club Med: Tips are included in cruise fare.
Lindblad Expeditions: $8 to $10, pooled.
Sea Cloud: $15, pooled.
Star Clippers: $5 for waiters, $3 for cabin steward.

THE FLEET

The company began operating small U.S.-flag coastal cruise ships in 1983 on itineraries in North and Central America. While for several years Clipper chartered Society Expeditions' 138-passenger *World Discoverer,* it was not until 1997 that the company bought its own expedition ship, the Russian-flag *Alla Tasasova,* which it rebuilt into a 122-passenger expedition ship with American standards and renamed *Clipper Adventurer.* In November 1999, Clipper took on the similar-size *Oceanic Odyssey,* which the company renamed the *Clipper Odyssey* and deployed for cruises in Asia and Australasia. The U.S.-flag fleet of two coastal vessels (*Yorktown Clipper* and *Nantucket Clipper*) carries an American crew while the two oceangoing expedition vessels have American and international crews.

PASSENGER PROFILE

Clipper's passengers are mostly mature Americans who have traveled quite a lot but are not risk-takers and prefer the intimacy of small ships with American management. The European programs attract a wider age range and more active passengers than do the U.S.-flag coastal ships. The passengers are not status-seeking but rather easygoing types who enjoy the company of like-minded travelers. Children are generally not part of the passenger profile, though those who enjoy adult company are likely to have a good time.

DINING

All Clipper chefs have been trained at the Culinary Institute of America at Hyde Park, New York, and they cater to American passengers who like well-prepared (but not overly rich) food, attractively presented and using top ingredients, rather than overly abundant or showy displays.

In Europe, where food supplies are varied, the menus will feature fresh, local ingredients, but prepared in a sophisticated style. Steaks and roast beef will be top quality, and the seafood dishes will run to Atlantic salmon, sea bass, and lobster tails. Salads change daily, and all the breads, pastries, and desserts are freshly prepared on board.

The dining room, with large picture windows, operates with a single seating for all meals, and there are tables for mostly four and six, none far from a good view. The dining staff is American and Filipino, and at peak times during dinner there can be some delays as the serving kitchen is much too small.

The **buffet offerings** for breakfast and lunch are displayed in the observation lounge, and they are limited to continental breakfast items and soup, salads, and sandwiches at lunch, with an occasional hot entree.

Clipper Fleet Itineraries

Ship	Home Ports & Season	Itinerary
Clipper Adventurer	8-day Spain and Portugal, Lisbon (Apr); 8-day W. Europe, Bordeaux (France) (May); 9-day British Isles, Amsterdam (May); 11-day Scandinavia/Norway, Amsterdam (May); 10-day Scotland, Bergen (Norway) (June); 11-day British Isles/Norway, Edinburgh (Scotland) (June); 8-day Norway, Tromsø (Norway) (July)	**8-day Spain and Portugal:*** Port calls include Leixoes (Portugal), La Coruña, Santander, Bilbao and San Sebastian (Spain), St-Jean-de-Luz (France); **8-day W. Europe:*** Port calls include La Rochelle, Belle-Ile, Saint-Malo, Honfleur, and Rouen (France), and Oostende (Belgium); **9-day British Isles:*** Port calls include Oostende (Belgium), Honfleur and Saint-Malo (France), St. Peter Port (Guernsey, U.K.), Isles of Scilly, Glangarriff (Ireland), and Fishguard and Holyhead (Wales); **11-day Scandinavia/Norway:*** Port calls include Ronne and Copenhagen (Denmark), Gdansk (Poland), Stockholm and Visby (Sweden), and Kristiansand and Ulvik (Norway); **10-day Scotland:*** Port calls include Flam (Norway), Shetland Islands, Orkney Islands, Kirkwell, Outer Hebrides, Loch Ewe, and Iona Island (Scotland); **11-day British Isles/Norway:*** Port calls include Orkney Islands, Shetland Islands (Scotland), Bergen, Flåm, Geiranger, Lofoten Islands, Hammerfest, Honningsvag, and Tromso (Norway); **8-day Norway:*** Port calls include Honningsvag, Bjornoya, and Longyearbyen (Norway)

* Sold as a cruisetour with 1 or 2 hotel nights.

Vegetarians and others following special diets can be accommodated with advance notice.

ACTIVITIES

Onboard activities are limited to daytime **lectures** at sea, and games and puzzles in the library. There is an excellent reference book collection and passengers display considerable interest in educating themselves. The captain has an open-bridge policy at all times, and talking with the officers is an integral part of life aboard the *Clipper Adventurer* day and night. You can send and receive e-mail through the ship's radio officer for $4 for the first page, and $1 for every kilobyte (1,000 characters) after that.

CHILDREN'S PROGRAMS

There are no special programs for children, but if there are a few aboard, the lecture staff will see that they have a good time, especially on trips ashore. However, children really need to enjoy adult company to enjoy this ship.

ENTERTAINMENT

The only entertainment would be **local groups** coming aboard in a few ports and destination-related **films** screened in the lounge after dinner. The ship does not have a casino or regular after-dinner shows.

SERVICE

The hotel staff is American and Filipino with Americans as bar and some of the dining crew. The cabin stewardesses are Filipino. Service is polite and low-key, though some of the older passengers will bond with some of the younger crew and, at the end of the cruise, will want to adopt them.

Bar service in the main lounge, the social center, is very personal, and after a few days, the bartenders will remember what the regulars like to drink.

You may send out laundry for the crew to do, but there is no self-service laundromat, and there is no dry cleaning.

Clipper Adventurer

The Verdict

A well-received addition to the expedition scene, the ship has rapidly gained a top reputation among cruisers who want a well-run, destination-oriented experience in their own language and with like-minded passengers.

Clipper Adventurer *(photo: Clipper Cruise Lines)*

Specifications

Size (in tons)	4,575	Officers	Scandin. & Filipino
Number of Cabins	61	Crew	58 (American & Filipino)
Number of Outside Cabins	61	Passenger/Crew Ratio	2.1 to 1
Cabins with Verandas	none	Year Built	1975 (rebuilt 1998)
Number of Passengers	122	Last Major Refurbishment	1998

Frommer's Ratings (Scale of 1–5)

Cabin Comfort & Amenities	4	Pool, Fitness & Spa Facilities	2
Ship Cleanliness & Maintenance	5	Children's Facilities	N/A
Public Comfort/Space	5	Decor	4

The *Clipper Adventurer* is an ideal-size ship for exploring the smaller ports in Europe without taking the masses with you. She is comfortable in a clubby way and was designed from scratch to appeal to homey Americans who would like to visit seriously interesting places in an informal atmosphere. While the ship is relatively new to the European market, the cruise staff and officers are as experienced as those aboard any ship of the type.

Cabins & Rates

Cabins	Brochure Rates*	Bathtub	Fridge	Hair Dryer	Sitting Area	TV
Outside	$4,880–$7,660	no	no	no	no	no
Suites	$7,080–$8,750	yes	yes	no	yes	no

Rates are based on 8-day itineraries and include all excursions, port charges, airfare from New York, pre- or post-cruise hotel nights, and transfers to and from the ship.

CABINS   All cabins are outside, and the nine on Promenade Deck look through two sets of glass to the sea, while those on A Deck have portholes. Most cabins are of average size, all with twin beds, showers, toilet, decent storage space in closets and on shelves and flat surfaces, and phones. They are designed for sleeping and resting between trips ashore, are plainly furnished with a chair and vanity-cum-desk, and have attractive wood-grain wainscoting and trim. One deluxe cabin and three suites are clustered on Boat Deck in a private section. Soundproofing throughout is good.

The cabins on the Promenade Deck, while roomy, look onto the narrow side promenade that is lighted at night, meaning that curtains must be drawn after dark and especially when sleeping. During the day there is little traffic.

PUBLIC AREAS   The ship has three main public rooms, plus the bridge, which is open 24 hours a day. The forward lounge slopes upwards with the ship's shear and can seat all passengers at once. The lectures and films take place here, plus continental breakfast and light lunch buffets. Though very comfy, the room suffers from being dark unless you are seated next to a window. Aft is a clubby lounge bar that sees little use except for card players or for a brief private chat. The library is the best of the lot, a cheerful space with a lighter atmosphere and away from any through foot traffic, of which there is very little on this ship. Passengers use the library for reading, research, games, and having coffee or a cold drink.

The dining room, located well aft on the Promenade Deck, is most attractive when you're seated next to a window; in the center it's slightly gloomy. The best tables are a pair with four places all the way aft. If something worth seeing suddenly appears outside, two doors allow passengers access directly onto the after deck.

Outside space includes a wide Boat Deck with deck chairs and a covered after section, but it is not possible to walk around this deck on one level. Forward of the bridge, there is a step down to an observation deck constructed as the deck roof to the extended lounge below. On the ship's more expeditionary itineraries, "Thar she blows" will bring scores to this open space, as will the sighting of an iceberg, but for most, the view forward is enjoyed from the bridge.

The very highest deck is wide open for sunning, something not much done on this ship. The forward staircase foyers exhibit some very attractive sculpture and artwork. The ship is entirely nonsmoking within.

ALTERNATIVE DINING   None.

POOL, FITNESS & SPA FACILITIES   The tiny gym has weights, treadmill, and stationary bicycle, and adjacent is a sauna. There is no swimming pool or whirlpool.

2 Club Med Cruises

SHIPS IN EUROPE   Club Med 2

75 Valencia Ave., Coral Gables, FL 33134. ☎ 800/CLUBMED. Fax 305/925-9052. www.clubmed.com.

French-style fun in the sun is what you'll get on this floating Club Med resort, a five-masted, engine-powered sailing ship where the crowd is international and the good times are universal.

Club Med's one ship, the *Club Med 2,* is a stable, high-tech version of an 18th-century clipper ship, with five masts, seven computer-operated sails, and a vague and sometimes far-fetched self-image as a private yacht. While the ship's sails add a lovely grace note, that's mostly all they do—in actuality, the ship relies almost entirely on its diesel engines for propulsion.

In Europe, Club Med carries a scant few Americans (between 5%–10%), though you can count on some Brits being aboard as well. The language on board is French and the currency is the euro. Just as at Club Med's land resorts, the ship is staffed by a cadre of *gentils organisateurs* (GOs), an army of cheerleaders who function as quasi-passengers, participating in the activities and encouraging passengers to do the same. Many guests love these GOs, but others find them irritating.

Note that the "club" in Club Med isn't just a word: You really have to join, with a one-time initiation fee of $30 per family (which includes travel insurance coverage) and an annual fee of $50 per adult and $20 for each person under 12.

Pros

- **International ambience.** Francophiles and anyone who particularly enjoys mingling with Europeans will appreciate the *Club Med 2*'s international mix of passengers.
- **Water sports.** A retractable water-sports platform lowers from the ship's stern and allows guests to conveniently windsurf, kayak, water-ski, snorkel, and swim.
- **Comfortable cabins.** For a small ship, these cabins are comfy and come stocked with a TV, a minibar, a couple of terry-cloth bathrobes, and a hair dryer.

Cons

- **International ambience.** Overkill. For some cruisers, the entire Club Med *savoir faire* misses the mark, fostering a cliquish rowdiness that reminds them of a summer camp for adults. Potential passengers who suspect they'd feel this way would be better off sailing with Windstar.
- **Amateurish entertainment.** It's Club Med's hallmark, but you won't find anything but talent-show-caliber stuff.

Compared with other Alternative lines, here's how Club Med rates:

	Poor	Fair	Good	Excellent	Outstanding
Enjoyment Factor				✓	
Dining				✓	
Activities					✓
Children's Program	✓				
Entertainment				✓	
Service				✓	
Overall Value			✓		

Club Med Fleet Itineraries

Ship	Home Ports & Season	Itinerary
Club Med 2	3- to 7-day W. Med, Port calls may include Portofino, Cannes (May, June, Sept), Capri, Elbe, Lipari, Taormina, Portofino, Portovenere, and Bonifacio (Italy), St.-Tropez, Calvi, and Propriano (France), Valletta (Malta). **7-day E. Med,** Valletta, Athens, Kuşadasi (June–Aug); 7-day Croatia/Italy Split Croatia and Ravenna (Italy)	**7-day E. Med:** Port calls may include Katakolon, Gythieon, Nauplia, Santorini, Lindos, Lesvos, Kithira, Delos/Mykonos, and Paros (Greece), Alanya, Kekova, Kaunos, and Istanbul (Turkey); **7-day Croatia/Italy:** Port calls include Trogir, Rovinj, Dubrovnik, and Hvar (Croatia), Venice and Ravenna (Italy)

THE FLEET

The 392-passenger, 14,745-ton *Club Med 2* was built in 1992 and is the sole ship of the famous vacation resort company. It's outfitted with masts and sails, but these accoutrements are just that: auxiliaries to the ship's engines, aesthetic ornaments aboard a vessel that usually diesels its way between ports. On some cruises, if the wind isn't cooperative, the sails are hoisted only occasionally, perhaps during exits and entrances from harbors, or at the beginning and end of a cruise.

Unlike actual sailing ships, the *Club Med 2* heels only slightly, and then only in the strongest of winds; sometimes CM captains actually induce a slight tilt to simulate the feeling of a ship under sail. The crew seems eerily absent from the minute-to-minute trimming of sails, and that's because the lines, ropes, riggings, and sails are set and fine-tuned via computer monitors from the bridge.

Despite all this mechanization, many passengers are awed by the vessel's sheer beauty, which adds to the romance of sailing through European waters. The ship's five masts and seven sails are merely a grace note, beautiful and evocative when viewed from the decks but far too small in proportion to the bulk of the ship's hull when seen from afar.

PASSENGER PROFILE

Many passengers are alumni from Club Med villages; others like the company's concept of relaxed informality but prefer the ship's more luxurious accommodations to the bare-boned CM villages on land. Most passengers are couples over 40 years of age. Many are French-born. On its European cruises the line also attracts passengers from Italy, Belgium, Germany, and England, as well as a handful from the U.S. and Canada (on most Europe sailings, 70% of the passengers are European).

Announcements and activities are conducted in English, German, French, and Italian.

Passengers tend to be sports- and fitness-conscious, and appreciative of luxury without insisting on formality (as aboard Windstar, no jackets are ever required). They like to visit exotic ports of call, are not particularly upset by any shortcomings in cuisine, and spend a lot of time playing at water sports.

Children under 10 are not permitted to sail aboard the Club Med vessel.

DINING

Two dining areas both allow sea views, and dinners are held in a single open seating. Officers and staff dine with the passengers, contributing to the clublike ambience. Tables for two are widely available; conversely, if you're looking for company, one of the GOs will quickly bustle you to a communal table.

Cuisine is—you guessed it—**French,** with a few hints of Italian and other continental traditions showing through occasionally. Charming touches include **cheese carts** featuring café au lait, espresso, and a selection of fine French cheese. Food is not superlative, but it is plentiful and prepared and served with style. Meals are always accompanied by **complimentary beer or red and white wine** (usually one of Club Med's private-label wines). A surcharge is imposed for more esoteric vintages.

Substantial and somewhat formal fare is served during breakfast and lunch hours in an indoor-outdoor bistro called the Odyssey. At lunchtime, both a la carte sit-down service and **buffet spreads** are featured. On some days a crew sets up a buffet, usually with lobster, on whatever beach happens to be nearby.

Dinners are more proper events capping otherwise more relaxed days. As in France itself, they can last for up to 3 hours. Diners opt for meals served between 7:30 and 9:30pm in the Odyssey or the more formal Le Louisiane Restaurant. The dress code is usually casual or informal, with the exception of two gala Captain's dinners offered during the course of each 7-night cruise. At these, men can wear a blazer but don't need a tie, while women can wear a skirt, dress, or nice pants outfit.

Room service is available 24 hours a day, although some items carry a supplemental charge and the menu is limited. Continental breakfast is always available in cabins. Upon request, **special diets** such as low-calorie, nonfat, or vegetarian are accommodated.

ACTIVITIES

The teakwood decks support an ongoing cross-cultural carnival that tries to be all things to all passengers. The outdoor areas invite sunbathing, although the ship's sails sometimes block the rays. **Deck games** with the GOs come with unbounded enthusiasm that can be a bit much, particularly if you don't feel as youthful as the GOs.

One benefit of the ship's relatively small size is the *Hall Nautique,* a **private marina** created by opening a massive steel hatch at the ship's stern, allowing windsurfers, sailboaters, water-skiers, and snorkelers direct access to the open sea. Gear for all of these sports is provided free. Scuba diving is reserved for certified divers, and all equipment is provided on board. A flotilla of tenders carries day-trippers to the sands of isolated beaches.

Bridge is popular aboard ship, and a GO will organize lessons and tournaments for whoever is interested. The **casino,** offering blackjack and roulette along with the inevitable slot machines, is small but generally adequate for the number of players.

There's also a gym with his-and-hers saunas and a beauty center. Aerobic, stretch, and water exercise classes are offered.

CHILDREN'S PROGRAM

Only children ages 10 and over are allowed on board, and even those who make the grade are not particularly welcome. Club Med does not advertise that it accepts children and does not encourage it, as the ship, in theory at least, is for

---

Supplemental Charges

Port Charges: For most itineraries, port charges are an additional 140€ ($126) per person.
Single Passengers: Single occupants of double cabins pay a 30% surcharge.

"sophisticated adults." If teenagers make it aboard, GOs will supervise daytime activities for them, but otherwise there are no special activities.

ENTERTAINMENT

By design, it's rather amateurish. GOs entertain on every cruise, lip-synching their way through the usual repertoire. Sometimes **local bands** come aboard for the evening at various ports of call. On the do-it-yourself front, the **karaoke** microphone is a popular staple.

There's a **piano bar** on board, and a **nightclub** that's staffed by GOs who may sing, dance, and tell jokes. Later, beginning around 10:30pm, the ship's **disco** swings into action. Sheathed in mirrors and chrome, it's hidden away behind an unmarked door on the vessel's bottom deck, a little too close to the engine room for anything approaching real glamour, but far from any cabins where passengers might be sleeping.

SERVICE

The staff is much more laid-back than your typical professional waiters and other service staff. In some ways, the army of GOs function on board as reliably energetic guests rather than as hotel staffers in the traditional sense, so service relies on cooperation and cheerful coexistence. The illusion is maintained that whoever is serving you is doing so as a favor. In some cases, if the staff finds a request inconvenient, you may find that they deliberately forget it.

Laundry service is available for a supplemental fee, but dry cleaning is not.

Club Med maintains a "no tipping" policy at each of its resorts and on board its ship, a policy that's consistent with the company's all-inclusive price structures. Despite that, many staff members are pleased to discreetly accept a gratuity for exemplary service.

Club Med 2

The Verdict

This sleek, five-masted, French-flavored ship offers an exotic international passenger mix and a truly unique cruise experience.

Club Med 2 *(photo: Club Med Cruises)*

Specifications

Size (in tons)	14,983	Officers	French
Number of Cabins	191	Crew	184 (International)
Number of Outside Cabins	191	Passenger/Crew Ratio	2.1 to 1
Cabins with Verandas	0	Year Built	1990
Number of Passengers	386	Last Major Refurbishment	N/A

Frommer's Ratings (Scale of 1–5)

Cabin Comfort & Amenities	4	Pool, Fitness & Spa Facilities	3
Ship Cleanliness & Maintenance	3	Children's Facilities	N/A
Public Comfort/Space	3	Decor	3

The decor and amenities aboard *Club Med 2* are on par with the chain's finest, most stylish, and most upscale resorts. Within the Club Med subculture, this is about as good as it gets.

Every upper deck on this vessel is affected by the very masts, riggings, and sails that make it distinct—even the understated smokestacks, with funnels that pivot so as to direct smoke away from the sails.

Cabins & Rates

Cabins	Brochure Rates	Bathtub	Fridge	Hair Dryer	Sitting Area	TV
Outside	$1,422–$1,700	no	yes	yes	no	yes
Suite	$1,638–$1,793	no	yes	yes	yes	yes

CABINS   A prime incentive for a cruise aboard the *Club Med 2* is the care and attention devoted to cabin accoutrements. All cabins are outside, and have their own pair of brass-trimmed portholes, climate control, music channels, minibar, safe, surprisingly generous closet, and telephone.

Significantly, regardless of the deck on which it's located, each cabin is almost exactly identical to every other one on board. None of the units has a private balcony. Most cabins measure a generous 188 square feet. There are also five suites, each with 258 square feet and a rectangular picture window. Other than the additional space, they differ little from the cabins. Cabin decor includes high-tech detailing, mahogany trim, and white walls offset by at least one other color, often navy blue. Bathrooms come equipped with a hair dryer and a pair of terry-cloth robes. Cabins have both 110- and 220-volt current, allowing appliances from Europe and North America to be used without converters or adapters.

Some cabins contain upper bunks for a third passenger. There are no single cabins, and no cabins are especially suited for passengers with disabilities.

PUBLIC AREAS   Various decorative details, including the use of Burmese teak as sheathing for all decks and a mixture of high-tech lines with lots of hardwoods, maintain the illusion that the vessel is, indeed, a small-scale yacht rather than a 14,000-ton ship. Scattered over its eight decks are four bars and lounges, a nightclub, a casino, and a medical center staffed by a doctor and nurse. One large lounge serves as an all-purpose bar, lecture hall, and rendezvous point. Lounges are soothing if colorful, often done up with unusual murals and designs in a sort of postmodern interpretation of Art Deco. Large windows bring views of the sea indoors. Two elevators connect the eight decks.

ALTERNATIVE DINING   None.

POOL, FITNESS & SPA FACILITIES   The ship contains a pair of medium-size saltwater pools, a small gym with ocean views, a sauna, and massage facilities. Aerobics classes are offered, and for joggers and walkers there's an uninterrupted jogging circuit around the ship.

3 Lindblad Expeditions

SHIPS IN EUROPE **Endeavour (formerly Caledonian Star)**

720 Fifth Ave., New York, NY 10019. ☎ 800/EXPEDITION. www.expeditions.com.

Lindblad Expeditions offers soft-adventure/educational cruises that transport passengers to places of natural beauty and compelling history away from the crowded tourist stops.

Company founder Sven Olof Lindblad, son of legendary expedition travel pioneer Lars Erik Lindblad, is a long-time advocate of environmentally responsible tourism, and Lindblad Expeditions' crew and staff emphasize respect for the local ecosystem in their talks with cruise passengers. A Lindblad cruise is built around frequent excursions off the ship on Zodiac landing craft that enable passengers to get off almost anywhere at a moment's notice. Flexibility and spontaneity are keys to the experience as the route may be altered at any time to follow a pod of whales or school of dolphins. There are usually two or three excursions every day (included in the cruise fare).

Camaraderie develops between passengers through participation in excursions and through sharing their experiences at lively recap sessions every evening before dinner. These sessions feature presentations by expert naturalists and historians who greatly enhance the cruise experience by sharing their knowledge of a particular region as well as acting as guides on shore excursions.

Pros

- **Great expedition feeling.** Innovative, flexible itineraries, outstanding lecturers/guides, casual dress policy, and a friendly, accommodating staff help make the *Endeavour* one of the top expedition vessels sailing today.
- **Excursions included.** All shore excursions are included in the cruise fare.
- **Few passengers.** Due to the small number of passengers, everyone can get on and off the Zodiacs with minimal waiting.

Cons

- **Small cabins.** While most passengers don't seem to mind their cramped quarters, the spartan, no-frills cabins are far from the most comfortable at sea.
- **Not much in the way of entertainment.** There is little to do in the evenings, and most passengers turn in after dinner to rest up for the next day's explorations.

Compared with other Alternative lines, here's how Lindblad rates:

	Poor	Fair	Good	Excellent	Outstanding
Enjoyment Factor				✓	
Dining			✓		
Activities				✓	
Children's Program	N/A				
Entertainment	N/A				
Service			✓		
Overall Value				✓	

Special Expeditions Fleet Itineraries

Ship	Home Ports & Season	Itinerary
Endeavour	**12-day British Isles,** Portsmouth (England) and Glasgow (Scotland) (May and June); **7-day Norway,** round-trip from Longyearbyen (Norway) (July and Aug); **10-day Norway,** Tromso to Norway (Aug); **13-day Med,** Seville (Spain) to Venice (Italy) (Sept)	**12-day British Isles:** Dartmouth and Isle of Scilly (England), Skellig Islands, Aran Islands, and County Donegal (Ireland), Staffa, Isle of Skye, Isle of Rum, St. Kilda, the Outer Hebrides, and Iona Islands (Scotland); **7-day Norway:** Exploring Svalbard;* **10-day Norway:** Exploring the North Cape, cruising the Barents Sea, Bear Island, exploring Svalbard; **13-day Med:** Cadiz and Granada (Spain), Tunis and Carthage (Tunisia), Agrigento (Italy), Valletta and Gozo (Malta), Olympia (Greece), Kotor Fjord (Yugoslavia), Dubrovnik and Korcula (Croatia)*

Includes overnight at a hotel.

THE FLEET

The largest ship in the Lindblad Expeditions fleet, the 110-passenger *Endeavour* (formerly *Caledonian Star*) is a former North Sea trawler that was completely rebuilt for expedition cruising in 1990. It is the only Lindblad Expeditions ship with stabilizers. In 1998, its cabins and public areas were treated to a $3 million renovation.

PASSENGER PROFILE

Lindblad Expeditions tends to attract well traveled and well-educated professional couples 55+ who have "been there, done that" and are looking for something completely different in a cruise experience. The passenger mix may also include some singles, a few honeymooners, and a smattering of younger couples. There is often a substantial contingent of British passengers on European itineraries. While not necessarily frequent cruisers, many passengers are likely to have been on other Lindblad programs (land and/or cruise). They tend to share common interest in wildlife (whale-watching, bird-watching) and are also intellectually curious about the culture and history of the regions they're visiting.

A Lindblad Expeditions cruise will not appeal to couch potatoes and other sedentary types expecting a big ship lineup of fun and games.

DINING

Hearty buffet breakfasts and lunches and sit-down dinners feature a good choice of both hot and cold dishes with plenty of fresh fruits and vegetables. Many of the fresh ingredients are obtained from ports along the way, and meals may reflect regional tastes. Another plus is the selection of freshly baked breads, pastries, and cakes.

While far from haute cuisine, dinners are well prepared and presented; varied menus feature primarily continental cuisine with a choice of fish and meat entrees. All meals are served at single open seatings that allow passengers to get to know each other by moving around to different tables. Lecturers and other staff members also dine with passengers.

ACTIVITIES

During the day most activity takes place off the ship on Zodiac and/or land excursions. The ship's new fleet of kayaks is available to passengers who wish to explore shoreside locations on their own. Thanks to an Undersea Program introduced in late 2000, passengers can hear live vocalizations from whales (via a hydrophone) or watch (thanks to underwater filming) a penguin swimming below the sea. The program includes a full-time Undersea Specialist on board who oversees activities, as well as a Video Chronicler who captures daily events (copies of the video are for sale at the end of the trip for about 50 or more, depending on the length of the cruise). While on board, passengers entertain themselves with a good book or a game of bridge, Scrabble, or Trivial Pursuit (the ships carry a good selection of board games). E-mail is available for a charge of $4 for the first kilobyte of text sent (1,000 characters), and $1 for each additional kilobyte. There is no charge for incoming e-mail.

CHILDREN'S PROGRAM
There are no organized programs, as there are few children aboard.

ENTERTAINMENT
Lectures and slide presentations are scheduled throughout the cruise and documentaries or movies may be screened in the evening in the main lounge. Extensive reading material is available in each ship's well-stocked library.

SERVICE
Dining room staff and room stewards are affable and efficient and seem to enjoy their work. Recommended tips of $8 to $10 per person per day are pooled and divided among the staff.

There's no room service unless you are ill and unable to make it to the dining room.

Endeavour

The Verdict

Well-run expedition ship with terrific staff and unique itineraries provides one of the richest overall cruise experiences available today.

Endeavor *(photo: Lindblad Expeditions)*

Specifications

Size (in tons)	3,132	Officers	Scandinavian
Number of Cabins	62	Crew	International
Number of Outside Cabins	62	Passenger/Crew Ratio	2 to 1
Cabins with Verandas	0	Year Built	1966 (rebuilt 1990)
Number of Passengers	110	Last Major Renovation	1998

Frommer's Ratings (Scale of 1–5)

Cabin Comfort & Amenities	3	Pool, Fitness & Spa Facilities	2
Ship Cleanliness & Maintenance	3	Children's Facilities	N/A
Public Comfort/Space	3	Decor	2

While far from a luxury liner, the newly renamed *Endeavour* (Lindblad Expeditions previously called the vessel *Caledonian Star*) is a solid, sturdy, fully stabilized vessel with a long track record of success as a pacesetter in expedition cruising. After a recent renovation, which included reinforcing the hull, the ship is more shipshape than ever before as it sails year-round on an ambitious schedule of itineraries from the North Cape of Norway to the British Isles and the Mediterranean (Europe) to the fjords of Chile and the white continent of Antarctica.

Cabins & Rates

Cabins	Brochure Rates*	Bathtub	Fridge	Hair Dryer	Sitting Area	TV
Outside	$4,900–$6,400	no	no	yes	no	no
Suites	$8,400	no	yes	yes	yes	yes

For 12-day British Isles; rates include all shore excursions.

CABINS   All cabins are outside and located above the waterline with a total of 46 double cabins, 14 single cabins, and two suites. There are five price categories ranging from Category 1 cabins on the lower deck to two suites on the upper deck. Cabins in categories 1 to 4 are simply furnished with two lower beds, a writing desk with chair, toilet/shower, and either a porthole or windows for outside lighting. Single cabins have one lower bed. The suites are the only accommodations with separate sitting and sleeping areas and large view windows.

Pack judiciously as there is minimal storage space except in the two suites.

PUBLIC AREAS   The two largest public spaces are the main lounge/bar and the spacious dining room. There are also a small swimming pool and fitness room plus a library, gift shop, hair salon, laundry, and small medical facility with full-time doctor. The navigation bridge is open to passengers.

ALTERNATIVE DINING   None.

POOL, FITNESS & SPA FACILITIES   There are no spa facilities and only a tiny, postage-stamp-size pool and small exercise room.

4 Sea Cloud Cruises

SHIPS IN EUROPE Sea Cloud • Sea Cloud II (preview)

32–40 N. Dean St., Englewood, NJ 07631. ℂ **888/732-2568** or 201/227-9404. Fax 201/227-9424. www. seacloud.com.

A week aboard the historic, fully rigged *Sea Cloud* is the closest most of us ever will get to sailing aboard someone's private yacht. Once owned by cereal heiress Marjorie Merriweather Post, it's the most elaborate and luxurious sailing vessel ever built.

Dinners are elegant affairs served at formal tables in the wood-paneled dining room and original salon, both with beamed ceilings and handsome oil paintings. As is true aboard most cruise experiences like this, there are few activities other than those that have to do with sailing itself. In port, there are low-key shore excursions, some independent and some organized. Passengers sailing aboard *Sea Cloud* are mostly well-heeled and well-traveled Americans, plus some Europeans. Most are attracted by the classic sailing ship experience, and many own their own sailboats.

To keep up with demand, the line also introduced a new ship, *Sea Cloud II,* christened in the winter of 2001, and modeled after the first *Sea Cloud,* down to the bathrooms with gold fittings. The owners have been able to market both ships mostly through alumni, museum, and affinity groups, and tour companies such as Abercrombie & Kent (ℂ **800/323-7308;** www.abercrombiekent.com), with some loyal organizations returning year after year. Individual travelers are also welcome aboard when there's space.

Pros

- **An authentic four-masted sailing yacht.** The *Sea Cloud* has a proud history that includes famous owners and passengers, a sterling war career, a rescue, and a complete refit by a group of investors.
- **Friendly social atmosphere.** Passengers know exactly what they're looking for in a cruise, and that's why they choose a cruise on the *Sea Cloud.* A great spirit of camaraderie soon develops.
- **Beautiful interiors.** The wood paneling, oil paintings, lighting fixtures, and plush furnishings create an opulent setting that exists on no other cruising vessel.

Cons

- **Not always under sail.** The *Sea Cloud* has an itinerary to keep, and though it is a relaxed one, the ship is subject to wind conditions, hence the need to use the engines more than passengers may expect.

Compared with other Alternative lines, here's how Sea Cloud rates:

	Poor	Fair	Good	Excellent	Outstanding
Enjoyment Factor					✓
Dining					✓
Activities			✓		
Children's Program	N/A				
Entertainment			✓		
Service				✓	
Overall Value				✓	

Sea Cloud Fleet Itineraries

Ship	Home Ports & Season	Itinerary
	Complete itineraries for *Sea Cloud* were not available at press time. However, the *Sea Cloud* will offer a series of **7- and 8-day W. Med** sailings from such ports as Monte Carlo (Monaco), Civitavecchia/Rome, Catania, and Venice (Italy), Valletta (Malta), and Malaga (Spain) (Apr–Nov); and a series of **7- and 8-day E. Med** sailings from Antalya, Kuşadasi, and Istanbul (Turkey), and Piraeus/Athens (Greece) (Apr–Oct)	**7-day W. Med:** Port calls may include Portofino, Naples, Palermo, and Porto Vecchio (Italy), Monte Carlo (Monaco),Dubrovnik (Croatia), Valletta (Malta), Mahon, Motril, and Palma de Mallorca (Spain), and Gibraltar; **7-day E. Med:** Port calls may include Santorini, Rhodes, Lesbos, Patmos, Crete, Kos, and Mykonos (Greece), and Bodrum, Dikili, and Cannakkale (Turkey). **For exact itineraries, individual travelers should call the company at ℂ 888/732-2568.**

THE FLEET

The **Sea Cloud** and *Sea Cloud II*'s itineraries vary from year to year but for the most part the ships are based in the Mediterranean for the summer and fall, and the number of cruises available for individual bookings depends on those dates not block-booked for groups. Even then, some groups will accept individuals if there is space.

Sea Cloud Cruises has also expanded into European river cruises, where they operate two high-class riverboats (see chapter 9), known as *River Cloud* and *River Cloud II.*

PASSENGER PROFILE

Mostly well-heeled and well-traveled Americans, and some Europeans, who have a distinct interest in sailing and an affinity with the sea. Some passengers own their own sailboats, and others come because the *Sea Cloud* is so well-known in certain circles.

Simply being aboard the *Sea Cloud* engenders good will and camaraderie amongst passengers.

DINING

Dinner is an elegant affair with open seating at formal tables set with silver napkin rings, candlelight, fresh flowers, and china embossed with the ship's logo. Both the wood-paneled dining room and original salon with their beamed ceilings and handsome oil paintings are set up for the evening meal. The food is **nouvelle cuisine,** with dinner starting with a soup or salad and entrees such as rack of lamb with cassoulet or sole roulade with leek and rigatoni.

Cruise Tips

Don't worry if you cannot afford one of the original cabins aboard the *Sea Cloud*. You will get to see them on a tour on the next to the last evening during an open house. Also, if you have a sailing date in mind and it turns out to be a charter, find out if the group has taken all the space. They may be happy to take you on, but check to see if their interests coincide with yours.

Complimentary red and white wines accompany the set menu. Guests share invitations to the **captain's table.**

Lunch is presented as a **buffet** on the Promenade Deck, and the staff will help passengers carry their trays to the Lido Lounge one deck above, where tables are set under a blue awning. The tasty fare includes assorted salads, spring rolls with sweet-and-sour sauce, carrot soup, cold poached salmon, saltimbocca with artichoke polenta, a selection of cheeses, and fresh waffles with cherry compote.

Vegetarians and others following special diets can be accommodated with advance notice.

ACTIVITIES

Watching the sail-handling and ship navigation is the chief pastime at sea. Few activities are organized other than **skeet shooting** or learning the ropes—just trying to remember the names of the 35 sails is an activity itself. Many passengers simply enjoy relaxing and reading, playing games, hanging out around the bridge, or staring at the sea. In port, there are low-key **shore excursions,** some independent and some organized.

CHILDREN'S PROGRAMS

Children will have to be happy in the company of adults, as there are no special children's facilities.

ENTERTAINMENT

The ship carries a **pianist** who plays in the Lido Lounge, and some of the crew sing salty sea chanteys. Visiting artists are also sometimes on board. Usually the cruise director or a **lecturer** who comes with a group will talk about the history of the ship and the glory days of sailing.

SERVICE

Service is professional and friendly, and some of the crew have been with the *Sea Cloud* for years and consider it to be a second home. The crew hails mostly from Europe.

Ship's laundry will do laundry and pressing (no self-service facilities). No dry cleaning.

Sea Cloud

The Verdict

The *Sea Cloud* is a one-of-a-kind, cared-for historic treasure offering an intimate sailing experience as part of an extended family of passengers who "own" the ship for a week.

Sea Cloud *(photo: Sea Cloud Cruises)*

Specifications

Size (in tons)	2,532	Officers	American/Polish/ European
Number of Cabins	34	Crew (mostly European)	60
Number of Outside Cabins	34	Passenger/Crew Ratio	1.15 to 1
Cabins with Verandas	None	Year Built	1931
Number of Passengers	69	Last Major Refurbishment	1993

Frommer's Ratings (Scale of 1–5)

Cabin Comfort & Amenities	5	Pool, Fitness & Spa Facilities	N/A
Ship Cleanliness & Maintenance	4	Children's Facilities	N/A
Public Comfort/Space	5	Decor	5

The *Sea Cloud* is all about history: Marjorie Merriweather Post and E. F. Hutton, the first owners; the guests who came aboard, such as the Duke and Duchess of Windsor; a wartime career as the navy's first integrated ship; a floating embassy moored in Leningrad's harbor by Mr. Joseph Harris, Marjorie's third husband; ownership by Santo Domingo's dictator Rafael Trujillo; and abandonment and then rebirth as the cruise ship we see today. The varnished wood, shiny brass, organized tangle of lines, multiplicity of sails, and ship's beautiful lines cannot fail to impress.

Cabins & Rates

Cabins	Brochure Rates*	Bathtub	Fridge	Hair Dryer	Sitting Area	TV
Outside	$3,500–$8,590	no	no	yes	some	no

*These rates are for cruise-only. Some tour operators may sell the cruise only with extras such as hotel stays, sightseeing, and transfers, so the actual prices may be higher.

CABINS   There are 8 original cabins, and 26 more were added when the ship was converted from a yacht to a cruise vessel in 1979. Marjorie's Suite (No.1) owner's cabin is fitted with a blue canopied bed in antique white with gold leaf ornamentation, Louis Phillippe chairs, a marble fireplace with an elaborate mantel, a plaster ceiling, and a grand Carrara marble bathroom with swan-shaped gold faucets. E. F. Hutton's Suite (No. 2) owner's cabin is dark paneled with deep red furnishings and a large mahogany secretary and high-backed chairs. French country fabrics decorate the twin beds in daughter Dina Merrill's room. The cabins added in 1979 are nautically styled with wood paneling, brass fittings, and marble bathrooms with shower. All cabins have telephone, safe, hair dryer, music channel, and bathrobes. The original cabins have portholes and the added cabins have windows.

Preview: *Sea Cloud II*

Christened in February 2001, the 96-passenger *Sea Cloud II* was modeled after the historic and elegant *Sea Cloud,* and offers traditional details, including lots of mahogany, combined with modern comforts. The 48 cabins include 2 luxury Owner's Cabins on the Lido Deck, 16 courtly junior suites on the Promenade Deck, and deluxe cabins on the Promenade and Cabin decks. Each cabin has a sitting area, minibar, TV/VCR unit, safe, phone, hair dryer, bathrobes, and marble bathroom with gold fittings.

Meals are open seating in the dining room. The Lido Deck is the main meeting place, accommodating the Lounge, Lido Bar, and Library, and is the setting for lectures and entertainment offerings. On the Bridge Deck are enough lounge chairs for all guests. The ship has a small fitness room and sauna, as well as a water-sports platform, with snorkel and dive gear available on a complimentary basis. There's also a library.

Which *Sea Cloud II* itineraries will be open to individual travelers was also unclear at press time, but officials said the ship would offer 4- to 12-day sailings in the Western Med, from ports including Barcelona and Palma de Mallorca (Spain), Lisbon (Portugal), Palermo, Venice, and Civitavecchia/Rome (Italy), Nice (France), and Monte Carlo (Monaco) (Apr–Nov); 10- to 13-day Northern Europe sailings from ports including Dartmouth (England), Edinburgh (Scotland), Copenhagen (Denmark), Helsinki (Finland), Stockholm (Sweden) Lübeck (Germany), Dublin (Ireland), London (England), and Zeebrugge (Belgium) (May–Aug); as well as a couple of Eastern Med sailings in October. The vessel's charterers include New York's Metropolitan Museum of Art. Rates were not available at press time.

PUBLIC AREAS   The decor of the dining room and lounge is marked by dark paneling, oil paintings, and fireplaces. There are a library corner, VCR, tables for playing cards and board games, and a small souvenir and gift shop. The wide promenade runs fore and aft outside this pair of rooms, and on the deck above there's an awning-covered lounge with bar. There are wooden deck chairs and isolated outdoor areas for reading and communing with the sea.

ALTERNATIVE DINING   None.

POOL, FITNESS & SPA FACILITIES   The *Sea Cloud* provides free use of the snorkeling, windsurfing, and water-skiing equipment. Zodiacs take passengers to beaches for snorkeling and swimming.

5 Star Clippers

SHIPS IN EUROPE   Star Flyer • Royal Clipper

4101 Salzedo Ave., Coral Gables, FL 33146. ℭ **800/442-0553** or 305/442-0550. Fax 305/442-1611. www.star-clippers.com.

With the sails and rigging of classic clipper ships and surprisingly nice amenities, a cruise on this line's ships offers adventure with comfort.

On Star Clippers, you'll have the better of two worlds. On one hand, these cruises espouse an unstructured, let-your-hair-down, hands-on ethic—you can climb the masts (with a harness, of course), pull in the sails, crawl into the bow netting, or chat with the captain on the bridge, and generally pretend you are Errol Flynn (even if you're not wearing a billowing shirt with a sword tucked in your belt). On the other hand, the ship offers comfortable, almost cushy public rooms and cabins; you'll think you're on a private yacht.

On board, leaning against railings just feet above the sea, and watching sailors work the winches or climb the masts and the captain and his mates navigate from the open-air bridge, passengers are reminded they are on a real working ship. Listening to the captain's daily talk about the history of sailing, knot-tying, or some other nautical subject from his forward perch on the Sun Deck, you'll feel like you're exploring Europe's seas and ports in a ship that belongs there. In today's world of look-alike megaships, the *Star Flyer* and *Royal Clipper* stand out, recalling a romantic, swashbuckling era of ship travel.

Pros

- **Hands-on experience.** While you don't have to do a darned thing if you don't want to, you're free to help pull in the sails or even climb the masts (wearing a harness and with much assistance from the crew, of course).
- **Rich in atmosphere.** On these wood-bound clipper ships, it's a real treat to just wallow in the ambience.
- **Off-beat itineraries.** In concert with popular, must-see ports, the ships visit more offbeat places like Lipari, Italy, and Patmos, Greece.

Cons

- **Rolling.** Even though the ships have stabilizers and ballast tanks to reduce rolling, you'll feel the motion if you run into rough seas, as is the case with any small ship.
- **Few activities.** Don't expect nonstop action. Most passengers are content to explore ports, partake of water sports, or sit up on deck with a good book.

Compared with other Alternative lines, here's how Star Clippers rates:

	Poor	Fair	Good	Excellent	Outstanding
Enjoyment Factor					✓
Dining					✓
Activities				✓	
Children's Program	N/A				
Entertainment					✓
Service					✓
Overall Value					✓

THE FLEET

The *Star Flyer,* built in 1991, will spend summer 2002 in France and Italy, and its twin, the *Star Clipper,* will stay in the Caribbean for 2002. The twin vessels are at once traditional and radical. They're the tallest and among the fastest clipper ships ever built, and with dimensions about 100 feet longer than the average 19th-century clipper, they're so beautiful that even at full stop they seem to soar. The *Royal Clipper,* 228-passenger, five-masted, debuted in the spring of 2000. At 439 feet in length, the ship is one of the largest sailing ships ever built.

Star Clipper's ships look like they should sail under wind power, and generally rely on sails for about 25% to 35% of their propulsion (on some sailings more and others less) and on engines for the rest. Still, whether engines are running or not, sails are up nearly the entire trip, creating a beautiful effect. And to top off the salty experience, the ships have live parrots on board as mascots.

PASSENGER PROFILE

While you're likely to find a handful of late-20-something honeymooners, the majority of passengers are well-traveled couples in their late 40s to 60s, active and intellectually curious. Many will be leisure sailors, and you may even encounter some retired seamen.

With only 170 to 228 passengers on board, each cruise seems like a triumph of individuality and intimacy. The line's unusual niche appeals to passengers who might recoil at the forced enthusiasm of cruises aboard larger, resort-style vessels (passengers on these ships would pass at bingo to sit on deck chatting or reading a good book). About 20% of any passenger roster is composed of people who have never cruised before, perhaps for this very reason. On the flip side, according to a company spokesperson, 80% of passengers have cruised before on big ships, like Holland America or Princess, and appreciate a "premium" soft-adventure cruise like Star Clippers. Many passengers are repeaters (overall, repeaters make up a whopping 60% of passengers, according to the company). About half are European, the remainder North American. The line's founder and owner, Mikael Krafft, may even be on board, in many cases with his wife and children, traveling as a low-key guest.

DINING

Overall, food is good and presented well. Breakfast and lunch are served **buffet-style,** with dinner being the sit-down meal of the day (except for a buffet the first night of the cruise). Star Clippers' cuisine has evolved and improved through the years as the line has poured more time and effort into it. In fact, in the spring of 1999, an executive chef was hired to enhance the overall quality of meals fleetwide, shifting from ship to ship to implement an enhanced menu. There have been great improvements. All meals are open seating and

---

(Fun Fact **Going to Great Lengths**

Introduced in 2000, the $55 million *Royal Clipper* is the largest sailing ship ever built, and the first five-masted sailing ship built since 1902 (it was modeled after the previous largest and fastest, the *Preussen,* built in 1902).

Star Clippers Fleet Itineraries

Ship	Home Ports & Season	Itinerary
Royal Clipper	7-day W. Med 1, round-trip from Cannes (May–Oct); 7-day W. Med 2, round-trip from Cannes (May–Sept)	7-day W. Med 1: Sardinia, Livorno, and Portovenere (Italy), Monte Carlo and Corsica (France); 7-day W. Med 2: Mahon, Palma de Mallorca, Cap Creus, and Barcelona (Spain), and St-Tropez (France)
Star Flyer	7-day Rivieras, round-trip from Civitavecchia/Rome (May–Oct); 7-day Italy, round-trip from Civitavecchia/Rome (May–Oct)	7-day Rivieras: Corsica (France), Monte Carlo, Portofino, Livorno, and Portoferraio (Italy); 7-day Italy: Paestum, Taormina, Lipari, Sorrento, and Palmarola (Italy)

served in the restaurant at tables of four, six, and eight, and the dress code is always casual (people dress up slightly at night). Catering to European as well as North American clienteles, all buffets include a better-than-average selection of cheeses, several types of salad, cold cuts, and fish. At breakfast, in addition to a cold and hot buffet spread, there's an **omelet station** where a staff member will make your eggs the way you like them, and the nifty feature of separate hot plates for crispy and limp bacon. Late afternoon snacks served at the Tropical Bar include items like tacos, spring rolls, or ice-cream sundaes with fresh coconut and pistachio toppings.

At dinner, four main entrees (seafood, meat, vegetarian, and a light dish), appetizers, and dessert courses are offered as well as a soup and salad. Choices include, for example, lobster and shrimp with rice pilaf, beef curry, and pasta dishes. When the ship is at full capacity, things can feel a bit frenetic (breakfast and lunch don't get as crowded as passengers tend to eat at staggered times). Waiters and bartenders are efficient and friendly, and dress in costume for several theme nights each week.

There's a worthwhile selection of **wines** on board, with a heavy emphasis on medium-priced French, German, and California selections. Coffee and tea are available from a 24-hour coffee station in the piano bar.

Room service is available only for guests who are sick and can't make it to the dining room, and those in the top suites.

ACTIVITIES

If you're looking for action, shopping, and dozens of organized tours, you won't find much on these ships and itineraries. For the most part, socializing among passengers and with the crew is the main activity (as it is on most any ship of this size). In fact, the friendliness starts the moment you board, with the captain and hotel director personally greeting passengers and inviting them to have a complimentary cocktail and some hors d'oeuvres.

Many activities involve simply exploring these extraordinary ships. The captain gives **informal talks** on maritime themes, and at least once a day the cruise director speaks about the upcoming ports and shipboard events. Knot-tying might be the topic of the day, or you might get to participate in a man-overboard drill. Within reason, passengers can lend a hand with **deck-side duties,** observe the mechanics of navigation, and have a token try at handling the wheel or pulling in the ropes when circumstances and calm weather permit. E-mail is available using a computer in the library of each ship: You buy a 50-unit card for $35, enough to send 5 to 7 messages from the shipboard account (when satellite connections are good). You cannot check your own account at home or go on the Internet. Calls from in-cabin phones are $6.50 a minute, which is quite reasonable by shipboard standards.

Each ship maintains an **open-bridge policy,** allowing passengers to wander up to the humble-looking navigation center at any hour of the day or night.

Port Charges
Port charges are $175 per person in addition to the cruise fares for Star Clippers' 7-day cruises.

Partly because ID "owner" Mikael Krafft is an avid scuba diver and partly because itineraries try to focus on waters that teem with marine life, each ship offers (for an extra charge) the option of PADI-approved scuba diving. Certified divers will find all the equipment they'll need on board. Even uncertified/inexperienced divers can begin the certification process on board.

Other activities may include a brief engine-room tour, and **massages** are available too (a great deal at $48 an hr.), doled out in a spare cabin or a small cabana on deck. Of course, sunbathing is a sport in and of itself, and crawling in the bowsprit netting to do so is a thrill and an effective way to try and spot sea creatures just feet below you.

Activities in port of course revolve around exploring the historic and romantic ports that cling to the Mediterranean's shores, with a limited number of organized shore excursions offered. And, wherever possible (usually more often in the Aegean than the French or Italian Rivieras), activities will also include beaches and water sports, which are all complimentary. **Snorkeling** equipment is issued at the beginning of the week for anyone who wants it, and for water-skiing and banana boat rides the young surfer-boy sports staff operates four Zodiacs that are carried on the ship. Being that everything is so laid-back, there are no sign-up sheets, so guests merely hang out and congregate by the gangway or on the beach until it's their turn.

Ships tend to depart from their ports of call early enough so they can be under full sail during sunset. Trust us on this one: Position yourself at the ship's rail or dawdle over a drink at the deck bar to watch the sun melt into the horizon behind the silhouette of the ships' masts and ropes. It's something you won't forget.

CHILDREN'S PROGRAM
This is not a line for young children, and there are no supervised activities. That said, an experience aboard a sailing ship can be a wonderful educational and adventurous experience, especially for children at least 10 years old.

No babysitting is available, unless a well-intentioned crew member agrees to volunteer his or her off-duty hours.

ENTERTAINMENT
Some sort of featured entertainment takes place each night after dinner by the Tropical Bar, which is the main hub of activity. And nearly everyone comes out

to join in the fun. There's a fashion show one night featuring the hunky sports crew (sometimes in drag), modeling items from the gift ship. Another night offers a **crew talent show,** which may include an Elvis impersonation by a singing bartender. Other events may include a trivia contest or a dance or music performance by **local entertainers** on board for the night. A keyboard player is on hand to sing pop songs before and after dinner, and there may be a pianist playing jazzy tunes in the Piano Bar. Some nights, disco music is put on the sound system and the deck between the deck bar and library becomes a dance floor. The highlight event, however, is the Crab Races, which involves betting on live crabs.

A couple of **movies** are available every day on cabin TVs, if you feel like vegging.

SERVICE

Service is congenial, low-key, unpretentious, cheerful, and reasonably attentive. Expect efficient but sometimes slightly distracted service in the cramped dining room, and realize that you'll have to fetch your own ice, bar drinks, and whatever else you might need during your time on deck.

The crew is international, hailing from places like Poland, Switzerland, Russia, Germany, Romania, Indonesia, and the Philippines, and their presence creates a wonderful international flavor on board. Crew members are friendly and indulgent and usually good-natured about clients who want to tie knots, raise and lower sails, and keep the deck shipshape. As English is not the mother language of some crew members, though, certain details might get lost in the translation.

Officers typically dine with guests at every meal, and if you'd like to have dinner with the captain, just go up to the bridge one day and ask him.

You may send laundry out, but there is no self-serve laundry. No dry cleaning.

Star Flyer

The Verdict

With the sails and rigging of classic clipper ships and the creature comforts of modern megas, cruises on the 170-passenger *Star Flyer* (and its twin, the *Star Clipper,* pictured) offers the best of two worlds and a wonderful way to explore the Mediterranean.

Star Clipper *(photo: Star Clippers)*

Specifications

Size (in tons)	2,298	Officers	International
Number of Cabins	84	Crew	70 (International)
Number of Outside Cabins	78	Passenger/Crew Ratio	2.5 to 1
Cabins with Verandas	0	Year Built	1991
Number of Passengers	172	Last Major Refurbishment	N/A

Frommer's Rating (Scale of 1–5)

Cabin Comfort & Amenities	3	Pool, Fitness & Spa Facilities	3
Ship Cleanliness & Maintenance	4	Children's Facilities	N/A
Public Comfort/Space	4	Decor	4

Life aboard the *Star Flyer* means life on deck. Since there are few other hideaways, that's where most passengers spend their days. Made from teakwood, these decks were planned with lots of passenger space, although some of it is somewhat cluttered with the winches, ropes, and other equipment of these working ships. There are lots of nooks and crannies on deck, and even with a full load the ship rarely feels overly crowded (except at dinner). More sail-trimming activity occurs mid-ship and near the bow, so if you're looking to avoid all bustle, take yourself off to the stern, where readers and nappers grab lounge chairs in an area shaded by a canopy.

Cabins & Rates

Cabins	Brochure Rates*	Bathtub	Fridge	Hair Dryer	Sitting Area	TV
Inside	$1,675–$1,875	no	no	yes	no	no
Outside	$1,875–$2,795	no	no	yes	no	yes
Suite	$3,795	yes	yes	yes	no	yes

Port charges are an extra $175 per person.

CABINS   Cabins feel roomy for a ship of this size and feature a pleasant nautical motif—blue fabrics and carpeting, portholes, brass-toned lighting fixtures, and a dark wood trim framing the off-white furniture and walls. The majority of cabins are outside and measure from about 120 to 130 square feet. They have two twin beds that can be converted into a double, a small desk/vanity with stool, and an upholstered seat fitted into the corner. Storage space is more than adequate for a 7-night casual cruise in a warm climate, with both a slim floor-to-ceiling closet and a double-width closet of shelves; there is also storage below the beds, desk, nightstand, and chair. Each cabin has a telephone, hair dryer, and safe, and all but the four smallest inside cabins (measuring a compact 95 sq. ft.) have a color television showing news and a selection of popular movies.

Standard bathrooms are small but functional, with marble walls, a nice mirrored storage cabinet that actually stays closed, and a narrow shower divided from the rest of the bathroom by only the curtain (surprisingly, the rest of the bathroom stays dry when the shower is being used). The sinks are fitted with annoying push valves, which release water only when they're compressed. The only real difference between the cabins in categories two and three is about a square foot of space. The eight deluxe cabins measure about 150 square feet, open right out onto the main deck, and have minibars and whirlpool bathtubs. Because of their location near the Tropical Bar, though, noise can be a problem.

None of the units is a suite, except for one carefully guarded (and oddly configured) owner's suite in the aft of the Clipper Deck that's available to the public only when it's not being set aside for special purposes.

Take note: The ship's generator tends to drone on through the night; cabins near the stern on lower decks are the most susceptible to this. Also, you may hear dishes clanging in cabins near the dining room.

PUBLIC AREAS   The handful of public rooms include the dining room, a comfy piano bar with banquette seating, the outside Tropical Bar (sheltered from the sun and rain by a canopy), and a cozy, paneled library with a decorative, nonfunctioning fireplace and a good stock of coffee-table books, tracts on naval history and naval architecture, and a cross-section of general titles. The piano bar and outdoor Tropical Bar are the ship's hubs of activity.

Throughout, the interior decor is pleasant but unmemorable, mostly white with touches of brass and mahogany or teakwood trim—not as upscale-looking as vessels operated by Windstar, but cozy, appealing, well designed, and shipshape.

ALTERNATIVE DINING   None.

POOL, FITNESS & SPA FACILITIES   Two small pools are meant more for dipping than swimming; one has glass portholes peering from its depths into the piano bar (and vice versa). The pool near the stern tends to be more languid, the favorite of sunbathers, whereas the one at amidships is more active, with more noise and splashing and central to the action. While there's no gym, aerobics and stretch classes are frequently held on deck between the library and Tropical Bar. PADI diving instruction is offered. There's also snorkeling (complimentary equipment is distributed at the start of the cruise), water-skiing, windsurfing, and banana boat rides offered by the ship's water-sports team in all ports (the ships carry along Zodiac motorboats for this purpose).

Royal Clipper

The Verdict

Star Clipper's newest ship is also its biggest and most fabulous.

Royal Clipper *(photo: Harvey Lloyd)*

Specifications

Size (in tons)	5,000	Officers	International
Number of Cabins	114	Crew	106 (International)
Number of Outside Cabins	108	Passenger/Crew Ratio	2.1 to 1
Cabins with Verandas	14	Year Built	2000
Number of Passengers	228	Last Major Refurbishment	N/A

Frommer's Rating (Scale of 1–5)

Cabin Comfort & Amenities	4	Pool, Fitness & Spa Facilities	4
Ship Cleanliness & Maintenance	4	Children's Facilities	N/A
Public Comfort/Space	5	Decor	4

The *Royal Clipper* is Star Clippers' biggest, newest, and plushest ship. The fully rigged, 439-foot vessel was launched in July 2000, and it's the largest full-rigged sailing ship in the world. With five masts flying 42 sails that together stretch to 56,000 square feet, it can hit 13 knots under engine power and 20 knots under sail power only. Size and power aside, the ship is extremely well accoutered, with a windowed disco, a three-story glass atrium, a three-story restaurant, and 14 suites with private deck patios.

Cabins & Rates

Cabins	Brochure Rates*	Bathtub	Fridge	Hair Dryer	Sitting Area	TV
Inside	$1,775	no	no	yes	no	yes
Outside	$1,875–$2,795	no	no	yes	no	yes
Suite	$3,795–$4,795	yes	yes	yes	yes	yes

Port charges are an extra $175 per person.

CABINS   All but six cabins are outside, with the average measuring 148 square feet. All have such accoutrements as brass light fixtures and mahogany furniture. And all come with hair dryers, safes, telephones, and TVs. About a fourth of the cabins have a third berth. Fourteen deluxe suites are located on the Main Deck forward, and boast private balconies, sitting areas, minibars, and whirlpool tubs. Two owner's suites measure 320 square feet and each has two double beds and two marble bathrooms. Bathrooms are small but all are marble and a little more luxurious than on the other Star Clipper vessels. There is a little more storage space on the Royal Clipper as well.

PUBLIC AREAS   The Observation Room offers a 90-person lounge with forward views that is used for meetings and lectures; it's a quiet place to read during the day. Like the other ships there is a central indoor/outdoor bar area (with a piano in the indoor portion). The nice-size library is dressed in Edwardian-style furnishings. Captain Nemo is a combination fitness–massage area, and sometimes doubles as a bar for private functions. It boasts underwater portholes, and when the ship is at anchor lights are turned on so you can see fish swimming around. The vessel boasts a three-story glass atrium and a three-level restaurant with a grand spiraling staircase. The ship's decor includes lots of wood accents and polished brass, as well as nautical paintings.

ALTERNATIVE DINING   None.

POOL, FITNESS & SPA FACILITIES   Unlike the earlier vessels, this one does have a small gym and massage area, with the neat feature of portholes below the waterline (see Captain Nemo, above), and featuring about a dozen machines including bikes and treadmills. The ship also has three pools. The biggest and most active pool is in the center of the ship and has an outdoor bar; for quieter times head aft. The *Royal Clipper* boasts a retractable swimming, diving, and water-sports platform. Outdoor deck space is expansive. There are even hidden balconies on either side of the bow, for those who want to get away from it all.

9

River Cruises

Cruising on Europe's rivers, canals, and lakes affords a pleasant alternative to inland bus tours or car treks and allows you to see a good deal of each country you visit. Whether aboard **river ships** or small converted commercial **barges,** the pace is leisurely, the ambience generally informal and, just like on an oceangoing cruise ship, you only have to unpack once, and meals and accommodations (and sometimes shore excursions) are included in the cruise fare. Also, a river cruise is perfect for those worried about getting seasick on an oceangoing vessel, as the waters are calm.

RIVER SHIPS

River ships are popular in Europe, especially with European travelers, although increasing numbers of Americans are discovering their virtues as well, leading the ship companies to add more English-speaking crew members (if you are cruising in Russia, it's a good rule of thumb to make sure the hotel and food service is also overseen by a non-Russian firm), plus amenities like suites and even some cabins with balconies.

On these long, low (usually no more than three or four decks) vessels, you and up to 250 fellow passengers will comfortably enjoy the passing scenery from a famous waterway like the Danube, Seine, or Rhine, visiting ports such as Budapest, Hungary; Vienna, Austria; and beautiful venues like Speyer and Koblenz, Germany. The vessels may cruise during the day or night, and some spend the night in key cities so you can get off and enjoy the local nightlife.

These floating hotels typically offer comfortable (though small) **cabins,** usually with a window. On the newer ships, the cabins may have TVs and minibars. **Cuisine** is hearty and in some cases gourmet, as aboard the Peter Deilmann ships and KD River Cruises' *Deutschland* and *Britannia.* **Public rooms** are limited, since these are small vessels, but they will include a nice lounge and dining room, and some ships have a separate bar, large viewing decks, and sometimes small splash pools, spas, and gyms. Light entertainment may be provided by a piano player or cabaret singer or trio.

Most passengers on these ships will be adults, ages 55 and up. Itineraries range from 2 nights to more than 2 weeks. The season is March to November. Some lines also offer pre- and post-cruise land options. The rates for some are under $100 per day, making them an affordable way to visit several countries on one trip.

BARGES

Barges are tiny vessels—many carry fewer than 12 passengers—and are pretty much the floating equivalent of a stay at a New England B&B—even to the extent that some barges are crewed by the families that own them. Americans are drawn to these products in particular because they're one of the most relaxing and pampered vacation experiences you can find. Intimate surroundings, gourmet food, and fine wine are what barge cruising is all about. Also, because the

Piloting Your Own Barge

The British **Crown Blue Line** is among a number of companies offering self-skippered barges. The easy-to-handle boats allow you the freedom to go where you want and eat where you want, with whomever you want. No previous boating experience is required. The barges, which accommodate two to 12 passengers, can be rented for as little as $780 (for a boat for two) for a 1-week outing. You can book the product through Abercrombie & Kent, Le Boat, MaupinWaterways, and Premier Selections (see below).

vessels are small, some people opt to rent the entire barge with a group of family and/or friends.

The barges move very slowly through the countryside—so slowly you can, if you choose, grab one of the bikes the barge will carry and pedal alongside. They move on historic canals that are navigated using a series of locks. When you stop at a town or city, you will be whisked away in a van for a private tour. The barges dock at night, allowing you additional opportunity to explore.

The passenger mix on board is all-important, as you'll get to know everyone very well during the course of a week, dining together, touring together, and relaxing together. **Meals** are a big part of the barge experience and are worth lingering over. Lunch and dinner will include complimentary wine, often from the region you are visiting.

Most barges have had an earlier life as supply vessels. Many are antiques and have been rebuilt to accommodate passengers. **Public rooms** typically include a dining room/lounge with a bar area, and the barges are configured to allow for a good amount of deck space. Some have tiny swimming pools and gyms. **Cabins** will be on the small side but comfortable, and some barges have larger suites available. Most cabins, but not all, have private bathrooms and windows or portholes.

Passengers will mostly be adults, although a few barges specialize in hosting families. A fun option for families is the self-drive barge (see above). **Shore excursions** are usually included in the cruise fare, with the exception of the popular option of hot air ballooning, available for an extra charge.

Barges are most popular in France, but you can also cruise in Holland, Ireland, England, and elsewhere, as noted below. The season is spring to fall (reduced rates are offered in Apr and Oct–Nov), and most itineraries are 6-night.

BOOKING A RIVER CRUISE

Both river ships and barges are typically represented in the U.S. by **brokers** who market a number of different vessels (it's these companies we've included in this chapter). Sometimes the same vessel may be booked by several different companies. A few also operate their own vessels, as noted. All rates listed are the lowest available per diems (multiply them by the number of days covered on the itinerary), are per person, are based on double occupancy, and vary by itinerary. You can book through a travel agent, or contact the numbers listed.

Abercrombie & Kent   Upscale tour operator A&K offers barge cruises on a fleet of 23 vessels in England, France, Belgium, Holland, Germany, Ireland, and

Scotland, including Continental Waterways' vessels *l'Abercrombie* and *Lafayette*. The company also offers the Crown Blue Line self-skippered product (see "Piloting Your Own Barge," above), plus it offers river cruises on ships in France, also operated by Continental Waterways, as well as river cruises in other locations, including Russia, sold as part of a cruisetour package. The barge cruises are 6-day, with rates ranging from $1,690 to $5,625. Rates for 6-day river cruises in France are $1,990 to $2,690.

1520 Kensington Rd., Oak Brook, IL 60523. © 800/323-7308. www.abercrombiekent.com.

The Barge Lady   The Barge Lady represents more than 50 6- to 12-passenger barges that cruise throughout France (including some departing from Paris), Belgium, Holland, Scotland, Germany, England, Ireland, Italy, and Austria. The company also represents a few bigger barges, as well as river ships including a 130-passenger vessel that cruises the Danube. Barge cruises are 6-day, with rates ranging from $1,690 to $5,695.

101 West Grand Ave., Ste. 200, Chicago, IL 60610. © 800/880-0071. www.bargelady.com.

Continental Waterways   This firm, which is bookable through other companies mentioned in this chapter (as noted above), was co-founded by a British journalist working on a story in France for Reuters in 1966, and helped pioneer the concept of hotel barges on European waterways. Its dozen barges (including the *Abercrombie* and *Lafayette,* operated exclusively for Abercrombie & Kent) carry 20 to 51 passengers each. Newer vessels include the 47-passenger *Chardonnay,* which debuted in 2000 as Europe's first all-suite river vessel, and *Princess Royale,* carrying 22 passengers.

Cruising areas include the Alsace, Burgundy, Champagne, Franche-Comte, Ile de France, and eastern and upper Loire. Call the operators listed below for rates.

c/o Abercrombie & Kent, © 800/323-7308; Barge Lady, © 800/880-0071; EuroCruises, © 800/688-3876; Ewaterways.com, © 800/546-4777; or Premier Selections, © 800/234-4000.

EuroCruises   EuroCruises represents the river ships *Arlene, Viking Peterhof, Viking Normandie, Venezia, Viking Rhone,* and *Viking Bordeaux,* plus the vintage steamers *Diana, Wilhelm Tham,* and *Juno.* Carrying from 60 to 180 passengers, they operate throughout Europe, with cruises on the Danube, Rhine, Moselle, Seine, and Po rivers; on Dutch canals; on Russian waterways; and elsewhere. The firm also represents the *Delphin Queen,* a 196-passenger upscale catamaran that operates on the Danube, offering large (173 sq. ft.) cabins with balconies on two of its three decks, and four cabins equipped for those with disabilities (rare on other river ships). Most river ship itineraries are 7-day. Rates range from $1,600 to $2,600 for weeklong sailings. EuroCruises also represents Fred. Olsen Cruise Lines (see chapter 6) and Continental Waterways barge vessels (see above).

303 W. 13th St., New York, NY 10014. © 800/688-3876. www.eurocruises.com.

Ewaterways.com (formerly B&V Waterways)   Ewaterways.com books cruises aboard about 35 privately owned barges sailing in Ireland, Holland, Belgium, England, and France (including Burgundy, Provence, the Armagnac, and the upper Loire and Loire Valley regions). Special theme cruises include golf, gardens, bicycling, wine, bird-watching, and photography. The line also offers river barge cruises in Beaujoules and Provence (France) on 20- to 50-passenger luxury vessels, and river cruises on bigger vessels (up to about 200-passenger) in

Germany, France, and Holland. Rates for 6-day barge cruises are $1,300 to $5,000.

140 E. 56th St., New York, NY 10022. ℂ **800/546-4777**. www.ewaterways.com.

French Country Waterways   This firm owns and operates the luxury barges *Espirit, Horizon II, Liberte, Nenuphar,* and *Princess,* accommodating 8 to 18 passengers. The company's seven mostly French itineraries include Burgundy, the Upper Loire Valley, the Champagne region, and Alsace/Lorraine. Cruises are 6-day, and rates range from $3,195 to $4,795.

P.O. Box 2195, Duxbury, MA 02331. ℂ **800/222-1236**. www.fcwl.com.

Global Quest (formerly OdessAmerica)   Global Quest operates 130- to 270-passenger river ships including the *Peter the Great, Viking Pakhomov,* and *Viking Kirov* on the waterways of Russia, including cruises between Moscow and St. Petersburg. More unusual offerings include a cruise in Siberia down the Lena River to the Arctic Sea. The company also offers cruises on the Danube. Itineraries are from 11 to 14 days, with rates for 11-day cruises ranging from $1,598 to $1,898 outside, and around $3,398 for suites.

50 Glen St., Ste. 206, Glen Cove, NY 11542. ℂ **800/221-3254**. www.globalquesttravel.com.

Intrav   Intrav, parent company of Clipper Cruise Line (see chapter 8), also charters the 76- to 240-passenger *Novikov Priboy, Switzerland II, Amadeus,* and three large barges, the *Vincent Van Gogh, Lord of the Glens,* and *Chardonnay,* offering cruises on the Danube and Rhine, as well as in Holland, Belgium, Germany, Portugal, Scotland, Slovakia, Hungary, Russia, the Czech Republic, Austria, and France. Intrav cruise directors and local experts in history and culture accompany the sailings, which range from 11 to 17 days (the 17-day Great Rivers and Waterways of Europe itinerary explores the Rhine, Main, and Danube). All cruises include round-trip airfare from New York, and all sightseeing and shore excursions. Some itineraries are sold as cruisetours with hotel nights. The voyages are offered April to October, depending on the destination. Rates range from $3,095 to $7,095, depending on the itinerary.

7711 Bonhomme Ave., St. Louis, MO 63105-1961. ℂ **800/456-8100**. www.intrav.com.

KD River Cruises   See Viking River Cruises, below.

Le Boat   Le Boat represents six self-drive barge companies, 45 independent barges, and Continental Waterways, operating in France, England, Ireland, Holland, Germany, Belgium, Italy, and Scotland from April to October, with some barges operating into December. All self-skippered trips are 7 days; crewed trips are 6 days. Rates for crewed barges are $1,790 to $4,500 per person, and self-skippered barges are from $900 to $4,000 per boat, per week.

45 Whitney Rd., Ste. C5, Mahwah, NJ 07430. ℂ **800/992-0291**. www.leboat.com.

MaupinWaterways   Operated by tour operator Maupintour, this firm offers cruises on 32 barges and river ships carrying 6 to 150 passengers in France, England, Ireland, Holland, and Italy. Cruises are 6 days. Rates range from $1,990 to $4,300.

1421 Research Park Dr., Ste. 300, Lawrence, KS 66049. ℂ **800/255-4266**. www.maupintour.com.

Peter Deilmann EuropeAmerica Cruises   This German firm, which also operates oceangoing vessels (see chapter 6), has eight deluxe river ships: the *Cezanne, Mozart, Danube Princess, Prussian Princess, Princess de Provence, Dresden,*

Konigstein, and *Katharina,* new *Casanova* (introduced in 2001), and brand-new *Frederic Chopin* (due in Mar 2002) on the Danube, Rhine, Moselle, Po, Oder, Seine, and Elbe rivers, as well as on Belgian and Dutch canals. Each carries 58 to 207 passengers. The company markets extensively in the U.S., and about 50% of the passengers on Danube cruises (40% on the others) are American. Itineraries for the river cruises are 7 to 14 days. Some of the ships have inside cabins and suites (others are all outside cabins). Rates for 7-day cruises range from $1,020 to $1,525 inside, $1,450 to $2,995 outside, and $2,950 to $4,550 suite.

1800 Diagonal Rd., Ste. 170, Alexandria, VA 22314. ℭ **800/348-8287**. www.deilmann-cruises.com.

Premier Selections   This firm represents more than 50 barges including those in the Continental Waterways fleet, and 50- to 100-passenger riverboats, as well as self-skippered barges in France, Belgium, Holland, Italy, England, Scotland, Germany, and Ireland. Barge cruises are 6 days; self-skippered 7 days. Barge cruises range from $1,490 to $4,150 per person; self-skippered are $1,120 per boat (for boats that sleep two) to $4,370 (for boats that sleep 10).

342 Madison Ave., Ste. 916, New York, NY 10173. ℭ **800/234-4000**. www.premierselections.com.

Uniworld   Uniworld is a California-based firm that offers 40 river cruise itineraries in Russia and other European destinations aboard the 75- to 140-passenger river ships including *Amadeus II, River Queen, Swiss Pearl, Douro Princess, Douro Prince, River Empress, Swiss Coral, Rhone Princess, River Princess, Michelangelo, Victor Hugo,* and *Seine Princess.* The company designs itineraries for American tastes, and the crew is English-speaking. Sailing areas include the Douro River in Portugal; the Po River in Italy; the Rhone, Saone, and Seine in France; assorted Dutch waterways; the Rhine and Moselle (Amsterdam to Basel); the Danube; and assorted waterways in Russia. A 14-day European Grand Cruise goes from Amsterdam to Vienna. Some cruises are packaged as cruisetours (including a hotel stay). The cruises range from 9 to 14 days. Rates for 9-night sailings are $1,998 to $2,348.

Uniworld Plaza, 17323 Ventura Blvd., Encino, CA 91316. ℭ **800/733-7820**. www.uniworld.com.

Viking River Cruises   In 2000, this firm bought German company KD River Cruises, the oldest and largest river cruise line in Europe (having begun offering cruises on the Rhine in 1857). The company operates 28 river ships in Europe—including the new, 150-passenger *Viking Neptune,* introduced in the summer of 2001, and sister ships *Viking Spirit, Viking Pride,* and *Viking Europe,* introduced in the spring of 2001. These hotel-like ships were designed with U.S. passengers in mind, and offer such unusual river ship amenities as picture windows that open. Cabins come with TVs, phones, hair dryers, and safes. The vessels cruise on the Rhine, Main, Danube, and Elbe rivers in Germany, as well as in Russia, France, Italy, Holland, Austria, Hungary, and the Czech Republic. Cruise fares include round-trip air to Europe and daily sightseeing, and there are English-speaking crew and guides. Rates for 7-day cruises range from $1,798 to $2,902.

21820 Burbank Blvd., Los Angeles, CA 91367. ℭ **877/66-VIKING** (877/66-845460). www. vikingrivercruises.com.

Part 3

Ports of Call

With information and advice on things you can see and do in dozens of ports of call, whether on your own or as part of an organized tour.

10

The Port Experience: An Introduction

The ports are likely the reason you've chosen to cruise in Europe. Nearly all offer historical attractions, in some cases truly ancient historical attractions (it's amazing how young 1776 is in the scheme of things!). In addition, the ports offer cultural attractions, shopping opportunities, and, in many cases, beaches. And some of them allow you access to famous cities like London, Rome, Amsterdam, and Paris.

In the next two chapters we describe the ports in the Mediterranean and Northern Europe on a country-by-country basis. In each we've noted distances of attractions from the port as well as the availability of transportation to help you decide whether to take a shore excursion or tour on your own. For more detailed information on each port, consult the appropriate Frommer's guide, a listing of which appears at the back of this book.

1 Debarkation in Port

Generally, ships on European itineraries stop at a port a day, with some spending 1 day at sea (without stopping at a port). On longer cruises you will have more than 1 day at sea, during which the emphasis will be on smooth sailing and providing you with pretty views of the coastline while you relax and enjoy the onboard facilities.

Coming into port, ships generally arrive right after breakfast, allowing you the morning and afternoon to take a shore excursion or explore on your own. Your ship will either dock right at the pier or tie-up slightly offshore, in which case the ship will tender passengers ashore in small boats. In either case, there is a fair amount of time (sometimes as much as 2 hr.) between when the ship stops and when you can actually get off. That's because local authorities have to board and clear the ship, a process that allows you to leave the vessel without going through Customs. Despite the logic of it, it can be frustrating to see a city laid out in front of you and have to wait to be told when you can step off the ship.

If you're on a large ship, the process may be further delayed because thousands of passengers will want to get off at the same time. In these cases, you may be assigned to a specific group and be requested to wait to leave the ship until your group is called. Those on shore excursions usually get to disembark first. Ship officials will keep you well-informed of the process.

Remember, whether on a shore excursion or touring on your own, to bring your **boarding pass** when you leave the ship, since you won't be able to get back aboard without it. Remember also to bring **money**—after a few days in the cashless atmosphere of a ship, it's remarkably easy to forget. Some ships offer currency exchange services on board. You can also usually find an ATM, bank, or other money exchange within walking distance of the pier where you can

Currency Conversion Chart

	U.S. $1	Canada $1	British £1	Australia $1	NZ $1
Belgium (euro)	1.11	.70	1.60	.57	.46
Croatia (kuna)	8.16	5.21	11.92	3.97	3.29
Denmark (krone)	8.25	5.28	10.06	4.29	3.59
England (pound)	.68	.43	-	.33	.27
Estonia (kroon)	17.03	10.86	24.82	8.26	6.86
Finland (euro)	1.11	.70	1.60	.57	.46
France (euro)	1.11	.70	1.60	.57	.46
Germany (euro)	1.11	.70	1.60	.57	.46
Greece (euro)	1.11	.70	1.60	.57	.46
Ireland (euro)	1.11	.70	1.60	.57	.46
Italy (euro)	1.11	.70	1.60	.57	.46
Malta (lira)	.44	.28	.64	.21	.17
Netherlands (euro)	1.11	.70	1.60	.57	.46
Norway (krone)	8.86	5.65	12.9	4.55	3.78
Portugal (euro)	1.11	.70	1.60	.57	.46
Russia (ruble)	29	18	42	14	11
Spain (euro)	1.11	.70	1.60	.57	.46
Sweden (krona)	10.82	6.91	15.80	5.26	4.36
Turkey (lira)	1,413,500	904,466	2,065,689	739,260	615,862

exchange a few dollars (though don't exchange too much or you'll end up having to change it back).

We also advise you to wear **comfortable shoes** (cobblestones and uneven surfaces are common in Europe) and bring along some **bottled water** (available on the ship), a hat, and sunscreen, especially in the summer months. If you are visiting churches or other religious sites, women may be required to cover their arms and legs. Your ship tour director should be able to offer you advice in this regard.

TAKING THE TRAIN

More intrepid travelers may want to save a few bucks by taking a train to get beyond the port city rather than booking the ship's pricier shore excursion or transfer options. Convenient service is offered in ports including Livorno (to get to Pisa or Florence) and Civitavecchia (to get to Rome), and we've indicated this in the following port chapters. Keep in mind, though, the train station may not be right near the pier (a cab or bus ride may be required to get there). For train schedules consult **www.raileurope.com**.

REBOARDING

Whether you do go off to explore on your own or are just puttering around in the port after your excursion, you'll need to carefully pay attention to the ship's **departure time** and be back at least a half-hour before that time. If your shore excursion runs late, the ship will be held, but if you're off on your own and miss the boat you will be responsible for paying your way to the next port. (If you do miss the boat, immediately contact the ship's representative at the pier.)

Ships usually depart in the early evening, giving you an hour or two to rest up before dinner. Small ships may even stay in port each evening to offer you a chance to sample the local nightlife, and some large ships will overnight in major ports such as Venice, Istanbul, or Monaco.

2 Shore Excursions

The cruise lines offer shore excursions to various sites of historical or cultural value or natural or artistic beauty, all designed to help you make the most of your limited time at each port of call. In general, excursions that take you well beyond the port area are the ones most worth taking—you'll get professional commentary and avoid hassling with local transportation. In ports that have attractions within walking distance of the pier, however, you may be best off touring on your own. If you are not a good walker, look for a shore excursion that does not involve much footwork (most lines have offerings in this regard).

Shore excursions typically involve buses, with a guide assigned to each bus. Even when you are on a European ship, you will have an English-speaking guide. However, if there are not enough English speakers to fill a whole bus, you may have to hear the commentary repeated in another language as well. Some of the more upscale and educational lines have expert lecturers who accompany shore excursions, and some offer tours in limos and minivans rather than in big buses.

Tours include entrance fees to attractions, and some include lunch or local folklore performances, as well as time for shopping either on your own or at a local crafts center (where you may be not so subtly encouraged to buy souvenirs). In some cases, you may have the option of lingering in a town and returning to the ship on your own.

The tours are usually conducted by local outside contractors and not by the cruise lines themselves. In some countries, including Greece and Turkey, the guides are required to be licensed and are thus very knowledgeable about their subject matter. Elsewhere, we have also generally been impressed with the level of the tours offered, with a few notable exceptions: Fran had a guide in Monaco, for instance, who tried to entertain us on our way to St-Paul-de-Vence with a combination of inane commentary on the scenery ("Oh, look at the sea, isn't it blue?") and gossip about Monaco's royal family, and who dropped us off telling us she would offer a historical walking tour if we wanted, but she knew we would all rather go shopping instead. All told, though, such lack of performance by guides in Europe is rare.

Shore excursion rates were accurate at press time, but are subject to change. Some lines, including Princess and Royal Caribbean, also offer reduced rate

Going Nowhere

At all the ports your ship will visit, you have the option of staying on the ship and relaxing. The restaurants usually remain open (even if you do get off, you can come back to eat, although we highly recommend in Europe that you try the local cuisine), and limited onboard activities may be offered.

shore excursions for kids. **Tipping** of the guides after the tour is at your discretion, but as a general rule of thumb, you should tip $2 per person for a half-day tour and $4 per person for a full-day tour.

BOOKING SHORE EXCURSIONS

The cruise lines detail their excursions in brochures you'll likely receive in the mail with your cruise documents, to allow you to preselect excursions that appeal to you; however, in all but a few cases you must book the tours aboard ship (preferably on the first day, since some will sell out). Excursions are sold on a nonrefundable first-come, first-served basis (some have capacity restrictions). Some lines allow bookings in advance on European cruises, and some include shore excursions in their cruise fares. If you want to learn more about the shore excursions, the excursions staff will give talks aboard ship to fill you in. Honestly, they're sometimes more like sales pitches (the cruise lines do, after all, make money off the tours), but they do give more background than the one- or two-paragraph summations in the brochures.

3 Touring the Ports on Your Own

If you're an independent-minded traveler and/or hate bus tours, skip the organized shore excursions and head off on your own—though bear in mind that some ports (such as Civitavecchia in Italy and Le Havre in France) are not much to look at in and of themselves, and serve primarily as seaports for large and sometimes distant cities (Rome and Paris, respectively, in this instance). Where this is the case, you're probably best off taking the organized excursions, since they're already structured to maximize your limited time. The cruise line may also offer a bus transfer option to a distant city that drops you off and picks you up at a designated time. Taking a train (see above) may be another option.

Walking is, of course, the most enlightening way to see a port, but when you want to visit a site that's not within walking distance, you'll have to find transportation. In most ports it's both a hassle and expensive to rent a car on your own, so you're better off either taking a taxi or public transportation such as buses or subways, or arranging to hire a car and driver—if you get together a small group to do this you can split the price and save money. Your ship's tour office should be able to offer recommendations.

Mediterranean Ports of Call

The ports in the Mediterranean include Lisbon and Barcelona in the west and Athens and Turkey in the east, and everything in between. Here you'll find history from B.C. on, folk culture, high culture (think French Riviera), beaches, shopping, and above anything else, great diversity: the riches of Venice and Rome; the glistening beaches of the French Riviera (populated by chic, equally glistening bodies); tiny Monte Carlo with its famous casino; the unbelievably scenic Italian Riviera; Dubrovnik, with its medieval ramparts and role in modern history; and the Greek Isles, with their incredible archaeological and local cultural offerings.

In the Med, you can follow the path of ancient mariners and find history around every corner, or you can just sit back in the sun to admire the incredibly blue sea and fabulous scenery. There's something for everyone.

1 Croatia

Heavily damaged during the shelling of 1991 and 1992 by Serbs and Montenegrins, the beautiful city of **Dubrovnik** has been restored—thanks in good part to donations made to the Rebuild Dubrovnik Fund—and cruise passengers name it as one of their favorites. Unfortunately, because of its geographic location on the same side of the Adriatic as Kosovo, most lines dropped Dubrovnik from their schedules for much of the 1999 season, though some returned after the war there ended.

The Croatian city is a jewel to be sure (it's even classified as a world heritage treasure by UNESCO), encircled by medieval ramparts, with ancient streets, historic buildings and stone houses, and a rich cultural heritage, not to mention a fine position on the blue sea. The surrounding countryside provides glimpses of life the way it used to be.

CURRENCY   The basic Croatian currency unit is the kuna. It is made up of 100 lipa. The exchange rate at press time was $1 = 8.16 kuna.

LANGUAGE   Croatian.

FROMMER'S FAVORITE DUBROVNIK EXPERIENCES
- **Walking the Placa (also called Stradun) and the side streets of Old Town.** Enter at the 16th-century Pile Gate and go exploring in this area, which has remained virtually unchanged since the 13th century.
- **Taking a ride in the country.** Shore excursions are offered to the pretty Konavle valley.

COMING ASHORE & GETTING AROUND   Ships dock about 10 minutes by car or bus from the Old Town. Taxis are usually available at the pier. There are also buses to Old Town.

THE BEST SHORE EXCURSIONS

Half-Day Historic Dubrovnik (3–4 hr., $31–$39): Travel by motor coach from Gruz Harbor to Pile Gate, one of the entrances to the old town. Visit the Sponza Palace, Dominican church and monastery, Rector's Palace, Church of St. Blaise, Dubrovnik Cathedral, and 14th-century Franciscan Monastery. Walk the centuries-old streets of the Placa (Stradun).

Dubrovnik, Konavle Valley & Konavoski Dvori (5–6 hr., $129–$138): Visit the Konavle region, 30 minutes south of Dubrovnik, to spend time in a natural setting. Enjoy a welcome of brandy and dried figs at the Konavoski Dvori restaurant, situated in an old water mill next to the Ljuta River, and enjoy a lunch of traditional food including grilled roast lamb, veal, and trout. It also includes a tour of historic Dubrovnik.

Dubrovnik, Konavle Valley, Artist's Studio & Glavic House (5–6 hr., $127–$138): Travel 30 minutes south of Dubrovnik to the Konavle region and the village of Mihanici. Visit the studio of local painter Mijo Sisa Konavljanin, who paints themes of daily life in Konavle. Stop at Glavic House, a traditional family home. The family produces brandy, wine, and olive oil. Lunch is served here, featuring Croatian specialties. It also includes a tour of Dubrovnik's Old Town.

THE TOP ATTRACTIONS

Cathedral Treasury   Contains such religious treasures as the St. Blaise Reliquary, a reliquary of the Holy Cross from Jerusalem, and an array of paintings and works of art.

Kneza Damjana Jude 1. ℂ 385/411-715. Admission 5.71kn (70¢). Weekdays 9am–5:30pm, Sun 11am–5:30pm.

City Walls   The walls run around part of the city for about a mile and a quarter. They were built between the 8th and 16th centuries. Walkers can visit five bastions and 15 lookout towers along the way. Entrance is on the north side, near St. Spasa Church.

Sv Dominika 3. ℂ 385/25-942. Admission 5.71kn (70¢). Daily 10am–6pm.

Dominican Monastery   Construction began on this monastery and church complex in 1228, but it wasn't completed till some 200 years later. Some of the city's most renowned citizens are buried here, and the treasury is worth a look.

Sveti Dominika 4. ℂ 385/26-472. Admission 5.71kn (70¢) adults, 3.27kn (40¢) children. Daily 9am–6pm.

Dubrovnik Museum—Rector's Palace   The rector of Dubrovnik lived here, but the palace, constructed beginning in 1435, was also a seat of government. The rector was not allowed to leave the palace during his short, 1-month term unless he was engaged in state business. The architecture combines Gothic and early Renaissance styles, and the palace today houses a museum with furnished rooms, historical exhibits, and baroque paintings.

Pred Dvorom 3. ℂ 385/26-469. Admission 10.2kn ($1.25). Mon–Sat 9am–1pm.

Franciscan Monastery   Dating from the 14th century, the monastery has an impressive cloister, a rich library with a beautiful reading room, and a pharmacy that dates back to 1317.

Placa 2. ℂ 385/26-345. Admission 5.71kn (70¢) adults, 3.27kn (40¢) children. Daily 8am–noon and 4–7pm.

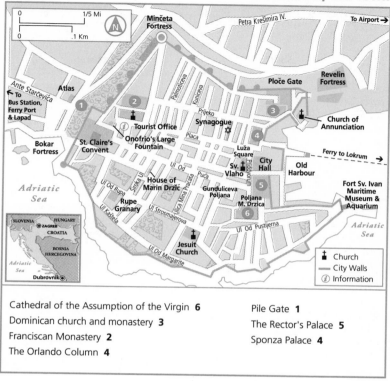

Cathedral of the Assumption of the Virgin **6**

Dominican church and monastery **3**

Franciscan Monastery **2**

The Orlando Column **4**

Pile Gate **1**

The Rector's Palace **5**

Sponza Palace **4**

Sponza Palace   This is one of the most beautiful buildings in the city, featuring a mix of late Gothic and early Renaissance styles, with impressive stone carvings. Construction started in 1516, and the luxurious building was used as a sort of customhouse. The atrium, with its arched galley, was said to have been the liveliest commercial center and meeting place for businessmen in the city. One wing of the palace housed the state mint. And intellectuals gathered here as "The Academy of the Learned."

Luza Square.

The Synagogue   The second-oldest Sephardic synagogue in Europe and home of the Jewish Community of Dubrovnik.

Zudioska 5. ⓒ **385/412-219.** Free admission. Mon and Thurs–Fri.

LOCAL FLAVORS

Local favorites include scampi and other seafood dishes, *manistra od bobica* (a bean soup), and *strukle* (rolls made with cottage cheese). Wash your meal down with a local Croatian wine (they're pretty good).

BEST BUYS

Shop here for lace, embroidery, woodcarvings, carpets, ceramics, tapestries, jewelry, and leather and woolen products. There are also a number of art galleries throughout the city. Stores generally close for lunch.

2 The French Riviera & Monte Carlo

The French Riviera is less than 125 miles long and is located between the Mediterranean and a trio of mountain ranges. **Cannes, Nice, Villefranche, St-Tropez,** and **Monte Carlo** are all so close together geographically that they offer nearly the same shore excursions, although each port has its own special flavor and charms. They are all located on the scenic Côte d'Azur, where the natural beauty includes coastal mountains and a very blue sea, and the man-made beauty includes yachts, diamond jewelry, and other reminders that the French Riviera is a playground of the rich and famous. Artists who have captured the glorious landscape here include Matisse, Cocteau, Picasso, Léger, Renoir, and Bonnard. Their works can be found at numerous museums throughout the area.

All the ports are crowded with tourists in the summer months, particularly in July and August. The scenic drive between the ports is gorgeous but can be slow, depending on the traffic.

Cannes is a bustling commercial center. The grand hotels made famous during the International Film Festival can be found on the seafront boulevards, but it's Coco Chanel, not the festival, who's credited with putting the city on the map when she came, got a suntan, then went back to Paris and started a trend. Cannes beaches today continue to be more for exhibitionism and voyeurism than swimming.

The city offers great shopping opportunities, including outlets of major Paris names such as Saint Laurent, Rykiel, and Hermés, which be found on La Croisette. More reasonable shopping can be found a few blocks inland on rue d'Antibes.

The 370-acre principality of **Monaco** became the property of the Grimaldi clan, a Genoese family, in 1297, and has maintained something resembling independence ever since. Its capital, **Monte Carlo,** has for a century symbolized glamour—and the 1956 marriage of Prince Rainier and the American actress Grace Kelly after their meeting at the Cannes film festival only enhanced that status. Their children, Caroline, Albert, and Stephanie, have lived their entire lives in the spotlight, and the bachelor status of Albert, the heir, has the entire principality concerned.

Visitors are always surprised at how small Monaco is. The second smallest state in Europe (Vatican City is smaller), Monaco consists of four tightly packed (we're talking prime real estate here) parts: the old town, setting for the royal palace (where a 10-min. changing of the guard ceremony is held daily at 11:55am) and the Monaco Cathedral (where the tomb of Princess Grace is located); La Condamine, the residential area; Monte Carlo, where the fancy hotels and famous casino are located; and Fontvieille, the commercial area.

When exploring the city, you can walk up hills or use Monaco's somewhat bizarre system of public elevators that take you, for instance, from the harbor to the casino. There is also a tram service that operates on a circuit between the palace, aquarium, and casino, that is priced at a reasonable 5.50€ ($5).

Nice, while once a Victorian playground of the aristocracy, is today a big middle-class city. It's the capital of the Riviera and the largest city between Genoa and Marseille. It's also one of the most ancient cities in the region, founded by the Greeks, who called it Nike, or Victory.

Artists and writers have long been attracted to the city, including Dumas, Nietzsche, Flaubert, Hugo, Sand, and Stendahl. Henri Matisse made his home here.

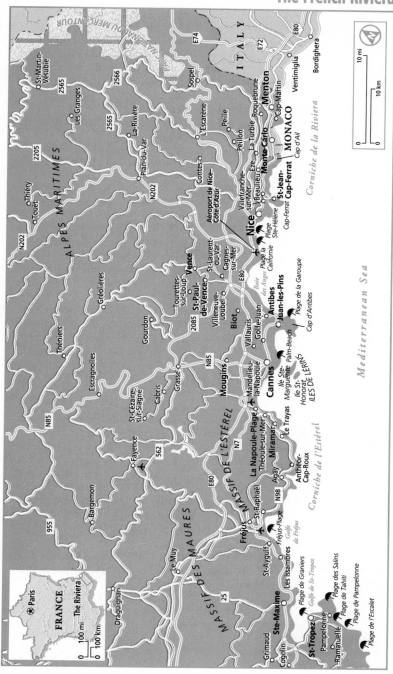

ITALY

St-Martin-Vésubie
2565
Les Granges
2566
2565
La-Rivière
Plan-du-Var
2205
Thiéry
Touët
ALPES MARITIMES
N202
N202
N85
Thénies
Gréolières
Escragnolles
Gourdon
St-Cézaire-sur-Siagne
Cabris
Fayence
N85
562
N7
Bargemon
955
Le Muy
Draguignan
MASSIF DES MAURES
25
Grimaud
Cogolin
St-Ayguif
Les Issambres
Ste-Maxime
St-Tropez
Ramatuelle
Pampelonne

Sospel
L'Escarène
Peille
Contes
Peillon
La Turbie
Èze
Beaulieu
Roquebrune
Cap-Martin
Ventimiglia
Bordighera
Menton
Monte-Carlo
MONACO
Cap d'Ail
St-Jean-
Cap-Ferrat
Cap-Ferrat
Villefranche-sur-Mer
Plage Ste-Hélène
Cap-Ferrat
Aéroport de Nice-
Côte d'Azur
Nice
Plage la
Californie

Vence
St-Paul-
de-Vence
Tourrettes-sur-Loup
2085
Villeneuve-
Loubet
Biot
Vallauris
Grasse
Mougins
N85
Mandelieu-
la-Napoule
La Napoule-Plage
Théoule-sur-Mer
Miramar
Le Trayas
Agay
Anthéor-
Cap-Roux
St-Raphaël
N98
Fréjus
Fréjus-Plage
Golfe
de Fréjus

St-Laurent-
du-Var
Cagnes-
sur-Mer
E80
Baie
des Anges
Golfe-Juan
Antibes
Juan-les-Pins
Plage de la Garoupe
Plage de l'Antibes
Cap d'Antibes
Cannes
Palm-Beach
Île Ste-
Marguerite
Île St-
Honorat
ÎLES DE LÉRINS
MASSIF DE L'ESTÉREL
Corniche de l'Estérel

PARC NATIONAL DU MERCANTOUR

E74
E80
E72

Corniche de la Riviera
Cap d'Ail

Mediterranean Sea

Golfe de St-Tropez
Plage de Graniers
Plage des Salins
Plage de Tahiti
Plage de Pampelonne
Plage de l'Escalet

FRANCE
Paris
The Riviera
0   100 mi
0   100 km

0   10 mi
0   10 km

Our favorite activity here is museum-hopping, especially in nearby Cimiez, home of the Musée National Message Biblique Marc-Chagall and the Musée Matisse. It's also fun to explore Nice's old town, with its colorful houses and narrow streets. The area around the Flower Market is full of outdoor cafes and a great place to people-watch. As bizarre as it may seem, it's also worth a trek uphill to the old graveyard of Nice, where great views and an interesting setting can be found, including lavishly sculpted monuments.

The promenade des Anglais is a wide boulevard on the bay, stretching several miles, and is a lovely walking spot past cafes and historic buildings, and, on the beaches, bronzed bodies in teeny-weeny bikinis.

Brigitte Bardot made the St-Tropez resort famous when she was filmed here in 1957 by her husband, Roger Vadim, in *And God Created Woman;* fun-in-the-sun is still the word in this thriving artists' colony. While the reputation is for hedonism (and you will see topless and even bottomless sunbathers on the beach), there is also a bit of quaint mixed in. Among the recent celebrities spotted here are Barbra Streisand, Jack Nicholson, Robert DeNiro, Sylvester Stallone, Oprah Winfrey, and Elton John.

The town was destroyed by the Germans in 1944, but the local residents, working from old plans and photos, rebuilt the small village to look exactly as it had before. In addition to the beaches, St-Tropez offers good shopping, including a wealth of antiques dealers and art galleries in Old Town.

Villefranche-sur-Mer is a lovely little port town, located only 4 miles from Nice. According to legend, Hercules opened his arms and Villefranche was born. But it is also home to the U.S. Sixth Fleet, and when the fleet's in, the quiet town takes on a decidedly different flavor, turning into a bustling Mediterranean port.

The town is a haven for artists (many of whom take over the houses on the hillside in summer), and provides a nice setting for a quiet day of walking and exploring. But Villefranche is also a good starting point for shore excursions to Nice, Eze, St-Paul-de-Vence, and Monaco.

One artist who came to Villefranche was Jean Cocteau, who left a legacy in the form of frescoes on the 14th-century walls of the Romanesque Chapelle St. Pierre. Also of particular interest is the Rue Obscure, a vaulted street.

Away from the coast, **St-Paul-de-Vence,** visitable by shore excursion, is the best known of the region's perched villages, a feudal hamlet growing on a bastion of rock, almost blending into it. Its ramparts overlook a peaceful setting of flowers and olive and orange trees. Outside the walls is the **Foundation Maeght** (✆ **04-93-32-81-63**), considered by some to be the best art museum on the Riviera. Its contemporary art collection includes works by Calder, Giacometti, Miró, Chagall, Matisse, and more. Admission is 7.75€ ($7) adults, 6€ ($5.50) kids 12 to 18, free for under 12.

Some people visit St-Paul-de-Vence solely to dine at **La Colombe d'Or** (✆ **04/93-32-77-78**), once the stomping ground of some of the most important artists of the 20th century. They would trade art for meals and rooms, and the walls and gardens contain works by Picasso, Braque, Miró, Matisse, Léger, Calder, Chagall, and others. Unfortunately, you can't view the collection unless you spring for a meal here. Main courses are 23€ to 36€ ($21 to $33). Reservations are required.

For the port of **Le Havre,** see chapter 12, "Ports of Call in Northern Europe & the British Isles."

CURRENCY   As of February 2002, France switched entirely to the euro (€) for its currency. One euro is made up of 100 euro cents. The exchange rate at press time was $1 = 1.1€.

LANGUAGE   French.

FROMMER'S FAVORITE FRENCH RIVIERA EXPERIENCES

- **Shopping for high fashion in Cannes.** Look for famous Paris brands on La Croisette, and more affordable shopping on rue d'Antibes and the streets in between.
- **Heading to the beach in Cannes.** Free public beaches include Plage du Midi and Plage Gazagnaire. There are also private beaches where you pay a fee (usually 18€–20€ or $16–$18), for which you get a mattress and a sun umbrella.
- **Visiting the Aquarium in Monte Carlo.** We went to the Oceanographic Museum just to kill some time one day, and discovered a fascinating place with exhibits that include sea dragons and other rare and exotic species. See description below for more info.
- **Playing James Bond at the Monte Carlo Casino.** Put on your tux and indulge in the opulence.
- **Exploring Nice's Old Town.** You'll find a maze of streets teeming with local life, inexpensive restaurants, and boutiques.
- **Climbing up to the cemetery in Nice.** It's a fascinating and scenic place and well worth a visit. Really!
- **Checking out the beaches in St-Tropez.** They're the Riviera's finest. The most daring are the Plage des Salins, Plage de Pampellone, and Plage de Tahiti. If you ever wanted to go topless or bottomless (or just want to gawk at people who are), this is the place.
- **Taking a shore excursion** or spending quiet time in sleepy Villefranche. Close by are Nice, St-Paul-de-Vence, and Eze.

COMING ASHORE & GETTING AROUND   Small ships can dock at Monte Carlo, St-Tropez, or Nice. Large ships at the French Riviera ports usually tender passengers ashore. Taxis are available at the pier, but are expensive (you may want to double up with other passengers if you're planning to go any distance). You can walk from all the ports to many local attractions. There is also great train service from Nice to other locations on the Côte d'Azur.

THE BEST SHORE EXCURSIONS

The best way to explore the French Riviera ports is on foot. You needn't book a shore excursion unless walking is a problem, or you wish to travel to a port other than the one your ship is visiting. If you're looking for something different, you may want to try one of the following.

St-Paul-de-Vence (4 hr., $52–$58): This medieval walled city offers art galleries and shops, cobblestoned streets, cafes, and gorgeous country views. The town has long attracted celebrities, and Gene Wilder and Gilda Radner were married here. The trip may be combined with a visit to Grasse, birthplace of the French perfume industry, and a stop at a perfume factory.

Medieval Eze (3–4 hr., $45–$68): Eze literally clings to the rocks above the sea, and is a medieval village worth exploring. This tour includes a guided walk through the narrow streets, with their lovely restored houses and stunning views. Time is allowed for shopping in the town's boutiques and artists' studios.

Visit to both St-Paul-de-Vence and Eze may be combined, for a higher fee, with a tour of Nice.

THE TOP ATTRACTIONS
CANNES

Musée de la Castre   The collection here includes 19th-century paintings, sculptures, decorative arts, and ethnography, including a gallery devoted to relics of ancient Mediterranean civilizations.

In Château de la Castre, Le Suquet. ☎ **04/93-38-55-26.** Admission 1.55€ ($1.40) adults, free for students and children. Apr–June Wed–Mon 10am–noon and 2–6pm; July–Sept Wed–Mon 10am–noon and 3–7pm; Oct Wed–Mon 10am–noon and 2–5pm.

MONTE CARLO

Monte Carlo Casino   The Casino was built in 1878 by Charles Garnier, the architect who also created the Paris Opera House. It is a very ornate building, but those used to Las Vegas casinos will be surprised at its small size. The atrium is surrounded by 28 Ionic columns made of onyx. The gaming rooms, one leading into the next (you pay more for admission the deeper into the casino you go), feature equally elaborate decor, including gilt, frescoes, and bas-reliefs. Games offered include baccarat, roulette, craps, and blackjack, as well as slot machines (in Salle Américaine).

Place du Casino. ☎ **377-92/16-21-21.** Admission 7.75€–15€ ($7–$14), depending on where in the casino you go. Opens daily at noon. No one under 21 is permitted inside. A passport is required to get in, and at night men must wear a jacket and tie.

Musée de l'Océanographie   This is one of the best aquariums in Europe, displaying rare and unusual sea creatures. The upper floor offers a history of underwater exploration, complete with early scuba gear and a submarine mockup from the 1700s. On the main floor is an aquarium with more than 90 tanks containing such endangered species as the fascinating leafy sea dragon. The museum building is an impressive structure in itself.

Av. St-Martin. ☎ **377-93/15-36-00.** Admission 11€ ($9.50) adults, 5.20€ ($4.70) children 6–18, free for children 5 and under. July–Aug daily 9am–8pm; Apr–June and Sept daily 9am–7pm; Oct daily 9:30am–7pm.

Palais du Prince   Visit the royal palace for a peek into the lifestyle of the ruling Grimaldi family. While the exterior is fortlike, the interior offers an Italianate courtyard and the kind of decorative grand rooms with gold gilt, lush fabrics, and frescoed ceilings that one would expect to find in a royal residence. The tour consists of a recorded commentary, with the tour guide simply pressing a button at each stop (make sure you get on a tour in English). You can buy a combo ticket that includes the adjacent museum and archives, but it's hardly worth the time or extra money to do the latter unless you are really into Napoleonic-era relics, of which the museum seems to have an abundance.

Place du Palais. ☎ **377-25-18-31.** Admission 6€ ($5.50) adults, 3€ ($2.70) children (for palace only). June–Sept daily 9:30am–6:30pm; Oct daily 10am–5pm.

NICE

Musée des Beaux-Arts   Housed in the former residence of the Ukrainian princess Kotchubey, this important gallery is devoted to the masters of the Second Empire and the Belle Epoque, with an extensive collection of 19th-century French artists, including Monet, Renoir, and Rodin.

33 av. Des Baumettes. ℭ **04/92-15-28-28.** Admission 3.75€ ($3.40) adults, free for 18 and under. Tues–Sun 10am–noon and 2–6pm.

Musée Matisse   Matisse spent the last years of his life in Nice, and the museum offers works donated by the artist and his heirs. Included are *Nude in an Armchair with a Green Plant, Nymph in the Forest,* and *Portrait of Madame Matisse,* as well as practice sketches and designs, and items from the artist's own collection and home.

In Cimiez. Villa des Arénes-de-Cimiez. 164 av. Des Arénes-de-Cimiez. ℭ **04/93-81-08-08.** Admission 3.75€ ($3.40) adults, 2.25€ ($2.05) children. Wed–Mon 10am–6pm.

Musée National Message Biblique Marc-Chagall   Located in the hills above Nice, this museum is dedicated to the artist's treatment of biblical themes. Chagall and his wife donated the works, which include oils, gouaches, drawings, pastels, lithographs, and sculptures, as well as a mosaic and stained-glass windows. A helpful brochure, available in English, describes biblical themes.

In Cimiez. Av. Du Dr.-Ménard. ℭ **04/93-53-87-20.** Admission 5.50€ ($5) adults, free for children. Rates may be higher for special exhibitions. July–Sept Wed–Mon 10am–6pm; Oct and Apr–June Wed–Mon 10am–5pm.

ST-TROPEZ

L'Annonciade Musée St-Tropez   This museum, housed in a former chapel, has one of the best modern-art collections on the Riviera, and includes Van Dongen's *Women of the Balustrade* and paintings and sculpture by Bonnard, Matisse, Braque, Utrillo, Seurat, Derain, and Maillol.

Place Georges-Grammont. ℭ **04/94-97-04-01.** Admission 4.50€ ($4.05) adults, 2.25€ ($2.05) children. June–Sept Wed–Mon 10am–noon and 3–7pm; Oct and Dec–May Wed–Mon 10am–noon and 2–6pm. Closed Nov.

VILLEFRANCHE

Romanesque Chapelle St-Pierre   Jean Cocteau left his mark here in the form of frescoes paying tribute to gypsies, St. Peter, and the young women of Villefranche.

Quai de la Douane/rue des Mariniéres. ℭ **04/93-76-90-70.** Admission 2.25€ ($2.05). July–Sept Tues–Sun 10am–noon and 4–8:30pm; Oct Tues–Sun 9:30am–noon and 2–5pm; Apr–June Tues–Sun 9:30am–noon and 3–7pm.

LOCAL FLAVORS

Definitely try bouillabaisse, fish stew, and salade Niçoise. Other local specialties include pizza served with onions or olives. Be sure to sample some French wine with your meal. If you have very big bucks (we're talking set-price dinner for 129€–148€/$117–$134 and lunch for 75€/$68), you'll want to eat at **Le Louis XV** in the **Hôtel de Paris** in Monte Carlo (ℭ **377-92/16-30-01**), where Alain Ducasse does his six-star magic (both this and his restaurant in Paris received three stars from Michelin). Make reservations well in advance, and expect a good dose of attitude from your wait staff.

Try **Le Safari** (ℭ **04/93-80-18-44**), overlooking the Flower Market, for a fun, inexpensive place to dine in Nice. It's open for lunch and dinner. Main courses run 10€ to 23€ ($9 to $21). Reservations are highly recommended.

BEST BUYS

Shop at these ports for high-fashion items, artwork, antiques, and items made of colorful Provençal fabrics.

3 Greece

Greece is a spectacular country where ancient sites and architectural treasures join forces with the sun, scenery, and food to make one of the best vacation spots on Earth. It's a feast for the mind and the senses, a place that is exotic but at the same time friendly and familiar, and where there is always something to remind visitors of the past.

CURRENCY As of March 2002, Greece switched entirely to the euro (€) for its currency. One euro is made up of 100 euro cents. The exchange rate at press time was $1 = 1.1€.

LANGUAGE Greek is the official language, but English and French are widely spoken.

ATHENS

This fabled metropolis is a delightful mix of modern and ancient. The Parthenon and the treasures on display at the National Archaeological Museum best personify the image most of us have of ancient Greece, but interspersed among the ancient monuments, tavernas, and neoclassical buildings are highrises, fast-food outlets, and plenty of souvenir shops. Modern Athens is crowded, teeming with inhabitants, traffic, and taxis (although getting one can be a challenge). The city is also polluted and grows unbelievably hot during the summer. To appreciate both sides of Athens, explore it slowly, and get resigned to the fact that you won't have time to see everything. Climb to the Parthenon, enjoy a leisurely lunch at an outside cafe, get caught in the hustle and bustle of the streets, and savor the moments spent in the birthplace of western civilization.

FROMMER'S FAVORITE ATHENS EXPERIENCES

- **Strolling around the Plaka.** The Plaka is the oldest neighborhood in Athens. As you wander its narrow streets you will come upon quaint single-story homes, neoclassical buildings, tavernas, nightclubs, and souvenir shops. It's easy to get lost in the maze of streets here, but along the way you may spot an ancient monument or a fascinating neighborhood church.
- **Going museum-hopping.** The National Archaeological Museum is enormous and can easily occupy a few hours. There are also several small museums worth a look (see below).
- **Visiting the National Gardens.** Located next to the Parliament House is the former royal family's palace garden. Visitors will find a park, a small zoo, shady trees, benches, a cafe, and small lakes and ponds with ducks, swans, and even peacocks. The garden is open daily from 7am to 10pm, but don't linger here alone at night.

COMING ASHORE & GETTING AROUND Cruise ships dock at the port city of **Piraeus,** about 7 miles southwest of Athens. There's not much to do in Piraeus, so you'll want to head into Athens. You can take a metro train or taxi into the city, and most cruise lines also offer a bus service (for a fee). We recommend the train, which you can walk to from the pier. It costs about a quarter. If you're taking a taxi, try to bargain with the driver. The average fare from Piraeus to Syntagma Square in Athens should be about 7.75€ ($7), but many drivers will quote a flat rate, which can be as high as 19€ ($17). You can pay it or try to find another taxi driver willing to turn on the meter. The trip can take a while if there's bad traffic (which there often is here).

Note that drivers here will not always accept you as a fare. They will ask where you are going and are free to decline if they are not going your way. Consequently, it sometimes takes a fair amount of time to find a cab (so plan accordingly). It is also not uncommon for a driver to stop and pick up two or three different parties to fill the cab. If this happens, you are only responsible for your leg of the journey.

THE BEST SHORE EXCURSIONS

Athens City Tour (3½–4 hr., $38–$44): Includes a guided tour of the Acropolis; a drive past other Athens highlights, including Constitution Square, the Parliament, the Temple of Zeus, Hadrian's Arch, and Olympic Stadium; and time for souvenir shopping. A full-day city tour (8½ hr., $92) also includes a visit to the National Archaeological Museum, time to shop in the Plaka, and lunch.

A Day Tour of Delphi (9½–10½ hr., $96–$109): If you've been to Athens before or just aren't into big cities and crowds, you may want to try this day trip to one of the great sights of antiquity. The tour visits the ruins of the Temple of Apollo, located in a stunning setting on the slope of Mount Parnassus. Lunch is included.

THE TOP ATTRACTIONS

The Acropolis   For many centuries, the Acropolis—the heights above Athens—was the religious center of Athens, and in various times it's served as the seat of a king and the home of gods and goddesses. The most striking structures are the Parthenon (the most recognized Greek monument, dedicated to Athena), the Propylaea (the gateway to the Acropolis), the Temple of Athena Nike (built in the 5th century B.C. and restored in the 1930s), and the Erechtheion (honored by Athenians as the tomb of Erechtheus, a legendary king of Athens, and noteworthy for its delicate carving). Visitors may be disappointed to find that they cannot enter the Parthenon due to preservation and restoration efforts. However, leave plenty of time to explore the Acropolis and the museum. In the summer, if possible, start out early in the morning, when the sun is not at its strongest and the crowds are not as overwhelming.

Enter on the west end of the site, accessible from a path off Dioskouon and Theorias sts. 🕐 01/321-0219. Admission 12€ ($10.50), which includes same-day admission to the National Archaeological Museum. Free admission on Sun. Admission includes entrance to the Acropolis Museum, which is sometimes open different hours than the site. Open daily in the summer (8am–7pm) and winter (8:30am–2:30pm).

Ancient Agora   The Agora, a jumble of ancient buildings, inscriptions, and fragments of sculpture, served as a political and commercial center of Athens. The two best ruins are the Hephaisteion (a temple to Hephaisos built in the 5th century B.C.) and the reconstructed Stoa of Attalos, which serves as a museum.

Below the Acropolis on the edge of Monastiraki. 🕐 01/321-0185. Admission 4.40€ ($4) adults, 3.30€ ($3) seniors, 2.20€ ($2) students. Tues–Sun 8:30am–3pm.

Greek Folk Art Museum   This small museum showcases pieces dating from 1650 to the present, including embroidery, costumes, silver and metal works, pottery, and wood and stone carvings, as well as paintings by Theophilos Hatzimichail.

Odos Kidathineon 17, Plaka. 🕐 01/322-9031. Admission 1.40€ ($1.30) adults, .85€ (78¢) students. Tues–Sun 10am–2pm.

Athens

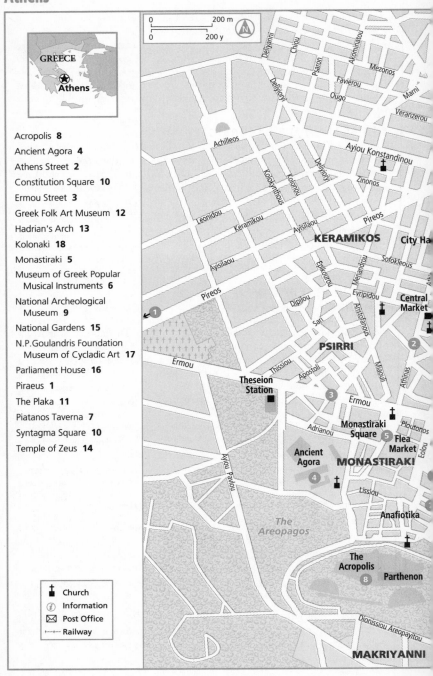

GREECE

Athens

0   200 m

0   200 y

✝ Church

ⓘ Information

✉ Post Office

┝━ Railway

Deliyanni

Chiou

Psaron

Akominatou

Mezonos

Marni

Favierou

Ougo

Veranzerou

Achilleos

Deliyoyi

Ayiou Konstandinou

Deliyoyi

Zinonos

Kolokynthious

Kolonou

Pireos

Leonidou

Keramikou

Ayisilaou

KERAMIKOS   City Ha

Ayisilaou

Epikourou

Sofokleous

Pireos

Menandrou

Evripidou

Dipilou

Aristofanous

**Central
Market**

Sari

Thissiou

PSIRRI

Miaouli

Athinas

Ermou

Apostoli

**Theseion
Station**

Ermou

Adrianou

**Monastiraki
Square**

Ploutonos

**Flea
Market**

Eolou

Ayiou Pavlou

**Ancient
Agora**

MONASTIRAKI

Lissiou

**The
Areopagos**

Anafiotika

**The
Acropolis**   **8**   **Parthenon**

Dionissiou Areopayitou

MAKRIYANNI

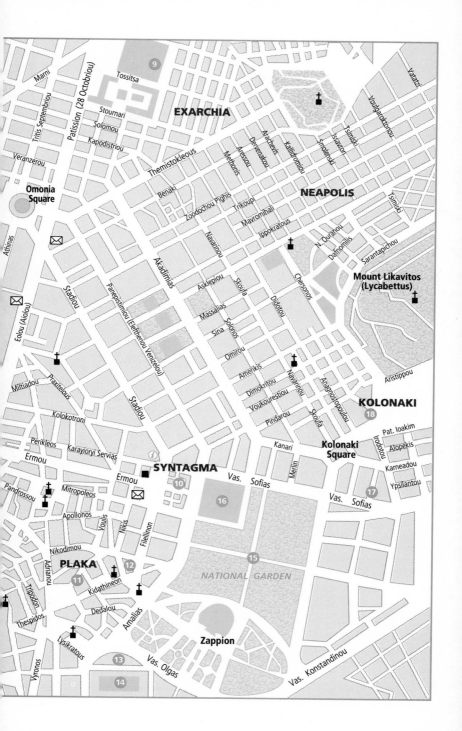

EXARCHIA

NEAPOLIS

Omonia
Square

Mount Likavitos
(Lycabettus)

KOLONAKI

Kolonaki
Square

SYNTAGMA

Vas. Sofias

Vas. Sofias

PLAKA

NATIONAL GARDEN

Zappion

Tossitsa

Marni

Tritis Septembriou

Patission (28 Octobriou)

Stournari

Solomou

Kapodistriou

Veranzerou

Themistokleous

Benaki

Zoodochou Pighis

Navarinou

Akadimias

Asklepiou

Skoufa

Massalias

Sina

Solonos

Omirou

Amerikis

Dimokritou

Voukourestiou

Pindarou

Skoufa

Navarinou

Didotou

Chesonos

Anagnostopoulou

Aristippou

Panepistimiou (Eleftheriou Venizelou)

Stadiou

Stadiou

Miltiadou

Praxitelous

Kolokotroni

Perikleos

Ermou

Pandrossou

Mitropoleos

Apollonos

Voulis

Nikis

Filellinon

Nikodimou

Adrianou

Kidathineon

Tripodon

Thespidos

Dedalou

Amalias

Lysikratous

Vyronos

Vas. Olgas

Karayioryi Servias

Ermou

Kanari

Merlin

Vaiatzi

Youkouridonou

Tsimiski

Issavron

Smolenski

Kallidromiou

Dervenakou

Aracheris

Aresou

Methonis

Trikoupi

Mavromihali

Ippokratous

N. Ouranou

Dafnomilis

Sarantapichou

Tsimiski

Pat. Ioakim

Irodotou

Alopekis

Karneadou

Ypsilantou

Vas. Konstandinou

287

Museum of Greek Popular Musical Instruments   There are about 1,200 popular Greek musical instruments in the collection (dating from the 18th century to present). The museum is housed in the Lassanis Mansion, built in 1842. Recitals are held in the museum's garden.

Odos Dioyenous 1–3. ℭ 01/325-0198. Free admission. Tues and Thurs–Sun 10am–2pm; Wed noon–6pm.

The National Archaeological Museum   This large museum takes time to navigate and is quite popular, so it's best to get there early so you'll be able to see the exhibits rather than the backs of fellow museum-goers. The museum contains collections from prehistoric times, pottery and Minoan art, sculpture, bronzes, and Egyptian art.

Odos Pattision 44. ℭ 01/821-7717. Admission 12€ ($10.50), which includes same-day admission to the Acropolis. Summer daily 8am–7pm; winter daily 8am–3pm (but double-check, as hours are subject to change).

N. P. Goulandris Foundation Museum of Cycladic Art   This attractive museum is the home of the second largest collection of art from the Cyclades, a group of about 200 islands in the Aegean, between the years 3200 and 2000 B.C. The Greek artifact collection includes jewelry, glass, and metal ware, pottery, and figurines from the 3rd millennium B.C. to the 4th century A.D.

Odos Neofytou Douka 4. ℭ 01/722-8321. Admission 2.20€ ($2) adults, .70€ (65¢) children. Mon and Wed–Fri 10am–4pm; Sat 10am–3pm.

LOCAL FLAVORS

Most Greek meals start off with *mezedes* (appetizers). Items can range from grilled *oktapodi* (octopus) to *keftedes* (meatballs) to *tzatziki* (yogurt dip with cucumber and garlic). Other items include *kalamaraki* (squid), feta (white goat cheese), and *spanakopita* (spinach pies).

Typical main dishes are *moussaka* (layers of eggplant, minced meat, and potatoes topped with a cheese sauce and baked), *pastitsio* (macaroni baked with minced meat and bechamel sauce), *gemista* (either tomatoes or green peppers stuffed with minced meat or rice), *dolmades* (cabbage or vine leaves stuffed with minced meat or rice and served with an egg and lemon sauce), and *souvlaki* (pieces of meat on small skewers).

Baklava, a honey-drenched pastry with nuts, is a popular dessert that is sticky and sweet. Ouzo is a traditional Greek liquor.

Some of the quaintest restaurants in the city can be found in the Plaka, but there are also some real tourist traps in that area. Don't frequent a place where waiters are standing outside to pull you in. Also avoid places with floor shows.

A good traditional taverna is **Platanos Taverna,** Odos Dioyenous 4 (ℭ **01/ 322-0666**), which is open for both lunch and dinner and offers outdoor tables in good weather. "Home cooking" has been served here since 1932. Especially great are the artichokes or spinach with lamb, and the house wine is pretty good too. Main courses are about 7.20€ to 9.95€ ($6.50 to $9.00).

BEST BUYS

Shop Athens for gold and silver jewelry, icons, leather goods, ceramics, kitchenware, *komboloi* (worry beads), and blue-and-white amulets (for warding off evil spirits).

Ermou Street is the place for women's fashion. **Kolonaki** is the place to head for designer boutiques and shoe stores. Kitchenware and household items can be found on **Athenas Street,** while **Monastraki,** the area adjacent to the Plaka, is

The Greek Isles

Skýros
SOUTHERN SPORADES
GREECE
Athens
Paralía Kímis
Izmir
ÉVVIA
AEGEAN ISLANDS
TURKEY
Híos
Kárystos
← Athens
Sámos
Ándros
Tínos
Sýros
Délos   Mýkonos
Sérifos
Páros   Náxos
Antíparos
Sífnos
KOS
CYCLADES
Mílos
Íos
Folégandros
Santoríni
DODECANESE
Rhodes

0   50 Mi
0   80 Km

known for its flea market, most lively on Sundays (but open every day). Keep in mind that not everything sold as an antique is genuine. Also, it's illegal to take antiquities and icons more than 100 years old out of the country without an export license, which is difficult to obtain.

MYKONOS

The landscape of this island's main town, **Hora,** dazzles with whitewashed homes, their doors and window frames painted brightly, and a harbor lined with fishing boats. Pelicans, the mascots of Mykonos, greet passengers at the pier.

There is a charming quality here despite the large numbers of sunseekers, the party-town reputation (especially in July and Aug), and the inevitable souvenir shops. As you navigate the cobblestone streets, you'll encounter windmills; small, blue-domed churches; and outdoor cafes.

Unlike other Greek islands visited by cruise ships, Mykonos is not a setting for ancient ruins. Those starving for sacred sights of note can catch a shore excursion to nearby **Delos,** the birthplace of Apollo.

Mykonos's second town is **Ano Mera,** about 4 miles east of Hora, where you'll find a more traditional ambience and some religious sites of note. The **Monastery of Panayia Tourliani** dates to 1580 and has a handsomely carved steeple, as well as a small religious museum inside. Nearby is the 12th-century **Monastery of Paleokastro,** one of the greenest spots on the island.

Hora (Mykonos Town)

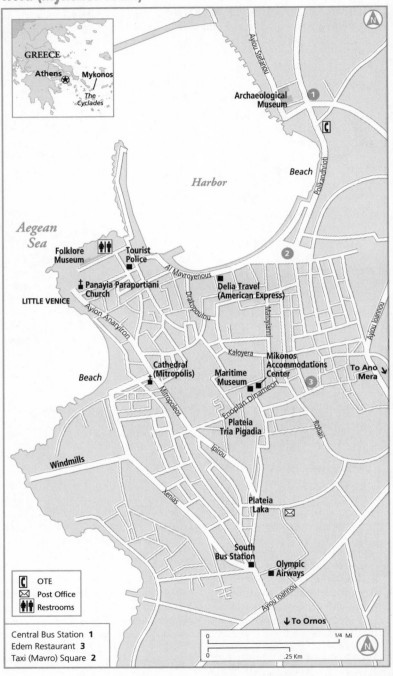

GREECE

Athens

Mykonos

The Cyclades

Aviou Stefanou

Archaeological Museum

1

C

Harbor

Beach

Aegean Sea

Folklore Museum

Tourist Police

Al Mavroyenous

2

Panayia Paraportiani Church

LITTLE VENICE

Delia Travel (American Express)

Drafopoulou

Avion Anaryiron

Matoyianni

Kaloyera

Mikonos Accommodations Center

Beach

Cathedral (Mitropolis)

Maritime Museum

To Ano Mera

3

Enoplan Dinameon

Mitropoleos

Plateia Tria Pigadia

Ipirou

Rohari

Aviou Ioannou

Windmills

Xenias

Plateia Laka

South Bus Station

Olympic Airways

Aviou Ioannou

↓ To Ornos

C OTE
⊠ Post Office
🚻 Restrooms

Central Bus Station **1**
Edem Restaurant **3**
Taxi (Mavro) Square **2**

0 _____ 1/4 Mi
0 _____ .25 Km

FROMMER'S FAVORITE MYKONOS EXPERIENCES

- **Hitting the beach.** Paradise, the island's original nude beach, is its most famous. Other notable stretches include Kalafatis and Ayios Sostis.
- **Having an undersea adventure.** Mykonos is the place for diving in the Aegean, especially in September. The best-known diving center is at **Psarou Beach** (ⓒ/fax **0289/24-808;** diving_center_psarou@ myk.forthnet.gr).

COMING ASHORE & GETTING AROUND   Ships tender passengers to the main harbor area along the Esplanade in Hora. The best way to get around town is to walk. Much of the rest of the island is served by a good **bus** system. The central bus station is located off the left of the harbor. Bus routes go to all the beaches from Hora. There are also two types of **taxis.** The standard cab, which you can find at Taxi (Mavro) Square, can take you outside of town. There's a notice board at the square with rates. Small motor scooter taxis also zip through the narrow streets of Hora, which by government decree is an architectural landmark where cars are not allowed. These can be found at the pier.

THE BEST SHORE EXCURSIONS

Delos Apollo Sanctuary (3–4½ hr., $37–$63): Travel by small boat from Mykonos harbor to Delos for a 2-hour guided walking tour of the tiny island that was once the religious and commercial hub of the Aegean, but now is home only to ancient ruins and their caretakers. View the Agora; the Sacred Way, which leads to the Temple of Apollo; and the Avenue of Lions, where five marble beasts from the 7th century B.C. guard the now-dry Sacred Lake. View the remains of the Hellenistic Quarter with its harbors, waterhouses, and villas, including the House of Cleopatra, and the renowned mosaic floors in the House of the Dolphin, the House of the Masks, and the House of Dionysos. Also visit the Archaeological Museum.

THE TOP ATTRACTIONS

The town of Hora itself, with its quaint houses, churches, and labyrinth of alleys, is the main attraction here. The best thing to do is simply wander about, heading inland from the pier and meandering along the labyrinth of streets, getting lost in the alleys, looking at the art galleries, jewelry, and other gift shops, or stopping at a cafe or bar. The town is like a picture postcard.

LOCAL FLAVORS

There are many quaint cafes and charming restaurants. Worth visiting is **Edem Restaurant** in Hora (ⓒ **0289/22-855**). It is known both for its meat dishes and great service, and is located above Panahrandou church—walk up Matoyianni, turn left on Kaloyera, and follow the signs up and to the left. Open for lunch and dinner. Main courses cost 11€ to 18€ ($10 to $16).

BEST BUYS

Mykonos boasts a large community of artists, with many galleries selling their work. Gold jewelry can be found throughout the island.

RHODES

The island of Rhodes is rich in history, and its landscape is dotted with beautiful beaches, mountain villages, and fertile plains. Its most famous inhabitants were the Knights of St. John, who arrived in 1291 after fleeing Jerusalem. They reigned for more than 2 centuries, and their legacy lives on in **Rhodes Town.**

The city is now made up of the New Town and the Old Town; within the medieval walls of the Old Town are treasures from the Knights, while the New Town boasts a happening nighttime scene with its bars, discos, and tavernas.

Lindos, a picturesque village about 50 minutes from Rhodes Town, boasts the Acropolis at Lindos, which rises about 400 feet above the town on a beautiful bay.

FROMMER'S FAVORITE RHODES EXPERIENCES

- **Exploring Old Town.** This section of the city is home to medieval treasures, charming rooftop cafes, and plenty of shops. To appreciate its many offerings, walk though its maze of streets. Main attractions include the Hospital of the Knights, the Streets of the Knights, and the Palace of the Grand Masters.
- **Visiting Lindos.** This picturesque village boasts the island's top archaeological site (the Acropolis) as well as traditional white-walled homes and cobblestone streets.
- **Soaking up the sun.** The island is known for its great beaches. Some of the best are located on the east coast. Faliaraki, about 20 minutes from Rhodes Town, is one of the island's most popular (admission is 3.90€/$3.50).

COMING ASHORE & GETTING AROUND   Ships dock at the commercial harbor, which is within walking distance of Rhodes Town's old section. The New Town is also within walking distance, but there is more to see in the Old Town.

To explore the island of Rhodes, transportation is required. Buses, rental cars, or motor scooters are available near the harbor. **Taxis** wait at the end of the pier. Negotiate fares with taxi drivers for sightseeing; the hourly rate is 28€ to 39€ ($25 to $35).

THE BEST SHORE EXCURSIONS

Rhodes & Lindos (4–4½ hr., $40–$56): Travel by bus through the scenic countryside to Lindos, an important city in ancient times. At Lindos, view the medieval walls, which were constructed by the Knights of St. John in the 14th century. Walk or ride a donkey up to the ancient Acropolis, where there are ruins and great views (you'll pass souvenir shops on the way). The trip may include a walking tour of Old Town Rhodes (see description above), a stop at a workshop selling Rhodian ceramics, and/or a visit to Mount Smith to view the ruins of ancient Rhodes, the Temple of Apollo, and Diagoras Stadium.

Lindos with Lunch by the Beach (8 hr., $65–$89): Drive to Lindos and explore the city (see above). Continue on to a secluded beach for some swimming and sunning. Changing facilities, restrooms, and showers are available. Lunch is at a beachfront restaurant. Return to Rhodes, driving along the walls of the medieval city and stopping at Port d'Amboise for a walk through Old Town. View the Palace of the Knights and the medieval houses, as well as the Hospital of the Knights of St. John. The tour may stop at a ceramics workshop to view how Rhodian ceramics are made.

THE TOP ATTRACTIONS

The Hospital of the Knights   The 15th-century Hospital of the Knights is now the home of the Archaeological Museum, whose collection features fine works from the Mycenaean and Roman eras.

Old Town. ✆ 02/41-276-57. Admission 2.20€ ($2). Summer daily 8:30am–6pm; winter daily 8:30am–3pm.

Alexis Taverna **4**
Faliaraki Beach **5**
Hospital of the
   Knights **3**
Palace of the Grand
   Masters **1**
Street of the Knights **2**

Mandraki Harbor   The Colossus of Rhodes, a 100-foot-tall bronze statue of the sun god Helios and one of the Seven Wonders of the Ancient World, was erected somewhere here. (Legend has it that the statue straddled the harbor, but more likely it was erected off to one side.)
New Town.

The Palace of the Grand Masters   This is the palace and fortress that dominates the Old Town. The floors are covered with mosaics from the island of Kos, and the palace features two permanent exhibitions about Rhodes.
Old Town. ℃ **02/41-233-59.** Admission 3.50€ ($3.15). Summer Tues–Sun 8am–6pm; winter Tues–Sun 8:30am–3pm.

The Street of the Knights   The cobblestoned street (noted on maps as "Ippoton") leads to the Palace of the Grand Masters and is where the inns of the various nations of the Knights of St. John were located. The inns served as clubs and meeting places for the knights, and their facades mirror the architectural styles of the various countries.
Old Town.

LOCAL FLAVORS

There are plenty of places in the Old Town and New Town to enjoy a meal, and the best bet at any of the restaurants is seafood. One of the best is **Alexis Taverna,**

Odos Sokratous 18, in Old Town (© **0241/29-347**). Among those who have dined here are Winston Churchill and Jacqueline Kennedy, as well as assorted royalty. Reservations are recommended. Specially designed dinners run about 44€ ($40) without wine.

BEST BUYS

Head to the Old Town for good buys on gold and silver jewelry, leather goods and furs, sea sponges, lace, and carpets and kilims.

SANTORINI

Dotted with whitewashed homes, black-pebble beaches, rich vineyards, and ancient ruins, Santorini is one of the most breathtaking islands in the world, and approaching it by ship is a dramatic experience. Ships enter the *caldera,* a central crater that was formed when a volcano erupted in 1500 B.C. Ash fell on the remaining land, burying the cosmopolitan city of **Akrotiri,** an event that some believe sparked the legend of the lost continent of Atlantis.

Fira, the capital of Santorini, lives up to its picture-postcard reputation. The city is about 1,000 feet above sea level. Along its winding streets are shops, cafes, and art galleries.

Ia, about 10 to 15 minutes from Fira, is an artist's colony. The city is quite picturesque, with charming homes and galleries showcasing modern and folk art and traditional handicrafts.

FROMMER'S FAVORITE SANTORINI EXPERIENCES

- **Watching the sunset.** The best spots are from the ramparts of Lontza Castle in Ia, the *volta* (stroll) in Fira, or the footpath between Fira and Ia (see below).
- **Walking from Fira to Ia.** If you're a hiker, there's a 6.2-mile pedestrian path that follows the edge of the caldera and offers stunning views. Along the way, you pass several churches and climb two substantial hills.

COMING ASHORE & GETTING AROUND   Ships tender passengers to the port of Skala, and visitors have three options to reach town: by donkey, by cable car, or on foot. The **donkey and cable car rides** cost about 2.75€ ($2.50) each way. The walk up the 587 steps is the same route the donkeys take. Word to the wise: Donkeys are fed at the bottom of the hill, so they tend to run down whether they are carrying someone or not. They are also very smelly. Cable cars run every 20 minutes; walking takes about 30 minutes (depending on the individual). Donkey rides take about 20 to 30 minutes depending on traffic and availability.

The city of Fira can be easily explored by foot. **Taxis** and **buses** are available to take you to other parts of the island. A cab ride to Ia takes about 10 to 15 minutes and costs 11€ to 13€ ($10 to $12) one-way; a cab ride to the ruins of Akrotiri is about 30 minutes (make sure you make return arrangements with the driver). Buses cost 1.70€ to 3.30€ ($1.50 to $3) each way. You can also rent a **moped** (11€–22€/$10–$20 a day), but it is not the safest way of getting around—the roads on this island are notoriously treacherous.

THE BEST SHORE EXCURSIONS

Akrotiri Excavations & Fira Town (3 hr., $45–$57): This tour takes you to Akrotiri, an excavation site that dates back to the second millennium B.C. You

are then dropped off in Fira, where you'll have time to shop or stroll through town before catching a cable car ride or mule back down the slope to the ship.

THE TOP ATTRACTIONS

Ancient Akrotiri   Excavations at Akrotiri, an ancient city that was preserved under a layer of volcanic ash 3,600 years ago, began in 1967 and are ongoing, giving visitors a glimpse of urban life in the Minoan period. Archaeologists have uncovered streets, houses, art, and magnificent frescoes, which are now on display at the National Archaeological Museum in Athens. It's best to take a guided tour here (as offered by the cruise lines), but guidebooks are available at the site. Also, try to visit in the morning, when it's cooler.

Akrotiri. ✆ **0286/81-366.** Admission 3.50€ ($3.15) adults, 1.70€ ($1.55) students. Tues–Sun 8:30am–3pm.

Ancient Thira   The extensive Hellenic, Roman, and Byzantine ruins of Ancient Thira stand on Mesa Vouna, and can be brought to life with the assistance of a good tour guide. From this perch, you get incredible views of Santorini and its neighbor islands. Two popular beaches, Kamari and Perissa, lie on either side of the mesa.

Kamari, 84700. ✆ **0286/31-66.** Admission 3.50€ ($3.15) adults, 1.70€ ($1.55) students. Tues–Sun 8:30am–3pm.

LOCAL FLAVORS

Watching the sunset from a cafe on the caldera is a popular pastime in Santorini. **Franco's** is the most popular spot, but drinks are expensive (nearly 8.85€/$8 a pop). Nearby, **Tropical** also has a good view but charges less. Arrive early to get a good seat outside: Have a drink, and wait for the show to begin.

In Fira, prices are higher at restaurants near the cable car station. Some of the city's finer establishments are located near the cathedral on Odos Ipapantis.

BEST BUYS

Jewelry prices in Fira are a tad higher than those in Athens, but there is a good selection. One of the better-known jewelers is **Kostas Antoniou** on Odos Ayiou Ioannou, north of the cable car station (☎ **0286/22-633**).

4 Italy

If you ask 10 people what their favorite country is in Europe, our guess is that 8 of them will say Italy. You can eat great food, talk to friendly people, and shop for the latest fashions; see some of the ancient world's most famous ruins, like the Forum in Rome and the ancient city of Pompeii; immerse yourself in the Renaissance in Florence; and be part of living history in Venice.

This is the land of Leonardo and Michelangelo, of Caesar and the Popes. And whether you are drawn to the treasure trove of artwork, the incredible architecture, the religious significance, the gorgeous scenery, the wonderful pasta, or all of the above, Italy, with its sense of *la dolce vita,* is bound to deliver.

CURRENCY   As of March 2002, Italy switched entirely to the euro (€) for its currency. One euro is made up of 100 euro cents. The exchange rate at press time was $1 = 1.1€.

LANGUAGE   Italian.

CIVITAVECCHIA/ROME

Civitavecchia has served as the port of Rome since Emperor Trajan declared it such in A.D. 108.

Cruise ships shuttle passengers from here to Rome, about 90 minutes away by bus. Civitavecchia itself, with its mostly post–World War II architecture, hasn't attracted much tourist attention. But the city did invest big bucks during the Jubilee Year (2000) in its cruise facilities and renovating its few landmarks, including the Vanvitelli fountain, the Roman dock of Lazaretto, and its ancient walls.

There is also shopping in town (keep in mind most shops close in the afternoon for a long lunch period) as well as some decent restaurants on the waterfront.

FROMMER'S FAVORITE CIVITAVECCHIA EXPERIENCES

• **Taking a shore excursion to Rome.** There is nothing in Civitavecchia that comes close to the Roman Colosseum, the Vatican, and other amazing landmarks.

COMING ASHORE & GETTING AROUND   From the pier, it's about a 15-minute walk to town, or a 5-minute cab ride. **Taxis** are usually available at the pier. The drive to Rome is about 90 minutes. There is also **train** service to Rome. The train station is in town, and the train ride takes about an hour (depending on the time of day, service is hourly or twice hourly).

THE BEST SHORE EXCURSIONS

In addition to the excursion below, most ships offer a bus transfer so you can explore Rome on your own for $56 to $69. Some offer the option of a half-day on your own and a half-day of group touring for $75 to $92.

Rome City Tour (9½ hr., $135–$182): This comprehensive tour includes visits to the Colosseum, the greatest architectural remnant of ancient Rome; and the Vatican, including the Bernini-designed Piazza San Pietro, magnificent St. Peter's Basilica, and the Vatican Museum, with its remarkable Sistine Chapel (bring binoculars). Also drive past such landmarks as the remains of the Roman Forum, Trajan's Column, the Arch of Constantine, and the Circus Maximus. The tour may also include a short walk to see Trevi Fountain.

THE TOP ATTRACTIONS

There's not really much to see in Civitavecchia. Head to Rome instead to see the attractions mentioned above.

LOCAL FLAVORS

There are restaurants and trattorias on Civitavecchia's waterfront, serving pasta, seafood, and pizza.

BEST BUYS

Shop in Civitavecchia for shoes and other leather goods. There are a number of good stores on the main street (though not as good as what you'll find in Rome). In the morning, it's also fun to poke around the market, located behind the main street.

LIVORNO

This major port city is the gateway to Florence, the birthplace of the Italian Renaissance, about a 2-hour drive away. It is also a port of choice for cruise lines because of its close proximity to Pisa and the leaning tower thereof, and as an entry to the Tuscany region with its famous Chianti vineyards, cypress trees, and olive groves.

There's not much happening in the way of tourist attractions in Livorno itself, but you can shop here for olive oil and Chianti and enjoy a typical Tuscan meal.

FROMMER'S FAVORITE LIVORNO EXPERIENCES

- **Taking the shore excursion to Florence.** Or you can take the shuttle and explore Florence on your own.

COMING ASHORE & GETTING AROUND   Ships dock about a mile from the center of town. **Taxis** are usually available at the pier. Florence is a 2-hour drive, or about an hour and a quarter by train (the train station is about a 15-min. cab or bus ride from the pier). Pisa is only 12 miles away, and also accessible by train (the ride takes about 25 min.).

THE BEST SHORE EXCURSIONS

Florence City Tour (9–10 hr., $89–$165): It's a 2-hour drive to the edge of the city center, where buses have to park, with the rest of the tour on foot. Visit the Galleria dell'Accademia, Europe's first drawing school, to view Michelangelo's sculptures, including *David;* the Duomo, the tremendous cathedral (it's the fourth largest church in the world); the Campanile, the 15th-century bell tower; Piazza della Signoria, the city's main square; and the 13th-century Church of Santa Croce. Lunch and shopping time are included. Some tours also make a

Rome

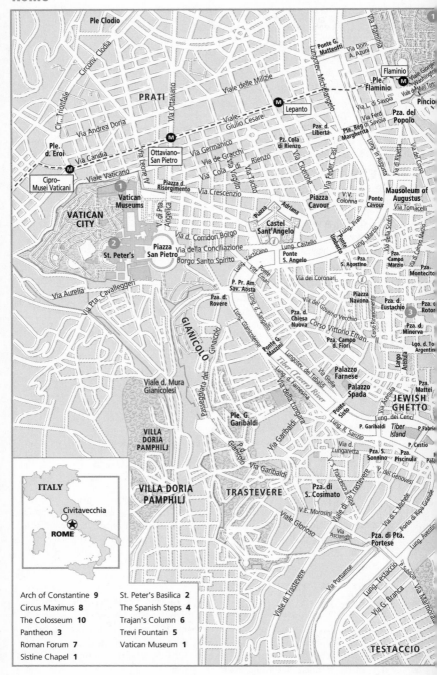

Ple Clodio

PRATI

Via Andrea Doria

Viale delle Milizie

Ponte G. Matteotti

Lungotev. Michelangelo

Lungotev. A. Azuni

Via Dom. A. Azuni

Via Flaminia

Viale Giorgio

Viale di Washington

Viale del Muro Torr

Flaminio

Ple. Flaminio

Pincio

Pza. del Popolo

Lepanto

Viale Giulio Cesare

Via L. di Savoia

Via Fer. di Savoia

Pza. d. Libertà

Pte. Reg di Savoia

Via di Rinetta

Via di Corso

Circonv. Clodia

Cir. Trionfale

Via Ottaviano

Ple. d. Eroi

Via Candia

Ottaviano-San Pietro

Via Germanico

Via de Gracchi

Via Cola di Rienzo

Via Cicerone

Pz. Cola di Rienzo

Rienzo

Via Virgilio

Via Feder. Cesi

V.V. Colonna

Ponte Cavour

Mausoleum of Augustus

Via Tomacelli

Cipro-Musei Vaticani

Viale Vaticano

Via Leone IV

V. di Pta Angelica

Piazza d. Risorgimento

Via Crescenzio

Piazza Cavour

Lung. Prati

Via di Ripetta in Augusta

VATICAN CITY

Vatican Museums

St. Peter's

Piazza San Pietro

Via d. Corridori Borgo

Via della Conciliazione

Borgo Santo Spirito

Piazza Adriana

Castel Sant'Angelo

Ponte S. Angelo

Lung. Castello

Ponte Umberto

Lung. Marzio

Pza. S. Agostino

Via dei Coronari

Pza. Campo Marzio

Pza. Montecito

Via Aurelia

Via Pta. Cavalleggeri

P. Pr. Am. Sav. Aosta

Lung. d. Tebaldi

Ponte Vitt. Eman.

Via Vaticano

Pza. d. Rovere

Lung. d. Sangallo

Piazza Navona

Pza. d. Chiesa Nuova

Corso Vittorio Eman. II

Corso Rinascimento

Piazza Cavour

Pza. d. Eustachio

Pza. d. Rotor

Pza. d. Minerva

GIANICOLO

Lung. Gianicolense

Ponte G. Mazzini

Via d. Governo Vecchio

Pza. Campo d. Fiori

Via Giulia

Lgo. d. To Argentina

Largo Arenula

Viale d. Mura Gianicolesi

Passeggiata del Gianicolo

Tiber (Tevere) River

Lungotev. dei Tebaldi

Via della Lungara

Via Farnesina

Palazzo Farnese

Palazzo Spada

Pza. Mattei

JEWISH GHETTO

VILLA DORIA PAMPHILJ

Ple. G. Garibaldi

P. d. Gianicolo

Via Garibaldi

Ponte Sisto

Lung. R. Sanzio

Lung. dei Cenci

P. Garibaldi

Tiber Island

P Fabric

P. Cestio

VILLA DORIA PAMPHILJ

Via Garibaldi

Via d. Lungaretta

V. S. Francesco a Ripa

Pza. S. Sonnino

Pza. Piscinula

Pala

TRASTEVERE

Pza. di S. Cosimato

V. dei Genovesi

Via di S. Michele

Ponte di Ripa Grande

Lung. Aventin

Viale Glorioso

V.E. Morosini

Viale Trastevere

Via Ascianghi

Pza. di Pta. Portese

ITALY

Civitavecchia

ROME

Viale di Trastevere

Via Portuense

Lung. Testaccio

Subicio Grande

Via G. Branca

Via Marmorea

TESTACCIO

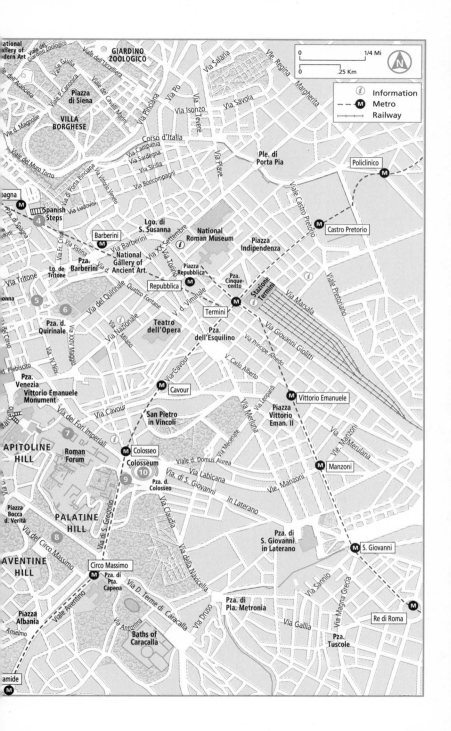

photo stop at Pisa. (Ships also offer transfers to Florence for 76€–83€ [$69–$75], for those who want to explore on their own.)

The Leaning Tower of Pisa (3 hr., $37–$46): Only 12 miles from Livorno is Pisa, home of the famous Leaning Tower. Galileo is said to have used the 180-foot tower for his gravitational experiments. On this tour you'll also explore the Baptistery and Campo Santo. Time is also allowed for souvenir shopping. As of November 2001, the tower is to be opened to visitors, but on a limited basis (30 people at a time), and it remains to be seen whether cruise passengers will have the opportunity to do the dizzying climb.

LOCAL FLAVORS

You can try Livorno's excellent, hearty Tuscan cuisine at one of the trattorias or at the fancier hotels. Sample pastas, cheeses, and simply prepared meat and fish, a main ingredient being the region's wonderful olive oil. Complement your meal with a glass of Chianti, especially the highly regarded Chianti Classico, or other Tuscan wines.

BEST BUYS

There are shops along the Via Grande, Livorno's main street; most close from 12:30 to 3:30pm. In addition to Chianti, best buys include the locally produced amber-colored olive oil.

SORRENTO

Known as the City of Sirens (those lovely mermaids who lured seamen to death with their pretty songs), Sorrento has for centuries been a favorite resort of wealthy Romans. It's dramatically located on top of a cliff overlooking the ocean. It's a charming town with great shops and quaint streets, although it can get very crowded and snarled with traffic in the summer high season.

Though most ships stop here more for the easy access Sorrento provides to the ancient city of Pompeii, the scenic Amalfi Coast, and the nearby romantic isle of Capri, Sorrento itself makes for a pleasant stroll, especially among the pretty lemon groves, and is a good place to do some shopping or sit in an outdoor cafe to people-watch.

FROMMER'S FAVORITE SORRENTO EXPERIENCES

- **Taking the shore excursion to Pompeii or to Capri.** That's really why your ship has stopped here.
- **Strolling around town and having a coffee in an outdoor cafe.** The shops are worth a look (especially those featuring inlaid wood and other local crafts) and this is a great place to people-watch.

COMING ASHORE & GETTING AROUND   Ships tender passengers to the pier, where you'll usually find **taxis.** The center of town is about a 15-minute uphill walk. **Minibuses** operated by the city also make the uphill climb.

THE BEST SHORE EXCURSIONS

The Ruins of Pompeii (4½ hr., $48–$57): Tour this once prosperous ancient city of 20,000, which was buried when Vesuvius erupted in A.D. 79. Today, nearly two-thirds of the city has been excavated and the ruins are amazing. On your guided walk through the rocky ruins you'll visit the baths and theaters, the wrestling ground and the restored villas. During the drive you can view Vesuvius, the still-active volcano.

Capri (5 hr., $55–$79): Board a hydrofoil for a cruise to Capri. Transfer by bus to Anacapri for magnificent views and a tour of Villa San Michele, with its collection of antiquities. Return to town for a walking tour of Capri to visit the Gardens of Augustus Park and explore the town's narrow streets and central square. The tour includes time to shop or visit a cafe.

Amalfi Coast (5–7 hr., $66–$85): Drive about 2 hours along the scenic Amalfi Coast to Amalfi town, a romantic little town that was a major shipping port during the Middle Ages. Take a guided tour of the town's center, including the Cathedral of St. Andrea, built in a combination of Moorish and early Gothic design. Time is allowed for souvenir shopping. From the bus, you'll see Positano with its white houses, terraced gardens, and fishing fleet, and other scenic coastal sights.

THE TOP ATTRACTIONS

Chiesa di San Francesco (The Cloister of St. Francis)   While few people come here to look at churches, this one is worth a peek. It dates from the 14th century, and offers pretty archways and a lovely garden. The convent is also an art school that regularly offers exhibits.

Via San Francesco. © 081/878-1269. Free admission. Daily 9am–6pm.

LOCAL FLAVORS

Pasta with seafood and fish cooked in salt crust are popular selections here. One of the best places to sample the local cuisine is the 200-year-old **L'Antica Trattoria,** Via P.R. Giuliani 33 (© 081/807-1082). Reservations are recommended. The restaurant's specialty is its antipasti. Open for lunch and dinner. Reservations are recommended. Main courses run 12€ to 24€ ($11 to $22).

BEST BUYS

The best areas for strolling and window-shopping are **Piazza Tasso** and **Via San Cesareo.** Locally made wooden inlaid items make a great souvenir, although prices are steep. The region's best-known maker of inlaid furniture is **Gargiulo & Jannuzzi,** Piazza Tasso (© 081/878-1041), which opened in 1863. Employees demonstrate the technique to tourists in the shop's basement. Embroidery and lace are two of the best bargains in Sorrento, and **Luigia Gargiulo,** Corso Italia 48 (© 081-878-1081), is recommended for embroidered sheets and tablecloths; the shop also offers children's clothing. Other popular souvenir items include coral jewelry, and lemon liquor (called limoncello).

VENICE

Everywhere you look in Venice there's something worth seeing, whether it's the Gothic and Renaissance structures this city seems to have grown like trees, or the construction efforts aimed at stopping said buildings from sinking.

Our favorite activity here is simply exploring the maze of canals and side streets, crossing the medieval bridges, people-watching, and getting lost (and finding our way back home again). That activity, in summer, can help you avoid some of the hordes of other visitors who crowd together at St. Mark's Square.

Sorrento

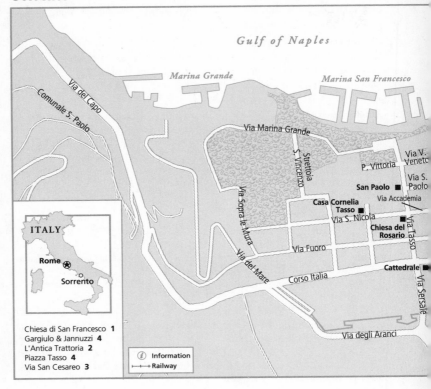

Gulf of Naples

Marina Grande

Marina San Francesco

Via del Capo

Comunale S. Paolo

Via Marina Grande

Strettoia S. Vincenzo

P. Vittoria

Via V. Veneto

Via S. Paolo

San Paolo ■

Via Accademia

Casa Cornelia Tasso ■

Via S. Nicola

Chiesa del Rosario ■

Via Sopra le Mura

Via del Mare

Via Fuoro

Corso Italia

Cattedrale ■

Via Tasso

Via Sersale

Via degli Aranci

ITALY

Rome ✪

Sorrento

Chiesa di San Francesco **1**
Gargiulo & Jannuzzi **4**
L'Antica Trattoria **2**
Piazza Tasso **4**
Via San Cesareo **3**

ⓘ Information
⊢——⊣ Railway

Getting out on the **Grand Canal,** a water version of a main city boulevard, is a must-do, whether you go the touristy route on a gondola (negotiate upfront with the driver and expect to pay through your teeth) or on equally overpriced water taxis, or if you go like most Venetians do on a vaporetto (water bus). The S-shaped canal curves for 2 miles past historic buildings, ornate bridges, and palaces. And as you check out the sights, you'll share the main waterway with ambulances, delivery barges, and other vessels going about the tasks of ordinary life here.

Everywhere you look there will be something artistic or otherwise fascinating to see. Like Florence, Venice has a treasure trove of paintings, statues, and frescoes in its churches (including the famous St. Mark's) and in its palaces. And the Peggy Guggenheim museum houses one of the best collections of 20th-century art in the Western world.

Check out the shops and cafes in and around **St. Mark's Square.** Enjoy the fact there are no cars, and ignore the fact there are too many other tourists (especially if you visit in July or Aug). Also ignore the fact that the prices for food and souvenirs have gotten ridiculously high. Have a meal, the favorite Italian pastime; grab a coffee or gelato in a cafe; or have an overpriced Bloody Mary at Harry's Bar.

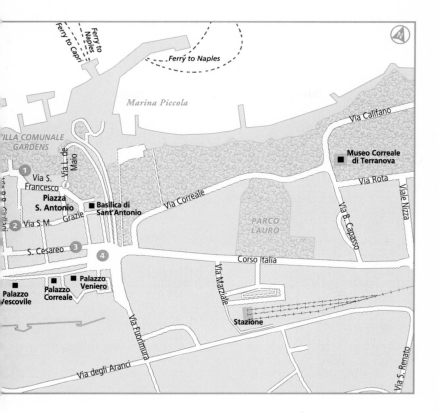

FROMMER'S FAVORITE VENICE EXPERIENCES

- **Going exploring.** The maze of historic streets and canals offers fascinating sights at nearly every turn.
- **Going shopping.** The selection of locally produced glass and other crafts is amazing, and the Italian designer shops tempting, even if the prices can be steep. And Prada is less expensive here than in New York.
- *Mangia!* Venetian cuisine, especially the seafood, is excellent, and worth the splurge.

COMING ASHORE & GETTING AROUND   Ships generally dock about 15 to 20 minutes by boat from St. Mark's Square. Travel here is on the water, by **water taxi** (which will be pricey) or on the **water buses** called *vaporetti* (which are cheap).

THE BEST SHORE EXCURSIONS

Venice City Sightseeing (3 hr., $48–$72): Take a motor launch to St. Mark's Square for a guided walking tour of St. Mark's Cathedral, one of the world's most famous churches. Tour the Doge's Palace, the former residence of the Duke of Venice. Tour also includes the Golden Staircase, where you can enjoy the views of St. Mark's Basin. Cross the famous Bridge of Sighs. Stop at the small workshops of glass manufacturers.

Venice

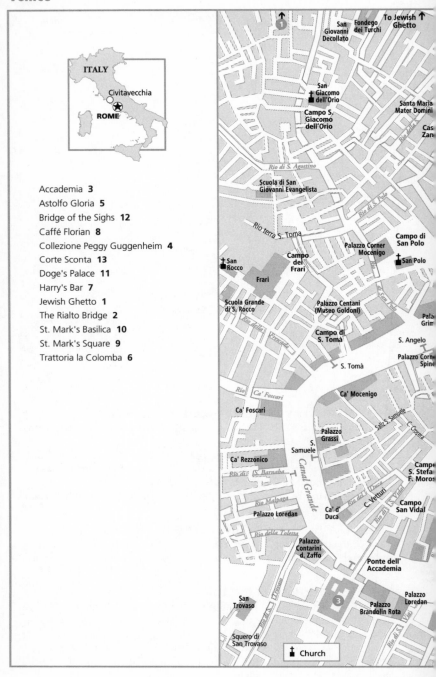

ITALY

Civitavecchia

ROME

To Jewish Ghetto

San Giovanni Decollato

Fondego dei Turchi

San Giacomo dell'Orio

Campo S. Giacomo dell'Orio

Santa Maria Mater Domini

Cas Zan

Rio di S. Agostino

Scuola di San Giovanni Evangelista

Rio di S. Polo

Rio terra S. Toma

Campo di San Polo

Palazzo Corner Mocenigo

San Polo

San Rocco

Campo dei Frari

Frari

Scuola Grande di S. Rocco

Palazzo Centani (Museo Goldoni)

Pala Grim

Rio della Frescada

Campo di S. Tomà

S. Angelo

Palazzo Corne Spine

S. Tomà

Rio Ca' Foscari

Ca' Mocenigo

Salta S. Samuele

C. Crosera

Ca' Foscari

S. Samuele

Palazzo Grassi

Ca' Rezzonico

Rio di S. Barnaba

Camp S. Stefa F. Moros

Canal Grande

Rio del Duca

C. Vetturi

Campo San Vidal

Rio Malpaga

Palazzo Loredan

Ca' d' Duca

Rio di Vidal

Rio della Toletta

Palazzo Contarini d. Zaffo

Ponte dell' Accademia

Palazzo Loredan

San Trovaso

Palazzo Brandolin Rota

Squero di San Trovaso

✝ Church

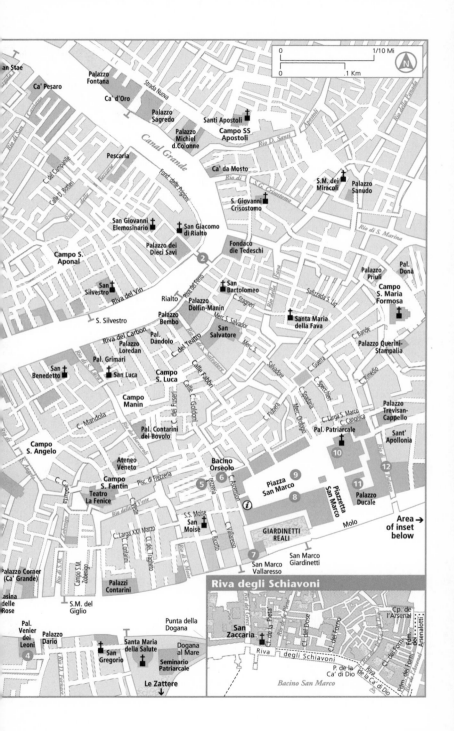

an Stae

Ca' Pesaro

Palazzo
Fontana

Strada Nuova

Ca' d'Oro

Palazzo
Sagredo

Palazzo
Michiel
d.Colonne

Santi Apostoli †

Campo SS
Apostoli

Canal Grande

Pescaria

Ca' da Mosto

Rio di

N. Cannaregio

S. Giovanni
Crisostomo

S.M. dei †
Miracoli

Palazzo
Sanudo

Rio di S. Marina

San Giovanni †
Elemosinario

† San Giacomo
di Rialto

Palazzo dei
Dieci Savi

Campo S.
Aponal

2

San †
Silvestro

Riva del Vin

Rialto

S. Silvestro

† San
Bartolomeo

Fondaco
die Tedeschi

Palazzo
Dolfin-Manin

Palazzo
Bembo

Riva del Carbon

Pal.
Dandolo

Palazzo
Loredan

C. del Teatro

San
Salvatore

Palazzo
Priuli

Pal.
Donà

Campo S.
Maria
Formosa

† Santa Maria
della Fava

Palazzo Querini-
Stampalia

Pal. Grimani

San †
Benedetto

† San Luca

Campo
S. Luca

Campo
Manin

Calle Fabbri

Calle G.Goldoni

C. dei Fuseri

Salvadore

Merc S.

Palazzo
Trevisan-
Cappello

Sant'
Apollonia

Pal. Contarini
del Bovolo

Campo
S. Angelo

Ateneo
Veneto

Pal. Patriarcale

10

12

Campo
S. Fantin

Pisc. di Frezzeria

Bacino
Orseolo

5

6

Frezzeria

Ascension

9

Piazza
San Marco

8

i

11

Piazzetta
San Marco

Palazzo
Ducale

Teatro
La Fenice

Rio delle Veste

C.Larga XXII Marzo

C. del Traghetto

Ridotto

Vallaresso

S.S. Moisè
San
Moisè †

GIARDINETTI
REALI

Molo

Area →
of inset
below

Palazzo Corner
(Ca' Grande)

asina
delle
Rose

Campo S.M.
Zobenigo

S.M. del
Giglio

Palazzi
Contarini

7

San Marco
Vallaresso

San Marco
Giardinetti

Riva degli Schiavoni

Cp. de
l'Arsenal

Pal.
Venier
dei
Leoni

Palazzo
Dario

Santa Maria
della Salute

Punta della
Dogana

San
Zaccaria †

Cl. de la Pietà

Cl. del Dose

Cl. del Forno

Arsenalotti

4

† San
Gregorio

Dogana
al Mare

Seminario
Patriarcale

Riva degli Schiavoni

P. de la
Ca' di Dio

Bacino San Marco

Le Zattere
↓

0   1/10 Mi

0   .1 Km

The Grand Canal & the Inside Canal (2½ hr., $83–$118): Travel by motor-boat with a guide and 10 to 12 other people and see the way the city works—the police, fire brigade, even wedding and funeral processions travel by boat. From the water you'll get a wonderful view of St. Mark's Square and other sights, including palaces and the Guggenheim Museum. You'll also go under the famous Rialto Bridge.

The Historic Jewish Ghetto (3½ hr., $41–$61): In the 16th century, the Jews of Venice were restricted to the Ghetto unless they were doctors. They had to wear distinctive clothing and could not own land. The Ghetto has been preserved and offers a fascinating glimpse of what life was like for the people who lived there, and of the modern Jewish culture in Venice (several synagogues in the Ghetto still have active congregations). You take a motor launch to the entrance and tour on foot.

THE TOP ATTRACTIONS

Palazzo Ducale (Doge's Palace) & the Bridge of Sighs   This Venetian Gothic palazzo is Italy's grandest civic structure. And it literally gleams. While it dates back to 1309, most was destroyed by a fire and rebuilt in the 16th century. Many of the greatest Venetian painters of that century helped with the restoration. After climbing the Sansovino stairway of gold, proceed to the Anti-Collegio salon to view Veronese's *Rape of Europe* and Tintoretto's *Three Graces* and *Bacchus and Ariadne*. Downstairs you can visit the apartments of the Doges and the grand Maggior Consiglio, with its allegorical *Triumph of Venice* by Veronese on the ceiling. Tintoretto's *Paradise* over the Grand Council chamber is said to be the largest oil painting in the world.

Follow the arrows to the Bridge of Sighs, which links the Doge's Palace with the Palazzo delle Prigioni, where you'll find cell blocks—the sighs refer to the laments of those tortured here.

Piazzetta San Marco. ☎ **041/522-4951**. Admission 9.40€ ($8.50) adults, 5.15€ ($4.65) students with ID, 3.10€ ($2.80) children 6–13, free for under 5. Apr–Oct daily 9am–7pm.

St. Mark's Basilica (Basilica di San Marco)   The "Church of Gold" is one of the greatest and most elaborate churches in the world, built in a conglomeration of styles, though Byzantine predominates (it looks like it would be just as at home in Istanbul). The basilica is capped by a dome that can be seen from your ship as you cruise down the Grand Canal. On the facade are replicas of the four famous St. Mark's horses (see more below). One mosaic depicts the entry of the evangelist's body into Venice, hidden in a pork barrel (the body was smuggled out of Alexandria in 828).

In the atrium are six cupolas with mosaics depicting scenes from the Old Testament, including the story of the Tower of Babel. The basilica's interior, once used as the private chapel of the doges, is stunning, with marbles, alabaster, pillars, and an ocean of mosaics.

Climbing the Bell Tower

For about 6€ ($5.50) you can climb to the top of the bell tower of St. Mark's, and you don't even have to brave a dark, steep, winding staircase to do it—there's an elevator. From the top you can get a bird's-eye view of the city, and a nice view as well of the basilica's cupolas.

The **treasury** contains skulls and bones of ecclesiastical authorities as well as goblets, chalices, and Gothic candelabra. In the presbytery rests the alleged sarcophagus of St. Mark.

The **Marciano Museum** upstairs contains the Triumphal Quadriga, the four famous horses looted from Constantinople by Venetian crusaders in 1204. The horses used to be outside, but were moved indoors due to pollution damage and subsequently restored. They're the only quartet of yoked horses to have survived from the classical era. It is believed they were cast in the 4th century. Napoléon once carted these horses off to Paris, but they were returned to Venice in 1815. From the museum, which also contains mosaics and tapestries, you can walk out onto the loggia for a view of Piazza San Marco.

Piazza San Marco. ℂ 041/522-5205. Basilica free; treasury 2€ ($1.85); presbytery 1.50€ ($1.40); Marciano Museum 1.50€ ($1.40). Basilica Apr–Sept Mon–Sat 9:30am–5:30pm, Sun 2–5:30pm; Oct–Mar Mon–Sat 9:30am–5pm, Sun 1:30–4:30pm. Note: Men and women are barred from wearing shorts or exposing bare arms and shoulders, and women may not wear skirts above the knee in the basilica. Silence is required, and you may not take photos.

St. Mark's Square (Piazza San Marco)   This square is the cultural hub of the city. You can easily spend hours here, watching people and feeding the pigeons, sitting at a cafe, visiting the Basilica and Doge's Palace (see above), and shopping. But the square is also a tourist hub that can be very crowded during the day, especially in the high summer tourist season. To see the square with fewer crowds, go very early in the morning (watch the sun come up) or in the evening. At night, there are music performances by chamber orchestras and other groups.

PORTOFINO

For quaint fishing villages you can't beat Portofino, known as the "Pearl of the Riviera," even if the harbor is almost overrun with luxury yachts in the summer. The village offers frescoed houses and lush vegetation and is absolutely picture-postcard perfect.

Ships tender passengers right into town (some offer Portofino as a shore excursion from Genoa). The town is tiny, and you can easily explore the narrow streets on foot. There are wonderful waterfront cafes, art galleries, and jewelry shops (be aware that prices can be hefty), but we highly recommend a hike up the hill above the harbor (you can also take a cab) for lunch on the terrace at the **Hotel Splendido,** Viale Baratta 13 (ℂ **800/223-6800** in the U.S., or 0185/269-551; reservations recommended). It may be the most expensive lunch you've ever eaten (be prepared to spend about 111€/$100 a person), but the splendid food, service, and views are worth every penny (or make that every C-note). Illustrious guests at the hotel have included the duke and duchess of Windsor, Ernest Hemingway, Greta Garbo, Ingrid Bergman, Clark Gable, and John Wayne.

Accademia   The glory of old Venice lives on in this museum, with its remarkable collection of paintings from the 14th to the 18th century.

Campo della Caritá, Dorsoduro. ℂ **041/5222-2247.** Admission 6€ ($5.50) adults, free for children 17 and under and seniors 60 and over. Mon–Sat 9am–7pm; Sun 9am–2pm.

Collezione Peggy Guggenheim   Ms. Guggenheim's former home, an impressive palazzo on the Grand Canal, now houses a comprehensive and brilliant modern art collection. In the tradition of her family, Guggenheim, who died in 1979, was a lifelong patron of contemporary painters and sculptors. Displayed are works by Pollack, Ernst, Picasso, Braque, Magritte, Duchamp,

Chagall, Mondrian, Brancusi, Dalí, Giacometti, and others. Some ships offer the opportunity to tour the museum on a private basis, on special shore excursions.

Ca' Venier dei Leoni, Dorsoduro 701, Calle San Cristoforo. © 041/520-6288. Admission 6€ ($5.50) adults, 4.10€ ($3.70) students and children 16 and under. Wed–Mon 11am–6pm.

LOCAL FLAVORS

Papa Hemingway liked **Harry's Bar** (Calle Vallaresso, San Marco; © 041/ 528-5777), but the fame has made the prices here downright shocking (main courses run 41€–55€/$37–$50), especially given the rather simple food. Still, those wishing to pay tribute to Hemingway should at least order a Bloody Mary at the bar.

A more reasonable choice is **Trattoria la Colomba,** Piscina Frezzeria, San Marco 1665 (© 041/522-1175; reservations recommended). The history of this restaurant is linked to some of Venice's leading painters, who traded art for meals. Modern paintings adorn the walls today (they change seasonally and are for sale). You can also dine outside. The cuisine is Venetian and includes wonderful seafood and pasta dishes and locally grown vegetables; main courses run from 18€ to 39€ ($16 to $35). For a more casual restaurant with excellent seafood, try **Corte Sconta,** Calle del Pestrin, Castello 3886 (© 041/522-7024; reservations required). Main courses are in the 13€ to 22€ ($12 to $20) range.

One of the most famous cafes for a light lunch, coffee, or sweet snack is **Caffé Florian** in St. Mark's Square, built in 1720 and romantically decorated with plush red banquettes and elaborate murals. Casanova is on the list of famous customers.

BEST BUYS

Venice is a shopper's delight, as long as you don't mind the steep prices, and it's fun exploring the winding streets of shops around St. Mark's Square and the Rialto Bridge. Generally, the farther away from the square you go, the more reasonable the prices become.

You'll find plenty of locally produced items including glassware, lace, linens, masks, leather goods (including shoes), and knitwear. Shops in tourist areas stay open long hours (many close for lunch, however), and some are even open on Sundays. One of Fran's favorite shops is the tiny **Astolfo Gloria,** Frezzeria, San Marco (© 041/520-6827), which features reasonably priced jewelry made of Venetian glass beads.

5 Malta

The former home of the Knights of St. John, the island nation of Malta, located on the southernmost tip of Europe (about 60 miles from Sicily and 180 miles from North Africa) has at one time or another been dominated by all its neighbors, including the British and the French.

Visitors to its bustling capital, **Valletta,** will find cathedrals, palazzos, and fortifications, mostly from the period of the knights, which started in the 16th century and ended when they were driven off the island by Napoleon Bonaparte in 1798. It is said that the city was built "by gentlemen, for gentlemen."

Malta became part of the British Empire in 1800, was granted independence in 1964, and became a republic in 1974. A must-see in Valletta for those interested in the island's history is *The Malta Experience* audiovisual presentation (see "Frommer's Favorite Malta Experiences," below).

> **Tips** **Diving in Malta**
>
> There are great diving opportunities in Malta and numerous water-sports and diving centers that hire equipment. For more information, contact the Malta National Tourism Organization in Valletta, ✆ **356/22-44-44.**.

Valletta is quite compact and easy to explore on foot. In addition to historic sights, the city offers a wealth of museums, restaurants, and shopping opportunities. Other parts of the island offer quaint towns, ancient sites (including the oldest known freestanding prehistoric temple structures in the world), and historic churches, all easily accessible.

The sea offers excellent opportunities for divers. For sun worshippers, there are a number of sandy beaches, the best of which, including Mellieha Bay, Golden Sands, and Armier, can be found in the north of the island.

Valletta's Grand Harbour is very impressive; you'll want to be on deck as the massive fortifications come into view.

CURRENCY   The official unit of currency is the Maltese lira. The rate of exchange at press time was $1 = .44 lira.

LANGUAGE   Maltese and English (Malta is a former British colony and English is widely spoken).

FROMMER'S FAVORITE MALTA EXPERIENCES

- **Seeing *The Malta Experience.*** This audiovisual presentation offers a look at the island's fascinating history. (Mediterranean Conference center, Old Hospital Street. Admission is about 2.50€ ($2.25). The 40-min. presentation is offered on the hour, Mon–Fri 11am–4pm; Sat–Sun 11am and noon.)
- **Exploring Mdina.** The island's medieval capital, about a 30-minute drive from Valletta, is a quaint, pedestrians-only walled city perched atop a plateau.
- **Visiting a museum.** You have numerous choices here, including museums of fine arts, archaeology, war, folklore, maritime (in Fort St. Angelo), science, and even toys.
- **Strolling Republic Street.** This is the place to be seen and to meet Malta's friendly populace. You can also view historically interesting buildings.

COMING ASHORE & GETTING AROUND   Ships dock close to the center of town. It's about a 15-minute walk or a 5-minute ride. **Taxis** are available at the pier. Malta's public transportation system is cheap and efficient. **Buses** cost less than 50¢, with the longest bus journey taking only 50 minutes.

THE BEST SHORE EXCURSIONS

Malta's Capital (4 hr., $36–$42): This bus and walking tour of Valletta (stopping at City Gate) visits St. John's Co-Cathedral, Palace of the Grand Masters, after which you drive by bus to the medieval fortified city of Mdina, where you'll find quaint winding streets and beautiful homes as well as a cathedral dedicated to St. Peter and St. Paul.

Full-Day Tour of Malta (7–7½ hr., $69–$76): A look at the island's history from the Bronze Age to the reign of the Order of the Knights of St. John. Visit Mdina; stop at the nearby town of Rabat, famous for its catacombs and Roman

Valletta

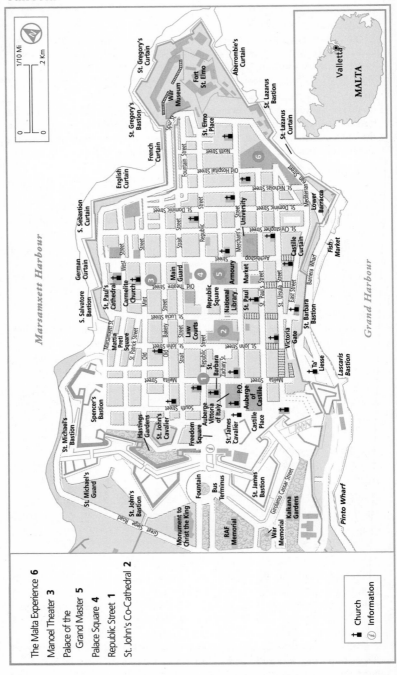

The Malta Experience **6**

Manoel Theater **3**

Palace of the
Grand Master **5**

Palace Square **4**

Republic Street **1**

St. John's Co-Cathedral **2**

✝ Church

ⓘ Information

MALTA

Valletta

Marsamxett Harbour

Grand Harbour

St. Gregory's Curtain

St. Gregory's Bastion

Abercrombie's Curtain

Fort St. Elmo

War Museum

St. Elmo Place

North Street

St. Lazarus Bastion

St. Lazarus Curtain

French Curtain

English Curtain

Old Hospital Street

Fountain Street

St. Nicholas Street

St. Dominic Street

S. Sebastion Curtain

St. Dominic Street

Lower Barracca

German Curtain

St. Christopher Street

University

Merchant's Street

Mediterranean Street

Fish Market

Castille Curtain

S. Salvatore Bastion

St. Paul's Cathedral

Carmelite Church

West Street

Strait Street

Republic Street

Archbishop

Market

National Armoury

Main Guard

Republic Square

St. Paul Street

Castille

East Street

Barriera Wharf

Old Theatre Street

Mint Street

St. Lucia Street

Strait Street

Bakery Street

Republic Street

St. John Street

Law Courts

St. Paul's Street

St. Ursula Street

St. Barbara Bastion

Marsamxett St.

Mattia Preti Square

St. Patrick Street

Old Bakery Street

St. Lucia Street

St. Barbara

Zachari St.

Victoria Gate

Melita Street

South Street

St. John Street

Melita Street

Ta' Liesse

Lascaris Bastion

Spencer's Bastion

St. John's Cavalier

Hastings Gardens

Freedom Square

Auberge Vittoria of Italy

P.O.

Auberge of Castille

Castille Place

St. Michael's Bastion

St. Michael's Guard

St. John's Bastion

Great Siege Road

Monument to Christ the King

RAF Memorial

St. James Cavalier

St. James Bastion

Bus Terminus

Fountain

War Memorial

Girolamo Cassar Street

Kalkara Gardens

Pinto Wharf

N

1/10 Mi

.2 Km

ruins; visit a parish church completed in 1860 and boasting the fourth largest unsupported dome in the world; visit the prehistoric Tarxien Temples; and visit Valletta, with a stop at the Palace of the Grand Masters with its Tapestry Room and Throne Room. Includes lunch and a stop at a crafts center (to watch glassblowers and traditional lacemaking, weaving, and silver filigree art).

Tour of the Temples (4 hr., $42): This tour includes some of the world's most impressive prehistoric temples, driving by bus to the Cottonera region; visiting the Malta Maritime Museum, which houses relics of Malta's history; visiting the temples of Hagar Qim with its decorated pillar and two altars, all constructed in the late megalithic period on a slope facing the tiny island of Filfla; then visiting Tarxien Temples, where the archaeological remains date back to 2,500 B.C.

THE TOP ATTRACTIONS

Manoel Theatre   This is one of the oldest theaters in Europe still in operation, built by the Portuguese Grand Master Antonio Manoel de Vilhena in 1731.

Old Theatre Street. ℂ **356/22-26-18.** Admission about .64L ($1.45). Tours Mon–Fri at 10:30am and 11:30am; Sat 11:30am; no tours Sun.

Palace of the Grand Master   This grand 500-year-old residence was completed in 1574 and today is the seat of the president and Parliament of the Republic of Malta. Inside are portraits of European monarchs and the Grand Masters of the Order of St. John, a furniture collection, Gobelin tapestries, frescoes, friezes, and other works of art.

Republic Street. ℂ **356/22-12-21.** Admission about .2L (45¢), free for seniors and students under age 19. 1-week ticket (valid for 10 visits) 1L ($2.25). June 16–Sept 30 Mon–Fri 8am–2:45pm; at other times, Mon–Wed 8:30am–3:45pm, Thurs–Fri 8:30am–4pm.

St. John's Co-Cathedral   The outside of this church, built between 1573 and 1577, is rather austere, but the interior is gorgeous and holds art treasures that include the Caravaggio masterpiece *The Beheading of St John*. The museum houses a collection of Flemish tapestries, silver objects, and church vestments.

St. John's Square. ℂ **356/22-05-36.** Admission about .25L (55¢). Mon–Fri 9:30am–12:30pm and 1:30–4:30pm; Sat 9:30am–12:30pm.

LOCAL FLAVORS

The food here is close to Italian, with a liberal use of garlic and olive oil. Fish is a favorite, as is rabbit.

BEST BUYS

Local, traditional crafts include hand-blown glass and lace, ceramics, silver and gold jewelry, metalwork, pottery, and tiles. Shops can be found on Republic Street and the small streets near Palace Square.

6 Portugal

Lisbon is Europe's smallest capital but this city of seven hills is also a cosmopolitan place offering a pleasing combination of history, cultural arts, modern amenities, and visual treats. Some areas might remind visitors of Paris, with street painters and the like, yet other areas resemble hilly San Francisco.

The city is alternately believed to have been founded by Ulysses and the Phoenicians, and was inhabited by Romans and later the Moors. In 1755, a great earthquake destroyed much of the city, killing some 40,000 people. The rebuilding was carefully planned based on a neoclassical grid. Areas untouched by the earthquake include Belém, on the banks of the Tagus River, and Alfama.

Lisbon offers historical sights, museums, and, thanks to the city's hosting of Expo '98, new attractions such as the Lisbon Oceanarium, billed as Europe's largest aquarium.

CURRENCY As of March 2002, Portugal switched entirely to the euro (€) for its currency. One euro is made up of 100 euro cents. The exchange rate at press time was $1 = 1.1€.

LANGUAGE Portuguese. Young people may also speak Spanish, English, or German.

FROMMER'S FAVORITE PORTUGAL EXPERIENCES

- **Exploring the Alfama.** Houses in the alleys are so close together you can't stretch your arms in some places to their full length. (Claustrophobics, look out!) Visit the 12th-century Sé (cathedral), check out the goods at the markets, and climb up to the Castelo Saño Jorge (St. George's Castle) to enjoy the views.

- **Shopping for handicrafts.** Although prices aren't as good as they used to be, look for colorful ceramics, embroidery, silver, porcelain, crystal, tiles, handwoven rugs, leather goods, and hand-knit sweaters.

- **Feeling like an explorer.** Belém, where the River Tagus meets the sea, is where Portuguese explorers like Magellan launched their missions. Check out Belém Tower and Jerónimos Monastery. Also explore the National Coach Museum.

- **Listening to fado.** Singers accompanied by 12-stringed Portuguese guitars can be heard nightly performing these melancholy songs in the little houses of the Bairro Alto.

- **Spending quiet time in Sintra.** Byron called this delightful village "glorious Eden." The area around village is known colloquially as Serra de Sintra. A drive around the loop is only about 36 miles, but plan to spend a day stopping off at such scenic delights as the remote Franciscan monastery (ca. 1560) known as Convento dos Capuchos and the old lighthouse at Cabo de Roca, the most westerly point on the European mainland.

COMING ASHORE & GETTING AROUND Cruise ships dock at the Port of Lisbon, about 15 minutes by car from the city center (2 miles/3km to the Alcantara district; 3 miles/5km to Belém Tower).

Lisbon itself is a walking city and is easy to get around, although the hills may prove challenging to some. **Taxis** are among the cheapest in Europe and are generally available outside the terminal building. They are usually diesel Mercedes. The ride to the central sightseeing and shopping districts is likely to be between 12€ and 19€ ($11 and $17). Traffic can be congested, so allow extra time. The city also has a good **bus and tram service** as well as Metro **subway** to get around. There's a **funicular** (elevator) connecting the Baixa area (where you'll find shopping) with the Bairro Alto (where you'll find nightlife).

THE BEST SHORE EXCURSIONS

Lisbon City Tour (3½ hr., $37–$45): This bus tour hits a number of city highlights, including Avenida da Liberdade with its mosaic-lined sidewalks and the magnificent views at Black Horse Square of the River Tagus. Tour the impressive Jerónimos Monastery. Also visit the National Coach Museum, or the Convent of Madre de Deus, founded in 1509 and containing samples of religious architecture.

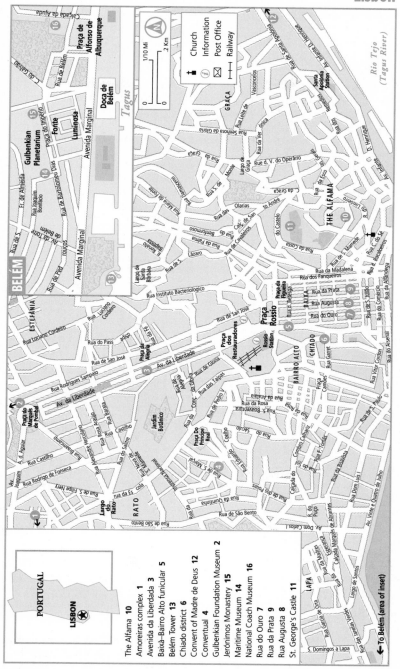

Lisbon

PORTUGAL

LISBON

The Alfama **10**
Amoreiras complex **1**
Avenida da Liberdada **3**
Baixa–Bairro Alto funicular **5**
Belém Tower **13**
Chiado district **6**
Conventual **4**
Convent of Madre de Deus **12**
Gulbenkian Foundation Museum **2**
Jerónimos Monastery **15**
Maritime Museum **14**
National Coach Museum **16**
Rua do Ouro **7**
Rua da Prata **9**
Rua Augusta **8**
St. George's Castle **11**

BELÉM

Church
Information
Post Office
Railway

0   1/10 Mi
0   .2 Km

Rio Tejo
(Tagus River)

GRAÇA

THE ALFAMA

BAIXA

CHIADO

BAIRRO ALTO

ESTEFÂNIA

RATO

LAPA

Praça de
Afonso de
Albuquerque

Gulbenkian
Planetarium

Doca de
Belém

Tagus

← To Belém (area of inset)

313

Sintra & Estoril (4 hr., $43–$47): This tour along the famous and scenic Estoril coast includes such memorable highlights as Sintra, a serene, historic resort nestled in the forested hills of Serra de Sintra. The tour continues inland to Queluz, to visit the magnificent 18th-century palace built in the style of Versailles.

Fatima & Batalha (8–9 hr., $106–$117): Located 100 miles from Lisbon is the place known to Roman Catholics as the "Lourdes of Portugal." Here, according to legend, three shepherds in 1917 claimed they saw the Virgin Mary in an oak tree. The town has since become a center of the Christian faith and of world pilgrimage. You will have time here to explore the imposing modern basilica, and on some tours you'll also visit the homes, just outside Fatima, where the three shepherds lived (their remains are kept inside the basilica). Lunch will be served at a local restaurant or hotel. Afterwards, continue on to Batalha for a visit to the impressive Gothic church of Santa Maria da Victoria.

THE TOP ATTRACTIONS

Belém Tower (Torre de Belém)   Scenically located on the banks of the Tagus River, the 16th-century tower is a monument to Portugal's age of discovery and its famous explorers.

Praca do Imperio, Belém district. ✆ **21-362-00-34**. Admission 2.10€ ($1.90) adults, 1.15€ ($1.05) children and seniors. Tues–Sun 10am–5pm.

Gulbenkian Foundation Museum (Museu de Fundacao Calouste Gulbenkian)   Deeded by Armenian oil tycoon Calouste Gulbenkian, who died in 1955, this museum houses one of the world's finest private art collections, including Egyptian, Greek, and Roman antiquities; Islamic art; and vases, prints, and lacquerwork from China and Japan. There are also European manuscripts, 15th- to 19th-century paintings and sculptures, and important collections of 18th-century French decorative works, French impressionist paintings, Lalique jewelry, and glassware. Notable are two Rembrandts, Rubens's *Portrait of Hélène Foourment,* and *Portrait of Madame Claude Monet* by Pierre-August Renoir.

Av. De Berna 45, Saldana district. ✆ **21-795-02-36**. Admission 2.75€ ($2.50) adults, free for children 9 and under and seniors. Free admission for all on Sun. Wed–Sun 10am–6pm; Tues 2–6pm.

Jerónimos Monastery (Mosteiro dos Jerónimos)   Built in 1502, the monastery is a masterpiece of Manueline architecture, built in the 16th century to commemorate the discoveries of Portuguese navigators, and one of the finest sights in the city.

Praca do Imperio, Belém district. ✆ **21-362-00-34**. Free admission to church; to cloisters 2.50€ ($2.30) for adults, free for children and seniors. Tues–Sun 10am–5pm.

The Maritime Museum (Museu de Marinha)   Located in the Jerónimos Monastery's west wing, this museum is one of the most important of its kind in Europe, and contains hundreds of ship models, from 15th-century sailing ships to 20th-century warships.

Praca do Imperio, Belém district. ✆ **21-362-00-19**. Admission 2.10€ ($1.90) adults, 1.15€ ($1.05) students, free for children under 10 and seniors. Tues–Sun 10am–6pm.

St. George's Castle (Castelo Saño Jorge)   This hilltop fortress is believed to have predated the Romans. Many of the walls still standing were erected by the Moors. The finest view of the Tagus and the Alfama can be had from the castle's esplanades and ramparts. On the grounds you'll also find olive, pine, and cork trees, and may encounter swans and rare white peacocks.

Rua Costa do Castelo, Alfama district. No phone. Free admission. Apr–Sept daily 9am–9pm.

LOCAL FLAVORS

Fresh seafood is a best bet. Typical dishes include fresh *bacalhau* (codfish), steamed mussels with ham and sausages cooked in white wine, and *acorda de marisco,* a spicy seafood soup. Meat-eaters will want to try the roasted lamb. Try your meal with a Portuguese wine. The cafes (such as those around the Rossio, the city's main square) are great places to people-watch. A nice Lisbon restaurant with a friendly owner is **Conventual,** Praca das Flores 45 (© **21-390-91-96**), decorated with panels from baroque churches, religious statues, and other bric-a-brac. It's open for lunch and dinner, and main courses run about 13€ to 22€ ($12 to $20). Reservations are required.

BEST BUYS

Handicrafts, ceramics, and embroidered linens are all good buys. Also look for gold filigree and silver jewelry, knitwear, leather goods, colorful Portuguese wall tiles, and items made out of cork. Many smaller shops close from 12:30pm to 3pm. There are more than 200 shops in the modern **Amoreiras complex,** located in the Amoreiras district (take a taxi), and upscale shopping can be found downtown on Rua Garrett in the **Chiado district.** Other shopping districts include **Baixa** (between the Rossio and the Tagus), **Rua do Ouro, Rua da Prata,** and **Rua Augusta.** The new shopping complex Colombo is located in the Benfica district and is the largest shopping mall on the Iberian Peninsula.

7 Spain

Spain offers fascinating history, pretty beaches, Moorish palaces, quaint villages, and, of course, Picasso, but the country is also full of modern-day vitality. Things began to change with the death of Generalissimo Francisco Franco and the country's 1986 entry into the European Union, and today the nation is undergoing a cultural renaissance that visitors will delight in, with cities like Barcelona, home of the 1992 Olympics, getting used to a new-found prosperity.

CURRENCY   As of March 2002, Spain switched entirely to the euro (€) for its currency. One euro is made up of 100 euro cents. The exchange rate at press time was $1 = 1.1€.

LANGUAGE   Spanish; Spanish and Catalan in Barcelona; Castilian Spanish and Catalan in Palma de Mallorca. Many young people also speak English or German.

BARCELONA

Barcelona, Spain's second largest city and the capital of Catalonia, was developed as a port by the Romans and has long been a Mediterranean center of commerce. Recently it's been discovered by the cruise lines, which are attracted by the city's prime location on the Iberian Peninsula and by its wealth of historical, cultural, and artistic offerings. Nearly every major cruise line visits here today, and many use the Port of Barcelona as a turnaround point.

Once home to Picasso, Miró, and Dalí, Barcelona mixes medieval architecture with Modernism, a style for which the city is world-renowned. Roman ruins, the narrow streets of the Gothic Quarter, buildings from the 13th and

Barcelona

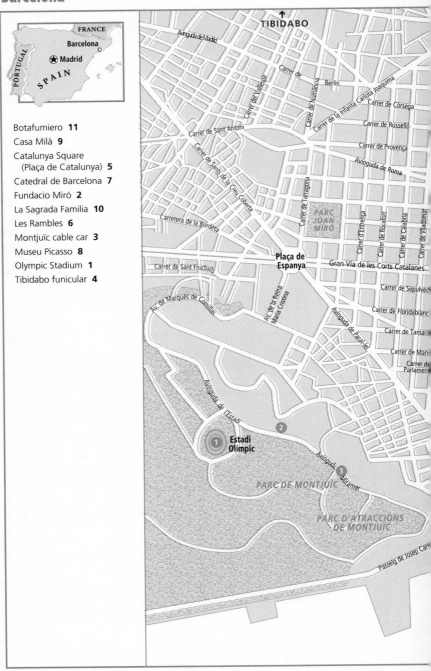

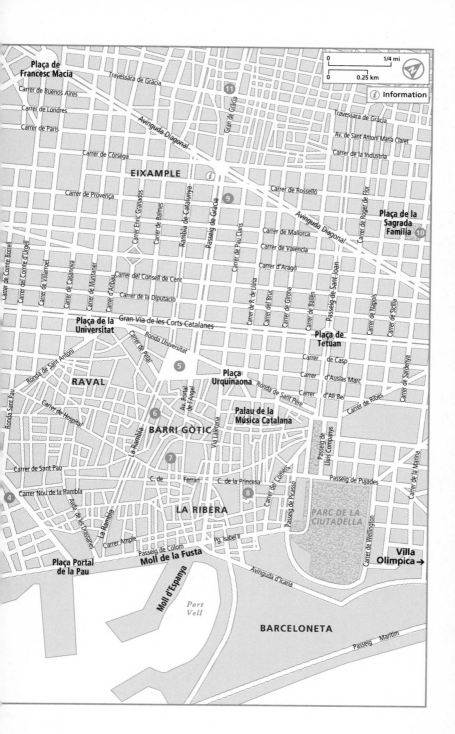

Plaça de
Francesc Macià

Carrer de Buenos Aires

Carrer de Londres

Carrer de Paris

Travessara de Gràcia

Avinguda Diagonal

Carrer de Còrsega

EIXAMPLE

Carrer de Provença

Carrer d'Enric Granados

Carrer de Balmes

Rambla de Catalunya

Passeig de Gràcia

Carrer de Pau Claris

Gran de Gràcia

Travessara de Gràcia

Av. de Sant Antoni Maria Claret

Carrer de la Indústria

Carrer de Rosselló

Avinguda Diagonal

Carrer de Mallorca

Carrer de València

Carrer d'Aragó

Carrer de Roger de Flor

Plaça de la
Sagrada
Família

Carrer de Comte Borell

Carrer del Comte d'Urgell

Carrer de Villarroel

Carrer de Casanova

Carrer de Muntaner

Carrer d'Aribau

Carrer del Consell de Cent

Carrer de la Diputació

Gran Via de les Corts Catalanes

Carrer R. de Llúria

Carrer del Bruc

Carrer de Girona

Carrer de Bailèn

Passeig de Sant Joan

Carrer de Nàpols

Carrer de Sicília

Plaça de la
Universitat

Carrer de Pelai

Ronda Universitat

RAVAL

Ronda de Sant Antoni

Carrer de Hospital

Ronda Sant Pau

Carrer de Sant Pau

Carrer Nou de la Rambla

La Rambla

Avda de les Drassanes

La Rambla

Av. Portal de l'Àngel

Plaça
Urquinaona

Ronda de Sant Pere

BARRI GÒTIC

Via Laietana

Palau de la
Música Catalana

C. de   Ferran

C. de la Princesa

Carrer del Comerç

Passeig de Picasso

LA RIBERA

Carrer Ample

Passeig de Colom

Moll de la Fusta

Pg. Isabel II

Plaça de
Tetuan

Carrer   de Casp

Carrer   d'Ausias Marc

Carrer   d'Ali Bei

Carrer de Ribes

Carrer de Sardenya

Passeig de Lluís Companys

Passeig de Pujades

PARC DE LA
CIUTADELLA

Carrer de Wellington

Carrer de la Marina

Villa
Olímpica →

Plaça Portal
de la Pau

Moll d'Espanya

Avinguda d'Icària

Port
Vell

BARCELONETA

Passeig   Marítim

0   1/4 mi
0   0.25 km

ⓘ Information

15th centuries, and a Bohemian atmosphere exist side by side with I. M. Pei designs and the whimsical creations of Gaudí. In addition to beautiful architecture, the city boasts great museums, friendly people, pleasant cafes, and a very active nightlife, with bars and late-night clubs.

Barcelona even has sandy beaches thanks to a recently reclaimed waterfront.

FROMMER'S FAVORITE BARCELONA EXPERIENCES

- **Walking through the Barri Gótic (Gothic Quarter).** You can wander for hours getting lost—that's part of the fun—and seeing the great cathedral, fountains, vintage stores, cobblestones, and cafes. Exercise caution here at night, however.
- **Strolling along the Ramblas.** Victor Hugo called the Ramblas "the most beautiful street in the world." It runs from Placa de Catalunya to the sea, and is a tree-lined boulevard boasting 24-hour performers, flower vendors, birds in cages, cafes, and shops.
- **Checking the views from Montjuïc or Tibidabo.** Both of these mountain parks are accessible by funicular.
- **Exploring the Museu Picasso.** Two converted palaces on a medieval street hold an impressive collection of the artist's works.
- **Enjoying the fantastical work of Antoni Gaudí.** The designer's creations in Barcelona include his masterpiece apartment building on Paseo de Gracia and the Templo Expiatorio de la Sagrada Familia.
- **Fundacio Joan Miró.** Miró's brilliant colors and abstracts made him one of Spain's beloved painters. This comprehensive display of his work is well worth a visit.

COMING ASHORE & GETTING AROUND   Your ship may dock close enough to the Old Port area to walk to shopping and restaurants, but getting from the port, which is on a long peninsula, requires a circuitous route and can be tricky. The city's notorious pickpockets make the task a bit risky, too. A bridge (opened in 2000) cuts about a quarter-mile from the walk; however, it's a drawbridge that opens several times a day, which sometimes causes delays. Our recommendation is that you take a cab or use the shuttle service provided by the cruise line. **Taxis** are available outside the terminal. The rate begins at about 2.10€ ($1.90), and there's a charge of about 83€ (75¢) per kilometer after that. There is a special supplement if the taxi is taken inside the pier area.

The city also has a good **Metro** and **bus system.** During the summer, there is also **Bus Turistic,** which passes by a dozen of the most popular sights. You can get on and off as you please and also ride the **Tibidabo funicular** and the **Montjuïc cable car** and funicular (both for panoramic city views) for the price of a single ticket. Tickets can be purchased on the bus or at the transportation booth at Placa de Catalunya, for about 13€ ($12) for a 1-day pass, 18€ ($16) for 2 days.

La Rambla is about 1 to 2 miles from the pier, depending on where your ship docks.

THE BEST SHORE EXCURSIONS

City Highlights (3½–4½ hr., $31–$53): This bus and walking tour includes the Gothic Quarter, a stop at Montjuïc for the views, the Olympic Stadium, Gaudí's whimsical Sagrada Familia, La Rambla, and Catalunya Square.

Museums Tour (3½–4 hr., $35–$45): Includes a visit to the Picasso Museum and the medieval "Ribera" quarter and/or a drive to Montjuïc for the impressive views, and/or the Miró Foundation, and/or a drive past buildings created by Antoni Gaudí.

Pilgrimage to Montserrat (5–6 hr., $69–$87): This tour heads north of Barcelona 36 miles to the sacred Mountain of Montserrat, one of Spain's natural wonders. The highest peak of this jagged mountain range reaches 4,072 feet. Approximately halfway up the mountain stands the famous Montserrat Monastery, built by Philip II between 1563 and 1592. It is world-famous for its shrine of the Virgin Mary, Our Lady of Montserrat. The shrine was dedicated to the image of the Virgin and has been considered for many years one of Spain's most significant places of pilgrimage. Afterward, listen to the famous Escolania choir from the monastery's School of Music. After returning to Barcelona, enjoy a brief tour of the city before returning to the ship. Lunch is included.

THE TOP ATTRACTIONS

La Sagrada Familia   Antoni Gaudí's creation was begun in 1882 and has never been finished, but the Church of the Holy Family is a bizarre wonder and should be at the top of everyone's list of landmarks to visit. The designer's style has been described as Art Nouveau run wild, and it is on full display here. Some predict it will be completed by the mid–21st century.

Majora, 401. ℂ **93/207-30-31.** Admission 4.90€ ($4.40), including a 12-min. video; 1.20€ ($1.10) extra for the elevator to the top. Apr–Aug daily 9am–8pm; Mar and Sept daily 9am–7pm.

Miró Foundation (Fundación Joan Miró)   This museum, located in Montjuïc park, pays tribute to one of Spain's greatest artists, and contains some 10,000 of the surrealist's works. Included are paintings, graphics, and sculptures.

Placa de Neptú, Parc de Montjuïc. ℂ **93/329-19-08.** Admission 4.90€ ($4.40) adults, 2.75€ ($2.50) students, free for children 14 and under. July–Sept Tues–Wed and Fri–Sat 10am–8pm, Thurs 10am–9:30pm, Sun 10am–2:30pm; Oct–June Tues–Wed and Fri–Sat the museum opens at 11am.

Museu Picasso   Barcelona's cathedral is Gothic in style. The basilica, except for the 19th-century western facade, was begun at the end of the 13th century and completed in the 15th century. The cloister offers a museum of medieval art. The three naves have wonderful Gothic details.

Montcada 15–19. ℂ **93/319-63-10.** Admission 4.25€ ($3.85) adults, 1.80€ ($1.65) students, free for 17 and under. Tues–Sat 10am–8pm; Sun 10am–3pm.

LOCAL FLAVORS

The big meal of the day here is lunch (*comida*) and is served at mid-afternoon. Fresh seafood is a best bet, and a good place to try it is **Botafumiero,** Gran de Grácia 81 (ℂ **93-218-42-30**). Main courses run 17€ to 42€ ($15 to $38); reservations are recommended for the dining rooms, but not necessary if you dine at the bar. In general, late afternoon or early evening is a good time to try tapas, or Spanish hors d'oeuvres. Dinner is served late. Try the local wines, including *cava,* the Barcelona version of bubbly (the kind marked "brut" is sweeter than the one marked "brut nature").

BEST BUYS

Shop in Barcelona for leather goods including shoes, jewelry, high fashion, artworks, and straw products. The main shopping area surrounds the **Plaça de Catalunya.** Upscale shopping can be found on **Passeig de Gracia** from the Avinguda Dagonal to the Plaça de Catalunya (upper Rambla). Traditional shopping can be found between the Rambla and Via Laietana. Dozens of galleries are located in the **Gothic Quarter** (Barri Gótic) and near the Picasso museum. Most shops, with the exception of some large department stores, close from 1:30 to 4pm.

CADIZ

Cádiz is 3,000 years old, making it the Western world's oldest continuously inhabited city. It's a venerable seaport, where thousands of ships embarked for the New World. Christopher Columbus started his second and fourth voyages here.

Today, as in years past, it's a bustling port. The city is geographically divided into two, one side the modern city, lying on the isthmus, with its busy commercial area, the other with the historic districts of El Populo and Santa Maria, with narrow streets and ancient stone walls, and plenty of local characters.

Despite the city's age, there are few remnants of antiquity here, although you'll find an impressive cathedral and some good museums. The Oratorio de San Felipe Neri, where the first Spanish constitution was drafted in 1812, has the painting *Immaculate Conception* by Murillo, and the Santa Cruz Chapel has three frescoes by Goya.

Cádiz also has nice beaches and two world-class golf courses, Montecastillo (designed by Jack Nicklaus) and Novo Sancti Petri (designed by Steve Ballesteros).

Despite all this, the cruise lines view Cádiz as more of a jumping-off point to explore **Seville,** one of Spain's prettiest cities and also, thanks to Don Juan and Carmen (aided by Mozart and Bizet), one of its most romantic. It's located about 75 miles from Cádiz. Shore excursions are also offered to **Jerez,** home of Spanish sherry and Andalusian horses.

FROMMER'S FAVORITE CADIZ EXPERIENCES

- **Sitting at a sidewalk cafe and people-watching.** The best spot in Cádiz is the Plaza de San Juan de Dios.
- **Strolling through Old Cádiz.** Explore the narrow streets of this pedestrian zone. You might also want to check out the city's parks, such as Parque Genoves, which looks onto the Atlantic.
- **Taking a shore excursion** to Seville or Jerez. (See below.)

THE BEST SHORE EXCURSIONS

Cádiz & Puerto de Santa Maria (3½ hr., $40–$50): This city-highlights tour includes a visit to a local winery. From the bus, you'll see the monument to the Constitution of 1810, the city's ramparts, the historic Castle of San Sebastian, the Cathedral of Cádiz, and other city highlights. Cross the harbor to Puerto Santa Maria to visit an elegant estate and renowned winery.

Cádiz, Jerez & the Royal School of Equestrian Art (7½ hr., $89; or visit the horse farm separately, 4½ hr., $63; or Jerez separately, 4½ hr., $42.) After a brief drive past the highlights of Cádiz, travel for about an hour to the old town of Jerez, where white mansions are guarded by historic walls and towers. Stop at a local cellar for a taste of brandy and sherry. Visit the equestrian school to see the Andalusian horses put through their training. Includes lunch.

Romantic Seville (8 hr., $99–$124): A full-day excursion takes you to this historic and beautiful city. Travel by bus for 2 hours through the countryside. In Seville, visit the Cathedral de Sevilla, the world's third largest cathedral, where you can see the tombs of King Fernando III and Christopher Columbus. Also

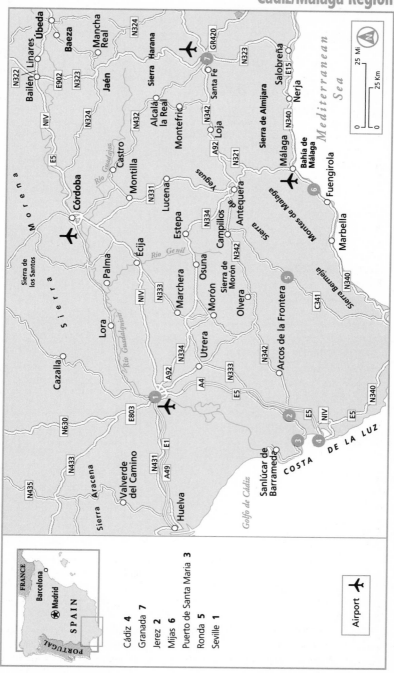

Mediterranean Sea

N322
Úbeda
Baeza
Mancha Real
N324
Linares
Bailén
E902
N323
Jaén
Sierra Harana
GR420
Santa Fe
7
N323
Salobreña
Nerja
E15
N322
NIV
N324
Alcalá la Real
N432
Montefrío
N342
Loja
A92
Sierra de Almijara
N340
E5
Río Guadalquivir
Castro
Montilla
Córdoba
N331
Lucena
Yeguas
N321
Antequera
Málaga
Bahía de Málaga
6
Fuengirola
Sierra Morena
Estepa
N334
Campillos
Sierra
Montes de Málaga
Marbella
Sierra de los Santos
Écija
Palma
Río Genil
Marchera
Osuna
N342
Olvera
Arcos de la Frontera
5
Sierra Bermeja
N340
Sierra
N333
Sierra de Morón
C341
NIV
Lora
Río Guadalquivir
Utrera
N334
A92
A4
N333
N342
Cazalla
1
E803
E5
2
E5
NIV
E5
N340
N630
E1
A49
N431
Valverde del Camino
Sanlúcar de Barrameda
3
4
COSTA DE LA LUZ
N433
Sierra Aracena
N435
Huelva
Golfo de Cádiz

25 Mi
25 Km

FRANCE
Barcelona
Madrid
SPAIN
PORTUGAL

Cádiz **4**
Granada **7**
Jerez **2**
Mijas **6**
Puerto de Santa Maria **3**
Ronda **5**
Seville **1**

Airport ✈

visit Seville's Alcazar, a 14th-century Mudéjar palace, and the Jewish quarter. Time is allowed to stroll Seville's charming streets. Enjoy lunch at a local restaurant or hotel.

COMING ASHORE & GETTING AROUND   It's about a 10-minute walk from the pier to the city center. **Taxis** are available at the pier. **Buses** and **trains** run regularly to Seville, about 2 hours away.

THE TOP ATTRACTIONS

Catedral de Cádiz   This magnificent 18th-century baroque building has a neoclassical interior. Music lovers come here to pay respects at the tomb of Cádiz-born Manuel de Falla. The cathedral's treasury/museum offers a collection of Spanish silver, embroidery, and paintings.

Plaza Catedral. ℂ **956/28-61-54.** Free admission to cathedral; museum admission 3.05€ ($2.75) adults, 1.20€ ($1.10) children. Tues–Sat 10am–12:30pm.

Museo de Cádiz   This museum contains one of Spain's most important Zurbaran collections, as well as paintings by Rubens and Murillo. The archaeology section displays Roman, Carthaginian, and Phoenician finds. There are also exhibits of pottery, baskets, textiles, and leatherwork.

Plaza de Mini. ℂ **956/21-22-81.** Admission 1.55€ ($1.40); free on Sun. Tues 2:30–8pm; Wed–Sat 9am–8pm; Sun 9:30am–2:30pm.

Oratorio de San Felipe Neri   The Cortes (Parliament) met here in 1812 to proclaim its constitution. There's a history museum, and Murillo's *Immaculate Conception* is on display.

Santa Ines. ℂ **956/21-16-12.** Free admission. Aug–June daily 8:30am–10am and 7:30–9:45pm. Closed July.

LOCAL FLAVORS

Seafood is big here and sardines are a favorite local treat. Try them, or any other fine fish dish, with local wine at **Achuri,** Calle Plocia, 15 (ℂ **956-25-36-13**), a favorite family-run restaurant since 1947.

BEST BUYS

Best buys are wine of the Jerez region, Andalusian handicrafts, leather, and ceramics. The main shopping area is on Columela and San Francisco streets.

MALAGA

Málaga is the Costa del Sol region's historic capital, and is today a bustling commercial and residential center. The city's most famous citizen was none other than Pablo Picasso, born here in 1881 at Plaza de la Merced, in the city center. Unfortunately, Picasso left little of his spirit and only a small selection of his work in his birthplace. The city does offer some interesting historical sights, however, including a 16th-century cathedral and the Moorish Alcazaba Fortress, and is a pleasant place to explore on your own, although the town can be quite crowded with tourists in the summer.

Málaga is also the port for nearby Granada, the famed Alhambra, and other inland sights.

COMING ASHORE & GETTING AROUND   Ships dock at a pier close to town, or at another pier that's a short cab ride away. **Taxis** are usually available pier-side. Watch out for purse-snatchers as you walk around the town, since Málaga has one of the highest crime rates in Spain. It's not recommended you walk alone around the area of the Castillo de Gibralfaro in particular.

FROMMER'S FAVORITE MALAGA EXPERIENCES

- **Checking out the Alcazaba.** Ferdinand and Isabella slept at this Moorish palace, the remains of which are within easy walking distance of the city center.
- **Trying some local wine.** Sweet dessert wines are a Málaga specialty.
- **Taking a bus or cab to the beach.** Depending on how much time you have in port, you can head to Torremolinos, about 9 miles west of Málaga, or other resort areas on Costa del Sol.
- **Heading inland to Granada.** (See below.)

THE BEST SHORE EXCURSIONS

Granada & the Alhambra (8½ hr., $112–$127): This tour highlights historic Granada and includes a number of interesting sights along the 2-hour drive, such as the town of Casabermeja, with its white houses, and Las Pedrizas, a scenic mountain pass. In Granada, visit the Muslim-Hispano complex known as the Alhambra, a spectacular example of Moorish architecture encircled by walls and towers. Also visit the nearby Generalife, the royal residence surrounded by water gardens, and El Vino Gate, commissioned by Carlos V in the 16th century. Includes lunch.

Granada Transfer (8½ hr., $52–$64): A 2-hour bus ride to Granada, where you will have free time to explore on your own and still be guaranteed to get back to the ship on time.

Málaga City Tour (4 hr., $32–$39): On this tour you will see the Alcazaba and the Gibralfaro. Also visit the city's Renaissance-style cathedral. Drive past the Roman theater, the facade of the bullring, and the 19th-century post office and City Hall. The tour may include a stop at a local tavern to taste the region's sweet wine, or a side trip to Mijas.

Mijas & Countryside (4½ hr., $32): This tour highlights Spanish country life and visits Mijas, a classical village with beautiful views of the coast. Visit San Sebastian church in the old part of town and the Barrio Santa Ana, with its whitewashed houses. Also check out the bullring, built in 1920. You can, if you want, explore the streets on donkey. Or you can visit a local cafe or souvenir and handicraft shops.

THE TOP ATTRACTIONS

Alcazaba   The remains of a Moorish palace are within easy walking distance of the city center (look for the signs pointing the way up the hill). The fortress was erected mostly in the 9th or 10th century, and among those who have stayed here were Ferdinand and Isabella. The Alcazaba now houses an archaeological museum. The grounds are beautiful, offering orange trees, purple bougainvillea, and some of the best views on the Costa del Sol.

Plaza de la Aduana, Alcazabilla. ✆ **95/221-60-05.** Free admission to grounds, admission to museum .22€ (20¢). Tues–Fri 9:30am–1:30pm and 5–8pm; Sat 10am–1pm; Sun 10am–2pm.

Málaga Cathedral   This vast and impressive 16th-century Renaissance cathedral, located in the city center, has been declared a national monument. Its most notable interior feature is the richly ornamented choir stalls.

Plaza Obispo. ✆ **95/221-59-17.** Admission 1.20€ ($1.10). Mon–Sat 10am–12:45pm and 4–6:30pm.

Museo de Bellas Artes (Málaga Fine Arts Museum)   A former Moorish palace located behind the cathedral, this art museum has a gallery devoted to native son Pablo Picasso, as well as works by Murillo, Ribera, and Morales, and Andalusian antiques, mosaics, and sculptures.

Calle San Agustín, 8. ℂ **95/221-83-82**. Admission 1.20€ ($1.10). Tues–Fri 10am–1:30pm and 4–7pm; Sat–Sun 10am–1:30pm.

LOCAL FLAVORS

Tapas are served here at typical tapas bars. Or, you may consider ordering hors d'oeuvres parador, a tableful of the small dishes, at **Parador de Málaga-Gibralfaro,** Monte Gibralfaro (ℂ **95-222-19-02**), a government-run restaurant with wonderful views from its mountainside setting.

BEST BUYS

Shop here for the region's rustic pottery, leather goods, silver and gold jewelry, and local wine. Most shops close between 1 and 5pm. An exception is **El Corte Ingles** department store. Small mall shops and boutiques can be found along **Calle Larios.** Outside the town limits, the most comprehensive collection of ceramics and pottery can be found at **La Vistillas,** Carretera Mijas, Km 2 (about 1¼ miles from the center of Málaga).

PALMA DE MALLORCA

Mallorca (also spelled Majorca), known as "the Island of Tranquility," is the largest of the 16 Balearic Islands, offering some 310 miles of coastline. The other main islands in the chain are Ibiza (which is also visited by some cruise ships) and Menorca.

Lying about 60 miles from the Spanish mainland and 130 miles from Barcelona, Mallorca offers a lush (some trees are more than 1,000 years old) and rugged landscape, and picturesque villages (and also some big high-rise hotels). It is a popular resort area, particularly with northern Europeans. Millions of tourists come here each year. Juan Carlos, king of Spain, has a residence in Marivent in Cala Mayor.

Palma, the capital, is a cosmopolitan city with a population of 300,000, and relies on tourism for its economy. There are big hotels and fast-food restaurants, but there are also sights of historical interest left by the Romans, the Arabs, and later Spanish kings who at one time occupied the island. The Gothic Quarter of Palma offers a maze of narrow alleys and cobblestone streets.

Outside the city are mountains, lush valleys, fine beaches, and little fishing villages where life is still simple. It's not surprising that writers, painters, and musicians have found inspiration here.

Arrival by sea here is particularly impressive, with the skyline characterized by the Bellver Castle and the city's Gothic cathedral. Plan to be on deck so you can catch the view.

FROMMER'S FAVORITE MALLORCA EXPERIENCES

- **Renting a car and heading to the mountains.** Drive west on C-719, then north on C-710, and back on C-711 (at Sóller) to pass through some of the most beautiful coastal and mountain scenery on the island.
- **Heading to the beach.** The best are Ca'n Pastilla and El Arenal, although they can get crowded. Another good bet is Cala Mayor.
- **Exploring the Gothic Quarter.** Palma's Gothic Quarter offers narrow streets and cobblestones and interesting sights such as the Moorish baths (**Banys Arabs,** Carrer Serra, 7).
- **Spending some quiet time in Deia.** This serene little Mallorcan village is located about 17 miles from Palma (it's accessible by bus) and offers

Cala Mayor beach **4**
Ca'n Pastilla beach **5**
Cartuja (Carthusian Monastery) **2**
Caves of Drach (Porto Cristo) **7**
Deia **1**
El Arenal beach **6**
La Granja de Esporlas **3**

mountain and sea views, stone houses, olive trees, and creeping bougain-villea. It's long been an artist's retreat, and notables who have lived here include Robert Graves, the English poet and novelist.

- **Visiting the Carthusian Monastery in Valldemossa.** Chopin and George Sand wintered here. See "Valldemossa & Chopin" under "The Best Shore Excursions," below.

COMING ASHORE & GETTING AROUND   Ships dock about 15 minutes (by vehicle) from the center of town. **Taxis** are generally available at the pier. **Buses** run from Palma to popular destinations that include Valldemossa, Deia, and Sóller. There are also **trains** to Sóller. **Rental cars** are available from **Atesa** at Passeig Marítim (© 971/78-98-96) and range from about 45€ to 91€ ($41 to $82) per day. **Avis** at Passeig Marítim (© **971/73-07-20**) offers cars 55€ to 169€ ($50 to $153) per day. Reservations for either are strongly recommended.

THE BEST SHORE EXCURSIONS

Valldemossa & Chopin (3½–4 hr., $39–$44): This tour explores the west side of the island. Drive 45 minutes to the quaint village of Valldemossa, located at the foot of the Northern Mountain Range, where the history dates back to the 14th century. Visit **Cartuja,** a former royal residence turned monastery in the Middle Ages. In 1838, both George Sand and Frederic Chopin came to live at

Gibraltar

The famous rock at the entrance to the Mediterranean is visited by some ships and simply pointed out by others (as in, "We do a daylight passing of the Rock of Gibraltar").

If you do set foot on the limestone rock—which is technically a peninsula rather than an island—you will find a small British colony from which you can view Africa on a clear day. In addition to spectacular views, Gibraltar offers a small town (also called Gibraltar) with Victorian architecture, natural caves, historical sights, museums, lovely botanical gardens, and the famous Barbary apes, as well as beautiful beaches.

In town, the **duty-free shops** are a big attraction. Best buys here include English china, crystal, Lladro and Nao figurines, English woolens, electronics, jewelry, watches, cosmetics, and perfume. And you can stop at one of the pubs on Main Street for fish-and-chips or steak-and-kidney pie, and a pint of ale.

The official language is English and the currency is the Gibraltar pound, which is equivalent to pound sterling. But U.S. dollars are also readily accepted.

Ships dock about 1 mile, or a 20-minute walk, from the center of town. And taxis and a shuttle service are both usually available at the pier.

The **Rock of Gibraltar tour** (2–2½ hr., $37–$51) offered by many cruise lines includes a scenic drive, with a stop at **St. Michael's Cave,** a natural grotto with spectacular stalagmites (you have to climb a lot of steps to see them), and the **Apes' Den,** inhabited by some 20 semi-wild Barbary apes (there are some 140 others in a pack in the Great Siege area). The apes were introduced as pets on the island by the British more than 200 years ago, and, according to legend, Gibraltar stays British as long as the apes remain here. The tour also includes time to shop in town. Some tours add a ride on the **Gibraltar Cable Car,** which takes you up the face of the Rock to the very top, and some include a visit to the **Great Siege Tunnels,** an ingenious defense system dating back to the 18th century.

the monastery. Sand later wrote a book titled *A Winter in Majorca* about that time, and Chopin composed "Raindrop Prelude" and other works here. The tour includes a short piano recital.

Palma de Mallorca City Tour (4 hr., $36–$46): Explore the capital of the Balearic Islands, including the Bellver Castle, Spanish Village, Almudaina Palace, cathedral, and Gothic Quarter. The drive back to the ship passes La Rambla, Paseo Mallorca, and the Maritime Promenade.

La Granja (4½ hr., $39–$46): This tour follows a scenic route past lovely villages and popular resort areas, and includes a visit to La Granja de Esporlas, a 17th-century manor house set on what is considered one of the most idyllic spots on the island. There are beautiful fountains and formal gardens, and the house offers a museum of daily life and a wine cellar. The tour may also include a visit to Puerto Andraitx, a quaint fishing port. A tasting of regional specialties is included.

THE TOP ATTRACTIONS

Art Espanyol Contemporani   This art museum features Picasso, Miró, Dalí, and Juan Gris in its collection, along with other 20th-century Spanish artists. The best-known work here is Picasso's *Head of a Woman.*

Carrer Sant Miquel 11. ✆ 971/71-35-15. Admission 3.05€ ($2.75) adults, 1.55€ ($1.40) seniors and children. Mon–Fri 10am–6:30pm; Sat 10am–1:30pm.

Castell de Bellver   Erected in 1309, this hilltop castle with its double moat was once a summer palace of kings and now houses the Museu Municipal, which offers a collection of archaeological objects and coins. But it's the view that attracts visitors. In fact, *Bellver* means beautiful view.

Between Palma and Illetas. ✆ 971/73-06-57. Admission 1.60€ ($1.45 adults), .95€ (85¢) children, students, and seniors. Mon–Sat 8am–8pm.

Catedral (Le Seu)   The Gothic cathedral is located in old town, and overlooks the sea. It was started during the reign of Jaume II (1276–1311) and completed in 1610. Of note is the scalloped-edged, wrought-iron canopy by Gaudí over the main altar. The treasury contains pieces of the True Cross and relics of St. Sebastián.

Carrer Palau Reial. ✆ 971/72-31-30. Free admission to cathedral; museum and treasury admission 3.05€ ($2.75). Mon–Fri 10am–6pm; Sat 10am–2pm. Museum and cathedral hours are often subject to change.

Palau de l'Almudaina   This fortress is a reminder that the island was once ruled by Muslims, and was used as a royal residence by Mallorcan kings. Inside is a museum with antiques, arts, suits of armor, and Gobelin tapestries. The grounds offer Moorish-style gardens and fountains, as well as panoramic views of the harbor of Palma.

Carrer Palau Reial. ✆ 971/72-71-45. Admission 2.45€ ($2.20) adults, 1.40€ ($1.25) children; free on Wed. Apr–Oct Mon–Sat 10am–2pm and 4–6:30pm; Nov–Mar Mon–Sat 10:30am–2pm and 4–6pm.

LOCAL FLAVORS

Meat-eaters will want to try the Mallorcan specialty, pork loin (*lomo*), or sausage (*sabrasada*). Other favorites include fish pie. Finish your meal with a *café carajillo* (coffee with cognac).

BEST BUYS

Shop here for Mallorca pearls, inlaid wood products, needlework, pottery, hand-blown glass, olive wood carvings, and leather goods (including shoes). The upscale shops are located along **Avenida Jaume III** and the **Paseo del Borne.** Good shopping opportunities can also be found on San Miguel, carrer Sindicato, Jaume II, carrer Platería, and Via Roman. Most shops close between 1:30 and 4:30pm, as well as on Sundays.

8 Turkey

Turkey is literally where East meets West (Istanbul sits where Europe and Asia touch) and is probably the most exotic country you'll visit on your European cruise. It's a land of mosques and minarets, sultans' treasures and crowded bazaars, unmatched Greek and Roman archaeological sites and holy Christian landmarks. While its cities teem with the energy of a modern nation looking to the West, its villages remain much as they've been for the past several hundred years.

> (*Tips*   **A Sign of Respect**
>
> Visitors to religious sites should dress respectfully: for men and women, no shorts or exposed bare arms or shoulders, and women may not wear skirts above the knee. It is best not to visit mosques during prayer times or on Friday, the holy day.

CURRENCY   Turkish lira (TL) notes are issued in 10,000-, 50,000-, 100,000-, 250,000-, 500,000-, 1 million, and 5 million denominations. The rate of exchange at press time was $1 = 1,413,500 TL. Because of the wide fluctuation of Turkish currency, prices are often quoted in U.S. dollars or other more stable currencies, and it is best to only exchange what you intend to spend.

LANGUAGE   Turkish and Kurdish are spoken here as well as English, French, and German.

ISTANBUL

The city where the continents of Asia and Europe meet is chaotic and congested, yet bold and exciting. A diverse mix of architectural styles, religions, and people form the backdrop and backbone of this cosmopolitan city, where modern cars careen through the streets past historic monuments that reveal a rich and ancient history. The senses spring to life here—the smell of the spice market, the sound of prayer, the taste of traditional Turkish dishes, the feel of a Turkish carpet, and the sight of awe-inspiring treasures at every turn. Istanbul served as the capital of three successive empires—the Roman, Byzantine, and Ottoman—and this legacy lives on. Everywhere you look, museums, churches, palaces, grand mosques, and bazaars attest to the city's glorious history.

FROMMER'S FAVORITE ISTANBUL EXPERIENCES

- **Exploring the old section.** Most of the major attractions are located in this area and are within walking distance of each other.
- **Shopping at the Grand Bazaar.** It's a sight to behold as 4,000 shopkeepers hawk their wares and patrons browse and bargain through a labyrinth of passageways.

COMING ASHORE & GETTING AROUND   Ships drop anchor on the Bosphorus on the European side of the city. **Taxis**—yellow, metered, and relatively inexpensive—wait to pick up passengers, and you'll also find plenty of them traveling throughout the city. The starting rate is about $1, and there is a surcharge after midnight. Tip drivers to the nearest lira. **Bus and tram service** are also available, and cruise lines usually provide shuttle buses to downtown (which usually drop you off near the expensive rug shops).

The best way to explore the old section of the city is by foot. All of the monuments are within walking distance of each other. It's a healthy walk from the pier to the Blue Mosque, and with all the crazy drivers and the generally hectic pace, you're best off taking the shuttle offered by the cruise line, or a cab.

THE BEST SHORE EXCURSIONS

Highlights of Istanbul (7–9 hr., $89–$97): Includes the Hippodrome, once the largest chariot race grounds of the Byzantine Empire; Sultan Ahmet Mosque, also known as the Blue Mosque for its 21,000 blue Iznik tiles; the famous St. Sophia, once the largest church of the Christian world; and Topkapi Palace,

Old Istanbul

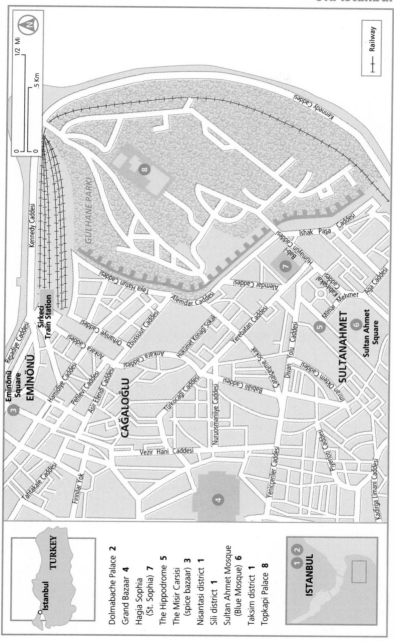

— | — | Railway

Kennedy Caddesi

GÜLHANE PARKI

Ishak Paşa Caddesi

Alemdar Caddesi

Taya Hatun Caddesi

Babı Hümayun Caddesi

Sirkeci
Train Station

Eminönü
Square
EMİNÖNÜ

Reşadiye Caddesi

Hamidiye Caddesi

Ankara Caddesi

Orhaniye Caddesi

Ebussuut Caddesi

Pehlevi Caddesi

Asir Efendi Caddesi

CAĞALOĞLU

Türkocağı Caddesi

Hükümet Konağı Sokak

Yerebatan Caddesi

Babıali Caddesi

Çatalçeşme Sokak

Nuruosmaniye Caddesi

Vezir Hani Caddesi

Taktakale Caddesi

Fırınlar Yok

Divan Yolu Caddesi

Imran Öktem Caddesi

SULTANAHMET

Mimar Mehmet

Sultan Ahmet
Square

Yeşebakçı Caddesi

Nga Caddesi

Piyelloji Caddesi

Yeniçeriler Caddesi

Kadırga Limanı Caddesi

Istanbul **TURKEY**

ISTANBUL

Dolmabache Palace **2**
Grand Bazaar **4**
Hagia Sophia
 (St. Sophia) **7**
The Hippodrome **5**
The Misir Carsisi
 (spice bazaar) **3**
Nisantasi district **1**
Sili district **1**
Sultan Ahmet Mosque
 (Blue Mosque) **6**
Taksim district **1**
Topkapi Palace **8**

329

the official residence of the Ottoman Sultans and home to treasures that include Spoonmaker's Diamond, one of the biggest in the world. Also visit the Grand Bazaar, with its 4,000 shops. Some tours bring you back to the ship for lunch while others include lunch in a first-class restaurant. (Shorter tours are also available that include some, but not all, of the above.)

THE TOP ATTRACTIONS

Topkapi Palace   Topkapi Palace served as the residence of sultans from the 15th century to the mid–19th century. The Ottoman complex includes the chamber of the Sacred Mantle, harem quarters, crown jewels, holy relics, the throne room, and other treasures. From the verandas of the palace, guests get panoramic views of the city. In the summer it's wise to get a ticket to the harem tour after arriving at the palace. Tours are conducted every half-hour.

Kennedy Cad. Sultanahmet. ✆ 212/512-0480. Admission $6; the guided harem tour costs $3. Wed–Mon 9am–5pm.

St. Sophia   The 6th-century basilica is famous for its gigantic domes and magnificent mosaics. St. Sophia was commissioned by Emperor Justinian, who was looking to restore the greatness of the Roman empire. It was later converted to a mosque by the Ottomans. Also known as the Church of the Divine Wisdom, Hagia Sophia is regarded as one of the best examples of Byzantine architecture.

Yerebatan Cad. Sultanahmet. ✆ 212/522-1750. Admission $6. Tues–Sun 9am–5pm.

The Blue Mosque   Also known as the Imperial Sultanahmet Mosque, the mosque was built in the 17th century and features dazzling blue and white Iznik tiles and six minarets. Guests must remove their shoes and leave them at the entrance.

Free admission. Daily 9am–6pm.

Hippodrome   This park was once the site of great chariot races and Byzantine civic life. What remains from those times are three monuments, the Obelisk of Theodosius, the bronze serpentine column, and the column of Constantine. Nearby is the Museum of Turkish and Islamic Arts.

Sultanahmet (in front of the Blue Mosque).

Dolmabache Palace   The 19th-century palace is sometimes referred to as the Ottoman Versailles because of its extravagant pieces, such as a 4-ton Baccarat chandelier that was a gift from Queen Victoria. The palace boasts a mix of architectural designs, including European, Hindu, and Turkish elements.

Dolmabache Cad. ✆ 212/258-5544. Admission $13 for a long tour; $7 for a short tour. Tues–Wed and Fri–Sun 9am–4pm. Camera fee $7; videocamera fee $15.

Grand Bazaar   The Kapali Carsi (Grand Bazaar) contains 4,000 vendors selling carpets, leather goods, jewelry, antique reproductions, and other items. The oldest part of the market is Cevahir Bedesteni, which specializes in gold and silver works. To help you find your way around, maps are on sale at newsstands for $5.

Yeniceriler Cad and Fuatpasa Cad. Free admission. Mon–Sat 9am–7pm.

Museum Closings

Most museums are closed on Mondays, except Topkapi Palace, which is closed on Tuesdays.

LOCAL FLAVORS

Turkish meals generally start with *meze* (hors d'oeuvres). Main courses usually feature fish, beef, and lamb dishes. One of the most popular items here is the kebab (either lamb or beef, skewered and grilled on a spit). The most common dessert is fresh fruit. The national drink is raki, which is flavored with anise. For a meal fit for a sultan, try **Asitane,** in the Kariye Oteli, Kariye Camii Sok 18 (adjacent to the Church of St. Savoir in Chora; ✆ **212/534-8414**), where meals are prepared using historical recipes from Topkapi Palace. Reservations are suggested. Main courses run $5 to $19.

BEST BUYS

Shop here for carpets and kilims, onyx, leather goods, meerschaum pipes, and jewelry—and be ready to bargain. While browsing or bargaining, a shopkeeper may offer a cup of tea or a cold drink. This is part of the Turkish hospitality, so don't feel obliged to make a purchase. Bargaining is a serious business here, and it is considered bad form to start bargaining if you are not serious about buying the item.

Istanbul's legendary Grand Bazaar (see above) boasts 4,000 shops selling everything from copperware to carpets to cologne. Tucked in the bazaar's narrow alleys and passageways are cafes and restaurants.

The **Taksim, Nisantasi,** and **Sili districts** boast the most fashionable shops. Flea markets are open daily in the **Topkapi** district. The Misir Carsisi or **spice bazaar** is located next to Yeni Mosque at Eminouno.

KUŞDASI

Once a sleepy port town, Kuşadasi (which means "bird island" in Turkish) has become a bustling seaside resort. The city is used as a starting-off point for excursions to archaeological sites in Ephesus, Priene, Didyma, and Miletus as well as trips to beaches and Dilek National Park. *Note:* If possible, explore Kuşadasi's sights early in the day, before the sun is at its strongest.

FROMMER'S FAVORITE KUŞADASI EXPERIENCES

- **Visiting Ephesus.** An excursion to one of the best-preserved ancient cities in the world is a must.
- **Shopping.** As you wander through the streets, shopkeepers will try to lure you into their stores by promising you the best deal. It's fun to peruse, bargain, and buy, whether it is a small trinket or an expensive carpet.

COMING ASHORE & GETTING AROUND   Ships dock right downtown. Stores and restaurants are within walking distance of the harbor. **Minibuses** (available from the town center) and **taxis** (yellow and metered) can take you to attractions and the beach.

THE BEST SHORE EXCURSIONS

Ephesus (3–4 hr., $35–$44): Visit one of the best preserved ancient cities in the world. Your guide will take you down the city's actual marble streets to the Baths, the theater, and the incredible library building, and along the way you will pass columns, mosaics, monuments, and ruins. The tour may include a stop at a shop for a demonstration on Turkish carpets—with the emphasis on getting you to buy.

Ephesus & The House of The Virgin Mary (3½–4½ -hr., $44–$52): This tour combines a visit to Ephesus with the House of the Virgin Mary, a humble chapel located in the valley of Bulbuldagi, on the spot where the Virgin Mary is believed to have spent her last days. The site was officially sanctioned for pilgrimage in 1892.

Ephesus, St. John's Basilica & House of the Virgin Mary (4½ hr., $56): This tour combines the two tours above with a visit to St. John's Basilica, another holy pilgrimage site. It is believed to be the site where St. John wrote the fourth book of the New Testament. A church at the site, which is now in ruins, was built by Justinian over a 2nd-century tomb believed to contain St. John the apostle. This tour may also be offered as a full-day excursion, including lunch at a local restaurant, and a visit to the museum of Ephesus (7½ hr., $72–$98).

Three Ancient Cities (6–7 hr., $68–$89): This tour takes in the ruins that surround the region of Ephesus, including Priene, known for its Athena Temple (bankrolled by Alexander the Great); Didyma, known for the Temple of Apollo; and Miletus, which includes a stadium built by the Greeks and expanded by the Romans to hold 15,000 spectators. A light lunch at a restaurant in Didyma is included.

THE TOP ATTRACTIONS

Basilica of St. John & the House of the Virgin Mary   It's said that the grave of St. John the Divine is located under the ruins of the church, which was one of the largest Byzantine churches in Turkey. It's believed that Mary spent the last days of her life in a house on a nearby hillside. Today, the house is a church, with the main altar where the kitchen was located.

5 miles southwest of Selçuk. Admission to the park and house $2.10. Dawn to dusk.

Ephesus   The city of Ephesus was built in the 11th century B.C. by the Ionians. The region thrived as a powerful trading port until silt accumulation over the course of centuries destroyed its harbor. Today, what remains of the city (and there's an amazing amount that remains) lies 3 miles from the sea. During its heyday, Ephesus also served as a center of worship. Its Temple of Diana was considered one of the Seven Wonders of the Ancient World. When touring the site (and we recommend you see Ephesus on a shore excursion, with a licensed guide, as you'll get more out of the experience), visitors walk down a street paved in marble to agoras, a theater, public toilets (a real must-see!), and Ephesus's most striking monument, the two-story Celsus Library. Temples, baths, columns, and a 25,000-seat amphitheater—which is still used today for concerts and other theatrical productions—are among the other attractions. *Note:* Ephesus is about 13 miles from Kuşadasi, and you are best off visiting on a shore excursion with a professional guide. But if you are on your own, hire a guide at the site (shop around for the price that suits you).

© 232/892-6402. Admission $5 adults. Summer daily 8am–6:30pm; winter daily 8:30am–4:30pm.

Kadinlar Denizi   Kuşadasi's most popular beach also goes by the name of Ladies Beach. The small stretch attracts a large crowd.

About 5 miles from the port, via taxi.

LOCAL FLAVORS

During the summer, restaurant prices tend to climb. The best place to eat is along the waterfront, where many establishments offer great views. Seafood dishes are particularly good in this area as well as fresh fruits like apricots, cherries, and figs.

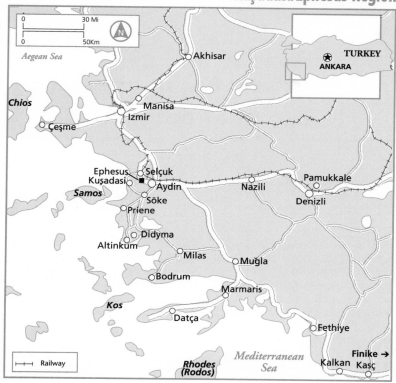

Kuşadasi/Ephesus Region

(Map labels)

Aegean Sea

Chios

Çeşme

Akhisar

TURKEY
ANKARA

Manisa

Izmir

Ephesus   Selçuk

Kuşadasi   Aydin

Samos

Söke

Priene

Nazili

Pamukkale

Denizli

Didyma

Altinkum

Milas

Muğla

Bodrum

Marmaris

Kos

Datça

Fethiye

Mediterranean
Sea

Finike →

Kalkan   Kasç

Rhodes
(Rodos)

0   30 Mi
0   50Km

N

⊢—⊣ Railway

BEST BUYS

There are plenty of places to shop and haggle both in town and immediately outside Ephesus. You will find Turkish carpets, brass, leather goods, copper, jewelry, meerschaum pipes, and onyx. Prices are generally bumped up when cruise ships are in port. It is a common practice for shopkeepers to offer tea or soft drinks to customers, so don't feel obligated to make a purchase.

12

Ports of Call in Northern Europe & the British Isles

A northern European cruise is a different animal than a Mediterranean cruise, offering you the opportunity to explore the stunning fjords of Scandinavia; the windswept shores of the British Isles; historic port cities like Amsterdam, Copenhagen, and Stockholm; and even such lovely capital cities as London, Paris, and Berlin, accessible via shore excursions from the nearest ports. Some itineraries will also visit cities like St. Petersburg, Russia, with its czarist treasures, and Tallinn, in the former Soviet bloc country of Estonia, where you can see firsthand a country attempting to modernize while also preserving tradition.

All the big cities offer history, museums (including some of the best art museums in the world), and great shopping and dining opportunities, and if it's scenery you're after, you'll find it in droves, especially in Norway, the land of the midnight sun, whose fjords are unbelievably gorgeous and where, on some itineraries, you can even go all the way up to the Arctic Sea.

1 Belgium

The medieval city of **Antwerp** is the world's fifth largest port and comes complete with all the liveliness, sophistication, and occasional seediness you would expect to find in any large port. Coming into Antwerp, ships cruise the Scheldt River from the North Sea, a distance of about 60 miles, passing a 12 mile–long stretch of port activity.

Shoppers will know Antwerp is the "Diamond Center of the World"—it's the leading market for cut diamonds and second only to London for raw and industrial diamonds. A visit to a diamond factory is an obligatory tourist attraction. Antwerp also offers a fine arts museum with Flemish masterpieces—the city was the home town of Rubens and other famous artists—a stunning cathedral, and a maze of medieval streets to explore.

The cruise lines use Antwerp as a starting-off point for shore excursions into Brussels, about 30 miles away; Bruges, about 65 miles away; and Ghent, about 31 miles away.

CURRENCY   As of March 2002, Belgium switched entirely to the euro (€) for its currency. One euro is made up of 100 euro cents. The exchange rate at press time was $1 = 1.1€.

LANGUAGE   The official languages are French, Dutch, and (in one small area of eastern Belgium) German. Many Belgians speak English.

Antwerp
BELGIUM

Cathedral of Our Lady **5**
De Keyserlei **10**
Diamondland **12**
The Diamond Quarter **12**
Druon and Brabo Fountain **3**
Flea Market **7**
Groenplaats **6**
The Grote Markt **3**
Leopoldstraat **13**

The Meir **9**
Minderbroedersrui **1**
Royal Museum of Fine Arts **14**
Rubens House **11**
St. Jacobskerk
(St. Jame's Church) **8**
Stadhuis (Town Hall) **4**
Steen Castle **2**

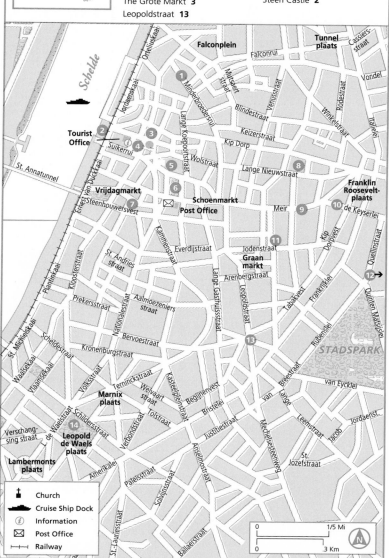

FROMMER'S FAVORITE ANTWERP EXPERIENCES

- **Eating Belgian chocolate.** Favorite handmade brands include Wittamer, Nihoul, Godiva, Leonidas, and Neuhaus.
- **Visiting a diamond factory.** The cutters in the Diamond Quarter are renowned worldwide for their skills.
- **Exploring Antwerp's medieval town center.** This is the most colorful part of the city, and the warren of winding streets fans out from the Grote Markt, a lively 16th-century square right near the ship pier.

COMING ASHORE & GETTING AROUND   It's about a 5-minute walk to the city center from the pier. **Taxis** cannot be hailed on the street but can be found at stands throughout the city. Antwerp also has a user-friendly network of **trams.** A single fare is about 1.40€ ($1.25).

THE BEST SHORE EXCURSIONS

Antwerp City Tour (3½–4 hr., $46–$64): Take a 15-minute bus ride to the pedestrian center of the city for a guided walking tour through the old town section and Grote Markt, including Town Hall, the gabled guild houses, cafes, and more. Visit the Vlaaikensgang alley, Our Lady's Cathedral, and Groenplaats, to see the statue of Rubens. Back in the bus, stop outside the house where Rubens lived. Visit Diamondland, a showroom where you can see diamond cutters do their thing and buy a special souvenir.

Brussels Sightseeing (4½–5½ hr., $50–$57): About an hour's bus ride takes you to Belgium's capital city, visiting Heysel Stadium and the site of the 1958 World's Fair. Walk through the city's historic center to see the St. Hubert Gallery, the world-famous Grand Place with its decorated guild houses, and the statue of the little Manneken Pis, which is exactly what you think it is (who says this translation business is difficult?). Shopping time at Grand Place is included. Also pass by the Royal Palace, the Court House, and the European parliament, as well as the NATO headquarters building. If you want to tour Brussels on your own, you can get a bus transfer through the cruise lines for about $63.

Bruges (8½ hr., $98–$127): After about a 2-hour bus ride from Antwerp, you will walk with a guide along the cobbled streets of this city's beautiful historic section. See the Town Hall, the Chapel of the Holy Blood, and the Market Place with its guild houses and belfry tower. At the boat dock, take a 30-minute trip on the canals for the best view of this medieval city. You'll have some free time to shop at the chocolate and lace shops at Market Place. Tour includes lunch.

Medieval Ghent & Belgian Chocolate (4 hr., $67): Take a guided walk through this historic city, visiting St. Nicholas Church, St. Bavo's Cathedral, and

---

A Girl's Best Friend

There are more than 12,000 expert diamond cutters and polishers at work in Antwerp's Diamond Quarter. Most belong to the Orthodox Jewish community that has traditionally handled the trade. To learn about the process, stop in at **Diamondland,** Appelmansstraat 33A (© **03/234-36-12**), which offers a guided tour and glittering souvenirs that you can buy to take home (at prices considerably lower than you will pay elsewhere). The workrooms are open Monday through Saturday, from 9am to 6pm. Admission is free.

The Legend of Druon & Brabo

The fountain in the center of Antwerp's Grote Markt recalls the legend of Druon and Brabo. According to the story, there was an evil giant named Druon who cut off the head of any Scheldt River boatman who refused to pay him a pricey toll. Brabo, a Roman centurion, eventually slew Druon and tossed his hand into the river. The Flemish word *handwerpen* (throwning of the hand) is where the name Antwerp derives from (or at least that's what they say).

the Belfry Tower, a 14th-century belfry with a 54-bell carillon, located across from St. Bavo's. Learn the fine art of making chocolates through a video presentation and a visit to a Belgian chocolate factory.

THE TOP ATTRACTIONS

Cathedral of Our Lady   This magnificent church was begun in 1352. The architecture includes seven naves and 125 pillars, making it the largest church in Belgium. In addition to a splendid interior architecture, the cathedral houses three Rubens masterpieces: *Raising the Cross, The Descent From the Cross,* and *The Resurrection.* There's also an impressive stained-glass window by Rombout, dating from 1503.

Handschoenmarkt. ✆ **03/213-99-40.** Admission 1.55€ ($1.40). Mon–Fri 10am–5pm; Sat 10am–3pm; Sun 1–4pm.

Royal Museum of Fine Arts   This neoclassical building houses a collection of works by Flemish masters (Rubens included) that is second to none, as well as paintings by more modern artists.

Leopold de Waelplaats 2. ✆ **03/238-78-09.** Admission 3.80€ ($3.45). Tues–Sun 10am–5pm.

Rubens House   Rubens built this mansion in 1610 with the tidy fortune he amassed by selling his paintings (no starving artist, he). There are examples of his works throughout the house, as well as works by his contemporaries, some master painters in their own right.

Wapper 9–11. ✆ **03/232-47-51.** Admission 3€ ($2.75) adults, 1.55€ ($1.40) students. Tues–Sun 10am–4:45pm.

Stadhuis (City Hall)   The town hall, which dominates the Grote Markt square, contains frescoes by Hendriks Leys, an important 19th-century painter; interesting murals; and, in the burgomaster's room, an impressive 16th-century fireplace.

Grote Markt. ✆ **03/221-13-33.** Guided tours .75€ (70¢). Mon–Wed and Fri at 11am, 2pm, and 3pm.

Steen Castle   Antwerp's oldest building is on the banks of the River Scheldt and dates back to the 13th century. The fortress houses the National Maritime Museum, which offers models of clipper ships and an extensive library on nautical subjects.

Steenplein 1. ✆ **03/232-08-50.** Admission 2.65€ ($2.40) adults, 1.30€ ($1.20) students. Tues–Sun 10am–4:45pm.

St. Jacobskerk (St. James's Church)   Rubens is buried in this majestic church, and several of the painter's works are here, as well as some by Van Dyck (also an Antwerp native) and other prominent artists.

Lange Nieuwstraat 73. (📞) **03/232-10-32.** Admission 1.30€ ($1.20) adults, .75€ (70¢) children. Apr–Oct Mon–Sat 9am–noon and 2–5pm; Nov–Mar Mon–Sat 9am–noon.

LOCAL FLAVORS

Belgian cuisine is much like French (some people actually like it better). Mussels and eel are specialties; other favorite dishes include steak and french fries, *tomates aux crevettes* (tomatoes stuffed with tiny shrimp and homemade mayonnaise), and Belgian endive (known here as *witloof*). Wash it all down with Belgian beer. There are some 400 brands, but we particularly like the dark, monk-brewed Trappist ales. Trendy bars and restaurants (and art galleries too) can be found south of the town center, around Vlaamsekaai and Waalsekaai streets.

BEST BUYS

Shop here for high fashion, lace, chocolate, Belgian beer, and diamonds. Expensive shops, boutiques, and department stores can be found on De Keyserlei and the Meir. For haute couture try Leopoldstraat; for lace, the streets surrounding the cathedral; for antiques, Minderbroedersrui; and for diamonds, Applemansstraat and other streets near Centraal Station. Bargain-hunters should head to the **Flea Market,** held on Wednesday and Friday mornings on Vrijfdagmarkt, facing the Plantin-Morteus Museum, for deals on household goods, especially.

2 Denmark

The Royal City of **Copenhagen** was founded in 1167 and is the capital of the oldest kingdom in the world. It's the largest city in Scandinavia, with a population of more than 1.5 million, and offers history and culture, lots of green city parks, and much charm, reflected as much in its friendly, fun-loving people as in its antique architecture.

This is a lively city where people like to have fun and the good times roll, especially at **Tivoli Gardens,** an extraordinary amusement park that's a must-visit attraction. In the summer, Copenhageners come outdoors (the winters are long), and that means lots of **outdoor cafes,** and people sunbathing (sometimes topless) in the city's parks.

The city's most famous resident was Hans Christian Andersen, whose memory still lives on here. All visitors seem to want to see **The Little Mermaid statue.** It's considered an almost obligatory stop.

You can easily cover Old Copenhagen, with its narrow cobbled streets and old houses, on foot. Especially pedestrian-friendly is the Strøget, Europe's longest and oldest walking street.

The name Copenhagen comes from the word *københavn,* meaning "merchants' harbor," and this is a city where you're often on the water, be it the sea or canals. The cruise pier is just a few minutes away from the city center. The entrance to the city through The Sound (the Øresund) that separates Denmark and Sweden is worth a view.

CURRENCY The Danish krone (crown), or kroner in its plural form, is made up of 100 øre. The international monetary designation for Danish kroner is DKK. Banknotes are issued in 50, 100, 500, and 1,000 Kr. The rate of exchange at press time was $1 = 8.25DKK.

LANGUAGE Danish. English is commonly spoken, especially by young people.

Copenhagen

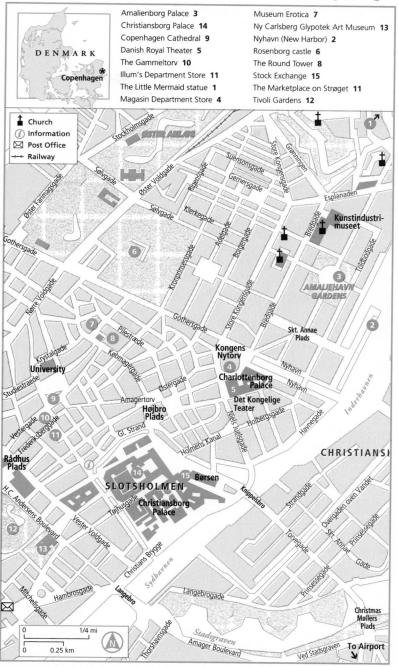

Amalienborg Palace **3**
Christiansborg Palace **14**
Copenhagen Cathedral **9**
Danish Royal Theater **5**
The Gammeltorv **10**
Illum's Department Store **11**
The Little Mermaid statue **1**
Magasin Department Store **4**

Museum Erotica **7**
Ny Carlsberg Glypotek Art Museum **13**
Nyhavn (New Harbor) **2**
Rosenborg castle **6**
The Round Tower **8**
Stock Exchange **15**
The Marketplace on Strøget **11**
Tivoli Gardens **12**

DENMARK

Copenhagen

- ✠ Church
- (i) Information
- ✉ Post Office
- ┼┼┼ Railway

Stockholmsgade

ØSTER ANLÆG

Grønningen

Store Kongensgade

Suensonsgade

Sølvgade

Øster Voldgade

Rigensgade

Gernersgade

Sølvgade

Klerkegade

Esplanaden

Øster Farimagsgade

Adelgade

Kunstindustri-museet

Gothersgade

Kronprinsessegade

Borgergade

Store Kongensgade

Bredgade

Toldbodgade

Nørre Voldgade

Gothersgade

AMALIEHAVN GARDENS

Pilestræde

Skt. Annae Plads

Krystalgade

Københavnsgade

Kongens Nytorv

University

Østergade

Charlottenborg Palace

Nyhavn

Studiestræde

Amagertorv

Det Kongelige Teater

Nyhavn

Vestergade

Højbro Plads

Niels Hemmingsensgade

Holbergsgade

Havnegade

Inderhavnen

Frederiksberggade

Gl. Strand

Holmens Kanal

Rådhus Plads

SLOTSHOLMEN

Børsen

CHRISTIANSH

H.C. Andersens Boulevard

Christiansborg Palace

Knippelsbro

Strandgade

Overgaden oven Vandet

Tøjhusgade

Vester Voldgade

Torvegade

Skt. Annae Gade

Prinsessegade

Mitchellsgade

Christians Brygge

Sydhavnen

Langebro

Langebrogade

Christmas Møllers Plads

Hambrosgade

Stadsgraven

Thorshavnsgade

Amager Boulevard

Ved Stadsgraven

To Airport

0 ___ 1/4 mi
0 ___ 0.25 km

N

FROMMER'S FAVORITE COPENHAGEN EXPERIENCES

- **Spending a day (and a night, too) at Tivoli.** These 150-year-old gardens offer a unique brand of fun.
- **Strolling the Strøget.** Europe's oldest and longest pedestrian street is a shopper's paradise.
- **Sitting at an outdoor cafe.** Have a beer and watch the scenery. The best spot is at Nyhavn (New Harbor), beginning at Kongens Nytorv, where the scenery includes tall ships.
- **Visiting Helsingør (Elsinore) and the Kronborg Castle.** "To be, or not to be . . . ." Shakespeare set his *Hamlet* here.
- **Taking a barge ride along Nyhavn Canal.** The comfortable little craft leave from right in the heart of town and pass much of historic Copenhagen in less than 2 hours.

COMING ASHORE & GETTING AROUND   It's about a 20-minute walk from the pier to the city center. **Taxis** are available at the pier. Make sure the cab is metered. Tips are included in the metered rate, which begins at about 21DKK ($2.65) and adds about 10DKK ($1.25) for each kilometer thereafter. Weekday nights and all day Saturday and Sunday, the fare is 11DKK ($1.35) per kilometer. The city also has an excellent **bus** system. It is easy to get from Copenhagen to sights in North Zealand by train.

THE BEST SHORE EXCURSIONS

City Tour (3 hr., $38–$59): Visit Christiansborg, the seat of Denmark's government since 1918, and Christiansborg Palace. Drive past the Stock Exchange with its stunning spire of entwining dragons' tails, built by King Christian IV; the Danish Royal Theater, home of the Royal Ballet Troupe, built in 1824; and Nyhavn, the sailor's district. Stop briefly outside the Amalienborg Palace to photograph the Queen's guards. Then check out the famous Little Mermaid statue. You'll also pass Tivoli Gardens, the Glyptotek Art Museum, the Round Tower, Copenhagen Cathedral, and the Gammeltorv, a marketplace and the oldest part of the city.

Copenhagen's Royal Palaces (4 hr., $52–$55): This tour includes Rosenborg castle, home of the Danish crown jewels; and Christiansborg Palace, a massive 12th-century fortress surrounded by canals on three sides; followed by a brief city tour.

North Zealand & Helsingør (7 hr., $82–$135): After a brief city tour of Copenhagen, travel by bus through the lush Danish countryside to Frederiksborg Castle in Hillerod. This magnificent Renaissance castle is now the National Museum of History. In the small chapel, you will find the oldest organ in the world, still in use today. Next stop is the Fredensborg Palace, summer residence of the Royal Family. Continue north to the town of Helsingør (Elsinore) where you'll explore the courtyard and ramparts of Kronborg Castle, which dates back to the 16th century. The castle is better known as Hamlet's Castle, immortalized when Shakespeare chose it as the setting for his play (even though Hamlet would have lived long before the castle was built). Return to Copenhagen along the coast, known as the Danish Riviera. Lunch featuring Danish specialties is included.

THE TOP ATTRACTIONS

Christiansborg Palace   The queen officially receives guests in the Royal Reception Chamber at the palace, located on the island of Slotsholmen (you go over a bridge to get there). Housing the Parliament House and the Supreme Court, the baroque structure is impressive, even by European standards, and you can tour the richly decorated rooms, including the Throne Room, Queen's Library, and banqueting hall. Before entering, you'll be asked to put on slippers to protect the floors. Under the palace, you can visit the well-preserved ruins of the 1167 castle of Bishop Absalon, the founder of Copenhagen.

Christiansborg Slotsplads, Prins Jørgens Gård 1. (*) 33/92-64-92. Admission to the Royal Reception Rooms 40DKK ($4.85) adults, 10DKK ($1.25) children; free admission to parliament; castle ruins 20DKK ($2.45) adults, 5DKK (60¢) children. Reception rooms guided tours given May to late Sept daily at 1pm and 3pm; Jan–Apr Tues, Thurs, and Sat at 11am and 3pm.

Kronberg Slot   This is the castle that Shakespeare made famous in *Hamlet* (although Shakespeare never actually visited here). The 16th-century Renaissance castle includes a Great Hall that is one of the largest in Europe. A new exhibit gives the history of plays performed at the castle, explains how the venue came to inspire Shakespeare, and describes the performances of various actors who have taken on the difficult Hamlet role. The castle's church with its original oak furnishings is also worth a peek.

Note: It is very easy to combine a trip to the Louisiana Museum and Helsingør. Buy a day ticket at the central station in Copenhagen, stop at the art museum, and then reboard the train for the 10-minute ride to Helsingør (from where you can catch the train back to Copenhagen).

In Helsingør (Elsinore), about 25 miles north of Copenhagen, or an hour by train. (*) 49-21-30-78. Admission 40DKK ($4.85) adults, 15DKK ($1.85) children, free for children under 6. Mar–Sept daily 10:30am–5pm; Oct–Apr Tues–Sun 11am–4pm.

The Little Mermaid (Den Lille Havfrue)   The one thing every visitor to Copenhagen wants to see. The famous statue is a life-size bronze of the character in Hans Christian Andersen's fairy tale of the same name. It was unveiled in 1913, and is located on rocks right offshore. The statue has been attacked more than once, losing an arm in one misadventure, and beheaded in another. The statue is near the cruise ship docks, no more than a 10-minute walk.

Langelinie.

Louisiana Museum of Modern Art   Take the train to Humlebæk, on the Copenhagen-Helsingør train line. The trains leave every half-hour. From the train stop in Humlebæk it's about a 10- or 15-minute walk (the direction is well marked), or take a shuttle bus.

A favorite of ours, the museum offers a collection that includes Giacometti and Henry Moore, located in an idyllic setting on the Danish Riviera. The museum is located about 20 miles north of Copenhagen and easily accessible by train.

About a 40-min. train ride outside the city. Admission 60DKK ($7.50) adults, 20DKK ($2.45) children 4–16, free for children under 4. Thurs–Tues 10am–5pm; Wed 10am–10pm.

Ny Carlsberg Glypotek   The Glypotek, located near Tivoli Gardens, was founded in the 19th century by Carl Jacobsen, also founder of the Carlsberg Brewing Company. It is one of Scandinavia's most important museums. The collection includes French and Danish art, mostly from the 19th century. Sculptures by Rodin can be found on the ground floor, and works of the Impressionists, including van Gogh's *Landscape from St. Rémy*, on the upper floors. There are also Greek, Roman, Etruscan, and Egyptian collections.

Museum of S-e-x

For a little something different, visit the **Museum Erotica,** the only museum in the world where you can learn about the sex lives of such luminaries as Freud, Nietzsche, and even Duke Ellington. The collection surveys erotica through the ages, and includes Etruscan drawings, Chinese paintings, and Greek vases, all depicting sexual activity. The museum is within walking distance of Tivoli, at Købmagergade 24. ℂ **33/12-03-11.** Admission is 70DKK ($8.50). May to September, daily 10am to 11pm.

Dantes Plads 7. ℂ **33/41-81-41.** Admission 30DKK ($3.65) adults, free for children under 16. Free admission Wed and Sun. Tues–Sun 10am–4pm.

Rosenborg Castle   The red-brick Renaissance castle, built in 1607 by King Christian IV as a summer residence, was converted into a museum in the 19th century. It houses the Danish crown jewels, costumes, and other impressive royal memorabilia.

Øster Voldgade 4A. ℂ **33/15-32-86.** Admission 50DKK ($6) adults, 10DKK ($1.25) children under 15. May–June daily 10am–4pm; July–Sept daily 10am–5pm; Oct daily 11am–3pm; Nov–Dec Tues–Sun 11am–2pm; Jan–Apr Tues–Sun 11am–2pm.

Tivoli Gardens   Since it opened in 1843, this garden and amusement park has been a must-do in Copenhagen. The garden offers thousands of flowers, and the fun includes a merry-go-round of tiny Viking ships, pinball arcades, slot machines, shooting galleries, bumper cars (populated at night mostly by businesspeople out for a night of fun), and a Ferris wheel of hot air balloons. There are more than two dozen restaurants located in an Arabian-style fantasy palace, and a lake with ducks, swans, and boats. Entertainment includes parades, regimental band concerts, and pantomime performances.

Vesterbrogade 3. ℂ **33/15-10-01.** Admission 50DKK ($6) adults, 30DKK ($3) children. Rides are 17DKK ($2) each; all-day wristband, which allows unlimited access to rides, is about 190DKK ($22). Sun–Thurs 11am–midnight; Fri–Sat 11am–2am. Closed mid-Sept to May (except for Christmas market hours).

LOCAL FLAVORS

The favorite dish at lunch is **smørrebrød,** meaning open-faced sandwiches, and it's practically a national institution. Our favorite is piled with tiny Danish shrimp, but other popular favorites are sliced pork loin, roast beef, and liver paste. Wash the sandwiches down with Carlsberg or Tuborg (beer). For a good selection of restaurants including outdoor eateries, head to **Tivoli Gardens** or the **Nyhavn** harbor area.

BEST BUYS

Best shopping buys here include stainless steel items, porcelain, china, glassware, toys, textiles, and jewelry (decorative, silver, and semi-precious stones). The Strøget provides the most shopping opportunities. In addition to numerous boutiques, there are two main department stores, Illum's and Magasin.

3 England

London is the largest city in Europe and one of the best tourist cities in the world. Known for pageantry and tradition, the city offers numerous monuments to its elaborate past, but it's also a hip and lively city, very up on the latest fashion, food, and music trends, and culturally and economically diverse. There is something for everyone here—history, magnificent palaces, medieval churches, literary shrines, culture, nightlife, parks and gardens, great museums (more than 300 of them), the best theater scene in the world, and fabulous shopping (a stop at Harrods is obligatory).

It's difficult to see everything in this sprawling city, but pick a few neighborhoods and walk around. Get yourself by tube (subway, to Americans) to Trafalgar Square and walk in any direction from there. Pall Mall, Buckingham Palace, St. James's Park to the southwest, The Strand, Fleet Street, St Paul's Cathedral are to the northeast. Big Ben, Whitehall, 10 Downing Street, the Houses of Parliament, and Westminster Abbey are due south. And so on. History, greenery, culture at every turn. Sightseeing from a double-decker bus is also a good choice. And the city's subway system (called the Underground) is very user-friendly and easy to negotiate, although it is admittedly in need of a major upgrade.

Take a picture of **Big Ben** (at the Houses of Parliament, Westminster Palace, Old Place Yard, SW1), and while you're in the neighborhood, check out **Westminster Abbey** and **10 Downing Street** (home of the prime minister). **Buckingham Palace,** home to the queen, is now open in the summer, and even when the gates are closed, the spectacle of the Changing of the Guard is worth fighting the crowds for. And for something different, listen to the speeches at the **Speaker's Corner** in Hyde Park (anyone can stand up and speak here), down a pint at a traditional pub, eat some fish-and-chips wrapped in paper, and make sure to experience afternoon tea.

There are restaurants everywhere, and even some good ones—it may be time to stop picking on British cuisine!

CURRENCY   The British unit of currency is the pound sterling (£), which is divided into 100 pence (p). Banknotes are issued in 1, 5, 10, 20, and 50 pound denominations. The rate of exchange at press time was $1 = £.68.

LANGUAGE   English.

FROMMER'S FAVORITE LONDON EXPERIENCES

- **Enjoying a traditional tea.** If you've never experienced scones with clotted cream, now is your chance—they're heavenly!
- **Attending a play at a West End theater.** London is the theater capital of the world, with more plays produced here than anywhere else.
- **Museum-hopping.** You have hundreds to choose from, including the Tate, National Gallery, Victoria & Albert, and British Museum, and many offer free admission.
- **Visiting a pub.** The traditional ones in central London have long mahogany bars, dark-wood paneling, and Victorian accessories, and are a great place to meet the locals.
- **Going shopping at Harrods.** Harrods in Knightsbridge is spread across 15 acres and proudly proclaims its motto *Omnia Omnibus Ubique* (or "everything for everyone"). Someone who didn't believe that claim in 1975 called the store at midnight and ordered a baby elephant to be sent to the home of the governor of California. The gift arrived safely, and Nancy Reagan sent a thank you note on behalf of herself and her husband, Ronald.

COMING ASHORE & GETTING AROUND   Some small ships, like those operated by Seabourn, Silversea, and Radisson, actually sail up the Thames and

Central London

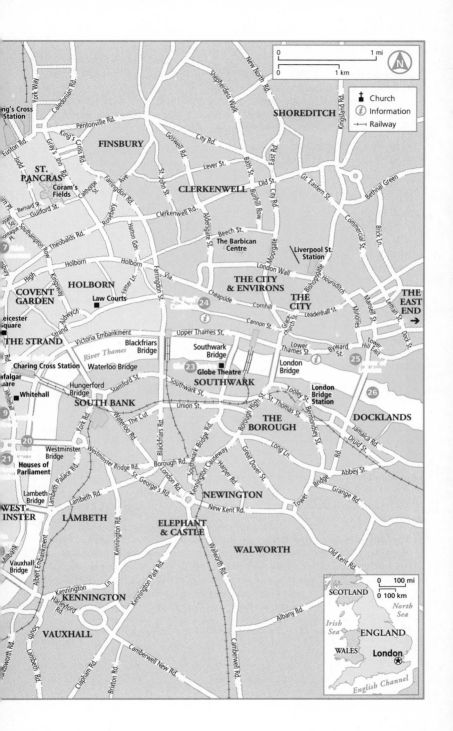

dock adjacent to Tower Bridge (opposite the Tower of London). *That* is a visual treat equal to sailing under San Francisco's Golden Gate Bridge or into Sydney Harbor! Other ships dock at further-out ports including Southampton, Dover, and Harwich, and bus passengers to London.

Getting around London is not difficult at all. There are **taxis** everywhere. There's also a great **Underground** (subway) system, referred to here as the "tube." Or you can ride on one of the famous red **double-decker buses.**

THE BEST SHORE EXCURSIONS

Our recommendation is for you to take the transfer to London offered by the cruise line and then go it on your own.

THE TOP ATTRACTIONS

The British Museum   This museum houses one of the most comprehensive collections of art and artifacts in the world. It would take days to explore, so we suggest you start with the Asian, Chinese porcelain, Indian sculpture, Prehistoric, and Romano-British collections (on your first visit, anyway).

Great Russell St., WC1. (€) **020/7323-8599** (or 020/7636-1555 for recorded message). Free admission. Mon–Sat 10am–5pm; Sun 2:30–6pm.

Buckingham Palace   This massive yet graceful palace is the official residence of the queen. If Her Majesty is at home the Royal Standard flag will be flying outside. When she is not at home, visitors are allowed to tour parts of the palace, including the state apartments, Throne Room, grand staircase, and picture galleries. The Changing of the Guard, the world's most famous military ritual, takes place in the palace's forecourt.

At the end of The Mall (the street running from Trafalgar Sq.). (€) **020/7839-1377.** Palace tours, about £12 ($17) adults to age 60, £9 ($13) seniors, £6 ($9) children under 17. Free admission to Changing of the Guard. Tours only in summer, usually Aug–Sept 9:30am–4:15pm, the months in which the Royal Family is not in residence. For tour hours check with your ship's shore excursions desk or consult the local tourist publications when you arrive in London. Do the same for the Changing of the Guard which, when it takes place, is offered at 11:30am, and is a must-see spectacle.

National Gallery   The neoclassical building itself is impressive, and the collection houses a comprehensive collection of Western paintings representing all the major schools from the 13th to the early 20th century.

On the north side of Trafalgar Square, WC2. (€) **020/7839-3321.** Free admission. Mon–Tues 10am–6pm; Wed 10am–9pm; Thurs–Sat 10am–6pm; Sun noon–6pm.

St. Paul's Cathedral   After the great fire of 1666, the old St. Paul's was razed, and Christopher Wren designed this impressive Renaissance structure with its massive classical dome. Inside are many monuments, including a memorial chapel to American service personnel who lost their lives during World War II. Wren lies in the crypt, as do the Duke of Wellington and Lord Nelson.

St. Paul's Churchyard, EC4. (€) **020/7236-4128.** Cathedral £5 ($7) adults, £2.30 ($3.40) children 6–16. Galleries £2.50 ($6) adults, £1.75 ($2.55) children. Guided tours £2.50 ($6), recorded tours £3.40 ($5). Free for children 5 and under. Mon–Sat 8:30am–4pm; galleries, Mon–Sat 10am–4:15pm. No sightseeing Sun (services only).

Tate Britain   The national gallery of British art from the 1500s until today, Tate Britain boasts a collection of works by Constable, Blake, Gainsborough, Hogarth, Hockney, and many more.

Millbank, London (in the Lambeth area on the north side of the Thames, near Vauxhall Bridge). (€) **020/ 7887-8008.** Free admission. Daily 10am–5:50pm.

Remembering Diana

A sea of flowers and other tributes were left at the beautiful Kensington Gardens (which adjoin Hyde Park at Kensington Palace) after the death of Princess Diana. Even today, mourners leave flowers at the gates of the palace, where Diana resided when she was in London. The palace is open to visitors from 10am to 5pm daily June through September, by guided tour, 10am to 4pm other months. Admission is £9 ($13) adults, £7 ($10) students and seniors, and £6 ($9) children (✆ 020/7937-9561). Princess Diana is buried on a picturesque island on the Oval Lake at Althorp, the Spencer family estate in Northamptonshire, about 75 miles from London. The grounds are open to visitors on a limited basis. Advance reservations are required. Call ✆ 01604/592-020.

Tate Modern   Opened in the Spring of 2000 in what was originally the Bankside Power Station, the magnificent Tate Modern is home to a collection of international art (1900 to the present) including works by Dalí, Picasso, and Warhol and more contemporary modern artists such as Susan Hiller and Dorothy George.

25 Summer St., Bankside (in the Southwark area, on the south side of the Thames, near Tower Bridge). ✆ 020/7887-8000. Free admission. Sun–Thurs 10am–6pm; Fri–Sat 10am–10pm.

Tower of London   Exhibits at this ancient fortress include the Armouries (that's how the Brits spell it) which date back to the time of Henry VIII (check out his suit of armor!); a display of instruments of torture recalling some of the more gruesome moments in the Tower's history; and the Jewel House, where the crown jewels are kept. Go early, as the Tower is extremely popular with Brits and tourists alike, and you're likely to encounter long lines.

Tower Hill (on the north bank of the Thames). ✆ 020/7709-0765. Admission £12.25 ($18) adults, £8.85 ($13) students and seniors, £8 ($11.75) children, or £36 ($53) for a family ticket for 2 adults and 3 children. Mar–Oct; Mon–Sat 9am–5pm, Sun 10am–5pm.

Westminster Abbey   An abbey was founded on this spot in 1065 by the Saxon king, Edward the Confessor. The first English king crowned in the abbey was Harold in 1066. William the Conqueror followed, and the coronation tradition has continued to the present day, broken only twice (Edward V and Edward VIII). Today's structure owes most to Henry VIII's plans, but many architects, including Christopher Wren, contributed. Noted spots include the shrine of Edward the Confessor (who was canonized in the 12th century) and the Poet's Corner, where you'll find monuments to Chaucer, Shakespeare, Ben Jonson, Samuel Johnson, the Brontë sisters, Thackeray, Dickens, Tennyson, Kipling, and even the American Longfellow.

Broad Sanctuary, SW1. ✆ 020/7222-7110. Free admission to cloisters. Abbey, £6.12 ($9) adults, £3.40 ($5) students, £2.30 ($3.40) children 11–18, free for 10 and under. Mon–Fri 9am–3:45pm; Sat 9:15am–1:45pm and 4–4:45pm.

Victoria and Albert Museum   This museum features fine and decorative arts, including medieval items, Islamic carpets, and the largest Renaissance sculpture collection outside of Italy, including a Donatello marble relief.

Cromwell Rd., SW7. ℰ **020/938-8500.** Admission £5 ($7.30) adults, £3 ($4.50) students and seniors, free for children under 18. Mon noon–5:30pm; Tues–Sun 10am–5:45pm.

LOCAL FLAVORS

You can find all the international favorites here—Indian is cheap and favored by locals—along with British specialties like **fish-and-chips,** which you can buy as take-out wrapped in paper—though, thanks to tougher health regulations, it's no longer yesterday's newspaper—and steak-and-kidney pie. Food is also served in pubs, where you can wash down your meal with a pint of ale.

If you want to experience **high tea,** head to a tea house or one of the better hotels. A traditional tea includes a choice of sandwiches and cakes, and scones with clotted cream.

BEST BUYS

You name it, you can buy it here, but there aren't many bargains to be found. You can find deals on some fashion items, British and Scottish woolens, and china. Food items make great gifts, especially English biscuits (cookies).

Major West End shopping streets include **Oxford Street** for affordable items (the flagship brand of the **Marks & Spencer** department store is here); **Regent Street** for more upscale shopping (including the famed **Liberty of London** department store, worth seeing even if you're not in a buying mood); and **Bond Street,** for luxury designer shopping.

In Knightsbridge, you'll find the world-famous **Harrods** department store and lots of other shopping opportunities as well, including designer shops on **Sloane Street.** Harrods is a must-do stop (check out, especially, the food hall on the lower levels).

King's Road, the main street of Chelsea, was hip in the '60s, and even today is frequented by young people. Shops including **The Conran Shop,** which sells household goods, can be found nearby at **Brompton Cross.**

For a fun, typically London experience, head on Saturdays to the **Portobello Market** in Notting Hill. You'll find a little bit of everything for sale there, including antiques.

4 Estonia

Located on the Baltic Sea, only about 37 miles (60km) across the Gulf of Finland from Helsinki, Estonia spent 2 centuries as one of Russia's Baltic Provinces before becoming an independent republic in 1918. Little over 2 decades later, it fell back under Russian control when Soviet troops rolled in and incorporated the country into the Soviet Union. It became independent once again in 1991. Separated from the west for 50 years, the capitol city of **Tallinn** is now visited frequently by tourists sailing aboard hydrofoils and other vessels from Helsinki and Stockholm.

Tallinn, a UNESCO world heritage site, was founded in the 12th century and has been under the rule of Denmark, Sweden, and Germany as well as Russia, and all left their mark on the city's architecture. It is one of the best preserved medieval towns in northern Europe, and makes a beautiful impression from the sea, with its ancient city walls, church spires, and red-tile roofed homes. At the Old Town, you pass beneath the arches of Tallinn's ancient stone walls and enter a world of cobblestones, narrow alleys, and medieval buildings. It's a fun place to explore on foot.

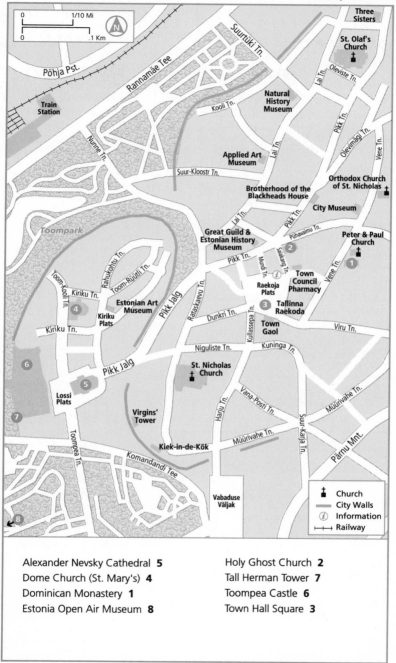

Tallinn, Estonia

0   1/10 Mi

0   .1 Km

Three Sisters

St. Olaf's Church

Suurtüki Tn.

Oleviste Tn.

Lai Tn.

Pikk Tn.

Pöhja Pst.

Rannamäe Tee

Olevimägi Tn.

Vene Tn.

Train Station

Kooli Tn.

Natural History Museum

Nunne Tn.

Lai Tn.

Applied Art Museum

Suur-Kloostr Tn.

Brotherhood of the Blackheads House

Orthodox Church of St. Nicholas

Lai Tn.

Pikk Tn.

City Museum

Toompark

Rahukohtu Tn.

Toom-Rüütli Tn.

Great Guild & Estonian History Museum

Pühavaimu Tn.

Peter & Paul Church

Toom-Kooli Tn.

Kiriku Tn.

Pikk Tn.

Mundi Tn.

Saiakäng Tn.

Vene Tn.

Estonian Art Museum

Pikk Jalg

Ratsakaevu Tn.

Raekoja Plats

Town Council Pharmacy

Kiriku Plats

Tallinna Raekoda

Kiriku Tn.

Dunkri Tn.

Kullassepa Tn.

Town Gaol

Viru Tn.

Pikk Jalg

Niguliste Tn.

Kuninga Tn.

Lossi Plats

St. Nicholas Church

Müürivahe Tn.

Toompea Tn.

Virgins' Tower

Harju Tn.

Vana-Posti Tn.

Suur-Karja Tn.

Pärnu Mnt.

Kiek-in-de-Kök

Müürivahe Tn.

Komandandi Tee

Vabaduse Väljak

- ✝ Church
- — City Walls
- ⓘ Information
- ⊢—⊢ Railway

Alexander Nevsky Cathedral **5**

Dome Church (St. Mary's) **4**

Dominican Monastery **1**

Estonia Open Air Museum **8**

Holy Ghost Church **2**

Tall Herman Tower **7**

Toompea Castle **6**

Town Hall Square **3**

While under German occupation in 1944, the city was bombed and 1,100 people were killed or wounded. Also at that time, about 11% of the old town was destroyed, and was replaced afterward by bleak Soviet architecture. Today, the city is growing rapidly, with modern buildings joining the old.

CURRENCY   The national currency is called the kroon, abbreviated as EEK, and is made up of 100 sents. The kroon is pegged to the German mark, 1DEM = 8EEK. The rate of exchange at press time was $1 = 17.03 kroons.

LANGUAGE   Estonian.

FROMMER'S FAVORITE TALLINN EXPERIENCES

- **Exploring Old Town.** Start at the Tall Herman Tower and explore the medieval world behind the old stone walls. Views to catch include the Baroque Toompea Castle, now the residence of the Estonian Parliament; Town Hall Square and Tallinn's Gothic Town Hall; and the Holy Ghost Church, which dates to the 14th century.

COMING ASHORE & GETTING AROUND   The pier in Tallinn is 0.5 to 1 mile (1–2km) from the city center, depending on where the ship berths, and you can walk or take a **taxi,** which you'll find waiting at the pier. However, some ships dock in Muuga, which is about a 35-minute drive from Tallinn. You can explore Old Town on foot.

THE BEST SHORE EXCURSIONS

Historic Walking Tour (4 hr., $32–$35): Visit Old Town, including Toompea Castle, the Russian Orthodox Church of Alexander Nevsky, the Holy Ghost Church, the Gothic Town Hall, and the partly ruined historic Dominican Monastery, where you'll hear a concert of medieval music before a final walk. Time is allowed for shopping in shops and from local vendors.

THE TOP ATTRACTIONS

Alexander Nevsky Cathedral   This lovely Russian Orthodox church is a dominating feature of Upper Town's city skyline. Inside are numerous golden icons and mosaics.

Lossiplats 10. ✆ **64/43-34-84**. Daily 8am–7pm.

The Dome Church (also known as St. Mary's)   This church is of Gothic design. Inside are more than 100 medieval coats of arms.

Toom-Kooli 6. ✆ **64/44-140**. Tues–Sun 9am–5pm.

Estonian Open Air Museum   This open-air museum, located in a picturesque bayside park, features Estonian village architecture from the 18th and 19th centuries. The country buildings include windmills, churches, and farms, all situated in a pleasantly wooded park. A folkloric show troupe performs traditional dances here.

Vabaõhumuuseumitee 12. ✆ **65/49-100**. Admission 25EEK ($1.50). Buildings daily 10am–6pm (grounds open until 8pm daily).

LOCAL FLAVORS

Estonian food is pretty plain. Local favorites include trout (smoked, pickled, or salted). The city is also home to a surprising array of international cuisine, including even Mexican and Asian food. One of the best local spots in Old Town is **Restaurant Laguun,** Vene 10 (✆ **63/14-727**), noted for its historic building (it's located in well-preserved medieval living quarters), as well as for its mostly seafood cuisine. Crayfish is caught locally and a good choice when in season, and the restaurant also offers both hot and cold tasting plates with several items for those who can't settle on one choice.

BEST BUYS

Shop here for handicrafts, hand-knit woolen sweaters, ceramics, leather goods, amber jewelry, and artwork. Small shops can be found in the center of town.

5 Finland

Although not technically in Scandinavia, **Helsinki** acts very Scandinavian. The city was founded by Swedes in 1550 and became the capital of Finland in 1812, acting as such during Finland's time as an autonomous Grand Duchy of Russia and remaining so when Finland became independent in 1917. Today, Helsinki is a business and industrial center, but is also an intellectual town with a major university and many cultural institutions. Locals still refer to it as "a big village," but the city is actually a pretty sophisticated place, offering tourists a clean environment with great museums, nice harbor views, and lots of shopping opportunities. Surrounded by water on three sides and including in its territory a number of islands, it's notable for its parks and squares and for its neoclassical city buildings, dating from the 19th century and planned out by German-born architect Carl Ludvig Engel.

CURRENCY   As of March 2002, Finland switched entirely to the euro (€) for its currency. One euro is made up of 100 euro cents. The exchange rate at press time was $1 = 1.1€.

LANGUAGE   Finnish. English is also commonly spoken.

FROMMER'S FAVORITE HELSINKI EXPERIENCES

- **Taking a boat to the Suomenlinna Fortress.** Fortresses and parks here are located on five interconnecting islands.
- **Going shopping.** The department store Stockmann offers the latest in Finnish design. Market Square is a fun market scene.
- **Remembering Sibelius.** Visit the composer's home in the country, or view the tribute to him in Sibelius Park, where there's a monument constructed of 527 steel pipes.

COMING ASHORE & GETTING AROUND   Ships dock near Market Square. It's easy to walk around central Helsinki to see such sights as Senate Square, where there's a monument to the Russian czar Alexander II; the 19th-century Lutheran Cathedral; Parliament House; and Alvar Aalto–designed Finlandia Hall.

Helsinki has an efficient transportation network that includes buses, trams, subway (metro), and ferries. **Taxis** are available at the pier. The fare begins at 3.25€ ($2.95). Surcharges are imposed in the evening and on Sunday.

THE BEST SHORE EXCURSIONS

Art & Architecture (4 hr., $72–$84): This tour combines a city tour with a visit to the charming Finnish countryside, including the coastal road, woodlands, and lake country. Visit Hvittrask, once the home of the famous Finnish architects Eliel Saarinen, Armas Lindgren, and Herman Gesellius. Built in 1902 of natural stone and logs, situated on a hill overlooking a lake and surrounded by

Helsinki

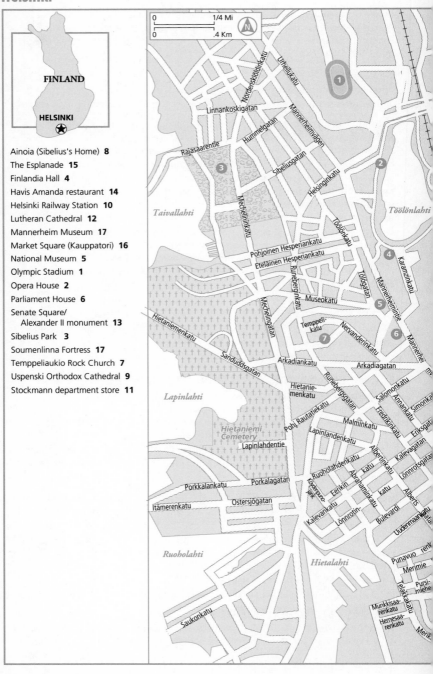

FINLAND

HELSINKI

Ainoia (Sibelius's Home) **8**
The Esplanade **15**
Finlandia Hall **4**
Havis Amanda restaurant **14**
Helsinki Railway Station **10**
Lutheran Cathedral **12**
Mannerheim Museum **17**
Market Square (Kauppatori) **16**
National Museum **5**
Olympic Stadium **1**
Opera House **2**
Parliament House **6**
Senate Square/
  Alexander II monument **13**
Sibelius Park **3**
Soumenlinna Fortress **17**
Temppeliaukio Rock Church **7**
Uspenski Orthodox Cathedral **9**
Stockmann department store **11**

Eläintar-
hanlahti

Kaisan-
iemen-
lahti

Siltavuoren-
salmi

Pohjoissatama

Eteläsatama

Valksaari

Luoto

Ryssasaari

Puolimatkansaari

Kaivopuisto

Cruise Ship Dock
Railway

woods, Hvittrask is an outstanding example of Finnish residential architecture, and is now an exhibition center for Finnish art and handicrafts. Tour Saarinen's magnificent home before continuing on to Tarvaspaa, the former home and studio of Finland's national painter, Akseli Gallen-Kallela. The house was built around 1912 and designed by the artist himself, and the park-like setting is on the sea. Gallen-Kallela's works and the story of his colorful life are on display here, as are exhibits by other famous artists depicting the Finnish way of life.

City Tour (3 hr., $28–$45): Pass the famous Uspenski Orthodox Cathedral with its brilliant gold onion domes en route to the Senate Square, site of several important buildings attributed to the neoclassic architect Carl Ludwig Engel. On Mannerheim Street, view the Parliament House, the National Museum, and Finlandia Hall, designed by the famous architect Alvar Aalto. Continue through lovely residential districts to the Olympic Stadium, site of the 1952 Olympic Games. You'll also pass the opera house, completed in 1993; stop at the Tempeliaukio Rock Church, a unique house of worship blasted into solid rock and topped by a copper dome; then make a photo stop at Sibelius Park, where you can photograph a monument constructed of 527 steel pipes honoring the great Finnish composer Jean Sibelius. The tour includes shopping time.

Porvoo & Highlights (6½ hr., $108–$136): Drive 45 minutes along the picturesque, shipyard-lined coastal road to Porvoo, a popular artistic center that's the second-oldest town in Finland, dating back to 1346. Here you will visit the majestic 1418 medieval cathedral and walk along the cobblestone streets of the Old Quarter, with its ancient, multi-colored wooden houses. Time is allowed for some shopping. The tour also stops at Haikko Manor, one of the country's leading spas and a place of history, elegance, and romance, overlooking the Gulf of Finland and dating back to 1362 and the Royal era. Lunch and a brief city tour of Helsinki are included.

Suomenlinna Island Fortress (3½ hr., $60): Travel by boat for 15 minutes to the island of Suomenlinna, the Gibraltar of the North, reputed to be the largest sea fortress in the world and one of Finland's most remarkable sights (it's included on UNESCO's list of World Heritage Treasures). See "The Top Attractions," below, for details. Time is allowed to explore the museum or visit one of the island cafes. Also includes a stop at the colorful market in Helsinki.

THE TOP ATTRACTIONS

Ainoia The Finns are very proud of composer Jean Sibelius, who lived here from 1904 until his death in 1957. He and his wife, Aino, for whom the house is named, are buried on the property.

Ainolantie, in Järvenpää. ✆ **09/287-322.** Admission 3.50€ ($3.20) adults, 1.10€ ($1) children. June–Aug Tues–Sun 11am–5pm; May and Sept Wed–Sun 11am–5pm. Closed Oct–Apr. Buses and trains run from Helsinki to Järvenpää, about 24 miles away.

Mannerheim Museum Once the home of Baron Carl Gustaf Mannerheim, marshal of Finland and president of the republic from 1944 to 1946, this museum houses his collection of European furniture, Asian art, and personal items including swords and decorations.

Kallionlinnantie 14. ✆ **09/635-443.** Admission, including a guided tour, 6.80€ ($6.20) adults, 5.10€ ($4.65) children 12–16, free for children 11 and under. Fri–Sun 11am–5pm.

Suomenlinna Fortress Known as the Gibraltar of the North, the fortress dates back to 1748, when Finland was part of Sweden, and lies on five interconnected islands that guard maritime approaches to Helsinki. The main attractions include a well-preserved bastioned fort on the island of Kustaanmiekka, and another larger fortress on Susisaari, where you can also find a number of parks, squares, and gardens.

Suomenlinna. 📞 **09/684-1800.** Guided tours offered during the peak summer months (June–Sept), at 12:30 and 2:30pm, are 4.30€ ($3.90) adults, 1.75€ ($1.60) children. At other times, tours are conducted on a private basis. Accessible by ferry from Market Square, with boats running about once an hour. The round-trip ferry ride costs about 4.80€ ($4.35) for adults, 2€ ($1.85) for children.

LOCAL FLAVORS

Typical ingredients of a Finnish **smörgåsbord** included herring, lightly salted fish and roe, smoked and cold fish dishes, reindeer meat, and desserts including fresh berries. Crayfish are in season late July to September (you'll need a bib when you eat them). An upscale city center tavern that's a good pick for lunch or dinner is **Havis Amanda,** Unioninkatu 23 (📞 **09/666-882**), named after the heroic female statue near its entrance. Finnish seafood is the main menu attraction (including the crayfish mentioned above). A two-course fixed-price lunch is 15€ to 22€ ($13.75 to $20); or a four-course dinner 52€ to 56€ ($47 to $51). Reservations are required. If a picnic is your fancy, get the fixings at Market Square (see below).

BEST BUYS

Best buys here include ceramics and glassware, handwoven articles, hand-carved wood, fashions (Fran bought a nifty pair of boots here once), rugs, and jewelry. Stores are open Monday to Friday 9am to 5pm and Saturday 9am to 2pm (sometimes until 4pm in the summer). The best places to shop include the **Esplanadi,** for more upscale Finish design offerings; **Market Square** (Kauppatori), an open-air market open Monday to Saturday, where you can find food, souvenirs, and gift items; and, beginning at the Esplanadi and extending to the famous Helsinki Railway Station, is the area simply known as **Central,** where the Stockmann Department Store and other big name shops can be found.

6 Le Havre, France

This is the leading port on France's west coast, and is popular with cruise lines for the access it offers to the rest of Normandy, the D-Day beaches, and Paris, which is about a 3-hour drive away.

The city itself is a modern (it was almost completely destroyed during World War II) and bustling town, and is not really worth hanging around, Instead, book one of the shore excursions listed below.

Le Havre has been an important port since at least 1066, when the Normans conquered England. In the earlier part of the 20th century, ocean liners— including those operated by the French Line, United States Line, Cunard Line, and Holland America Line—linked Le Havre with New York.

For France's Mediterranean ports, see chapter 11.

CURRENCY   As of mid-February 2002, France switched entirely to the euro (€) for its currency. One euro is made up of 100 euro cents. The exchange rate at press time was $1 = 1.1€.

LANGUAGE   French.

FROMMER'S FAVORITE LE HAVRE EXPERIENCES

- **Taking a shore excursion.** There's not a lot to see or do in Le Havre itself, so plan to take one of the shore excursions that leaves from the port. See below.

COMING ASHORE & GETTING AROUND   The port is about 1 mile from the center of town. If you're not booking a shore excursion, take the **transfer** offered by the cruise line to Paris (priced at $72–$99) and explore on your own. If you want to stay closer by, take a **taxi** to Honfleur, the quaint nearby fishing port (about 13 miles/21km from Le Havre). You can also take a boat from Le Havre to Deauville, the chic beach resort. *Note:* It is not easy to get from Le Havre to Paris by train, so if you want to visit The City of Eternal Light, you are better off taking the transfer mentioned above or a shore excursion.

THE BEST SHORE EXCURSIONS

Note: Similar tours may be offered from Honfleur, France.

Paris Highlights (10½–11 hr., $105–$165): Spend the day in the magnificent city of Paris, a 3-hour drive away. View the Arc de Triomphe, Champs Elysees, Place de la Concorde, Obelisk of Luxor, and Eiffel Tower, and visit the Cathedral de Notre Dame. Also includes lunch, and in some cases a boat ride on the Seine. (Transfers are also offered to Paris for those who want to explore on their own; 10 hr., $85–$99.)

Landing Beaches of Normandy (9–10 hr., $142–$166): On June 6, 1944, the 50th British Division towed a massive prefabricated port across the English Channel as part of the D-Day invasion, and installed it at the small fishing port of Arromanches-les-Baines, enabling supplies to be brought in for the Allied forces. The wreckage of the artificial harbor lies just off Arromanches Beach, which you'll visit on this tour, along with the Museum of the Landing, also in town. Also included are visits to Omaha Beach and the American Cemetery (cemetery of Colleville-Saint Laurent); Point du Hoc, site of a memorial to the three companies of the 2nd Ranger Battalion who climbed the 100-foot cliffs on D-Day to capture the strategic position; and a drive past Sword, Juno, and Gold beaches.

The Sights of Rouen (4½–5 hr., $60–$76): Take a guided walking tour of historic Rouen, including the imposing Gothic cathedral, dating from 1201, made famous by Claude Monet's Impressionist studies of its facade. Also view the Gros Horloge clock tower; Rue du Gros Horloge, where you'll find 15th- and 16th-century timber-framed houses; and Vieux Marchae, the area in which Joan of Arc was sentenced to death and burned at the stake in 1431. You will also see the nearby 15th-century Saint Maclou church. Time is allowed for shopping.

THE TOP ATTRACTIONS

Honfleur   This old Norman fishing village dates from the 11th century. Early in the 17th century, colonists set out from here for Quebec. The town was later popular with artists including Daubigny, Corot, and Monet. Stroll the old harbor, with its fishing boats and slate-roofed narrow houses, stop for a bite to eat at a sidewalk cafe, and browse in the art galleries and craft shops.

About 13 miles from Le Havre.

Deauville   This chic resort is where beach-lovers should head for a day of fun-in-the-sun.

On the coast, just east of Honfleur.

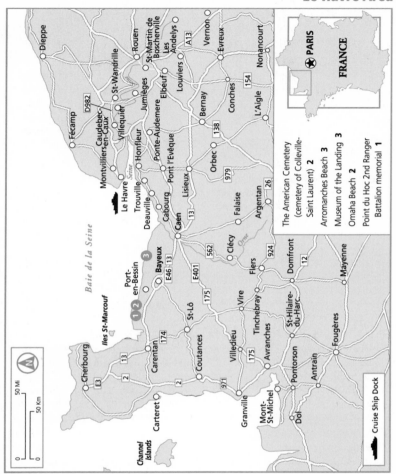

The American Cemetery (cemetery of Colleville-Saint Laurent) **2**

Arromanches Beach **3**

Museum of the Landing **3**

Omaha Beach **3**

Point du Hoc 2nd Ranger Battalion memorial **1**

➤ Cruise Ship Dock

LOCAL FLAVORS

Regional specialties include cider, Calvados brandy, and Camembert cheese. Sauce normande is a rich white sauce. Tripe is a popular dish.

BEST BUYS

Shop here for ceramic ware, antiques (especially in Rouen), Calvados, and Camembert.

7 Germany

Germany is one of Europe's most complicated and diverse countries, wealthy and industrial but at the same time possessed of beautiful natural scenery. Though World War II took its toll on many of the nation's older buildings, much remains and has been restored—including much of Berlin, which has been essentially one big construction site over the past several years as the city geared up to once again become the capital of Germany in 2000, after a 50-year hiatus.

CURRENCY As of January 2002, Germany switched entirely to the euro (€) for its currency. One euro is made up of 100 euro cents. The exchange rate at press time was $1 = 1.1€.

LANGUAGE German. English is also commonly spoken, particularly by young people.

HAMBURG

Hamburg, located on the River Elbe, is known as both "the Venice of the North" for its numerous bridges (2,100 of them) and as "Sin City" for its famous Red Light district, St. Pauli. The Port of Hamburg, stretching nearly 25 miles, is the world's fifth-largest harbor and has been one of the busiest centers of trade on the Continent since 1189. Today, more than 1,500 ships from all over the world call here each month—including cruise ships, which visit mostly to give passengers an opportunity to see Berlin, 177 miles away. If you choose not to make that trek, though, there's still plenty to see in Hamburg itself.

The 1,200-year-old city was nearly destroyed during World War II. Old Hamburg still has buildings that date back to medieval times, but a new city with parks (it's the greenest city in Europe) and impressive buildings grew out of the rubble. Sights worth seeing include the neo-Renaissance Rathaus (town hall), which dominates Hamburg's main square, and the baroque St. Michael's Church.

FROMMER'S FAVORITE HAMBURG EXPERIENCES

- **Taking the shore excursion to Berlin,** or heading to Berlin on your own on the high-speed train. With its fascinating history, Berlin is one city you really shouldn't miss.
- **Walking around Hamburg, comparing old architecture with new.** Because of the damage caused by World War II bombing, many of the buildings are relatively new, an interesting counterpoint to what little was left of the old.

COMING ASHORE & GETTING AROUND Ships dock in Hamburg, about 0.5 mile (1km) from the city center. The most convenient way to get to Berlin is to book the shore excursion offered by the cruise line. There is also high-speed train service that takes about 150 minutes; by bus, it's about 3 hours.

For those who want to stay in Hamburg, the city has a **subway** system (the U-Bahn), which is one of the best in Germany. **Buses** offer a good alternative, and **taxis** are available at the pier, with metered fares that begin at about 2.50€ ($2.30).

THE BEST SHORE EXCURSIONS

Berlin City Tour (13 hr., $219–$298): The Berlin tour includes the fascinating Checkpoint Charlie Museum, which provides an overview of how the Wall divided East and West Berlin for more than 40 years. The display here includes descriptions of how people tried to escape from East Berlin (many didn't make it). Other highlights include a visit to the impressive 19th-century Berlin Cathedral; a photo stop at the famous Brandenburg Gate; and a tour of the lavish Charlottenburg Palace, built as a summer palace in 1695 for the first Prussian king (it was heavily damaged during World War II but rebuilt in the 1950s). The tour includes lunch and shopping time.

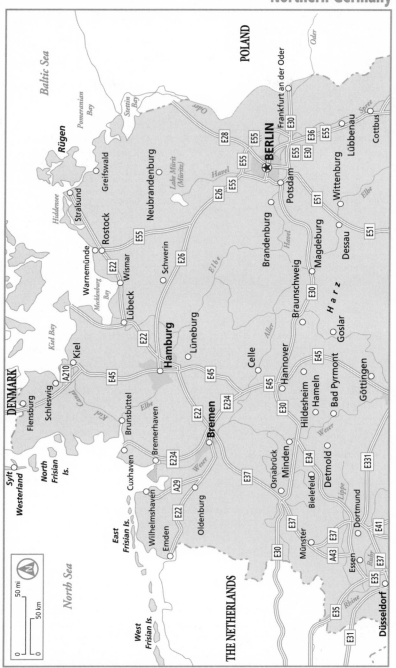

Alster Lake Boat Tour

A boat trip on Alster Lake affords views of villas and sailing boats set against a panorama of towers and church spires, and of the beautiful **Alsterpark,** on the northwest banks of Alster Lake and encompassing 175 manicured acres of shade trees and gardens. **ATG-Alster-Touristik,** Am Anleger Jungfernstieg (📞 **040/3-57-42-40**), has departures about every 30 minutes from 10am to 6pm. The trip lasts about 50 minutes. Cassettes are available with a description of the sights in English, and a brochure in four languages (including English) is available from the captain. Offered April to October (Nov to Mar tours at 10:30am, noon, and 1:30pm), the trip costs about 8.25€ ($7.50) for adults, 4.15€ ($3.75) for children under 16.

Your cruise line may offer special-interest shore excursions in Berlin as well. The Berlin Jewish Heritage Tour (12 hr., $275) combines a Berlin city tour with a drive through the former East Berlin to visit the New Synagogue/Centrum Judaicum, which offers a look at historic and modern Jewish life in the city. The tour also passes the Jewish school and the Jewish cemetery, a reminder of the violent times of the Nazi regime in Berlin. Also visited are several memorials and a train station used by the Nazis for deportation purposes. Berlin's Allied Life (12 hr., $275) offers a city tour with a special emphasis on the 45 years of Allied presence in Berlin. Included is the Glienicker Bridge, where American and Russian spies were exchanged; the former American residential areas of Berlin; and a stop at the new Allied Museum, where displays show the city from the Allied point of view. Lunch is served at Schoneberg Town Hall, where John F. Kennedy made his famous Berlin speech.

Hamburg City Tour (3 hr., $48): This tour takes in the town hall, St. Michael's Church, and other sights including scenic Alster Lake.

THE TOP ATTRACTIONS

Hauptkirche St. Michaelis (St. Michael's Church) Baroque St. Michaelis church is Hamburg's favorite landmark. Take the elevator or climb the 449 steps to the top of the hammered-copper tower for a sweeping view. The crypt, one of the largest in Europe, contains the tombs of famous citizens including Carl Philipp Emanuel Bach. There's also an audiovisual show that tells the history of the city.

Krayenkamp 4C, Michaeliskirchplatz. 📞 **040/3767-8100.** Entrance to the church is free, but to use the stairs or elevator costs about 2.40€ ($2.20). A combined ticket to the tower, show, and crypt costs about 4.70€ ($4.25). Apr–Sept daily 9am–6pm (until 10pm Thurs).

Rathaus Rathausplatz Hamburg's 647-room town hall is a Renaissance-style structure built in the late 19th century (modern compared to many of Germany's town halls). Its clock tower overlooks the city's largest canal.

📞 **040/36-81-24-70.** Guided tours 1.55€ ($1.40). Guided tours are offered in English Mon–Thurs hourly 10:15am–3:15pm; Fri–Sun 10:15am–1:15pm. No tours are offered during official functions.

St. Pauli The Red Light district is the nightlife center of Hamburg. The most famous street in the district is Reeperbahn. In addition to erotica in many forms (including sex shows), the district boasts cafes, bars, discos, and music halls. About a half-mile from the Elbe, and split by the Reeperbahn.

LOCAL FLAVORS

Seafood is a best bet, including lobster from Helgoland; shrimp from Büsum; turbot, plaice, and sole from the North Sea; and fresh oysters. For those interested in trying traditional local cuisine, a favorite is the sailor's dish, *Labskaus,* made with beer, onions, cured meat, potatoes, herring, and pickle. If you're adventurous, try the eel soup, another local favorite.

Among the leading restaurants is **Peter Lembcke,** Holzdamm 49 (© **040/ 24-32-90**), which has been in operation since 1910. You can get both *Labskaus* and eel soup here. The restaurant also serves excellent steaks. Reservations are recommended. Another good bet is the **Old Commercial Room,** Englische Planke 10 (© **040/36-63-19**), in St. Pauli. The restaurant was founded in 1643, and is considered a premier sailors' stopover. The Labskaus here is considered the best in the city, and those ordering it get a numbered certificate proclaiming you are a genuine Labskaus-eater.

BEST BUYS

Clocks, cutlery (especially **J. A. Henckels**), and fashion items are good buys here. Two of the major shopping streets are **Grosse Bleichen** and **Neuer Wall.** Big department stores, including Horton and Karstadt, can be found on **Mönckebergstrasse.** The more upscale (think Bloomingdale's) **Alsterhaus** can be found on **Jungfernsteig,** Hamburg's main artery and shopping district.

WARNEMÜNDE & ROSTOCK

Like Hamburg, the seaside cities **Warnemünde** and **Rostock** in the former East Germany are visited by the cruise lines because they are fairly close to Berlin (about 3 hr. by bus). There is not much to do in Warnemünde, so if you land there we recommend, if you're not making the trek to Berlin, that you head to Rostock, which is about 5 miles away.

Rostock was founded in 1218. During the Cold War period it was East Germany's major seaport. The town still bustles with maritime activity, and there's a good maritime museum. St. Mary's Church has a famous astrological clock, which dates back to the 1400s. You can also climb to the tower for a panoramic city view. Other sights worth seeing include Kröpeliner-Strasse, a pedestrian-only walkway lined with shops and restored historic buildings.

FROMMER'S FAVORITE WARNEMÜNDE EXPERIENCES

- **Taking a shore excursion to Berlin,** or heading to Berlin on your own. It's a city that shouldn't be missed.

COMING ASHORE & GETTING AROUND   In both Warnemünde and Rostock, ships usually dock within walking distance of town. **Taxis** can be found at the taxi stand at the train station; your ship's shore excursions desk can also advise on taxis and may be able to make arrangements for you in advance of arrival. If you are not going to Berlin, and arrive in Warnemünde, take a taxi or train (there's frequent service) to Rostock, about 5 miles away, and then explore Old Town on foot.

THE BEST SHORE EXCURSIONS

Berlin City Tour: See description under Hamburg shore excursions, above.

Rostock City Tour (3½–4½ hr., $50–$68): The tour includes Old Town, St. Mary's Church, and City Hall. Some tours also visit a local brewery that makes German Pilsner, or include a boat ride up the River Warnow.

THE TOP ATTRACTIONS

St-Marien-Kirche (St. Mary's Church) This Rostock church has a famous clock that dates back to the 1400s, with astrological figures on its face. You can also climb the tower for a panoramic city view.

Am Ziegenmarkt. (*) 0381/4-92-33-96. Admission 1.30€ ($1.15). Mon–Sat 10am–5pm; Sun worship at 10am.

Schiffahrtsmuseum (Navigational Museum) This Rostock museum contains exhibits related to the town's nautical history, from the Vikings on up to the early 20th century.

August-Bebel-Strasse 1. (*) 0381/4-92-26-97. Admission 2.50€ ($2.30) adults, 1.30€ ($1.15) children. Tues–Sun 10am–6pm.

LOCAL FLAVORS

The oldest sailor's pub in Rostock is **Zur Kogge,** where the decor includes all kinds of nautical items. Fish is the chef's specialty. Located at Wokrenterstrasse 27, on the harbor ((*) **0381/4-93-44-93**).

BEST BUYS

There are small shops in Warnemünde offering maritime souvenirs. In Rostock (to which you'll have to take a taxi), head to the pedestrian zone for a larger selection of stores, both traditional and modern.

8 Ireland

Ireland is a mass of contradictions. It's ancient, filled with Bronze-age forts, Viking walls, and Norman castles, but it's an adolescent in terms of its nationhood, having only severed its last constitutional ties to Britain in 1948; it's the land of poets and priests, but it has been embroiled in factional struggle over the fate of the North for the better part of a century; it's a land from which the best and brightest fled for decades due to limited opportunities, but it's now the possessor of a massively booming "Celtic Tiger" economy.

And it really is green. Remarkably green, in hues you hardly see elsewhere. In the countryside you can still see whitewashed thatch-roof houses sitting among verdant fields and cozy pubs warmed by turf fires, where the Guinness on tap was delivered fresh that morning from the brewery. In the cities, especially Dublin, you can find a mix of Georgian architecture and new development, and even some places (like Dublin's Temple Bar district) that are considered among the trendiest in Europe.

CURRENCY As of mid-February 2002, Ireland switched entirely to the euro (€) for its currency. One euro is made up of 100 euro cents. The exchange rate at press time was $1 = 1.1€.

LANGUAGE English. Irish Gaelic is spoken as well in some rural areas.

COBH

The port city of Cobh (pronounced "Cove"), formerly known as Queenstown, was once a regular stop for famous liners like the *Queen Mary,* and was the last port of call for the ill-fated *Titanic.*

Today, Cobh is used mostly as a jumping-off point for various excursions around Ireland's southeast, including Cork, the second largest city in the Irish Republic, offering period buildings and churches and plenty of shopping opportunities; County Waterford, known for producing Waterford Crystal; Blarney Castle, home of the famous Blarney Stone; and the scenic environs of Killarney.

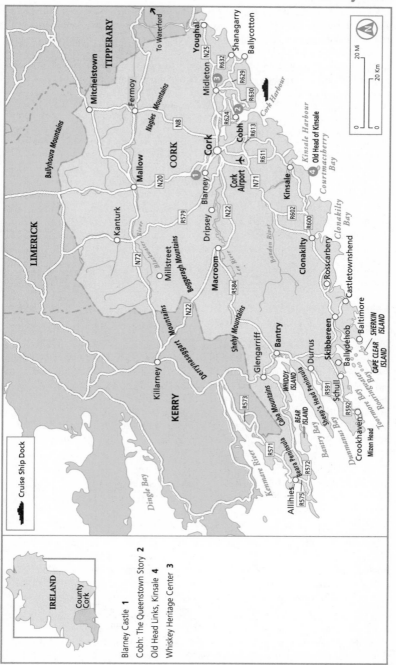

County Cork

TIPPERARY

To Waterford

Mitchelstown

Fermoy

Nagles Mountains

Ballyhoura Mountains

Mallow

N8

CORK

Cork

N20

Kanturk

LIMERICK

N72

Blackwater River

Millstreet

R579

Dripsey

Boggeragh Mountains

N22

Macroom

R584

Lee River

KERRY

N22

Derrynasaggart Mountains

Killarney

Shehy Mountains

Bandon River

R573

Glengarriff

Caha Mountains

Bantry

Dingle Bay

Kenmare River

R571

R575

R572

Allihies

Beara Peninsula

WHIDDY ISLAND

BEAR ISLAND

Sheep's Head Peninsula

Bantry Bay

Durrus

R591

Schull

R592

Dunmanus Bay

Crookhaven

Mizen Head

Toormore Bay

Roaring Bay

Skibbereen

Ballydehob

Baltimore

SHERKIN ISLAND

CAPE CLEAR ISLAND

Youghal

N25

R632

Shanagarry

Ballycotton

Midleton ③

R629

R630

Cork Harbour

R624

Cobh ②

R613

Kinsale Harbour

R611

Old Head of Kinsale

④

Cork Airport

N71

Kinsale

R602

R600

Courtmacsherry Bay

Clonakilty

Clonakilty Bay

Rosscarbery

Castletownshend

Blarney ①

Cruise Ship Dock

IRELAND

County Cork

Blarney Castle **1**

Cobh: The Queenstown Story **2**

Old Head Links, Kinsale **4**

Whiskey Heritage Center **3**

20 Mi

20 Km

363

Outside of Cobh, the picturesque town of Kinsale is famed for its fine cuisine. And the East Cork town of Youghal (pronounced "yawl") is a leading beach resort and fishing port.

In the days before airline travel, Cobh was Ireland's chief port of entry and departure, and hosted about three or four transatlantic liners each week. More than 2½ million emigrants departed Ireland here for new lives in the U.S., Canada, and Australia, most in the post-famine years of the early 20th century. A new visitor center, called **Cobh: The Queenstown Story,** tells the city's history as an emigration port. Photos of some of the early ocean liners that visited here can be found around town.

FROMMER'S FAVORITE COBH EXPERIENCES
- **Visiting picturesque Kinsale.** The town is picture-perfect, with a gorgeous harbor and narrow hilly streets dropping to the sea. Kinsale also has the largest concentration of fine restaurants outside of Dublin, and a nifty fort to explore.
- **Golfing at Old Head Links in Kinsale.** This is a world-class young course, and a legend in the making. The setting couldn't be more gorgeous, with the sea on three sides (greens fees for 18 holes are 320€/$292, and the caddy fee is 39€/$35 per bag).
- **Kissing the Blarney Stone.** Oh come on, you know you want to!
- **Sharing a pint of Guinness** or porter with the locals in any pub.

COMING ASHORE & GETTING AROUND   You can walk into Cobh from the pier, but it's about 15 miles to Cork city. **Taxis** are available at the pier.

THE BEST SHORE EXCURSIONS
Cork & Blarney Castle (4½ hr., $45–$65): Drive by bus to Cork, passing St. Anne's Cathedral, noted for its Shandon bells hung in 1752, and visiting St. Finbarr's Cathedral, located near the site where St. Finbarr founded his famous monastic school around 650. Then drive to Blarney, home of the magical Blarney Stone (which you can kiss if you're willing to walk up 100-plus steps to do so). Time is allowed to enjoy the formal gardens around the castle or to visit the Blarney Woolen Mills, where you can buy something to bring home.

A Visit to Cork, Kinsale, & Charles Fort (4–6½ hr., $58–$76): A quick tour of Cork is followed by a bus trip through the countryside to Kinsale, known as the gourmet capital of Ireland. Enjoy a sample of "good taste" at a quaint waterfront cafe. Also at Kinsale's harbor, enjoy the views at the 17th-century Charles Fort, named for King Charles II. The views are breathtaking.

Whiskey Heritage Center & Youghal (3½–4½ hr., $44–$49): Drive by bus to Midleton, a small market town best known as the home of the Jameson Irish Whiskey Heritage Center. Although the Midleton distillery is one of the most modern in Europe, relics of its 19th-century origins remain, including the old waterwheel and a gleaming 30,000-gallon copper pot, said to be the largest in the world. On the way back, visit Youghal (pronounced "yawl"), a historic seaport where Sir Walter Raleigh was once mayor (and where he purportedly first tried tobacco). A whiskey tasting is included in the distillery tour.

A Day in Killarney (8½ hr., $109–$124): Drive past the highlights in Cork, then continue on to Killarney, in County Kerry. The unrivaled beauty of Killarney's lakes and mountains make this region one of the most celebrated attractions in Ireland. The tour here includes a visit to the restored Victorian

Muckross Manor House and Gardens, located in a magnificent setting in Killarney National Park. Lunch at the Killarney Park Hotel is included, and time is allowed for exploring the beautiful town.

Waterford & Waterford Crystal (9 hr., $109–$115): From Cobh, cross the agricultural plains of east Cork to Youghal, an old fishing port with fine sandy beaches that somewhat resembles a New England seaport (it was so chosen as the setting for the 1950s film of *Moby-Dick*). Cross the Blackwater River into scenic County Waterford. At the Waterford Crystal Works, watch master craftspeople demonstrate glassblowing, cutting, polishing, and engraving. Also visit the gallery, where the largest collection of Waterford crystal in the world is displayed. The tour may also include the 12th-century Waterford Castle or a stop at a typical country pub in the heritage town of Lismore. The excursion includes lunch and shopping opportunities.

THE TOP ATTRACTIONS

We recommend you take one of the shore excursions above, but if you do stay in town, check out the following:

Cobh   This new heritage center, located in a former railway station, commemorates the days when Cobh, then known as Queenstown, was a vital link in transatlantic traffic. The center tells the story of the city, the harbor, and the Irish exodus in a series of displays with an audiovisual presentation. The center also offers exhibits that re-create the age of luxury-liner travel. A genealogical referral service is in the works.

The Queenstown Story. Cobh Railway Station. ⓒ **021/813591.** Admission 5.10€ **($4.65)** adults, 2.60€ ($2.35) children. Daily 10am–6pm (last admission at 5pm).

LOCAL FLAVORS

It's not just meat and potatoes, although Irish beef is quite popular. The star of most menus these days is seafood, including wild Irish salmon, Dublin Bay prawns, Galway oysters, Kinsale and Wexford mussels, Kerry scallops, Dingle Bay lobster, and Donegal crab. Wash it all down with a Guinness or two. If you try an Irish breakfast, you'll be presented with a feast of eggs, bacon and other pork products, traditional brown bread, and more.

BEST BUYS

Shop here for Waterford crystal, Irish linens, crafts, woolens, pottery, and whiskey. In Cork, try **Patrick Street,** the main shopping thoroughfare, or look for antiques on **Paul's Lane.** The legendary department store **Cashs** at 18 Patrick St. dates back to the 1830s.

Fun Fact **Kiss and Tell: The Legend of the Blarney Stone**

Here's the real deal with the Blarney Stone kissing tradition. Back in the 1830s, one Father Prout wrote: "There's a stone there / That whoever kisses / Oh! he never misses / To grow eloquent." From that line, a tourist attraction was instantly created. The stone is wedged underneath the battlements of Blarney Castle. It's kind of hard to reach—you have to lie on your back and slide your head under the wall—but that doesn't stop countless tourists from coming up for a smooch.

DUBLIN

Divided into north and south by the River Liffey, Ireland's capital offers noble public buildings, superb museums and art galleries, magnificent St. Patrick's Cathedral, lovely Trinity College (where the 8th-century Book of Kells is displayed), and tempting shopping. Once barely passable as a European capital, Dublin is on the fast track these days, a hub of computer software development and booming with the roar of Ireland's "Celtic Tiger" economy. With such prominence comes the key components to any major city: money, young people, and flair. So, to the last generation's surprise, Dublin is now a hip, young place with excellent international cuisine, five-star hotels, and posh nightclubs. The Dublin of old—struggling and dilapidated even just 10 years ago—has become one of the hottest up-and-coming places to live in Europe.

The city retains its original charm and history in the middle of all this modernizing, though. In fact, it's the booming economy that has allowed Dublin to clean up its act and drop money into restoring public buildings and historical exhibits. The writer, Dubliner James Joyce, once characterized it as "our dear, dirty Dublin." You wonder what he would think of the place today, in all its modern finery. Not that the city has lost its charm of olden days, mind you. Far from it. You can still find remnants of Georgian splendor, medieval churches and imposing castles, broad boulevards and picturesque parks. Worth exploring on foot are the Temple Bar area (Dublin's self-proclaimed Left Bank) and the Trinity College and St. Stephen's Green/Grafton Street areas.

FROMMER'S FAVORITE DUBLIN EXPERIENCES

- **Pub crawling.** The pub has for centuries been the mainstay of Irish social life, and there are more than 1,000 of them in the city, literally on every street and at every turn. See "Local Flavors" below, for suggestions of a few of the city's best.
- **Exploring.** Don't forget Grafton Street for great shopping, St. Stephen's Green for a bucolic moment, Trinity College for historical splendor, and Temple Bar for one of the hippest scenes in Europe.
- **Playing golf.** A quarter of Ireland's top courses are within an hour's drive of the city, including the **Portmarnock Golf Club** (© **01/846-2968**) and the **Royal Dublin Golf Club** (© **01/833-6346**).
- **Taking a scenic shore excursion** to Glendalough and Powerscourt or Malahide Castle (see below).

COMING ASHORE & GETTING AROUND   Ships dock about 1.5 miles (2.4km) from the city center at the Dublin Port. Smaller ships may come right up the River Liffey into the city center. **Taxis** are available at the pier. Double-decker **buses,** single-deck buses, and minibuses operate throughout the city and suburbs.

THE BEST SHORE EXCURSIONS

In addition to the excursions listed below, several private companies offer escorted walking tours of note in Dublin. One of the best is the **Jameson Literary Pub Crawl** (© **01/670-5602;** tickets $7 per person; operated year-round; times vary), which follows in the footsteps of Joyce, Behan, Beckett, Kavanagh, and other Irish literary greats, visiting a number of pubs with literary connections. Actors provide appropriate performances and commentary at the stops. The tour assembles at the Duke Pub on Duke Street (off Grafton).

Dublin Highlights (4 hr., $48): Accomplished mostly by bus, this tour takes you past the Customs House, one of James Gandon's architectural triumphs (he also designed the Parliament House, which now houses the Bank of Ireland), Trinity College, Merrion Square and Fitzwilliam Square, the National Gallery, St. Stephen's Green and Dawson Street, City Hall and Dublin Castle, St. Patrick's Cathedral, the Guinness Brewery, the homes of the president of Ireland and the American ambassador, Ireland's Courts of Justice (Four Courts), and the General Post Office, headquarters of the 1916 uprising and birthplace of the Irish nation.

Powerscourt Estate and Gardens (4½ hr., $49–$64): Travel to Enniskerry, one of Ireland's prettiest villages, and the gardens of Powerscourt Estate. The 34,000 acres of this majestic estate extend along both shores of the River Dargle. The house at Powerscourt has recently been refurbished to include both an exhibition of the history of the estate and a shop for quality Irish goods, such as crystal and linen. The tour includes shopping time.

Coastal Drive & Malahide Castle (3½ hours, $52–$54): Drive along the coast to Malahide, about 8 miles (13km) north of Dublin, to visit one of Ireland's oldest castles. Malahide Castle was occupied by the aristocratic Anglo-Irish Talbot family from 1185 to 1973. Fully restored, the interior offers one of the finest collections of Irish period furniture, dating from the 17th through the 19th centuries, and one-of-a-kind historic portraits on loan from the National Gallery. After touring the house, you can explore the 250-acre estate, which includes 20 acres of prized gardens with 5,000 varieties of plants and flowers. Also includes a stop at the quaint fishing port of Howth.

THE TOP ATTRACTIONS

Trinity College & the Book of Kells   Trinity is the oldest university in Ireland, and was founded in 1592 by Queen Elizabeth I. It sits in the heart of the city on a beautiful 40-acre site just south of the River Liffey. The college is home to the Book of Kells, an 8th-century version of the four Gospels with elaborate scripting and illumination. One page per day is turned for public viewing.

College Green. ✆ **01/608-1688.** Admission to see the book about 5.95€ ($5.40) adults, 5.10€ ($4.65) seniors and students, free for children under 12. Mon–Sat 9:30am–5pm; Sun (June–Sept) 9:30am–4:30pm.

National Gallery   This gallery, which opened its doors in 1864, offers one of Europe's finest collections including paintings, drawings, miniatures, prints, sculpture, and objets d'art. Every major school of European painting is represented. A new extension is scheduled to open this year.

Merrion Sq. W. ✆ **01/661-5133.** Free admission. Mon–Sat 10am–5:30pm; Sun 2–5pm.

National Museum   Established in 1890, the National Museum complex comprises the **Natural History Museum,** the **Archaeological Museum,** and **Collins Barracks,** all within a 4-block area. The Archaeological Museum exhibits a collection of Irish heritage items from 2000 B.C. to the present (it toured the U.S. in the 1970s), and includes the Ardagh Chalice, Tara Brooch, and Cross of Cong. Restored Collins Barracks, said to be the oldest military barracks in Europe, has a display of weaponry, Irish silverware, and antique furniture.

Kildare St. (Natural History), Merrion St. (Archaeological), and Benburb St. (Collins Barracks). ✆ **01/677-7444.** Free admission. Tues–Sat 10am–5pm; Sun 2–5pm.

Dublin

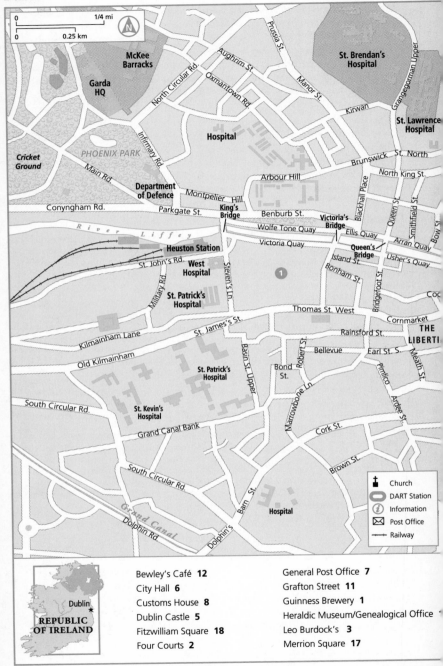

Church
DART Station
Information
Post Office
Railway

REPUBLIC
OF IRELAND

Dublin

Bewley's Café **12**
City Hall **6**
Customs House **8**
Dublin Castle **5**
Fitzwilliam Square **18**
Four Courts **2**

General Post Office **7**
Grafton Street **11**
Guinness Brewery **1**
Heraldic Museum/Genealogical Office **1**
Leo Burdock's **3**
Merrion Square **17**

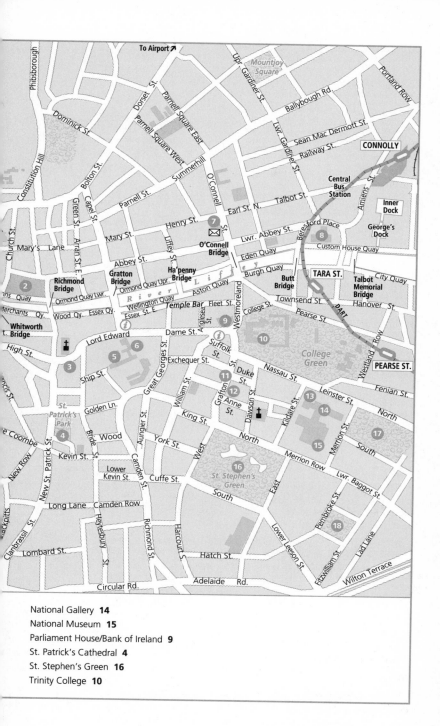

To Airport ↗

Mountjoy Square

Phibsborough

Dominick St.

Constitution Hill

Church St.

Dorset St.

Parnell Square East

Parnell Square West

Bolton St.

Green St.

Capel St.

Arran St.

Parnell St.

Summerhill

Upr. Gardiner St.

Ballybough Rd.

Sean Mac Dermott St.

Lwr. Gardiner St.

Railway St.

Portland Row

Amiens St.

CONNOLLY

Central Bus Station

Inner Dock

George's Dock

Henry St.

Mary St.

Mary's Lane

Earl St. N.

Talbot St.

Beresford Place

Custom House Quay

Liffey St.

O'Connell St.

7

☒

O'Connell Bridge

Abbey St.

Lwr. Abbey St.

Eden Quay

8

City Quay

2

Quay

Richmond Bridge

Gratton Bridge

Ormond Quay Lwr.

Ha'penny Bridge

Ormond Quay Upr.

Burgh Quay

TARA ST.

Talbot Memorial Bridge

Hanover St.

Church St.

Ormond Quay Lwr.

River Liffey

Butt Bridge

erchants Qy.

Wood Qy. Essex Qy.

Wellington Quay

Essex St. E.

Temple Bar

Fleet St.

Aston Quay

Townsend St.

Whitworth Bridge

Anglesea St.

College St.

Westmoreland

Pearse St.

DART

t. Bridge

High St.

Lord Edward

Dame St.

9 ℹ

Suffolk St.

10

College Green

PEARSE ST.

Westland Row

✝

ℹ

5 **6**

3

Ship St.

Exchequer St.

Great Georges St.

Duke St.

Nassau St.

Leinster St.

Fenian St.

St. Patrick's Park

Golden Ln.

William St.

King St.

Grafton St.

Anne St.

Dawson St.

✝

Kildare St.

Merrion St.

13

14

North

South

17

ncis St.

4

Bride

Wood

York St.

West

North

15

Merrion Row

e Coombe

New Row

New St. Patrick St.

Kevin St.

Aungier St.

Camden St.

Lower Kevin St.

Cuffe St.

16

St. Stephen's Green

South

East

Lwr. Baggot St.

Lower Leeson St.

Clanbrassil St.

Long Lane

Camden Row

Richmond St.

Harcourt S.

Heytesbury St.

Pembroke St.

Fitzwilliam St.

Lad Lane

18

ckpitts

Lombard St.

Hatch St.

Adelaide Rd.

Wilton Terrace

Circular Rd.

National Gallery **14**

National Museum **15**

Parliament House/Bank of Ireland **9**

St. Patrick's Cathedral **4**

St. Stephen's Green **16**

Trinity College **10**

Heraldic Museum/Genealogical Office   The museum boasts a unique collection of heraldry, including shields, banners, coins, paintings, porcelain, and stamps depicting coats of arms. This is also the place to start tracing your Irish roots (for a fee of about $31).

2 Kildare St. ✆ 01/603-0200. Free admission. Mon–Fri 10am–12:30pm and 2–4:30pm.

St. Patrick's Cathedral   Founded in 1190 (though a church has actually stood at the site since 450), St. Patrick's is the largest Protestant cathedral in Dublin and the national cathedral of the Church of Ireland. The most famous of St. Patrick's many renowned deans was Jonathan Swift, author of *Gulliver's Travels.*

Patrick's Close, Patrick St. ✆ 01/475-4817. Admission about 3.40€ ($3.10) adults, 3€ ($2.70) students and seniors, 8.50€ ($7.75) for families. May and Sept–Oct Mon–Fri 9am–6pm, Sat 9am–5pm, Sun 10am–11am and 12:45pm–3pm; June–Aug Mon–Fri 9am–6pm, Sat 9am–4pm, Sun 9:30am–3pm and 4:15–5:15pm.

The Guinness Storehouse   Learn everything you never knew you wanted to know about the "black stuff," and at the end of your tour you can try a complimentary pint. The $35 million museum opened in 2000 (it replaced an older visitor center) and is located in the Guinness factory complex. Several floors of exhibit space are devoted to the history of the 250-year-old beer and much detail given about the brewing process, but our favorite display is about Guinness advertising, which includes commercials with the old tag line "Guinness is good for you." There's also a rooftop bar and a big gift shop (where you can buy really cool Guinness poster reproductions for about $6).

St. Jame's Gate. ✆ 01/408-4800. Admission 11.55€ ($10.50). Apr–Sept daily 9:30am–7pm; Oct–Mar daily 9:30am–5:30pm.

LOCAL FLAVORS

Dining in Dublin offers great variety that includes Old World hotels, casual bistros, wine bars, and ethnic cuisine. Non-Irish offerings tend towards French and Italian, and you can find a good concentration of trendy spots in the Temple Bar area. One place you can enjoy a quintessential Dublin experience is **Bewley's Café,** 78/79 Grafton St. (✆ **01/677-6761**), a three-story landmark opened in 1840, done up in traditional, if a bit decayed, decor, and specializing in coffees and teas, home-baked scones, pastries, and sticky buns. If you've got a craving for fish-and-chips, **Leo Burdock's,** 2 Werburgh St. (✆ **01/454-0306**), offers the best take-out.

Pubs are everywhere, and we urge you to just pick one close by and walk in. But for those shy about doing that, a few suggestions: For conversation and atmosphere try **The Stag's Head,** 1 Dame Ct., off Dame St. (✆ **01/679-3701**), which is done up with stags' heads on the walls; **The Long Hall,** 51 S. Great George's St. (✆ **01/475-1590**), pretty and oft-photographed for its Victorian decor; and **Brazens Head,** 20 Lower Bridge St. (✆ **01/679-5186**), which claims to be the city's oldest pub. For traditional music, head to **Mother Red Caps Tavern,** Back Lane (✆ **01/454-4655**), where people just show up with their instruments or voices at midday on Sundays; or **Kitty O'Shea's,** 23-25 Upper Grand Canal St. (✆ **01/660-9965**), where Irish music is on tap most nights.

BEST BUYS

Grafton Street, which is open to pedestrians only, offers a parade of boutiques, department stores, and specialty shops, as well as a festive atmosphere complete with street performers and sidewalk artists. In nearby **Temple Bar** are interesting boutiques as well as art and music shops. (See Cobh for the best Irish products.)

9 The Netherlands (Holland)

Is it Holland or the Netherlands? Actually, it's both, and before that it was Batavia. But whatever you call it, this small country offers a lot more than wooden shoes, tulips, and windmills. There's incredible art for one—this is the home country of van Gogh, not to mention the Dutch masters. It's also the home of dikes and canals, of historic towns, of beautiful and raucous Amsterdam, of the Hague and the International Court of Justice, and of a cultured populace that appreciates history and the outdoors and also knows how to have a good time.

CURRENCY   As of February 2002, the Netherlands switched entirely to the euro (€) for its currency. One euro is made up of 100 euro cents. The exchange rate at press time was $1 = 1.1€.

LANGUAGE   Dutch. English is also commonly spoken.

AMSTERDAM

Amsterdam is spread out over 70 islands and boasts 60 miles of canals, 1,000 bridges, and the largest Old Town in Europe. It's a city with a history—boats have sailed from here since the 13th century, and its 17th-century town houses and Floating Flower Market are full of old-world charm—but Amsterdam is also a young and exciting place offering a little bit for every taste, from the erotic sights of the Red Light District, to a plethora of shopping and nightlife options, to world-renowned art museums—it's been a big art city since the time of Rembrandt. Anne Frank and her family hid in a house here for 2 years, and visitors can tour the attic where she wrote her famous diary before being discovered by the Nazis. It's a very moving experience.

On the outskirts of the city are quaint villages worth exploring, including Delft, a historic town where the famous blue and white pottery is made.

COMING ASHORE & GETTING AROUND   Your ship will dock at one of the three terminals: Amsterdam Passenger Terminal (APT), about a 15-minute walk to the city center; Felison Terminal, a 30-minute drive; or Scandia Terminal, a 15-minute drive. In any case, Centraal Station, near Dam Square, is a good start-off point.

Amsterdam is an easy city to explore, either by foot or boat. **Biking** is another option. It's the mode popular with the Dutch, but you need to exercise caution if you go this route: Riding on cobblestones can be particularly tricky. You can rent bikes for about 5.50€ ($5) a day (with a deposit required) from **Mac Bike,** Mr. Visserplein 2 (℗ **020/620-09-85**), or **Mac Bike Too,** Marnixstraat 220 (℗ **020/626-6964**).

Or if you really want something to talk about, rent a **water bike** to pedal along the canals. A two-seater goes for about 6.5€ ($6) per person, per hour; a four-seater for about 5.5€ ($5) per person, per hour. Moorings are at Centraal Station, Leidseplein, Westerkerk (near the Anne Frank house), Stadhouderskade (between the Rijksmuseum and Heineken Brewery Museum), and Toronto Bridge on the Keizersgracht, near Leidsestraat.

Taxis are available at the pier. Officially, you are not supposed to hail a cab on the street (although they may stop for you anyway) but should instead call **Taxi Centrale** (℗ **020/677-7777**). The city also has an extensive **bus** and **tram** network, as well as two **subway** lines.

FROMMER'S FAVORITE AMSTERDAM EXPERIENCES

- **Strolling the red light district.** The architecture is neat and the ladies in the windows rather fascinating (from the outside, anyway).

Central Amsterdam

HOLLAND

Amsterdam

THE JORDAAN

Lindengracht

Westerstraat

Angeliersstraat

Eglantiersstraat

Egelantiersgracht

Bloemgracht

Rozengracht

Rozenstraat

Laurierstraat

Lauriergracht

Elandsstraat

Elandsgracht

Lindengracht

Marnixstraat

Nassaukade

Singelgracht

Marnixstraat

Reestraat

Hartenstraat

Berenstraat

Wolvenstraat

Runstraat

Huidenstraat

Prinsengracht

Keizersgracht

Raadhuisstr.

Herengracht

Singel

Dam
Square

Spuistraat

N.Z. Voor burgwal

Kalver-

Spui

Rol

Looiersgracht

Houseboat
Museum

Muntplei

Nassaukade

Singel gracht

Leidsegracht

Leidsestraat

Keizersgracht

Kerkstraat

Prinsengracht

Reguliers dwarsstraat

Herengracht

Leidseplein

Overtoom

Vondelstraat

Vondelpark

Stad houderskade

Nieuwe Spiegelstraat

Vijzelstraat

Constantijn Huygensstraat

Vossiusstraat

P. C. Hooftstraat

Jan Luykenstraat

Museumplein

Museumstraat

Hobbemakade

Hobbemastraat

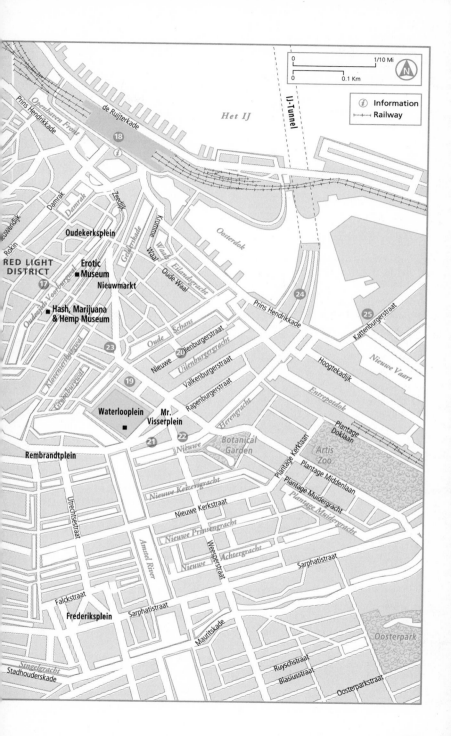

Het IJ

de Ruijterkade

Prins Hendrikkade

Openhaven Front

18

Oosterdok

IJ-Tunnel

ⓘ Information
⊢—⊣ Railway

0   1/10 Mi
0   0.1 Km

Oudekerksplein

Zeedijk

Damrak

Damrak

Nieuwendijk

Rokin

Kromme Waal

Geldersekade

Wolle

Oude Waal

Eilandsgracht

Oosterdok

Prins Hendrikkade

24

25

Kattenburgerstraat

RED LIGHT
DISTRICT

Erotic
■ Museum

Nieuwmarkt

17

Oudezijds Voorburgwal

■ Hash, Marijuana
& Hemp Museum

Oude Schans

Nieuwe Uilenburgerstraat

20

Uilenburgergracht

Valkenburgerstraat

Hoogtekadijk

Nieuwe Vaart

Kloveniersburgwal

Groenburgwal

23

19

Rapenburgerstraat

Entrepotdok

Waterlooplein
■

Mr.
Visserplein

Berengracht

Plantage
Doklaan

Rembrandtplein

21

22

Nieuwe

Botanical
Garden

Artis
Zoo

Nieuwe Keizersgracht

Plantage Kerklaan

Plantage Middenlaan

Utrechtsestraat

Nieuwe Kerkstraat

Plantage Muidergracht

Plantage Muidergracht

Amstel River

Nieuwe Prinsengracht

Nieuwe Achtergracht

Weesperstraat

Sarphatistraat

Falckstraat

Sarphatistraat

Frederiksplein

Mauritskade

Oosterpark

Singelgracht

Stadhouderskade

Ruyschstraat

Blasiusstraat

Oosterparkstraat

- **Visiting Anne Frank's house.** You'll find it a moving experience.
- **Taking a canal boat trip.** The boat's-eye view is the best for seeing the city's famed gabled houses and numerous bridges (you can catch a boat at key locations around town, including along Damrak or Prins Hendrikkade near Centraal Station, on the Rokin near Muntplein, and near Liedseplein; the cost is 5.50€–8.25€/$5–$7.50 for adults, 4.50€–5.50€/$4–$5 for children, for a 1-hr. ride).
- **Museum-hopping.** This is one of the best cities in the world for this activity. Start with the van Gogh Museum.
- **Photographing the floating flower market.** The market on the Singel at Muntplein is a photographer's delight, with rows of barges selling fresh-cut flowers, plants, and tulip bulbs.

THE BEST SHORE EXCURSIONS

Amsterdam City Tour (3½–4 hr., $36–$42): This highlights tour passes Dam Square, the Royal Palace, the 550-year-old Nieuwe Kerk (New Church), the Portuguese Synagogue, and Rembrandt's House. Then you board a glass-topped motor launch for a canal ride past historic sights including the narrowest house in Amsterdam, the skinny bridge over Amstel River, and the Anne Frank House. Some tours also include a visit to the Rijksmuseum.

Traditional Fishing Villages (4 hr., $34–$40): This bus and walking tour visits the quaint towns of Marken, Monnikendam, and Volendam. Highlights include views of the lush countryside, cobblestone streets with colorful homes, boat-filled harbors, and a visit to a cheese factory.

Grand Holland (7–8 hr., $112): This tour visits Holland's Royal City, the Hague. Drive past the Royal Palace, Houses of Parliament, and Peace Palace. Also visit Delft, one of the oldest cities in Holland and home of the Delft pottery factory, famous for its blue and white pottery. Lunch is included. Some tours include a stop at Aalsmeer to view the flower auction, or a stop at Madurodam, a reproduction in miniature of a typical Dutch city.

THE TOP ATTRACTIONS

Anne Frankhuis (Anne Frank House)   No one should miss this moving experience. The young Jewish girl Anne Frank wrote her diary here while hiding from the Nazis from 1942 to 1944. There's a small exhibit on the Holocaust, and you can view the famous attic where Anne and her family lived. The house is so small groups are not allowed, so you can only visit on your own (and not on shore excursions).

Prinsengracht 263 (just below Westermarkt). © 020/556-7100. Admission about 4.60€ ($4.20) adults, 2.30€ ($2.10) children 10–17. Apr–Aug daily 9am–9pm; Sept–Mar daily 9am–5pm.

Stedelijk Museum of Modern Art   This museum offers a collection of contemporary art that includes such modern Dutch painters as Karel Appel, Willem de Kooning, and Piet Mondrian, as well as works by Chagall, Cézanne, Picasso, Renoir, Monet, and Manet, and Americans Calder, Oldenburg, Rosenquist, and Warhol.

Paulus Potterstraat 13 (at Museumplein). © 020/573-2911. Admission about 4.15€ ($3.75) adults, 2.10€ ($1.90) children 7–16, free for children under 7. Daily 11am–5pm.

Van Gogh Museum   This museum houses the largest collection of Vincent van Gogh's work in the world: The permanent collection includes more than 200 paintings and 600 drawings. Notable parts of the collection include *The*

The Ladies of the Night

The Walletjes (Red Light District), the warren of streets around Oudezijds Achterburgwal and Oudezijds Voorburgwal by the Oude Kerk, is one of the city's major tourist attractions. The district's ladies represent a cross-section of nationalities, displayed in windows and doorways in various stages of undress.

There's plenty to see during the day, but if you choose to tour this area at night, you should exercise extreme caution. Watch out for pickpockets and don't let the more aggressive ladies pull you into their rooms (unless you want to be so pulled). Also keep in mind that taking pictures here is a no-no—if you violate the rule your camera may be grabbed from you and broken.

Potato Eaters, Self Portrait as a Painter, Still Life with Sun Flowers, and *Cornfield with Rows.* The museum's collection also includes works by other notable Dutch artists and paintings by van Gogh's contemporaries, including Gauguin, Monet, and Toulouse-Lautrec.

Paulus Potterstraat 7–11 (at Museumplein). ✆ **020/570-5200.** Admission about 7.15€ ($6.50) adults, 2.30€ ($2.10) children ages 13–17, free for children under 13. Daily 10am–6pm.

Rijksmuseum   This major art museum houses the largest art collection in the Netherlands, with paintings from the 15th century to the 19th century, including 22 Rembrandts (*Night Watch* is the most famous), Vermeer, Frans Hals, Alvert Cuyp, and Jan Steen. The print room houses one million prints and drawings.

Stadhouderskade 42 (at Museumplein). ✆ **020/673-2121.** Admission about 6.90€ ($6.25) adults, 3.50€ ($3.15) children 6–18, free for children under 6. Daily 10am–5pm.

Koninklijk Paleis (Royal Palace)   Built in the 17th century as the City Hall, the building was turned into the palace in 1808 by Napoleon when he came to Amsterdam. It's decorated in Empire Style, and is still used for receptions and official ceremonies by her majesty the queen.

Dam Square. ✆ **020/624-8698.** Admission about 7€ ($3) adults, 2.30€ ($2.10) seniors and children 13–18, 1.20€ ($1.05) children 12 and under. June–July daily 10am–5:30pm; Aug–Oct daily 12:30–5pm; otherwise, generally Tues–Thurs 12:30–5pm. Closed mid-Dec to mid-Feb.

Joods Historisch Museum (Jewish Historical Museum)   This museum, located in the city's old Jewish Quarter, in a renovated Ashkenazi synagogue, offers a view of the social and cultural history of the Jewish community in the Netherlands, including both good times and bad.

Jonas daniël Meijerplein 204 (near Waterlooplein). ✆ **020/626-9945.** Admission about 4.60€ ($4.20) adults, 2.10€ ($1.90) children 13–18; 1.20€ ($1.05) children 6–12, free for children under 6. Daily 11am–5pm.

LOCAL FLAVORS

The restaurant choices here go across the international spectrum. A favorite is the **Indonesian rijstafel** (a sampling of various dishes). Distinctive Dutch dishes include white asparagus (in season in May), raw herring (in May or early June), and Zeeland oysters and mussels (in Sept). You can enjoy your meal with the local brew, Heineken. You'll see people on the street (in shopping areas) eating french fries and mayonnaise. It's a local treat that sounds gross but is really very good—just make sure you spend some time in your ship's gym afterward to work off the calories.

BEST BUYS

Best buys here include Delft pottery, wooden shoes, cheese, antiques, and diamonds. Main shopping streets (many pedestrian-only) are **Kalverstraat** near Dam Square (for inexpensive items); **Rokin,** parallel to the above (for quality fashions, art, and antiques); **Leidsestraat** (for upscale clothing, china, and gifts); **P. C. Hooftstraat** and **Van Baerlestraat,** near Museumplein (for hip fashion and gifts); and **Nieuwe Spiegelstraat,** near the Rijksmuseum (for antiques). **De Bijenkorf,** at Dam Square, is a top department store. If you're flying out of Holland, keep in mind the Amsterdam airport has some of the best duty-free shopping you'll find anywhere.

If you're in the market for diamonds, the following are members of the Amsterdam Diamond Foundation, and offer both showrooms and diamond-cutting and polishing demonstrations: **Amsterdam Diamond Center,** Rokin 1 (© 020/ 624-5787); **Coster Diamonds,** Paulus Potterstraat 204 (© 020/676-2222); **Gassan Diamonds,** Nieuwe Uilenburgerstraat 173–175 (© 020/622-5333); **Stoeltie Diamonds,** Wagenstraat 13–17 (© 020/623-7601); and **Van Moppes Diamonds,** Albert Cuypstraat 2–6 (© 020/676-1242).

ROTTERDAM

Rotterdam is a bustling metropolis and a major port city, sometimes referred to as "the gateway to Europe." It's located only a half-hour from the Hague and 1 hour from Amsterdam.

The city is one of contrasts, with only one tiny area, historic Delfshaven, retaining its historic structures (as well as museums and art galleries). Elsewhere in the city, big, well-designed modern buildings have taken the place of those destroyed during World War II.

Of special interest to Americans in Delfshaven is the old church in which the Pilgrims said their last prayers before boarding the *Speedwell* to the New World in 1620. When the ship did not prove seaworthy, they switched to the *Mayflower* at Southampton.

The city's museums include Boymans–Van Beuningen, an outstanding museum with a collection of ancient and modern art and design work. The old Holland America Line passenger terminal on Wilhelmina Quay has been completely renovated and serves as the city's cruise terminal. Located in the heart of the city near the new Erasmus Bridge and only a 10-minute walk from the city center, it's a tourist destination all its own.

Rotterdam is only a half hour away from major Holland tourist attractions including the historic cheese town of Gouda, which you can visit on a shore excursion.

FROMMER'S FAVORITE ROTTERDAM EXPERIENCES

- **Taking a harbor boat ride.** Spido Havenrondvaarten, on Willemsplein (© 010/413-5400), offers 1-hour cruises with fascinating narration for about 9.25€ ($8.40) per person.
- **Stopping by the Pilgrim Fathers Church.** This church (on Voorhaven) is where the pilgrims said goodbye to the Old World before heading off to the New.
- **Going museum hopping.** The Maritime Museum and Museum Boymans–Van Beuningen art museum are both worth a look.

Rotterdam

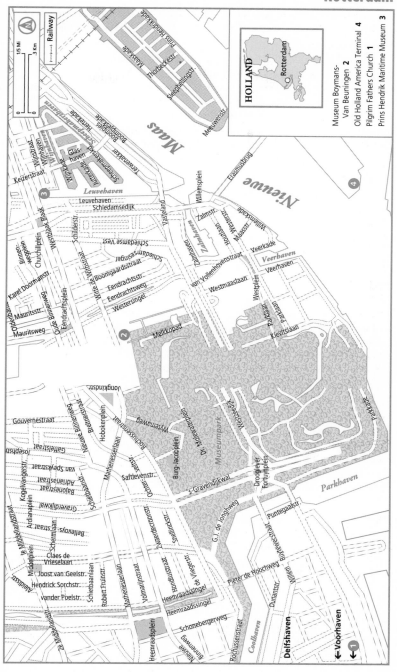

HOLLAND

Rotterdam

Museum Boymans-
Van Beuningen **2**
Old Holland America Terminal **4**
Pilgrim Fathers Church **1**
Prins Hendrik Maritime Museum **3**

⊕

15 Mi

3 Km

┼─┼─┼ Railway

Maas

Nieuwe

Erasmusbrug

Pieter Hendrikkade

Thorbeckestr.

Stiephellingstr.

Maaskade

Boompjeskade

Boompjes

Terrekade

Willemsplein

Meeuwenstr.

Zalmhaven

Willemskade

Leuvehaven

Leuvehaven

Schiedamsedijk

Vasteland

Zalmstr.

Veerkade

Veerhaven

Veerhaven

Keizerstraat

Scheepmakershaven

Wijnstraat

Wijnhaven

Glas-
haven

Wijnstraat

Wijnhaven

Westblaak Blaak

Schilderstr.

Schiedamse Vest

Schiedamsesingel

van Vollenhovenstraat

Hotlaansestraat

Westerstraat

Maasstr.

Westmaaslaan

Westplein

Parkaan

Parklaan

Binnen-
wegplein

Churchillplein

Wite de Withstraat

Wite de Boomgaardstraat

Eendrachtsstr.

Eendrachtsweg

Westersingel

Melkkopad

Kievitslaan

Karel Doormanstr.

Mauritstr.

Oude Binnenweg

Eendrachtsplein

Mauritsweg

Oldebane

Jongkindstr.

Gouvernestraat

Hobokenplein

Nieuwe Binnenweg

Rochussenstr.

Wytemaweg

Museumpark

Westzeedijk

Parkkade

Gaffelstraat

Josephstr.

van Speykstraat

Mathenesserlaan

Kieler

Saftlevenstr.

Burg.-Jacobplein

Dr. Molewaterplein

Westzeedijk

Bajonetstraat

Adrianastraat

Schiebanlaan

Oddman str.

Kogelvangerstr.

Gravelijnkwal

Bellevoys-
straat

Schiertan

's Gravendijkwal

Droogleever
Fortuynplein

Parkhaven

te Middellandstr.

Ardianaplein

Schier-
laan

Zwaertecronstr.

Spellinckstr.

G.J. de Jonghweg

Puntegaalstr.

Claes de
Vrieselaan

Middellplein

Joost van Geelstr.

Schietbaanlaan

Robert Fruinstr.

Mathenesserlaan

Yolmarijnstraat

Hindulusstraat

de Vliegertstr.

Heemraadssingel

Droogleever
Fortuynplein

Pieter de Hoochweg

Dunantstr.

Willen

Buytevestraat

Aleidisstr.

2e Middellandstr.

Hendrick Sorchstr.

vander Poelstr.

Nieuwe
Binnenweg

Heemraadssingel

Schoneberger weg

Rochussertstraat

Coolhaven

Voorhaven

Delfshaven

← Voorhaven

Heemraadsplein

377

COMING ASHORE & GETTING AROUND It's about a 10-minute walk to the city center. **Taxis** are available at the pier, but are expensive. Rotterdam also has an extensive public transportation network of **buses, trams,** and **subways** (Metro).

THE BEST SHORE EXCURSIONS

Ships that dock in Rotterdam do so as an alternative to Amsterdam, so shore excursions are also offered to Amsterdam, the Hague, Delft, and other locations described in the Amsterdam section, above.

Rotterdam City & Harbor Tour (3 hr., $46): View from the bus the city's acclaimed modern architecture, and pass historic landmarks. Then take a harbor cruise of the busy port.

Zeeland & The Delta (5 hr., $54): In 1953, the Province of Zeeland was the scene of a major flood that covered more than 260,000 acres, killing nearly 1,900 people. As a result of the disaster, water management techniques were developed to reclaim the land. Dams, canals, and dikes were constructed along with a storm surge barrier. The massive project actually shortened Holland's shoreline by more than 300 miles. Visit the Delta Expo for an explanation of the fascinating hydro-engineering project. On the way, you'll pass scenic countryside and the historic city of Zierrikzee.

Gouda & Oudewater (5 hr., $39): Gouda, about half an hour from Rotterdam, is best known for producing cheese. This tour brings you to town for a walking tour that visits the market, the Gothic town hall (the oldest in the Netherlands), and the weighing house, which dates back to the 17th century. You then reboard the bus to travel to Oudewater, where you'll visit the Witches Weighing House, the only remaining such place in Holland. Last used in 1729, this is where people were weighed to determine if they were witches.

THE TOP ATTRACTIONS

Museum Boijmans–Van Beuningen. Museumpark 20 Dutch and Flemish artists from the 16th and 17th centuries are featured here, including Rubens, Hals, Rembrandt, and Steen. Separate galleries boast international modern art, applied arts, ceramics, and sculpture. There are also regular exhibitions of the museum's extensive collection of drawings and prints. The museum has recently been renovated.

© **010/441-9400.** Admission about 3.70€ ($3.35) adults, 1.90€ ($1.70) children. Tues–Sat 10am–5pm; Sun and holidays 11am–5pm.

Maritime Museum Rotterdam This museum is devoted to the history of Rotterdam harbor and is full of nautical lore. It's located in the harbor area, and consists of a main building and *De Buffel,* a beautifully restored 1868 warship.

Leuvehaven 1. © **010/413-2680.** Admission about 3.30€ ($3) adults, 1.65€ ($1.50) children. Tues–Sat 10am–5pm; Sun and public holidays 11am–5pm.

LOCAL FLAVORS

Favorites here include raw herring and *jenever* (Dutch gin). Henkes' Brasserie, Voorhaven 17 (© **010/425-5596**), is a great place to enjoy the wonderful atmosphere of old Delfshaven. The interior, formerly Henkes' Jenever, has been transformed into a beautiful dining room.

BEST BUYS

Head to Delfshaven for galleries and craft shops. The central shopping area is called the Beurstraverse.

10 Norway

Norway offers visitors an embarrassment of riches, from majestic glacier-born fjords and mountain views, to charming and remote towns and villages, to summer's Midnight Sun. Both seafaring and tradition are important parts of what this natural frontier is all about—Norway's name is even nautical, deriving from *Norvegr*, a 1,000-year-old Viking term meaning "the way north," describing the shipping route along the Norwegian coast. But Norway is also a modern and technologically advanced nation with a well-educated and amazingly athletic populace—where else does nearly every child learn to ski?

CURRENCY   The Norwegian currency is the krone (plural kroner), and there are 100 øre in 1 krone. Banknotes are issued in denominations of 50, 100, 200, 500, and 1,000 kroner. The exchange rate at press time was $1 = 8.86 NOK.

LANGUAGE   Norwegian. English is also widely spoken.

BERGEN

Bergen is the capital of Norway's fjord district, and the largest city on the west coast, an area known for its awesome natural beauty. The city is an ancient one, nearly 1,000 years old, squeezed between mountain ranges and bounded by water. Until the 14th century it was the seat of the medieval kingdom of Norway. Today, it's a commercial capital, but it's also a town with important traditions, including in shipping. Besides being a starting-off point for exploration, Bergen has its own sightseeing attractions, including the historic medieval district of **Bryggen,** which is on UNESCO's list of World Heritage sites.

FROMMER'S FAVORITE BERGEN EXPERIENCES

- **Visiting Bryggen.** This quarter of historic timbered houses, rebuilt on the waterfront after a disastrous fire in 1702, is what remains of medieval Bergen. The buildings (some open to the public) now house workshops of painters, weavers, and craftspeople. Bryggen is on UNESCO's World Heritage List as one of the world's most significant cultural and historical re-creations of a medieval settlement.
- **Taking the Fløibanen funicular to Fløien.** The view is worth every øre.

COMING ASHORE & GETTING AROUND   Ships dock within walking distance of the city center. **Taxis** are available at the pier, but you can easily explore the city on foot.

THE BEST SHORE EXCURSIONS

Bergen City Highlights & Troldhaugen (3 hr., $40–$49): Drive past the historic row houses and other city sights, then visit Troldhaugen, a Victorian house in rural surroundings outside of Bergen that was the home of Norway's famous composer Edvard Grieg. The house contains Grieg's own furniture, paintings, and other mementos, and it was here that he composed many of his famous works. The tour may also include a piano recital at the nearby turf-roofed Concert Hall.

THE TOP ATTRACTIONS

Bergen Art Museum   The works of Norwegian and international artists—among them Picasso, Braque, Miró, Kandinsky, and Paul Klee—are displayed at this museum in the city center. The museum also contains some of Edvard Munch's most important works.

Norway

Bergen

Railway ┼┼

Store
Lungegårdsvann

Nya Nygårdsbroen

Wolffs gt.

Hans Tanks gt.
Jonas Reins gt.
Lyder Sagens gt.

Michael Krohns gt.

Puddefjordsbroen

Kalfarveien

Lungegårdskaien

Vestre Strømkaien

Fosswinckels gt.
Allégaten Harald Hårfagres gt.

Nygårdsgaten

Dokkeveien

Strømgaten

Prof. Hansteens gt.

Fjellveien

Sparebanken

Kong Oscars gt.

Markén

Lille
Lungegårdsvann

allé
Christies gt.

Olav Kyrres gt.
Vestre Torggate

Rosenberggaten

Bispenggaten

Lille Øvregt.

Nygårdsgaten
Kaigaten
Landsbroen
Strandkaien

Torgallmenningen
Ole Bulls plass

Håkons gt.

Fløibanen

Skansen

Øvregaten
Rosenkrantzgate

Vetrlidsallmen.
Valkendorfsg. C.

Neumanns gate
Engen
Markveien

Nøstet

Finnegårdsgt.

Bryggen

Henrik Wergelands gt.
Øvre Blekeveien

Skansemyrsveien

Nye Sandviksveien

Klostergaten
Klosteret

Strandgaten C.
Strandgaten C.

Kroharsenggaten

Ladegårds gt.

Skuteviksstorget

Nordnesveien

Helen

Nordnesbakken

Sandviksveien

Nordnes
parken

Byfjorden

NORWAY

OSLO

Bergen

Bergen Aquarium **6**
Bergen Art Museum **5**
Det Hanseatiske Museum **2**
Fløibanen funicular **1**
Galleriet shopping complex **4**
Torget Marketplace **3**

Rasmus Meyers Allé 3–7. © **55-56-80-00.** Admission 35NOK–50NOK ($3.95–$5.65) adults, free for children. May 15–Sept 15 daily 11am–5pm; Sept 16–May 14 Tues–Sun 11am–5pm.

Det Hanseatiske Museum This museum, housed in one of the best-preserved wooden buildings at Bryggen, illustrates what life was like on the wharf centuries ago. The museum is furnished with authentic articles dating from 1704.

Finnegårdsgaten 1A, Bryggen. © **55-31-41-89.** Admission May–Sept 4ONOK ($4.50) adults; Oct–Apr 25NOK ($2.85) adults; free for children. June–Aug daily 9am–5pm; May–Sept daily 11am–2pm.

Fløibanen Funicular A short walk from the fish market, the funicular heads up Fløien, the most famous of Bergen's seven hills, from which you can view the city, the neighboring hills, and the harbor. The ride takes about 8 minutes in each direction.

Vetrlidsalm 23A. © **55/31-48-00.** Round-trip ride 4ONOK ($4.50) adults, 20NOK ($2.25) children. May 25 to Aug, Mon–Fri 7:30am–midnight, Sat 8am–midnight, Sun 9am–midnight; Sept–May 24, Mon–Thurs 8am–11pm, Fri and Sat 8am–11:30pm, Sun 9am–11pm.

Bergen Aquarium This aquarium is one of the largest and nicest in Scandinavia. Marine life includes seals, penguins, lobsters, and piranhas. An especially popular attraction is seal and penguin feeding time (they eat daily in the summer at 11am, 2pm, and 6pm; in the winter, daily at noon and 4pm).

Nornesbakken 4. © **55/55-71-71.** Admission 80NOK ($9) adults, 50NOK ($5.65) children. May–Sept daily 9am–8pm; Oct–Apr daily 10am–6pm.

LOCAL FLAVORS

Traditional favorites include fish and game dishes (including reindeer). Smoked salmon (*laks*) is a local delicacy. Nice cafes can be found near the harbor.

BEST BUYS

Head to the **Marketplace** (Torget) for bargains on local handicrafts from the western fjord district, including rugs and handmade tablecloths. The best time to visit is between 8am and noon. Bargaining is welcomed. The most important shopping complex in the city is **Galleriet** (Torgalmenningen 8), located near the fish market. Here you'll find 70-some stores offering tax-free shopping. Hand-knit Norwegian sweaters are a good buy in Bergen.

THE NORWEGIAN FJORDS

On a North Cape cruise, as you explore the Norwegian fjords, you will make several port calls. Following are two of our favorites.

HAMMERFEST

The world's most northernmost town, and subject to long, dark winters, Hammerfest bought a generator from Thomas Edison in 1891 and became the first European town with electric streetlights. Much of the town was destroyed during World War II, and it is today a modern port with nice shops catering to tourists on their way to the North Cape.

In the basement of the town hall is the **Royal and Ancient Polar Bear Society** (© **78-41-31-00**). Stop by and become a member for 150NOK ($17). The money is used to protect endangered Arctic animals. There's also a small museum. The center is open June to August, Monday to Friday 10am to 5pm, Saturday and Sunday 9am to 5pm.

THE BEST SHORE EXCURSIONS

Arctic Fishing (3 hr., $58): A typical fishing boat will take you about an hour outside of town, where you'll find so much cod, catfish, and other fish you're almost guaranteed to catch something. Ask the chef on your ship if he or she will prepare your catch for dinner.

HONNINGSVAG

This is the world's northernmost village, and gateway to the North Cape. It is a completely modern fishing harbor (only the chapel withstood the German destruction of 1944) and has a museum called Nordkappmuseet, in the **Nordkapphuset,** Fergeveien 4 (© 78/47-28-33), right at the harbor and town center, that offers exhibits relating to the cultural history of the North Cape. (Admission is 25NOK/$2.85 adults, 5NOK/60¢ children, free for children under age 6. Hours June 15–Aug 15 are Mon–Sat 9am–8pm, Sun 1–8pm. At other times, Mon–Fri 12:30–4pm.) But we most recommend you take the shore excursion to the North Cape (see below).

THE BEST SHORE EXCURSIONS

The North Cape (3½ hr., $57–$60): Drive about 45 minutes to the Nordkapp, the actual northernmost point in Europe. Here the Nordkapphallen visitor center offers a video presentation and museum exhibits on the history of the North Cape, including a visit by King Oscar (king of Norway and Sweden) in 1873, and the arrival of King Chulalongkorn of Siam (now Thailand) in 1907. Stop by the post office for a Nordkapp postmark. And if it's not foggy (as it was on our recent visit), check out the incredible sea views from the top of the world (or at least the top of Europe). The main attraction here is Mother Nature, but the center also has a huge gift shop.

TROMSØ

This "Gateway to the Arctic" island has been a starting-off point for exploration of the North Pole. It's the capital of Norwegian Lapland, and a popular destination with tourists who come in summer to celebrate the midnight sun. Local sights include the **Arctic Cathedral,** built in the shape of an iceberg. **Polaria,** Hjalmar Johansengst. 12 (© 77-75-01-00), is a seaside adventure center with a Polar and Barents Region theme. The building itself is worth a peek, as it is uniquely shaped like ice floes. Inside is a wide-screen video presentation as well as an aquarium with seal and sea life exhibits, and interactive exhibits. Admission is 70NOK ($8) adults, 35NOK ($4) children. The attraction is open May to August, 10am to 7pm, and September to April, noon to 5pm. Another key Tromsø attraction is **Nordlysplanetariet,** the world's most northernmost planetarium.

THE BEST SHORE EXCURSIONS

Tromsø City Tour (3 hr., $45): This tour includes the Tromsø Museum, which offers zoology, geology, cultural history, and botany displays and a special exhibit on the Sami, the region's original inhabitants. Also visited are the Arctic Cathedral and Polaria.

TRONDHEIM

Founded by the Viking king Olaf I Tryggvason in the 10th century, Trondheim is Norway's third largest city and was the country's capital until the early 1200s. It's scenic, pleasant, and an active university town, noted for its timbered architecture and links to its medieval past, which include the Gothic-style **Nidaros Cathedral** and **Archbishop's Palace,** Bispegaten 5 (© 73/50-12-12). Admission to both is 35NOK ($4) adults, 20NOK ($2.25) children. The cathedral is open Monday to Friday 9am to 6pm, Saturday 9am to 2pm, and Sunday 1 to

4pm June 20 to August 18 (closes earlier other times of the year). The palace is open June to mid-August only, Monday to Friday 9am to 3pm, Saturday 9am to 2pm, Sunday noon to 3pm.

THE BEST SHORE EXCURSIONS

City Tour with Open-Air Folk Museum (3 hr., $40): This tour visits the Nidaros Cathedral as well as the Trøndelag Folk Museum, one of Norway's major folk-culture complexes. The collection includes farmhouses, churches (including the northernmost stave church in Norway), and town buildings, surrounded by a nature park.

OSLO

Oslo is one of the oldest Scandinavia capitals, founded in the mid–11th century by a Viking king and named as the nation's capital around 1300. Though it's never been on the mainstream tourism circuit, Oslo is a growing city permeated by a kind of Nordic joie de vivre, and offers a wealth of sights and activities and numerous new restaurants, cafes, and shopping options. It's also a starting point for easy excursions along the 60-mile-long Oslofjord or to nearby towns and villages.

Oslo residents love nature and are proud of the nearby forests and fjords. It takes only a half-hour by tram to get from the Royal Palace, at Drammensveien 1, to **Tryvannstårnet Lookout Tower,** where you can enjoy the lushness of Oslo Marka, the giant forest, and look down from the 390-foot tower onto hundreds of sailboats, motorboats, and windsurfers among the numerous islands of the Oslo archipelago. For information, phone ℂ **22/14-67-11.** Admission is about 35NOK ($4) adults, 20NOK ($2.25) children. Hours are May and September, daily 10am to 5pm; June, 10am to 7pm; July, 9am to 10pm; August, 9am to 8pm. Nearby is the **Holmenkollen Ski Jump,** the site of Olympic competitions in 1952, worth looking at if for no other reason than to see how crazy ski jumpers really are (it's tall!).

FROMMER'S FAVORITE OSLO EXPERIENCES

- **Taking a ferry to the Bygdøy peninsula.** This is where some of Oslo's major attractions, including the Viking Ship Museum, polar ship *Fram,* and Norwegian Folk Museum are located.
- **Admiring outdoor sculptures** at the Vigeland Sculpture Park.
- **Exploring the Edvard Munch Museum.** But don't Scream!
- **Enjoying the street musicians.** They flock here by the hundreds in the summer, and can be found along Karl Johans Gate or at the marketplace.
- **Eating a bag of shrimp on the harbor.** See "Local Flavors," below.

COMING ASHORE & GETTING AROUND   Ships dock right in the city center, which is small, compact, and easy to walk around. **Taxis** may be difficult to come by. The city, however, has an efficient system of **buses, trams** (streetcars), and **subways.**

THE BEST SHORE EXCURSIONS

Oslo Highlights (3 hr., $39–$49): Drive through the capital, passing Akershus Castle, the Parliament building, the National Theater, the university, the Royal Castle, and Karl Johan Street, Oslo's main thoroughfare. Continue on through Oslo's beautiful residential areas to Holmenkollen Ski Jump. Continue on to Vigeland Sculpture Park for a walking tour, then to Bygdøy Peninsula, a former royal preserve, now the site of some of Oslo's most important museums, including the Viking Ship Museum.

Maritime Oslo (4 hr., $44–$46): A city tour with stops at the Fram Museum, featuring a polar ship; the Maritime Museum, offering a video presentation with spectacular views of Norway's coastline and a depiction of life on the high seas; and the Viking Ship Museum. May also include a visit to Vigeland Sculpture Park (see "The Top Attractions," below).

THE TOP ATTRACTIONS

Edvard Munch Museum This museum is devoted exclusively to the works of Edvard Munch (1863–1944), Scandinavia's leading painter and creator of *The Scream*. The artist's gift to the city, the collection contains some 1,100 paintings, 4,500 drawings, and 18,000 prints, numerous graphic plates, six sculptures, and documentary material. Exhibits are changed periodically.

Tøyengate 53. ✆ 23/24-14-00. Admission 60NOK ($6.80) adults, 30NOK ($3.40) children. June to mid-Sept daily 10am–6pm; May Tues–Wed and Fri–Sat 10am–4pm, Thurs and Sun 10am–6pm.

Henie-Onstad Kunstsenter (Henie-Onstad Art Center) This museum on the Oslofjord, about 7 miles west of Oslo, displays the art collection of skating champion Sonja Henie and her husband, Niels Onstad, a shipping tycoon. There are some 1,800 works by Munch, Picasso, Matisse, Léger, Bonnard, and Miró. Also on display are Miss Henie's three Olympic gold medals and other trophies. There's also a top-notch, partly self-service grill restaurant, The Piruetten, on the premises.

Høkvikodden, Baerum. ✆ 67/54-3050. Admission 60NOK ($6.80) adults, 40NOK ($4.50) children 16 and under. Tues–Thurs 10am–9pm; Fri–Mon 11am–6pm. Take a bus to Høvikodden.

Kon Tiki Museum *Kon Tiki* was the flimsy balsa raft on which intrepid Norwegian explorer Thor Heyerdahl and five companions sailed 4,300 miles across open seas from Peru to Polynesia. Why? To prove a theory that it might have been done centuries ago.

Bygdoynesveien 36. ✆ 23-08-67-67. Admission 33NOK ($3.75) adults, 11NOK ($1.30) children, 80NOK ($9) for family ticket for 4. Apr–May and Sept 10:30am–5pm; June–Aug 9:30am–5:45pm.

Norwegian Folk Museum This open-air folk museum features 140 original buildings, transported here from all over Norway. Included are medieval dwellings, a stave church, and rural buildings grouped together by region of origin. Inside, the museum has exhibits capturing every imaginable facet of Norwegian life, past and present. There's a particularly outstanding exhibit on Norway's Lapp population.

Museumsveien 10. ✆ 22/12-36-66. Admission 70NOK ($7.90) adults, 50NOK ($5.65) children 16 and under; 20NOK ($2.25) for barn. June–Aug daily 9am–6pm; May and Sept daily 10am–5pm. Take a ferry from Pier 3, facing the Rådhuset, or hop a city bus.

Vikingskiphuset (Viking Ship Museum) On display here are three Viking burial vessels that were found preserved in clay on the shores of the Oslofjord. The most spectacular is the 9th-century dragon ship, which features a wealth of ornaments and was the burial chamber of a Viking queen and her slave.

Huk Aveny 25, Bygdøy. ✆ 22/43-83-79. Admission about 40NOK ($4.50) adults, 20NOK ($2.25) children. May–Aug daily 10am–6pm; Sept daily 11am–5pm. Take a ferry from Pier 3, facing the Rådhuset, or hop a city bus.

Vigeland Sculpture Park This 75-acre park displays the work of Gustav Vigeland, Norway's greatest sculptor. There are some 211 sculptures of humans and animals in stone, bronze, and iron. The nearby museum is the sculptor's former studio, and contains more of his works, sketches, and woodcuts.

Oslo

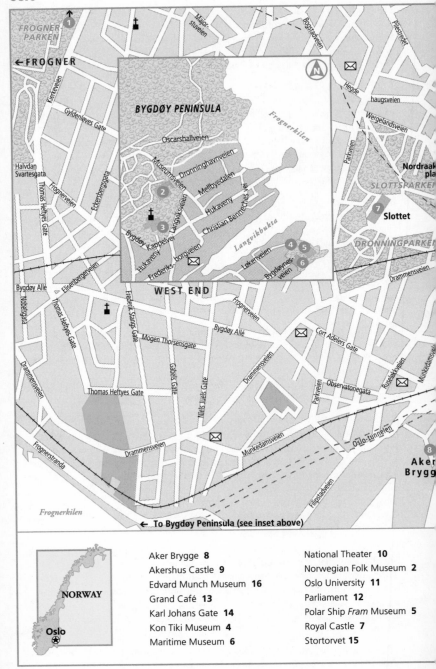

FROGNER PARKEN

← FROGNER

Kerkeveien

Gyldenløves Gate

Halvdan
Svartesgata

Thomas Heftyes Gate

Frognerveien

Eckersbergsgata

Majorstuveien

BYGDØY PENINSULA

Oscarshallveien

Museumsveien

Dronninghavnveien

Meltbyedalen

Hukaveny

Christian Benneches vei

Langviksveien

Bygdøy Kappelvei

Hukaveny

Frederiks-borgveien

Langvikbukta

Løkeriveien

Bygdøynes
veien

WEST END

Frognerveien

Frognerkilen

Boostedveien

Hegde

haugsveien

Wergelandsveien

Parkveien

Nordraak
pla

SLOTTSPARKE

Slottet

DRONNINGPARKE

Drammensveien

Bygdøy Allé

Elsenbergveien

Thomas Heftyes Gate

Nobelsgata

Frederik Stangs Gate

Mogen Thorsensgate

Gabels Gate

Thomas Heftyes Gate

Bygdøy Allé

Niels Tuels Gate

Drammensveien

Cort Adelers Gate

Parkveien

Observatoriegata

Ruselokkveien

Munkedamsveien

Drammensveien

Frognerstranda

Frognerkilen

Munkedamsveien

Filipstadveien

Oslo-Tunnelen

Aker
Brygg

← To Bygdøy Peninsula (see inset above)

NORWAY

Oslo

Aker Brygge **8**
Akershus Castle **9**
Edvard Munch Museum **16**
Grand Café **13**
Karl Johans Gate **14**
Kon Tiki Museum **4**
Maritime Museum **6**

National Theater **10**
Norwegian Folk Museum **2**
Oslo University **11**
Parliament **12**
Polar Ship *Fram* Museum **5**
Royal Castle **7**
Stortorvet **15**

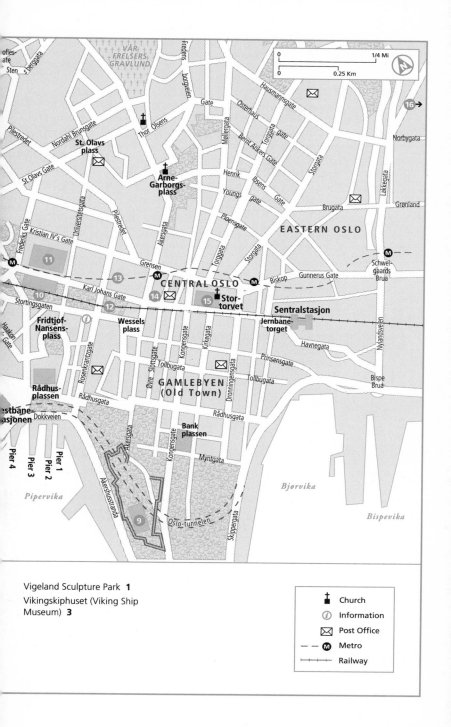

Vigeland Sculpture Park **1**
Vikingskiphuset (Viking Ship
Museum) **3**

Church
Information
Post Office
Metro
Railway

Frogner Park. Nobelsgate 32. (📞 **22/44-23-06.** Free admission to the park; museum 30NOK ($3.40) adults, 15NOK ($1.70) children. Park daily 24 hr. Museum May–Sept Tues–Sat 10am–6pm, Sun noon–7pm; Oct–Apr noon–4pm, Thurs noon–7pm.

LOCAL FLAVORS

At the harbor, in front of the Rådhuset, you can buy a bag of freshly caught and cooked **shrimp** from a shrimp fisherman and shell your meal as you check out the harbor scenery. Those looking for smart restaurants serving Norwegian food and foreign food (especially American) should also head to the waterfront, in particular **Aker Brygge,** the former shipbuilding yard, now a restaurant and shopping complex. The **Grand Café** in the Grand Hotel, Karl Johans Gate 31 (📞 **22/42-93-90**), is where Edvard Munch and Henrik Ibsen used to hang out (reservations are recommended).

BEST BUYS

Though Oslo is one of the most expensive cities in Europe, best buys here include sportswear, silver, enamelware, traditional handicrafts, pewter, glassware, teak furniture, and products made of stainless steel. Oslo has many pedestrian streets for shoppers. A good place to start is the **Stortorvet.** Another large cluster of stores can be found along **Karl Johans Gate.** For sweaters, check out the shop at the SAS Radisson hotel, where they have been known to negotiate (especially if you are buying more than one).

11 Russia

Fascinating **St. Petersburg,** founded in 1703 and named for Peter the Great, had a tough 20th century, with much trauma and bloodshed. The 1917 Russian Revolution that ushered in the Soviet era also ushered in a new name for the city: Leningrad, in honor of Vladimir Lenin. In the early 1940s, Nazi troops seized Leningrad for 900 days during World War II, leaving approximately a million dead and the city badly battered.

In 1991, the city, under the new non-communist Russian government, returned to its original name, and today the one-time capital of Imperial Russia is a cosmopolitan city of five million that's both an industrial and a cultural center. It's the second largest city in Russia and the country's largest port. But the signs of age and warfare are obvious at close range. The walls of many buildings that, seen from afar, seem architecturally appealing, close up look tattered and worn, graffiti-stained, with paint blistered and just, well, sort of tired. Putting this gorgeous city in order is going to take determination—and lots of cash.

The Neva River cuts through the city, which was once swampland, and there are some 360 bridges crossing the river and canals, a layout that's earned the city the nickname "Venice of the North." The canals are lined with opulent baroque and neoclassical palaces, cathedrals, and monuments. The city's ongoing restoration project requires that all existing facades in the downtown area be retained.

Top sights in St. Petersburg include the Hermitage museum, which has one of the richest art collections in the world; the Peter and Paul fortress, the burial place of the Romanov dynasty; and St. Isaac's Cathedral, the fourth largest cathedral in the world. Outside the city, you can visit the lavish summer homes of the czars.

Cruise lines also typically offer nighttime shore excursions here to see ballet, opera, folk performers, or a circus.

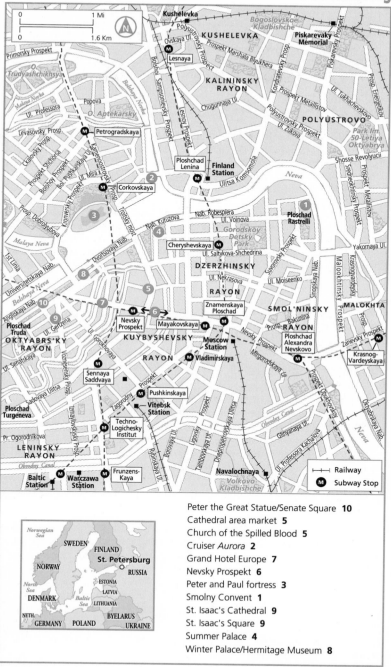

Peter the Great Statue/Senate Square **10**

Cathedral area market **5**

Church of the Spilled Blood **5**

Cruiser *Aurora* **2**

Grand Hotel Europe **7**

Nevsky Prospekt **6**

Peter and Paul fortress **3**

Smolny Convent **1**

St. Isaac's Cathedral **9**

St. Isaac's Square **9**

Summer Palace **4**

Winter Palace/Hermitage Museum **8**

Important Visa Information

Passengers who participate in St. Petersburg shore excursions or arrange for private transportation through the ship's shore excursions desk (see "Coming Ashore & Getting Around," below) do not need to obtain a visa.

Those who wish to go ashore on their own, however, do have to obtain a tourist visa prior to departure. To receive a Russian visa, you must have a valid passport which remains valid at least 30 days past the last day of the cruise. Visa application forms are available from the Russian consulates in Washington, New York, San Francisco, or Seattle, or from travel agencies or visa services. The visa processing fee is $70 for not less than 2 weeks' processing time. Additional fees are charged for quicker processing.

For information, contact the Embassy of the Russian Federation in the United States (℗ **202/939-8913** or 202/939-8918; http://russian embassy.org), open Monday through Friday, 9am to 1pm and 2:30 to 6pm. But take our advice: You are better off taking the visa-less shore excursion.

CURRENCY   Rubles, but street vendors will readily accept dollars. The rate of exchange at press time was $1 = 29 rubles.

LANGUAGE   Russian.

FROMMER'S FAVORITE ST. PETERSBURG EXPERIENCES

- **The Hermitage** wins hands down. Even though the building itself is one of those that could do with a face-lift, what's inside is memorable. And you needn't be an art snob to appreciate the beauty of the exhibits.
- **Strolling the Nevsky Prospekt.** St. Petersburg's main thoroughfare (and the most famous street in Russia) offers historic squares, bridges, buildings, shopping, cafes, crowds, and even the occasional scam artist and black marketeer (don't buy anything from someone who starts the conversation with "Pssst . . .").
- **Visiting a summer palace.** These historic estates of the czars are lavish and memorable.

COMING ASHORE & GETTING AROUND   The main cruise terminal is about a 20-minute drive from the city center. Small ships can come right into town up the Neva River, but you are still best off taking a **taxi,** especially at night. Official taxis are usually four-door Volvo sedans. In Russia, they also have what are known as "private" taxis. "Private," in this case, means virtually anyone can stop and pick you up, and you enter these cabs at your own risk (there have been incidents of robberies). If you want to tour the city without having to join a shore excursion, you are best off hiring a car, limo, or van with a **private guide.** Your cruise line shore excursion desk will be able to arrange this for you. The line may also provide **shuttle bus** service to the center of town.

THE BEST SHORE EXCURSIONS

City Tour (3–3½ hr., $40–$55): This introductory tour includes a view of the Peter and Paul Fortress with its gilded spire; the cruiser *Aurora,* the ship that fired a blank round in 1917 that signaled the start of the October Revolution; and the Winter Palace, which houses the Hermitage. You will see the famous Bronze Horseman statue depicting the city's founder, Peter the Great; the exquisitely decorated Church of the Spilled Blood; and the magnificent St. Isaac's Cathedral, one of the world's largest domed structures (it took 40 yr. to construct and was used as a museum under the Soviet regime; it's now an active church again). Some tours include a stop at 18th-century Smolny Convent, a crowning achievement of the renowned architect Rastrelli. Others include a stop at the Summer Palace, a beautiful example of 18th-century architecture.

The Hermitage (3½–4 hr., $49–$76): Take a short drive to the Winter Palace, along the banks of the Neva River, for a guided tour through parts of the vast Hermitage Art Museum. The former home of the imperial family, this 18th-century baroque palace and four adjacent buildings now house one of the most outstanding art collections in the world.

Peterhof (4 hr., $58–$60): Drive 22 miles through the suburbs of St. Petersburg to Peterhof, the former summer home of Peter the Great, built to rival Versailles. Construction began 300 years ago and spanned 2 centuries. The massive estate encompasses seven parks and more than 20 smaller palaces and pavilions. Your guided tour will include the grand staircase and a walk through some of the palace's lavish rooms, as well as the palace's grounds. The 300-acre park and spectacular fountains, some 129 in total, were designed by Peter himself.

Pushkin (Tsarskoye Selo) (4 hr., $45–$52): Drive 17 miles south of St. Petersburg to Pushkin (the village of Tsarskoye Selo was renamed Pushkin in 1937 after Russia's favorite poet, Alexander Pushkin) for a visit to the opulent summer residence of Catherine the Great. The estate was presented as a gift from Peter the Great to his wife Catherine in 1710 and was the main summer residence of the imperial family from Peter's reign until the fall of the monarchy in 1917. The palace was almost totally destroyed during World War II, but has been magnificently restored to its former splendor. You'll take a guided tour of several lavish rooms, including the Great Blue Room, Picture Gallery, and Amber Room. The surrounding park features Italian-designed grounds with numerous marble statues.

THE TOP ATTRACTIONS

Because of odd museum opening hours, long lines, labyrinthine corridors and display rooms, and a lack of English translations, you can literally get lost in the Hermitage, as Jerry did once while visiting with his wife and three other couples. Just plain got lost in a corridor with no hope of retracing his steps to link up with them again. It is best to see the top attractions here as part of shore excursions, or in a hired car—in both cases you get an experienced guide. Cruise lines offer a particularly large selection of shore excursions here, with something suited to nearly everyone's taste.

LOCAL FLAVORS

Restaurants in St. Petersburg are expensive and not all that great, although you may be surprised to find Chinese and Indian food in addition to the traditional Russian meat-and-potato offerings. Still, if you must try chicken Kiev and blinis and caviar, and you don't mind paying top dollar (we're talking Paris prices), you're best off heading to a top hotel such as the **Grand Hotel Europe,** Mikhailovskaya ul. 1/7 (© **329-60-00**).

BEST BUYS

Shop here for *matreoshka* dolls, hand-painted lacquer boxes, caviar, fur hats, vodka, and amber jewelry. Good places to hunt for souvenirs are around **St. Isaac's Square** and the **market** near Spilled Blood Cathedral.

12 Scotland

Edinburgh, situated on the south bank of the Firth of Forth (across the water, due south of the historic golf complex at St. Andrews), has been Scotland's capital since the 600s. Its status as Scotland's seat of power took on renewed significance a couple of years ago when the country was granted a modified form of independence. The Act of Union (with England) in 1707 essentially disbanded Scotland's parliament and left Edinburgh a capital within the framework of Great Britain and answerable to Whitehall. The union is intact but Scotland now has greater authority to govern its own affairs, and many believe that complete independence is only a matter of time.

Edinburgh's primary tourist attraction is its 1,000-year-old castle, which dominates the city center. The rock on which it stands towers over Princes Street and the stunningly beautiful gardens there. The Royal Mile runs from the castle to Holyroodhouse, one of the Queen's Scottish palaces from which she left by horse-drawn carriage on that historic day in 1999 to open the Scottish Parliament, sitting for the first time in 300 years.

The city, while hip enough in its own way, especially during the Edinburgh Festival each August, reeks of history. Dark, ancient "closes" (narrow tenement hallways) along the High Street have given rise to a flourishing trade in late-night ghost tours. Lesser castles, now in ruins, offer mute testimony to the battles that raged in the area over the centuries, mostly between the Scots and the English and sometimes between the Scots and the Scots! The Tron Kirk, where John Knox, leader of the Protestant Reformation, held sway, displays architecture dating back to the 1600s. It's hard to turn round in Edinburgh without rubbing shoulders with the past. And how different the world might be today without some of those born and/or raised in the tity: Alexander Graham Bell (no telephone), James Simpson (no anesthesia), Sir Walter Scott, John Buchan, Robert Louis Stevenson, Arthur Conan Doyle (think of the great literature lost). Perish the thought, there might have been no James Bond movie series had it not been for Edinburgher Sean Connery making the on-screen character famous.

CURRENCY   Although the country is now somewhat independent, the Scottish currency is still the British pound, exchangeable at press time at the rate of $1 = £.68

LANGUAGE   English.

FROMMER'S FAVORITE EDINBURGH EXPERIENCES

- **Strolling along Princes Street.** The castle and the massive Walter Scott Monument are on one side, Victorian and more modern architecture on the storefronts on the other.
- **Visiting during Edinburgh Festival month.** During the annual event, not all of the entertainment is of the paid variety. Walk on Princes Street or Charlotte Square or the West End and you may find a German youth choir singing *a cappella* on one street corner, a juggler on another, a mime farther along, or a harpist outside a department store. They'll take donations but essentially it's a street show for free.

The Military Tattoo, an integral part of the festival, displays military precision marching, Highland dancing, massed bands, and all kinds of pomp and ceremony. It's held in the evening on the forecourt in front of the castle on which seating is erected. We defy anybody not to be moved by the finale: A lone piper on a parapet over the castle main gate—illuminated by the only light in the entire forecourt—playing "Amazing Grace."

- **Sampling the pubs along Rose Street.** The street parallels Princes Street, a block south, and is reputed to contain more public houses than any other of its length. They used to say in Scotland that you were not a man until you had had one drink in every pub in Rose Street.
- **Visiting Deacon Brodie's Tavern.** On the Royal Mile, near the castle. Brodie was a prominent Edinburgher, a city councilor who also happened to be a burglar in the wee hours. He was said to have inspired Stevenson's *The Strange Case of Dr. Jekyll and Mr. Hyde.* He was hanged in 1788.

COMING ASHORE & GETTING AROUND   Most ships are too big to enter Edinburgh's docks (at Leith, a couple of miles from the city center) because of a narrow lock at the entrance. Smaller ships, such as Silversea's *Silver Cloud* and *Silver Wind* (but not the company's newer, somewhat bigger vessels) can negotiate the lock. Others must anchor offshore or dock on the other side of the Firth of Forth and bus their passengers into town, a drive of an hour or so.

THE BEST SHORE EXCURSIONS

We recommend that you take the cruise line's shuttle into town (it'll almost certainly drop you off near Princes Street) and do your own thing. The city bus service will take you anywhere you want to go and cabs are plentiful. There are also double-decker buses (open upstairs) that offer tours of the historic Royal Mile, Holyroodhouse, the King's Park, the Grassmarket, and so on that leave from the side of the Waverley Railway Station. But much of Edinburgh is for walkers, anyway.

THE TOP ATTRACTIONS

Princess Street Gardens   View Hundreds of acres of greenery, flowers, trees, a bandstand where summer lunchtime concerts are often to be found, a fabulous floral clock, picnic areas, leafy glades, and walkways. And it's all free.

Edinburgh Castle   The castle's past, in part, is shrouded in mystery; but there's more confusion due to inadequate history-keeping. It may have taken roughly its present form during the reign of Malcolm III, in the 11th century. Mary, Queen of Scots, gave birth to James (later James VI of Scotland and James I of England) in Edinburgh Castle and her chambers are still visitable. The castle also houses the Scottish Crown Jewels and the famed Stone of Scone (say *Skoon*) on which Scottish kings were crowned for centuries.

Castle Hill. ☎ **0131/225-9846.** Admission £7.15 ($10.50) adults, £2 ($3) children 15 and under. Apr–Sept 9:30am–5:15pm; Oct–Mar 9:30am–4:15pm.

Walter Scott Monument   The views from this Gothic-style tower are stunning, but be forewarned: It's a tought slog up those stairs.

Princes St. (overlooking the gardens). ☎ **0131/529-4068.** Admission £2.75 ($4) adults. Open daily at varying times.

The National Gallery   This is small as national galleries go but contains some fine works, including some Titians, Gainsboroughs, and others alongside the works of Scottish artists such as Henry Raeburn and Alexander Naysmith.

2 The Mound (which runs north off Princes St.). Free admission. Mon–Sat 10am–5pm; Sun 2–5pm.

Edinburgh

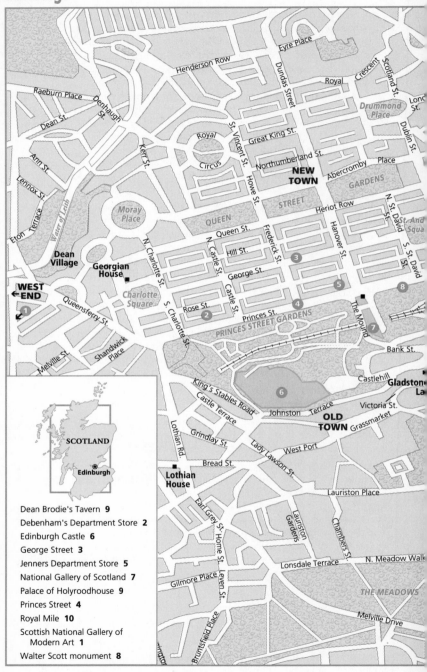

Dean Brodie's Tavern **9**

Debenham's Department Store **2**

Edinburgh Castle **6**

George Street **3**

Jenners Department Store **5**

National Gallery of Scotland **7**

Palace of Holyroodhouse **9**

Princes Street **4**

Royal Mile **10**

Scottish National Gallery of
   Modern Art **1**

Walter Scott monument **8**

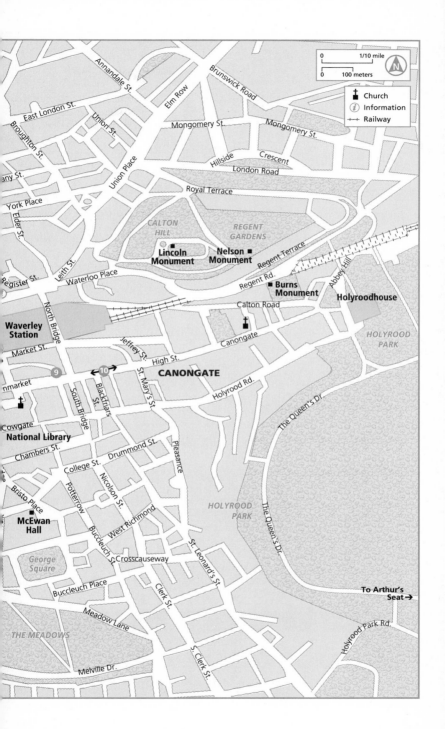

Palace of Holyroodhouse   Holyroodhouse is an official residence of Queen Elizabeth II and Prince Philip. It has for centuries been home to a succession of royal figures, including Mary, Queen of Scots, whose Italian secretary (and, some say, lover) was slain there by her husband, Lord Darnley, and numerous accomplices, in 1566. Bonnie Prince Charlie threw a gala affair in its main room during the Jacobite Rebellion years of the mid-1700s. *Note:* The palace is closed to the public for 2 weeks in May and 3 in late June and early July. The exact dates vary, so check in advance.

Canongate, at the eastern end of the Royal Mile. ℭ 0131/556-7371. Admission £5.5 ($8) adults, £3 ($4.50) children 15 and under. Mon–Sat 9:30am–4:45pm; Sun 10:30am–4:40pm.

Scottish National Gallery of Modern Art   This former school building, which dates from 1828, offers an international collection that includes Henry Moore and Barbara Hepworth sculptures, Picasso, Braque, Matisse, Miró, Ernst, Lichtenstein, and Hockney, as well as English and Scottish artists including William Turner, John Constable, Henry Raeburn, and David Wilkie, to name a few.

Belford Rd. ℭ 0131/556-8921. Free admission except for some temporary exhibits. Mon–Sat 10am–5pm; Sun 2–5pm.

LOCAL FLAVORS

Scotch broth, a beef, barley and vegetable soup, tastes great in the right atmosphere—like in the shadow of Edinburgh Castle. The very Scottish dish of **haggis** reflects the necessities and culinary capabilities of the poor who tilled the highland soil and tended the sheep in olden times. Time was, it comprised all kinds of low-grade animal parts and oatmeal (some people would say sawdust) cooked in the stomach of a sheep. Fortunately, those days are long gone and haggis is made under strictly hygienic conditions, using only government-approved cuts of meat and filler. Try it; you might like it! If you find yourself in a really traditional Scottish restaurant, you might come across another odd-sounding item—**skirlie** (or skurlie)—a side dish of potatoes or oatmeal fried with onions.

BEST BUYS

Needless to say, one of the prime products is tartans—kilts, scarves, bonnets, jackets, pants. Some of the sellers will also offer to trace your genealogy for you or at least to tell you what clan you're affiliated with. (Believe us, they'll find one!) Edinburgh Crystal is another fine product, as are woolen goods.

Princes Street is one of the major shopping areas with very good stores including the city's two best: Debenham's and Jenners. **George Street** and the **Royal Mile** also offer plenty of shopping opportunities, as do **Leith Walk,** at the east end of Princes Street; **The Bridges,** also nearby; and **Lothian Road** and the **Haymarket** area, in the west.

13 Sweden

Stockholm, a city of Renaissance splendor mixed with very modern skyscrapers, is built on 14 bridge-connected islands in Lake Mälaren, which marks the beginning of an archipelago of 24,000 islands, skerries, and islets stretching all the way to the Baltic Sea. Definitely plan to be on deck as your ship cruises through the archipelago.

While the medieval walls of Stockholm's Old Town are no more, the winding cobblestone streets, dating to the 13th century, are well preserved and a real treat to visit. Here, within walking distance of the cruise ship pier, you'll find the Royal Palace, ancient churches, historic merchant houses, and dozens of restaurants and shopping opportunities (including art galleries and antique stores).

Another must is Djurgården (Deer Park), the site of many of the city's popular attractions, including the open-air museums of Skansen and the *Vasa* man-of-war. You can get there easily by ferry. If you want to further explore the archipelago, or are just looking for some quiet time, boats leave frequently in the summer from the harbor for the bathing resort of **Vaxholm** and other scenic islands.

CURRENCY   Sweden's basic unit of currency is the krona (plural kronor). One krona is divided into 100 öre. Banknotes are issued in denominations of 20, 50, 100, 500, 1,000, and 10,000 kronor. The rate of exchange at press time was $1 = 10.82 kronor.

LANGUAGE   Swedish. English is also commonly spoken.

FROMMER'S FAVORITE STOCKHOLM EXPERIENCES

- **Exploring Gamla Stan (Old Town), especially at night.** The narrow cobblestone streets are specially lit. It's like going back in time.
- **Taking a ferry to Djurgården.** Here you'll find the Vasa Ship Museum and other popular attractions.
- **Watching the summer dawn.** If you can get yourself out of bed at 3am in midsummer, you're in for a treat.
- **Fishing.** You can even fish in downtown Stockholm, casting a line within view of the king's palace for some of the finest salmon in the world.

COMING ASHORE & GETTING AROUND   Cruise ships dock about 1 mile (1.5km) from the city center, and within easy walking distance of the Royal Palace and Gamla Stan (Old Town). You can get around by **bus, subway** (T-bana), and **tram** (streetcar). **Taxis** are available at the pier, but are expensive. The meter starts at about 37SEK ($3.45). A short ride can easily cost more than $11.

THE BEST SHORE EXCURSIONS

City Tour (3 hr., $40): This comprehensive city tour includes districts of Gamla Stan, Normalm, Østermalm, Djurgården and Sødermalm, each with its own special character. Begin with a short drive up to Fjällgatan, for a panoramic view of the city, then head through Gamla Stan, the medieval Old Town, and pass the Royal Palace.

Proceed past the Royal Dramatic Theater along Strandvägen to the island of Djurgården for a tour that includes the Vasa Museum. Continue through Diplomatic town to Østermalm, a fashionable neighborhood of stately apartment buildings, then on to Hamngatan and Sergel's Torg, the focal point of modern Stockholm. Proceed south past the Parliament Building, past the House of Nobility, and via the narrow canal at Slussen to Sødermalm, the large island on Stockholm's south side, where you'll find a number of small, closely integrated neighborhoods. An alternative tour substitutes a visit to Stadshuset, Stockholm's imposing, red-brick city hall (where they hold the Nobel Prize Banquet) in place of the Vasa Museum.

Historic Stockholm & Sigtuna (6½ hr., $115): This tour offers a driving tour of the city, a walk through Old Town, a stop at the Vasa Museum, and a drive through the scenic countryside to visit Sigtuna on Lake Mälaren. This religious village was founded approximately 1,000 years ago by the first Christian king of Sweden, and even today is a bastion of religion and education. Includes lunch and shopping time.

THE TOP ATTRACTIONS

Royal Flagship Vasa This 17th-century man-of-war is the world's oldest identified and complete ship and the biggest tourist attraction in Stockholm. It capsized and sank on its maiden voyage in 1628. The ship was salvaged in 1961 and has been carefully restored. Some 97% of its original sculptures were also retrieved.

Galärvarvet, Djurgården. (© 08/519-54-800. Admission 65SEK ($6) adults, 35SEK ($3.50) seniors and students, 15SEK ($1.50) children. June 10–Aug 20 daily 9:30am–7pm.

Skansen Referred to as "Old Sweden in a nutshell," this open-air museum offers more than 150 dwellings from Lapland to Skaøne, most from the 18th and 19th centuries, that have been reassembled on about 75 acres of parkland. The exhibits range from a windmill to a manor house to a complete town quarter, plus folk dancing and open-air concerts.

Djurgården. (© 08/442-80-00. Admission 35SEK–55SEK ($3–$5) adults, $1.50 children 14 and under. May–Aug daily 11am–6pm; Apr and Sept daily 11am–4pm. Take ferry from Slussen.

Kungliga Slottet (The Royal Palace) This 608-room Italian baroque palace is one of the few official residences of a European monarch open to the public (though the king and queen prefer to live and bring up their children at Drottningholm—see below). A changing-of-the-guard ceremony is offered here Monday to Saturday at noon and on Sunday at 1pm. You can also tour the State Apartments. The Treasury exhibits a celebrated collection of crown jewels, while the Royal Armory has weapons, armor, gilded coaches, and coronation costumes from the 16th century. The Museum of Antiquities has Gustav III's Roman sculpture collection.

Kungliga Husgerådskammaren. (© 08/402-61-32. Admission to apartments, Museum of Antiquities, and Treasury: each museum, 55SEK ($5) adults, 40SEK ($4.50) seniors and students; Royal Armory, 65SEK ($6) adults, 40SEK ($4.50) seniors and students. Apartments May–Aug daily 10am–4pm; Sept Tues–Sun noon–3pm. Museum of Antiquities June–Aug daily noon–4pm; Sept and May noon–3pm. Royal Armory, daily 11am–4pm.

Drottningholm Palace Modeled on Versailles, this palace, built on an island about 7 miles (11.25km) from Stockholm, is the actual home of Sweden's Royal Family. Inside are courtly art, royal furnishings, and Gobelin tapestries; outside are fountains and parks. Nearby is Drottningholm Court Theater (© **08/ 759-04-06**), the best preserved 18th-century theater in the world.

Drottningholm. (© 08/402-62-80. Admission 55SEK ($5) adults, 35SEK ($3) people under 26. May daily 11am–4:30pm; June–Aug 10am–4:30pm; Sept noon–3:30pm. Catch the ferry from City Hall (also reachable by bus or subway).

National Museum (National Museum of Art) One of the oldest museums in the world (it celebrated its 200th birthday in 1992), the collection here offers a treasure trove of rare paintings and sculpture, from Rembrandt to Rubens, Bellini to van Gogh.

Sødra Blasieholmshamnen. (© 08/519-54-300. Admission about 65SEK ($6) adults, 40SEK ($4) seniors and students, free for children 15 and under. Tues and Thurs 11am–8pm; Wed–Sun 11am–5pm. The museum is located a short walk from the Royal Opera House.

LOCAL FLAVORS

The best place to sample Sweden's legendary smörgåsbord is **Operakällaren** (© **08/676-58-00**), which is part of the Royal Opera Complex on Kungsträdgården and dates from 1787. The emphasis is on fresh fish, but you'll also find smoked eel, reindeer, Swedish red caviar, and grouse. There's a regular menu as well. The price tag for the smörgåsbord is around $38.25, and reservations are required. For a different kind of experience, try **Lisa Elmquist** (© **08/660-92-32;** reservations recommended), a cafe and oyster bar located in the produce market (Østermalms Saluhall). A favorite here is shrimp with bread and butter for 135NOK to 186NOK ($12.75 to $17.25).

BEST BUYS

It seems like anything of Swedish design is gorgeous, including housewares, hand-blown glass, wood items, and handicrafts, but they can all be pricey. Items to watch for include kids' clothes, silver jewelry, reindeer gloves, stainless-steel utensils, Swedish clogs, hand-woven items, and woolens. Everybody's favorite shopping area is **Gamla Stan** (Old Town). The main street for browsing is **Västerlånggatan.**

Index by Ship Name

continued

Ship	Cruise Line	Page
Marco Polo	Orient Lines	94
Melody	Mediterranean Shipping Cruises	144
Minerva	Swan Hellenic Cruises	179
Mistral	First European Cruises (Festival Cruises)	131
Monterey	Mediterranean Shipping Cruises	146
Noordam	Holland America Line	81
Nordkapp	Norwegian Coastal Voyage	153
Nordlys	Norwegian Coastal Voyage	153
Nordnorge	Norwegian Coastal Voyage	153
Norwegian Dream	Norwegian Cruise Line	87
Odysseus	Royal Olympic Cruises	168
Olympia Countess	Royal Olympic Cruises	170
Oriana	P&O Cruises	159
Polarlys	Norwegian Coastal Voyage	153
Prinsendam	Holland America Line	82
Queen Elizabeth 2	Cunard Line	202
Radisson Diamond	Radisson Seven Seas Cruises	208
Rhapsody	Mediterranean Shipping Cruises	147
Richard With	Norwegian Coastal Voyage	153
Royal Clipper	Star Clippers	261
Royal Princess	Princess Cruises	102
Sea Cloud	Sea Cloud Cruises	253
Sea Cloud II	Sea Cloud Cruises	254
Seabourn Legend	Seabourn Cruise Line	217
Seabourn Pride	Seabourn Cruise Line	217
Seawing	Airtours	181
Seven Seas Mariner	Radisson Seven Seas Cruises	209
Silver Cloud	Silversea Cruises	224
Silver Shadow	Silversea Cruises	225
Silver Whisper	Silversea Cruises	225
Song of Flower	Radisson Seven Seas Cruises	211
Splendour of the Seas	Royal Caribbean International	108
Star Flyer	Star Clippers	259
Stella Solaris	Royal Olympic Cruises	171
Sunbird	Airtours	181

FROMMER'S® MEMORABLE WALKS

Chicago   New York   San Francisco
London   Paris

FROMMER'S® GREAT OUTDOOR GUIDES

Arizona & New Mexico   Northern California   Vermont & New Hampshire
New England   Southern New England

SUZY GERSHMAN'S BORN TO SHOP GUIDES

Born to Shop: France   Born to Shop: Italy   Born to Shop: New York
Born to Shop: Hong Kong,   Born to Shop: London   Born to Shop: Paris
  Shanghai & Beijing

FROMMER'S® IRREVERENT GUIDES

Amsterdam   Los Angeles   San Francisco
Boston   Manhattan   Seattle & Portland
Chicago   New Orleans   Vancouver
Las Vegas   Paris   Walt Disney World
London   Rome   Washington, D.C.

FROMMER'S® BEST-LOVED DRIVING TOURS

Britain   Germany   New England
California   Ireland   Scotland
Florida   Italy   Spain
France

HANGING OUT™ GUIDES

Hanging Out in England   Hanging Out in France   Hanging Out in Italy
Hanging Out in Europe   Hanging Out in Ireland   Hanging Out in Spain

THE UNOFFICIAL GUIDES®

Bed & Breakfasts and Country   Florida with Kids   New Orleans
  Inns in: Golf Vacations in the   New York City
    California   Eastern U.S.   Paris
    New England   The Great Smoky &   San Francisco
    Northwest   Blue Ridge Mountains   Skiing in the West
    Rockies   Hawaii   Southeast with Kids
    Southeast   Inside Disney   Walt Disney World
Beyond Disney   Las Vegas   Walt Disney World for
Branson, Missouri   London   Grown-ups
California with Kids   Mid-Atlantic with Kids   Walt Disney World for Kids
Chicago   Mini Las Vegas   Washington, D.C.
Cruises   Mini-Mickey   World's Best Diving Vacations
Disneyland   New England & New York
                                  with Kids

SPECIAL-INTEREST TITLES

Frommer's Adventure Guide to Australia & New   Frommer's Exploring America by RV
  Zealand   Frommer's Gay & Lesbian Europe
Frommer's Adventure Guide to Central America   Frommer's The Moon
Frommer's Adventure Guide to India & Pakistan   Frommer's New York City with Kids
Frommer's Adventure Guide to South America   Frommer's Road Atlas Britain
Frommer's Adventure Guide to Southeast Asia   Frommer's Road Atlas Europe
Frommer's Adventure Guide to Southern Africa   Frommer's Washington, D.C., with Kids
Frommer's Britain's Best Bed & Breakfasts and   Frommer's What the Airlines Never Tell You
  Country Inns   Israel Past & Present
Frommer's France's Best Bed & Breakfasts and   The New York Times' Guide to Unforgettable
  Country Inns   Weekends
Frommer's Italy's Best Bed & Breakfasts and Country Places Rated Almanac
  Inns   Retirement Places Rated
Frommer's Caribbean Hideaways